Foreword

The hills and mountains of England are some of our greatest natural assets. They provide a vital livelihood to rural communities and the wild and dramatic scenery attracts visitors throughout the year. The spectacular landscapes are also widely recognised as being internationally important for the range of wildlife habitats and species they support. The best areas now form part of the European Natura 2000 series of sites. Furthermore, priority habitats such as upland oak woodlands and blanket bog and species such as black grouse are an important component of the UK Biodiversity Action Plan programme.

The upland landscape we see today has not been created overnight but is the product of centuries of human activity. Unfortunately serious wildlife losses over the past 50 years have occurred through intensive land management practices, and current overgrazing and damaging burning regimes continue to reduce the wildlife interest of the English uplands.

However, major changes are underway and land management practices that are more sympathetic to the needs of wildlife are now being promoted and integrated into the policies, programmes and practices of Government departments and the key sectors they influence. The Government's Biodiversity Action Plan programme has also set clear targets for restoring upland habitats and species and provides the framework for action. In addition, with the recent substantial increase in funding for agri-environment schemes there will be further scope to promote environmentally sensitive farming practices, and make an important contribution towards thriving rural communities.

The *upland management handbook* pools the expertise of many of the country's leading wildlife, farming and land management specialists to provide a blueprint for translating policies into the practical delivery of the land management that will benefit our upland wildlife.

It is the most comprehensive guide to the management needs of upland wildlife ever published and identifies the key priorities for action. We commend it to all those involved in the management of these important habitats and hope it can lead the way in demonstrating how environmentally sustainable land management practices can be integrated into the English uplands.

Michael Meacher — Minister for the Environment

Elliot Morley — Minister for Fisheries and the Countryside

ENGLISH NATURE

The upland management handbook

Edited by Joanne Backshall, Jayne Manley
and Michael Rebane

ISBN 1 85716 402 4

Authors and acknowledgements

A large number of authors have contributed to *The upland management handbook*. The major authors of the individual chapters are given below. Note: Where not employed by English Nature, their organisation is also listed. In addition the following also made significant contributions to the handbook: Andy Brown (bird sections), Martin Drake (invertebrate section - Chapter 9), Rob Fuller - British Trust for Ornithology (bird section - Chapter 8), Tony Gent* (mammal, amphibian and reptile sections), Roger Key (invertebrate sections) and Vicky Morgan - Environmental Consultant (vascular and lower plant tables). * indicates no longer with English Nature.

CHAPTER 1	INTRODUCTION TO THE HANDBOOK Joanne Backshall* and Michael Rebane
CHAPTER 2	WILDLIFE AND LAND USE OF THE UPLANDS Joanne Backshall, Siâron Hooper, Keith Kirby (Forestry section) and and Rigby Jerram, Environmental Consultant
CHAPTER 3	DECISION MAKING Rigby Jerram, Environmental Consultant and Michael Rebane
CHAPTER 4	EARTH HERITAGE FEATURES Natalie Bennett and Simon Webb (Karst sections)
CHAPTER 5	MONTANE AREAS Joanne Backshall*
CHAPTER 6	MOORLAND Joanne Backshall*
CHAPTER 7	MEADOWS AND ENCLOSED PASTURE Rigby Jerram, Environmental Consultant with assistance from Richard Jefferson and Joanne Backshall*
CHAPTER 8	WOODLAND AND SCRUB Keith Kirby with assistance from Christine Reid and Philip Horton*
CHAPTER 9	FRESHWATER HABITATS Tessa Harding and Sue Bell, both Scott Wilson Resource Consultants with assistance from Chris Newbold and Mary Gibson*
CHAPTER 10	CRAGS, SCREE AND LIMESTONE PAVEMENT Joanne Backshall*, Simon Webb and Rigby Jerram, Environmental Consultant
CHAPTER 11	BIBLIOGRAPHY AND FURTHER READING Compiled by Joanne Backshall* and Michael Rebane

GLOSSARY	Joe Murphy, Environmental Consultant
INFORMATION NOTE 1	Rigby Jerram, Environmental Consultant, Allan Drewitt and Joanne Backshall*
INFORMATION NOTE 2	Siâron Hooper, Chris Lloyd, National Sheep Association and James Cameron (illustrations)
INFORMATION NOTE 3	Joe Murphy, Environmental Consultant
INFORMATION NOTE 4	Joe Murphy, Environmental Consultant and James Cameron (illustrations)
INFORMATION NOTE 5	Joe Murphy, Environmental Consultant
INFORMATION NOTE 6	Joanne Backshall*
INFORMATION NOTE 7	Joe Murphy, Environmental Consultant
INFORMATION NOTE 8	Joe Murphy, Environmental Consultant
INFORMATION NOTE 9	Joe Murphy, Environmental Consultant
INFORMATION NOTE 10	Joe Murphy, Environmental Consultant, Peter Davies, Lake District National Park and Jim Loxham, National Trust

Acknowledgements

The many authors identified previously are due thanks for their major contributions to this handbook. A great many other individuals also provided comments on all or part of the draft of the handbook and provided further useful information. We would particularly like to thank the following persons from English Nature and many other organisations and individuals. * indicates no longer with English Nature.

English Nature: John Bacon, John Barrett, Alastair Burn, Alison Carter, David Clayden, Rob Cooke, Peter Corkhill, Alistair Crowle, Andrew Dalton*, Erica Donnison, Martin Drake, Allan Drewitt, Paul Evans, Adrian Gardiner, Mary Gibson*, Mike Harley, Andrew Hearle, Jon Hickling, Siâron Hooper, Sidika Hudda*, Richard Jefferson, Peter Lambley, Ben Le Bas, Gordon Leel, Chris McCarty, Frank Mawby, Ben Mercer, Roger Mitchell, Chris Newbold, Jacqui Ogden, Rob Petley-Jones, Ron Porley, Denise Ramsay, Rupert Randall, Mandy Richardson, Mary Roberts, Maggie Robinson, Karen Slater, Ian Slater, Ian Soane, Allan Stewart, Jon Stewart, Ian Taylor, Clare Trinder*, Andy Wagstaff, Tom Wall, Simon Webb, Terry Wells*, Peter Welsh, Will Williams, Richard Wilson, Robert Wolton, Flemming Ulf-Hansen.

Scottish Natural Heritage: Helen Armstrong, Philip Boon, Angus MacDonald, Des Thompson, Phil Whitfield.

Countryside Council for Wales: Marcus Yeo.

Joint Nature Conservation Committee: Nick Hodgetts, Stephen Ward, Martin Wiggington.

Others: Judy Allfrey (Ministry of Agriculture, Fisheries and Food), Simon Allday (Ministry of Agriculture, Fisheries and Food), Penny Anderson (Penny Anderson Associates), David Baines (Game Conservancy Trust), James Baker (Ministry of Defence), David Beskine (Rambler's Association), John Biggs (Ministry of Agriculture, Fisheries and Food), Don Brown, (Ministry of Defence), Roy Brown (Manchester University), Roger Buisson (Royal Society for the Protection of Birds), David Bullock (National Trust), Stephen Cane (Ministry of Agriculture, Fisheries and Food), Bob Cartwright (Lake District National Park Authority), Chris Chesterton (Farming and Rural Conservation Agency), Ian Condliffe (Farming and Rural Conservation Agency), James Cooper (Woodland Trust), David Crabtree (Yorkshire Dales National Park Authority), Jane Croft (Biological Record Centre, Monkswood), Andy Croxford (Environment Agency), Fred Currie (Forestry Commission), Alex Dasi-Sutton (Ministry of Agriculture, Fisheries and Food), Peter Davies (Lake District National Park Authority), Mervyn Edwards (Farming and Rural Conservation Agency), Andrew Fairey (Cumbria Business Link), Rob Fuller (British Trust for Ornithology), Martin Gillibrand (Moorland Association), David Glaves (Farming and Rural Conservation Agency), Sue Goodfellow (Dartmoor National Park Authority), Robert Goodison (Farming and Rural Conservation Agency), Mrs G Halliday (Ministry of Agriculture, Fisheries and Food), Geoffrey Halliday (University of Lancaster), David Harpley (Cumbria Wildlife Trust), Sally Hart (English Sports Council), Trevor Harwood (Ecological Consultant), Katherine Hearn (National Trust), Stuart Higham (Newton Rigg College, Cumbria), John Hooson (National Trust), Peter James (Environmental Consultant), Rigby Jerram (Environmental Consultant), Joe Johnson (Farming and Rural Conservation Agency), Sarah Jupp (Ministry of Defence), Miles King (Plant Life), Clive Kirkbride (Yorkshire Dales National Park Authority), Paul Kirkland (Butterfly

Conservation), Chris Lloyd (National Sheep Association), Jim Loxham (National Trust), Keith McDougall (National Sheep Association), Andrew Nicholson (East Cumbria Countryside Project), Henry Owen-John (English Heritage), John Phillips (Heather Trust), Derek Ratcliffe (British Association of Nature Conservation), Sue Rees (North York Moors National Park Authority), Tim Rich (National Museum of Wales), Roderick Robinson (Rhone Poulenc), Giles Rowe (Ministry of Defence), F. Rumsey, Ann Sansom (Environment Agency), Rosie Simpson (Countryside Agency), Roger Smith (University of Newcastle), Andy Stokes (British Trust for Conservation Volunteers), Lindsay Waddell (Moorland Gamekeepers Association), Chris Wheeling (Sutherland Estates), Alan Woods (Country Landowners Association).

Contents

Contents

Introduction to the handbook 1

1.1 Definition of the term upland

The distinction between upland and lowland habitats in England is often blurred with no precise dividing line between the two. The 250 m contour is the most commonly used cut-off between upland and lowland, but in reality this 'line' does not exist, and the two merge through a broad band of transitional vegetation and land management. Further complications arise with this means of rigid definition as one travels farther north and west in England, with 'upland' vegetation, species and land-use occurring at much lower levels in response to the harsher environment.

To use a precise altitudinal definition is therefore both inappropriate and constraining for a management handbook, particularly so as the land management systems in the uplands do not use high land in isolation; the management of the higher land is always integrated with the activities on the adjacent lower ground. In this handbook we have used the term 'upland' to refer to those Natural Areas (see 1.2) of England which fall within the Less Favoured Areas (LFA) boundary and are upland in character. By this we mean land from the valley bottoms with its streams and rivers, hay meadows and pastures right up to the mountain tops, incorporating the in-bye grassland, the unenclosed moor with its heaths and bogs along the way.

Natural Areas have been identified by English Nature and are parts of the country with similar types of wildlife and other natural features. In many cases they also share similar landscapes. Their boundaries do not follow administrative boundaries but are defined by their wildlife and natural features, their land use and human history. Their distinctive features have been described and long-term objectives have been identified which provide direction and focus for action to maintain or restore our natural heritage. Natural Areas provide a framework for much of English Nature's work and are the basis of our advice to others.

LFAs were introduced in 1975 (see 2.8.1) to 'ensure the continuation of farming, thereby maintaining a minimum population level or conserving the countryside' in recognition of the difficult farming conditions (such as low soil fertility, high rainfall, short growing seasons and steep slopes) and, in some cases, geographical remoteness. Although originally they were primarily a socio-economic designation, they closely relate to the extent of upland habitats in England.

1.2 Location and extent of the English uplands

Precise information on the distribution and extent of upland landscapes is not available because of the variety of ways in which the uplands have been defined, surveyed and classified (Manley & Smith 1994). However, in one study the Institute of Terrestrial Ecology (ITE), now the Centre for Ecology and Hydrology, developed a land classification system which identified 13 upland land classes. Estimated figures for these land classes put the total area of uplands (including forest and agricultural grass) at 39% of Britain, and the area of upland vegetation (bog, moorland and grassland) at 23% of Britain (Bunce & Barr 1988). Of the upland vegetation, 32% was estimated to comprise bog, 37% moorland and 31% grassland. In England the LFAs (see 2.8.1) encompass around 2.2 million ha and this correlates closely with the area of land predicted as being upland by the ITE land classification.

A more recent survey of the British countryside was carried out in 1990 under the title of the *Countryside Survey 1990* (Barr *et al* 1993). This was the first survey to be based on the integration of information from satellite imagery and traditional field survey methods. It reported that semi-natural vegetation covered over 73% of upland landscapes in GB. In England, open and dense scrub covered 25.6% of upland habitats (1,112 km^2), heath/moor grass 34.9% (1,515 km^2), bog 2.7% (119 km^2), bracken 5.6% (245 km^2), deciduous/mixed woodland 0.8% (37 km^2) and coniferous woodland 8.1% (353 km^2). *Countryside 2000* (Haines-Young *et al*) has since been published which provides more up to date information on the extent of upland habitats in England.

Natural Areas within the LFA with upland characteristics are listed below and are shown in Figure 1.1 (English Nature 1993b, 1994c; English Nature 1996c; English Nature & Countryside Commission 1996):

2. Border Uplands
4. North Pennines
8. Yorkshire Dales
10. Cumbria Fells and Dales
12. Forest of Bowland
14. Southern Pennines
15. Pennine Dales Fringe
17. North York Moors and Hills
26. Dark Peak
29. South West Peak
30. White Peak
41. Oswestry Uplands
42. Shropshire Hills
58. Clun & North West Herefordshire Hills
60. Black Mountains and Golden Valley
87. Exmoor and the Quantocks
92. Dartmoor
94. Bodmin Moor

1.3 Intended audience for the handbook

This handbook is written for people who advise farmers and other land managers in upland areas about the best management for wildlife and other natural features. It is also for people who actively manage upland areas and wish to accommodate or encourage wildlife and other natural features. It is equally applicable to all land in the uplands, not just nature reserves, and should be particularly helpful in the implementation of schemes such as Environmentally Sensitive Areas, the Countryside Stewardship scheme and other agri-environment measures. In addition, the handbook should be useful for training and educational purposes, such as agricultural and ecological courses within colleges.

It is intended for readers with some understanding of basic ecological processes and practical land management. Information on standard agricultural practices is included to assist those readers with limited agricultural training. In due course English Nature intends to produce management advice derived from the handbook in forms suitable for other audiences.

1.4 Aims of the handbook

The overall aim of *The upland management handbook* is to provide advice on the management of the English uplands for wildlife and other natural features. In pursuing this aim the handbook:

- identifies the features of nature conservation significance in the uplands of England;
- outlines the distribution of these features in England;
- explains the habitat and management requirements of these features;

- presents management options and guidelines for land with these features;
- recognises the need to integrate management for nature conservation with other land uses;
- assists in implementing the UK Biodiversity Action Plan;
- identifies sources of further information.

1.5 Wildlife and other natural features covered by the handbook

This handbook covers habitats, species and earth heritage features within the uplands of England, as defined above. These can be divided into the following broad categories:

- geological and geomorphological interests (Chapter 4 Earth heritage features);
- montane communities (Chapter 5 Montane areas);
- heaths (Chapter 6 Moorland);
- mires (Chapter 6 Moorland and Chapter 7 Meadows & enclosed pasture);
- grasslands (Chapter 6 Moorland and Chapter 7 Meadows and enclosed pasture);
- woodland and scrub (Chapter 8);
- freshwater habitats (Chapter 9);
- rock communities (Chapter 10);
- the constituent species of all these habitats (Chapters 5-10).

Many of the features covered are not exclusive to the uplands and also occur in Natural Areas which are more lowland in character and are not covered by this handbook.

Not all the habitats, species and earth heritage features of the uplands are of equal conservation value. This handbook concentrates on those features of recognised nature conservation importance.

While this handbook concentrates on the provision of information on the management of land with existing nature conservation interest, enhancement of areas of lesser interest is also covered. The handbook, however, does not cover the re-creation of features of wildlife interest, nor does it discuss survey and monitoring techniques, because these subjects warrant, and indeed have, publications in their own right.

1.6 How to use the handbook

The users of this handbook are likely to vary, from individuals already knowledgeable in this subject seeking small amounts of specialised information, to those wishing to find out more general information about the English uplands and their management for wildlife. Consequently, there are different ways in which to use this handbook. One option is to look through the contents list for the subjects covered, another is to look through the relevant chapter, or the reader can consult the index for key words. For example, moorland management is covered in Chapter 6 Moorland and grassland management in Chapter 7 Meadows and enclosed pasture. Information on grazing and burning is included in several chapters, such as Chapter 6 Moorland and Chapter 7 Meadows and enclosed pasture. Information on particular species, for example golden plover or bracken, is included in the most appropriate chapter for the species in question and can be found by consulting the index. A broad outline of the handbook structure and contents follows.

The handbook is divided into 10 main chapters, followed by a bibliography and further reading list, a glossary and 10 information notes of additional technical information. The second chapter describes the wildlife interest and land use of the English uplands. Chapter 3 describes the approaches to decision making. The handbook is then divided into chapters which cover the major earth heritage features and wildlife habitats of upland areas. These include montane areas, unenclosed moorland, enclosed meadows and pasture, woodland and scrub, freshwater habitats and rocky areas including crags, scree and limestone pavement. These chapters identify the habitats and species of nature conservation significance, together with management options, techniques and guidelines for land supporting these interests.

1.7 Sources of information for the handbook

The information contained in this handbook comes from published sources where they exist, as well as from unpublished sources and from people with particular species knowledge or practical experience of nature conservation in the uplands of Britain. Where information is derived from published material, the appropriate references are cited in the text. However, there are many areas where our knowledge is scant or absent, for example the distribution and ecology of many upland invertebrates. There are also many aspects of nature conservation management in the uplands about which little has been published, although a great deal of knowledge and expertise exists. Therefore, much of the information in the handbook is not from published sources but represents the best available knowledge from experienced nature conservation practitioners.

The National Vegetation Classification (NVC) provides a systematic classification of British vegetation and is used in this handbook.

1.8 How the handbook will be kept up to date, and feedback

It is intended that sections of the handbook will be updated as further experience and information is acquired. Management recommendations are likely to evolve with time as practical experience, monitoring and research identify more effective management techniques. We welcome suggestions and information which will assist us with the updating process. Please complete and return the enclosed feedback form to the English Nature Uplands Team in Peterborough.

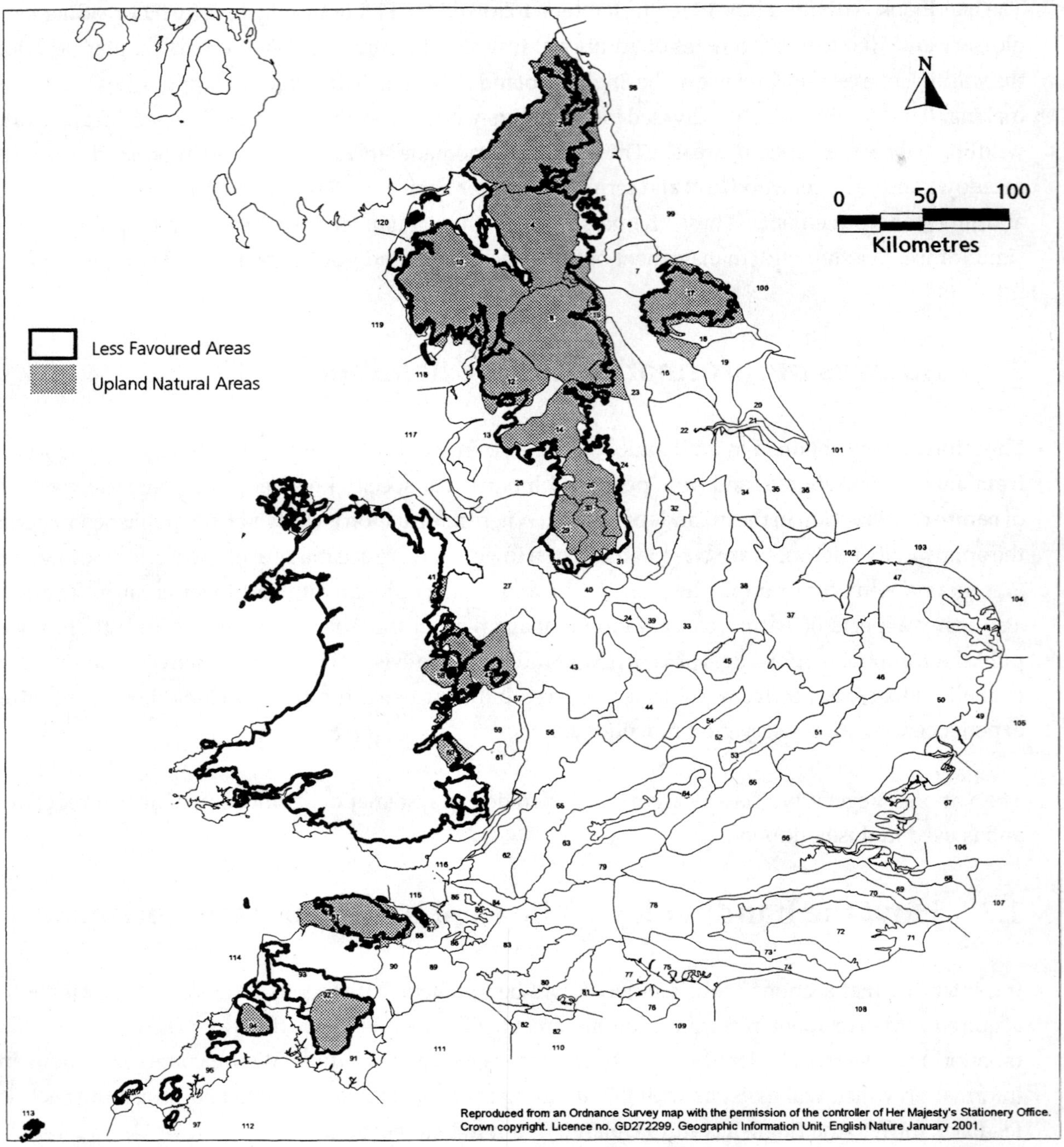

1 North Northumberland Coastal Plain
2 Border Uplands
3 Solway Basin
4 North Pennines
5 Northumbria Coal Measures
6 Durham Magnesian Limestone Plateau
7 Tees Lowlands
8 Yorkshire Dales
9 Eden Valley
10 Cumbria Fells and Dales
11 West Cumbria Coastal Plain
12 Forest of Bowland
13 Lancashire Plain and Valleys
14 Southern Pennines
15 Pennine Dales Fringe
16 Vale of York and Mowbray
17 North York Moors and Hills
18 Vale of Pickering
19 Yorkshire Wolds
20 Holderness
21 Humber Estuary
22 Humberhead Levels
23 Southern Magnesian Limestone
24 Coal Measures
25 Dark Peak
26 Urban Mersey Basin
27 Mosses and Meres
28 Potteries and Churnet Valley
29 South West Peak
30 White Peak
31 Derbyshire Peak Fringe and Lower Derwent
32 Sherwood
33 Trent Valley and Rises
34 North Lincolnshire Coversands and Clay Vales
35 Lincolnshire Wolds
36 Lincolnshire Coast and Marshes
37 The Fens
38 Lincolnshire and Rutland Limestone
39 Charnwood
40 Needwood and South Derbyshire Claylands
41 Oswestry Uplands
42 Shropshire Hills
43 Midlands Plateau
44 Midland Clay Pastures
45 Rockingham Forest
46 Breckland
47 North Norfolk
48 The Broads
49 Suffolk Coast and Heaths
50 East Anglian Plain
51 East Anglian Chalk
52 West Anglian Plain
53 Bedfordshire Greensand Ridge
54 Yardley-Whittlewood Ridge
55 Cotswolds
56 Severn and Avon Vales
57 Malvern Hills and Teme Valley
58 Clun and North West Herefordshire Hills
59 Central Herefordshire
60 Black Mountains and Golden Valley
61 Dean Plateau and Wye Valley
62 Bristol, Avon Valleys and Ridges
63 Thames and Avon Vales
64 Midvale Ridge
65 Chilterns
66 London Basin
67 Greater Thames Estuary
68 North Kent Plain
69 North Downs
70 Wealden Greensand
71 Romney Marshes
72 High Weald
73 Low Weald and Pevensey
74 South Downs
75 South Coastal Plain and Hampshire Lowlands
76 Isle of Wight
77 New Forest
78 Hampshire Downs
79 Berkshire and Marlborough Downs
80 South Wessex Downs
81 Dorset Heaths
82 Isles of Portland and Purbeck
83 Wessex Vales
84 Mendip Hills
85 Somerset Levels and Moors
86 Mid Somerset Hills
87 Exmoor and the Quantocks
88 Vale of Taunton and Quantock Fringes
89 Blackdowns
90 Devon Redlands
91 South Devon
92 Dartmoor
93 The Culm
94 Bodmin Moor
95 Cornish Killas and Granites
96 West Penwith
97 The Lizard
98 Northumberland Coast
99 Tyne to Tees Coast
100 Saltburn to Bridlington
101 Bridlington to Skegness
102 The Wash
103 Old Hunstanton to Sheringham
104 Sheringham to Lowestoft
105 Suffolk Coast
106 North Kent Coast
107 East Kent Coast
108 Folkstone to Selsey Bill
109 Solent and Poole Bay
110 South Dorset Coast
111 Lyme Bay
112 Start Point to Land's End
113 Isles of Scilly
114 Land's End to Minehead
115 Bridgewater Bay
116 Severn Estuary
117 Liverpool Bay
118 Morecambe Bay
119 Cumbrian Coast
120 Solway Firth

Figure 1.1. Upland Natural Areas and the Less Favoured Area boundary in England

Introduction

The upland management handbook feedback form

Name ....

Position ....

Name of organisation ....

Contact address ....

....

Post Code ....

Telephone .... E-mail ....

If you would like to receive information on revisions of *The upland management handbook* as they are produced, please tick here ☐

1. Are there any areas not covered or not covered in enough detail in the handbook?

....
....
....
....
....
....

2. Do you have any comments with respect to the format and style of the handbook, ie is it user friendly?

....
....
....
....
....
....

3. Please tell us or send us copies of any further information which you think should be included in future versions.

....
....
....
....
....
....

Please send completed forms to:

English Nature, Uplands Team, Northminster House, Peterborough, PE1 1UA

The uplands

Wildlife and land use in the uplands 2

Tables

Wildlife in the uplands

2.1 Introduction

The English uplands are important for their wealth of habitats and species, supporting unique combinations of plants and animals and including a blend of southern and northern elements (Ratcliffe 1988). They also contain diverse and widespread earth heritage interests. A summary of these interests, with reasons why they are considered to be important, is given below.

Wildlife and earth heritage interests are considered to be important for a variety of reasons. For example, they may be internationally or nationally:

- rare or scarce;
- threatened or fragmented;
- declining;
- restricted in distribution;
- limited in extent or number;
- at the edge of their range;
- important in England because a significant proportion of the UK or international habitat, population, or interest, occurs there;
- important in England because they are particularly well developed or representative in England when compared to Europe or the rest of the world.

Consequently, the nature conservation importance of different features is defined and expressed in different terms. For example, plants are identified as being nationally rare or scarce on certain criteria, birds are identified as being of conservation concern on different criteria, and the status of invertebrates is defined by other criteria again. Some species are legally protected and many habitats and species are included in the European Community (EC) Habitats and Species Directive and the UK Biodiversity Action Plan (see 2.5). Further details on the nature conservation interests of the uplands and their importance can be found in the chapters on specific habitats.

2.2 Habitats

The uplands of England represent the largest area of 'semi-natural' habitat remaining in England. Most of Britain's vegetation is generally referred to as 'semi-natural' (Tansley 1939) because it has been modified by people to some degree. Semi-natural vegetation is composed of native species with structural affinities and community processes corresponding to those of natural vegetation, although the abundance of species, and in some cases the actual species composition, has been changed by man's activities (Thompson & Horsfield 1990).

Upland dry and, to a lesser extent, wet heath, blanket mires and acid grasslands form some of the largest continuous tracts of semi-natural habitat in Britain. Because they contain these large areas of semi-natural habitat, the uplands have long been recognised as a resource of high nature conservation value. It is not just the extent of these habitats which gives them their importance; many of the communities present are internationally scarce and some are largely confined to the UK (see Table 2.1, Brown *et al* 1997; Drewitt & Manley 1997). These include National Vegetation Classification mire communities such as M17 *Trichophorum cespitosum-Eriophorum vaginatum* blanket mire, M16 *Erica tetralix-Sphagnum compactum* wet heath and M26 *Molinia caerulea-Crepis paludosa* mire; heath communities such as H4 *Ulex gallii-Agrostis curtisii* heath, H8 *Calluna vulgaris-Ulex gallii* heath and H21 *Calluna vulgaris-Vaccinium myrtillus-Sphagnum capillifolium* heath; CG9 *Sesleria caerulea-Galium sterneri* grassland and limestone pavement.

This unique representation and mosaic of habitats and vegetation structures, supporting many rare and unusual plant and animal species, results from the variation in altitude, climate, geography, geology, topography, soils and land use (Thompson *et al* 1995c). An altitudinal gradient of climate produces zones of vegetation in response to the changing conditions for plant growth. With increasing altitude, temperature is reduced, whereas wind speed, rainfall and cloud cover increase (Barry 1981). A typical upland vegetation zonation in England today would be represented by meadows, enclosed pastures and woodland in the valley bottom and on the lower slopes, through to sub-montane communities (dwarf shrub heaths, grasslands and blanket bogs) with occasional scrub and woodland on higher ground, and finally montane communities (grassland, moss- or lichen-heath) above the climatic tree limit, around 650 m (Ratcliffe 1991).

Further information:
All vegetation communities: Rodwell 1991, 1992, 1995 and 2000.
Grasslands: Jefferson 1996, Jefferson & Robertson 1996a.
Mountains & moorlands: Drewitt & Manley 1997; Ratcliffe & Thompson 1988; Thompson *et al* 1995c.
Woodlands: Reid, Kirby & Cooke 1996; Kirby & Reid 1997.
Scrub: Hopkins 1996.
Freshwater wetlands: English Nature 1997b; Gardiner 1996.

2.3 Species

Upland habitats support a wide range of vascular and non-vascular plants, invertebrates, birds, mammals, amphibians, reptiles and fish. Some of these are restricted to upland habitats while others have a wider altitudinal range and may be numerous in the uplands as a result of the lowlands becoming less suitable. Many species are of international, national or local importance. Some of these species are included in the UK Biodiversity Action Plan (see 2.5, UK Biodiversity Group 1998 and 1999; UK Steering Group 1995). The conservation status, distribution in England by Natural Area, and habitat and management requirements of significant upland plants and animals is given in more detail in Chapters 5-10.

2.3.1 Plants

Nationally rare and scarce plants occur throughout the uplands in a variety of habitats. These species are often restricted in their distribution because their usual habitats are now also restricted in extent and distribution, or have become unsuitable through management practices such as heavy grazing, fertiliser application or drainage.

Semi-natural calcareous grasslands, for example, support species such as Teesdale violet *Viola rupestris* and spring gentian *Gentiana verna*. Bird's-eye primrose *Primula farinosa* and bog orchid *Hammarbya paludosa* can be found in upland flushes. Blanket and valley mires can support species such as tall bog sedge *Carex magellanica* and small cranberry *Vaccinium microcarpum* and uncommon bryophytes like *Sphagnum austinii* and *Cephalozia loitlesbergeri*. Alpine catchfly *Lychnis alpina* and alpine saxifrage *Saxifraga nivalis* are present on some high altitude rock ledges. Heaths may have populations of dwarf cornel *Cornus suecica*, pale dog-violet *Viola lactea* and the rare eyebright *Euphrasia vigursii*. Woodlands, particularly those on limestone, may hold populations of species such as narrow-leaved helleborine *Cephalanthera longifolia*, angular Solomon's-seal *Polygonatum odoratum* and lady's slipper orchid *Cypripedium calceolus*, while acidic woods can be important for bryophytes, including English rarities like *Tritomaria exsecta* and *Jubula hutchinaiae*, and lichens.

Knowledge of the distribution, status and conservation needs of lichens and fungi is unfortunately patchy and therefore lichens are mentioned only briefly and fungi have not been considered at all in this edition of the handbook (but see Ing 1992).

2.3.2 Birds

The English uplands support an internationally important assemblage of breeding birds (Ratcliffe 1990a & b). Many of these are considered to be of conservation concern for reasons such as historical population decline (RSPB 1996). British breeding birds that are positively associated with the uplands are identified in Stillman & Brown (1998) and their definition of upland birds and list of species relevant to England are used in this handbook.

The bird communities on blanket bogs and in high mountain areas, which include waders such as golden plover *Pluvialis apricaria* and dunlin *Calidris alpina*, are unique in species mixture and as important outliers of largely Arctic Eurasian distributions. Heathlands support their own particular assemblage of birds, including red grouse *Lagopus lagopus scoticus* and merlin *Falco columbarius*. Many of the species associated with the uplands, such as the golden eagle *Aquila chrysaetos*, peregrine falcon *Falco peregrinus* and hen harrier *Circus cyaneus*, are of conservation concern in Europe and are listed on Annex 1 of the EC Birds Directive (see 2.5 and Brown & Grice 1993). The upland fringes support species such as twite *Carduelis flavirostris*, black grouse *Tetrao tetrix* and curlew *Numenius arquata*.

2.3.3 Invertebrates

Invertebrates are also an important part of the upland biological community, both on land and in freshwater systems. Although some species are common with widespread distributions that include lowland habitats, many species are unique to the uplands. Examples include the whorl snail *Vertigo geyeri* of base-rich flushes, the ground beetle *Nebria nivalis*, which lives on mountain top scree and boulder fields, the broad-bordered white underwing moth *Anarta melanopa* of high altitude heath, the crab spider *Clubiona norvegica* which lives among *Sphagnum* on moorland, the hoverfly *Platycheirus melanopsis* of high altitude grassland and the white-clawed crayfish *Austropotamobius pallipes* of calcium-rich rivers and streams.

In general, the invertebrates have not been studied as much as other species groups. Consequently, information on their populations, distribution and ecological requirements is more scant than for other species groups. Nevertheless, the invertebrates have important functions as herbivores, decomposers and food sources for other animals. For example, cranefly larvae are an important food for many moorland breeding birds. Rare and scarce invertebrates associated with the uplands are identified in the following chapters.

2.3.4 Mammals

There are relatively few species of mammal for which the upland habitats in England are of special conservation importance. The exception is the mountain hare *Lepus timidus*. This species, which is native to Scotland, is only present in the Peak District in England where it is an introduced species.

For some species, the uplands today are the significant strong-hold in England. However, these species, now restricted to a fragment of the former range, would once have been widespread in both lowland and upland habitats. Examples are the pine marten *Martes martes* and the red squirrel *Sciurus vulgaris*. These two species are now found in predominantly upland conifer forests, although there is currently some debate as to whether the pine marten occurs in England.

Upland habitats, especially moorland, can maintain very large populations of small mammals. Field voles *Microtus agrestis* can be found in large numbers in rough grassland areas of moorland, although they occur at only low densities in heather moorland. Shrews *Sorex* spp. can also be found in large numbers in moorland habitats, the pygmy shrew *Sorex minutus* more so than the common shrew *Sorex araneus*. These small mammals are widespread and abundant elsewhere in England, but have conservation significance as they form an important food source for many upland predators, eg short-eared owl *Asio flammeus*.

Deer, notably red deer *Cervus elaphus*, sika deer *Cervus nippon* (an introduction) and roe deer *Capreolus capreolus*, can be numerous in upland habitats, particularly in the south west, although in England, upland populations are not as large as they are in the Scottish Highlands. The conservation significance of deer relates primarily to their impact on vegetation structure and diversity, and the requirement to manage numbers to prevent damage to habitats.

2.3.5 Amphibians and reptiles

Amphibians and reptiles are found in the English uplands but no species are exclusive to upland areas; indeed most would typically be described as lowland species. However, the uplands do hold large populations of many species, such as the adder *Vipera berus*. Upland habitats, notably moorland and newly planted woodland, are valuable habitats for adders. These snakes are becoming scarcer in lowland habitats in part owing to disturbance and habitat loss and fragmentation. Grass snakes *Natrix natrix* also occur in the uplands.

Two species of lizard occur in upland habitats: the common (or viviparous) lizard *Lacerta agilis* and the slow worm *Anguis fragilis*. Both species occur in a wide range of habitats throughout England and can be common in moorland, open woodlands and grasslands.

Although six species of amphibian are found in the uplands, these habitats are more frequently associated with just three: the common frog *Rana temporaria*, common toad *Bufo bufo* and the palmate newt *Triturus helveticus*. Some upland areas, such as the Peak District, have important populations of great crested newts *Triturus cristatus*. The smooth newt *Triturus vulgaris*, although usually described as a 'lowland species', is also found in upland areas. The natterjack toad *Bufo calamita* is mostly associated with lowland heathland, coastal dunes and salt marshes, but a recent discovery of a population in the Cumbrian Fells and Dales Natural Area shows that this species too can inhabit upland habitats.

2.3.6 Fish

Fish are an important component of freshwater ecosystems and the English uplands contain some species of particular nature conservation importance. These include the rare vendace *Coregonus albula*, schelly *C. lavaretus* and arctic char *Salvelinus alpinus*, which are all relics of ice age populations. Other important species include the bullhead *Cottus gobio*, allis shad *Alosa alosa*, twaite shad *A. fallax*, grayling *Thymallus thymallus*, and the sea, river and brook lampreys *Petromyzon marinus*, *Lampetra fluviatilis* and *L. planeri*. Upland rivers also form important spawning grounds for Atlantic salmon *Salmo salar*.

Further information:
Vascular plants: Jermy *et al* 1978; Palmer 1994 & 1996; Perring & Farrell 1983; Stewart *et al* 1994; Wigginton 1999.
Non-vascular plants: Church *et al* 1996; Hodgetts 1992, 1993b; Palmer 1994 & 1996; Purvis *et al* 1992; Schumaker *et al*. 1993.
Fungi: Ing 1992.
Birds: Batten *et al* 1990; Brown & Grice 1993; Grice *et al* 1994; RSPB 1996.
Invertebrates: Bratton 1991; Hyman & Parsons 1992; JNCC Invertebrate Site Register (ongoing).
Mammals, reptiles and amphibians: Mitchell-Jones 1996; Mitchell-Jones & Gent 1997.

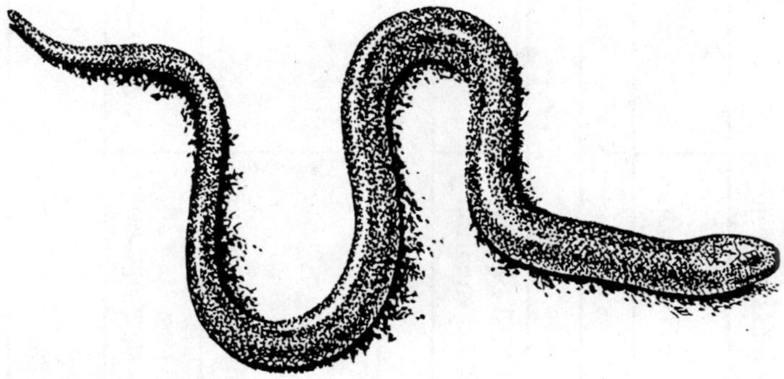

Slow worm

Table 2.1 Habitats Directive Annex 1 habitat types present in upland Natural Areas of England, with National Vegetation Classification and Biodiversity Action Plan equivalents

Habitats Directive Annex 1 habitats (by Corine habitat type)[1]	National Vegetation Classification[2]	UK Biodiversity Action Plan Broad habitats[3]
Heaths		
31.11 North Atlantic wet heaths with *Erica tetralix*	M14, M15, M16, H5	Dwarf shrub heath
31.2 Dry heaths (all sub-types)	H1-H4, H7-H10, H12, H16, H18, H21	Dwarf shrub heath
31.4 Alpine and sub-alpine heaths	Alpine heaths: H13-H15, H17, H19, H20, H22 Subalpine heaths: H10, H12, H16, H18, H21	Montane habitats
Scrub		
31.88 *Juniperus communis* formations on heaths or calcareous grasslands	W19, W21	Calcareous grassland Dwarf shrub heath
Grasslands		
34.2 Calaminarian grasslands	Not specified	-
34.31-34.34 Semi-natural dry grasslands and scrubland facies on calcareous substrate (*Festuco brometalia*) (important orchid sites*)	CG1-CG9	Calcareous grassland
35.1 Species-rich *Nardus* grasslands, on siliceous substrates in mountain areas (and sub-mountain areas in continental Europe)*	CG10, CG11	Calcareous grassland
36.32 Siliceous alpine and boreal grasslands	U7-U10	Acid grassland
37.31 *Molinia* meadows on chalk and clay (*Eu-Molinia*)	M24, M26	Acid grassland Fen, marsh and swamp
37.7-37.8 Eutrophic tall herbs	U17	Montane habitats
38.8 Mountain hay meadows (British types with *Geranium sylvaticum*)	MG3	Neutral grassland

Habitats Directive Annex 1 habitats (by Corine habitat type)[1]	National Vegetation Classification[2]	UK Biodiversity Action Plan Broad habitats[3]
Bogs, mires and fens		
51.1 Active raised bogs*	Not specified	Bogs
51.2 Degraded raised bogs (still capable of natural regeneration)	Not specified	Bogs
52.1 Blanket bog (active only*)	M17, M18, M19	Bogs
54.5 Transition mires and quaking bogs	M4, M5, M9, S27	Fen, marsh and swamp
54.12 Petrifying springs with tufa formation (*Cratoneurion*)*	M37, M38	Fen, marsh and swamp
54.2 Alkaline fens	M9, M10, M13	Fen, marsh and swamp
54.3 Alpine pioneer formations of *Caricion bicoloris-atrofuscae**	M10, M11, M12	Fen, marsh and swamp
Rocky habitats		
61.1 Siliceous scree	U18, U21	Inland rock
61.2 Eutric Scree	OV38 and other forms with no NVC equivalents	Inland rock
62.1 & 62.1A Chasmophytic vegetation on rocky slopes: Calcareous sub-types	OV40, OV39 and other forms with no NVC equivalents	Inland rock
62.2 Chasmophytic vegetation on rocky slopes: Silicicolous sub-types	U21 and other forms with no NVC equivalents	Inland rock
62.4 Limestone pavement*	Not specified	Inland rock
65 Caves not open to the public	N/A	
Woodland		
41.13 *Asperulo-Fagetum* beech forests	W12, W14	Broadleaved, mixed and yew woodland
41.4 *Tilio-Acerion* ravine forests*	W8d-g, W9	Broadleaved, mixed and yew woodland
41.53 Old oak woods with *Ilex* and *Blechnum* in the British Isles*	W10e, W11, W17	Broadleaved, mixed and yew woodland
42.A71-42.A73 *Taxus baccata* woodland*	W13	Broadleaved, mixed and yew woodland

Habitats Directive Annex 1 habitats (by Corine habitat type)[1]	National Vegetation Classification[2]	UK Biodiversity Action Plan Broad habitats[3]
Freshwater habitats		
Standing water		
22.11 & 22.31 Oligotrophic waters containing very few minerals of Atlantic sandy plains with amphibious vegetation: *Lobelia*, *Littorella* and *Isoetes*	*Littorelletalia*-type vegetation	Standing open water and canals
22.12 & (23.31 and 22.32) Oligotrophic to mesotrophic standing waters of plains to subalpine levels of the Continental and Alpine Region and mountain areas of other regions, with vegetation belonging to *Littorelletea uniflorae* and/or *Isoeto-Nanojuncetae*	Standing water Types 2 and 3 (oligotrophic) and Type 5 (mesotrophic) (Palmer 1989)	Standing open water and canals
22.12 & 22.44 Hard oligo-mesotrophic waters with benthic vegetation of *Chara* formations	Not specified	Standing open water and canals
22.13 Natural eutrophic lakes with *Magnopotamion* or *Hydrocharition*-type vegetation	*Hydrocharition* and *Magnopotamion*-type vegetation	Standing open water and canals
22.14 Dystrophic lakes	Not specified	Standing open water and canals
Running water		
24.2 Floating vegetation of *Ranunculus* of plain and submountainous rivers	*Ranunculus* community subtypes 1&2	Rivers and streams

Key
1. Listed on Annex 1 of the EC Habitats Directive.
* Priority habitat types from Annex 1 of the EC Habitats Directive
2 National Vegetation Classification (NVC, Rodwell 1991, 1992, 1995 and 2000). Interpretation of habitats taken from Brown *et al* (1997).
3 Broad habitats taken from Table 1 of UK Biodiversity Group (1998).

2.4 Earth heritage features

A vast range of geological and geomorphological interest is present in the uplands of England. For a relatively small country, England has a complex geological history, demonstrated by the diverse geology and landscape. The geological history of England is important worldwide because many of the names given to geological time units originate from place names or type localities (a reference site with which all rocks of a similar age and geological type can be compared) in England.

The English uplands contain examples of past geological conditions and processes, such as ice ages and glaciation, tropical seas leading to limestone formation, river deltas leaving coal deposits, deserts resulting in sandstones, and mountain-building activity creating folding, mineralisation, volcanic and metamorphic rocks. Areas where these processes and their results are well illustrated are valued for reference purposes, as well as for their potential for education and research.

The uplands have been continually evolving since their formation and are still undergoing modification by a series of geomorphological processes. Upland areas illustrating these processes, such as mass movement, fluvial activity, karst landscape evolution and a range of other eroding or depositing processes, represent further important examples for reference and education.

Further information: King *et al* 1996; JNCC Geological Conservation Review Series (ongoing); Chapter 4 Earth heritage features.

2.5 International, national and local nature conservation obligations

The uplands are covered by a range of international, national and local obligations in relation to nature conservation in England. These reflect and protect the significant nature conservation value of the English uplands, and are summarised below and in Table 2.2 .

2.5.1 The Habitats and Species Directive

The European Union (EU) has powers to make laws which apply across the Community. Directives are one of the most commonly-used types of European law. They generally set out a series of deadlines for action, which Member States must meet by creating or modifying their own legislation. The United Kingdom meets the obligations of European Directives by bringing in laws that are introduced into Parliament, either as Bills or Regulations (English Nature 1994d; HMSO 1994b; UK Steering Group 1995).

The Directive (Directive 92/43/EEC on the conservation of natural habitats and of wild fauna and flora) commonly known as the Habitats and Species Directive gives Europe-wide protection to certain rare and endangered habitats, plants and animals, on land and sea. Those which are particularly threatened are singled out as Priority Habitats or Species. The Directive was developed by the European Union to meet the commitments made by world leaders at the Earth Summit in Rio de Janeiro in 1992, where the Convention on Biological Diversity was signed. It builds on work already done under the Birds

Directive (see below) and provides for the creation of a network of protected areas across the European Union to be known as the 'Natura 2000' series.

The Natura 2000 series will contain some of the most outstanding wildlife sites in Europe. Together they will represent the range, variation, quality and biodiversity of the most endangered habitats and species in Europe (Brown *et al* 1997; European Communities 1992). The Natura 2000 network of protected sites will consist of Special Areas of Conservation (SACs) designated under the Habitats Directive and Special Protection Areas (SPAs) designated under the Birds Directive. In England, land which becomes part of the Natura 2000 series will also be notified as Sites of Special Scientific Interest (SSSIs).

The habitats included in the Habitats and Species Directive which occur in the English uplands are shown in Table 2.1. The animal and plant species listed in the Directive and relevant to the English uplands are indicated in the relevant chapters of the handbook. The Directive also gives certain species of flora and fauna strict protection prohibiting their deliberate capture, killing, disturbance, destruction or sale.

In England, proposed SACs include the North Pennine Dales Meadows, South Dartmoor Woods, the Asby Complex (limestone pavements, *Molinia* meadows and limestone grassland), Moorhouse-Upper Teesdale (blanket mire, limestone grassland, hay meadows, chasmophytic vegetation, eutric and siliceous scree, flushes, montane heath and juniper scrub) and The Stiperstones and The Hollies (dry heath). Further proposals were announced in 2000.

2.5.2 Birds Directive

The EC Birds Directive (Directive 79/409/EEC on the conservation of wild birds) requires Member States to take special measures to conserve the habitat of two categories of birds. These categories are (under Article 4.1 of the Directive) certain listed rare or vulnerable species, and (under Article 4.2) regularly occurring migratory species. Particular attention must be paid to the protection of wetlands, especially wetlands of international importance. Member States are required to designate the most suitable areas for the relevant species as SPAs and these also form part of the Natura 2000 series. Like SACs, the SPAs are also notified as SSSIs. The Directive has been in force for some years now and many SPAs have already been designated in Britain, including the Bowland Fells, North Pennine Moors and South Pennine Moors.

2.5.3 Wildlife and Countryside Act 1981

The Government's nature conservation policies are implemented mainly through the Wildlife and Countryside Act 1981 (as amended). The Act provides for the protection of endangered species of animals and plants and for the protection and management of important habitats. It does this through a series of Sites of Special Scientific Interest (SSSIs) of which there are now over 4,000 in England, covering more than 6% of the country. SSSIs are selected according to published guidelines reflecting the importance of features and species (Ellis *et al* 1996; Nature Conservancy Council 1989).

The Countryside and Rights of Way (CROW) Act, which received Royal Assent on 30 November 2000 replaces and revises parts of the Wildlife and Countryside Act. The new CROW Act is in five parts:

- Part I. Access to the Countryside.
- Part II. Public Rights of Way and Road Traffic.
- Part III. Nature Conservation and Wildlife Protection.
- Part IV. Areas of Outstanding Natural Beauty.
- Part V. Miscellaneous

From 30 January 2001, the CROW Act revises the site protection mechanisms of the Wildlife and Counryside Act within England and Wales. In respect of SSSIs the main aims of the CROW Act are to secure their better protection and management.

2.5.4 Ramsar Convention on Wetlands of International Importance

The Ramsar Convention (the Convention on Wetlands of International Importance especially as Waterfowl Habitat) agreed in Iran in 1971, was the first international nature conservation agreement to be concluded. The objectives are to stem progressive encroachment on, and loss of, wetlands now and in the future. A wetland is defined as being an area of fen, marsh, peatland or water, whether natural or artificial, permanent or temporary, with water that is static or flowing, fresh, brackish or salt. In signing the Convention in 1973 and ratifying it in 1976 (HMSO 1976), the UK Government accepted a commitment to promote both the conservation of particular sites and the wise use of wetlands within its territory. Under this Convention many sites in England, such as Esthwaite Water and Malham Tarn, have now been designated 'Ramsar sites'.

2.5.5 Biodiversity Action Plans

Biodiversity put simply is 'the variety of life'. Following the Earth Summit in Rio de Janeiro in 1992, the *UK Biodiversity Action Plan* was published two years later (Department of the Environment 1994a). This sets out a strategy for the next 20 years for conserving and enhancing the biological diversity within the UK, and contributing to the conservation of global biodiversity through all appropriate mechanisms.

As part of the UK Biodiversity Action Plan (BAP), a Biodiversity Steering Group was established which produced a report to initiate implementation of the UK BAP (UK Steering Group 1995). This identified habitats and species which were considered to require Habitat or Species Action Plans to further their conservation (see Table 2.1 for the BAP habitats identified; BAP species are identified in the following relevant chapters). Habitat Action Plans have been produced, including the following upland habitats (UK Biodiversity Group 1998; UK Steering Group 1995): limestone pavements, purple moor grass and rush pastures (*Molinia - Juncus*), upland hay meadows, upland oakwoods, upland mixed ashwoods, wet woodland, and various freshwater habitats. Further Habitat Action Plans were published in 1999 (UK Biodiversity Group 1999), including upland heathland, blanket bog and upland calcareous grassland. Species Action Plans have also been produced for a range of species, some of which are relevant to the uplands (UK Biodiversity Group 1998; UK Steering Group 1995). The lists of habitats and species have been amended since the initial report and Habitat and Species Action Plans continue to be produced and pursued.

Further information: Council of Europe 1996.

2.5.6 Sustainable land-use

Agenda 21 is the international action plan for sustainable development. It came out of the Earth Summit, held in Rio de Janeiro in 1992, and sets out the actions which national governments should implement to achieve sustainable development.

The UK Sustainable Development Strategy (Department of the Environment 1994b) sets out the future agenda for achieving sustainable development in the next century. 'Sustainable development' is defined as "development which meets the needs of the present without compromising the ability of future generations to meet their needs".

English Nature's approach to land use involves the concept of 'environmental sustainability'. This means maintaining the environment's natural qualities and characteristics and its capacity to fulfil its full range of functions, including the maintenance of biodiversity. To achieve environmental sustainability, environmental considerations must be integrated into all levels of policy formation, development and land use planning.

In Chapter 28 of Agenda 21, local authorities are encouraged to adopt a sustainable development strategy, a Local Agenda 21 for their community. This is essentially about community involvement and partnerships to get consensus and action towards sustainable development. Priority actions identified include integrating environment and development, changing consumption patterns, promoting sustainable human settlements, environmentally sound resource and waste management, and sustainable agriculture and rural development. Many local planning authorities have embarked upon putting Local Agenda 21 into practice through initiatives such as environmental strategies or audits, State of the Environment reports, environmental appraisal of development plans and urban initiatives.

Table 2.2 Main protection mechanisms for upland areas in England

Mechanism	Enabling legislation (where appropriate)	Principal organisation(s) involved
Site of Special Scientific Interest (SSSI)	S.28 1981 Wildlife & Countryside Act (1985 Amendment)	English Nature
National Nature Reserve (NNR)	S.19 1949 National Parks & Access to the Countryside Act S.35 1981 Wildlife & Countryside Act	English Nature
Local Nature Reserve (LNR)	S.21 1949 National Parks & Access to the Countryside Act	Local Planning Authorities, English Nature
Areas of Special Protection (Statutory Bird Sanctuary)	S.3 1981 Wildlife & Countryside Act (replaces Bird Sanctuary designated under 1954 Protection of Birds Act)	Department of the Environment, Transport and the Regions (DETR)
Wetland of International Importance (Ramsar site)	Ramsar Convention on Wetlands of International Importance especially as Waterfowl Habitats (Iran) 1971.	DETR, English Nature, Joint Nature Conservation Committee (JNCC)
Special Protection Area (SPA)	Article 4 of the EEC Directive on the Conservation of Wild Birds (79/409/EEC)	DETR, English Nature, JNCC
Special Area of Conservation (SAC)	Article 7 of the EC Habitats & Species Directive (92/43/EEC)	DETR, English Nature, JNCC
Local Plan Policies	Various	Local Planning Authorities, National Park Authorities

Land use in the uplands

2.6 Introduction

Farming, especially livestock production, has been the dominant force in shaping and creating upland landscapes and habitats. Field sport management and forestry have also been influential. In addition, recreation and public access have become increasingly important. Other land uses to have shaped the uplands include mining and quarrying, water supply and power generation. This section briefly outlines the historical background and the current situation regarding agriculture, field sports, forestry, recreation and other land uses in the English uplands.

2.7 Historical background to land use in the uplands

The uplands have been substantially modified by people, either directly, through activities such as tree-felling, burning, agricultural 'improvement' and livestock grazing, or indirectly, through pollution. All have resulted in structural and floristic changes to the vegetation and consequently the fauna. In the uplands, most widespread human activities have included intensifying natural processes, such as fire, and grazing the land with sheep, cattle and deer (Thompson & Horsfield 1990). It is these management practices that maintains and modifies many of the open communities now present in the uplands and prevents their reversion to woodland.

About 7,000 years ago, forest cover in Britain was at its greatest and most of the ground below 600 m in England was probably wooded. Thereafter, early man began to clear the forests to create arable and grazing land (Godwin 1975). Extensive deforestation occurred in the upland areas of England, other than the Lake District, between 2,600 and 2,100 years ago, in the pre-Roman Iron Age. Extensive deforestation in the Lake District occurred around 1,700 years ago (post-Roman). Local temporary clearances did, however, occur before these dates (Birks 1988). By a thousand years ago, the woodland cover in the uplands was probably less than 20% of the land area (see Chapter 8 Woodland and scrub).

During the early Bronze Age (*c.* 4,000-3,000 years ago), the British climate was warmer and drier than it is today and there was a considerable amount of farming in the uplands (Ingrouille 1995). This did not just involve livestock grazing, but included a good deal of arable cultivation as well. Following a population decline some 3,000 years ago, agricultural activity in the uplands declined. At about the same time, the climate became wetter and cooler. Upland soils started to change, becoming more acidic and podzolised as a result of the changes in vegetation cover initiated by forest clearance and in climate. In wetter areas and on higher ground, soils became waterlogged in the absence of trees to intercept and transpire rain water. These processes led to the development of the blanket peats and, in drier areas, the heaths seen today. There is no general date for blanket bog formation; it may have been initiated in different parts of England at any time between 7,500 and 2,000 years ago, depending on altitude and topography (Birks 1988).

From around 3,000 years ago onwards the distinction between the land use in the uplands and lowlands became increasingly marked, with most intensive agricultural activity occurring in the lowlands (below 300 m), and only extensive livestock rearing occurring in the uplands. The use of the uplands for sheep grazing intensified in the Middle Ages and some of the extensive areas of acid grassland probably originated from this period. Woodland clearance continued and by about AD 1800 little native woodland remained, the surviving relics being mainly of oak wood or mixed broadleaved forest (Ratcliffe 1988).

Stock rearing, particularly sheep although in some areas also cattle, now dominates over much of the uplands, but in some areas goats and cattle were once more important. The other main influence, dating from about 1840, has been the management of upland heath for red grouse *Lagopus lagopus scoticus*, which feed chiefly on dwarf shrubs, especially heather *Calluna vulgaris*. Management of moors for grouse increases the extent of dwarf shrubs, particularly heather, mainly by rotational burning. In the second half of the twentieth century, there has been considerable loss of heather moorland through overgrazing. Those moors still managed for grouse have also seen reductions in grouse populations.

Today's farming character has evolved rapidly over a relatively short time. Farming practices were transformed by the Enclosure Acts (1802 to 1844), and the subsequent industrialisation of Britain (Cole, Kernon & Knightbridge 1996). In the early part of the twentieth century, farming was in recession and during the 1930s much land was abandoned. But during World War II there was pressure for the UK to increase food production and thereby reduce the risk of shortages. Government policy and grant aid sought to increase the amount of agricultural production. The Agriculture Act 1947 provided, for the first time, guaranteed prices and markets for agricultural products. In addition, technological developments since the 1940s, particularly in machinery, use of pesticides and plant and animal genetics, have caused massive changes.

Agricultural land use intensified greatly as a result, especially in the lowlands and, later and more slowly in the uplands. The agricultural productivity of land was increased by draining, ploughing, reseeding and the use of fertilisers. Into the 1970s, fields were enlarged to accommodate new machinery, and hedgerows and trees were removed. Further agricultural 'improvements' were made through the use of herbicides and genetic manipulation of grass species, the most notable being perennial rye grass *Lolium perenne*. There has since been a wide scale switch from hay to silage making, owing to the latter's better feeding quality and reduced dependency on dry weather for a quality product. Financial incentives became available for farmers to 'improve' moorland by draining, and the use of supplementary feeding on moorland increased. This allowed stock to be kept on hill land at higher densities and for longer periods of time, leading to all year round and more intensive use of the uplands, with vegetation being grazed in spring and autumn when is it most susceptible to grazing damage. Technical advances in livestock farming led to larger, more productive stock being kept, and a reduction in the labour force employed on farms led to a decline in shepherding and appropriate burning management. The last half century or so has seen a further decline in the extent of arable crops, particularly cereals, but also root crops grown in upland areas.

The above, coupled with the introduction of Government subsidies, led to a progressive increase in the number of sheep on hill land. This is illustrated by MAFF census data, which indicates that, in 1977, 71% of moorland rough grazing in England and Wales was stocked at less than two ewes per hectare, whereas in 1987 71% of this land was stocked at between two and six ewes per hectare (Felton & Marsden 1990).

Changes in agricultural management practices have contributed to the decline in semi-natural vegetation. Awareness has increased of environmental problems caused by farming practice, and concerns about the negative effects of agriculture on the environment started at the official EU level in the mid-1980s (Brouwer & van Berkum 1996). Recognition of the indirect effects of agricultural support mechanisms available in the British Less Favoured Areas (LFA) on the biodiversity of the uplands is increasing (Egdell, Smith & Taylor 1993; Felton & Marsden 1990). The role of farmers in the protection of the rural environment and management of the landscape has also been recognised more fully, with farmers being increasingly rewarded for environmentally sustainable management (Brouwer & van Berkum 1996).

During the twentieth century, there has been a considerable expansion of the woodland cover in upland England. This has largely been government sponsored and implemented by the Forestry Commission. The majority of the woodland planted has been in the form of non-native coniferous tree species, particularly sitka spruce *Picea sitchensis*. In some parts of upland Britain, these recent conifer plantations cover very extensive areas of former moorland. The non-native broadleaved species, such as sycamore *Acer pseudoplatanus*, have also been widely planted on lower ground, but such plantations are rarely as large as those composed of conifers.

Further details of agricultural and forestry changes and policies, and their impact on the ecology of the uplands, are given in later sections. Since the 1980s, Agri-environment schemes have been implemented to provide incentives for land managers to conserve and enhance features of wildlife, landscape or archaeological interest. Details of these schemes are also given in the following sections.

2.8 Agriculture in the uplands

Agriculture is the dominant land use in the uplands. The main agricultural enterprises comprise sheep and beef, and the major influence on these enterprises is the implementation of the Common Agricultural Policy (CAP) in the UK including the system of LFAs. The chief vegetation types used by agriculture in the uplands comprise grassland, heathland, bog and woodland. Increasingly, the link between wildlife and land management is being made and Agri-environment schemes are being pursued.

Further information: English Nature 1997g.

2.8.1 Less Favoured Areas (LFAs)

LFAs were introduced in 1975 under the European Directive (75/268) on mountain and hill farming in certain areas. This Directive and its amendments have since been incorporated into Council Regulation (EC) 950/97, and are further amended by the Rural Development Regulation under Council Regulation (EC) 1257/99). The original objective of LFA policy was to "ensure the continuation of farming, thereby maintaining a minimum population level or conserving the countryside in certain less favoured areas".

Under the original Directive, three categories of LFA are defined. Broadly, these are mountain areas, areas in danger of depopulation, and other areas with specific handicaps. In the United Kingdom, all LFAs (with the exception of the Isles of Scilly) are designated under the second category (Article 24 of

Council Regulation (EC) 950/97. This essentially depends on the presence of land where agricultural productivity is low, economic results are lower than the national average, and there is a low or dwindling population reliant on agriculture.

For the purposes of UK legislation, there are two types of LFA, according to the severity of the handicaps of agricultural production. These are designated as the 'Severely Disadvantaged Areas' (SDA) and 'Disadvantaged Areas' (DA). In both types, agricultural production is either severely restricted or restricted in its range by virtue of the adverse soil, relief, aspect or climate, or by a combination of these. In England, 1,627,000 ha of the LFA are Severely Disadvantaged and 586,700 ha are Disadvantaged (I. Condliffe, pers comm).

Within the LFA boundary (Figure 1.1), farmers are eligible for financial assistance which is additional to the market support and structural incentives of the CAP. These include enhanced rates of grant and special payments for livestock farming (see 2.8.4 and Box 2.1).

LFA policy has recently been reviewed as part of the Rural Development Regulation under the EU's Agenda 2000 CAP reforms. This has led to a greater emphasis being placed on sustainable farming systems associated with maintaining and enhancing wildlife habitats in the uplands. Farmers will also have to follow "good farming practices compatible with the need to safeguard the environment and maintain the countryside". In line with the need to 'decouple' subsidy payments from production, the basis of payment for LFA subsidies (formerly the Hill Livestock Compensatory Allowances) will change under Agenda 2000. Payments under the new Hill Farm Allowance (HFA) Scheme will be made for each hectare of land rather than for each ewe or cow.

The English LFA covers some 2.2 million ha of which roughly 1.8 million ha is agricultural land. In total, the LFA covers around 17% of England, accounting for 19.6% of the agricultural area. The moorland line encloses some 0.8 million ha. Common land accounts for some 0.2 million ha of the agricultural land in the LFAs. There are approximately 17,000 agricultural holdings in the English LFA (MAFF 2000).

Further information: HMSO 1997; Glossary; National Economic Development Countil 1990; National Farmers Union 1997.

2.8.2 Grades and types of agricultural land

The MAFF Agricultural Land Classification (MAFF 1988) provides a framework for classifying land according to the extent to which its physical or chemical characteristics impose long-term limitations on agricultural use. The Agricultural Land Classification grades are described in Table 2.3 in terms of the types of limitation that can occur, typical cropping range and the expected level and consistency of yield.

Some 73.9% of all agricultural land in England and Wales is in Grades 1, 2 or 3, ie excellent to moderate quality (MAFF News Release 277/96). Within the LFA, agricultural land comprises a high proportion of Grade 4 and 5 land, ie poor or very poor agricultural land.

Land classification grades of increasing agricultural value generally represent decreasing nature conservation value, although there are important exceptions. For example, some of the very threatened and fragmented remnants of semi-natural habitat and associated populations occur on land of higher agricultural value. However, in general the environmental quality of a given piece of land will be strongly linked to its current use.

The following terms are frequently used to describe certain types of farmed land in the uplands:

- **In-bye land** - enclosed pasture and hay meadow, usually in the valley bottom and 'in by' the farm, which is accessible to farm machinery and may have been cultivated by ploughing, reseeding or fertilising.
- **Allotment or intake land** - enclosed land which usually consists of agriculturally poor- quality, unimproved pasture 'taken in' from the hill and consequently adjacent to moor or fell land (although it may also include some agriculturally improved land).
- **Moor or fell land** - unenclosed, unimproved grazings above the fell wall which consist of dwarf shrubs, blanket and other mires, grassland and montane vegetation.

Associations can be made between upland land-use types and the characteristic plant communities that appear within them. Table 2.4 identifies the vegetation types typically found within these land-use categories (Manley & Smith 1994), using the National Vegetation Classification (Rodwell 1991, 1992).

MAFF, the Department of the Environment, Transport and the Regions (DETR) and English Nature are currently examining alternative approaches to land classification in the uplands to more fully reflect the objectives of the Rural Development Regulation (RDR).

Further information: Section 2.10 on forestry in the uplands; Chapter 8 Woodland and scrub.

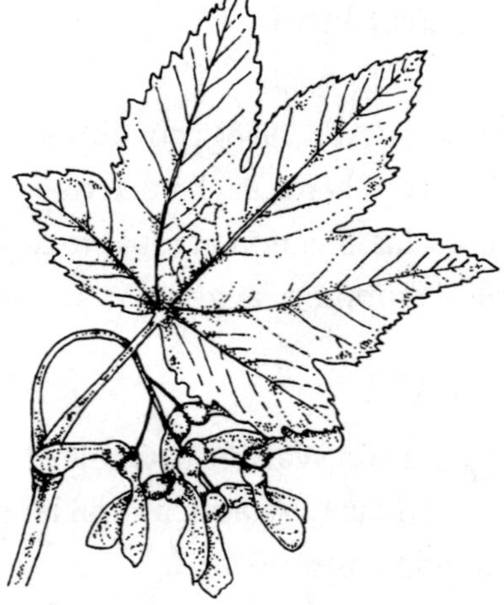

Table 2.3 **MAFF Agricultural Land Classification (ALC)**

Grade 1 - excellent quality agricultural land Land with no or very minor limitations to agricultural use. A very wide range of agricultural and horticultural crops can be grown and this commonly includes top fruit, soft fruit, salad crops and winter harvested vegetables. Yields are high and less variable than on land of lower quality. Estimated area of ALC grade within the LFA: 0.006%
Grade 2 - very good quality agricultural land Land with minor limitations which affect crop yield, cultivations or harvesting. A wider range of agricultural and horticultural crops can usually be grown, but on some land in the grade there may be reduced flexibility owing to difficulties with the production of the more demanding crops such as winter harvested vegetables and arable root crops. The level of yield is generally high but may be lower or more variable than Grade 1. Estimated area of ALC grade within the LFA: 0.5%
Grade 3 - good to moderate quality agricultural land Land with moderate limitations which affect the choice of crops, timing and type of cultivation, harvesting or the level of yield. Where more demanding crops are grown, yields are generally lower or more variable than on land in Grades 1 and 2. Estimated area of ALC grade within the LFA: 9.1% **Sub-grade 3a - good quality agricultural land** Land capable of consistently producing moderate to high yields of a narrow range of arable crops, especially cereals, or moderate yields of a wide range of crops including cereals, grass, oilseed rape, potatoes, sugar beet and the less demanding horticultural crops. **Sub-grade 3b - moderate quality agricultural land** Land capable of producing moderate yields of a narrow range of crops, principally cereals and grass, or lower yields of a wider range of crops, or high yields of grass which can be grazed or harvested over most of the year.
Grade 4 - poor quality agricultural land Land with severe limitations which significantly restrict the range of crops and/or level of yields. It is mainly suited to grass with occasional arable crops (eg cereals and forage crops) the yields of which are variable. In moist climates, yields of grass may be moderate to high but there may be difficulties in utilisation. The grade also includes very drought-prone arable land. Estimated area of ALC grade within the LFA: 37.5%
Grade 5 - very poor quality agricultural land Land with very severe limitations which restrict use to permanent pasture or rough grazing, except for occasional pioneer forage crops. Estimated area of ALC grade within the LFA: 46.6%

Source: MAFF 1988

2.8.3 Agricultural enterprises

Agricultural enterprises in the uplands depend primarily on hill sheep and suckler cows. However, dairy farming also occurs in some areas, particularly the White Peak and around the fringes of higher land in other Natural Areas. There is also limited arable, mixed and organic farming. The type of livestock farming practised depends heavily on the nature of the land available. For example, the North Pennines Natural Area contains nearly 60% Grade 5 agricultural land and supports mostly sheep and mixed sheep and cattle enterprises. In contrast, the Oswestry Uplands Natural Area comprises 60%

Grade 3 and above land, and this Natural Area supports predominantly dairy farms (information based on Parish Statistics).

Upland farming is generally a low input - low output system. The amount of energy, in terms of feed and chemicals, imported into the uplands is usually low, although this has been increasing since the World War II. Where winter feed cannot be made on the farm, it has to be bought in, or stock must be sold off in autumn or wintered away on lowland farms. This allows the maximum use of summer grazings while reducing the number of mouths to be fed in the winter (Haines 1982). Farms in the LFA generally do not produce animals for immediate slaughter (ie finished), but produce the store stock which is fattened, or used for breeding other stock for fattening, on lowland farms. However, increasingly in some areas, farms are finishing stock themselves rather than producing store animals.

In 1997 there were 22,056 LFA farms in England (Parsisson and Moxey 1999). Of these, some 46.2% were full-time and 53.8% were part-time holdings. Over the period 1990-1997, there was a reduction in the number of full-time farmers in the English LFA (Parliamentary Question 28/798). This trend is broadly consistent with the overall decline in the number of farmers in agriculture generally. Despite the large area covered by the average LFA farm, 40% had a business size less than the minimum considered sufficient to maintain a full-time holding (Parliamentary Question 24/5/97). Average net farm income (NFI) for LFA cattle and sheep farms in England has fallen by 76% from its peak in 1996/97. The continuing strength of the Pound relative to the European Currency Unit (later the Euro) over the period has been a factor in the drop in farm incomes.

For cattle and sheep farms in the LFAs in England, net farm income has fallen 27% in 1999/00 and 47% the previous year. The fall in incomes in 1999/00 was due in the main to a fall in sheep enterprise output, reflecting year on year declines in sheep prices and a fall in Sheep Annual Premium receipts. For dairy farms in England (including lowland), NFI fell by 35% in 1999/00, a fall of 78% from the peak of 1995/96. In addition to the strength of sterling, low market prices and the knock-on effects of BSE have all contributed to a continuing decline in upland farm incomes. Incomes on LFA farms are notoriously erratic and, when compared with other agricultural sectors such as dairy, cereals and cropping, remain low.

After land and buildings, livestock represent the bulk of the farmer's capital, and livestock subsidies, the sale of livestock and related products form the majority of the revenue. There is a mixture of financial support mechanisms for these enterprises and farm incomes in the LFAs are underpinned by European and UK agricultural policy.

Further information: 2.8.4 and Box 2.1; Glossary; Information Notes 2-5; Nix annual publication; Scottish Agricultural College annual publication.

Upland and hill farms

The farming systems prevalent in the uplands fall into two categories: hill farms and upland farms. These largely correspond to the productivity of the land; upland farms are more productive and more likely to support a mixed livestock enterprise.

In England, true hill farms are confined to the North Pennines, the Bowland Fells, Dartmoor, the North York Moors and the Lake District fells. These farms concentrate on sheep production through self-replenishing flocks. They consist predominantly of rough grazing land, mainly composed of unenclosed, unimproved moorland and allotment, perhaps with some permanent or long-term grassland, and little in-bye land.

Upland farms are more productive and are more likely to support a mixed livestock enterprise. These farms have a greater proportion of enclosed in-bye and agriculturally improved grassland; between 10-60% of the farm area (Felton & Marsden 1990). This makes them better able to support more demanding livestock than that found on hill farms, such as upland-lowland cross-bred ewes and suckler cows. Some dairy cattle may also be kept. In-bye land may also be used for making conserved fodder (silage, hay) and fattening lambs, although beef cattle are generally sold off for fattening on lowland farms.

For hill and upland sheep enterprises income typically comprises of:

- lamb, draft ewe and wool sales;
- Sheep Annual Premium (SAP);
- Hill Livestock Compensatory Allowances (HLCA) (now Hill Farm Allowance) – see 2.8.4.

For hill and upland beef enterprises, it is typically based on an income comprised of:

- calf sales;
- Suckler Cow Premium (SCP);
- Beef Special Premium (BSP);
- Hill Livestock Compensatory Allowances (HLCA) (now Hill Farm Allowance).

Payments from environmental schemes are becoming increasing important sources of income in some areas and farmers are increasingly looking to supplement incomes from diversification.

The sheep enterprise

Sheep production is the major agricultural activity in upland England and is central to the economy and ecology of these areas. Over the last 50 years, technical innovations and the implementation of government policy have combined to change the upland sheep industry.

Each of the British hill areas has its own breed of sheep, many of whose names indicate their origin - Swaledale, Scottish blackface, Welsh mountain. These produce hardy ewes which are able to survive in harsh conditions and have good mothering tendencies. They are not usually as productive as the sheep breeds found in the lowlands and lambing percentages are generally low.

The simplest sheep farming system practised is the rearing of store sheep, where lambs are born in spring and remain with their mothers until weaning in late summer. The lambs are then sold off the farm as store lambs at special sales held in the autumn. These animals are bought by farmers with land at lower altitudes and will be fattened there before slaughter. The rationale behind this system is that there is insufficient grazing available by late summer to bring lambs into a finished condition, ie fit for slaughter. In recent years some of these lambs have been sold for export and more upland farmers are finishing their own animals.

On hill farms, a proportion of the ewe lambs are normally kept for breeding in the home flock. This perpetuates the self-sustaining flock and only rams are bought in. Ewes are generally sold from the hill flock at between four and five years old, when they are considered too old to continue to thrive in the hills. These ewes are not sold for slaughter, but as draft ewes which go for further breeding on upland and lowland farms where they respond well to the improved conditions.

Although sheep graze hills with few or no stock proof boundaries, the flocks generally graze the same piece of land. The home range of a discrete group of sheep is called the heft (or heaf), and this term can also be used to describe a section of the flock. Lambs learn from their mothers to keep to this area. However, in some areas this hefting ability is being lost, exacerbated by the decline in shepherding and the increase in supplementary feeding. The result is that the nature and pattern of sheep grazing on the hills has radically changed since World War II. Along with increases in numbers of sheep, this has contributed to overgrazing.

The hefted flock is generally sold along with the farm, and is called 'bound to the ground' or 'a bound flock'. This is because a new flock would wander and not know where to find shelter or food in severe weather. During the winter, some flocks are moved on to lower ground, but many remain on the unenclosed land throughout.

Further information: 2.8.4 and Box 2.1; Information Notes 2 and 3 on sheep breeds and farming systems.

The beef enterprise

In the English uplands, beef farming usually involves producing suckler calves and rearing store cattle. Suckler calves are usually born in spring and remain with their mothers until weaning in late summer and sale in the autumn. Some are born in the autumn and remain with the cow for the next 6-10 months. At this stage, they are not fit for slaughter (not finished) because they are too small, and have to be fed for at least an extra year before being slaughtered. This is usually not possible on an upland farm, where there is insufficient feed to carry calves in addition to the breeding stock over the winter. The young animals are therefore sold as store cattle to lowland farms for finishing. The breeding cows are usually kept on in-bye land or housed over the winter.

Further information: 2.8.4 and Box 2.1; Information Notes 4 and 5 on cattle breeds and farming systems.

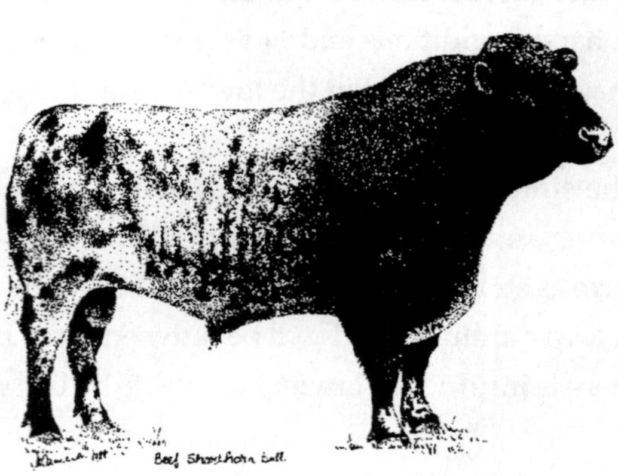

Table 2.4 Upland land use types and their associated semi-natural NVC communities (excluding woodland and scrub)

NVC code	NVC name	In-bye	Intake (Allotment)	Moor or Fell	Montane
	Heaths				
H4	*Ulex gallii-Agrostis curtisii* heath		✔	✔	
H8	*Calluna vulgaris-Ulex gallii* heath			✔	
H9	*Calluna vulgaris-Deschampsia flexuosa* heath		✔	✔	
H10	*Calluna vulgaris-Erica cinerea* heath		✔	✔	
H12	*Calluna vulgaris-Vaccinium myrtillus* heath		✔	✔	
H18	*Vaccinium myrtillus-Deschampsia flexuosa* moss-heath		✔	✔	✔
H19	*Vaccinium myrtillus-Cladonia arbuscula* heath				✔
H21	*Calluna vulgaris-Vaccinium myrtillus-Sphagnum capillifolium* heath		✔	✔	
	Mires				
M1	*Sphagnum auriculatum* bog pool community		✔	✔	
M2	*Sphagnum cuspidatum/recurvum* bog pool community			✔	
M3	*Eriophorum angustifolium* bog pool comunity			✔	
M4	*Carex rostrata-Sphagnum recurvum* mire		✔	✔	
M6	*Carex echinata-Sphagnum auriculatum/recurvum* mire		✔	✔	
M8	*Carex rostrata-Sphagnum warnstorfii* mire				✔
M10	*Carex dioica-Pinguicula vulgaris* mire	✔	✔	✔	
M15	*Scirpus cespitosus-Erica tetralix* wet heath		✔	✔	
M16	*Erica tetralix-Sphagnum compactum* wet heath		✔	✔	
M17	*Scirpus cespitosus-Eriophorum vaginatum* blanket mire		✔	✔	
M18	*Erica tetralix-Sphagnum papillosum* raised and blanket mire			✔	
M19	*Calluna vulgaris-Eriophorum vaginatum* blanket mire		✔	✔	
M20	*Eriophorum vaginatum* blanket and raised mire		✔	✔	
M23	*Juncus effusus/acutiflorus-Galium palustre* rush pasture	✔	✔	✔	
M25	*Molinia caerulea-Potentilla erecta* mire	✔	✔	✔	
M26	*Molinia caerulea-Crepis paludosa* mire	✔	✔		
M32	*Philonotis fontana-Saxifraga stellaris* spring		✔	✔	
	Acid grasslands				
U3	*Agrostis curtisii* grassland		✔	✔	
U4	*Festuca ovina-Agrostis capillaris*	✔	✔	✔	
U5	*Nardus stricta-Galium saxatile* grassland		✔	✔	
U6	*Juncus squarrosus-Festuca ovina* grassland		✔	✔	
U7	*Nardus stricta-Carex bigelowii* grass heath				✔
U10	*Carex bigelowii-Racomitrium lanuginosum* moss heath				✔
U15	*Saxifraga aizoides-Alchemilla glabra* banks				✔
U16	*Luzula sylvatica-Vaccinium myrtillus* tall herb community				✔
U17	*Luzula sylvatica-Geum rivale* tall herb community				✔

NVC code	NVC name	In-bye	Intake (Allotment)	Moor or Fell	Montane
U20	*Pteridium aquilinum-Galium saxatile* community		✔	✔	
	Calcareous grasslands				
CG9	*Sesleria albicans-Galium sterneri* grassland	✔	✔	✔	
CG10	*Festuca ovina-Agrostis capillaris - Thymus praecox* grassland	✔	✔	✔	
CG11	*Festuca ovina-Agrostis capillaris-Alchemilla alpina* grass heath				✔
	Mesotrophic grasslands				
MG3	*Anthoxanthum odoratum-Geranium sylvaticum* grassland	✔			
MG5	*Cynosurus cristatus-Centaurea nigra* grassland	✔			
MG6	*Lolium perenne-Cynosurus cristatus* grassland	✔			
MG7	*Lolium perenne* leys and related grasslands	✔			
MG8	*Cynosurus cristatus-Caltha palustris* grassland	✔			
MG9	*Holcus lanatus-Deschampsia cespitosa* grassland	✔			
MG10	*Holcus lanatus-Juncus effusus* rush pasture	✔			

Source: Manley & Smith 1994; Rodwell 1991b, 1992.

2.8.4 Agricultural policy

With agriculture the dominant force in the uplands and wildlife value very much dependent on the type of land management practised, agricultural policy is critical in maintaining and enhancing the natural heritage of the uplands. The links between agriculture and wildlife have become increasingly recognised and future developments in agricultural policy are likely to strengthen them still further.

In the UK, the agricultural support system is determined by the Common Agricultural Policy (CAP, see below) and the UK Government's policies. The CAP is influenced by the General Agreement on Tariffs and Trade (GATT) and the World Trade Organisation (WTO), and is implemented by the UK Government. The parts of CAP most relevant to the uplands are those relating to the beef and sheepmeat regimes, provisions on improving the efficiency of agricultural structures and the Rural Development Regulation. All these terms and their implications are explained below. Implementation of the Agenda 2000 agreement on CAP Reform will have considerable influence on agricultural and rural development policy in the future.

Further information: Box 2.1

The General Agreement on Tariffs and Trade (GATT)

The General Agreement on Tariffs and Trade (GATT) was first signed in 1947 by 23 countries and came into force in January 1948. The next round of discussions on the future of world trade will occur in the **World Trade Organisation (WTO)** talks, and commenced in 2000. The WTO is the body that was established following the conclusion of the GATT Uruguay Round in 1993 to progress the debate on the liberalisation of world trade. The WTO was set up in January 1995 as the new and more powerful successor to the GATT, which has now ceased to exist. GATT's functions have passed to the WTO, but the name is still used to refer to the 1994 trade agreement which resulted from the Uruguay Round. The GATT's membership has grown to 128 countries and several countries are currently going through the WTO process.

The next WTO round will cover further liberalisation measures for agriculture, including further cuts in agricultural support, tariffs and export subsidies. It will determine the policies that will apply to world trade, and therefore agriculture, thereafter.

The Common Agricultural Policy (CAP)

For more than 30 years, agricultural production in the European Union (EU) has been governed by the Common Agricultural Policy (CAP). The original objectives of the CAP are specified in Article 39 of the 1957 Treaty of Rome, and are as follows:

- to increase agricultural productivity by promoting technical progress and by ensuring the rational development of agricultural production and the optimal utilisation of the factors of production, in particular labour;
- to ensure a fair standard of living for the agricultural community, in particular by increasing the individual earnings of persons engaged in agriculture;
- to stabilise markets;
- to ensure stability of supplies;
- to ensure that supplies reach consumers at reasonable prices.

The main reason for such government intervention policies was (and still is) considered to be to encourage agricultural productivity so as to ensure farmers a satisfactory and equitable standard of living, and to stabilise agricultural markets and farmers' incomes (Brouwer & van Berkum 1996). No objectives relating to the environment and nature are specified in Article 39 of the Treaty of the European Union, nor in other Articles of the separate agriculture section of the Treaty (Articles 38-47).

Traditionally the CAP objectives have been achieved through a range of measures, such as guaranteed prices to farmers, quotas, tariffs on imports and subsidies for exports. It provides the financial support mechanisms for farmers and the framework within which they operate.

A number of important developments have occurred in recent years, including the MacSharry reforms of the CAP which were agreed in 1992, the GATT agreement in 1994 and the enlargement of the EU and now Agenda 2000. The 1992 reform of the CAP, together with the GATT agreement (see below), set firm rules which currently govern the trading relationships of the EU and the rest of the world.

The **MacSharry reforms** of the CAP in 1992 had wide-ranging implications throughout agriculture in Britain. Some of their aims were to improve the competitiveness of EU agriculture, to restore market balance and to stimulate less intensive production methods (Brouwer & van Berkum 1996). Measures adopted were aimed at reducing surplus production, reducing price support and improving the environmental soundness of agricultural production. In connection with the last aim, the reforms included a requirement for all European Union Member States to set into operation a programme to encourage environmentally sensitive farming, forestry and provisions for early retirement. These are the **Accompanying Measures** - the Agri-Environment Regulation, an Afforestation Regulation and an Early Retirement Regulation. In the UK, the Government decided not to implement the retirement option because it was not felt to be necessary. The forestry option was adopted, and was felt to be covered by existing woodland grant schemes. The **Agri-Environment Regulation** provides for a financial aid scheme to encourage farmers to introduce or continue farming practices which are compatible with the protection of the environment and management of the countryside. The UK Government is currently implementing this via the Agri-Environment Programme (see 2.8.5 on agri-environment schemes).

Currently, most of the funding available to agriculture goes directly to Commodity support, while the Accompanying Measures receive minimal funding by comparison. Spending in the UK under the CAP was £3,193 million in 1998/9 and was forecast to fall in 1999/2000 to £2,924 million. This reduction occurs mainly in connection with a fall in BSE-related expenditure. Other expenditure on agricultural support schemes in the UK is estimated to be £248.5 million in 1999/2000 compared with £388.7 million in 1998/99. This expenditure includes grants for conservation, exchequer funding of accompanying measures and assistance for agriculture in special areas. Included in this is expenditure on agri-environment schemes which, in England, are expected to reach £87.4 million in 1999/2000 compared with £44 million in 1996/97.

Successive governments have recognised the need to continue efforts to reform the CAP, with payment directed more towards the encouragement of environmentally beneficial and sustainable farming (Cole, Kernon & Knightbridge 1996). There also appears to be a growing consensus that a further liberalisation of agricultural trade is inevitable in the years ahead, which could require the dismantling of farm support policies. The major external pressures for CAP reform include future pressure from the WTO (see under GATT below) to remove production subsidies to balance world trade and the costs of accession of Central and Eastern European countries to the EU. Other factors exacerbating budgetary pressures are changes in consumption patterns and levels, the general constraints on government expenditure, and deficits and debt levels for the EU countries preparing for European Monetary Union.

Agenda 2000

In July 1997 the European Commission (EC) published *Agenda 2000: for a stronger and wider Europe*. The primary aim of Agenda 2000 was to deepen the reforms of the CAP started in 1992, in preparation for the next round of WTO negotiations and the enlargement of the EU. The UK Government published draft regulations for reform in this country in 1998 and a consultation process followed. Agenda 2000 is intended to run from 1 January 2000 through to 2006.

The Agenda 2000 CAP reform proposals were agreed in March 1999 and their implementation commenced on 1 January 2000. This has been an attempt by the EU to alter fundamentally the balance of subsidies away from production-based payments and towards an integrated approach to the rural economy. Minor reforms have been made to the arable, beef and dairy regimes although, unfortunately, there has been no reform of the sheepmeat regime. The new Rural Development Regulation or 'Second pillar' of the CAP includes changes to measures on LFAs, agri-environment measures and afforestation of agricultural land. Of particular note are:

- provision for the introduction of environmental conditions across all commodity regimes;
- provision for 'modulation' on direct payments to release money for agri-environment schemes;
- arrangements for changing LFA support from HLCA headage based payments to an area basis and linked to environmentally sustainable farming (the new Hill Farm Allowance Scheme);
- potential for using the 'beef national envelope' to encourage extensive beef production;
- extension of rural development measures, including in England new measures on enteprise and training beyond the farm-gate.

The main instruments of the European Union (EU) beef and sheepmeat regimes, as implemented in the UK, are the various livestock subsidies and the intervention arrangements for beef. These policies concentrate on maintaining the farming community through direct payments on livestock production, in the form of headage payments on breeding ewes and cattle, and price support measures. However, some elements of these have changed as a result of Agenda 2000 with a move away from headage payments towards area-based payments. Other elements will also change.

Further information: Brouwer & van Berkum 1996; English Nature *et al* 1998; English Nature, Countryside Agency and Countryside Council for Wales 1999.

Livestock quota

Livestock quotas form part of the CAP livestock commodity regimes and were introduced in 1993 to control the level of meat production and the cost of the CAP. Farmers can only claim Sheep Annual Premium and Suckler Cow Premium for the number of animals for which they hold quota (Box 2.1 and below).

Sheep and beef quota was originally allocated to producers, based on the number of animals they had at a given time (the reference year). A national quota reserve now operates to distribute surrendered quota. The quota is tied to the producer not the holding and is fully transferable by sale or lease. However, sheep quota is 'ring-fenced', which in the UK means that quota allocated to an LFA lamb producer cannot be transferred out of the LFA. The exception is quota made available through participation in an extensification programme (see Box 2.2). Farmers are then allowed to transfer sheep quota to lowland producers in other environmental schemes requiring the reversion of arable land to grass.

From 1998 onwards, producers were allowed to lease out sheep quota for a period of one, two or three years, and after the leasing period, there had to be a gap of at least two years. The intention of this rule was to ensure that producers used their quota for claiming premium, and to prevent them from leasing out quota indefinitely. Another rule prevented a recipient of national reserve quota from leasing out any quota in the year of receipt and in the following two years.

Sheep quota allocations are equal to the number of ewe premiums paid to a producer in 1991, provided that a claim was also made in 1992. There are rules relating to sheep quota sale and leasing, quota transfer, non-use of existing quota, and allocation of quota from the reserve. Special rules apply to those farmers who have reduced sheep numbers owing to participation in an environmental scheme, such as Environmentally Sensitive Area Schemes, the Countryside Stewardship Scheme and the now defunct Moorland Scheme (Box 2.2).

Suckler cow quota exists for Suckler Cow Premiums and individual producer's quotas were based on the number of eligible cows on the farm in 1992, minus 1% to provide for a national reserve. There is no upper limit to the amount of quota an individual producer can hold. As with sheep, transfers of quota without land or with part of a holding are subject to a siphon into the national reserve of 15%.

Member States are limited on the total number of animals receiving Beef Special Premium (see Box 2.1).

Overgrazing and environmental conditions

Environmental conditions are attached to all the main livestock and hill subsidy schemes (Hill Livestock Compensatory Allowances (now HFA), Sheep Annual Premium, Suckler Cow Premium and Beef Special Premium, see MAFF 1996b). The Government concluded in the early 1990s that headage payments could not be allowed to encourage overgrazing or the use of unsuitable supplementary feeding which would cause significant environmental damage. The UK, therefore, sought and obtained EU legislation to enable Member States to introduce environmental cross-compliance measures into livestock schemes.

For the purposes of the livestock schemes, overgrazing is legally defined as:

".... grazing land with livestock in such numbers as adversely to affect the growth, quality or species composition of vegetation (other than vegetation normally grazed to destruction) on that land to a significant degree."

Unsuitable supplementary feeding is defined as:

". . . . providing supplementary feed (other than to maintain livestock during abnormal weather conditions) in such a manner as to result in damage to vegetation through excessive trampling or poaching of the land by animals or excessive rutting of vehicles."

Before 1992, the term 'overgrazing' was used by agriculturalists to indicate when sheep health was threatened due to the inadequate provision of nutrition. Regulations governing the HLCA subsidies inferred 'overgrazing' when "poor animal condition and sustained undue recourse to supplementary feed" occurred. Since 1992, the definition of overgrazing was extended to cover damage to the quality or diversity of the vegetation, as defined above.

English Nature has devised a method for assessing whether heather moorland is being grazed sustainably (English Nature 1995b) and this is used by the Farming and Rural Conservation Agency (RCA) and MAFF as the basis for environmental cross-compliance measures.

Box 2.1 The main instruments of the European Union (EU) meat regime as implemented in the UK

Each of the main livestock schemes (Sheep Annual Premium, Beef Special Premium, Suckler Cow Premium and Hill Livestock Compensatory Allowance Scheme - now the Hill Farm Allowance Scheme) has rules that enable MAFF to reduce or withdraw premium payments if overgrazing or unsuitable supplementary feeding takes place.

Sheep Annual Premium (SAP)

Under the sheepmeat regime, premium payments come from the EU, and via MAFF, to producers in England. This market support mechanism aims to cover the difference between the representative market price of lambs, as calculated for the EU as a whole, and the annual support price set by the EU (the Basic Price). Advance payments are made based on estimated prices for the marketing year. There is an additional supplement payable to qualified Less Favoured Area (LFA) producers.

Payment of ewe premium is restricted by the amount of quota held by the producer. It is paid on a per head basis on eligible ewes at least 12 months old on the last day of the retention period (15 May) or which have given birth to a lamb by that date. Farmers must keep at least 10 sheep and they must be kept for the 100 days retention period which runs from midnight 4 February to midnight on 15 May.

SAP payments are not subject to a stocking rate limit. This makes it worthwhile for farmers to have as many sheep as is feasible (but subject to the overgrazing rules), given the quota, technical and financial limitations imposed by the individual business.

Beef special premium (BSP)

This scheme forms part of the beef regime and is administered in England by MAFF. The premium is paid on male beef cattle. Premium may be claimed twice in the life of a steer (castrated animal) and once in the life of a bull (uncastrated animal). The first application for a steer may be made when the animal is at least seven months old **and** under 20 months. For the second application steers must be at least 20 months old. Bulls must be at least seven months old when the application is made; there is no upper age limit. Producers may submit no more than 12 claim forms each year.

There is no upper limit on the number of animals, in each age range, claimed in any one year. The previous limit of 90 animals in each age roup has been abolished. Payment is conditional on cattle being retained on a holding for two months following a claim and on stocking density restrictions.

Member States are limited on the total number of animals receiving Premium, if the limit is exceeded the payments will be reduced to bring the claimed animals down to the UK limit.

Producers claiming on a total of 30 animals or less are exempt from this reduction.

Box 2.1 The main instruments of the European Union (EU) meat regime as implemented in the UK (continued)

Suckler cow premium (SCP)

The purpose of this scheme, which forms part of the EU beef regime, is to support the incomes of specialist beef producers. Premium is fully funded by the EC and is paid on suckler cows belonging to a herd used for rearing calves for meat production. For the 2000 scheme, the premium rate per suckler cow is £102.15. The scheme opens for claims each year generally on 1 July to 6 December, with late claims accepted up to 31 December subject to penalties. Eligible animals are cows of a meat producing breed or the offspring of a cross with at least one parent being an animal of a meat producing breed or beef/dairy cross. Dairy cows are not eligible for premium and farmers must not sell or deliver milk products from their holding. However, the scheme is open to small dairy producers who hold no more than 180,000 kg (174,780 litres) of milk quota.

Animals on which premium is claimed must be kept on the producer's holding for a retention period of 6 months. In-calf heifers can be used as replacements for suckler cows lost or disposed of during the retention period.

Premium payments are limited by the number of units of quota held by a producer and are also restricted by a maximum stocking density limit of 2 LUs per hectare of forage area. There is no LFA premium and MAFF administers the scheme in England.

Under Agenda 2000 reforms from 1 January 2000, UK SCP quota has been reduced by 5.5%. Also, claims can include up to 20% heifers.

Extensification Payment Scheme (EPS)

An extensification payment is available to farmers who receive Beef Special Premium (BSP) or Suckler Cow Premium (SCP), and who meet specific stocking density levels. Producers must indicate their intention to claim Extensification payments at Section 5 of form IACS 2 (2001) or Section 4 of form IACS 2 (F) (Forage) (2001) for 'Forage - Only Farmers'.

Claims are assessed on the basis of Livestock Units (LUs) per hectare (Ha). LUs are allocated to all bovine animals aged six months or over on farm and sheep claimed under the Sheep Annual Premium Scheme.

Two Scheme options exist: 'Standard' and 'Simplified'. The Standard option requires the average stocking density for the year to be equal to or below a specific level. This is determined by assessing the Livestock Units on a producer's holding on six census dates. Census dates are chosen randomly throughout the year within two month periods (ie a date for January/February, a date for March/April etc) and are announced retrospectively. The Simplified option requires the producer to maintain stocking density equal to or below a specified level throughout the year.

Box 2.1 The main instruments of the European Union meat regime as implemented in the UK (continued)

Slaughter Premium Scheme (SPS)

Introduced in January 2000, Slaughter Premium provides direct support to all producers of domestic cattle and operates on a calendar year basis.

The Scheme is divided into two categories: the Slaughter Premium Scheme (SPS) and the Veal Calf Slaughter Premium Scheme (VCSPS). Each scheme has a limit to the number of animals which may be claimed in the UK. If the limits are exceeded payments will be reduced to bring the claimed animals down to the UK limit.

SPS further divides by age: TUM (animals over eight and under thirty months of age) and OTM (over thirty month) animals. In England, MAFF Regional Service Centres (RSCs) operate the scheme for UTM cattle and the Intervention Board operates the scheme for OTM cattle.

To be eligible for SPS, cattle must be kept on the holding for a retention period of two months immediately prior to slaughter, must be slaughtered within one month of leaving the holding and must be claimed on within six months of leaving the holding for slaughter.

VCSPS is payable on calves of more than one and less than seven months of age, with a carcase weight of less than 160 kg. For calves more than one and less than three months old, the retention period is one month. Calves aged three to six months old (inclusive) must be retained on farm for two months immediately prior to leaving the holding for slaughter. The period in which slaughter must take place and claims be submitted is the same as for SPS. All claims in England must be submitted to Worcester RSC.

A maximum of 12 claim forms may be submitted for each element of the Scheme: ie 12 claim forms for VCSPS, 12 for under 30 month cattle and 12 for over thirty month cattle.

Hill Farm Allowance Scheme (HFA) in England

The new area-based HFA scheme replaced the headage-based Hill Livestock Compensatory Allowance Scheme in 2001 as part of Agenda 2000. Different arrangements apply in the different countries of the United Kingdom.

The HFA scheme is designed to supplement the income of farmers in the Less Favoured Areas. It aims to "contribute to the maintenance of the social fabric in upland communities through support for continued agricultural land use, and to help preserve the farmed upland environment by ensuring that land in LFAs is managed in a sustainable way". Payments are part-funded by the EU under the Rural Development Regulation 1257/1999.

Payments are made per hectare and have three elements: basic payment per hectare of eligible LFA forage land, 'environmental enhancement' payments of 10 or 20%, and extra payments under a 'safety net' for the first three years of the scheme. The basic payment is paid at different rates for moorland (as defined by the Moorland Line) and common land, non-moorland SDA and non-moorland DA land. Payments also differ according to farm size.

HFA claimants must be IACS-registered, have the use of at least 10 hectares of eligible LFA forage area and keep breeding sheep and/or suckler cows. In addition, there is a minimum stocking density of 0.15 LU/ha (although those in a recognised environmental scheme may stock at a lower density) and farmers must follow 'Good Farming Practice' as defined in the England Rural Development Programme.

Agenda 2000 reforms has focussed LFA payments more explicitly on environmentally sustainable farming systems. Payments under the new Hill Farm Allowance Scheme will be paid on an area-basis rather than per head of livestock as under current HLCAs to farmers following "usual good farming practices compatible with the need to safeguard the environment and maintain the countryside. . . ."

2.8.5 Environmental land management schemes

The largest environmental land management schemes are implemented under EC Regulation 1257/99 (the Rural Development Regulation) which aims to encourage agricultural production methods compatible with the requirements of the protection of the environment and the maintenance of the countryside. These schemes are operated under EC rules and have to be approved by the Commission but there is considerable national flexibility as to the details. Expenditure is funded partly by the EC and partly through national budgets. In 1999-2000 some £86 million was spent in England on payments to farmers under agri-environment schemes. The schemes are all subject to regular review.

Modulation, whereby Member States can 'recycle' a proportion of direct CAP payments to farmers into certain measures of the Rural Development Regulation, will provide significant additional resources for the agri-environment programme. For example, expenditure on agri-environment schemes in England is expected to total £1 billion over the seven years of the England Rural Development Programme.

Agri-environment schemes in the English uplands comprise:

- Environmentally Sensitive Areas Scheme (see also Box 2.2 and Table 2.5);
- Countryside Stewardship Scheme (including elements of the now defunct Moorland Scheme) (see also Box 2.2);
- Organic Farming Scheme (see also Box 2.2).

A number of other environmental land management schemes also are relevant to the uplands. These include nature conservation project grants and the Wildlife Enhancement Scheme operated by English Nature, woodland schemes operated by the Forestry Commission and MAFF and part funded by the EC, Objective 5b grants in designated areas funded by the EC (now replaced by the Rural Enterprise Scheme), LIFE funding from the EC and a wide range of grants and schemes from National Park Authorities and local authorities.

Agri-environment schemes are likely to become more important in the future; they are the only compulsory element of Agenda 2000's Rural Development Regulation.

Details of these environmental land management schemes and grants are given in Boxes 2.2 and 2.3.

Table 2.5 Upland Environmentally Sensitive Areas (ESAs) in England

ESA	Principal habitat types	Total eligible area (ha)
Tranche I - designated 1987		
Pennine Dales	Hay meadows, pastures & allotments	39,100
West Penwith	Moorland, in-bye pasture (plus archaeological interest)	6,900
Tranche II - designated 1988		
North Peak	Heather moorland, shrubby heath, in-bye grassland, rough grazing	50,500
Clun	Hay meadows, oak woods	18,900
Tranche III - designated 1993		
Exmoor	Heather & grass moorland, grassland	67,700
Lake District	Grass & heather moorland, meadows & pastures. lowland, wetland	219,300
South West Peak	Heather & grass moorland, grassland	27,000
Tranche IV - designated 1994		
Dartmoor	Heather & grass moorland, grassland	89,000
Shropshire Hills	Moorland, grassland	34,900

Box 2.2 Agri-environment schemes available in the English uplands

Environmentally Sensitive Areas (ESAs)

Aim:	Provide incentives for farmers to follow prescribed environmentally beneficial agricultural practices and to reduce pressure on 'traditional farming systems'.
Administration:	Designated, funded and administered by MAFF.
Date of launch:	First ESAs designated in 1987, followed by further designations in 1988, 1993 and 1994.
Target areas:	Nine existing upland ESAs (total number 22), covering a wide variety of habitats and features, as shown below.
Habitat types:	See Table 2.2.
Mechanism:	Voluntary management agreements with participating farmers, some covering the whole farm holding, others covering only part of the holding.
Agreement contents:	A wide range of management requirements and restrictions.
Additional options:	Conservation plan grants for capital works, eg tree planting, hedgerow management, repair of stone walls and traditional buildings, and bracken control. Public access tier to provide new opportunities for public access and other quiet recreation.
Agreement period:	10 years, with an optional break clause after five years.
Scheme review dates:	England Rural Development Plan (RDP) mid term, and at end of seven year plan.
Total area:	22 existing ESAs in England cover some 10% of the agricultural land area. See below for eligible areas in upland ESAs.
Percentage take up:	See Table 2.4.
Cost of scheme:	£41 m in 1999/2000 and likely to remain more or less constant in the next few years.

Box 2.2 Agri-environment schemes available in the English uplands (continued)

Countryside Stewardship Scheme

Aim:	Provide incentives for land managers to follow prescribed environmentally beneficial agricultural practices.
Administration:	Funded and administered by MAFF.
Date of launch:	First launched in 1991. Enhanced upland options launched in 1999.
Target areas:	Nationwide, landscape types rather than designated areas.
Habitat types:	Landscape types include uplands, chalk & limestone grassland, lowland heath, watersides, coast, historic landscapes, old traditional orchards, old meadows and pastures, the countryside around towns and Community Forests, traditional field boundaries and the margins of arable fields. Upland landscape category includes moorland restoration, conversion of agriculturally improved land to moorland, restoration and conservation of upland hay meadows, restoration and conservation of in-bye, intake or allotment pastures, protection of archaeological and historic remains, restoration of landscape features, eg hedgerows, stone walls & gill woodlands and improved opportunities for public access.
Mechanism:	Voluntary management agreements with participating farmers, covering the features concerned. While it is not a whole farm scheme, it does promote good conservation management on all land managed by the applicant.
Agreement contents:	A wide range of management requirements and restrictions to protect, enhance and re-create features on the land.
Additional options:	Capital grants, such as for the restoration of ponds and field boundaries such as stone walls and hedge banks, hedgerow management, tree and shrub planting and management, scrub management, bracken control and the provision of fencing and water supplies. Public access tier to provide new opportunities for public access and other quiet recreation. Under the new option introduced in 1999 a whole farm upland survey is required and must accompany any applications for Countryside Stewardship.
Agreement period:	10 years, with no five-year break clause.
Cost of scheme:	£35.5 million allocated for 2000/01, rising to £126 million in 2006/07.

Box 2.2 Agri-environment schemes available in the English uplands (continued)

Moorland Scheme

This scheme closed in 1998 and is now incorporated into the Countryside Stewardship Scheme under the upland options.

Aim:	To encourage the conservation and enhancement of heather and other shrubby moorland vegetation.
Administration:	Funded and administered by MAFF.
Date of launch:	First launched in 1995.
Target areas:	Available to producers farming heather moorland in LFAs but outside ESAs, with moorland grazing units shown on the Moorland Map of England 1992 (MAFF), of at least 20 ha in size and with at least 25% heather coverage (including other dwarf shrubs).
Mechanism:	Voluntary management agreements with participating farmers, who received an annual payment for the removal of each ewe eligible for HLCA payments.
Agreement contents:	Stocking levels at certain set limits and an agreed moorland management plan covering heather cutting and burning, shepherding, supplementary feeding and erection of temporary fencing. On non-heather moorland, further rules applied to the use of pesticides and fertilisers, cultivation operations, fencing, drainage, and to features such as farm buildings, boundaries, historic and archaeological features, watercourses, ponds, pastures and meadows, and woodland and hedges.
Additional options:	Additional stock reductions paid for if environmental benefits resulted. Capital grants for, eg temporary fencing, bracken spraying.
Agreement period:	Five years.
Scheme review dates:	Three years from launch, ie 1998.

Box 2.2 Agri-environment schemes available in the English uplands (continued)

Organic Farming Scheme

Aim:	To aid farmers who convert land to organic production.
Administration:	Administered by MAFF.
Date of launch:	1999.
Target areas:	Country-wide.
Mechanism:	Voluntary agreements with participating farmers.
Agreement contents:	Each hectare of land converted receives a certain sum over five years according to land type. There is a minimum eligible size of 1 ha. Participants are required to maintain the organic status of their unit while aid is being paid on any part of it. Participants must register for conversion with one of the organic inspection bodies or with the United Kingdom Register of Organic Food Standards (UKROFS), and provide a conservation plan. Payments are additional to other subsidies.
Agreement period:	Five years.
Cost of scheme:	£10 million in 2001/02 rising to £23 million in 2006/07.

Box 2.3 Environmental land management schemes and grants available in the English uplands

Wildlife Enhancement Schemes (WES)

Aim:	To secure the active management required to maintain and enhance the nature conservation interest of Sites of Special Scientific Interest (SSSIs).
Administration:	Established and run by English Nature.
Date of launch:	Pilot schemes in 1991 & 1992, became part of English Nature's management agreement approach 1996.
Target areas:	Sites of Special Scientific Interest (SSSI).
Habitat types:	A variety of habitats around the country, and current upland WES include: • North Pennines moorland; • Yorkshire Dales meadows and pastures; • Pennine Dales meadows, pastures and allotments; • North York Moors meadows and pastures; • Juniper in Northumbria; • Lake District Wethers pilot.
Mechanism:	Voluntary management agreements with participating farmers, who receive annual standard payments and/or fixed costs payments for capital works.
Agreement contents:	Standard management prescriptions for different habitats.
Agreement period:	Normally for an initial term of not more than three years.
Cost of scheme:	£3.66 m for 1999/2000 (total amount for all WES schemes, including lowland).

Nature Conservation Project Grants: These are grants up of to 50% of costs, available from English Nature for projects which further nature conservation. They are aimed at new projects for maintaining or managing sites and species of nature conservation importance. Examples include work on nature reserves, such as fencing, scrub control, water level management, coppicing, hire or purchase of equipment or materials, and interpretative facilities. The establishment of key posts in voluntary nature conservation bodies and other innovative projects which further nature conservation are also considered.

Wildlife and Landscape Conservation and Amenity Planting Grants: These are grants of up to 50% or more that are available from Local Authorities and National Park Authorities. Examples include hedgerow planting and improvement, heather management, bracken control, and work on ponds, green lanes and ditches. Grants are also available for archaeological and geological conservation.

Local Authority Management Agreements: Local Authorities and National Park Authorities have statutory powers to enter into environmental agreements with land owners and private individuals. These aim to maintain or enhance the landscape, protect wildlife, provide access and cater for recreation. Some Authorities have developed special schemes covering whole farms, for example, the North York Moors Farm Scheme.

Box 2.3 Environmental land management schemes and grants available in the English uplands (continued)

Woodland Grant Scheme: This scheme provides grants for a range of woodland management and establishment options and is available from the Forestry Commission. Applicants are required to work in accordance with a five year plan of operations approved by the Forestry Commission. Included in the scheme is a Woodland Improvement Grant aimed at helping to deliver the Habitat and Species Action Plans from the UK Biodiversity Action Plan in existing woodlands. In addition there is a native woodland challenge initiative in National Parks.

The Woodland Grant Scheme and related initiatives change regularly so for further current details, contact the Forestry Commission.

Farm Woodland Premium Scheme: This is open to farmers throughout England and encourages the planting of new woods on land currently in productive agriculture. It is run by MAFF although there is a joint application procedure with the Forestry Commission's Woodland Grant Scheme.

LIFE III (LIFE-Nature)

The third phase of the European Commission's Financial Instrument for the Environment (LIFE III).

Aim: The general objective of the LIFE fund is to contribute to the development of EU environmental policy, in particular the integration of the environmental concerns into other policies and the implementation and updating of environmental legislation. As under LIFE II, there are three areas of eligible activity, each with their own priorities and procedures. These are LIFE-Nature, LIFE-Environment and LIFE-Third Countries. This information relates to LIFE-Nature solely.

Administration: Funding comes from the European Union, from the European Structural Funds, via the Department of the Environment, Transport and the Regions (DETR). Completed applications to DETR by end September, and to Commission by October.

Date of Launch: LIFE III launched in 2000.

Mechanism: There are two sorts of projects eligible for funding under LIFE-Nature:

1. Nature conservation projects on SPAs, SACs and certain species. To be eligible under this category, projects will have to contribute to the implementation of the Birds Directive, the Habitats Directive and the Natura 2000 network and contribute to maintaining or restoring natural habitats and species populations to a favourable conservation status as defined by the Habitats Directive. These projects will have to relate to:
   - a site proposed by a Member State under the Habitats Directive, ie submitted formally by DETR to the Commission as a Candidate SAC; or
   - a site classified under the Birds Directive as an SPA; or
   - a species in Annex II or IV of the Habitats Directive or in Annex I of the Birds Directive.

2. In addition there are three new types of project that will be eligible, known as accompanying measures and include:
   - measures to prepare projects which involve partners in several member states (starter measures);

Box 2.3 Environmental land management schemes and grants available in the English uplands (continued)

- measures which exchange experiences between projects (co-op measures)
- measures to monitor and evaluate projects and disseminate their results, including the results of projects decided upon during the preceding phases of LIFE (assist measures).

Funding: Generally provide up to 50% funding of approved proposals (although this can rise to 75% in exceptional cases). Preparatory or exchange projects can receive a maximum 100%

Rural Enterprise Scheme

Aim: To provide assistance for projects that help to develop more sustainable, diversified and enterprising rural economies and communities.

Administration: The Rural Enterprise Scheme is part-funded by the EU and part-funded and administered by MAFF regional offices. A similar scheme operates in Objective 1 areas, part-funded by MAFF, part-funded by the EU and administered by Government Offices.

Date of launch: October 2000.

Target areas: England-wide, except in the Objective 1 areas of Cornwall and the Isles of Scilly, Merseyside and South Yorkshire.

Mechanism: Grant scheme based on a project plan jointly agreed between MAFF and the applicant. Funding varies depending upon the project and in particular its commercial return.

Measures available under the Rural Enterprise Scheme are:

- setting up of farm relief and farm management services;
- marketing of quality agricultural products;
- basic services for the rural economy and population;
- renovation and development of villages and protection and conservation of the rural heritage;
- diversification of agricultural activities and activities close to agriculture to provide multiple activities or alternative incomes;
- agricultural water resources management;
- development and improvement of infrastructure connected with the development of agriculture;
- encouragement for tourist and craft activities;
- protection of the environment in connecting with agriculture, forestry and landscape conservation as well as with the improvement of animal welfare.

Cost of scheme: Total funding available from MAFF and the EU is £152 over seven years.

NOTE: This just covers successor schemes to Objective 5b. It does not cover Objective 2 administered by the Department of the Environment, Transport and the Regions (DETR) or the Vocational Training Scheme which could help with training on environmental practices, nor grants offered by other bodies.

2.8.6 Agriculture and biodiversity

Agriculture has intensified over the last 60 years, encouraged by high levels of subsidy. Changes that have taken place since the 1940s include the agricultural improvement of in-bye, allotment and unenclosed moorland by fertilisers, herbicides, reseeding and drainage. One of the main changes in Britain is the loss of upland heath vegetation through agricultural improvement, usually to grassland (Bunce & Barr 1988). There has also been a large-scale switch from hay to silage making. Example statistics include the following (Cole, Kernon & Knightbridge 1996; Egdell , Smith & Taylor 1993; Fuller 1987; Parry, Bruce & Harkness 1981; RSPB 1984):

- an estimated 0.25 million hectares of upland semi-natural vegetation has been lost by mechanical cultivation to give agriculturally improved pasture;
- since 1930, the area of unimproved grassland in upland and lowland England and Wales has declined by 97%;
- the area of rough grazing (excluding commons) fell by 5% from 1979 to 1994, mostly as a result of conversion to improved grassland and forestry plantings in upland areas;
- the number of ewes in the Severely Disadvantaged Area (SDA) of England increased by around 40% between 1976 and 1994;
- the remaining area of rough grazing was stocked at a higher rate, with additional nutrition being provided by feed in the form of hay and silage.

Much of the biodiversity of the uplands depends for its survival upon low intensity or mixed vegetation management. The intensification which has occurred has had widespread effects on this biodiversity. There has been a significant loss of semi-natural vegetation in the uplands since the 1940s, and a decline in the distribution of moorland and other birds. Examples of the effect of agriculture on upland biodiversity are given below (Thompson *et al* 1995c).

- There has been a net loss of 20% of heather moorland in England and Wales between 1947 and 1980, with heavy grazing by sheep accounting for 67% of the total change in moorland cover. Grassland, bracken or forestry have generally replaced heather moorland.
- Of 40 bird species using moorland, 40% are declining in distribution in Britain.

Effects of grazing on vegetation

The type and breed of grazing animal influences the effect of grazing on the vegetation. This is because different animals select different plants in the vegetation and have different biting methods. Different types and breed of animals also vary in their habits and trampling impact. This is summarised in Box 2.4, but see Armstrong 1998 for further details.

The type, age and structure of vegetation being grazed also influences the impact of grazing. Upland vegetation communities vary in their appeal to grazing animals as well as their ability to withstand grazing, reflecting their species composition and growth form.

The mix of vegetation types in any upland area determines the pattern and seasonal variation in grazing. Areas dominated by palatable grasses will attract most grazing pressure, with surrounding vegetation types, such as dwarf-shrub heaths, being next in line. Small flushes, springs and grass under bracken can also be favoured by grazing animals, and a very high concentration of grazing may occur in a very small area, such as in base-rich locations in more acid or peaty soils.

In areas of mixed heather and grass, the majority of the heather grazing occurs in the autumn, winter and spring. This is before, and after, sufficient grass growth is available for the livestock. The morphology of the heather plant makes it relatively tolerant of moderate defoliation. Regular removal of heather shoots helps to stimulate and maintain the plant in a juvenile state in which growth is active and the development of potential competitors is suppressed (Gimingham 1972). However, although removal of 40% of the current season's shoots of healthy and vigorous heather by grazing may be tolerated, 80% removal cannot (Grant *et al* 1982). For example, the percentage flowering of heather, as well as the current year's growth increments, are much reduced by heavy grazing. For monitoring heather condition in ESAs, ADAS have used the following "suppression thresholds" which are derived from "desirable levels of utilisation" given by Sibbald *et al* (1987) and used in the MLURI Hill Grazing Management Model (Grant & Armstrong 1993).

Table 2.6 Suppressive levels of biomass utilisation

Heather type	Approximate age	Utilisation threshold
Young (pioneer stage)	0-5 years	40%
Intermediate (building stage)	5-15 years	10%
Old (mature/over mature)	> 15 years	5%
Blanket bog	-	15%

Source: P. Anderson

However, only the 40% figure is derived from experimental work (Grant *et al* 1978, 1982) and the determination of suppressive thresholds of biomass utilisation around the country is the subject of ongoing MAFF-funded research. Palmer (1997), using an empirical model of the annual shoot production of heather, suggests that ". . . . previously published estimates of the utilisation levels that heather can tolerate without a reduction in shoot production may be too high. For pioneer and early building heather, estimated threshold utilisation levels are 16% in summer and 24% in autumn. Furthermore, it is suggested that any level of utilisation will reduce the rate of increase of heather ground cover after burning".

It is also of note that shoot utilisation and threshold levels of utilisation may have different meanings. Shoot utilisation is generally used for the mean % by weight of the current/previous year's growth lost, but has sometimes been used for the % of shoots grazed (eg in some of the methods of MacDonald & Armstrong 1989). Suppression is normally defined as the level of utilisation at which heather is reduced in biomass or cover, or does not increase, but has sometimes been used for the levels at which heather production is reduced compared with ungrazed situations (eg Palmer 1997).

Heather is particularly vulnerable to damage from an excess of grazing in the spring and autumn when its reserves are being mobilised or stored, and to a slightly lesser extent in winter. The recent trend to overwinter stock on moorland is a significant cause of heather loss on moorland. Traditional grazing regimes tended to keep numbers which could be sustained by the heather present. Alternatively, stock were wintered on lower ground and off the hill. But recent trends have included an increase in the number of sheep being wintered on the unenclosed land and an increase in supplementary feeding.

Generally, species with growing points high above ground level suffer most from heavy grazing or repeated mowing. Heather *Calluna vulgaris* falls into this category and this makes it a useful indicator species. It produces characteristic growth forms indicative of the past grazing pressure (MacDonald 1993). Grasses with buried apical meristems, such as purple moor-grass *Molinia caerulea*, are ensured a degree of protection from grazing. Bilberry *Vaccinium myrtillus* also has growing points on its underground stems (rhizomes) and hence tends to be more resistant to grazing than heather.

Heather

Box 2.4 Grazing characteristics of large herbivores in the uplands

Sheep

Sheep graze by biting and shearing the vegetation and only have lower incisors. They are highly selective grazers and search for and select out the most palatable species. This may lead to the loss of some herb and grass species and the spread of unpalatable grasses. Where it is available, sheep will preferentially graze bent *Agrostis* spp., fescue *Festuca* spp., wavy hair-grass *Deschampsia flexuosa* and reseeded grassland. They tend to avoid grazing mat-grass *Nardus stricta*, except in early spring, unless little else is available or it is in an intimate part of a bent/fescue sward. When grazing pressure is high, sheep eat round the edges of *Nardus* tussocks and can keep it in check. Lowering the grazing pressure slightly can then cause it to spread, but lowering it further will allow other plant species to compete and the *Nardus* is likely to remain as it is, or even decline. This effect depends on the soils since *Nardus* does relatively better on more acid, moister soils (H. Armstrong, pers comm).

Sheep tend to avoid rushes and purple moor-grass when other vegetation is available. However, in the absence of more palatable grasses, *Molinia* may be grazed in spring and summer when a flush of new growth makes it more palatable and nutritious. Young heather is eaten regularly when it is intermittently mixed with grass, but sheep generally only move onto heather when live, green, palatable grasses are unavailable.

Wethers (castrated male sheep) are believed to be less selective in their grazing than ewes and are thought to eat rough vegetation more readily than ewes, although there is no documented evidence as yet. Hence they have the potential to limit the spread of less palatable grasses. They were traditionally kept as a proportion of hill flocks, because they tend to be more territorial than ewes and maintain the flock's heft or grazing area against intruding sheep. They were also used to occupy the worst ground of the farm. The practice of keeping adult wethers has declined, primarily due to the shift in public taste from mutton to lamb: mature wethers are too large and fat for today's markets. The move away from keeping wethers has also been influenced by the subsidy and quota systems, which are based on ewes.

Cattle

Cattle are less selective grazers than sheep and tend to wrap their tongues around vegetation and pull. They can also bite and shear vegetation, having only lower incisors, like sheep. They cannot graze short grassland efficiently but, because of their larger gut size, they have a greater ability than sheep to digest poor quality forage (Armstrong 1996). As a result they are more likely to move onto mat-grass or purple moor-grass in summer. They may be more effective in controlling mat-grass because they consistently ingest more of this species than do sheep (Grant *et al* 1985, 1987). They are also thought to be effective in controlling the spread of purple moor-grass, but only if grazing occurs early in the season when this grass is at its most palatable and susceptible to grazing effects.

Cattle readily graze rushes *Juncus* spp and at moderately high stocking levels can significantly reduce their extent in a field. They will graze sharp-flowered rush *Juncus acutiflorus* in preference to soft rush *J. effusus* and compact rush *J. conglomeratus* and this can lead to the replacement of the former by soft rush in some circumstances. Cattle grazing can be used to control rushes without eliminating them, which is beneficial to nesting waders, and may reduce the need to use pesticides or mowing to control them. However, high stocking levels during the breeding season may be damaging to wader populations because of the increased risk of nest and chick trampling. Cattle may also help to control the spread of bracken *Pteridium aquilinum* through trampling effects.

Box 2.4 Grazing characteristics of large herbivores in the uplands (continued)

Horses and ponies
Horses and ponies also occur on unenclosed hill land. They graze by biting the vegetation and have upper and lower incisors. They tend to graze more palatable species selectively, but will eat coarse grasses and scrub. Where it is present, they may graze heather in winter in the absence of more palatable vegetation. As with cattle, they can cause damage to dwarf shrubs through trampling, but may help to control the spread of purple moor-grass and bracken.

Red deer
Red deer, like sheep, graze by biting and shearing the vegetation and only have lower incisors. They are selective feeders, choosing particularly grass-dominated vegetation types (Reynolds 1998). Seasonal declines in grass abundance and digestibility, and the need for shelter, result in an increase in the use of other vegetation types during the autumn and winter. At this time, browsed vegetation, particularly dwarf-shrubs, predominates in the diet.

Source: Armstrong 1998

Grazing and changes in vegetation type

Grazing can affect the productivity and structure of vegetation, and may cause it to change from one type to another. For example, ericoid-dominated communities may be replaced by grass-dominated communities, such as *Agrostis/Festuca* (Welch 1974), or by *Nardus-*, *Molinia-* and *Juncus squarrosus*-dominated communities, depending on the conditions (eg King 1960; Welch 1984a, b & c). The direction of change of the vegetation owing to grazing is determined by the initial vegetation type, the underlying solid and drift geology, the resulting soil and hydrology, and the slope and aspect (see Rodwell 1991, 1992). It will also be affected by the impact of other management practices such as burning and drainage. Less extreme increases or a relaxation of the grazing pressure can alter the vegetation structure without actually causing a change from one type to another.

Even though heather and other dwarf shrubs are less palatable than grasses, utilisation rates by stock can be very high if there is nothing else to eat. The loss of heather from an area can occur very slowly, or it may happen relatively quickly, ie 5-10 years, particularly in the presence of heavy grazing and too frequent burning. Heather areas, where they abutt good grassland and grazing pressure is highest, can decline significantly from the edges of the dwarf shrub community in that time (H. Armstrong, pers comm). Receding heather edges occur because sheep tend to graze predominantly on grassy swards and so heather adjacent to the grassland will receive the most grazing once grass growth slows and stops. The reason heather decline does not happen instantly is because this species has good root reserves and only the current year's shoots are generally eaten. Bracken may also predominate over heather when it is heavily grazed and burnt.

Where the grazing pressure is relatively low, heather and other plants mature and this can give rise to greater stand heterogeneity (Gimingham 1972). Shrubs may become established or the heath may be replaced by other vegetation types, such as bracken-dominated stands. However, degeneration of heather does not always occur in the absence of management, as heather can regenerate vegetatively by layering (adventitious rooting of stems) and stable stands of heather can develop (MacDonald *et al* 1995).

The effects of grazing (and burning) on moorland habitats, particularly the replacement of dwarf shrub heath and mire communities by grasses, heath rush *Juncus squarrosus* and cotton-grass *Eriophorum* spp. dominated communities have been documented (Ratcliffe 1959; Rawes & Williams 1973; Tansley 1939) and more recently reviewed (Felton & Marsden 1990; Thompson *et al* 1995c). Increasing grazing pressures have been shown to have a major influence on moorland condition and to have contributed to changes from dwarf shrub moor to grass moor.

Anderson and Yalden (1981) found that the upland vegetation of a large part of the Peak District, mapped in 1913 as having 36% of the vegetation dominated by heather, was dominated by graminoids. Similarly, aerial photographs have indicated that in Cumbria since the 1940s 70% of heather-dominated vegetation has been replaced by unimproved vegetation dominated by graminoids (Nature Conservancy Council 1987).

Dwarf shrubs are not the only group to decline in the face of heavy grazing. Tall herb and fern communities become restricted to cliff ledges and other inaccessible sites, while the regeneration of any shrubs or woodland is also prevented. The plants and animals typically associated with heather moorland, tall herb communities, scrub and woodland are generally more highly prized, in nature conservation terms, than those associated with the acid grassland or bracken *Pteridium aquilinum* communities which replaces them (Evans & Felton 1987). However, this does depend on the particular interest being considered and the way the heather moorland is being managed.

Further information: Stewart & Eno 1998; Chapter 6 Moorland; Chapter 7 Meadows & enclosed pasture.

Effects of agricultural burning on vegetation

Man has influenced upland vegetation using fire for a long time, perhaps since the Mesolithic period (Mowforth & Sydes 1989). Burning has been practised for the management of vegetation, principally for stimulating new growth of grasses or heather. The most commonly burnt upland vegetation type is dwarf-shrub heath, although some burning of blanket bog, enclosed and unenclosed grassland, bracken and scrub is also undertaken. It is strictly controlled by law and can only be conducted in winter (see Chapter 6 Moorland).

Like grazing, burning can have a major effect on the species composition of moorland communities, particularly when the vegetation is burnt more frequently than once every eight or so years. At high burning frequencies, particularly when combined with moderate to high grazing levels, the dwarf-shrub component of heath and blanket mire communities can be substantially reduced or even eliminated. On dry heath this will result in mat-grass becoming dominant, or bristle bent *Agrostis curtisii* in the south west of England, while on wet heath and blanket mire hare's-tail cotton-grass *Eriophorum vaginatum* or purple moor-grass will be favoured.

Grassland burning, or 'swaling' is traditionally practised in some areas of the English uplands and in general, 'individual' burns are much more extensive than those upland areas managed for grouse (see 2.9.1). In the south west, for example on Exmoor, large areas of unenclosed land are dominated by purple moor-grass. These areas are traditionally used as summer pasture for sheep and cattle. They are stocked fairly heavily during the summer months and large areas are burnt every spring to produce younger, more palatable herbage. *Molinia* is relatively unpalatable except when young, when it can be of high quality feeding value, and is able to regenerate vigorously after being burnt. Such a high frequency of burning is probably responsible for the dominance of *Molinia* here, because it gives this species a competitive advantage on wet soils, and has resulted in the agricultural and ecological impoverishment of these moors. Small-scale burning combined with early summer grazing may be the best way to diversify such areas (see Chapter 6 Moorland).

In addition, shrubs such as gorse *Ulex* spp are burnt to help stock to move around the land and encourage an initial flush of grass growth. Further information on burning is included in Chapter 6 Moorland. The effects of burning for grouse moor management are discussed in the next section and in further detail in Chapter 6 Moorland.

2.9 Field sport interests in the uplands

2.9.1 Grouse shooting

In northern England, the principal shooting interest on moorland is for grouse. The large-scale management of heather moorland for red grouse first started in the early nineteenth century and reached a peak towards the end of that century and the beginning of the twentieth. There has been some decline in management for grouse in some areas, but it still remains a major land use in the North Pennines, Yorkshire Dales, Forest of Bowland and North York Moors.

Grouse moor management involves regular burning to maintain heather in the young, highly productive age-class on which grouse prefer to feed. This young growth has to be in close proximity to taller heather, which is used for nesting and cover. As a result, moors managed for grouse tend to be burnt to produce a mosaic of stands of heather of different ages, rather than the more extensive pattern of large burns associated with management for grazing alone. Grouse moors tend to be burnt on an eight- to fifteen-year cycle.

Moorland management for grouse has had an important role to play in maintaining the extent of open heath and some of its wildlife. Grouse shooting helped to retain the dwarf shrub cover of grouse moors after the Second World War when agricultural pressures converted much moorland to grass moor. In many areas, heather moorland survived where the shooting interest has provided the incentive, the will and the money to retain it.

Some grouse moors support a range of vegetation structures, from areas of short heather and bare ground to unburnt areas. Additional wildlife benefits can be gained from grouse moors which maintain areas of unmanaged or less intensively managed moor, which retain or encourage native woodland and scrub, and which reverse moorland drainage.

However, rotational and relatively frequent burning involved in grouse moor management has a profound effect on the vegetation present and can lead to swards dominated by heather with few other species and only limited areas of taller and older stands of dwarf shrubs. Repeated burning also affects the species composition of the invertebrate fauna. Therefore, burning will benefit some species and disadvantage others. Whether or not it is beneficial for wildlife will depend upon the nature conservation interests present and the objectives for the area concerned.

Moorland drainage used to be widely practised, with the intention of improving the heather cover for grouse, but this trend has now declined. The benefits for grouse are debatable and it has adverse effects on wildlife, including the loss of wet habitats and the erosion of peat, which causes undesirable changes in freshwater habitats.

A number of pests and diseases cause problems on grouse moors, particularly the parasitic ticks and worms that affect grouse, and are controlled to maximise grouse populations. Grouse moor management also involves a high degree of predator control which may benefit some other breeding birds. The unnaturally low population size of many birds of prey in upland England, eg hen harrier, is widely attributed to their persecution as predators of grouse. The illegal killing of birds of prey still occurs on grouse moors, despite the protection afforded by the Wildlife and Countryside Act 1981.

Further information: Hudson & Newborn 1995; Chapter 6 Moorland.

2.9.2 Deer management

During the nineteenth century many estates in the uplands of Britain began to be managed primarily for red deer. Originally creatures of the woodland, these animals were forced to adapt to the open upland habitat as the area of woodland decreased and management of it intensified. In the moorland situation, there are herds of red deer on Exmoor, in the Lake District and the Southern uplands of Scotland, but the greatest numbers are to be found in the Scottish Highlands. Here herds are only partly managed as a field sport resource, with venison being an additional source of income. Numbers are controlled to some extent by annual culling, which is necessary in the absence of natural predators such as the wolf *Canis lupus*. Outside Scotland, populations are also controlled to some degree in certain areas, and in the south west they are managed as a field sport resource.

Native deer (roe *Capreolus capreolus* and red) still occur in upland woods and can have very great impacts on the conservation management of the woods in both a positive and negative way. Browsing, antler damage, and grazing of ground vegetation can cause local, and sometimes widespread effects. Deer damage is probably a more significant problem in woodlands than in open upland habitats. Control can be by shooting, or a combination of different approaches such as fencing, using tree guards and shelters, applying chemical and physical repellents and providing alternative feeding areas. Fencing can, however, cause mortality in game birds, and many deaths, particularly in Scotland, occur when black grouse *Tetrao tetrix* and capercaillie *Tetra urogallus* fly into these fences.

Further information: Langbein 1997; Chapter 8 Woodland and scrub; Chapter 6 Moorland.

2.9.3 Pheasant shooting

Pheasant releases for shooting occur in some upland woods for field sport purposes. This practice can have implications for nature conservation interests where non-native shrubs are planted within native broadleaved woodlands; where release pens are sited in areas of nature conservation interest or where they can cause soil erosion; and where straw bales are used to provide cover in areas of nature conservation interest.

Further information: Carrol & Robertson 1997; Chapter 8 Woodland and scrub.

2.10 Forestry in the uplands

Three main woodland and forestry management systems can be distinguished in the English uplands. These are:

- plantation forestry based mainly on large-scale conifer forests;
- broadleaved woods actively managed for timber or wood products, mainly as high forest, but with small areas of worked coppice;
- other mainly broadleaved woods (including most of the semi-natural woodland) which is not actively managed for wood products, but may be contributing to other outputs such as landscape, recreation and sheltered grazing.

There will also be some woods which do not fit into any of these woodland and forestry management systems but these are thought to be less than 10% of the whole (K. Kirby, pers comm).

Further information: English Nature 1994b; Chapter 8 Woodland and scrub.

2.10.1 Plantation forestry

Some of the earliest large-scale conifer plantations in England were established by water companies in the uplands around reservoirs, such as Thirlmere in the Lake District. The main expansion occurred, however, following the establishment of the Forestry Commission in 1919.

Key points:

- predominantly coniferous with sitka spruce *Picea sitchensis* as the main tree species;
- large-scale forests forming the matrix of the landscape, either private or state-owned depending on location;
- stands managed as high forest with clear fells for the most part probably between 10 and 50 ha, of rotations 30-60 years, with re-stocking by planting, and the process heavily mechanised and with relatively little thinning;
- there is some conservation interest attached to the plantations (eg raptors in places) but is more often associated with the non-plantation elements (eg open spaces, remnant broadleaved stands, the woodland interface with other habitats);

- negative nature conservation attributes include loss of open ground habitats and possible increased predation of breeding birds on adjacent open land caused by predators using plantations as cover and for breeding;

- commercial/production-orientated as they are the main source of home-grown timber in England.

2.10.2 Broadleaved woods actively managed for wood production

Most broadleaved woods in the uplands have been managed for wood or timber in the past. Important products included charcoal, swill baskets and bark, as well as wood for buildings, farm implements, fencing and so on. Frequently the woods were coppiced, but this system was virtually extinct by about 1930 except in a few places. Many woods were last cut over in the two World Wars. Recently, there has been a small-scale revival of coppice, for example in Cumbria, and of interest in managing broadleaved woods generally for timber as high forest. Initiatives such as Coed Cymru in Wales have had particular success with encouraging farmers to manage their woods. Nevertheless, the proportion of broadleaved woods in the uplands where wood production is a significant or the main objective is always likely to be relatively small, not least because growth rates are much lower than in lowland broadleaved woods.

Key points:

- predominantly native broadleaves but beech and sycamore are locally important as timber trees;

- relatively small woods (less than 50 hectares) forming patches in the landscape, mainly in the upland fringe, and mainly privately owned (but often large estates);

- mainly now treated as high forest, but with some worked coppice, eg in south Cumbria, and small scale (1-10 ha) clear-fells or group felling, with rotations of 15-30 years for coppice or 100-150 years for high forest, and re-stocking mainly by planting (except for coppice), with a low level of mechanisation;

- conservation interest (if any) associated with the woodland itself or with the interface between woodland and other habitats, and may or may not be improved by management;

- protection against grazing and browsing animals essential especially during re-stocking;

- commercial/production considerations significant but unlikely to be sole driving force in management of the woodland - conservation, landscape or field sport issues also likely to be important.

2.10.3 Broadleaved woods not managed primarily for wood production

Probably 50-70% of broadleaved woods in the uplands receive no management or else management is driven by objectives other than wood production (eg grazing, shelter, field sports, amenity, conservation), with any timber harvested regarded as a bonus. In many instances, very little management is required to maintain their nature conservation value.

Key points:

- predominantly semi-natural;
- mainly small (less than 20 ha), forming patches and linear features in the upland fringe (but extending to higher altitudes and poorer soils than the previous category), mainly privately owned (frequently farmers with no particular woodland interest or experience, but locally organisations such as the National Trust and County Wildlife Trusts are important);
- conservation value associated with the wood itself or with the interface between woodland and other habitats;
- very little financial return from the woods, but often very high conservation or landscape value and some agricultural value as sheltered grazing (but this has never been quantified).

2.10.4 Forestry systems and other land uses

Commercial upland forestry is almost totally independent of the upland agriculture system except in so far as they compete for land and can provide employment in the overall rural economy. Forested areas are important in terms of the landscape, field sport interests, recreation and other aspects of upland land use, while being set within an agricultural context, often with field sport interests. Decisions about whether and how the woods are managed may be influenced by implications for the farming business. For example, removing the woodland from the grazing area will affect the subsidy payments received by farmers. Decisions will also depend on whether farmers have the capital to pay for fencing or the skill and time to manage the wood themselves.

Commercial forestry can be important locally in the context of pheasant, fox and stag hunting. The value of the forest for different species depends on the growth stage, for example black grouse are mainly found in the younger stages of the plantation growth. Both plantations and semi-natural stands may be important for other forms of recreation, such as walking, cycling and bird watching.

Forestry may provide some potential for farmers to shift the balance of their productive output away from food products, but in most cases this is only likely to be undertaken by those with a strong interest in forestry. More often, new forest plantings are likely to occur on large estates or when land changes ownership.

2.10.5 National forestry policies

Forestry in the uplands is covered by national forestry policies which, amongst other things, aim for:

- a steady expansion of the tree cover of Great Britain, to increase the many diverse benefits that forests provide;

- the sustainable management of existing woods and forests;
- woods that are currently broadleaved to remain so;
- the special interest of ancient semi-natural woods to be maintained.

The main way these policies are promoted is via the grants and regulatory activities of the Forestry Commission. All felling (with small exceptions) requires a licence from the Forestry Commission and a re-stocking condition is normally imposed. This may cause problems where substantial tree removal is desirable, for example, on bogs or heaths, but it is generally advantageous. Re-stocking and new planting on open ground attract grants with a variety of special supplements for particular situations (see Box 2.3). Any forestry work coming before the Forestry Commission is also expected to meet basic environmental standards and guidelines which to varying degrees take account of nature conservation requirements. A public register of new planting and felling applications is maintained by the Forestry Commission.

2.10.6 Forestry and biodiversity

Modern plantations can have a significant effect on the biodiversity of upland areas. For example RSPB (1995) summarised the effects of afforestation on blanket bog

- hydrological disruption due to intensive drainage;
- peat wastage resulting from drainage;
- peat drying owing to drains and increased evapo-transpiration;
- generally lowered water table;
- shading by the canopy and accumulation of needles;
- fertiliser application;
- acidification of ground water;
- vegetation changes;
- loss of open moorland species;
- changes in rates, sedimentation loads, nutrient content or pH of run-off from afforested peatlands affecting associated freshwater systems.

Similar effects are produced on drier moorland habitats.

Large conifer plantations do have some nature conservation interest and they can be important for some birds, particularly goshawk *Accipter gentilis,* siskin *Carduelis spinus* and crossbill *Loxia curvirostra.*

Nightjars *Caprimulgus europaeus* have also colonised some upland plantations. This interest, however, is more often associated with the establishment and re-stocking phases, and the non-plantation elements such as open spaces and rides, which frequently contain semi-natural habitats such as dry heath, blanket mire, raised mire, grasslands or limestone pavement and remnant broadleaved stands. Conifer plantations also extend the available habitat for red squirrel and pine marten.

2.11 Public access and recreation in the uplands

Visitors have long been attracted to upland areas. Increasingly in urbanised societies, people feel the need to escape to areas that are perceived to be wild and natural landscapes (Poore 1992). These areas provide a source of inspiration and recreation which satisfies the more spiritual values of solitude, enjoyment and enrichment, the feelings of physical excitement, exhilaration, healthiness and contentment.

The uplands are used for a variety of recreational activities. These include hill walking, fell running and orienteering, mountain biking, horse riding, rock climbing, gill scrambling, caving, paragliding and handgliding. Motor cycles and four-wheel drive vehicles are also used, and in water environments, canoeing and angling are popular. Visitor support is beneficial to the local economy of upland areas, and there is great potential for raising visitor awareness of and support for the various land uses present, as well as nature conservation.

The majority of people involved in recreation in the uplands arrive by car. This means that the areas around car parks are often the most heavily visited, and in some areas further parking provision is required. The concentration of visitors around car parks provides an ideal opportunity to inform the public about the wildlife and land use of the area, via visitor centres for example. However, large visitor numbers can increase footpath erosion, the incidence of accidental fires and other problems associated with recreational activities.

When compared with factors such as climatic change, grazing or fire, recreational impacts may be of little long-term conservation significance. Nevertheless, in some situations they may be the critical last link in a chain of limiting factors (Ratcliffe 1990b). Mountains and hills can be vulnerable to the impacts of recreation. Some habitats, such as those in wet areas and on rock outcrops, are fragile and of high nature conservation value for the plants and animals they support. Many areas are valued for their aesthetic appeal as well as their wildlife interest. Activities such as hill walking have led to a loss of vegetation, erosion and discernible scars in the last few decades, but this tends to be on a rather localised basis. Damage can be exacerbated by four-wheel drive vehicles, motor cycles, horse riding, mountain bikes and runners using unsurfaced rights of way.

Erosion and scars are readily seen, but less obvious, and more difficult to quantify, is the long-term effect of disturbance on birds, mammals and invertebrates. However, there is currently little evidence to suggest that disturbance leads to anything other than localised problems for animals.

Although more of a problem in Scotland, skiing occurs in certain places in the English uplands and can damage the vegetation. More widespread activities in England are rock climbing and gill scrambling, which can adversely affect fragile and rare plant communities and disturb breeding birds. Another recreational activity, caving, can damage underground features and disturb bats.

It is possible to manage recreation, to help the general public gain access to and a greater understanding of the uplands, without putting the special value of these areas at risk. The managers of upland areas can build on an alliance between users' interests and their own aims, remembering the importance of the contribution made by visitors to rural economies.

Significant proportions of the uplands are designated as National Parks where two equal statutory purposes apply. These are, "to conserve and enhance natural beauty, wildlife and cultural heritage", and, "to promote opportunities for the understanding and enjoyment of" their special qualities. It should be possible to reconcile any conflicts by cooperation between the relevant interests and the National Park Authorities, through careful planning and management. This is being actively pursued and achieved in many National Parks in England. A great deal of recreation can take place without causing problems, provided that it is well planned and managed. Good planning of visitor management is essential, relating the type of management to the type of recreation in the area concerned.

Nature reserves exist in the English uplands and are owned and managed by a variety of bodies, such as English Nature, the RSPB and Wildlife Trusts. They support a variety of wildlife interests and have various arrangements for public access and recreation.

The Countryside and Rights of Way Act embraces major new legislation on access, and follows a long consultation period (Department of the Environment, Transport and the Regions 1998a).

Further information: Countryside Commission & Countryside Council for Wales 1997; Federation of Nature & National Parks of Europe 1992; Sports Council & Countryside Commission 1995; Scottish Natural Heritage 1997; Ramblers Association 1998; English Nature 2000a, 2000b; Information Note 10 Management of public access; The Association of National Park Authorities and individual National Park Authorities.

2.12 Other land uses in the uplands

2.12.1 Mineral extraction

Quarrying for stone and, locally, mining are significant land uses in the uplands. Quarrying can result in the loss of semi-natural habitats and earth heritage features, affect adjacent habitats through changes in the water table and result in increased sediment loading of watercourses, which can damage freshwater ecosystems. However, some quarries may have wildlife value once extraction has ceased, either in their own right or where habitat re-creation opportunities exist. They may also expose geological strata of scientific interest.

Mining was once a major feature of many upland areas and while the majority of mines are now abandoned many moorlands are littered with old mine shafts, adits and spoil heaps. Some areas of mine spoil are of significant nature conservation interest. This is principally where the mining has been for metals such as lead or copper. Here the toxic spoil supports characteristic metalliferous grassland communities which are entirely restricted to these situations and include a number of rare and scarce plant species.

Further information: English Nature 1997a, 1998a.

2.12.2 Water supply

Water companies now own or manage substantial areas of ground in the uplands. Upland areas provide the principal water catchment areas for much larger geographical regions. Rainfall is usually greater at these altitudes than in adjoining lowlands and water from mountains provides the source of most rivers and streams on which lowland peoples depend for water supplies. The quality, quantity and timing of water yield from mountain catchments are therefore of considerable social and economic importance. These are all affected by the land use in the catchment.

Different types of vegetation intercept and impede the flow of rainwater to differing extents. Woodland and scrub, for example, slow the passage of water from hill sides to rivers to a far greater extent than grasslands as trees have a greater surface area onto which rain will fall, preventing it reaching the ground immediately. Some of this water then evaporates back into the atmosphere without ever reaching the ground. Of the water that does reach the ground, trees will take up a greater proportion through their roots than grasses and herbs because of their size, and again this is passed back into the atmosphere via evapo-transpiration. Because rainwater takes longer to reach the ground in woodland than in grassland there are fewer rapid fluctuations in river levels where catchments are wooded than there are in unwooded catchments. As a result there is less erosion and sediment load in water from wooded catchments than from unwooded ones.

The urbanisation of the population in the nineteenth century led to a need for increased water supplies in towns and cities which could not be met from local supplies. As a result a number of large valleys were flooded and water levels in existing lakes were raised to create reservoirs. The majority of these reservoirs were created in upland areas and today water companies are major landowners in the uplands. One consequence of the building of reservoirs was the loss of areas of semi-natural habitat and in some instances this has resulted in the loss of areas of very high nature conservation interest, such as in upper Teesdale and on Bodmin Moor.

Many upland stream, rivers and water bodies have been developed as a source of drinking water for private and public supply. Water is abstracted directly from surface or ground waters, thereby posing a threat to water levels and flow regimes downstream of the abstraction point. Water may also be abstracted for non-consumptive use, for example by hydro-electric power stations or by fish farms. Abstraction can lead to significant impacts on the wildlife of freshwater systems and wetlands.

Further information: Chapter 9 Freshwater habitats

2.12.3 Power generation

Since the late 1980's there have been increasing numbers of wind power farms built in upland locations as they are consistently windy. Wind farms require some land take, though this is usually small, but it can lead to loss of semi-natural habitat. Semi-natural habitat may also be lost during the construction phase. Concern has also been raised as to the effect of wind farms on bird populations, both breeding and migratory, in their vicinity owing to increased disturbance and loss of habitat and the potential for increased risk of bird strikes where wind farms are built in heavily used flight paths. Many upland areas are protected from wind farm developments to a certain degree as they lie within National Parks, the planning committees of which are currently vigorously opposed to such schemes, primarily on landscape grounds.

Further information: English Nature 2000c.

2.12.4 Military training in the uplands

The Ministry of Defence (MoD) owns a significant area of the uplands, managed primarily for military use. Examples include training areas on Dartmoor, at Otterburn in Northumberland and at Warcop in the North Pennines. Large parts of these areas are largely free from human disturbance because they are overshoot zones for firing ranges. The majority of military ranges and training areas are closed to the public for at least part of the time. For this reason, they can be extremely valuable for wildlife, particularly breeding birds, and can contain rare plant species. The MoD is also actively pursuing management for wildlife on its training grounds.

Parts of specific training areas can be subject to heavy use and certain types of military machinery, eg tanks, or types of training activity, are monitored to help reduce damage or repair predicted damage. All large training areas have Conservation Groups and sustainable military training use is the overall target of the MoD.

A number of military radar establishments are also located on areas of moorland. There are usually areas in the immediate vicinity of the radar that are fenced off from livestock and are largely unmanaged owing to potential radiation hazards. Areas of moorland habitat which are unmanaged, such as these, are uncommon and are useful in research into moorland ecological processes.

Further factors influencing the uplands

2.13 Pollution

Atmospheric pollution, effluent discharge and eutrophication of fresh waters all affect upland ecosystems.

Atmospheric pollution has been a major cause of recent vegetation change in the uplands (Birks 1988). Oxides of sulphur and nitrogen are released during the combustion of fossil fuels and are deposited either dry or, combined with moisture in the atmosphere, as acid rain. Brown & Farmer (1996) have found that sulphur and nitrogen deposition exceed their critical loads in many upland Natural Areas and that this is likely to be having a significant impact on their nature conservation interest. The widespread development of infertile, acidic soils is the principal ecological factor characterising the long-term ecological history of the uplands. These soils result from the acidic nature of much of the local bedrock, coupled with intensive leaching under a cool, moist climate. Long-term, natural soil acidification has been greatly increased by recent, rapid acidification caused by acid atmospheric deposition in certain upland areas.

Certain ecological changes in the Southern Pennines, for example, are almost certainly responses to the atmospheric pollution of the industrial revolution. These changes include the virtual disappearance of

Sphagnum from blanket mires (Lee, Tallis & Woodin 1988; Tallis 1964). Atmospheric pollution may be partly to blame for the recent increase in the extent and rate of blanket mire erosion in the Southern Pennines (Tallis 1985), as well as intense land use, although some of this erosion is thought to be part of natural processes. It has also been suggested that the high deposition of soot after the start of the industrial revolution may have been involved in the change from heather moor to the dominance of purple moor-grass in South Wales (Chambers, Dresser & Smith 1979). Atmospheric pollution may also affect species of montane heaths such as woolly hair-moss *Racomitrium lanuginosum* and stiff sedge *Carex bigelowii* that obtain nutrients from water droplets in cloud and fog (occult deposition) (Lee, Tallis & Woodin 1988).

In areas where the soil cannot counteract the acid depositions, surface waters can become acidified. Other pollution effects on fresh waters include localised nutrient enrichment from stock faeces, or eutrophication of water bodies resulting from the run-off of organic and inorganic fertilisers applied to the surrounding land. Effluent discharges into fresh waters include organic effluent such as farm waste or sewage, and toxic effluent such as sheep dip, pesticides and herbicides. All these pollution effects can alter the fauna and flora of freshwater systems.

Further information: Bobbink *et al* 1998; Kirkbride 1996; Lee 1998; New Phytologist 1998; Woodin & Farmer 1993; Chapter 9 Freshwater habitats.

2.14 Erosion and sedimentation

Erosion of upland soils, resulting in vegetation loss and increased amounts of sediments in water systems, arises from natural causes and various activities such as drainage, burning, bracken control, heavy grazing, forestry and recreational activities such as walking, mountain biking and off-road driving. Erosion and the sediment it produces disrupt the natural hydrology of the adjacent water courses and surrounding catchment area, altering flow rates and changing patterns of deposition and flooding. Sediment in the water can affect the aquatic flora and fauna, by shading plants and silting rocky habitats used by invertebrates and spawning fish.

The erosion of soil by water is caused when rainfall is so intense that the soil cannot absorb it by infiltration. It then runs over the surface as sheets or is concentrated in runnels and streams. Where there is no vegetation cover the water picks up soil particles as it moves over the surface. Gullies soon form and once present they will continue to eat back at their heads into previously uneroded soils and can cause the further loss of vegetation cover (Dasmann & Poore 1979).

Stock trampling on banks and shores of freshwater systems can also lead to erosion and increased levels of suspended solids in fresh waters. This can reduce light levels in the water, smother plant and animal species, and alter the constituent communities.

Erosion is, however, a natural process and scree slopes, for example, are a result of natural erosion caused by freeze-thaw action. Erosion tends to become a problem when human activities exacerbate natural processes.

Further information: MAFF 1997c, 1998e; Tallis 1997; Chapter 9 Freshwater habitats.

2.15 Climate change

It is possible that upland habitats may be influenced by climatic changes associated with the greenhouse effect (Bardgett *et al* 1995). There is a growing consensus that increasing amounts of carbon dioxide and other greenhouse gases (eg methane and nitrous oxide) in the atmosphere will lead to an increase in average temperature of 2.5 °C by the year 2100 (Hadley Centre 1997). It is also estimated that by the 2050s average summer temperatures in the UK might have increased by about 1.4 °C and winter temperatures by 1.5 °C (Climate Change Impacts Review Group 1996). Increasing temperatures may influence the future extent and distribution of upland vegetation, both directly through changes in the productivity of moorland soils and vegetation, and indirectly through increased opportunities for land improvement and cropping, and an extension of the grazing season. This could have fundamental consequences for agriculture, wildlife and recreation.

It is possible, for example, that changes in the geographical distribution of heather-dominated vegetation will occur (Bardgett *et al* 1995). One model predicts a reduction of approximately 25% in the current extent of blanket bog with increases in temperature in the order of 3 °C. It is thought that the loss in area of blanket bog is likely to result from increased evapo-transpiration from peat soils and a subsequent increase in peat decomposition rates, producing a shift in vegetation type to more productive dry heath and acid grassland. Another model predicts that bracken could expand its altitudinal range as a result of global warming and become more difficult to control (Marrs & Pakeman 1995).

Sophisticated computer models of the global climate system are used as the basis for predicting climate change. A new set of climate change scenarios for the UK has recently been developed and provides greater detail than the CCIRG study referred to above (Hulme & Jenkins 1998). However, it must be recognised that although climate models are driven by the best available scientific evidence, they do still contain an element of uncertainty.

Further information: Department of the Environment, Transport and the Regions 1998b; Loh 1997.

Decision making

Decision making 3

3.1 Introduction

3.1.1 The context of decision making

The aim of this chapter is to set out a structured way of making decisions about upland management for wildlife. However, as most of the uplands are not managed as nature reserves, these decisions are unlikely to be taken in an vacuum and will need to be set within the context of, for example, a farming business, sporting enterprise, forestry concern or water catchment management.

The decision making process can involve a number of individuals and agencies especially where there are public monies involved. The process will also follow a number of stages, which are described in detail in the following sections. The stages one has to go through will be similar for a small parcel of land, such as a single field like a hay meadow, a management unit of a moor, or a whole farm. However, the larger the area and the greater the variety of habitats then the greater the likelihood is that more decisions will need to be taken. The stages to follow will:

- identify and describe the features of the land in question;
- evaluate these features in an international, national and local context;
- gain an understanding of how much of the site's features is dependent on land management practices;
- formulate land management objectives and prescriptions based on the requirements of the habitat and species , and factors influencing those objectives such as current farming practices;
- prepare a work plan that addresses the above to deliver biodiversity targets and hopefully integrates such management successfully within the wider land management context;
- review the effectiveness of the management regime and implement adjustments as required.

3.1.2 Economic realities

Given the precarious position of many family hill farming businesses and the long-term need to retain environmentally sustainable livestock farming in the uplands, conservation decisions need to be balanced alongside other important factors such as livelihoods. Financial incentives for agricultural products account for the great majority of support for hill farmers and these incentives have encouraged an intensive approach to farming which has had severe impacts on both semi-natural habitats and the species that depend on them. However, while still only a small proportion of the total Common Agricultural Policy (CAP) budget, agri-environment incentives attempt to address these problems by funding and encouraging a more environmentally friendly and sustainable form of land management.

A more integrated approach has been tested in the Forest of Bowland and Bodmin Moor, and through other Structural funded initiatives such as the Northern Uplands Moorland Regeneration Project in the

North Pennines. For all of these areas the economic, environmental and social aspects are considered together, and advice and funding is given in the form of an integrated package.

3.1.3 Upland and hill management for biodiversity

Land management, for whatever purpose, can require a large number of decisions to be made and it is therefore necessary to determine the aims for the site, or farm or estate. This is as important for conservation as it is for agriculture or sport. A structured approach to the decision making process will result in a clearer understanding of the management priorities of the land, and the implications such priorities have on current management of the land in question and within the wider farm or land management context. It will enable farmers, land managers and funding agencies to direct their resources where they are most needed.

For many farmers, land managers and landowners detailed information on the requirements of habitats and species will come 'second-hand' from organisations such as English Nature in relation to the management of land on Sites of Special Scientific Interest (SSSIs), Farming and Wildlife Advisory Group (FWAG) for general and specific advice on farmland management for wildlife, and Farming and Rural Conservation Agency (FRCA) for advice particularly in association with funding through agri-environment schemes such as Environmentally Sensitive Areas (ESAs) or Countryside Stewardship. For the appropriate decisions to be made the individual or agency providing that advice must be aware of:

- the importance of the existing feature;
- the condition of that feature or resource;
- the conservation priorities at a both national and local level;
- the ecological requirements of the habitats and species in question;
- the management needs and how these may impact on the current land use;
- the potential to restore or recreate features;
- the potential for integration of biodiversity needs into broader land management practices.

The following sections provide a structured guide to the information required and factors that should be considered by a land manager/adviser when deciding on an appropriate management regime or restoration programme. Although it is targeted to the provision of guidelines towards management for biodiversity, similar thought processes will be required in situations where nature conservation is not the primary land use but which may be in receipt of funds to maintain or increase biodiversity.

3.1.4 Nature conservation objectives and targets for the English uplands

Nature conservation objectives, be it for small hay meadows or large moorland blocks should always take into account the wider picture and the evaluation of land holdings and individual 'sites' are described in detail under section 3.2.2.

The main reason for having objectives and targets is that they:

- clearly identify the relative importance of features so that conservation actions are driven by sound conservation priorities which safeguard these features and produce biodiversity gains;
- inform government departments, other agencies and organisations in order to gain support and share an understanding of upland priorities and issues;
- prioritise work and resources to increase biodiversity and provide a framework to make the best use of opportunities through, for example, scheme targeting of Stewardship and Wildlife Enhancement Schemes;
- relate international to national to local objectives.

English Nature proposes to produce nature conservation objectives and targets for the English uplands. They will contain the national priorities, objectives and biodiversity targets for upland habitats, species and earth heritage interests. A parallel exercise is also being undertaken by English Nature to use these objectives to identify priorities and targets for each upland Natural Area. The refinement and development of objectives has been undertaken in a framework and in parallel with other work, for example the implementation of Biodiversity Action Plans and the implementation of the Habitats and Species Directive, and addresses England's obligations regarding internationally and nationally significant habitats, species and earth heritage interests.

The relative importance of the habitats, species and earth heritage interests of the English uplands are determined by a number of criteria. They evaluate features in an international, national and local context as to whether they are:

- rare or scarce;
- threatened;
- declining;
- restricted in distribution;
- limited in extent or number;
- fragmented;
- at the edge of their range;
- representative of a particular interest;
- important in England because a significant proportion of the international or UK population, habitat or interest occurs there.

A number of common principles guide the implementation of upland nature conservation objectives for the English uplands. These are:

- to maintain the overall distribution, extent and the full range of variation of upland habitats, species and earth heritage interests;
- to ensure that the resource is maintained in a favourable condition (see Information Note 1);
- to restore areas that have been damaged in the past and seek to achieve favourable condition;
- to recreate areas of the resource with a particular emphasis on reducing fragmentation.

The following chapters describe and identify the key components and species for upland habitats along with, where known, their requirements and management prescriptions.

3.1.5 Management plans

While a structured approach to land management decision making is more likely to deliver biodiversity gains, it need not become bureaucratic or time consuming. Management plans can assist in the formulation of objectives and prescriptions, and provide a work plan over a specified period. They do provide a written record of why particular management decisions were taken and can be useful at a later date, if only to act as a reminder to oneself. Such records will also allow for continuity of thought processes when there is a change in personnel, crucial when a farmer or tenant moves on or where there are changes in land management adviser. This handbook is, however, not intended to be a guide to the production of management plans.

It is not always necessary to adopt a very formal approach or lengthy format. Even on National Nature Reserves English Nature has moved away from time consuming and lengthy processes required to formulate management plans. It has now adopted the 'minimum format' (Nature Conservancy Council 1991) as the standard format for writing management plans. Other situations will necessitate a slightly different approach although the similar principles will still drive the preparation of the plan or management proposals.

For SSSIs, English Nature defines Conservation Objectives which defines the nature conservation interest of the site. The next stage involves the production of a Management Statement, which is intended to provide a framework to capture the short- and medium- term management needs. These are brief documents that focus on the core management necessary to protect the SSSI but are not intended to replace management plans where more detail may be required. They are in effect a summary of a management plan's key elements. Like all plans, however, they are intended to be updated and amended in the light of new knowledge and experience. They contain a number of sections - introduction, nature conservation importance, nature conservation objectives, objectives of owner/occupier, agreed objectives, agreed management actions, management records, effectiveness of agreed management actions, and maps. Changes in legislation relating to SSSI notification management are contained in the Countryside and Rights of Way Act.

For farmers and landowners considering applying for Countryside Stewardship an *Upland Survey* (MAFF 1999) is required. This is to assist in the identification of all features of environmental interest on the land holding and much of the information can be supplied in map form. Guidance is given on the amount of detail needed, which in addition to environmental features includes legal, agricultural and land use information. Scheme objectives are set out and county target statements explain which objectives apply locally and which type of land or features are a priority. Specific conservation objectives and work are then identified for individual land holdings that are eligible for the scheme.

Figure 3.1 summarises the decision making process required that will apply to most situations and which is described in Section 3.2.

Further information: Andrews & Rebane 1994; Countryside Council for Wales 1996; Hirons, Goldsmith & Thomas 1995; Nature Conservancy Council 1988; Tait, Lane & Carr 1988.

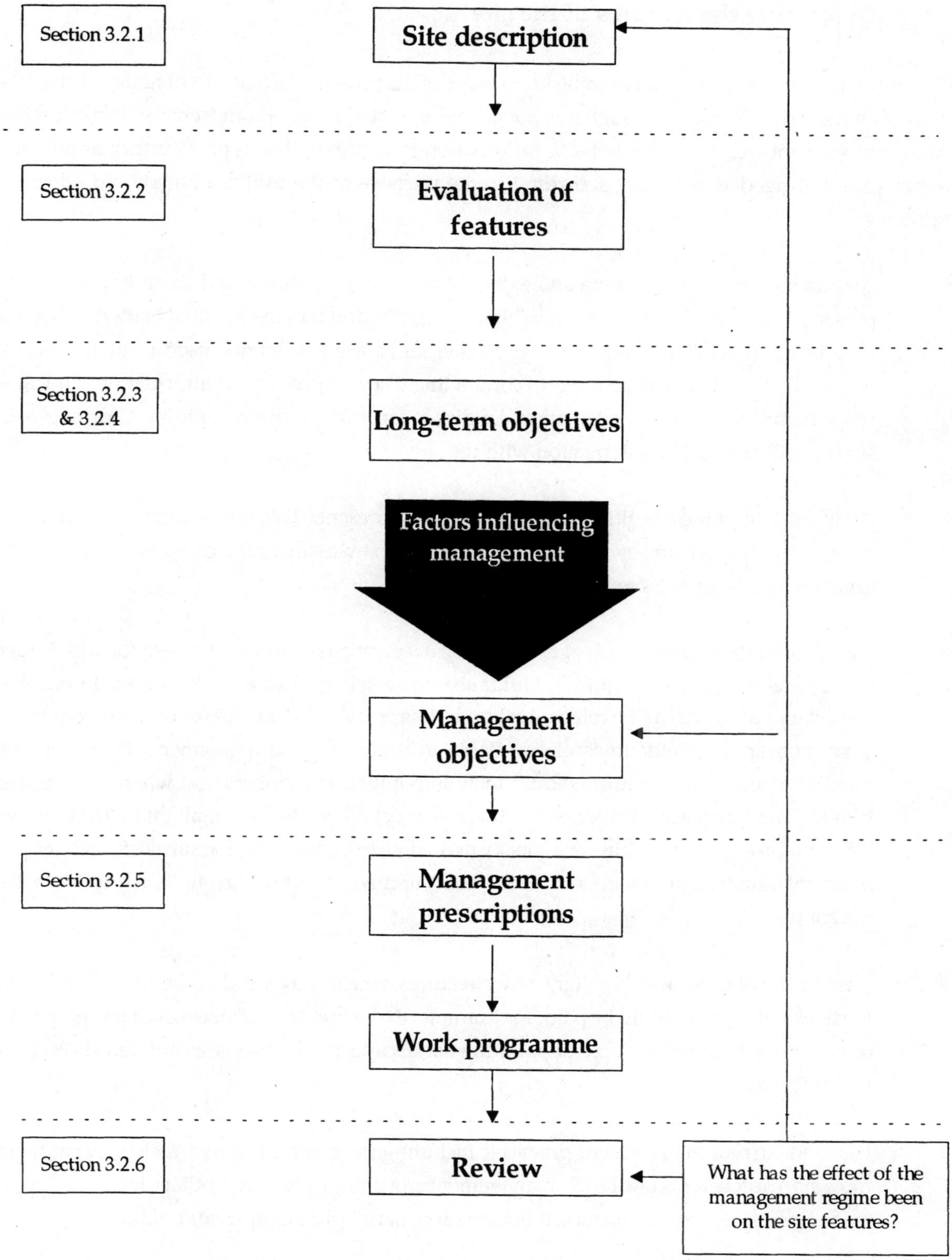

Figure 3.1. The decision making process

3.2 The decision making process

3.2.1 Describing the features of the site

The first step in the process requires some knowledge of the presence of features of nature conservation interest on the land holding. Although it is not always essential to have comprehensive information to make management decisions, some basic information is required. The type of information and the degree of detail needed will vary according to the purpose of the exercise but should address the following:

- An annotated map of the type and extent of the wildlife habitats and earth heritage features present. This can vary from broad habitat categories down to the detail of National Vegetation Classification (NVC) community types (the latter are sometimes useful but not normally essential). It is almost always worth conducting a new survey as old information is not always reliable and habitats and vegetation condition can change quite rapidly. Carrying out the survey will also aid familiarisation with the site.

- An indication of the condition of wildlife habitats present. This can be carried out at the same time as the habitat survey. Guidance on condition assessment for certain upland habitats is given in Information Note 1.

- Details (and location map) of *species of nature conservation significance* present for which specific management might be required. Guidance on which species are considered to be of such importance are given in the relevant tables in Chapters 5-10. The degree of detail required will vary with species and timescale available to undertake the assessment. However, where possible, species information should include population numbers and where known, recent trends. The presence of species of note is most likely to be highlighted from previous information and surveys but occasionally may come to light during the survey for higher plants, birds, mammals, amphibians and reptiles and certain invertebrate groups such as butterflies or dragonflies.

- The survey should also highlight other features which may need to be taken into account. Particular attention should be paid, for example, to the presence of stockproof fences, condition of boundary features, sources of pollution, landscape and archaeological interests and public rights of way.

- Past and current management practices, including information on livestock, grazing regimes, mowing practice, woodland management, burning practice, other farm or sporting management, sources of historical information, aerial photographs and old maps.

- Legal obligations associated with the land, such as sporting rights, tenancies, access, land designations such as SSSI or archaeological monuments, areas of ground covered by schemes such as ESAs, Countryside Stewardship.

- Land with the potential for restoration or recreation of wildlife features.

A number of initiatives are now adopting a whole farm/estate approach. This does not mean that all land has to be entered into an agreement but encourages a wider assessment of features of note on the holding. This can be particularly relevant when changes to the livestock regime are proposed as there may be implications for other parts of the estate through, for example, reducing grazing pressures elsewhere.

Possible sources of site records/information: Country nature conservation agencies (English Nature, CCW, SNH, DoENI), County RSPB, Wildlife Trusts, County/District Councils, the Environment Agency or equivalent, the County Biological Records Centre, ADAS, FRCA, ESA & Countryside Stewardship project officers, FWAG advisers, the County Bird Recorder and local museums.

Further information: MacDonald *et al* 1998; Nature Conservancy Council 1990a; Pollard 1977; Rodwell 1991 to 2000; Thomas 1983; Information Note 1.

3.2.2 Evaluating the site's features

Once a description of the site or land holding has been compiled, an evaluation of the wildlife (habitats, communities and species) and earth heritage features present should be made. This is essential as it will assist in identifying the conservation priorities and consequently the management objectives later. Each habitat, species of nature conservation significance or other interest feature should be assessed as to its international, national, regional or local significance. In addition assessments should include:

- the rarity of the feature in terms of each of these four geographic scales;
- the extent of the habitat or size of the species population on the site;
- to what extent the feature has been modified by man, ie how natural is it?
- how diverse are the various species groups/communities/habitats present?
- how susceptible to change is the feature?

At the end of the evaluation a picture should appear of how significant each of the individual site features is, and in relation to each other.

Further information: Batten *et al* 1990; Countryside Council for Wales 1996; Nature Conservancy Council 1988 & 1989; Perring & Walters 1990; Ratcliffe 1977; Rodwell 1991 to 2000; Stewart, Pearman & Preston 1994; UK Steering Group 1995; county floras, the records/information sources given in Section 3.2.1.

3.2.3 Formulating management objectives

A frequent mistake is to begin to make detailed decisions about upland management before the broad objectives for management have been defined. Objectives will need to be determined for each significant interest feature, to give a clear idea of what the management of that feature is meant to achieve. The nature of the objective will depend on the condition of the vegetation or population trend of a species. Where, for example, the vegetation condition is unfavourable, or a species is in decline, then the objective is likely to want to bring about a change in the current management to bring about a recovery. In contrast, where habitats appear to be in favourable condition and species populations are stable or increasing then the objective is likely to be to maintain the current management regime. For example, where an area of heath is losing dwarf-shrub cover then the objective might be: 'to return dwarf-shrub cover to >75%'. For upland heath and blanket bog, for example, the criteria for favourable vegetation condition given in Information Note 1 could be used to identify objectives, where vegetation is the principal management concern.

Where a specific species is in decline it is useful to include specific habitat requirements in the objective, such as sward height, sward structure or species composition in addition to population levels or overall distribution on the site. This provides clearer guidelines for the management and provides a number of targets that will be easier to monitor.

3.2.4 Factors influencing management

Before arriving at final management objectives, it is necessary to take into account those factors which will influence the achievement of the long-term objectives. Factors that need to be considered include the following:

- natural processes, including natural succession, erosion and sedimentation;
- national trends in species populations - a species may be in decline for reasons that are beyond the control of a land manager, including climate change, acid deposition, cyclical fluctuations or disease outbreaks;
- the ecological requirements of species or communities;
- external factors such as pollution or grazing pressure from wild animals such as deer or rabbits;
- legal obligations - the need to maintain public rights of way, conditions in tenancy agreements, SSSI obligations;
- conflicting management objectives - management for one feature might threaten the existence of another;
- practical considerations, such as off wintering facilities required to reduce winter grazing pressure;
- conflicts of interest with other land users including other commoners;

- the availability of resources, financial and labour and conditions attached to public monies received for management.

Once those factors which influence the management have been taken into consideration it might be necessary to modify the long-term objectives or, where resources are limited, prioritise these objectives in which case the following factors should be taken into account:

- the evaluation of the national and local significance of the features present;

- the significance of the features, in terms of the site's overall nature conservation interest. For example, how do the features compare in terms of extent/population numbers? How do they rank in terms of national/local scarcity? A site may, for example support a significant proportion of the national population of a particular species, or a large area of a nationally rare plant community. A small area of a rare community might be more important than a larger area of a more common one;

- how susceptible each feature is to changes in management, or changes in the structure or composition of the habitat in which it occurs. Consider what would happen if nothing is done to halt or reverse unfavourable conditions;

- how successful the possible management options are likely to be in achieving the desired effect. For example, if vegetation condition or species numbers are in decline, or a problem species is increasing in numbers or extent, will the management option redress the problem?

By taking all the above factors into account it should be possible to arrive at a set of management objectives which can then be turned into a work programme.

3.2.5 Work programme

For each management objective appropriate management prescriptions need to be selected and followed which will achieve the desired result. Management prescriptions should be chosen after referring to the relevant sections of this handbook and other references listed in each chapter. Choices will need to be made as to stocking rates, mowing regimes and burning programmes, together with ancillary requirements such as repair of stock boundaries, blocking of grips, degrees of bracken clearance or footpath maintenance.

Once management prescriptions have been selected and the details of the prescription identified, a work programme can be drawn up. This should outline what needs to be done at what time of year and, in some instances, in what year it should be done. It is conventional for work programmes to cover five year periods although some schemes offering financial incentives for management may require land managers to enter into a 10 year agreement with a corresponding work programme. Whatever period is used a review of the effectiveness of the management is standard at the end of that period so that any shortcomings can be taken into account. In some instances reviews may be undertaken more frequently.

Some management objectives and prescriptions may, however, involve much longer time scales so it may be necessary to have a short- to medium-term work programme running together with a more long-term programme covering, say, burning rotations and woodland restoration schemes relying on natural regeneration.

Annotated sketch maps of the site are often an effective way of keeping a record of the condition of the site when management decisions were made, the site condition which management is aiming to achieve and the management required to achieve this state. Figures 3.2, 3.3 and 3.4 give examples of this type of map.

3.2.6 Reviewing the effectiveness of the work programme

Managing land for nature conservation is not an exact science. Many of the management recommendations contained in this handbook are guidelines rather than precise prescriptions. There are many variables involved in land management, such as local climate or soil productivity, which makes it difficult to draw up rules that will fit every situation. There are, however, basic principles that will apply to most situations and that, with a little fine tuning, can be adapted to individual circumstances. For this reason alone it is important for there to be feedback from the effects of the management.

Some monitoring of the effects of management prescriptions on the vegetation and animal groups considered to be of importance should take place. Depending on the resources available and the objectives of the management, this can vary from a photographic record, through assessments of vegetation condition using, for example, the method in Information Note 1 or MacDonald *et al* (1988), to detailed monitoring programmes using quadrats and statistical analysis or surveys of specific species or groups of species. Information from monitoring should be fed back into the decision making and planning process so that modifications can be made to prescriptions where they are required. It is important to take into consideration when interpreting monitoring results that ecological change is not necessarily linear. There may be a lag period of several years before pronounced effects are noticed following a change in management regime. Some systems, however, may respond quite quickly. Also, detected changes may be caused by external factors such as abnormal weather conditions. It is usually best to monitor over a reasonable period before jumping to conclusions, unless it is very obvious that something is drastically wrong.

Record keeping can also be an invaluable aid to land management and can greatly aid the interpretation of unexpected outcomes to management operations. At the very least, basic records of what was done when, or, often more importantly, what wasn't done, and where, should be kept. The more detail that is recorded (stock type, number, timing of grazing, area burnt or felled/planted, date of mowing), the more useful the information is likely to be. Again any management that is missed in a given year should be recorded so that it can be fed into the following year's work programme.

Further information: Brooks & Stoneman 1997; Byrne 1991; Goldsmith 1991; Moore & Corbett 1990; Nature Conservancy Council 1988; Pollard 1977; Rowell 1988; Sutherland 1996; Thomas 1983.

3.3 Decision making example

The example used in this chapter to demonstrate the decision making process is a 3.75 ha field of wet grassland on the edge of a lake (see Figure 3.2). It is owned and managed by a National Park Authority (NPA). Its management comes within the remit of a Park Ranger. The field lies within an SSSI, so English Nature must be consulted about appropriate management practices.

This site consists of a section of ungrazed canary reed-grass *Phalaris arundinacea* tall fen lakeshore hydrosere vegetation, with scattered willow *Salix* bushes, and a damp field of soft rush *Juncus effusus* and sharp-flowered rush *Juncus acutiflorus* marshy grassland, with stands of bladder sedge *Carex vesicaria* swamp, plus drier grassland and hawthorn *Crataegus monogyna* bushes on the landward edge. The uncommon water sedge *Carex aquatilis* grows in the lakeshore tall herb fen. An invertebrate survey has established the presence of several uncommon species in the damp grassland. There are no breeding birds present in the grassland.

The lakeshore vegetation is in good condition. The rush pasture, however, is thought to be too heavily dominated by bulky species, such as soft rush, meadowsweet *Filipendula ulmaria*, tufted hair-grass *Deschampsia cespitosa* and purple moor-grass *Molinia caerulea*.

Management of the field has varied considerably both prior to and since the NPA's acquisition in 1984. It is known to have been grazed and possibly mown prior to 1984 but was not grazed or otherwise managed in the two years immediately preceding this date. In 1985 the north-east corner was mown but the field was not cut again until 1989, when it was also intermittently grazed.

The field has been summer grazed since 1990 using beef cattle from a nearby farm. The inception of grazing has varied each year and has tended towards June or, in some years, July. Stocking density has also varied considerably, with nine beef cattle in 1990 and four in 1998. In 1999 stocking varied from seven cattle initially, to three later on in the year. In addition to grazing the field is occasionally mown in August. The cuttings are normally baled and taken off site. However, in 1994 the baled cuttings were left to decay on the upper edge of the field.

The NPA's principal management objective has been to diversify the sward and create a sward structure suitable for breeding waders such as curlew *Numenius arquata*, snipe *Gallinaga gallinaga* and redshank *Tringa totanus*.

The following pages and boxes discuss the long-term objectives for the field (Box 3.2); the factors that influence the management (Box 3.3); the identification and formulation of management objectives (Box 3.4); the identification of management prescriptions to deliver the above (Box 3.5); and the production of a work programme (Box 3.6). Figure 3.3 shows the desired state of the field, and Figure 3.4 identifies the management required to achieve the desired state of the field.

Box 3.1 Example: Evaluation of nature conservation significance of features present

1. Vegetation types

Four vegetation types are present. These have the following nature conservation interest:

Rush pasture:	Relatively widespread locally, but nationally has undergone a significant decline in extent. Moderately species-rich stands are present, but no notable plant species present. This habitat can be of importance for breeding waders but none present. This is the most extensive vegetation type present, its composition is largely the result of grazing with livestock and, probably, annual mowing. Both practices also prevent natural succession to tall herb fen and eventually wet woodland.
Bladder sedge *Carex vesicaria* swamp:	A localised vegetation type, both within the county and nationally. Stands are restricted to the wetter parts of the field. It is more natural in terms of species composition than the rush pasture but grazing is preventing succession to willow carr.
Canary reed-grass *Phalaris arundinacea* tall herb fen:	A widespread vegetation type around water bodies, but of high ecological interest. Present as a broad strip along the lakeshore. Largely natural in species composition, but will develop into willow carr in the medium to long term without management.

2. Plant species

Water sedge *Carex aquatilis*:	A very rare species in the county, with only ten known sites. Nationally uncommon, but not classified as Nationally Scarce.

3. Animal species

Platypalpus unicus	A nationally rare Red Data Book fly
Geomyza apicalis	A nationally scarce fly
Platycheirus perpallidus	A nationally scarce hoverfly
Apion spencei	A locally distributed beetle
Themira annulipes	A locally distributed fly

Summary of nature conservation significance:

Site features		International	Significance National	Regional	Local
1. Vegetation types					
Rush pasture			Moderate	High	
Bladder sedge swamp			Moderate	High	
Canary reed-grass tall-herb fen				Moderate	High
2. Species					
Plants:	*Carex aquatilis*		Moderate	High	
Invertebrates:	*Platypalpus unicus*		High		
	Geomyza apicalis		Moderate	High	
	Platycheirus perpallidus		Moderate	High	
	Apion spencei				High
	Themira annulipes				High

Box 3.2 Example: Formulation of objectives – 1. Long-term objectives

The lakeshore tall herb fen vegetation appears to be in an acceptable condition. There are one or two willow bushes, which if allowed to become more numerous would result in a loss of open vegetation and its conversion to willow carr, a habitat which predominates around the rest of the lakeshore. At their present extent, however, these bushes provide perching and feeding sites for birds such as sedge and reed warbler and reed bunting. A suitable long-term objective would be *the maintenance of the open tall herb fen vegetation, with no more than 5% cover of willow bushes.* Preventing succession to woodland will retain diversity to the lakeshore as a whole.

There appears to be scope for improving the condition of the rush pasture as it is largely dominated by coarse species, such as soft rush *Juncus effusus*, meadowsweet *Filipendula ulmaria*, tufted hair-grass *Deschampsia cespitosa* and purple moor-grass *Molinia caerulea* at the expense of less competitive species. Additionally there is potential for waders to breed in the field, but none are currently present. This may be due to the sward structure being uniformly tall. A suitable long-term objective would be *to create and maintain a more diverse sward, with reduced abundance of coarse species and with a structure more suitable for breeding waders, such as curlew, redshank and snipe (a mosaic of short swards and tussocks with vegetation height ranging from 5-50+cm).* In addition to this *the existing populations of rare and uncommon invertebrates should be maintained.*

Box 3.3 Example: Formulation of objectives – 2. Factors influencing the management

- The main constraining factor which has hindered the achievement of the NPA's management objectives for this field is the difficulty of finding a grazier. This is due to the poor grazing quality of the land. The NPA does not own any stock itself. The NPA currently has a grazier for the land, but it has not always proved possible to maintain the desired grazing intensity throughout the grazing period, as the grazier periodically removes stock to better land to maintain their condition. As a result the vegetation is not grazed as hard as is desired so that little change in structure or species composition has occurred since grazing was re-introduced in 1990.

- The current management prescription is attempting to create conditions suitable for species which have not bred here for at least 10 years, possibly much longer, and does not take into account the requirements of species already present, which might have equivalent or greater nature conservation importance. Both heavy summer grazing and mowing, particularly the latter, are potentially detrimental to the invertebrate populations present as they result in a sward with few flowers, so reducing the abundance of nectar which is one of the major food sources for adult invertebrates. A recent survey identified one nationally rare hoverfly and two nationally scarce flies, along with a number of locally important species. While this could be said to be a reflection of general under-recording of invertebrates, it may also be indicative of a diverse invertebrate fauna at this site. Some of these species are nectivorous as adults.

- The size of the field dictates that it will never attract more than a few (less than five, and more likely two or three) pairs of breeding waders.

- No waders breed in the field at present.

- Scrub encroachment will occur in the ungrazed lakeshore unless management is carried out to interrupt the process of natural succession.

Box 3.4 Example: Formulation of objectives – 3. Taking the factors influencing management into account and formulating operational management objectives

Having considered the factors discussed in **2**, a clarification of the management objectives and methods on the field is required:

The principal objective of the management of the field is to diversify the sward structure and reduce the dominance of species such as soft rush *Juncus effusus*, meadowsweet *Filipendula ulmaria*, tufted hair-grass *Deschampsia cespitosa* and purple moor-grass *Molinia caerulea*.

Attracting breeding waders should not be considered to be the primary objective of the management of this field as the numbers of waders that could be attracted would never be of major significance. It could, however, be a beneficial side-effect of the management and the sward structure required by curlew, redshank and snipe (a mosaic of tussocks and short turf, ranging in height from 5-50cm) would meet the requirements of diversifying the sward structure and provides a suitable guide as to what constitutes the desired sward structure.

Grazing with cattle is the best method of creating and maintaining a tussocky sward. Initially grazing should be heavy in order to effect a change in the sward structure. A minimum stocking rate of 350 Lu/ha/yr (13 cattle) from 1 June until 31 October (153 days), with the grazing density being maintained throughout this period should achieve this. Taking half the cattle off half way through, as has happened in the past, will reduce the effectiveness of this remedial management considerably. To reduce the likelihood of this taking place, a hardy breed of cattle, that will not lose condition on this poor quality grazing, is required. This high level of grazing should not need to be maintained for more than a few years (probably no more than five) before the desired sward structure has been attained. It will be important to monitor both the sward structure and species composition during this period, so that the effectiveness of the management can be assessed and changes made if undesirable changes are occurring to the species composition or the sward structure is not seen to be developing in the desired way.

Once the sward has acquired the desired structure of a mosaic of short patches and tussocks with vegetation height ranging from 5-50+cm then the stocking rate should be reduced to a maintenance level. Some experimentation, with close monitoring of the sward structure and species composition, will be required to establish exactly what the appropriate maintenance stocking rate is, but initially a rate of 200 Lu/ha/yr (seven or eight cattle) between 1 June and 31 October is suggested. Should waders start to breed in the field then the stocking rate up to mid-July will need to be reviewed and, perhaps, reduced to decrease the chance of trampling damage to nests and chicks.

Annual mowing has been used to supplement grazing in bringing about a change in sward structure, but it is not a suitable long-term management technique as it will tend to produce a uniform sward rather than a tussocky one and the sudden change in sward height that it brings about is likely to be detrimental to the invertebrate interest. Occasional mowing may, however, aid the remedial management when stock numbers fall short of levels required.

An alternative and more effective, though more labour intensive, method of enhancing the effect of grazing with mowing during the remedial management phase is to use a brush cutter to cut the vegetation around preferentially grazed areas to lead the cattle into the coarser vegetation. This would need to be done at least monthly throughout the grazing period. This should not need to be continued once the required vegetation structure is achieved. It is thought at present, however, that this would require too great an input of labour. Topping the coarser vegetation on a regular basis throughout the growing season might also be considered as an alternative. However, there would be difficulty in removing the cut material and this would be essential.

The use of mowing in any form should cease as soon as the required vegetation condition is achieved. In all cases where mowing is used the cuttings should be removed from the site. Mowing should also cease if waders start breeding in the field.

Vegetation monitoring and the use of the resulting data to direct the future course of the management regime is essential here, as the management is attempting to produce a change in the vegetation. Recording quadrats in each stand type over the remedial management phase is especially important.

It should be noted that the management is primarily aiming at changing the structure of the sward, rather than its species composition. It would be undesirable for the management regime to result in a reduction in species diversity, a general loss of characteristic fen species or a marked shift in the species composition away from the current M23 *Juncus effusus/acutiflorus-Galium palustre* rush pasture communities towards a more grassy less diverse community such as MG10 *Holcus lanatus-Juncus effusus* rush pasture, or for it to result in the replacement of *J. acutiflorus* by *J. effusus* in stands where the former is currently dominant. If monitoring detects that any of these trends are occurring then changes in the management regime should be considered.

Monitoring of the sward structure may best be done using fixed point oblique stereo photography.

Monitoring of invertebrate groups should also be carried out to ensure that the management is not having an adverse effect on the uncommon species present. In addition to this monitoring, consideration should be given to carrying out surveys of the surrounding fields to ascertain the distribution of the uncommon invertebrate species that have been recorded in the NPA's field so that the local significance of the field for these species can be assessed.

If the desired sward structure has not been achieved within five years of inception of this regime then the management of this field should be thoroughly reviewed. It should not take ten years to achieve the required sward condition; five years of the appropriate management should suffice.

The lakeshore is largely a non-intervention zone. However, invasion by willow, which is more or less absent at present, needs to be monitored and cleared on a regular basis with treatment of stumps and the removal of felled trees.

Box 3.5 Example: An action plan with management prescriptions

Objective	Prescription	Specification	Priority
Main field			
1. To maintain and enhance the wet meadow vegetation and provide breeding habitat for wading birds.	1. Graze to create tussocky sward structure.	13+ cattle between 1 June & 31 October	High
	2. Top sward to reduce vigour of *Juncus effusus*.	Regular (monthly/ bimonthly) topping of vegetation at a height of 15 cm and removal of cuttings during remedial management phase.	Moderate
	3. Check for presence of breeding waders.	During last two weeks of May. If waders present reduce stocking level and cease mowing between 1 June & 15 July.	High
	4. Maintain fence and water hole.	Repair/renew as required.	High
	5. Once required sward structure achieved reduce stocking to a maintenance level.	Seven or eight cattle between 1 June & 31 October.	High
	6. Monitor effect of grazing regime on vegetation composition and adjust stocking as appropriate.	Record quadrats every three years during course of remedial grazing regime. Monitor every five years once maintenance regime established.	High
	7. Monitor effect of grazing regime on invertebrate assemblage and consider adjustments to stocking if a decline in notable species is detected.	Survey unrecorded groups and repeat surveys of uncommon species every five years.	High
	8. Review management objectives and methods after five years.	If management has been unsuccessful in creating desired sward structure consider alternative management regime.	High
Lakeshore			
1. To maintain and enhance the lakeshore vegetation.	1. Prevent encroachment of willow into lakeshore compartment.	Monitor extent of willow scrub and clear willow as required. Treat stumps with a herbicide approved for use near water, eg Fosamine Ammonium. Willow scrub not to exceed 5% cover.	Moderate
	2. Continue exclusion of stock.	Maintain fence between lakeshore and main field and adjacent fields.	High

Box 3.6 Example: A five year work programme*

	Year				
Job	**1**	**2**	**3**	**4**	**5**
Main field					
Monitor for presence of breeding waders (Late May)	✓	✓	✓	✓	✓
Graze with cattle at remedial stocking rate (June – October)	✓	✓	✓	?	?
Reduce stocking rate if waders breeding (June – mid July)	?	?	?	?	?
Mow sward (June/mid-July if waders breeding – October)	✓	✓	✓	?	?
Maintain fence and water hole (when required)	✓	✓	✓	✓	✓
Graze with cattle at maintenance stocking rate (June – October)				?	?
Monitor vegetation (late June/early July)	✓		✓		✓
Monitor invertebrate populations (summer)	✓		✓		✓
Review management			?		✓
Lakeshore					
Monitor willow scrub (summer/autumn)					✓
Control scrub encroachment (winter)					?
Maintain fence and water hole (when required)	✓	✓	✓	✓	✓

***Note**

The example management prescriptions and work programme shown above include monitoring of the vegetation structure and species composition and invertebrate populations. The results of these programmes are used to review the effects of the management and to modify prescription specifications when necessary. A five yearly review is built into the work programme to ensure that the prescriptions are achieving the management objectives.

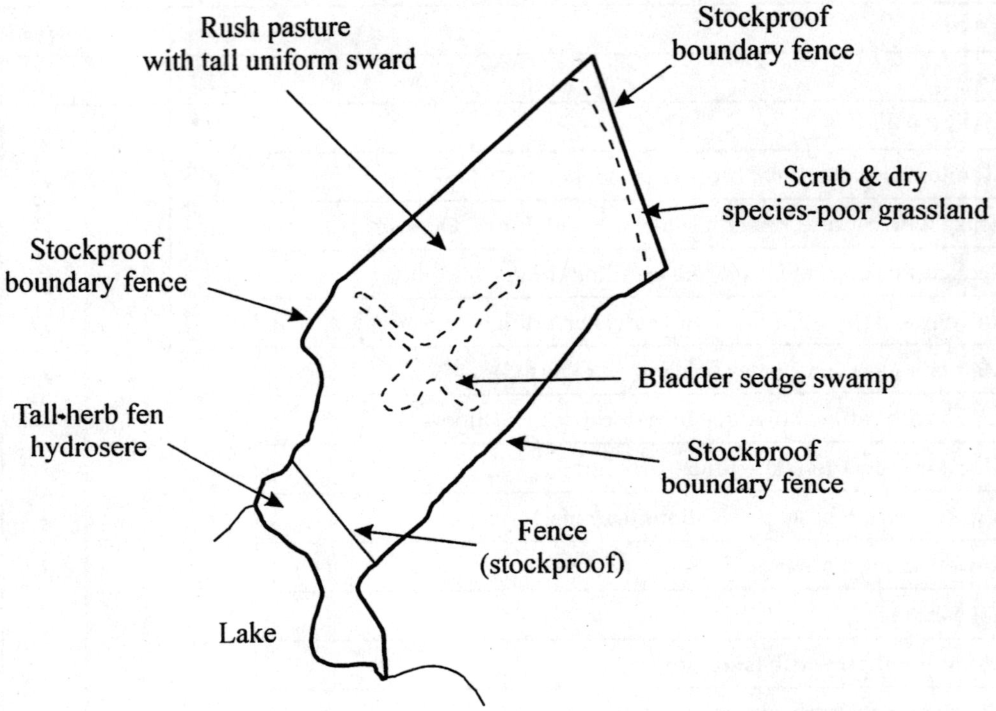

Figure 3.2. Existing state of example field

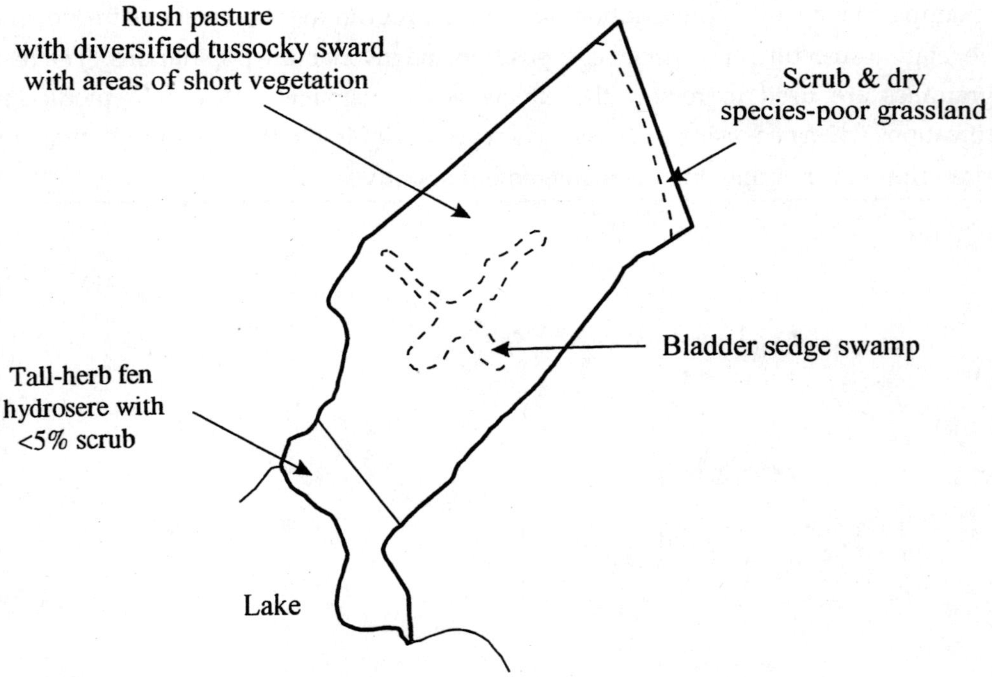

Figure 3.3. Desired state of example field

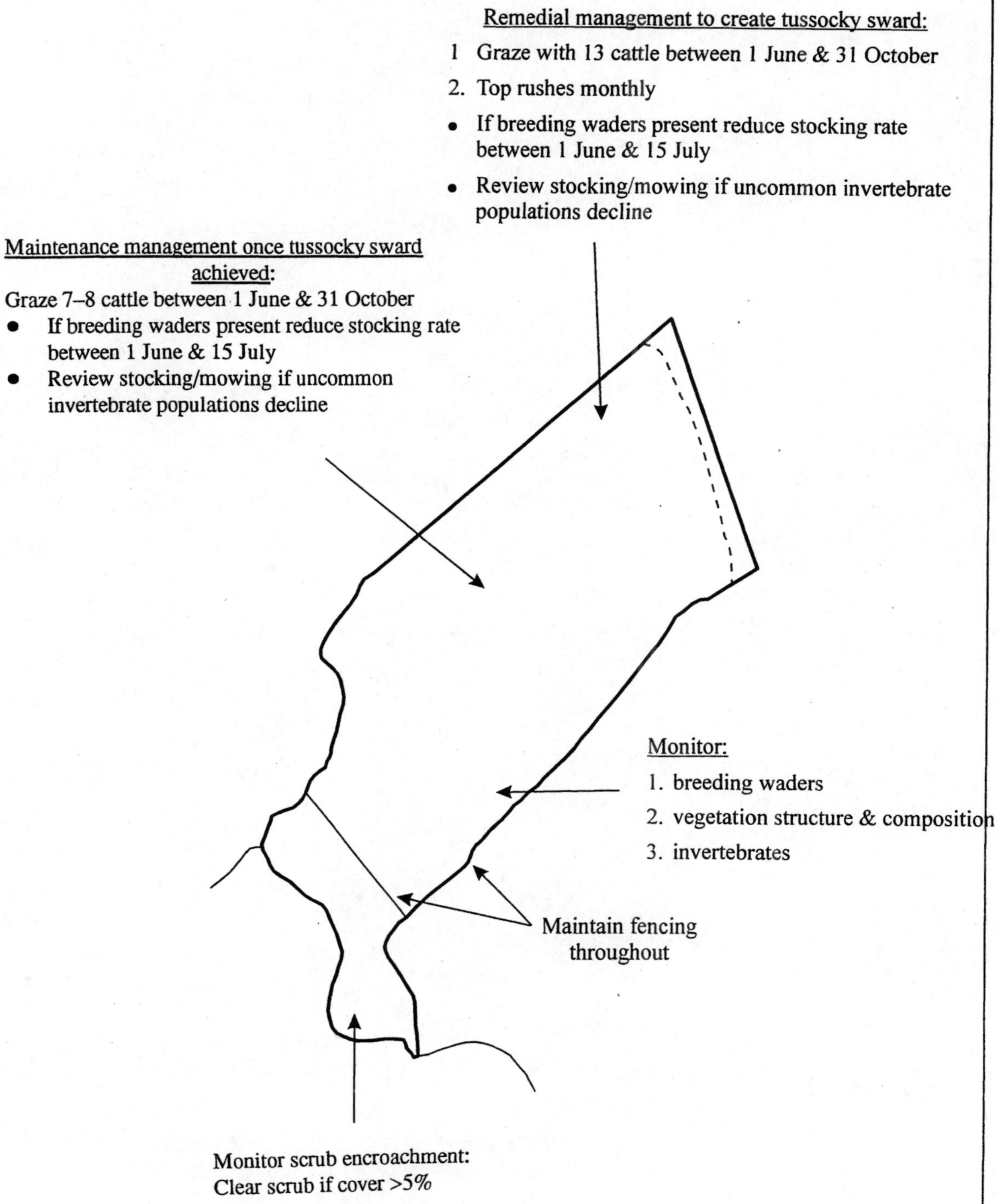

Figure 3.4. Management required to achieve desired state of example field

Earth heritage features 4

Table

4.1 The geological history of England and its landscape

The geological evolution of the earth began around 4.6 billion years ago and the oldest rocks found in Britain are older than 570 million years. The geological timescale is sub-divided into eras, periods and stages. Many of the names given to world-wide geological time units originate from English place names or type localities (reference sites with which all rocks of a similar age and geological type can be compared). As such the geological history of England is internationally significant.

Upland areas are the result of millions of years of geological activity. Some upland areas were created by the uplift, folding and faulting of rocks as oceans closed and continents collided during the geological evolution of Britain. Others were never affected by these mountain building episodes and exist as uplands simply because they are formed of rock that is more resistant to erosion than the surrounding geology. All of them have been affected by the Ice Age that swept across the country.

A vast range of geological and geomorphological interest is found within the uplands and the link between landscape and geological form and process is inescapable. Upland areas are characterised by their sub-surface geology and the level of resistance of each of the rock types to erosion. Superimposed onto this is a series of geomorphological processes that sculpt the shape of the land surface. In turn the geology and geomorphology of the landscape also dictate the nature of the soil cover, which determines the range of flora and fauna that the land is able to sustain.

For a relatively small country, England has a complex geological history clearly demonstrated by the diverse geology and landscape. In general the uplands of England comprise igneous rocks (crystallised from magma from the earth's centre) or metamorphic rocks (rocks recrystallised under heat or pressure) as they are more resistant to erosion than sedimentary rocks. However, more durable sedimentary limestones of the Pennines and the sandstones of the North York Moors.

4.2 The importance of earth heritage conservation

Britain was the birthplace of a great deal of geological thinking and research during the eighteenth and nineteenth centuries. Interpretation of geological history provides us with important information concerning climatic and environmental changes and demonstrates the link between geology and biology. Understanding our geological past is the key to interpreting our geological and environmental future. As such the conservation of a network of sites that interprets the evolution of our land mass is critical for our scientific, educational, cultural, aesthetic and economic development.

The geological evolution of the English uplands is demonstrated in Table 4.1.

Table 4.1 Geological evolution of the English Uplands

Geological Age (millions of years)	General rock types	Geo-environment and geological events relevant to the uplands	Upland area
Quaternary 'The Ice Age' 1.6-0.01	Screes, wind-blown and eroded material Boulder clays, river and melt-water deposits Peat, soils, river deposits	Ice sheet cover with tundra-like conditions, erosion of the landscape and deposition of eroded material Temperate, non-glacial conditions	All areas All areas
Tertiary 65-1.6	Sands and muds	Tropical weathering of sediments, karst development and the formation of the pre-Quaternary landscape	Landscaping effect on all uplands. Pockets of Tertiary sediments eg: Peak District.
Cretaceous 140-65	Chalk deposition under marine conditions	Pulling apart of the super-continent	Little impact on uplands as they were 'land' areas at this time.
Jurassic 195-140	Marine limestones and shales Non-marine sandstones	Flooded by warm seas Delta encroachment	North York Moors.
Permian & Triassic 280-195	Evaporates, sands and other desert deposits	Desert conditions with inland sea development	Pockets of sediments in uplands, eg: Penrith Sandstone, Cumbria.
Upper Palaeozoic - Carboniferous 345-280	Flooded peat beds (later transformed into coal seams), limestones and sandstones Volcanic rocks, folding and mineralisation	Sea-level rise flooded much of the land surface The Variscan mountain building episode, continued into early Permian	N. Pennines, S. Pennines Peak District, Forest of Bowland, Yorkshire Dales Dartmoor, Bodmin Moor, Pennines and the Peak District.
Upper Palaeozoic - Devonian 395-345	 Marine muds and fossil-rich limestones Non-marine sandstones	Erosion of land after Caledonian Orogeny and the opening of the Rheic Ocean	Igneous activity in the Cheviots and Lake District Exmoor Cheviots and Lake District

Geological Age (millions of years)	General rock types	Geo-environment and geological events relevant to the uplands	Upland area
Lower Palaeozoic - Cambrian, Ordovician & Silurian 570-395	Limestones, shales and sandstones	Widening and then closing of 'Iapetus', an ancient ocean which formed the proto-Atlantic'	Welsh Borders, Lake District
	Metamorphic rocks and igneous activity. Conversion of shales to slates by metamorphic activity	Caledonian mountain building episode	Slatey rocks of the Lake District. Igneous activity and folding in Shropshire, Pennines and the Lake District, with associated mineralisation.
Precambrian >570	Metamorphic rocks and volcanics. Sediment deposition		Welsh Borders

4.3 The evolution of England's upland landscape

The uplands have been continually evolving ever since their formation. They have been modified by the Ice Age and a series of geomorphological processes, such as the movement of material down-slope, river activity, karst landscape evolution and a range of other erosional and depositional processes. This modification occurs by way of breakdown of the rock or sediments by weathering agents, such as frost, wind and rain, and the redistribution of this eroded sediment by transporting agents, such as rivers, mass movement and wind. The result is a two-fold landscape; one that is dominated by erosion-forming the mountain areas, and another dominated by the deposition of material, on the valley sides and floors. These processes may change the form of the landscape slowly over centuries or through relatively rare catastrophic events, such as the landslip at Mam Tor, Derbyshire which caused the re-routing of the A625.

Human activity may also be regarded as a geological agent as it has had a tremendous impact on the British landscape. Mineral extraction, forest clearance, farming, transport, urbanisation and recreation have produced a 'cultural landscape' reflecting human intervention, even in the most remote upland areas.

As a result of this landscape evolution England's uplands may be divided broadly into six distinct areas of different geological character, all of which reflect the geological development of the English landscape. These are as follows:

- **Granite uplands.** This group includes Bodmin Moor and Dartmoor in the West Country, which are dominated by granite intrusions and mineral-rich deposits. During the Quaternary the area was subject to tundra-like conditions, which helped to sculpt the characteristic tor and boulder strewn landscape.

- **Precambrian and Lower Palaeozoic uplands.** This group includes the Shropshire Hills and Central Marches. The landscape comprises resistant Carboniferous rocks and early Palaeozoic sedimentary rocks and was subject to tundra-like conditions during the Quaternary period.

- **Late Palaeozoic uplands.** This group includes Exmoor and the Quantocks, Oswestry, Staffordshire Uplands, Black Mountains and the Golden Valley. The geology is solid Carboniferous and Devonian bedrock, overlain by Permo-Triassic deposits. The area was proximal to the ice sheets during the Quaternary and it is considered that localities such as The Golden Valley were formed through ice scouring the landscape. There are extensive deposits associated with the melting of ice and melt-water rivers.

- **Carboniferous Limestone and Millstone Grit uplands.** This group includes the Pennines, Peak District, Forest of Bowland and the Yorkshire Dales and is, in reality, a subset of the Late Palaeozoic Uplands, but has been placed in a second group due to its different management requirements. Mineral-rich water flowing through the limestone bedrock resulted in the formation of mineral rich veins. The landscapes in these areas are exposed and rugged with surface streams on the Millstone Grit and cave systems and potholes within the limestone bedrock. Ice sheets scoured the rock surface during the Quaternary, leaving it susceptible to weathering which aided the formation of characteristic limestone pavements.

- **Jurassic uplands.** This group includes the North York Moors with fossiliferous muds, shales and sandstones dominating the landscape. During the Quaternary the ice sheets deposited boulder clays, melt-water channels scoured deep into the bedrock and there is evidence of tundra conditions at the ice margins.

- **Caledonian uplands.** This group includes the Cumbrian Fells and Dales. The area has a mixed geology. Extensive erosion by the Quaternary ice sheets left only the most resistant rocks outstanding, for instance the Lake District Borrowdale Volcanic Group which forms the central Lake District hills.

4.4 The identification and selection of sites for earth heritage conservation

From the late 1940s until 1977 the most important earth heritage sites were identified by the Nature Conservancy, and then the Nature Conservancy Council, using information supplied by earth scientists. In 1977, the Geological Conservation Review (GCR) developed a systematic approach to site selection in Britain by identifying a network of sites that reflected the range and diversity of geology and geomorphological processes. Sites were selected between 1977 and 1990 and of all of the sites are notified as SSSIs. The criteria developed for site selection can be synthesised as follows:

- sites of importance to the international community of earth scientists;

- sites that are scientifically important because they contain exceptional features;

- sites that are nationally important because they are representative of an earth science feature, event or process which is fundamental to Britain's earth history.

The GCR classification scheme corresponds to seven 'categories' which correspond to periods of geological time or processes. Within these, individual 'sites' fall into subject 'blocks', so breaking the category down into more specific time periods or processes. For instance, the geomorphology category includes 10 'blocks' that allow subdivision of the geomorphological processes. A site such as the Mam Tor landslide, Derbyshire, would fall into the geomorphological 'category' and the mass movement 'block'. A full account of the GCR classification scheme can be found in the GCR Introductory Volume (Ellis *et al* 1996).

All earth heritage sites are classified as either *integrity* or *exposure* sites under the Earth Science Conservation Classification (ESCC). Integrity sites are those where the geology or landform is irreplaceable if removed or damaged and includes sites of limited extent and geomorphological sites. Exposure sites are those where the deposit is extensive and there is no immediate threat of the resource being lost.

4.5 Earth heritage objectives

Geological objectives for upland areas are derived from several sources including the English Nature Strategy, generic Natural Area geological objectives and key geological objectives for specific upland Natural Areas.

4.5.1 Earth heritage strategy

The English Nature leaflet entitled *Conserving England's Earth Heritage* is a good introduction to geological conservation highlighting English Nature's strategy for future work, under five headings:

- Managing and safeguarding the resource

  Including the completion of the SSSI and GCR site notification programme, site enhancement schemes and guidance for local Regionally Important Geological/Geomorphological Sites (RIGS) groups.

- Integrating earth heritage and the holistic approach

  Establishing closer working relationships with site owners and international partners to develop and share best practice.

- Influencing the influencers

  Production of best practice guidelines for Local Authorities and the inclusion of earth heritage conservation within the hierarchy of local plans.

- Raising awareness

  Striving to enhance the public's awareness of earth heritage through site interpretation schemes and publication at a range of levels of understanding.

- Involving the public

  Through public involvement we strive to increase public enjoyment and understanding, use established resources such as RIGS, the Geologists Association, local community and conservation groups.

4.5.2 Key geological objectives for upland areas

The key geological objectives for upland Natural Areas are as follows:

- maintaining and enhancing the geological resource through the enhancement of existing exposures, the use of site safeguard policies and the continued assessment of the scientific importance of sites;
- including earth heritage conservation features within Local Authority plans, National Park plans and the development of long-term conservation packages;
- promoting the English Nature position statement on fossil collecting (English Nature 1996) and emphasis of the need for responsible collecting at other sites including mines and tips, quarries and, where applicable, geomorphological sites;
- raising public awareness of the vulnerability of limestone pavements and the mechanisms in place to ensure their protection;
- supporting local caving groups in producing and implementing cave conservation plans and encouragement of local groups to take responsibility for specific cave systems;
- establishing initiatives for strengthening the links between English Nature and local communities through earth heritage conservation;
- establishing joint biological/geological management strategies for mixed interest sites and raise awareness of the link between geology and habitat development;
- promoting of the geological resource through the assessment of site educational value, on-site interpretation and the development of thematic trails.

More specific geological objectives have been developed for individual Natural Areas and may be found in the relevant Natural Area profiles which have been produced by English Nature.

Site classifications and examples of management options for earth heritage sites are outlined below. As with all conservation strategies, management needs to be site specific to take account of the uniqueness of the interest represented at each SSSI. Detailed management options for earth heritage sites are discussed more fully in the appendices of the *Earth Science Conservation in Great Britain, A Strategy* (Nature Conservancy Council 1991).

4.6 Site classification and examples of site management

4.6.1 Geomorphological sites

Geomorphological sites include three sub-groups of scientific interest in upland areas, active process sites, relict landform sites and karst landscapes. These are discussed in more detail below. Geomorphological sites are designated to provide examples of geological processes and systems that sculpt our landscape, and to conserve examples of rivers, slope failures, landforms, limestone pavements and caves. Sites in all three categories are classified as integrity sites as the interest may be easily damaged and is irreplaceable.

Active process sites

Active process sites include river and mass movement interest blocks. The management emphasis for active geomorphological sites is placed on maintaining the 'natural evolution' of the system. By their very nature geomorphological sites are active and evolving sites that may have social implications, for instance changing river patterns resulting from natural channel evolution or slope failure as a result of geological evolution of the landscape. As it is the natural evolution of the system that is important to the scientific interest of a site, management strategies should seek to minimise impacts on or changes to the natural system.

Human intervention is often incompatible with the effective conservation of these active sites as it is the naturalness of the geomorphological system that is scientifically important. In the uplands, rivers are generally free from the major human intervention common in lowland areas and are often accompanied by well documented histories in terms of local knowledge, historical records and photographs. In some cases it may be necessary to alter the natural system in some way, for instance engineering works to stabilise dangerous slopes in the interest of public safety or damage to property. In such cases the effects on the integrity of the site should be minimised and any changes that take place in the system should be recorded and monitored.

Some geomorphological activity is so catastrophic that attempts to curb the natural processes are abandoned and the sites are left to evolve naturally. At the well documented landslip site at Mam Tor, Derbyshire, the A625 road was destroyed during a series of landslips (Skempton, Leadbeater & Chandler 1989). Due to the extent of the movement and the likelihood of future activity, the road was diverted and the old road closed to traffic. The site, designated as an SSSI, is still an active landslip and has become a popular walking route with considerable educational opportunities.

Relict landforms

Relict or static geomorphological landforms are those that were formed during the Quaternary or Ice Age. They include glacial landforms such as tors and glacial ridges and features such as patterned and hummocky ground.

These sites require an integrated approach to management, taking account of the way in which the surrounding environment affects the site and ensures that development does not impinge on the scientific interest. Activities such as mineral extraction, tipping, in-filling, development and forestry are all likely to influence the scientific interest of these sites and appropriate consultation should be undertaken to ensure that alternatives are considered.

Karst

Karst sites are particularly vulnerable to damage and as such considerable detail has been paid to them in this handbook. Karst landscapes are those where the underlying geology is generally limestone. They are created by solution of limestone bedrock and are characterised by a landscape of surface hollows and depressions together with underground (rather than surface) drainage. The term karst derives from the German form of the Slovene word *kras*, meaning bare stony ground.

British karst landscapes can be found on both hard and soft limestones and include features of the chalk downlands as well as the hard limestone uplands. The most important karstic rock of Britain is the Carboniferous Limestone (Waltham *et al* 1997) which forms the upland blocks of Mendip, the White Peak, the Pennines and the Lake District fringes. A variety of features develop in karst topography of the uplands and these are discussed below.

- **Limestone pavements** are level or gently inclined bare limestone surfaces that are fissured by natural erosion demonstrating a pattern of blocks and fissures known as clints and grikes. Their basic structure results from glacial scouring but fine detail and patterning is a result of continuing geomorphological evolution. There is only 2,600 ha of pavement in Britain (Webb 1995) and it is known that only 3% of British pavements are undamaged (Ward & Evans 1976). Limestone pavements support a characteristic flora including a number of rare and scarce species (see Chapter 10 Crags, scree and limestone pavements). Over 90% of British pavements are found in northern England within Cumbria, North Yorkshire and the northern parts of Lancashire.

  Limestone pavements have been extensively damaged by the removal of stone for decorative garden rockeries. Provision was made in the Wildlife and Countryside Act 1981 for the protection of these features. Limestone Pavement Orders can be made under Section 34 of the Act which makes disturbance of the limestone a criminal offence. The orders have been very effective in reducing the amount of damage to the remaining limestone pavements in northern England. However, illegal damage and damage within areas with planning permission for quarrying continues. In 1995 the Limestone Pavement Action Group was established to reduce the demand for the water-worn rockery stone. Focusing on education and publicity the group has been very successful and has helped to secure revocation of two pavement quarrying planning permissions. Techniques to protect pavement have thus been focused on both preventing supply and reducing demand.

The management of limestone pavement and the impact of various agricultural regimes is discussed in Chapter 10. It is essential that the biological and geological interest of these features are considered together when devising management and protective strategies, as the conservation management of limestone pavements in the uplands must attempt to integrate the biological and geological interest of the features. In practice this is not difficult to achieve. Optimal management requirements for upland pavements are discussed in Chapter 10 but in general will centre on a reduction of grazing pressure. Ingleborough and Great Asby Scar National Nature Reserves are examples where grazing stock have been excluded from pavement areas. These sites are nationally important for both their botanical and geological features. The change in vegetation resulting from the exclusion of the grazing stock has not resulted in the loss or obscuring of geological features. It is important to remember that these pavements are active geomorphological sites which display a relationship between vegetation cover and physical form.

- **Cave systems** are an important feature of upland karst areas. They are formed where there is an available flow of water with the potential to dissolve limestone and a hydraulic gradient between the top and bottom of a cave. The cave passages, and the sediments and speleothems (stalactites, etc) within them, are fragile features and as such are regarded as integrity sites. They have taken thousands of years to form and many pre-date the last ice age. The sediments and speleothems within the caves, as well as the physical form and shape of the passages, add significantly to our understanding of the geological evolution of the English uplands. Caves often contain important environmental and archaeological deposits that improve our knowledge of past climates. Caves also support rare fauna such as bats or troglobites (species adapted to living in permanent darkness).

  Cave entrances and catchments are generally included within the SSSI boundary. Caves are important local drainage routes and changes to the hydrological catchment (drainage, abstraction, etc) can have an impact on the condition of the cave, its sediments and decorative speleothems. It is therefore important that caves are viewed as systems, together with their catchment areas rather than as isolated passages.

  Damage to cave environments can be averted through appropriate management of the cave catchment area. Practices such as moor gripping, afforestation, deforestation or modification to water courses can all affect the cave, its sediments and speleothems. Threats to caves include recreational damage, physical loss (through quarrying, mining or waste disposal) and changes in hydrology or catchment.

  Damage caused by recreational use by cavers generally has an impact on sediment deposits and speleothems rather than on the physical form of the cave itself. The National Caving Association (NCA) published a conservation policy in 1995 and has a code of conduct for cavers. The conservation policy, which was supported by English Nature, identifies cave conservation plans as a valuable tool to secure the conservation interest of caves. These site-specific plans are devised, supported and implemented by the cavers who know and use the site. The NCA policy also addresses external threats to caves such as quarrying, landfill and water abstraction. The threats are best addressed through the minerals planning process, development plans and responses to individual planning applications.

In the cave conservation plan produced for Lathkill Head Cave, Derbyshire two levels of threat were identified: internal and external. The internal threats came from usage of the cave system while external threats were identified as changes in the catchment hydrology and therefore water movement within the system. As a result recommendations were made to safeguard the areas of the cave system that were most at risk and a number of issues were highlighted for further investigation, including the use of information boards to inform cavers of the threats to the system and moves to limit the amount of litter left within the system.

- **Other karst features** found in the uplands include shakeholes or depressions, scars, scree and dry valleys. These features are separate parts of a mosaic which makes up the karst landscape. They are often physically linked and in many cases the processes are still active and the features are still evolving. As well as providing information about the evolution of the post-glacial landscape these features are often of botanical importance with thin soils, species-rich grasslands and a variety of rock habitats (see Chapter 10).

Karst features such as shakeholes or depressions, scars and scree are vulnerable to agricultural impacts especially where they lie within enclosed land. Infilling of depressions and shakeholes with agricultural rubbish has been a continuing problem especially on the Mendip Hills (Stanton 1992) where these depressions form convenient receptacles for a variety of farmyard waste. The result is a permanent loss of the landform and a potential pollution threat, as many of the depressions link directly to underground drainage.

Scars, screes and limestone pavements form a useful source of hardcore or building stone. Whilst it may be acceptable to find material for wall gapping or track maintenance from these features, the scale of removal needs to be balanced with a permanent loss of feature. Best practice will centre on management agreements and discussing stone sources with the landowner or tenant.

Further information: Watson 1997

4.6.2 Mines and mine dumps

Igneous activity and the movement of water through rocks can leave behind mineral-rich deposits. For centuries man has exploited these mineral veins. Mines and their associated waste material are of geological significance as they provide us with information relating to the formation of the surrounding area and the geological evolution of Great Britain. The associated waste material often provides a safe study site as an alternative to abandoned mines, which may be flooded or too dangerous to enter. Consequently mine dumps are often the only possible location to study and collect certain rocks and minerals.

To maintain the geological interest of these sites access to and direct contact with the mineralised deposits is critical. Close examination of the mined material can be achieved by utilizing spoil tips. In cases where development pressures result in damage to the scientific interest of these spoil heaps it may be necessary to move the spoil tip to another location. However, although this will conserve some of the scientific interest, it is less desirable than maintaining the interest *in situ*. Responsible collecting of material is encouraged by English Nature and the Geologists Association code of conduct should be adhered to when visiting such sites.

4.6.3 Disused quarries

Disused quarries have the potential to provide excellent geological exposures which may have been difficult to access during normal quarrying operations. These exposures provide us with information relating to the geological evolution of Britain. In general these quarries are classified as exposure sites, as an area of the scientifically important material remains as an unexcavated reserve on the quarry margin. In those localities where the deposits are of outstanding importance or are limited in their extent, the sites are classified as integrity sites.

A range of after-uses is possible for disused quarries, including nature conservation, development, landfill and reservoir formation. If the entire quarry is being used as a geological nature reserve, the rock faces should be kept safe and cleared of vegetation and slumped material (scree) as and when necessary. If an application is made to fill a site it is usual that English Nature will enter into negotiations with the landowner to secure a permanent exposure within the quarry which is representative of the interest at the site.

Positive management of the geological interest requires that physical and visual access to the geological sections should be maintained. Commonly in disused quarries, the geological face and scree may become a haven for wildlife and any works undertaken to re-expose the geological section should be balanced with all conservation interests at the site, including any biological or entomological interest. In addition operations considered as normal practice during mineral extraction may now be found on the list of operations likely to damage the scientific interest.

A good example of earth heritage conservation as an after-use is Burrator, Dartmoor, where a series of disused quarries has been designated as an SSSI. The site is accompanied by a geological trail which examines the range of landforms associated with tor formation and the evolution of the Dartmoor landscape. The trail is designed for both specialists and interested non-specialists. Further information about the site may be found in the Nature Conservancy Council publication *Burrator, Dartmoor landform trail* (Keene & Harley 1987).

4.6.4 Active quarries

Active quarries are important for earth heritage conservation as the exposures provide us with information relating to the geological evolution of Britain. Mineral extraction creates new geological sections, so revealing new material and scientific information on a regular basis and provides the opportunity to create a permanent conservation face for study. It is acknowledged that active quarries may modify the landscape unacceptably. Mineral extraction may be compatible with geological conservation provided that discussion is entered into concerning the location, size and management of permanent sections.

Active quarries are generally classified as exposure sites. As with disused quarries site management should address maintaining access to the geological interest. Early consultation with English Nature can help to ensure that geological conservation is integrated with extraction and restoration schemes for the site and to identify the optimum location for a permanent section that displays the necessary information for site interpretation.

At Shap Quarry, Cumbria, the zoned mineralisation seen in the rocks is the result of igneous and metamorphic activity. Owing to the nature of the extraction process and the danger of falling rocks the quarry company has allowed limited access to the site and provides a 'safe' area where prepared blocks of the material can be viewed. It is hoped that when quarrying is completed a permanent exposure will be left in the quarry face.

4.6.5 Natural upland exposures and outcrops

Natural upland exposures and outcrops include sites of geological interest ranging from natural rock outcrops, through to peat deposits and frost shattered material. Next to coastal cliff sections England's uplands provide the most extensive natural exposures and are therefore critical to developing our understanding of the geological evolution of Great Britain.

As with many geological sites, once the interest has been damaged or destroyed it can not be replaced. Due to the range of geological sites included within this group it is difficult to generalise about appropriate site management. However, the general emphasis should be placed on assessing the scale of the impacts, maintaining natural exposures and restricting damage to the geological interest. Examples are given below:

- Recreational activity, such as rock climbing, can be severely damaging to upland geological exposures. The British Mountaineering Council (BMC) is researching techniques to minimise rock edge erosion and is campaigning to educate climbers about responsible climbing techniques and the scientific importance of sites.

- Peat erosion can occur for a number of reasons including footpath erosion and vegetation loss. The restoration of eroded peat may be ecologically beneficial but for sites designated for their geological interest the scientific importance lies in the actual organic material contained within the peat which provides important climatic information, some of which would have already been lost through erosion. Revegetating the peat to slow down the rate of erosion is the most effective restoration technique and would be the preferred geological management option. Some peat exposure and erosion may be the result of natural processes and evolution of the geological system and for this reason management decisions should be site specific based on the extent of the deposit and the causes and rates of erosion.

- Scree deposits are susceptible to footpath erosion. Repair and restoration of scree slopes should be by natural recharge from the higher areas, as the import of 'fresh' material will destroy the structure of the slope, the slope angle and down-slope sorting of material.

Moor House and Cross Fell SSSI, Cumbria is a large geological site with a range of interests including karst, fluvial and peat sites. Part of the site is also biologically important and is a NNR. Access to the peat bog area is restricted, which safeguards the scientific interest. The Pennine Way crosses the site and footpath erosion is therefore a potential threat, but early consultation with English Nature will allow management options to be discussed.

4.6.6 Road and railway cuttings

Roads and railway cuttings can provide extensive exposures often lacking in inland Britain. These exposures provide us with information relating to the geological evolution of Britain and may be temporary (occurring only during construction) or permanently designed cuttings, such as the Tebay Road cutting SSSI, Cumbria.

Cuttings are generally classified as exposure sites and in order to manage the scientific interest of the site, access to the geological faces should be maintained. Early consultation with English Nature and inclusion of the geological interest within the road design can be used to address issues of access and safety. The English Nature reports on Roads and Geological Conservation (English Nature 1994; Larwood & Markham 1995) discuss the use that cuttings play in earth heritage conservation and examines good practice and techniques available to overcome the geological and geomorphological complications that may arise as a result of creating permanent exposures.

Construction of the Tebay road cutting, Cumbria cut through marine sandstones deposited 415 million years ago. Permanent exposures were designed into the road scheme and exposures have been left along the M6 and the A685, with access made for study purposes along the A road site. Management of this site is minimal, mainly because the rocks are not subject to slumping or collapse.

4.7 Advice on earth heritage conservation

Advice on earth heritage conservation may be sought from both English Nature local area teams and the geological specialists in the Peterborough office. A number of documents are also available covering aspects of earth heritage conservation and these are referenced in Chapter11.

Local geological conservation can be addressed through the RIGs. Contact with groups relevant to upland issues, such as the National Caving Association or The Limestone Pavement Action Group, is also recommended.

Montane

Montane areas 5

Tables

Definition and location of montane areas

5.1 Definition of montane areas

Montane areas are defined here as the land above the natural tree-line, which is the climatically determined upper limit of tree growth. This area is also referred to as the alpine zone (Horsfield & Thompson 1996). In England this is generally found above 600 m, although the precise altitude of the potential tree-limit varies across the country and depends on local variations in temperature, shelter and humidity (Pearsall 1950; Ratcliffe 1977; Ratcliffe & Thompson 1988). In the Lake District, for example, the climatic tree-line is estimated to lie at about 535 m, while in the Brecon Beacons and Cairngorms it lies at about 640 m (Ratcliffe 1991). The tree-line is difficult to detect in the British Isles because it has been greatly modified by grazing and burning (Ingrouille 1995).

At the upper limits of tree growth there may be a zone of tall scrub, often composed of the same tree species (mainly oak, birch and pine) which dominate the woodland below. The upper limits of this tall scrub may be taken as the boundary between the sub-montane and montane zones, although the distinction between the two zones is often blurred. The two typically merge through a broad band of transitional vegetation which varies in exact altitude even across one mountainside. The transition between sub-montane and montane habitats can be particularly difficult to identify in England, because the limits of tree growth are often only revealed by scattered woody growth on cliff faces (Ratcliffe 1977).

The tall scrub gives way with increasing altitude to shrubs of medium height, of species such as juniper *Juniperus communis* and willows *Salix* spp., and then to dwarf-shrub heath (ericoids). Amongst or in place of ericoid heath are found moss- and lichen-heaths, dwarf-herb communities, sedge- and rush-heaths, and other grass-dominated communities.

5.2 Location and extent of montane areas

The majority of the montane area in Britain occurs in Scotland, but in England montane habitats are found on the highest mountains and hills in the north and west of the country. They occur in the central Lake District fells as well as the North Pennines, the Yorkshire Dales and the Cheviot Hills in Northumberland.

The extent of montane habitats in England is limited and where they occur they are local in their distribution. Along with examples in North Wales, they represent southern outliers in Britain of vegetation communities which are far more widespread and extensive in Scotland. It is estimated that montane heath, mire and grassland in England covers approximately 1,500 ha. For further details of the distribution of particular montane habitats and species in England, see section 5.4 below.

Habitats and species of montane areas

5.3 Why montane areas are important

Montane areas in Britain support a unique flora and fauna (Ratcliffe 1977). British montane habitats represent southern and oceanic outliers of habitats which are more extensive in continental Europe. They show considerable diversity and include several types which are either highly local or apparently absent elsewhere (Ratcliffe & Thompson 1988; Thompson & Brown 1992). For these reasons several plant communities of montane areas are of international significance and this is recognised by their inclusion in Annex 1 of the Habitats Directive (see Table 5.4).

The best examples of British montane habitats are found in Scotland, but English montane habitats are of significance because they represent examples of these communities near the southern-most extremity of their range in Britain. Most of the montane communities occurring in England extend farther south, into Wales. As might be expected from this southerly position, the English montane areas are relatively small in extent, rather fragmented in nature, and limited in terms of the species they contain. Nevertheless, they are still of considerable importance and support species, such as Arctic-alpine plants, which are specific to these conditions.

Yellow marsh saxifrage *Saxifraga hirculus* is threatened throughout its international range and is included in the Habitats Directive (Annex IIb). The majority of the British population occurs in England (Taylor 1994), where it is found in the North Pennines Natural Area.

Montane areas support many vascular and non-vascular plants and invertebrates that are nationally rare and scarce (Tables 5.1, 5.2 and 5.7). Montane habitats and certain species of these areas are included in the UK Biodiversity Action Plan (UK Biodiversity Group 1998; UK Steering Group 1995).

Montane areas are also valued for their geological and geomorphological interests (5.6.4), as well as their archaeological and historic interests (5.6.5).

5.4 Habitats and species of montane areas, their nature conservation status and distribution

5.4.1 Vascular plants

The plant species of nature conservation significance in montane areas of England are shown in Table 5.1, with their nature conservation status and distribution in upland Natural Areas. Many species of the montane zone, like the grasses and some of the heath plants, have a wide altitudinal distribution and are able to survive in the poor soils and unfavourable conditions of mountain tops. Other species, such as some of the saxifrages *Saxifraga* spp., are found most frequently in montane areas, but also occur further down the hill side. In addition, there are the specialised montane plants, including alpine species and Arctic-alpines, which are rarely or never found outside montane environments and make mountains places of particular interest to botanists (Pearsall 1950). (See Glossary for definitions of alpine, Arctic and Arctic-alpine plant species.)

Many scarce montane plants have a relict distribution (Stewart, Pearman & Preston 1994). Fossil evidence indicates that they were present in the last glacial period at sites in England and Wales which are now far south of their current range. They now grow in habitats such as wind-exposed summits, sheltered and shaded sites where snow accumulates in the winter and lies late into the spring and summer, rock-ledges on cliffs and sides of gullies, and among screes, springs and flushes. Species which can withstand grazing are also found in montane grassland communities.

5.4.2 Bryophytes

Montane areas of England support a range of nationally rare and scarce moss and liverwort species, some of which are restricted to this zone while others have a broad altitudinal range and are more widespread (Table 5.2). There are some species which can be unambiguously regarded as montane or upland, but there are many which are not so easily categorised this way.

Bryophytes can be very specialised in their niche requirements and often their distribution is determined by the distribution of suitable substrates or conditions. Many are associated with rocky situations, such as cliff ledges and crevices, ravines, mountain summits and areas of scree or boulders. These frequently provide moist, base-rich conditions which favour certain species. *Grimmia incurva* for example is principally a montane species but this is probably a reflection of the distribution of acidic rock outcrops. Although very rare, this species does occur in southern, lowland England on artificial substrates such as slate roofs and in churchyards.

5.4.3 Plant communities

The vegetation found at high altitudes in England includes dwarf-shrub heath, moss- and lichen-heath, grassland, mires, tall-herb and fern-dominated communities and low growing juniper and willow scrub. The National Vegetation Classification (NVC, Rodwell 1991, 1992) describes the montane plant communities of Britain. Those occurring in English montane areas are shown in Table 5.4, together with their nature conservation status and distribution in upland Natural Areas of England (Drewitt & Manley 1997).

Some of the montane zone is covered by communities which are more widespread in the sub-montane zone or have developed as a result of grazing and burning. These are discussed further in Chapter 6 Moorland. For example, bilberry *Vaccinium myrtillus*-wavy hair-grass *Deschampsia flexuosa* heath (NVC community H18) occurs in both the montane and sub-montane zones, naturally and in response to heavy grazing and/or burning. Much of what was the predominantly montane community of stiff sedge *Carex bigelowii*-woolly hair moss *Racomitrium lanuginosum* moss heath (NVC community U10) is now sheep's fescue *Festuca ovina*-common bent *Agrostis capillaris*-heath bedstraw *Galium saxatile* grassland (NVC community U4). This is due to grazing, the consequent enrichment and trampling, and this community is extremely widespread in the sub-montane zone.

5.4.4 Birds

Birds associated with the montane zone in England are shown in Table 5.5, with their current nature conservation status and distribution in upland Natural Areas. Of the small number of bird species which nest or feed in the montane zone of England, only one is confined to it - the dotterel *Charadrius morinellus*. The total dotterel population is now restricted to around two pairs in the North Pennines. In the nineteenth century and up to about 1860, it is estimated that the total annual breeding population in England was 50-75 pairs in good years (Ratcliffe 1973). Breeding dotterel in England are at the southern edge of their European and global range.

Ptarmigan *Lagopus mutus* would also be confined to the montane zone if they were present, but this species is extinct in England. The reason for their extinction in England is not known but it may have been due to a combination of climate change and over hunting (P. Whitfield, pers comm). It is likely that the species was never common in England. Evidence for its former occurrence is scant, but it seems probable that it formerly bred in the Lake District until the early eighteenth century (MacPherson & Duckworth 1886).

A number of other species nest and feed in the montane zone, but they also breed in the sub-montane zone and overall numbers there are far higher (Table 5.5). The English montane zone is consequently of lower conservation significance for these species when compared with other far more extensive upland habitats.

5.4.5 Invertebrates

Invertebrates of montane areas include beetles, moths, butterflies and spiders, many of which are more numerous or widespread in Scotland and Wales. The beetles and spiders at this altitude are particularly important, with several nationally rare and scarce species living in wet moss or under stones on mountain tops. Species of nature conservation significance in the montane areas of England are shown in Table 5.7. Further species which occur in montane areas but are more abundant at lower altitudes are covered in other chapters, for example, the nationally scarce mountain ringlet butterfly *Erebia ephiphron* (Chapter 6 Moorland).

Many of the montane invertebrate species in Britain exhibit a northern or western distribution and they are probably responding to the wetness and lower temperatures of these regions. This is reflected in their relatively larger populations in Scotland. Some of these species occur almost down to sea level in the far north west. For example, the snowfield ground beetle *Nebria nivalis*, which is restricted to late snow-lie areas and only occurs on Scafell Pike in England, occurs at sea level on Skye.

Alpine lady's mantle

5.5 Habitat and management requirements of montane species

The habitat and management requirements of nationally rare and scarce montane species are shown in Tables 5.1-5.8. For many species, their ecology is poorly understood and therefore very little information is available on their habitat requirements. This in turn makes it difficult to identify the most appropriate management, but some general guidelines have been provided.

Nationally rare and scarce plants of montane areas occur in a range of plant communities and situations, for example, in grassland and mires, on cliff ledges and scree. Many of these species require undisturbed conditions, while others appear to need particular grazing levels.

For many animal species, maintaining montane heath, mire and grassland communities, including their typical, natural diversity of plant species and vegetation structure, will be of benefit. Invertebrates living in moss or undisturbed stony areas will obviously suffer if these habitats are lost.

Yellow mountain saxifrage

Management of montane areas

5.6 Managing montane areas

Natural montane vegetation communities are generally climax types which require minimal management. However, the montane areas of England have been greatly modified by the influence of man. The main management practices conducted are grazing and burning, although management of public access and recreation is becoming increasingly important. These practices, together with the option of no management, are discussed below.

The information included here is only a guide, because the most appropriate management for any given area will depend upon its individual characteristics, as well as the particular farming system involved. Grazing regimes will vary from area to area and will affect the distribution and extent of many plants and animals, as well as the composition and structure of vegetation communities. Changes such as complete removal of stock may be detrimental for some species due to increases in tall vegetation.

Changing management in the montane zone may not always have the desired effect because of changing environmental factors. Global warming, for example, may affect the survival rates and future distribution of montane habitats and species. Nitrogen deposition, which has increased four-fold in some areas over the last 120 years (Lee, Tallis & Woodin 1988), could also exert effects on plant growth and community structure. Here the vegetation is often at the edge of its climatic range and is usually strongly nitrogen-limited (Ineson 1989). In these situations, the benefits of altering management regimes may be limited. For example, reducing grazing with the aim of expanding populations of montane species is unlikely to be successful with populations which are limited by climate. Similarly, attempts to restore montane heath may be unsuccessful if high levels of nitrogen deposition inhibit woolly hair moss regeneration and encourage competing species.

5.6.1 Grazing in montane areas

Montane areas present special problems for grazing because of the slow rate of plant growth. This results in carrying capacities which are lower than on similar areas of lower ground. Montane moss- and lichen-heaths in England and Wales have declined in extent and in their cover of moss and lichens, and this deterioration has corresponded with greater sheep grazing (Jerram 1992; Thompson, Whyte & Oswald 1988).

Sheep are the principal large herbivores found in the montane areas of England. However, a high proportion of vegetation at high altitude is also consumed by invertebrates (Heal & Perkins 1978). The numbers and breed of sheep using montane areas of hill land, in combination with the particular farming system used by the land manager, will influence the impact of the stock on the montane habitats.

Swaledale

Box 5.1 outlines options and techniques for grazing in the montane areas of England, depending on the current condition of the habitat. Where montane habitats have deteriorated owing to heavy grazing, recovery of moss- and lichen-heath will be dependent on the removal of sheep and any other large herbivores (D. Ratcliffe, pers comm). Once this vegetation has recovered, any return to stock grazing must be at sustainable levels if further damage is to be avoided. Maintaining certain areas of montane habitat permanently free of stock grazing is also an option.

Control of livestock movement, as well as numbers, is important in achieving appropriate grazing management in the montane zone. Regular shepherding is now very rare, but can help to spread the grazing pressure across an area. These areas are frequently grazed as part of a larger management unit. Although in practice stocking levels are often much lower at the montane level, sheep may still congregate locally on montane turves and damage the vegetation. Areas favoured by sheep include sheltered valleys and hollows and more palatable grassland such as on limestone. Animals may create bare ground where they concentrate, cause accelerated erosion, trample and damage vegetation and form bare tracks or trails. Where these tracks or 'trods' form near watering places they can act as drains leading to the drainage of wetlands. Local nutrient enrichment from urine and dunging can also occur where sheep gather.

Walling or fencing may be required to control stock numbers and movement. New stock proof boundaries require careful planning in montane areas to avoid conflict with landscape and public access objectives, as well as agricultural uses (see Information Note 7). Small fenced areas can be useful for monitoring the effects of removing or reducing grazing. Fencing larger areas, for example around or immediately below cliffs and rocky outcrops, may allow plants confined to these areas by grazing to spread further afield (see Figure 5.1). Temporary seasonal fencing on areas of turf is another option and allows plants to flower and set seed.

Where montane moss- and lichen-heaths and dwarf shrubs remain but local grazing pressure has reduced their cover, reducing grazing could have considerable benefits for montane species. Substantially reducing or removing grazing altogether may be desirable to allow remaining vegetation to at least stabilise and preferably improve in quality and extent. In the longer term, moderate grazing may be beneficial in promoting or maintaining preferred habitat mosaics and structures (R. Fuller, pers comm). However, reversing severe vegetation changes in montane areas of England may be extremely difficult, especially since they have been exacerbated by nitrogen deposition (Fuller 1996).

Further information:
Marrs & Welch 1991
Chapter 10 Crags, scree and limestone pavement
Information Note 1 Assessing vegetation condition in the English uplands
Information Note 2 Sheep breeds of the English uplands and their characteristics
Information Note 3 Sheep farming systems of the English uplands
Information Note 7 Fencing in the uplands

Box 5.1 Options for grazing in montane areas of England

To maintain vegetation in favourable condition
(See Information Note 1 to determine vegetation condition)

Maintain current grazing practices

- Provided grazing practice has not recently altered and is not causing a deterioration of the habitat.
- Remember that recent alterations may take several years to manifest themselves as a cause of habitat deterioration.
- As a guide, maximum stocking rates should not exceed 0.5 sheep/ha in summer, and in winter the whole flock should be removed from montane areas. Lower summer rates may be desirable in some areas, eg where dotterel nest.
- Favourable condition may also result from a complete absence of stock grazing.

Shepherd sheep to ensure the area is grazed evenly, or as desired.

- Consider incentives for shepherding where it is not currently practised.
- Consider concentrating shepherding effort at particular seasons.

Do not feed stock on montane habitats.

- Feed is generally only required in winter when most stock should be off montane areas.
- Feed may be used at lower altitudes on areas of no conservation interest, such as species-poor acid grassland, to assist in influencing grazing patterns on the management unit as a whole.

To bring vegetation into favourable condition

Where vegetation is unfavourable because of heavy grazing:
Off-winter stock from September to May-June.

- Stock are often removed from the hill or kept down below montane areas from October-November until after lambing in May or June, depending on the weather conditions. Montane habitats are particularly susceptible to grazing damage in the spring and autumn and would benefit from reduced grazing at these times.
- Consider additional sheep housing to facilitate increased off-wintering.
- Consider additional away-wintering to facilitate off-wintering. This involves stock leaving the farm and spending the winter on lower ground.

Reduce grazing

- Reduce grazing to 0.5 sheep/ha or less in summer, and in winter remove the whole flock from montane areas.

To bring vegetation into favourable condition where the above practices do not bring sufficient improvement

Remove grazing temporarily

- Small plots illustrate the effects of removing grazing and are useful for monitoring purposes.
- Larger areas allow a return to a more natural state, increasing overall habitat and species diversity.
- A range of grazing regimes across an area, from none to a variety of lightly grazed states, may provide maximum diversity.
- Only return stock to excluded areas when the vegetation has recovered, and at a lower stocking level than had previously caused the vegetation to deteriorate.

Remove grazing permanently

- Establish areas with no stock grazing, to allow recovery and enhance biodiversity, where appropriate in the context of the surrounding land and its management.

Introduce wethers (castrated male sheep) as a proportion of the flock.

- Consider incentives to encourage this practice, because wethers help to establish the territories of flocks and prevent other flocks encroaching on to their area of the hill. They also eat coarser vegetation, such as mat-grass *Nardus stricta* and heath rush *Juncus squarrosus*, and help to reduce its dominance.

Figure 5.1. Fencing around or immediately below cliffs and rocky outcrops may allow plants confined to these areas by grazing to spread farther afield. The position of the fence is critical as stock, particularly sheep, may be able to find their way into the exclosure by indirect routes! Fences can be permanent or temporary. Fence design should also allow for the easy removal of stock that find their way into the exclosure

Effects of grazing on montane communities and species

Montane plant communities are both changed and damaged by excessive stocking. It may alter the vegetation structure, eliminate plant species, change the plant community or remove the vegetation altogether. For example, sheep grazing increases the cover and frequency of grasses at the expense of lichens, mosses and other montane species such as stiff sedge. Continued heavy grazing can remove even the grass dominated communities and lead to bare ground. Maintaining plant diversity and cover is necessary to provide the appropriate habitat for many montane species, as well as helping to prevent soil erosion.

Moss- and lichen-heaths are not particularly palatable to grazing animals but over-stocking, good weather and feeding of sheep by tourists on regularly visited summits may encourage high numbers of sheep to congregate on mountain tops and utilise these habitats. Grazing animals also move to higher ground to escape being pestered by insects and to feed on the nutritious new growth which occurs later at higher altitudes. The demise from England and Wales of moss-heath has corresponded with increased sheep grazing (Thompson, Whyte & Oswald 1988).

Tall-herb communities and many of the **rarer montane and alpine plants** are restricted in their distribution to places out of reach of the mouths of herbivores. These are usually rocky habitats such as cliff faces and ledges or enclosed ravines and gills. Most tall herbs are palatable to grazing animals and, therefore, these communities can be eliminated by heavy grazing. Reduction or removal of grazing pressure in areas supporting herb-rich communities may be desirable in some places, in order to allow these plants to spread from their current refuges.

Further information: Chapter 10 Crags, scree and limestone pavement.

Bird populations in the montane zone are likely to be lost if the habitat deteriorates through, for example, heavy grazing or greater acidification. Loss of montane moss-heaths, for example, is ornithologically significant because dotterel *Charadrius marinellus* and ptarmigan *Lagopus mutus* are closely associated with the habitat. Dotterel may have been deterred from breeding in England by the loss of moss-heath communities (Galbraith *et al* 1993a & b; Thompson, Whyte & Oswald 1988; Thompson & Brown 1992).

Grazing can also adversely affect the breeding success of birds by trampling their nests and chicks. For example, there may be significant trampling effects on dotterel nests at stocking rates as low as 0.2 sheep/ha (A. MacDonald, pers comm).

Invertebrates suffer detrimental effects from heavy grazing pressure in montane areas. It leads to the loss of some plant species which may be important for shelter or food for invertebrates, such as woolly hair moss, ericoids, golden-rod *Solidago virgaurea* and saxifrage species. It also reduces the structural diversity of the habitat, with detrimental effects on the invertebrate fauna. In addition, extensive trampling by stock (and humans) on mountain summits disturbs stones and small boulders which provide important cover for beetles and spiders.

5.6.2 Burning in montane areas

Burning in the montane zone is uncommon and where it does occur it often arises from fires at lower altitudes being allowed to burn too far up hill or out of control. Burning is damaging to the nature conservation interest of montane habitats because recovery rates in this environment are extremely slow and erosion is likely to result. The same is true for the burning of blanket bogs at this altitude. There are no benefits from burning in the montane zone, for biodiversity or for agricultural or game management.

5.6.3 Managing public access and recreation in montane areas

Mountains are popular areas for public access and recreation, and are extremely valuable for providing enjoyment and appreciation of the countryside. In some areas, visitor pressure may disturb animal populations, trample the vegetation or cause erosion, because the soils and plant communities present are fragile and easily damaged. Such effects tend to be localised, but may cause concern for the wildlife and landscape interest of the area.

Protecting this environment and its vegetation is paramount because of the various animal and plant species it supports. Healthy vegetation also minimises erosion at low cost and maintains the scenic value of the area. In the often fragile soils of montane areas, vegetation helps to reduce the movement of sediments into water courses. Large sediment loads in water courses can cause damage in lower areas and impair water quality, both important aspects for aquatic life, reservoirs and people.

Measures such as footpath and bridleway repair can be employed to minimise adverse effects of activities such as walking, fell running and mountain biking (see Information Note 10). Other techniques may be required for some activities, such as rock climbing (see Chapter 10). Informing the public of the interest of montane areas and about ways to minimise the adverse effects of their visit would also be beneficial.

Further information: Countryside Commission & Countryside Council for Wales 1997; Scottish Natural Heritage 1997; Sports Council & Countryside Commission 1995; Chapter 10 Crags, scree and limestone pavement; Information Note 10 Managing public access and footpaths in the uplands; Figure 5.2.

Figure 5.2. Stone flags have been used to surface footpaths over peat in montane areas in the North Pennines and Cheviot Hills. The material used for the flags should be compatible with the geology of the area. The flags float on the peat surface and provide a smooth walking surface. They allow re-vegetation of the surrounding bare peat and the edges and joints also grow over to make the path less obvious (see Information Note 10).

5.6.4 Earth heritage features and management in montane areas

Montane areas contain a range of earth heritage interests, including periglacial features such as patterned ground including stone polygons, circles and stripes (fossil and modern), fossil solifluction lobes and terraces, frost-shattered bedrock (blockfields), ploughing blocks, nivation processes and earth hummocks (thufurs). Where present, these features have implications for management because some activities, such as heavy grazing or visitor pressure, may damage or destroy them. Care should be taken not to disturb features during footpath maintenance and paths can be directed away from fragile features.

Further information: Chapter 4 Earth heritage features; King 1976; O'Halloran *et al* 1994.

5.6.5 Archaeological and historical interests and management in montane areas

Montane areas contain archaeological and historical features such as trackways, beacons, cairns, and enclosures. These have implications for management, such as taking care not to disturb or destroy features during footpath maintenance, and directing paths away from fragile features. English Heritage and County Archaeologists hold records of important sites and features and can be contacted for further information and advice.

5.7 Techniques to restore montane habitats

Recovery of the shrub, moss- or lichen-rich heaths found in the montane zone, such as heather *Calluna vulgaris* or bilberry and lichen *Cladonia arbuscula* heath, is very slow, but recovery is possible if the disturbance ceases (Thompson *et al* 1987). The most obvious option to aid recovery is temporary or permanent removal of grazing, and in some cases management of public access (see 5.6) .

Damage and rehabilitation of ground in mountain areas has been studied in Scotland (Bayfield 1976, 1979, 1980, 1985, 1987; Bayfield & Brown 1985; Bayfield *et al* 1981, 1988). Techniques such as laying stone aggregates on some heavily used footpaths can reduce damage. For badly damaged areas, proposals include the use of mulches and soil stabilizers, repeated applications of nitrogenous fertilizer, sowing with macerated moss fragments and establishment with native species, as well as exclusion of grazing animals (Miller 1986). Other examples include restoration of bared and disturbed ground on Great Dun Fell in Cumbria and in the Cairngorm Mountains (Anderson & Radford 1988).

Further information: Bayfield & Miller 1988; Gilbert et al 1997; Information Note 10 Managing public access and footpaths in the uplands

Table 5.1 Nationally rare and scarce vascular plants associated with montane areas in England

(Note: Some of these species have a broad altitudinal range and also occur in sub-montane and lowland areas. See also Chapter 10 for species predominantly of crags, scree and limestone pavement, and Chapter 6 for species predominantly of sub-montane habitats.)

Plant species	Status	Habitat requirements	Management requirements	Distribution by Natural Area (including those not containing montane areas)
Ajuga pyramidalis pyramidal bugle	LR- ns	In montane areas, ledges of steep basic rock. See Table 6.1.	• Protect sites from habitat destruction.	Cumbria Fells and Dales
Alchemilla minima an alchemilla	VU, EE Priority	In montane areas, very short turf of base-rich *Festuca ovina* grassland amongst limestone boulders and debris. See Table 6.1.	• Maintain grazing. • Protect sites from habitat destruction. • See Species Action Plan (UK Biodiversity Group 1998)	North Pennines Yorkshire Dales
Alopecurus borealis Alpine foxtail	LR-ns	In oligotrophic mountain springs and flushes, often associated with late snow-beds, usually in the centres of flushes with percolating water. Found over a wide range of acidic or slightly basic substrates. It is vulnerable to heavy grazing and inflorescences may be most common on drier ground amongst taller vegetation which protects the plants from grazing.	• Protect populations from heavy grazing and from damage by trampling.	Border Uplands North Pennines
Betula nana dwarf birch	LR-ns	Wet upland heaths and blanket bogs on ground varying from moderately dry and sloping to completely flat and waterlogged.	• Protect populations from heavy grazing and burning, although judicious burning may improve seedling establishment. [1]	Border Uplands North Pennines
Carex atrata black Alpine-sedge	LR-ns	Scattered tufts or small clumps in dry and moist places on ungrazed faces and ledges of calcareous cliffs.	• More information is needed about the precise requirements, but it is likely that cessation of grazing may be required if the small populations are to increase.	Cumbria Fells and Dales

Plant species	Status	Habitat requirements	Management requirements	Distribution by Natural Area (including those not containing montane areas)
Carex capillaris hair sedge	LR-ns	A strict calcicole growing on limestone in short herb-rich grassland, closed marshes with low vegetation, open hummocky marshes and flushes and on steep rock faces and ledges. It can grow in very open boreal woodland. Although it is intolerant of competition from taller plants it grows well in short swards and withstands moderate grazing. Heavy grazing or the application of fertilisers to pasture may damage populations.	• Control grazing to moderate levels. • Prevent the enrichment of surface waters or soil by fertilisers.	Cumbria Fells and Dales North Pennines Yorkshire Dales
Cerastium alpinum Alpine mouse-ear	LR-ns	On ledges, scree and in base-rich grassland, always on a substrate rich in bases such as calcium.	• Protect sites from habitat destruction. • Protect populations from heavy grazing and burning.	Cumbria Fells and Dales
Circaea alpina Alpine enchanter's-nightshade	LR-ns	Open and usually shaded or north-facing seepage areas and stream sides. See Table 8.1.	• Protect sites from habitat destruction.	Cumbria Fells and Dales North Pennines White Peak Yorkshire Dales
Dryas octopetala mountain avens	LR-ns	Relatively exposed sites on basic rocks, where the soil is not too deep and the drainage is very good.	• Protect sites from erosion and grazing.	North Pennines Yorkshire Dales Cumbria Fells and Dales
Euphrasia frigida	LR-ns	On damp to wet, usually rather basic, ledges.	• Protect sites from habitat destruction. • Protect populations from heavy grazing and burning.	Cumbria Fells and Dales

Plant species	Status	Habitat requirements	Management requirements	Distribution by Natural Area (including those not containing montane areas)
Gentiana verna spring gentian	Sched. 8 of WCA LR-nt SCC	Upland limestone grassland, usually with short turf. Also sometimes on hummocks in turfy marshes. Growth and reproduction are suppressed by heavy grazing in spring or summer but plants can tolerate grazing in late summer and winter.[2] The species may still be vulnerable to unscrupulous collecting.	• Where possible, control grazing to moderate levels, especially in spring and early summer.	North Pennines
Juncus alpinoarticulatus Alpine rush	LR-ns	Base-rich mires over limestone, usually in open vegetation.	• Protect sites from habitat destruction. • Protect populations from heavy grazing and burning.	North Pennines Yorkshire Dales
Kobresia simpliciuscula false sedge	LR-nt	Grassland and open gravel flushes of sugar limestone.	• Protect sites from habitat destruction. • Protect populations from heavy grazing and burning.	North Pennines
Lychnis alpina Alpine catchfly	Sched. 8 of WCA VU SCC	Steep, shattered faces of a high crag of acidic, metalliferous Skiddaw slate, inaccessible to sheep or deer. The species is sensitive to grazing and vulnerable to damage by gully-scramblers. In the past it has been threatened by collecting.	• Access to the site should be controlled. • Consideration should be given to restricting grazing on potential sites nearby to encourage the spread of this species.	Cumbria Fells and Dales
Lycopodium annotinum interrupted clubmoss	LR-ns	A calcifuge of acidic grassland or heath, in exposed moist but well-drained situations, especially where there is only a thin covering of peat over rock debris, amongst rocks or on wet ravine edges.[3]	• This species requires protection from collecting. • Protect sites from habitat degradation. • Some sites may be threatened by heavy grazing, which should be controlled.	Cumbria Fells and Dales

Plant species	Status	Habitat requirements	Management requirements	Distribution by Natural Area (including those not containing montane areas)
Minuartia stricta Teesdale sandwort	Sched. 8 of WCA EN SCC	Over sugar limestone in open gravelly and stony flushes and eroding margins of sikes, and around the base of hummocks of moss. It is intolerant of competition from other plants.	• Continue to restrict access to the site to prevent damage by trampling visitors.	North Pennines
Minuartia verna spring sandwort	LR-ns	On Carboniferous limestone, in semi-open short grassland and among limestone rocks and scree. Also on basic Borrowdale Volcanic rocks. Frequent around old lead and zinc mines. See Table 10.1.	• Protect sites from habitat destruction. • Where possible, sites should be heavily grazed.	Cumbria Fells and Dales Dark Peak North Pennines Pennine Dales Fringe South West Peak White Peak Yorkshire Dales
Myosotis alpestris Alpine forget-me-not	LR-nt SCC	Heavily grazed limestone grassland on base-rich brown earth soils and rendzinas, sometimes flushed with water from limestone cliffs, usually in semi-open turf. It may be vulnerable to heavy grazing; the failure of one population to flower is thought to be due to grazing in spring.	• Protect sites from habitat destruction. • Where heavy grazing is thought to be adversely affecting the populations, this should if possible be controlled, especially in spring.	North Pennines
Phleum alpinum Alpine cat's tail	LR-ns	Open, rocky habitats or closed swards on base-rich substrates, usually in damp places. It can thrive under light grazing but heavy grazing appears to have restricted its distribution.	• Protect sites from habitat destruction. • Where heavy grazing is thought to be restricting the populations, this should if possible be controlled.	Cumbria Fells and Dales North Pennines
Poa alpina Alpine meadow-grass	LR-ns	Steep, open faces of calcareous rocks.	• To allow populations to spread from cliffs, grazing needs to be light.	North Pennines Yorkshire Dales Cumbria Fells and Dales

Plant species	Status	Habitat requirements	Management requirements	Distribution by Natural Area (including those not containing montane areas)
Poa glauca glaucous meadow-grass	LR-ns	Steep, open faces of calcareous rock and scree. It appears to be sensitive to grazing.	• Protect sites from habitat destruction. • Where heavy grazing is thought to be restricting the populations, this should be controlled.	Cumbria Fells and Dales
Polygala amarella dwarf milkwort	VU	Open sites in short turf over calcareous rocks in well-drained sites. Sometimes in mires, but then on tussocks raised above wetter areas. It is sensitive to heavy grazing.	• Protect sites from habitat destruction. • Where heavy grazing is thought to be restricting the populations, this should be controlled.	North Pennines Yorkshire Dales Cumbria Fells and Dales
Potentilla crantzii Alpine cinquefoil	LR-ns	Steep, dry rock faces, ledges and grassland over calcareous rocks, in both shaded and sunny aspects. See Table 10.1.	• Populations which are accessible to stock should be protected from heavy grazing.	Cumbria Fells and Dales North Pennines White Peak Yorkshire Dales
Potentilla fruticosa shrubby cinquefoil	LR-nt SCC	In Cumbria, growing on screes and cliffs of loose crumbly rock kept moist by surface water and high precipitation, often on ungrazed ledges. Also on base-rich river alluvium in Teesdale. See Table 10.1.	• Protect sites from habitat destruction. • Protect from grazing.	Cumbria Fells and Dales North Pennines Pennine Dales Fringe
Salix lapponum downy willow	LR-ns	On dry to moist rock faces, usually basic. It is susceptible to grazing, which has confined it to inaccessible cliffs and rocky sites. Male and female plants must be present in adequate proximity for seed to be set.	• Consideration should be given to increasing the chance of populations spreading, by removing grazing and if possible ensuring that there are enough male and female plants to set seed.	Cumbria Fells and Dales

Plant species	Status	Habitat requirements	Management requirements	Distribution by Natural Area (including those not containing montane areas)
Saxifraga hirculus yellow marsh saxifrage	Sched. 8 of WCA Annex IIb VU Priority	Low-growing, species-rich flush and mire communities, often fed by springs from Carboniferous limestone. It seems to require a moderate amount of grazing to keep down the surrounding vegetation and patches of bare ground in which seedlings can become established. Heavy grazing in summer suppresses flowering; the species can also reproduce vegetatively and seems able to persist for many years without flowering.	• Wherever possible, control grazing to prevent heavy grazing. • Protect sites from habitat loss and degradation such as by drainage, afforestation or other agricultural improvements. • See Species Action Plan (UK Steering Group 1995).	North Pennines
Saxifraga nivalis Alpine saxifrage	LR-ns	Periodically irrigated rocks or open vegetation on ledges of crags, usually in shaded sites on base-rich rocks. See Table 10.1.	• Protect sites from habitat destruction. • Protect populations from heavy grazing and burning.	North Pennines Cumbria Fells and Dales
Sedum villosum hairy stonecrop	LR-ns	In stony flushes that are only slightly base-rich, often on rather level ground beside streams amongst species-poor hill grassland or heather moorland.	• Protect sites from damage such as drainage or the effects of fertilisers.	Border Uplands Cumbria Fells and Dales North Pennines Yorkshire Dales.
Thlaspi caerulescens Alpine penny-cress	LR-ns	High calcareous rocks of the Cumbrian fells. Also a pioneer colonist of metalliferous mine wastes and river gravels. See Table 10.1.	• Protect sites from habitat destruction. • Where possible, sites should be heavily grazed.	Border Uplands North Pennines Cumbria Fells and Dales White Peak Yorkshire Dales
Viola rupestris Teesdale violet	LR-nt	In open turf on limestone. See Table 6.1.	• Ensure sufficient grazing to keep a short, open turf.	Cumbria Fells and Dales North Pennines Yorkshire Dales

Plant species	Status	Habitat requirements	Management requirements	Distribution by Natural Area (including those not containing montane areas)
Woodsia ilvensis oblong woodsia	Sched. 8 of WCA LR-nt Priority	Amongst hard, neutral igneous rocks.	• Populations of this species have been damaged by collecting in the past and are still considered to be vulnerable. Site confidentiality should be maintained. • See Species Action Plan (UK Biodiversity Group 1998).	Cumbria Fells and Dales

Key to Table 5.1

Annex IIb - listed on Annex IIb of the EC Habitats and Species Directive
Sched. 8 of WCA - listed on schedule 8 of the Wildlife & Countryside Act.

Red list categories

CR - critically endangered
EN - endangered
VU - vulnerable
DD - data deficient
LR -nt - Lower risk-near threatened
LR-ns - Lower risk-nationally scarce
E - endemic to Great Britain
EE - endemic to England.

Biodiversity Action Plan (BAP)

Priority - Priority species from UK Steering Group 1995 and UK Biodiversity Group 1998.
SCC - Species of conservation concern from UK Steering Group 1995 and UK Biodiversity Group 1998.

Sources

Most information from Stewart, Pearman & Preston 1994, Wigginton 1999., Hodgetts, Palmer & Wigginton 1996 and Porley & McDonnell 1997.

1. A. MacDonald, pers comm. 2. I. Taylor, pers comm. 3. Page 1982.

Table 5.2 Nationally rare and scarce bryophytes associated with montane areas in England

(Note: Some of these species have a broad altitudinal range and also occur in sub-montane and lowland areas. See also Chapter 10 for species predominantly of crags, scree and limestone pavement, and Chapter 6 for species predominantly of sub-montane habitats.)

Plant species	Status	Typical habitat	Distribution by Natural Area (including those not containing montane areas)
Amblyodon dealbatus	LR-ns	A calcicole of wet, open ground. On hills and mountains it occurs on tussocks in tufa springs and on stream banks, cliffs and gravel where flushed by calcareous water.	Border Uplands North Pennines Yorkshire Dales Cumbria Fells and Dales
Amblystegium jungermannioides	LR-ns	Damp basic rocks often in woodlands but also on montane rocks. See Table 8.2.	Yorkshire Dales White Peak
Amphidium lapponicum	LR-ns	Base-rich montane cliffs and crags, both on exposed rocks and in gullies, occasionally descending to lower altitudes in ravines and on stream-banks. It usually forms small isolated tufts in rock crevices and is indifferent to rock type provided there is adequate base-enrichment.	Cumbria Fells and Dales
Andreaea frigida	VU Priority	On wet, acid rock, flushed or periodically immersed.	Cumbria Fells and Dales
Andreaea mutabilis	LR-ns	On periodically to more continuously wet, more or less exposed acid boulders, crags or rubble (granite, andesite, basalt, quartzite); rarely on thin soil over rock.	Cumbria Fells and Dales
Anomobryum filiforme var. *concinnatum*	LR-ns	Dry earthy, often crumbling ledges of sun-exposed basic rocks. See Table 10.2.	Border Uplands Yorkshire Dales
Aplodon wormskjoldii	LR-ns	As pale green tufts or patches on dung in wet peaty places at high altitudes.	North Pennines

Plant species	Status	Typical habitat	Distribution by Natural Area (including those not containing montane areas)
Barbilophozia lycopodioides	LR-ns	Base-rich rocks at high altitude.	Border Uplands North Pennines Yorkshire Dales
Barbula icmadophila	LR-nt	Base-rich montane ledges.	Cumbria Fells and Dales
Brachydontium trichodes	LR-ns SCC	Rocks and cliffs. See Table 10.2.	Cumbria Fells and Dales North Pennines South West Peak
Bryum elegans	LR-ns	In dense red-green tufts on limestone rocks and in rock crevices, occasionally in thin limestone turf and on calcareous walls. See Table 10.2.	Forest of Bowland Yorkshire Dales
Bryum weigelii	LR-ns	As pink or greenish-pink patches in mountain springs and flushes, by snow patches and streams, avoiding lime.	Yorkshire Dales Cumbria Fells and Dales Shropshire Hills
Calypogeia integristipula	LR-ns	Montane and lowland rocks. See Table 10.2.	Border Uplands North Pennines South West Peak Yorkshire Dales
Catoscopium nigritum	LR-ns	Mountain ledge communities.	North Pennines
Conostomum tetragonum	LR-ns	On windswept summits and on humus over rock in north-east facing corries.	Cumbria Fells and Dales
Dicranoweisia crispula	LR-ns	Dry acidic rocks, usually in open sunny situations, often on boulders where it is sometimes the only bryophyte. In the Lake District it grows with *Cryptogramma crispa*.	Cumbria Fells & Dales

Plant species	Status	Typical habitat	Distribution by Natural Area (including those not containing montane areas)
Ditrichum zonatum var. *zonatum*	LR-ns	On acid skeletal soils and rocks on a mountain ridge. Particularly characteristic of hepatic mat communities of late snow-beds and flushes in relatively sheltered situations with north and east aspects.	Cumbria Fells and Dales
Encalypta alpina	LR-ns	Small tufts in dry or seasonally moist rock crevices and cliff-faces of limestone, calcareous schist or crumbling calcareous basalt. Favours, but is not restricted to N- or E-facing cliffs.	Yorkshire Dales
Encalypta ciliata	LR-ns	Dry or periodically damp, shaded crevices or cliff-faces of calcareous montane cliffs usually of limestone, calcareous schist, basalt, volcanic tuff or other basic igneous rocks. Also in shaded crevices on rock walls of Carboniferous limestone ravines and gills. Associated with high altitude woodland communities. Always in small quantity and seemingly indifferent to aspect.	Cumbria Fells and Dales Yorkshire Dales
Encalypta rhaptocarpa	LR-ns	Soft, basic igneous rocks. See Table 10.2.	North Pennines Yorkshire Dales
Eremonotus myriocarpus	LR-ns	On schistose, base-rich flushed rocks and crevices on soft lithosols. Also basic rocks in ravines and streams.	Cumbria Fells and Dales
Glyphomitrium daviesii	LR-ns	Dry, often sun-exposed or periodically irrigated, south or west facing basic igneous rock outcrops and stable block-litters.	Cumbria Fells and Dales
Grimmia atrata	LR-ns	One of the 'copper mosses' forming dark green tufts on the surface and in crevices of moist, sheltered or exposed, acidic heavy-metal-bearing rocks. On cliffs, rock outcrops, in scree and by lakes. See Table 10.2.	Cumbria Fells and Dales
Grimmia elongata	LR-nt	Forming small tufts on damp or dry acidic rocks.	Cumbria Fells and Dales
Grimmia incurva	LR-ns	On exposed acidic rock, mountains summits and block scree.	Border Uplands Cumbria Fells and Dales

Plant species	Status	Typical habitat	Distribution by Natural Area (including those not containing montane areas)
Grimmia montana	LR-ns	On hard, exposed, acidic, siliceous rocks.	Cumbria Fells and Dales Shropshire Hills Dartmoor
Hamatocaulis vernicosus slender green feather moss	Annex IIb DD Priority	Mainly a species of somewhat base-rich springs in upland districts. See Species Action Plan (UK Steering Group 1995).	Cumbria Fells and Dales Shropshire Hills
Hygrohypnum dilatatum	LR-ns	Forms green or yellow-green tufts on rocks in fast-flowing streams and rivers, usually in montane areas but sometimes at low altitude.	Border Uplands Cumbria Fells and Dales
Hypnum hamulosum	LR-ns	A calcicole of sheltered rocks, typically in cool situations with a north or east aspect, often growing directly on vertical rock-faces and also on rock-ledges, in rock crevices and in turf among rocks. See Table 10.2.	Cumbria Fells and Dales
Jungermannia subelliptica	LR-ns	In moist or periodically irrigated habitats in rock crevices, on cliff ledges, on disintegrating rock and on flushed gravelly banks and soil. Usually in base-rich situations but not confined to them. See Table 10.2.	Border Uplands Cumbria Fells and Dales Exmoor and the Quantocks Forest of Bowland
Kiaeria blyttii	LR-ns	Sides and tops of boulders in lightly sheltered block screes and on large boulders in streams above normal flood level, most frequently above 500 m.	Border Uplands Cumbria Fells and Dales North Pennines
Kiaeria falcata	LR-ns	Chionophilous communities, late snow lie, boulders and summit ridges.	Cumbria Fells and Dales

Plant species	Status	Typical habitat	Distribution by Natural Area (including those not containing montane areas)
Kiaeria starkei	LR-ns	Characteristic of late-snow areas, where it may grow on near-horizontal slabs, but more often occurs on detrital soils, especially where a thin layer of grit lies over sloping rocks at the foot of crags; also between larger stones and boulders in gullies and in block-screes. On most types of rock except limestone and the most acid rocks.	Cumbria Fells and Dales
Lophozia heterocolpos	LR-ns	Usually on damp calcareous rock outcrops in ravines, on stream sides and on shaded cliffs, typically creeping over cushions of other bryophytes. See Table 10.2.	North Pennines Yorkshire Dales
Lophozia opacifolia	LR-ns	On wet and dripping rocks in gullies and block-screes, especially by waterfalls, springs and flushes and on irrigated gravel and soil by streams, by lakes and in areas of late snow. It favours cool shaded north to east aspects.	Cumbria Fells and Dales
Lophozia wenzelii	LR-nt	In and beside springs, pools and flushes and on wet rocks, especially in areas of late snow.	Cumbria Fells and Dales
Marsupella adusta	LR-ns	Screes, exposed fell-fields, ridges, summits, stream sides, flushes and loch margins. Small stones of granite are the favoured substrate, more rarely basic schists or basalt. Less typically on moist rock-walls and slabs and rarely on moist gravel soil amongst rocks.	Cumbria Fells and Dales
Marsupella boeckii var. stableri	LR-ns	Forming distinctive purplish-brown or coppery mats on periodically flushed montane acid rock walls, boulders and gravelly soil, usually on north- to east-facing slopes and often in gullies.	Cumbria Fells and Dales
Marsupella sphacelata	LR-ns	A calcifuge of montane habitats such sheltered north- or east-facing gullies, where it grows on wet rock-slabs and boulders in and by streams and flushes.	Cumbria Fells and Dales

Plant species	Status	Typical habitat	Distribution by Natural Area (including those not containing montane areas)
Meesia uliginosa	LR-ns	Calcicole of wet, open ground, on seeping rocks, gravel and tufa in the mountains.	Border Uplands North Pennines Cumbria Fells and Dales
Oedipodium griffithianum	LR-ns	In loose, pale green tufts or as scattered plants on moist humus-rich soil in shady rock crevices and in block screes in mountain regions.	Cumbria Fells and Dales Border Uplands North Pennines
Oncophorus virens	LR-ns	On damp calcareous turf, especially in flushes and close to streams, often mixed with other species. Less often it occurs on base-rich rock faces.	North Pennines Cumbria Fells and Dales
Orthothecium rufescens	LR-ns	Occurs most frequently as dense, red, silky patches on damp, periodically flushed, north to east facing steep, often vertical, sheltered montane cliff-faces of limestone, volcanic or other basic rocks. Also on damp, shaded limestone walls of low-lying ravines and more rarely on the sides of turfy tufaceous hummocks in calcareous 'rich-fens' and springs.	Yorkshire Dales Cumbria Fells and Dales
Paraleptodontium recurvifolium	LR-nt	In more or less pure tufts or scattered among other plants on and at the base of cliffs, on rock ledges and banks and in rock crevices, often where water drips from above or within the spray zone of a waterfall. The aspect is usually between north and east and the substrate is probably always base-enriched.	Cumbria Fells and Dales
Plagiothecium cavifolium	LR-ns	On moist, basic mountain rock-ledges, where it may be associated with a wide variety of other calcicoles. Less often on siliceous rock-ledges at lower altitudes, sometimes where the basic influence is only slight.	Cumbria Fells and Dales Yorkshire Dales
Plagiothecium denticulatum var. *obtusifolium*	LR-ns	Among boulders and in rock crevices on mountains, where it is often a component of the vegetation of high-level boulder fields and late-lying snow patches. It also occurs in crevices on calcareous rock-ledges, usually on north- or east- facing cliffs.	Bodmin Moor Cumbria Fells and Dales Yorkshire Dales

Plant species	Status	Typical habitat	Distribution by Natural Area (including those not containing montane areas)
Pohlia elongata ssp. *polymorpha*	LR-ns	On skeletal peaty or gritty soils on rock-ledges, in crevices and occasionally on rocky stream-banks. It also grows on soil amongst boulders on mountain summits.	Cumbria Fells and Dales
Pohlia ludwigii	LR-ns	On moist or wet, sandy and gritty soils on banks and by streams. Also locally frequent in montane bryophyte springs	Cumbria Fells and Dales
Pseudoleskeella catenulata var. *catenulata*	LR-ns	Forms dense, dark- or olive-green patches on calcareous rocks. Prefers dry, open sites, often south facing, where there is little competition.	North Pennines Yorkshire Dales
Pterigynandrum filiforme	LR-ns	Forming neat yellow-green, green or brown mats on open sites in the mountains, on basic rocks or, rarely, branches and roots of trees.	Border Uplands Cumbria Fells and Dales
Racomitrium elongatum	LR-ns	On sandy or gritty soils. See Table 6.2.	Border Uplands Cumbria Fells and Dales
Racomitrium sudeticum	LR-ns	On dry or moist acid rocks, occasionally on soil in the mountains.	Cumbria Fells and Dales Dark Peak Dartmoor North Pennines Yorkshire Dales
Rhabdoweisia crenulata	LR-ns	Rocks from sea-level to high altitudes. Also associated with high altitude woodland communities. See Table 10.2.	Border Uplands Cumbria Fells and Dales Yorkshire Dales
Rhytidium rugosum	LR-ns	Calcicolous species of dry, short and often rather open grassland and turf on well-drained shallow rendzina soils developed over a range of substrates. Also occurs on dry south to south-west facing rock ledges.	North Pennines Yorkshire Dales Cumbria Fells and Dales White Peak

Plant species	Status	Typical habitat	Distribution by Natural Area (including those not containing montane areas)
Scapania aequiloba	LR-ns	On well-drained, strongly calcareous substrates, especially schists and limestones, often in rather exposed situations, such as mountain cliff-ledges, boulders and mossy turfs, but also on rocks in ravines. Less common in moister places such as boulders in streams and flushes.	Border Uplands Cumbria Fells and Dales North Pennines Yorkshire Dales
Scapania cuspiduligera	LR-ns	Forming small whitish-green patches on damp calcareous rocks in shady ravines and on rocks and detritus on stream sides, montane cliffs and rocky gullies. Also on soil and schistose gravel. Limestone and basic schist are the usual substrates but it is also recorded from Old Red Sandstone conglomerate and from Millstone Grit where subject to basic seepage or flooding.	Dark Peak North Pennines Yorkshire Dales
Scapania degenii	LR-ns	A strict calcicole favouring substrates derived from basic schist and limestone, in and beside stony flushes and on wet rock ledges and cliffs.	Cumbria Fells and Dales
Scapania ornithopodioides	LR-ns	As scattered stems amongst other bryophytes or as pure dark reddish-brown patches at moderate to high altitudes in mossy block-screes, on rocky well-drained slopes. Most common on acid substrates on open slopes or in mountain corries with a north to east aspect, where shade and humidity are maintained. It is a characteristic member of the 'hepatic mat' community.	Cumbria Fells and Dales
Scapania paludosa	LR-ns	In high altitude neutral to mildly basic bryophyte-dominated springs and flushes, and on wet rocks in gullies.	Cumbria Fells and Dales
Scapania uliginosa	LR-ns	High altitude springs and flushes, often submerged or emergent, usually in acid to neutral oligotrophic water. Also on wet rocks in late snow areas, in boggy ground, on lake shores and on constantly irrigated rocks on dripping cliffs and in shaded gullies.	Cumbria Fells and Dales North Pennines
Schistidium trichodon	LR-ns	Dry, often south- or west-facing, or seasonally damp limestone, calcareous schist or volcanic tuff cliffs.	North Pennines

Plant species	Status	Typical habitat	Distribution by Natural Area (including those not containing montane areas)
Sphenolobopsis pearsonii	LR-ns	In minute appressed green to blackish mats or as scattered stems on damp shaded rock-walls and boulders in sheltered ravines, on large blocks in scree and on vertical rock-walls on montane cliffs with a north to east aspect. Rocks are usually acid, eg granite and gneiss. Also associated with high altitude woodland communities. The plants may grow directly on rock or on a thin peaty, or mossy crust, sometimes with filamentous algae.	Cumbria Fells and Dales
Splachnum vasculosum	VU	In pale green loose patches on dung in springs and flushes at high altitudes.	Border Uplands North Pennines Cumbria Fells and Dales
Tomentypnum nitens	LR-ns	Open calcareous mires, flushes and wet fields, sometimes on gentle slopes flushed by water from steeper ones, at pH 5.8 or more.	Border Uplands Cumbria Fells and Dales North Pennines South West Peak Yorkshire Dales
Tetralophozia setiformis	LR-ns	Forming conspicuous mats, sometimes in quantity, on dry granite rocks and soil and amongst boulder scree, also rarely on tree roots.	Border Uplands

Key to Table 5.2

Annex IIb	- listed on Annex IIb of the EC Habitats and Species Directive
Sched. 8 of WCA	- listed on schedule 8 of the Wildlife & Countryside Act.
Red list categories	
CR	- critically endangered
EN	- endangered
VU	- vulnerable
DD	- data deficient
LR -nt	- Lower risk-near threatened
LR-ns	- Lower risk-nationally scarce
E	- endemic to Great Britain
EE	- endemic to England.
Biodiversity Action Plan (BAP)	
Priority	- Priority species from UK Steering Group 1995 and UK Biodiversity Group 1998.
SCC	- Species of conservation concern from UK Steering Group 1995 and UK Biodiversity Group 1998.

Sources

Most information from Hill, Preston & Smith 1991, 1992, 1994, Hodgetts, Palmer & Wigginton 1996 and Porley & McDonnell 1997.

Table 5.3 Habitat and management requirements of bryophytes associated with montane areas in England

Plants	Habitat requirements	Management requirements
Plants of rocks and block-scree	Relatively undisturbed rocks. Block-scree sometimes supports mixed hepatic mat communities (see below).	• Where relevant, protect sites from damage by climbing or trampling.
Plants of montane grassland and skeletal soil amongst rocks	Relatively undisturbed conditions.	• Where relevant, protect sites from damage by trampling.
Communities of Atlantic liverworts	These are related to the Scottish 'mixed hepatic mat' communities, which are very rare in England. Those constituent species which occur in Cumbria are mostly scattered through a variety of habitats, including rocky woodland and steep open rocks.[1] They are sometimes found beneath heathland of senescent *Calluna* and other ericaceous shrubs, or in block-scree. They can be badly damaged by fire.[2]	• Protect sites from burning.

Sources

1. D. Ratcliffe, pers comm.
2. N. Hodgetts, pers comm.

Also Hodgetts 1993b, P. Lambley and R. Porley, pers comm.

Table 5.4 **Plant communities associated with montane areas in England (National Vegetation Classification, NVC, Rodwell 1991, 1992)**

NVC code	NVC name	Inclusion in Annex 1 of Habitats Directive[1]	Significance in England[2]	Montane Natural Area of England where community occurs[2]
Heaths				
H13	*Calluna vulgaris-Cladonia arbuscula* heath	Alpine & sub-alpine heaths	I	North Pennines Cumbria Fells and Dales
H18 (Also sub-montane - see Ch 6)	*Vaccinium myrtillus-Deschampsia flexuosa* heath	Alpine & sub-alpine heaths Dry heaths	L	Border Uplands Yorkshire Dales Cumbria Fells and Dales North Pennines
H19	*Vaccinium myrtillus-Cladonia arbuscula* heath	Alpine & sub-alpine heaths	L	Border Uplands Yorkshire Dales Cumbria Fells and Dales
H22	*V. myrtillus-Rubus chamaemorus* heath	Alpine & sub-alpine heaths	UK	Border Uplands North Pennines
Mires				
M7	*Carex curta-Sphagnum russowii* mire	-	L	North Pennines
M8	*Carex rostrata-Sphagmum warnstorfii* mire	-	L	North Pennines
M31	*Anthelia julacea-Sphagnum auriculatum* spring	-	L	Cumbria Fells and Dales
M32	*Philonotis fontana-Saxifraga stellaris* spring	-	L	Cumbria Fells and Dales
Grasslands				
U7	*Nardus stricta-Carex bigelowii* grass heath	Siliceous alpine & boreal grassland	L	North Pennines Yorkshire Dales Cumbria Fells and Dales
U10	*Carex bigelowii-Racomitrium lanuginosum* moss heath	Siliceous alpine & boreal grassland	UK	North Pennines Cumbria Fells and Dales
U13	*Deschampsia cespitosa-Galium saxatile* grassland	-	I	Cumbria Fells and Dales

NVC code	NVC name	Inclusion in Annex 1 of Habitats Directive[1]	Significance in England[2]	Montane Natural Area of England where community occurs[2]
U15	*Saxifraga aizoides-Alchemilla glabra* banks	-	L	Cumbria Fells and Dales
U16	*Luzula sylvatica - Vaccinium myrtillus* tall herb community. See also Chapter 10 Crags, scree and limestone pavement	-	UK	Border Uplands North Pennines Cumbria Fells and Dales
U17	*Luzula sylvatica-Geum rivale* tall herb community. See also Chapter 10 Crags, scree and limestone pavement.	Eutrophic tall herbs	L	Border Uplands North Pennines Cumbria Fells and Dales Yorkshire Dales
CG11	*Festuca ovina-Agrostis capillaris-Alchemilla alpina* grass heath	Species-rich *Nardus* grassland on siliceous substrates*	UK	Cumbria Fells and Dales

Key

1 From Brown *et al* 1997:
* Priority habitat

2 From Drewitt & Manley 1997:
I Internationally scarce with UK representation;
UK Well developed in the UK but represented elsewhere;
L Widely developed in Europe.

Table 5.5 Breeding birds associated with montane areas in England

(Note: Some of these species have a broad altitudinal range and also occur in sub-montane and lowland areas. See also Chapters 6-10 for species predominantly of sub-montane habitats.)

Bird species[1]	Birds of conservation concern in the UK[2]	Listed on Schedule 1 of the Wildlife & Countryside Act 1981	Listed on Annex 1 of the EC Birds Directive	No of British 10-km squares with breeding records 1988-90	% of breeding records in upland ITE squares in Britain[3]	Main upland habitat associations	Principal upland Natural Areas supporting the species (including those not containing montane areas) *= major/important areas[4]
Golden eagle *Aquila chrysaetos*	Amber list	●	●	216	88.9	Moorland and montane areas	10* extinct elsewhere
Peregrine *Falco peregrinus*	Amber list	●	●	719	61.6	Moorland and montane areas	4, 8, 10*, 12, 14, 15, 25, 87*, 94
Red grouse *Lagopus lagopus scoticus*	-	-	-	749	78.6	Moorland	2*, 4*, 8*, 10, 12*, 14*, 15*, 17*, 25*, 29, 41, 42, 58(?), 87, 92
Ptarmigan *Lagopus mutus*	-	-	-	133	100	Montane areas	4, 10 but extinct in England
Dotterel *Charadrius morinellus*	Amber list	●	●	48	100	Montane areas	4*, 10
Golden plover *Pluvialis apricaria*	Amber list	-	●	630	84.1	Moorland and enclosed land	2*, 4*, 8*, 10, 12*, 14*, 15, 17*, 25*, 29, 92
Dunlin *Calidris alpina*	Amber list	-	-	353	78.8	Moorland	2, 4*, 8*, 12, 14*, 25*, 94
Meadow pipit *Anthus pratensis*	-	-	-	2,257	38.1	Moorland and enclosed land	All areas
Wheatear *Oenanthe oenanthe*	-	-	-	1,339	60.6	Montane areas, moorland and enclosed land	2*, 4*, 8*, 10*, 12, 14, 15, 17, 25, 29, 30*, 41, 42, 58, 60, 87, 92*, 94
Ring ouzel *Turdus torquatus*	Amber list	-	-	401	93.5	Moorland and scrub	2, 4*, 8*, 10*, 12, 14*, 15(?), 17, 25, 29, 30, 42, 87, 92*

Key to Table 5.5

1. Upland breeding bird species as identified in Stillman & Brown 1998.
2. Birds of conservation concern from RSPB 1996.
3. From Bunce & Barr 1988, using the 13 ITE land classes which were regarded as upland (information not available on an English basis).
4. The following 18 Natural Areas are classed as upland by English Nature:

No	**Natural Area name**		
2	Border Uplands	29	South West Peak
4	North Pennines	30	White Peak
8	Yorkshire Dales	41	Oswestry Uplands
10	Cumbria Fells and Dales	42	Shropshire Hills
12	Forest of Bowland	58	Clun and North West Herefordshire Hills
14	Southern Pennines	60	Black Mountains and Golden Valley
15	Pennine Dales Fringe	87	Exmoor and the Quantocks
17	North York Moors & Hills	92	Dartmoor
25	Dark Peak	94	Bodmin Moor

Natural Areas containing montane habitats to include the following:

2	Border Uplands	8	Yorkshire Dales
4	North Pennines	10	Cumbria Fells and Dales

Table 5.6 **Habitat and management requirements of birds associated with montane areas in England**

Montane birds	Habitat requirements	Management requirements
Ptarmigan (extinct in England)	• Nest on the ground in a range of montane plant communities, including *Racomitrium lanuginosum* heaths, but avoid areas of extensive grassland. • Feed in a range of montane habitats, but with a greater selection for dwarf shrub communities (primarily bilberry *Vaccinium myrtillus* but also crowberry *Empetrum nigrum*). • Cover in the form of rocks, heavily broken ground and hummocks is also an important feature of habitat selection. • Flushes and springs are particularly heavily selected by feeding birds, either with or without chicks. • A mosaic of small patches of dwarf shrub heath, flushes and rock is ideal. • Chicks feed on invertebrates (mainly flies), the flowers of herbs (eg bedstraw *Galium* spp., alpine lady's mantle *Alchemilla alpina* and saxifrage *Saxifraga* spp.) and bilberry shoot tips. As they grow, invertebrates decrease in importance and dwarf shrubs (eg crowberry) become more important as their diets change to those of adults. • Present in montane areas all year unless forced to descent by severe weather.	• Maintain and enhance montane dwarf shrub heaths by reducing grazing and encouraging non-intervention areas.
Dotterel	• Prefer flat or gently sloping ground. • Nest on the ground with strong selection for nesting on woolly hair moss *R. lanuginosum* heaths. • Areas of bare ground within *R. lanuginosum* heaths (up to 10% cover) important for nesting and feeding adults and chicks. • Feed mainly on beetles, sawflies and the adults and larvae of crane-flies *Tipula montana*. • Birds not present in uplands outside breeding season (mid-April – end August).	• Maintain and enhance *R. lanuginosum* heaths and montane dwarf-shrub heaths by reducing grazing and encouraging non-intervention areas. • Maintain a degree of heterogeneity in the appearance of the habitat as this is important for nesting.

Sources

Ratcliffe 1973, Galbraith *et al* 1993a & b and P. Whitfield, pers comm.

Table 5.7 **Nationally rare and scarce invertebrates associated with montane areas in England**

Invertebrate species		Nature conservation status	Typical habitat	Distribution in upland England (not currently available in terms of Natural Areas)
Scientific name	**English name**			
Moths				
Catoptria furcatellus	Micro-moth	Nationally Scarce B	Sparse turf at high altitude	Lake District (and a nineteenth century Cheviot record)
Xestia alpicola alpina	Northern dart moth	Nationally Scarce A Priority	Feeds on *Empetrum nigrum* at high altitude	North Pennines. Old records for Lake District and Northumberland
Xestia ashworthii	Ashworth's rustic moth	Nationally Scarce A Priority	On heather and other upland plants (including foxgloves) in montane and moorland areas	Northumberland
Butterflies				
Erebia epiphron	Small mountain ringlet	Nationally scarce B SCC	*Nardus* grassland, from around 400 m upwards	In England it is restricted to the Lake District only occurring at high altitudes.
Beetles				
Aphodius fasciatus	Dung beetle	Nationally Scarce B	Sheep and deer dung at high altitude on moorland and mountain habitats	North York Moors, Lake District and Pennines
Byrrhus arietinus	Pill beetle	Nationally Scarce B	Feeds on *Racomitrium lanuginosum* on moors and mountain tops	Pennines, Derbyshire Peaks, North York Moors and Lake District
Elaphrus lapponicus	Ground beetle	Nationally Scarce A	Wet moss at very high altitude, also by very high streams	Lake District

Invertebrate species		**Nature conservation status**	**Typical habitat**	**Distribution in upland England (not currently available in terms of Natural Areas)**
Eudectus whitei *	Rove beetle	Nationally Scarce A	Under stones and in moss on mountain summits	Only on summits of Three Peaks in Yorkshire Dales, although possibly now extinct there
Geodromicus longipes	Rove beetle	Nationally Scarce B	In *R. lanuginosum* and under stones on mountain tops	Cumbria and perhaps Staffordshire
Leistus montanus	Ground beetle	Nationally Scarce A	Under stones on mountain tops	Lake District
Miscodera arctica	Ground beetle	Nationally Scarce B	Under stones on mountain summits, moors and northern lowland heath	Cumbria, Northumberland, Pennines, North York Moors and Exmoor
Mycetoporus monticola	Rove beetle	Nationally Scarce B	In moss on mountain tops	Cumbria
Nebria nivalis	Ground beetle	Nationally Scarce A	Very cold areas – by late snow-lie beds, north facing gullies at high altitude and frost shattered summits among *Racomitrium* growing between stones	Scafell Pike
Olophrum assimile	Rove beetle	RDBI	Wet moss, litter and stream sides at very high altitude	The only recent GB record is from Dun Fell. Old records in Scotland
Oxypoda soror	Rove beetle	Nationally Scarce B	In moss and under stones on mountain tops	Old records from Skiddaw in Cumbria
Oxypoda tirolensis	Rove beetle	Nationally Scarce B	In moss and under stones on mountain tops	Old records for Scafell and Skiddaw in Cumbria
Stenus glacialis	Rove beetle	RDBK	In wet moss high on mountains	Single old record in England from summit of Cheviot

* Not recorded elsewhere other than the UK, but almost certainly not endemic – is in a poorly understood group of beetles

Invertebrate species		Nature conservation status	Typical habitat	Distribution in upland England (not currently available in terms of Natural Areas)
Spiders				
Entelecara errata	Money spider	Nationally Scarce B	Under stones on mountain tops	Northumberland
Lepthyphantes pinicola	Money spider	Nationally Scarce B	Mainly under stones on mountains but also on moorland	Yorkshire, Cumbria and Staffordshire
Lepthyphantes whymperi	Money spider	Nationally Scarce B	In cavities among rocks on mountains	Lake District
Pardosa trailli	Wolf spider	Nationally Scarce B	Under stones and in scree on mountains	Lake District
Rugathodes bellicosus	Comb-footed spider	Nationally Scarce B	Under stones on high ground (but at sea level in Scotland). Mountain tops and moorland in England	Yorkshire Pennines and the Lake District
Tiso aestivus	Money spider	Nationally Scarce B	Under stones above 600 m	Lake District

Key

RDB	Red Data Book (Shirt 1987; Hyman & Parsons 1992)
RDBI	Red Data Book - Indeterminate
RDBK	Red Data Book - Insufficiently known
Nationally Scarce A	15-30 10-km squares of national grid
Nationally Scarce B	30-100 10-km squares of national grid
Priority	Priority species in the UK Biodiversity Action Plan (UK Steering Group 1995; UK Biodiversity Group 1998)
SCC	Species of conservation concern in the UK Biodiversity Action Plan (UK Steering Group 1995; UK Biodiversity Group 1998)

Table 5.8 Habitat and management requirements of invertebrates associated with montane areas in England

Montane invertebrates	Habitat requirements	Management requirements
Moss-inhabiting species	Moss, especially woolly hair moss *Racomitrium lanuginosum* and moss in flushes and beside streams.	• Maintain minimal grazing and manage recreation on summits. • Encourage non-intervention areas.
Species living under stones (lapidicolous)	Undisturbed stony areas, fairly stable screes.	• Manage recreation. • Discourage opportunistic cairn-building by informing the public of the invertebrate interest and potential impacts.
Ground and rove beetles	Bare ground for hunting.	• Usually no necessity for management in montane areas where grazing occurs and paths are present.

Moorland

Moorland 6

Tables

Definition and location of moorland

6.1 Definition of moorland

In this handbook the term moorland is used to refer to the unenclosed land of the English uplands. This supports dwarf-shrub heaths (wet and dry), blanket mires, other mires, scrub and grassland. Woodland, freshwater, montane and rock habitats also occur in the unenclosed uplands, but are covered in separate chapters. Bracken *Pteridium aquilinum* is also very widespread in the unenclosed and enclosed uplands and is discussed in Information Note 6.

Dry dwarf shrub heath is a vegetation community in which ericoid dwarf shrubs (heather *Calluna vulgaris, Erica* spp., *Vaccinium* spp, and crowberry *Empetrum nigrum*) or western gorse *Ulex gallii* form more than 25% of the cover in relatively dry situations. Wet heath can be defined by the same cover of ericoid dwarf shrubs but in wet situations and where peat depth does not exceed 0.5 m. Mires are wetlands supporting vegetation which is normally peat-forming, and occur where the ground is permanently or periodically waterlogged (Lindsay 1995; Rodwell 1991). Blanket mires cover extensive areas of land, including slopes, and are found on blanket peat bodies usually deeper than 0.5 m. Grasslands, where grasses are the dominant species and where dwarf shrubs form less than 25%, are widespread.

These vegetation types frequently occur as an intimate mosaic of habitat types, and within them are also found areas of bracken, shrubs and occasional trees. The National Vegetation Classification (NVC, Rodwell 1991, 1992) describes the many plant communities of the moorlands of England and those covered by this chapter are listed in Table 6.4. A number of the mire communities found in the unenclosed as well as the enclosed uplands are covered in Chapter 7 Meadows and enclosed pasture.

6.2 Location and extent of moorland

Moorland areas are found throughout the uplands of England. They occur in all the upland Natural Areas of England identified by English Nature, a map of which is shown as Figure 1.1.

Countryside Survey 1990 (Barr *et al* 1993) reported that semi-natural vegetation covered over 73% of upland landscapes in Great Britain. In England, heath/moor grass covered 34% (1,515 km^2) of upland habitats with bog 2.7% (119 km^2) and bracken (5.6% (245 km^2).

The extent of moorland in the Less Favoured Areas (LFA) of England was estimated to be 798,969 ha (MAFF Moorland Map of England 1992). Moorland was defined as semi-natural rough grazings consisting mainly of plant species characteristic of grassy and shrubby heaths and moors. Open moors, enclosed land on the margins of the uplands which had reverted to a more natural state, and rock land associated with moorland vegetation were all included. As part of this study (but not recorded in the final report), the presence of dwarf shrub vegetation was also recorded. It was found to occur in 3,060 one kilometre grid squares (over 50% dwarf shrub cover) and 6,400 one kilometre grid squares (5-50% dwarf shrub cover, I. Condliffe, pers comm). The area of upland heath has also been estimated to be

269,000 ha (Felton & Marsden 1990). Blanket peat is thought to cover some 215,000 ha of England (UK Biodiversity Group 1999).

For further details of the location of particular moorland habitats and species, see section 6.5 below.

Habitats and species of moorland

6.3 Why moorland areas are important

A great number of moorland habitats and species are recognised as being of nature conservation importance, either internationally, nationally or at a more local level. Dwarf shrub heath, for example, is extensive in Britain, but has become fragmented and of limited extent in the rest of Europe (Gimingham 1975). Heathland containing gorse *Ulex* species is widespread in the uplands of south west England but no other continental hills have a comparable extent of vegetation dominated by *Ulex gallii*. Blanket mire is globally rare and 10-15% of the world resource is thought to occur in Britain, with the majority in Scotland (Lindsay *et al* 1988).

As well as being important for the plant communities present, moorland areas support many animal and plant species of conservation interest. Heather moorland in particular is rich in species of conservation value (Usher & Thompson 1993, see section 6.4 below). Moorlands are also important because they form the largest extent of undeveloped wildlife habitat remaining in the country (Ratcliffe & Thompson 1988).

The peat of blanket bogs represents a rich archaeological archive which, once lost, cannot be restored or rehabilitated (Brooks & Stoneman 1997). Moorland deposits also make an important contribution to the geological record, especially records of climate change (see Chapter 4).

6.4 Habitats and species of moorland, their nature conservation status and distribution

6.4.1 Vascular plants

The plant species of nature conservation significance in the moorland areas of England are shown in Table 6.2, with their nature conservation status and distribution in the upland Natural Areas. They range from species typical of heaths and blanket bogs to those characteristic of limestone grassland, flushes, ledges or metalliferous soils in the unenclosed uplands of England. While many have a wide altitudinal distribution and are also found outside the moorland environment, some are particularly associated with this situation.

Of particular note are those species identified as a priority for conservation action in the UK Biodiversity Action Plan (UK Biodiversity Group 1998; UK Steering Group 1995). These include an alchemilla *Alchemilla minima*, found in short, base-rich grassland in the North Pennines and Yorkshire Dales, and a euphrasia *Euphrasia rivularis* which occurs in bryophyte-rich flushes in Cumbria. Another euphrasia *E. vigursii* is found in damp, grassy heathland on Bodmin Moor and Dartmoor.

6.4.2 Bryophytes and lichens

Moorland areas support a range of bryophytes (mosses and liverworts) and lichens. In heathland and bogs, these can be very numerous and an important part of the plant community. *Sphagnum* moss, for example, is a vital component of bog vegetation because it acts as a sponge and retains water. Bryophytes are often the first plants to colonise newly exposed ground, such as burnt areas, and are important in stabilising the soil. They may also dominate in environments with heavy-metal-rich soil and some invertebrates depend on them for a food source.

Less is known about non-vascular plants of moorland than about the associated vascular plants, and consequently less information is included here. However, the important bryophytes in the moorland areas of England are identified in Table 6.3, along with their conservation status and distribution.

6.4.3 Plant communities

Heaths

Upland heathland lies below the montane zone (about 600 m in England) and usually above the upper edge of enclosed agricultural land, and is found across the uplands of England. Upland dry heath is dominated by ericaceous dwarf shrubs, particularly heather (also called ling). Other dwarf shrubs include bell heather *Erica cinerea*, bilberry *Vaccinium myrtilus*, crowberry, cowberry *Vaccinium vitis-idaea* and bearberry *Arctostaphylos uva-ursi*. Dry heaths tend to occur on mineral soils with humus-rich surface horizons or thin accumulations of peat.

Upland wet heath is also dominated by ericoid dwarf shrubs, and occurs on peat soils up to about 0.5 m deep, which isolates the plant roots from the underlying mineral soil and rocks (Nature Conservancy Council 1990a, for peat depths >0.5 m see blanket mire). Cross-leaved heath *Erica tetralix* is generally more frequent in wet heath, whereas it is usually no more than occasional in dry heath. Bryophytes, including *Sphagnum* spp., are generally abundant, although they may be absent in degraded stands. Purple moor-grass *Molinia caerulea*, heath rush *Juncus squarrosus* and deer grass *Scirpus cespitosus* may also be frequent or abundant. Wet heath can also occur in transitions from basin mires to heaths.

Dry heath communities are confined to the British Isles and the western seaboard of Europe. Those found in the UK are therefore of significance in an international context. The structure and function of these communities has developed over many generations of human influence in combination with specific local climatic and geological conditions. Of special significance are the communities found over calcareous strata in Cumbria.

Wet heath is restricted in its distribution to the Atlantic fringe between Scandinavia and Normandy. The majority of the wet heath resource in the EU is in the UK and it spans upland and lowland altitudes. Wet heath is usually found in a mosaic with blanket mire and dry heath communities, mainly in the western Pennines and in the south west.

The heaths of the English uplands are described by the National Vegetation Classification (NVC, Rodwell 1991, Table 6.4). Certain upland dry and wet heath communities are included in Annex 1 of the Habitats Directive. They are also included in the Biodiversity Action Plan programme (UK Steering Group 1995; UK Biodiversity Group 1999).

Heathland which occurs in lowland areas of England is covered elsewhere (English Nature & RSPB 1995; Gimingham 1992).

Mires

The uplands contain a great diversity of mire types, many of which are of significant nature conservation value. Many are included in Annex 1 of the Habitats Directive and they are also included in the Biodiversity Action Plan (UK Steering Group 1995; Blanket Bog Habitat Action Plan, DETR 1999).

Six basic types of mire can be distinguished (Heathwaite & Gottlich 1993, Table 6.1) and the National Vegetation Classification (NVC, Rodwell 1991) classifies mires into 38 categories, each further sub-divided (Table 6.4). They can also be sub-divided into fens, which are influenced by water from the surrounding land and range from nutrient poor to rich, and bogs, which are mires deriving their water exclusively from precipitation and generally having a low nutrient status (Tansley 1939).

Sphagnum

One particularly extensive mire type in the uplands is known as blanket bog which is really a misnomer for a wide range of unconfined peatlands. Blanket mire is a more accurate term, where a mire is any peat-forming ecosystem. It is worth noting that the NVC defines communities on the vegetation alone, so degraded blanket bog on blanket peat (> 0.5 m deep) may be inappropriately identified as heath or grassland communities.

Grasslands

The grasslands found in unenclosed moorland areas can be sub-divided into acid, calcareous and neutral grasslands. This sub-division assists the understanding and identification of the different types, which are described by the National Vegetation Classification (NVC) (Rodwell 1992, Table 6.4).

Acid grasslands are the most extensive grassland type in England, being generally derived from the heavy grazing of dwarf shrub communities. They occur from the lowlands to the montane zone and in the unenclosed uplands they may be dominated by such grass species as sheep's fescue *Festuca ovina*, common bent *Agrostis capillaris* or mat grass *Nardus stricta*, or by heath rush. These grassland types are mostly relatively species-poor, but where they are found in association with dwarf shrub and mire communities they can add to the diversity, structure and function of the habitat. Bracken over grassland, or dense stands of bracken alone, is another feature of the unenclosed (and enclosed) uplands.

More species-rich upland acid grassland communities also occur, eg NVC types U4c and U5c, but are restricted in distribution, occurring for example in the North Pennines. Another community, U3, *Agrostis curtisii*, also has a limited distribution and is confined to the south west of England. Other kinds of acid grassland present in the uplands of England are the purple moor-grass and rush pasture communities. These occur on poorly drained soils, particularly in Devon and Cornwall where the habitat is known as Culm grassland. Their vegetation consists of various species-rich types of fen meadow and rush pasture. Purple moor-grass and rushes, especially sharp-flowered rush *Juncus acutiflorus*, are usually abundant. The communities often occur in a mosaic with wet heath, dry grassland, swamp and scrub.

Purple moor-grass and rush pastures are highly susceptible to agricultural modification and reclamation. Only a small percentage of the original resource now remains in the UK and Europe, and fragmentation and isolation of stands have been common. Certain *Molinia*-dominated acid grasslands are included in Annex 1 of the Habitats Directive. Acid grasslands are also included in the Biodiversity Action Plan (UK Biodiversity Group 1998; UK Steering Group 1995).

Calcareous grasslands in the uplands are generally restricted to shallow soils that are derived from a variety of calcareous bedrocks. The majority of upland calcareous grassland is found on Carboniferous limestone in the North Pennines, Yorkshire Dales, Cumbria and Peak District, and the Corallian limestones of the North York Moors. It is inherently more species-rich than acid grassland and supports an exceptional diversity of plants, including rarities and species restricted to lime-rich soils such as blue moor-grass *Sesleria caerulea* and common rock-rose *Helianthemum nummularium*. It can be found as open or dense swards, with a tall and tussocky or short and tightly cropped structure.

Calcareous grasslands are thought to have been widespread at a European scale at the turn of the century. However, as they are particularly sensitive to changes in management, these grassland types are now rare in Europe. They are included in Annex 1 of the Habitats Directive and the Biodiversity Action Plan programme (UK Steering Group 1995; UK Biodiversity Group 1999).

Unimproved neutral grasslands are those which have not undergone agricultural improvement and are generally species-rich. They are usually enclosed and managed as traditional hay meadows or pastures and are covered in Chapter 7 Meadows and enclosed pasture.

Metalliferous communities

These are communities which have developed on metal-rich soils and are also called calaminarian grasslands. They are rare communities that should be maintained and their nature conservation importance is recognised by their inclusion in the Habitats Directive. The soil on which these communities exist can cause pollution problems, particularly by rivers, and if land owners and water companies want to remove the potential source of pollution the communities are threatened.

Examples include metalliferous grasslands in the Pennines, Yorkshire Dales, Peak District ('lead-rakes'), metalliferous mire communities with particular bryophyte interest on Bodmin Moor, and a metalliferous algae community in the River Nent in the Pennines. The communities on spoil-heaps of the Pennine lead mines, for example, have a very characteristic flora which is restricted by the presence of lead and other metals in the soil (Kelly & Perry 1990). Lead-tolerant species such as spring sandwort *Minuartia verna*, alpine penny-cress *Thlaspi caerulescens*, sheep's sorrel *Rumex acetosella* and various lichens and mosses thrive in the absence of competition from other plants. Lead-tolerant varieties of fescue *Festuca* spp. and bent grasses *Agrostis* spp. are also found, and these have proved useful in the reclamation of metalliferous spoil in industrial areas.

Metalliferous habitats are of some value for invertebrates. For example, the nationally scarce ground beetle *Notiophilus aesthuans* seems to favour lead mine spoil in the Yorkshire Dales, as well as occurring in montane areas in Scotland. In addition to their wildlife value, many old spoil-heaps are of considerable geological interest. See Chapter 4 Earth heritage features.

Further information: Antonovics *et al* 1971; Baker 1987; Sellers & Baker 1988; Stewart & Drewitt 1989; Rodwell 2000.

6.4.4 Birds

Unenclosed heaths, grasslands and mires can be important habitats for birds. British breeding birds that are positively associated with these habitats in the uplands are identified in Stillman & Brown (1998) and their definition of upland birds and list of species relevant to England are used here.

Black grouse

Heather is an important feeding and nesting habitat for red grouse *Lagopus lagopus*, and to a lesser extent black grouse *Tetrao tetrix*. Scrubby areas on heaths are also important for black grouse, as well as other birds such as whinchat *Saxicola rubetra* and stonechat *Saxicola torquata*. Ring ouzel *Turdus torquatus*, wheatear *Oenanthe oenanthe*, meadow pipit *Anthus pratensis* and skylark *Alauda arvensis* also breed in the unenclosed uplands, although the last species is more associated with lowland grasslands. Moorland areas provide hunting grounds as well as nesting sites for rare raptors such as merlin *Falco columbarius* and hen harrier *Circus cyaneus*. Peregrine *Falco peregrinus* and raven *Corvus corax* can be found nesting on cliffs within moorland. Few breeding bird species actually appear to be dependent upon heather moorlands (Fuller 1996).

Blanket bogs support breeding golden plover *Pluvialis apricaria* and dunlin *Calidris aplina* and waterlogged areas with pools and mossy hollows of *Sphagnum* are important feeding grounds for these birds. Many other birds also nest in heather and rough grazing areas while feeding in boggy patches, next to water or in agriculturally improved grassland near the moor. Redshank *Tringa totanus* and snipe *Gallinago gallinago* utilise unenclosed and enclosed damp grasslands for breeding and feeding, and twite *Carduelis flavirostris* are particularly associated with the moorland edge. The bird species associated with moorland areas in England are shown in Table 6.5.

6.4.5 Invertebrates

Northern and western British moorlands tend to have some elements of lowland heathland fauna reaching their northern limit and montane species reaching their southern limit. On the whole the diversity is fairly low when compared with lowland habitats, although spiders, ground beetles, rove beetles and craneflies can be diverse. Relatively few scarce species are restricted to moorland. The highest proportion of moorland species are among the moths, ground and rove beetles, money spiders and craneflies. The greatest biomass is in the form of cranefly larvae (leatherjackets) and click beetle larvae (wireworms), including several species of the former and three or four main species of the latter, as well as annelid worms (small white Enchytraeidae). Leatherjackets and wireworms are of particular value for upland birds. In grass moorland and bracken mosaics, the beetle *Phyllopertha horticolor* may also form a significant biomass. Nationally rare and scarce invertebrate species particularly associated with moorlands in England are listed in Table 6.7.

Particularly conspicuous and typical moorland beetles include click beetles and the common tiger beetle *Cicindela campestris*. Moths include the northern eggar moth *Lasiocampa quercus*, emperor moth *Pavonia pavonia* and common heath moth *Ematurga atomaria*. The mountain ringlet butterfly *Erebia ephiphron*, small heath butterfly *Coenonympha pamphilius* and the large heath butterfly *Coenonympha tullia* are also typical, the last only occurring on bogs. Other typical species include the mountain bumble bee *Bombus monticola*, northern darter *Sympetrum danae*, northern aeshna *Aeshna juncea* and golden ringed *Cordulegaster boltoni* dragonflies, immature stages of the last occurring in streams while the adults range widely over moors.

Further information:
Coulson, Fielding & Goodyear 1992; Fishpool & Usher 1989; Sanderson *et al* 1995; Sutherland & Hill 1995; Usher 1992; Usher & Thompson 1988.

6.4.6 Mammals

Moorland provides the only habitat of the mountain hare *Lepus timidus* in England (Table 6.9). It lives on the *Calluna-Eriophorum* areas at higher altitudes than the brown hare *Lepus europaeus*. This species, which is native to Britain, is found only in the Peak District in England, where it has been introduced.

Structurally diverse moorland can provide high densities of small mammals, notably field voles *Microtus agrestis* and shrews *Sorex* spp. (Butterfield, Coulson & Wanless 1981). Voles are herbivores and feed mainly on grasses. As such, they can be found in large numbers on grass moorland and in lower numbers in heather moorland. These form an important element in the food chain, being especially important prey items for birds of prey, such as short-eared owl *Asio flammeus*, hen harrier, buzzard *Buteo buteo* and other animals such as the adder *Vipera berus* and polecat *Mustela putorius*.

Moorlands provide valuable habitats where these are adjacent to woodland blocks. For example rocky, undisturbed moorlands provide valuable habitats for pine martens *Martes martes* when adjacent to large areas of conifer or deciduous woodland. Open moorland can also be a valuable buffer for preventing incursion of grey squirrels *Sciurus carolinensis* to woodlands occupied by red squirrels *S. vulgaris*.

Open moorlands provide areas for foraging for deer. The largest population of red deer in England occurs in the 'West Country' (Langbein 1997), with the best known herds found within Exmoor and the Quantock Hills. The increase in red deer numbers in the south west of England over recent decades has led to mounting concern about deer damage. This is particularly justified in woodland habitats, where regeneration can be significantly reduced. On moorlands the contribution by deer to overall grazing can be important in relation to appropriate levels of domestic stock.

6.4.7 Amphibians and reptiles

Moorlands can provide valuable habitats for both amphibians and reptiles (Table 6.9). Frogs, toads and newts may be more restricted in the use of these areas by the occurrence of suitable breeding ponds. Sometimes moorland ponds are naturally too acidic for successful breeding owing to surrounding peat. However, such ponds are also poorly buffered and can be particularly susceptible to anthropogenic acidification.

Common lizard

Large areas of natural and semi-natural habitat, with low levels of disturbance, favour the development of good and robust reptile populations. These areas can also support a high biomass of prey species (invertebrates for lizards; small mammals, lizards and amphibians for snakes). In such systems, local losses can be replenished by immigration.

Upland habitats, notably moorland and newly planted woodland, are valuable habitats for adders. These snakes are becoming scarcer in lowland habitats in part due to disturbance, as well as habitat loss and fragmentation. The large expanses of structurally diverse habitat, rich in both lizard and mammal prey, are therefore important for this species.

Two species of lizard occur in upland habitats, the common (or viviparous) lizard *Lacerta agilis* and the slow worm *Anguis fragilis*. Both species occur in a wide range of habitats throughout England and can be common in moorland, open woodlands and grasslands.

6.5 Habitat and management requirements of moorland species

Some habitat and management requirements of key moorland species are shown in Tables 6.2 (vascular plants), 6.6 (birds), 6.8 (invertebrates) and 6.10 (mammals, amphibians and reptiles). However, there is generally a shortage of adequate knowledge on the ecological and hence the management requirements of many upland species. Recommendations presented here are based on the best available information or, where there is little or no quantitative evidence, then the opinion of experienced workers in the field concerned. Such recommendations may change as further information becomes available.

Some nationally rare and scarce vascular plant species are particularly associated with dwarf-shrub communities while others occur in grassland, mires or rocky habitats in the unenclosed uplands. Many are not exclusive to moorland areas, and may even be considered to be more typical of enclosed or lowland areas, in which case cross-references to other chapters are made. However, all species require their particular habitat type to be maintained; for example, heaths should not be lost nor mires drained. Many require particular grazing regimes, although the most appropriate intensity varies with the species concerned.

For many non-vascular plants, their ecology is poorly understood and therefore very little information is available on their habitat and management requirements. Bryophytes of mires, wet heath and dwarf-shrub heath generally require minimal intervention, except possibly control of scrub development. Burning, particularly if frequent or intense, can be damaging to some non-vascular plants in these habitats (N. Hodgetts pers comm) and so particularly rich sites or sites with rare species should be protected from burning. Non-vascular plant diversity and abundance is likely to be greatest in unburnt areas or areas burnt on a very long rotation.

Certain rare bryophytes occurring on moorland have specialised habitat and management requirements. For example, slender green feather-moss *Hamatocaulis vernicosus* is found in base-rich lowland sedge-fens and upland flushes, where the development of scrub and coarse vegetation is prevented by management such as cutting or grazing. In this situation it is necessary to maintain the level and chemical quality of the water table and to maintain levels of grazing or cutting, as appropriate, to prevent the encroachment of tall vegetation. Another rare species, marsh earwort *Jamesoniella undulifolia* occurs in wet mineral-rich *Sphagnum* mires. To maintain this species it is necessary to prevent changes in hydrological conditions, including drainage and flooding for reservoirs. It is also necessary to prevent eutrophication of the habitat, including pollution from agricultural run-off and drift, and damage to the colonies by poaching by cattle.

Many birds typical of the unenclosed uplands rely on heather moorland and require extensive areas of this habitat in good condition to feed and breed. Blanket bog and bracken stands are also important for many bird species. Maintaining moorland habitat diversity, including mires, wet heath and grassland, scrub and trees, and freshwater habitats such as pools, rivers and lakes ensures that the maximum diversity of bird species can be supported.

Moorland areas containing habitat, floristic and structural diversity are particularly valuable for invertebrates. For example, mosaics including heath, wet flushes, grassland, scattered shrubs and trees and fresh water support a diverse invertebrate assemblage, as do areas with significant moss cover and a diversity of exposed substrates, such as bare peat, mineral soil, sand, rocks and stones. Dwarf-shrub communities containing all phases of heather growth, including young and mature heather with a build-up of litter, provide feeding, breeding and sheltering habitats for many types of invertebrates. A range and abundance of flowering plants, especially species with early flowers or a long flowering period, provide important pollen and nectar sources. Animal dung and small hydrological features such as peat pools, *Sphagnum* pools, seepages and stream headwaters, with varied margins to water bodies, are also of value.

Further information:
Birds: Dodds *et al* 1996; English Nature 1996a; Hudson & Newborn 1995; Mason & MacDonald 1999); Phillips 1997b.
Invertebrates: Coulson 1988; Coulson & Butterfield 1985; Gardner *et al* 1997; Gardner & Usher 1989; MacDonald & Haysom 1997; Usher 1992.

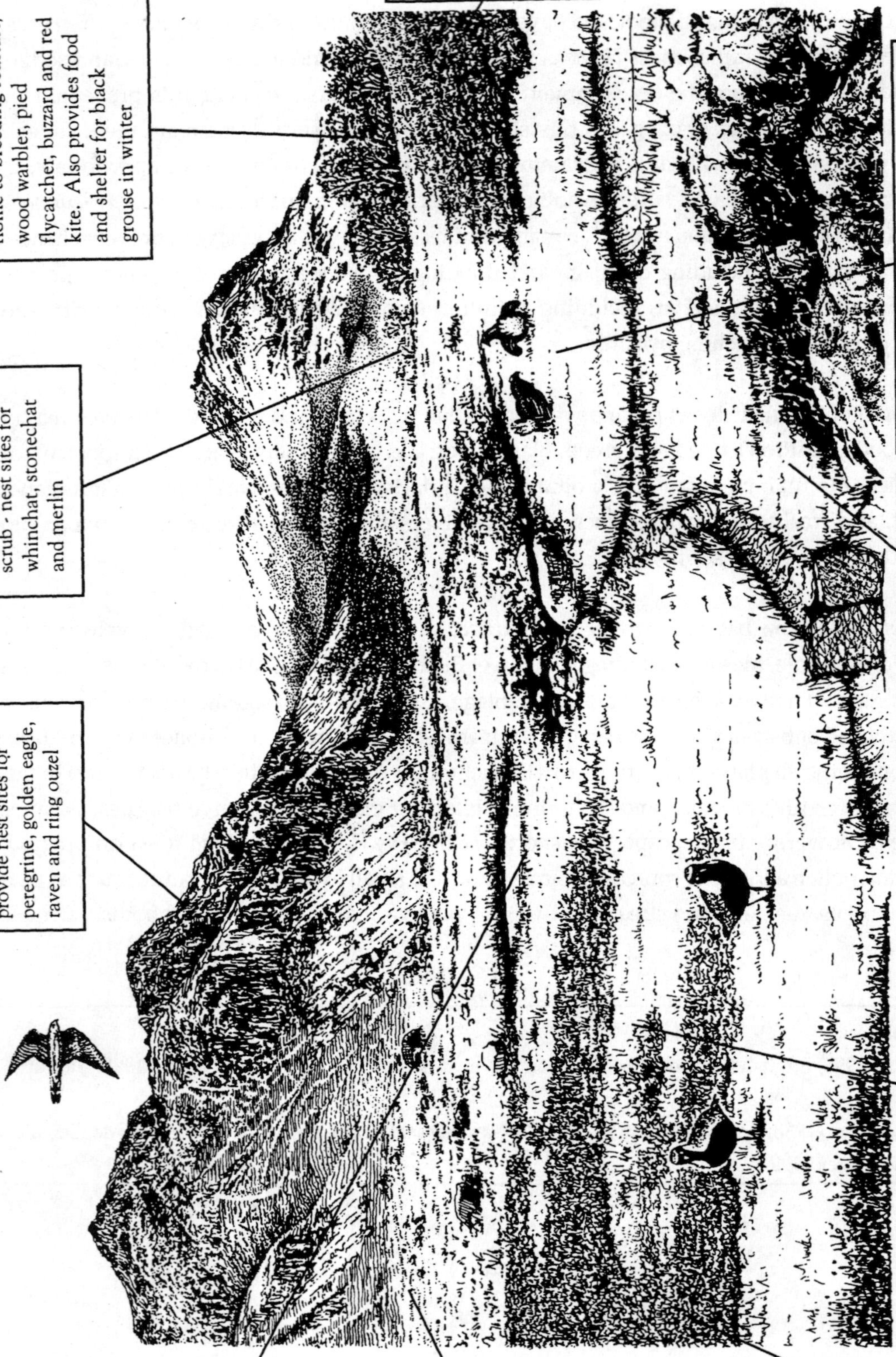

Figure 6.1 Stylised moorland for birds in the English uplands

Management of moorland

6.6 Managing moorland

The main agricultural and sporting management practices conducted in moorland areas include grazing, burning and cutting of heaths, mires and grasslands, and predator control. Other activities include bracken, scrub and rhododendron management, while agricultural improvement and moorland drainage has also been practised in the past. Grazing, burning and cutting are covered in this section, while other management activities, including predator control, reversing moorland drainage, applying surface treatments, managing shrub and recreation, are covered in the following sections (see 6.7). Bracken management is discussed in Information Note 6.

A diverse approach to management in the English uplands is desirable, to assist in maintaining and enhancing biodiversity. This also recognises that different approaches may be traditional and appropriate in different parts of the country, and management objectives may differ between sites.

6.6.1 Grazing of moorlands

Retaining a varied moorland resource requires a balance between high grazing pressure, which can lead to the spread of grasses and loss of dwarf shrubs, and low-grazing pressure, which can allow invasion of some trees and shrubs (Hester 1996; Ward, Macdonald & Matthew 1995).

The three main components of the grazing process are defoliation, trampling and manuring (Crofts & Jefferson 1994). The overall effect of grazing is to reduce the quantity of more palatable plant species and increase the frequency of less palatable and more grazing and trampling resistant species (eg grasses, low and rosette-forming species and distasteful plants). The specific effects of grazing will depend on a number of factors, including the following (Ausden & Treweek 1995):

- the types of vegetation present;
- the condition of the vegetation present (including the proportion of different age classes of heather, if present);
- the timing of grazing (whether year round, seasonal or occasional);
- the intensity of grazing (numbers of animals, length of grazing period);
- the type of grazing animal (species, breed, age, sex);
- the associated practices (supplementary feeding, presence and nature of shepherding practices, use of vehicles);
- the other management practices conducted (burning, cutting, bracken management);

- the existence and location of fences and other boundaries;
- the geographical location of the area;
- the underlying geology, soil type and wetness of the area;
- the climate, topography, altitude and aspect.

Cowberry

All grazing animals are to some extent selective in the plants they eat. Favoured elements of the vegetation are eaten first while less desirable plants are left until last or not eaten at all. There is considerable variation in grazing behaviour between different types of animals, different breeds of the same animal and different age classes within breeds. The grazing preferences of the stock employed will affect the species composition and structure of the vegetation.

Sheep and cattle are the main grazing animals on moorlands, with some horses, ponies and feral goats. Grazing animals other than domestic stock include deer and rabbits. The sheep and beef enterprises encountered in the English uplands are introduced in Chapter 2, with further details in Information Notes 3 (sheep) and 5 (cattle). The grazing characteristics of large herbivores in the uplands are given in Box 2.4. The characteristics of the different breeds of sheep and cattle are described in Information Note 2 (sheep) and 4 (cattle).

Further information: Hester 1996.

Livestock management on moorlands

Shepherding, also termed 'raking', is required for good grazing management of a hill sheep flock. It spreads the sheep and hence the grazing pressure over the hill and reduces the risk of localised overgrazing. It is a practice which has severely declined in recent years, as the number of people employed on upland farms has decreased. Where uneven grazing pressure is a problem for nature conservation interests and shepherding is not currently practised, incentives for shepherding may be an option. For example, moving stock away from the 'bottom edge' of the heather at least twice a week could be beneficial. All Terrain Vehicles are sometimes used by shepherds, but this is best kept to defined routes and only if continued use of a route does not lead to damage to the vegetation.

Appropriate burning management, producing a pattern of small patch burns, also encourages stock to move across an area (see 6.6.2 on burning).

Stock proof boundaries, such as fences and walls where they already exist, also help to control stock movement and hence grazing pressures on moorlands. Repairing or erecting walls or fences in certain areas can be used to reduce or remove grazing. However, new stock proof boundaries often need careful consideration to avoid conflict with landscape and public access objectives, as well as agricultural uses. On common land, permission is required from the Secretary of State to erect new boundaries.

Small fenced areas can be used for monitoring the effects of removing or reducing grazing, although these need to be large enough to avoid shelter effects. Fencing areas around the bases of cliffs may allow the spread of plants confined to these areas by grazing. Temporary fencing of areas will allow recovery of dwarf shrubs, flowering and seed set of moorland plants, and badly eroded areas to recover.

Fences have been known to kill birds because they can become entangled in wire netting or hit the wire in flight (particularly grouse). Fixing markers to the wire reduces the problem. For further details of fencing options and techniques, together with the associated problems, see Information Note 7 on fencing in upland areas.

Stock feeding is common in the English uplands, where livestock are provided with additional or 'supplementary' feed in winter. This may be in the form of hay, silage, pellets or solid feed blocks and licks. These are placed at various locations around the moor, some even being air lifted to more remote locations. Supplementary feeding is provided because sheep require a better nutrient source in the autumn before tupping and especially in the spring before lambing and during lactation. Alternatively, this nutrient source can be provided by grazing the ewes at these times on in-bye land, agriculturally improved hill pasture or grassland away from the farm.

Supplementary feeding is often crucial to the profitability of hill sheep, and relevant to the nature conservation issue because overgrazing and physical damage to dwarf shrubs is a recognised problem around feeding areas (Evans & Felton 1987). The resulting concentration of animals and the use of vehicles to bring feed can damage vegetation. A feed block, for example, lasts one or two weeks and heather damage adjoining a block can extend to 10 m with the heather taking up to 10 years to recover. Supplementary feeding introduces nutrients and potentially weed seeds into the system. It could also be argued to be unsustainable, because it artificially inflates the number of stock that a given area can support, and so may lead to generally higher grazing levels over the whole management unit. On the other hand, if sufficient feeding sites are used, nature conservation interests can benefit because sheep are encouraged to disperse over a wider area of land (provided stocking levels are not so high that grazing damage continues).

General recommendations concerning stock feeding and watering on moorlands are given below.

- If feed is required at times of year other than in winter, it suggests that the vegetation present is not sufficient to support the stocking levels employed.

- Do not feed stock on land with wildlife interest such as heaths and blanket mires.

- Where winter feeding is unavoidable, any feed, mineral supplements and blocks should be sited on areas with little wildlife interest, such as on acid grassland. It should not be on or ideally within 100 m of dwarf shrub heath, blanket mire or wet, flushed areas.

- Alternatively, rotate the feeding sites regularly to avoid damage. They can be used to aid the dispersal of sheep across the hill if sufficient sites are used.

- Locate water troughs in areas of low conservation interest.

Further information: Roberts *et al* 1996b.

Off-wintering of stock is another important aspect of livestock management in moorland areas. Many farmers remove their stock from unenclosed land for the winter, usually taking them off in October-November and returning them between March-June, depending on the timing of lambing and the weather conditions. Stock are either kept on in-bye land around the farm, or indoors where sufficient housing exists, or sent to other farms with spare grazing capacity for a fee (away-wintered).

Dwarf shrubs are most susceptible to grazing damage in the spring and most vulnerable to grazing in the autumn and benefit from this reduced grazing. For additional benefit, for example to allow recovery of degraded heaths and mires, stock can be removed from the management unit at the end of September and their return delayed until April, May or June. Where off-wintering is desirable for conservation purposes, incentives to increase or introduce this practice, may be an option. Similarly, where sheep housing is unavailable or inadequate, financial help may be needed for additional sheep housing to facilitate increased off-wintering. It is important that off-wintered sheep do not damage other important habitats on the farm or further afield, such as species-rich or wet grassland.

Further information: Chapter 2 , 2.8.3 and Information Notes 1-5.

The effect of grazing on moorland plant communities

The effect of grazing on moorland plant communities is a well documented but variable process (eg Anderson & Radford 1994; Armstrong & Milne 1995; Grant *et al* 1976, 1978, 1982, 1985, 1987, 1996; Hester 1996; Rawes 1983; Shaw *et al* 1996, 1997; Shaw, Wheeler & Backshall 1997; Welch 1974, 1984a,b&c, 1985, 1986; Welch & Scott 1995). Moorlands are usually composed of a mosaic of plant communities, such as heath, grass and mire, and each is differentially grazed and affected by grazing. They each have their own rates of production and utilisation, and these in turn vary with factors such as climate, altitude and geographic location.

The potential effects of grazing on moorland habitats include both ecological effects, such as:

- changes in the vegetation structure;
- changes in the plant species composition;
- changes in the fauna;
- the introduction of alien plant species;
- the loss of plant and animal species;

and physical effects, such as:

- poaching;
- nutrient enrichment from dung and feed;
- formation of bare ground, tracks and ruts;
- erosion.

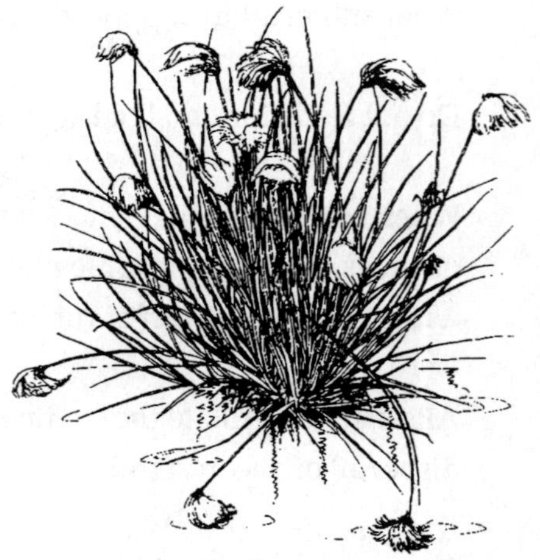

Hare's-tail cotton-grass

These effects can be both beneficial and damaging to moorland habitats, but sustainable grazing levels:

- maintain heathland communities and prevent the loss of the heathland fauna and flora;
- lengthen the burning or cutting cycle used to manage the heath;
- increase the diversity of the habitat because animals congregate and influence certain areas in particular ways;
- provide dung which is an important habitat for invertebrates and these in turn provide food for birds.

Moderate levels of grazing may lead to a change in dominance from heather to bilberry. Heavy grazing on poorer soils can bring about the replacement of heather with swards dominated by unpalatable mat-grass and heath rush. On better soils, finer grasses such as *Agrostis* and *Festuca* can replace heather under heavy grazing. Heather can be checked and bilberry encouraged by certain grazing pressures (Welch *et al* 1994).

Local variations in grazing density occur, and can be affected by environmental variations such altitude, aspect, rainfall, soil wetness and pH. These variables determine the type, productivity and hence the carrying capacity of the vegetation, and also affect the grazing behaviour of the livestock (Mowforth & Sydes 1989).

Metalliferous communities may require grazing in order to retain the characteristic metal-tolerant plants such as alpine penny-cress and spring sandwort.

The effect of grazing on moorland birds

Knowledge of the effects of grazing on moorland bird populations is extremely poor and very little is understood about how different grazing levels affect different bird species (Fuller 1996). There are various mechanisms by which grazing animals may influence breeding birds on unenclosed moorland, including effects on vegetation structure, trampling of nests and young, and dunging, which provides invertebrate food.

Certain grazing regimes may have benefits in terms of producing the appropriate vegetation structure. For example, grazing may create short or tussocky vegetation, depending on the vegetation and stock type involved, and both can be beneficial for birds. It can also lead to bare, sparsely vegetated or disturbed ground, which some birds require. However, too many grazing animals can destroy the vegetation and structure required by some birds, such as dwarf shrub heath with tall heather, and remove valuable food sources, such as cotton-grass *Eriophorum* flowers which are very nutritious and are favoured by sheep and black grouse. Grazing animals can also disturb and destroy the nests and young of ground-nesting birds, particularly waders.

A lighter summer grazing regime on flatter, unenclosed ground can provide a short sward of benefit for breeding waders such as golden plover, although different waders have different requirements (see

Ausden & Treweek 1995 and Table 6.6). In general, low levels of grazing on unenclosed land are most appropriate for the conservation of moorland bird populations including most ground-nesting waders.

Enclosed upland farmland is of outstanding importance for moorland birds. Not only can it support very high densities of breeding waders, but it is used for feeding before, during and after the breeding season by many of the birds which nest on adjacent moors. Its management is, therefore, likely to be a crucial factor in determining the health of populations of many moorland nesting birds.

Further information: Fuller 1996; Table 6.6; Chapter 7 Meadows and enclosed pasture.

The effect of grazing on moorland invertebrates

Grazing is a gradual form of vegetation removal when compared with burning or cutting, except at high densities. Its effects are therefore incremental rather than catastrophic, which is important for invertebrates. Catastrophic management, such as sudden periods of very intensive grazing, burning or cutting causes breaks in the continuity and the condition of habitats. This may lead to the loss of invertebrate species, although the scale is obviously important - how catastrophic an event may be depends on the amount of ground covered in relation to the dispersal distance of the invertebrate species.

A good diversity of vegetation structure, including tall and mature heather, tussocks and a build-up of litter, is particularly important for invertebrates. This is especially true for web-spinning spiders and grazing animals also directly destroy webs. Grazing creates or removes diversity in the structure and composition of vegetation, depending on the species and characteristics of the grazing animal and the stocking levels involved. For example, continuous grazing at high stocking densities is likely to create a uniformly short turf with few flowers, which is generally poor for invertebrates. Mammal herbivores also compete with phytophagous invertebrates for food.

For invertebrate conservation on moorland, the main management objective is to maintain or increase the habitat diversity and the structural diversity of the vegetation, which will assist in increasing the diversity of invertebrate species. The diversity of physical structure is particularly important in heathlands, including all phases of the heather cycle from young to mature and degenerate heather with its associated litter. It is also important to ensure continuity of all phases within relatively small areas. Establishing grazing levels which encourage patchiness in moorland swards, rather than even swards, is also beneficial, as is encouraging floral diversity, especially flowering nectar sources in addition to heather.

Grazing can be beneficial for invertebrates which require bare, sparsely vegetated or disturbed ground. Many invertebrates are also associated with the grazing animals themselves, in particular their dung, or with carrion. Other invertebrates are associated with undisturbed and ungrazed areas. See Table 6.8 for habitat and management requirements of moorland invertebrates.

Further information: Shaw *et al* 1996.

The effect of grazing on moorland mammals

The diverse vegetation structure required for small mammals can be maintained by light grazing by stock. In some areas it may even be maintained by 'natural grazing' by deer and voles, and also by climate. Overgrazing can remove the necessary vegetation structure and lead to the loss of small mammals (but see 6.4.6), as well as the species dependent upon them. Heavy stock grazing is likely to lead to competition for resources with deer where these are present. See Table 6.10 for habitat and management requirements of moorland vertebrates.

The effect of grazing on moorland amphibians and reptiles

Terrestrial habitats for the more widespread species of amphibians can be managed in a variety of ways with a view to maintaining structurally diverse conditions. Heavy grazing and frequent burning should be avoided as these remove the structure which benefits these animals and maintains their invertebrate food source. Light grazing can help to maintain an uneven vegetation structure. Natterjack toads *Bufo calamita,* on the other hand, which have now been found in the uplands, may benefit from localised heavier grazing pressures. This not only opens up habitats to provide bare ground and short vegetation for foraging, but also makes the area less suitable for the more widespread amphibians and the grass snake *Natrix natrix,* which is a predator on the natterjack.

Reptiles require a structurally varied ground cover, without heavy shading. The species composition is less important than structure. Management should therefore aim to maintain the latter. Often such vegetation would persist in the absence of management in nutrient poor soils or where grazing is light. Overgrazing or too frequent burning will reduce structural variation and both management techniques can kill animals (through trampling or burning).

Consideration may need to be given to reducing grazing pressure, at least at local 'hot-spots' often associated with southerly facing slopes. This can be achieved through erecting fences; these may be permanent or temporary features that may keep grazing stock off areas at all times or for only the most sensitive times of the year (ie April to September inclusive). See Table 6.10 for habitat and management requirements of moorland vertebrates.

The effect of removing or reducing grazing on moorland habitats

High grazing pressures tend to change dwarf shrub vegetation into grass, rush and sedge communities, which are of lower nature conservation value (Welch & Scott 1995). Much research work on the effects on upland vegetation of removing sheep grazing was reported in a literature review (Marrs & Welch 1991), which led to a number of conclusions.

- There was a large amount of variability in the results of such studies, with few clear trends.

- Where heather was already present in the vegetation it tended to increase in cover at a rate of between 0-5 % per year.

- Where heather was absent, its invasion and subsequent growth was difficult to predict. Grassy bog, tall grass, scrub and woodland vegetation communities developed in different places depending on initial floristic composition, nearness of seed sources, whether the soil was disturbed and the heather seed activated, and niche availability.

- Lichens tended to increase in some sites.

- There was evidence at many sites that when sheep densities were reduced, other herbivores, including deer, rabbits *Oryctolagus cuniculus*, hares and voles, increased.

Other observations are included below (P. Welsh, pers comm).

- Where a high frequency of suppressed plants remain, rapid (two to three years) recovery of good dwarf shrub cover can occur when the grazing pressure is reduced.

- If a low frequency of dwarf shrubs remains, heather recovery can be aided by light grazing in June to August, and/or by burning after a good seeding year. However, even light summer grazing can restrict bilberry growth.

- If few or no dwarf shrubs remain, the vegetation is likely to become dominated by the tallest growing grass or cotton-grass, with thick litter layers and a reduction in other herb and grass species.

- An absence of animal dung will lead to the loss of specialised invertebrate species, such as the nationally scarce dung beetle *Aphodius fasciatus*, which is associated with sheep and cattle dung in moorland and montane areas (R. Key, pers comm).

A summary table of the impacts of sheep keeping on habitats and landscape features can be found in Milne *et al* 1998.

The MLURI Hill Grazing Management model of the effects of sheep grazing

This computer based model is a means of assessing the effects of a given grazing management regime (stock type, numbers, seasonality) on the vegetation. It does this by predicting the degree of utilisation likely on different vegetation types at different times of year at a particular site (Armstrong & Milne 1995). It is particularly sensitive to estimates of grassland cover on the area concerned, because this forms the preferred grazing of sheep.

The model has proved to be useful as an educational tool and in providing site specific predictions (Armstrong & Milne 1995). These are useful in testing field assessments and expert opinion. Predictions made by the model are likely to become more reliable as further data on plant communities, species and grazing animals are added.

Further information: Armstrong 1993.

Sustainable grazing of moorland

The most appropriate stocking level for any particular moorland area will depend upon all the factors listed in 6.6.1, as well as the purposes of management.

Options for grazing of upland dry heath are shown in Box 6.1-6.3.

Box 6.1 Management options for grazing of upland heath and blanket mire in England

To maintain vegetation in favourable condition
(See Information Note 1 to determine vegetation condition)

Maintain current grazing practices
- Provided grazing practice has not recently altered and is not causing a deterioration of the habitat.
- Remember that recent alterations may take several years to manifest themselves as a cause of habitat deterioration.
- See Boxes 6.2-6.3 for guidelines on stocking rates.
- Favourable condition may also result from a complete absence of stock grazing.

Shepherd sheep to ensure the area is grazed evenly, or as desired
- Consider incentives for shepherding where it is not currently practised.
- Consider concentrating shepherding effort at particular seasons.

Do not feed stock on habitats of nature conservation interest
- Feed may be used at lower altitudes on areas of no conservation interest, such as species-poor acid grassland, to assist in influencing grazing patterns on the management unit as a whole.

To bring vegetation into favourable condition

Where vegetation is unfavourable because of heavy grazing:
Off-winter stock
- Heather is particularly susceptible to grazing damage in the spring and autumn and would benefit from a reduced grazing pressure at these times.
- Where off-wintering is not already practised, consider its introduction.
- Seek a longer off-wintering period, from September to May-June.
- Consider additional sheep housing to facilitate increased off-wintering.
- Consider additional away-wintering to facilitate off-wintering. This involves stock leaving the farm and spending the winter on lower ground.

Reduce grazing
- See Boxes 6.2-6.3 for guidelines on stocking rates.
- Encourage low-intensity farming on the upland unit as a whole and avoid moving large numbers of stock from the moor on to potentially important enclosed land.

Where vegetation is unfavourable because of too little grazing:
- Scrub and woodland development on moorland may be desirable for wildlife in certain situations. Therefore, an increase in grazing may not be required.
- Where the heath is deemed to be threatened by under-grazing, increase grazing to sustainable levels. See Boxes 6.2-6.3 for guidelines on stocking rates.

Box 6.1 Management options for grazing of upland heath and blanket mire in England (cont)

To bring vegetation into favourable condition where the above practices do not bring sufficient improvement

Remove grazing temporarily
- Small fenced plots illustrate the effects of removing grazing and are useful for monitoring purposes.
- Larger grazing exclosures allow a return to a more natural state, increasing overall habitat and species diversity.
- A period of three to five years of no grazing would allow restoration of vigour to suppressed heather plants, or 5-10 years for more badly affected areas.
- Consider temporary fencing out of retreating heather edges.
- A range of grazing regimes across an area, from none to a variety of lightly grazed states, may provide maximum diversity.
- Only return stock to excluded areas when the vegetation has recovered, and at a lower stocking level than had previously caused the vegetation to deteriorate.

Remove grazing permanently
- Where appropriate in the context of the surrounding land and its management, consider establishing areas with no stock grazing, to allow recovery and to enhance biodiversity.

Cross-leaved heath

Box 6.2 General points relating to stocking rates on all habitats of moorland areas

- The following stocking densities are guidelines only because the appropriate rate for a particular area will depend on many factors (see 6.6.1) and the individual characteristics of the site.
- Stocking rates are expressed in terms of Livestock Units (LUs, see Glossary) or sheep/ha (where a sheep is taken to be a ewe plus its followers, ie lambs), or cows/ha (where a cow is taken to be a male or female beef animal).
- Appropriate stocking rates will also depend on the type of stock used and the timing of grazing.
- Most areas contain an intimate mixture of vegetation types, and the proportions of each will affect the number of stock the management unit can support without damaging the habitats.
- When determining grazing levels, other relevant management activities on the land, such as burning and bracken management, will need to be taken into account.
- Cattle, horse or pony grazing can help to reduce the dominance of purple moor-grass, mat grass or heath rush, eg in *Nardus-Galium* (U5) grassland (Rodwell 1992). However, heavy stocking can damage dwarf shrubs and wet ground.
- Where cattle, horse or pony grazing is practised, overall stocking rates should not exceed those identified for sheep (see livestock unit, LU, equivalents in Glossary). A higher degree of caution will be required in addressing acceptable levels and timing of grazing by cattle and horses.
- Stocking rates should not lead to excessive poaching or any indicators of overgrazing (English Nature 1995b & c; MacDonald 1993.).
- An increase in the area of bare ground is a simple indicator of extreme overgrazing.
- High numbers of deer can have a significant effect on the vegetation.
- Consider the requirements of animal and plant species of nature conservation interest, in terms of the grazing regime and vegetation types needed. Generally, a more structurally and botanically diverse habitat will be of benefit.

As heather plants grow larger and more woody their growth rate and form change (MacDonald 1996a). The changes are described classically according to four developmental phases: pioneer, building, mature and degenerate. The vigour of heather plants is greatest during the first two phases while stand productivity is greatest when all the heather plants are in the building phase, when the heather canopy attains maximum coverage and density. In dense, even-aged stands each phase typically lasts from five to 10 years.

Grazing at low densities can benefit heather growth on dry heath by slowing down the rate of heather ageing. It can maintain the plants in the building or maximum phase of growth and prevent them from passing into the later, degenerate phase of growth (Gimingham 1995; Mowforth & Sydes 1989). However, too much grazing leads to the loss of dwarf shrub cover (Hester 1996). Heather cover on upland can also be maintained by other means. This is because heather is able to regenerate by layering, which is the development of adventitious roots and shoots on prostrate stems, particularly in damp conditions (Gimingham 1988a & b; MacDonald *et al* 1995; see 6.6.2).

Heather cover will generally decline if grazing animals utilise more than 40% of the season's growth (experimentally determined for building phase heather, Grant *et al* 1982). More recent research has indicated that even lower utilisation rates than previously thought may lead to suppression (see Table 2.7): There is generally a positive relationship between stocking rate and utilisation of heather, and a negative relationship with cover of heather (Nolan, Henderson & Merrill 1995). Just as importantly, the structural habitat features which dwarf shrubs provide are eliminated by heavy grazing and this occurs in advance of the loss of dwarf shrubs.

Heather is also grazed most in autumn, winter and spring. It is most vulnerable to grazing during the autumn, after the plants have expended energy on producing flowers and seed, and in the spring when plants are producing their first flush of growth. At these times both the carbohydrate reserves and overwintering shoots can be damaged (Mowforth & Sydes 1989). This covers the period of greatest nutritional demand for the sheep (ie prior to mating, lambing and lactation) and is also the time when grass availability and digestibility decline. Both sheep and heather will benefit if sheep are moved to more productive land during these critical periods, although this is likely to be a problem only if stocking levels are high.

To maintain dwarf shrub cover, stocking levels need to be appropriate to the type and age structure of the vegetation present, as well as the time of year. For example, heather can tolerate higher levels of grazing in the building phase of growth and in the summer months.

Levels of grazing damage to dwarf shrubs tend to be lower in the summer, because stock generally prefer to graze other herbage, which is usually plentiful at this time. Bilberry tends to be grazed most in September and October, with a secondary, lower peak in March and April (FRCA 1997). Bilberry is somewhat more tolerant of heavy grazing than heather, being rhizomatous. At moderate grazing levels heather increases at the expense of bilberry.

When determining appropriate stocking levels for upland heaths, other management practices and issues on the land in question will also need to be taken into account. These may include, for example, burning practices or the number of wild herbivores present, eg deer.

Assessment of grazing pressure on moorland was developed by English Nature using a 'Grazing Index', an easy to use and repeatable method developed for assessing the impact of grazing on heather moorland (Bullock 1997; English Nature 1995b & c). Further work has now been completed by Scottish Natural Heritage (MacDonald *et al* 1998a) and English Nature (see Information Note 1).

Appropriate grazing of upland wet heath

Heavy grazing on infertile wet soils replaces heather swards with indigestible and unpalatable highly acidic grassland dominated by mat-grass, purple moor-grass and heath rush (Hester 1996; Miles 1988). The previous history and stand structure of wet heather moorlands, such as whether and when it was burnt, can have an important effect on the response to stocking rate changes.

Options for grazing of upland wet heaths are outlined in Box 6.1, and stocking rate guidelines in Boxes 6.2 and 6.3.

Sustainable grazing of blanket mire

The sensitivity of blanket bog vegetation to grazing depends on the initial species composition of the sward and the age of the stand. Generally, the wetter the site the lower the productivity of the blanket mire plants and the greater the sensitivity to grazing (Coulson, Fielding & Goodyear 1992).

Hare's-tail cotton-grass *Eriophorum vaginatum* and heather form the majority of the sheep diet on blanket mire during the winter (Grant *et al* 1976). The former is also favoured in early spring, when the flower stems and leaf bases emerge from the dead tussocks (Mowforth & Sydes 1989). This is termed draw-moss or moss-crop in parts of England. It is also grazed in late summer in preference to heather when the productivity of the more palatable grasses falls (Rawes & Williams 1973).

Grazing can either maintain or reduce the cover of dwarf shrubs and other plants, depending on the situation and the grazing level. Light summer grazing, for example, can help to reduce heather domination, shrub invasion and cotton-grass competition in recovering situations. High levels of grazing can reduce the cover of *Sphagnum* and lichens, while *Eriophorum* species and/or purple moor-grass increase in dominance (Coulson, Fielding & Goodyear 1992; Rawes & Hobbs 1979). Light grazing by sheep, without burning, is likely to be an acceptable management for blanket bogs in the interests of conservation (Rawes & Hobbs 1979).

Sheep generally prefer the vegetation found on mineral soils to that occurring on areas of peat (Rawes & Welch 1964). Blanket bog vegetation is comparable in energy content with that on the mineral soils, but has lower digestibility and mineral content. The peat of blanket mires is incessantly leached by rain, is low in available nutrients, and is generally too deep to allow root penetration to the underlying mineral soil.

The density of sheep on blanket bog at Moor House in the northern Pennines, for example, was found to be low, in parts down to 0.02-0.2 sheep/ha (Heal & Perkins 1978). At this density they had little influence on total primary production on most of the bog, removing only a small fraction of the vegetation. Where sheep grazing intensity was increased on blanket bog either experimentally (Rawes & Williams 1973) or through long-term management (Welch & Rawes 1966), the major changes were a decline in the standing crop of heather and an increase in hare's-tail cotton-grass. The presence of heath rush in heavily grazed bogs (0.75 or more sheep/hectare) indicates that the *Juncus*-dominated sward is at least partially caused by heavy grazing pressure.

Taylor & Marks (1971) found that removal of grazing resulted in greater above-ground standing crop of cloudberry *Rubus chamaemorus* with an increased shoot density and larger shoots bearing many more flowers and fruits than grazed plots.

Options for grazing of blanket mire are outlined in Box 6.1, with stocking rate guidelines in Boxes 6.2 and 6.3. See also Box 6.4 for information on grazing of other upland mires.

Box 6.3 Stocking rates on moorland habitats

See options and general recommendations for grazing of moorland areas in Boxes 6.1 and 6.2.
See also examples of stocking rates in various environmental land management schemes (Chapter 7, Table 7.7)

Upland dry heath (NVC types H4, H8, H9, H10, H12, H15, H16, H17, H18, H21)

To maintain dry heath in favourable condition:

- year round stocking rates should not exceed 0.5-1.5 sheep/ha or 0.075-0.225 LUs/ha; (Edwards & Marsden 1991; MAFF 1998b-f); Nature Conservancy Council 1990b; Smallshire *et al* 1997);
- winter stocking rates should be reduced by 25%, with all hoggs, cattle and horses removed, and stocking should not exceed 1 sheep/ha or 0.15 LUs/ha (MAFF 1998b, d, & e);
- increasing altitude and wetness will reduce environmentally sustainable, year round grazing levels to below 1.0 sheep/ha or less than 0.15 LUs/ha.

To bring dry heath into favourable condition:

- year round stocking rates should not exceed 0.5-0.75 sheep/ha or 0.075-0.1 LUs/ha (Evans & Felton 1987; MAFF 1998c-e);
- winter stocking rates should be reduced by at least 25%, with all hoggs, cattle and horses removed, and preferably all stock should be removed in winter.

Upland wet heath (NVC types M15, M16) **and blanket mire** (NVC types M17, M18, M19, M20)

To maintain wet heath and blanket bog in favourable condition:

- undisturbed wet heaths and blanket mires require little management and should be left completely alone as far as possible (Burgess *et al* 1995), but few of these now remain in England;
- no grazing in the autumn or winter, with at most very light grazing in the summer, is the ideal grazing regime for wildlife on most wet heaths and blanket mires;
- year round stocking rates should not exceed 0.25-0.5 ewes/ha or 0.037-0.075 LUs/ha; (Mowforth & Sydes 1989; RSPB 1995);
- winter stocking rates should be reduced by at least 25%, with all hoggs, cattle and horses removed and preferably all stock should be removed in winter;
- year round stocking rates of up to 1.0 sheep/ha or 0.15 LUs/ha may be environmentally sustainable on degraded blanket bogs which lack *Sphagnum* or not do not show active *Sphagnum* growth.

To bring wet heath and blanket bog into favourable condition:

- a maximum year round stocking rate of around 0.1 sheep/ha or 0.015 LUs/ha has been recommended (Evans & Felton 1987), with winter levels again lower still;
- some recovery can be achieved with up to 0.5 sheep/ha or 0.075 LUs/ha in summer and/or complete off-wintering;
- if bare peat is exposed, it is very difficult to stabilise and any stocking will make matters worse;
- restoring high water levels may be the most important factor in reversing deterioration.

Box 6.3 Stocking rates on moorland habitats cont.

Mires other than blanket mire

- See Box 6.4

Unenclosed grassland

Stocking rates will depend on the type of grassland and the objective for the area, for example, whether restoration of heather cover or flowering of limestone grassland is being sought.

Acid grassland (NVC types U1-6)

- Unimproved upland grassland with more than 50% *Agrostis-Festuca* grassland: 5 sheep/ha or 0.75 cattle/ha or 0.5-0.75 LUs/ha all year, or equivalent during the summer only (Countryside Council for Wales 1992).
- Unimproved upland grassland with less than 50% *Agrostis-Festuca* grassland (ie *Molinia* or *Nardus* dominated): 2.5 sheep/ha or 0.5 cattle/ha all year or 0.37 LUs/ha, or equivalent during the summer only (Countryside Council for Wales 1992).
- Stocking should not normally exceed 0.25-0.6 LUs/ha on upland rough grazing pastures (MAFF 1997b, 1998d & f, 1999).

Calcareous grassland (NVC types CG2, CG3, CG6, CG7, CG9, CG10)

- Graze stock at no more than 1 sheep/ha or 0.15 LUs/ha for any continuous period of eight weeks between 1 May and 31 August (Mercer & Evans 1997).
- At any other time graze stock at no more than 2 sheep/ha or 0.3 LUs/ha. Grazing rates may be higher when gathering stock on up to five separate days per year (Mercer & Evans 1997).
- Encourage diversity of the habitat by having some areas only grazed in autumn and others ungrazed by stock.
- See also Chapter 7 Meadows and enclosed pasture.

Neutral grassland (NVC types MG2-10)

- Flower-rich pastures and hay meadows: 5 sheep/ha or 0.75 cattle/ha at any time (meadows must be closed for at least 8 weeks before mowing and the aftermath should be grazed, Countryside Council for Wales 1992).
- Damp and marshy grassland: 0.5 cattle/ha/year. (Lower stocking rates are recommended between 1 March and 30 June to reduce nest trampling, Countryside Council for Wales 1992.)
- See also Chapter 7 Meadows and enclosed pasture.

Upland habitat mosaics

- See Box 6.5

Sustainable grazing of other mires

The desirability of grazing on upland mires other than blanket mires depends on the nature of both the mire and the grazing regime. The mire types concerned (listed in Tables 6.1 & 6.4) comprise small sedge bryophyte fens, valley mires, *Molinia* and *Juncus* fens and springs. They vary in their response to grazing, and as in the grazing of the surrounding vegetation, the effect will depend on the four main variables - the timing of grazing, the duration of grazing, the type of animal conducting the grazing and the number of these animals. Many of these factors will be determined by the agricultural practices on the surrounding land, but some general principles aimed at maintaining the nature conservation interest of the different mire types are explained in Box 6.4.

Some mires, particularly certain flush communities, may benefit from light grazing which can maintain plant and invertebrate diversity by reducing the dominance of more aggressive species and creating gaps by trampling. As these community types almost always occur in mosaics with other vegetation types that are grazed, they are inevitably grazed to some extent.

There is insufficient knowledge and variety in mires to be able to recommend exact grazing levels for these communities. Even if this were possible, it would be difficult to achieve specific management for mires because they typically occur as intimate mixtures with other habitats. However, a range of grazing levels, from light to very light to none at all, would be desirable to obtain maximum habitat and species diversity.

Further discussion of management options for flushed grasslands and mires can be found in Chapter 7 (7.6.4).

Box 6.4 Recommendations concerning grazing of mires within unenclosed upland grasslands

Grazing of upland small sedge bryophyte fens
(NVC types M4, M5, M6, M9, M10, M11, M13)

Timing and length of grazing period

- Graze late in the summer and stop in autumn
  The best starting date is sometime in July, to allow flowering and seed set, with finishing dates in the autumn when the mires become too wet, which is generally in October.

- Avoid excessive poaching by being flexible in the deployment of grazing stock.
  Trampling creates an uneven surface which is pitted with holes created by hooves. At low levels this provides regeneration niches for plants, but at high levels it may result in fragmented vegetation and erosion.

Type of grazing animal

- Cattle are preferable for grazing these mire types.
  Some of the lighter traditional cattle breeds are most appropriate, and single suckler beef cows are also suitable.

- Sheep are not as desirable because they tend to produce a more uniform vegetation structure.

- Horses and ponies in enclosed grassland tend to crop certain areas more closely while leaving others untouched, principally latrine areas, and this may allow rank vegetation to develop (Burgess *et al* 1995).

Box 6.4 Recommendations concerning grazing of mires within unenclosed upland grasslands cont.

Number of grazing animals

- As a guide, use up to 2 cows/ha (or equivalent) for short periods (until the vegetation is eaten down), or lighter stocking rates for longer, and ideally only on mires where grazing is not damaging (see below).

The stocking rate for the whole grazing unit may be determined by the vegetation type surrounding the mires, but if possible consider the requirements of the mire types present, as outlined below (Rodwell 1991):

M4-5 Wet, fragile habitats that are typically too wet to be grazed and would be damaged by heavy stocking.

M6 Grazing determines the composition of this mire type. If too heavy, grazing may result in a switch from sedge- to more rush- or grass-dominated communities. Grazing alone, or in combination with other management practices such as drainage, burning and applications of fertiliser and lime, can have this effect, eg grazing and drainage combined can convert the community to grassland. Exclusion of grazing may lead to the loss of small plant species and invasion by scrub, with succession to wet scrub woodland in time.

M9 Wet, fragile habitats which are typically too wet to be grazed and would be damaged by heavy stocking.

M10 Most stands are grazed and this mire type requires light grazing and trampling by large herbivores to maintain the species diversity. Too much grazing is likely to be damaging, and grazing by cattle, or sheep and cattle in combination, is preferable. It may progress through tall-herb dominated communities to shrubs or woodland in the absence of grazing.

M11 Anything other than light grazing is likely to be detrimental. Found mainly at higher altitudes in England, where climate and water movement can maintain an open structure.

M13 Grazing, particularly in combination with other treatments such as burning, drainage, mowing, peat cutting and eutrophication, may eliminate this community. However, grazing or mowing can maintain the species diversity of some of the sub-communities, and prevent succession to woodland.

Grazing of upland valley mires (NVC type M21)

- Ideally very little grazing should occur on upland valley mires, although light grazing should not cause significant adverse effects and valley mires dominated by *Molinia* may benefit.

Box 6.4 Recommendations concerning grazing of mires within unenclosed upland grasslands cont.

Grazing of *Molinia* and *Juncus* fens
(NVC types M17, M22, M23, M24, M25, M26)

- Light spring/summer grazing and higher cattle grazing in late summer/autumn allows flowering of species-rich communities (but may conflict with heathland requirements in mosaics).

- In *Molinia*-dominated areas where a reduction in dominance of this species is desired, graze the area relatively intensively (see below), preferably with cattle, during the period of maximum growth and palatability of *Molinia*, ie mid-May to mid-July.

  Suggested grazing regimes for *Molinia* 'grass' moor are as follows:

Mid-May - Mid-September:	@ 1.0 cow/ha for M25/M15 @ 0.3 cows/ha for M17
Equivalent overall annual grazing level:	@ 0.33 cows/ha for M25/M15 @ 0.1 cow/ha for M17

  The overall grazing level could be achieved by grazing for a longer period with fewer stock, but the levels shown should be maintained from mid-May to mid-July.

  See also management of *Molinia* in Chapter 7 Meadows and enclosed pasture, and Boxes 6.11 and 6.12 for options concerning burning of *Molinia* grassland.

Sustainable grazing of upland unenclosed grassland

Virtually all sub-montane grasslands in England require some mechanism to prevent succession to shrubs and woodland if they are to remain as grassland. Where the grassland is of value for wildlife, halting this succession is obviously desirable although the presence of some trees and scrub can increase biodiversity. Many upland, unenclosed grasslands are species-poor but some species-rich grasslands also occur, particularly in limestone areas, and these are of value for the plants and invertebrates they support. All upland unenclosed grasslands represent an important agricultural resource.

Grazing is the most common means of maintaining grassland and the nature of the grazing will determine the form of the vegetation. At low stocking densities it will tend to produce a mosaic of tall and short vegetation, especially on larger areas. High stocking rates are more likely to create a uniformly short turf with few flowers (Ausden & Treweek 1995). However, this depends on the grazing animal involved and the timing of grazing. Grazing during the growing season (early spring to late summer) favours those plant species able to survive and reproduce under repeated defoliation. This usually means the more common and competitive grass species. The abundance of palatable tall herbs and species, whose populations rely on plants setting seed, can be considerably reduced.

Winter grazing is preferable for maintaining more grazing sensitive species. If carried out in October to March it can prevent the build-up of vegetation and arrest succession, but still allow plants to flower and set seed. However, grasses are at their least productive and palatable at this time and determining appropriate stocking rates can be difficult. In moorland mosaics, other vegetation types such as heaths may also be damaged by grazing at this time. Options concerning grazing on upland unenclosed grasslands are shown in Boxes 6.2 and 6.3 and discussed for different grassland types below. See also Chapter 7 Meadows and enclosed pasture.

Many areas of species-poor grassland have been derived from heavy grazing of dwarf-shrub communities. Conservation objectives for some upland areas may, therefore, focus on the restoration of an upland heath resource rather than the maintenance of a species-poor grassland community.

Acid grassland

Acid grasslands can be characterised by the dominant species present. On drier soils, bent *Agrostis* and fescue *Festuca* species can become dominant while on wetter soils rush *Juncus* species and purple moor-grass are more abundant. Mat-grass can also dominate, generally as a result of heavy grazing on the more species-rich types.

Grassland dominated by *Agrostis* (not *A. curtisii* - see below) and *Festuca* species is the most palatable and digestible acid grassland type when there is a high proportion of green material present (Armstrong 1996; Mowforth & Sydes 1989). Although growth of these grasses occurs in all seasons, most is in summer. This dies off in the autumn, resulting in a build up of dead material unless summer grazing is heavy. Dead material is of low digestibility and will build up in the sward if it is grazed lightly or not at all.

Mat-grass is one of the most widespread but least palatable grasses found in the upland grasslands of England. It is grazed by sheep, cattle and horses in late winter and early spring when other vegetation is scarce (Welch 1986), but its leaves are high in silicates and this makes it tough to eat (Armstrong 1996). New growth in spring, which has low silicate levels, can be quite digestible if the new growth can be separated from the previous year's dead material. Intensive grazing will increase the proportion of this grass in the vegetation because other grasses are favoured and grazed more intensively. However, removing grazing can also lead to an increase in *Nardus*-domination, at least in the short term, and will become tall and rank and overshadow other species. This is influenced by the previous grazing regime and soil type involved.

Wavy hair-grass *Deschampsia flexuosa* is less palatable than *Agrostis* and *Festuca* species and is mostly grazed during May to July. However, in grassland dominated by this species it may also be eaten in winter because it is evergreen (Mowforth & Sydes 1989). Grazing of wavy hair-grass generally tends to reduce its abundance.

Heath rush is less palatable and digestible to sheep than grasses but is grazed more readily by cattle and horses (Mowforth & Sydes 1989). It is only grazed in late autumn, winter and early spring when more palatable vegetation is scarce. The *Juncus-Festuca* grassland (U6) is strongly encouraged by particular kinds of burning and grazing treatments on blanket bog (eg in the South Pennines). Once established, *Juncus squarrosus* can be persistent and invasive, but it can decline due to competition from *Sphagnum* or taller vegetation if grazing is reduced or removed.

Purple moor-grass *Molinia caerulea* dominates large areas of poorly drained land in the uplands of Britain, particularly in the south west (Torvell, Common & Grant 1988). In traditional sheep production *Molinia* is usually little grazed, although it can provide a useful resource for the summer grazing of hill cattle. Ungrazed *Molinia* can develop very tall tussocks which are difficult to reduce or remove. Under continued heavy grazing pressure *Molinia* grasslands can spread (Welch 1984a), particularly on wetter soils and where burning is practised.

Molinia is deciduous and has a short but highly productive growing season. It is quite digestible between May and July when the new growth is available and it is readily grazed at that time (Welch 1984). Fresh growth of *Molinia* has the feeding value of cultivated grasses but a lower calcium content (Mowforth & Sydes 1989). However, the digestibility quickly declines and the swards generally contain a high proportion of dead matter which has negligible nutritional value (Armstrong 1996). As a consequence, these grasslands do not provide grazing in the winter (Grant *et al* 1963). See section on grazing and *Molinia* in Boxes 6.2 and 6.3 above, Grant *et al* 1996 and burning of *Molinia* in Boxes 6.11 and 6.12.

Bristle bent *Agrostis curtisii* dominates large areas of grassland on moors in the south west of England. On Dartmoor, for example, it is more abundant than *Nardus*, and governs the carrying capacity of the land for grazing stock. It is relatively unpalatable, of low agricultural value and particularly prevalent after burning.

Calcareous grassland

Calcareous grasslands are mostly found on shallow soils over limestone and are often species-rich and of considerable nature conservation interest. The various calcareous grassland communities found in the uplands are dependent on a certain balance of grazing for their maintenance (Rodwell 1992). In agricultural terms they are important for grazing of cattle and sheep, because they tend to be very palatable and the nature of the substrate or topography often renders cultivation impractical. Stock will graze them in preference to heaths or more acid grasslands where a choice is available, leading to the greatest grazing pressure and dung deposition occurring in these areas. See also Chapter 7 Meadows and enclosed pasture.

Further information: Roberts, MacDonald & Wood-Gee 1996b.

Grazing of habitat mosaics

Moorlands are generally very varied and rarely consist of just one habitat type. Vegetation mosaics of heath, grassland and mires are widespread and very valuable for wildlife interests. Hill grazing systems are usually made up of such mosaics, over which herbivores are able to range freely. Grazing animals have seasonal preferences for different types, typically preferring the more palatable grasses in spring and summer and switching to heather only in the winter when the growth of grass has declined. The utilisation of heather will vary for each management unit, depending on the area of palatable grass present and the grazing pressure exerted on it. The latter is determined by the seasonal stocking rate and the type, breed and size of the animals involved. Management units with a higher proportion of more palatable grass can generally support more stock.

Heather occurs in mixtures with other species and in mosaics with other vegetation types. The palatability of these other species, which may vary through the year, may affect grazing on the heather (Armstrong 1996; Hester & Baillie 1999; Mowforth & Sydes 1989). For example, local concentrations of heather grazing will occur near grassy areas and patches of palatable or reseeded grassland. Heather which is mixed with *Agrostis-Festuca* or *Deschampsia flexuosa* grassland is more likely to be eaten than heather which is mixed with grasses of poor forage value such as *Molinia caerulea* and *Nardus stricta*. Flushes are also preferentially grazed.

Apart from calcareous grassland where it occurs, *Agrostis-Festuca* grassland is the most preferred upland moorland vegetation of sheep. The presence of this grassland type increases the number of sheep that an upland grazing unit can support. However, it also attracts grazing animals, sometimes leading to localised damage to the vegetation when they have a free range and can congregate.

Vegetation mosaics may lead to conflicting management requirements. For example, cattle grazing may be desirable for flushes but less so for areas of dwarf shrub heath. In some cases, fencing may be an option, to allow different management regimes to be implemented on adjoining areas of land. In other situations, compromise regimes, or seasonal or annual variations in grazing, may be all that is practical. In reality, the vast majority of the English uplands comprise mosaics grazed under one regime. The Macaulay Land Use Research Institute model (MLURI, see) has the potential to help when determining appropriate grazing levels for upland habitat mosaics. See Box 6.5 for options for grazing upland habitat mosaics.

Box 6.5 Options for grazing of upland habitat mosaics

Grazing of *Agrostis-Festuca* grassland - heather mosaics

- Use the two pasture systems recommended by the Macaulay Land Use Research Institute (MLURI, Mowforth & Sydes 1989).

  If reseeded pastures or *Agrostis-Festuca* grasslands are available in upland areas, these are most usefully integrated into the moorland grazing programme by using them only when herbage quality is most important to the sheep, ie in the autumn prior to tupping and in the spring immediately before lambing and during lactation. In this way, lamb production can be maintained while damage to heather may be reduced.

- Adopt appropriate and different stocking levels for the *Agrostis-Festuca* grass and heather areas where it is possible to maintain them (see boxes above).

Grazing of poor grass - heather mixtures

- In areas of acid grassland dominated by mat-grass or purple moor-grass, measure or estimate the area of heath and calculate stocking rates on the area of heath alone (see stocking rates for wet and dry heaths above).

- Graze so as to allow scattered mosaics of shrubs and woodland to establish in poor grass areas, to increase the diversity of habitats and wildlife present (Usher & Thompson 1993).

6.6.2 Burning

The principles of moorland burning

Burning has been used to manage vegetation in Britain for centuries, principally for stimulating new growth of grasses or heather. Careful, periodic burning of upland vegetation can have advantages for agriculture, game rearing, wildlife conservation and intrinsic landscape appeal. However, inappropriate and careless fires in the uplands can be more damaging than a complete lack of burning management.

If vegetation is to be managed by burning then a range of burning regimes, from more intensive, to less intensive and no burning at all are best for biodiversity. This desirable range of regimes applies across an individual site as well as across the country. It will create a mosaic of habitat types with vegetation of different ages, composition and structure. These in turn will support a diversity of animal and plant species.

The most commonly burnt upland vegetation type is dwarf shrub heath, although some burning of blanket bog, enclosed and unenclosed grassland, bracken and shrubs is also undertaken. Burning alters the vegetation composition, pattern, physical and age structure, nutrient status and carrying capacity for herbivores, as well as the associated fauna. A summary of the advantages and disadvantages of burning for different land uses is given in Table 6.11.

Natural regeneration of heather

Heather moorland is the most commonly burnt habitat in the uplands and burning is particularly associated with grouse moors. Heather regenerates after burning by re-sprouting from the bases of the stems (if these survive and are not too old and woody), or by the exposure and germination of seeds which have lain dormant in the upper few centimetres of the soil. In both cases the new shoots produced grow more vigorously than on the bushes prior to burning, ie the plants are rejuvenated. Re-sprouting heather plants can grow much more quickly than heather seedlings. But re-sprouting from dormant buds on the stem bases declines as bushes become larger and more woody. Re-sprouting tends to occur best when stems are less than pencil thickness. So when older stands are burnt germination of seed can be the principal means of regeneration.

It is a common misconception that heather will disappear if it is not burnt (Macdonald 1996a). This is only likely to occur in old, even-aged heather stands, those which are heavily grazed, or in situations where prolonged, regular burning has reduced the capacity of stands to maintain themselves vegetatively. However, heather is able to regenerate vegetatively by layering under the right conditions without the need for burning (Gimingham 1988b).

Heather stems buried by the growth of *Sphagnum* and other mosses produce adventitious roots and these continue the growth of the heather stems. This process, known as layering, promotes natural regeneration without the necessity to burn. Layering tends to be associated more with deep peat and more sheltered conditions (MacDonald *et al* 1995), although it also occurs in dry heaths. It rejuvenates heather plants and stands in which vigorous layering is maintained will not become degenerate. High levels of productivity can be maintained for many decades and it can lead to a diverse age structure and mixture of species.

Hence heather cover can be maintained for many decades in the uplands by layering, without burning, even in drier eastern areas. However, regular burning (or cutting) is likely to reduce the capacity of stands to maintain themselves by layering should burning (or cutting) cease. In the absence of burning such stands may undergo successive degenerate phases while conditions conducive to layering slowly become established. In the absence of succession to woodland, heather cover is likely to stabilise eventually, with the formation of an uneven-aged and unevenly structured stand.

To burn or not to burn?

Whether burning is or is not appropriate for a piece of land will depend on the objectives for that particular area. These objectives may be for nature conservation, game, agriculture or landscape, although these land uses are not mutually exclusive. Achieving these objectives may or may not require burning. The advantages and disadvantages of burning various habitats for different land uses are shown in Table 6.11.

If it is decided that burning is necessary to achieve the desired objectives, the actual effects of burning on any particular area will depend on the following:

- the vegetation composition and condition, including the proportions of different communities, species distributions, age and structure;
- the previous management history, particularly whether the site has been burnt, drained or grazed;
- the current management regime, particularly the grazing intensity and whether shepherding is carried out;
- the method of burning, including frequency, patch sizes and pattern, and the time of year;
- the likely intensity of the fire, which is particularly influenced by the weather conditions;
- the nature of the substrate, such as mineral soil or peat, its depth, water content and organic content;
- the surrounding vegetation, such as bracken or woodland;
- the local physical conditions, such as climate, altitude, aspect, exposure and topography.

The decision to undertake burning should also consider the following points:

- the availability of appropriate labour, equipment and expertise to burn, because without these burning may be uncontrolled and damaging;
- the likelihood of a planned, appropriate burning programme being continued into the future, because sporadic burning may be worse than none at all.

Burning should not be carried out in areas where it would be the introduction of a new management practice. Additionally, it should be stopped in areas where its original introduction extended the practice into inappropriate locations and habitats (see Boxes 6.8, 6.11 & 6.12).

The creation of fire breaks may be necessary to prevent more extensive uncontrolled fires. These wildfires can lead to the loss of valuable wildlife habitats, threaten public safety and property, tie up the emergency services, cause erosion and scar the landscape for considerable periods of time. Large stands of woody heather or extensive areas of dense grass litter may develop in the absence of burning, and these can sometimes pose a fire hazard. In these situations, burning may be appropriate to reduce the fuel available to burn, to create fire breaks and generally reduce the likelihood of uncontrolled fires.

Maintaining some areas unburnt or burnt on a long rotation can be of great benefit for wildlife. Recommendations concerning burning of dry heath, wet heath, blanket bog and grassland for nature conservation purposes are given in the following sections.

Post-fire succession on dwarf shrub heath

After a fire on dry heath, heather and other dwarf shrub stands show a fairly regular pattern of succession, although this can be influenced by the grazing pressure. A typical pattern would start with a predominance of grass species and sometimes bilberry *Vaccinium myrtillus*, because they are able to grow and spread faster than heather after a fire. Eventually these are overtopped by heather and become only minor components of the sward. However, this pattern is affected by the frequency of burning. Heather itself may be lost if moorland is burnt too frequently, because this prevents it from out competing other species which are quicker to establish, particularly grasses (Mowforth & Sydes 1989). When an area has been left unburnt for a long time, the old heather bushes may not regenerate vegetatively when burning is reintroduced, but the presence of a seed source may allow successful seedling establishment if ground disturbance occurs.

Regular burning of peatland communities can cause a shift from *Sphagnum*-richness to a distinctly heathy vegetation (Rowell 1988). This depends on the nature of the fire and is most likely with particularly hot fires which can lead to drying of the peat and changes in its nature and structure. Light fires at longer return intervals may have little effect.

The effect of burning on moorland plants

Heather

Burning can maintain heather in the building stage of growth and prevent it from reaching the degenerative phase. The capacity of heather to recover from burning depends on:

- the age of the heather stand being burnt;
- the presence and age of a bank of dormant seed in the upper few centimetres;
- the presence of dormant buds at the base of the stem;

- the temperature of the burn;
- the intensity of grazing pressure.

Other plants

The balance of vascular plant species can be altered by burning. Some plants have adaptations which render them relatively resistant to fire, eg growing points at or below ground level. Purple moor-grass, deer grass *Trichophorum cespitosum* and hare's-tail cotton-grass are examples of such species (Rowell 1988). Other species are more adversely affected by burning and changes in the competitive balance are as important as the effects on the vigour of particular plants.

Non-vascular plants can be harmed by burning, although there has been little research on this subject (Shaw *et al* 1996). The intensity and frequency of the fire is critical. For example, damage to bryophytes can be avoided if a quick fire occurs when the ground is frozen (Rowell 1988). Some species, including certain, but not all, *Sphagnum* species, are also capable of rapid recolonisation following burning (Daniels 1991). Low intensity fires on blanket bogs at more than 20-year intervals may have little long-term effect on *Sphagnum* species, but moderate to high intensity fires at return intervals of less than 20 years can eradicate them.

Where the climate is appropriate, stable, layering stands which have experienced prolonged periods without any form of major disturbance provide a favourable habitat for certain liverworts (and invertebrates) which need high humidity and shelter (MacDonald 1996a). Many of these species are uncommon and/or have poor powers of dispersal and recolonisation, and may be lost if burning is introduced.

The effect of burning on moorland birds

Red grouse

Regular burning is undertaken on grouse moors to provide the mosaic of heather types required by red grouse. These birds require a mosaic of stands of heather of different ages for feeding, sheltering, nesting and rearing their young, and these conditions are provided by regular moorland burning. For example, young heather is utilised as food while older, taller heather provides good cover in which nesting grouse can avoid predation and find shelter in bad weather.

The purpose of burning on grouse moors is principally to restructure the vegetation so that feeding sites and nesting sites of appropriate height are provided for grouse or sheep (MacDonald 1996a). Red grouse need an intimate mixture of short heather (10 cm to 20 cm tall) for feeding and taller heather (20 cm to 30 cm) for nesting. They tend to avoid heather which is taller than 35 cm. For sheep, on the other hand, the principal management aim is to maintain most of the heather less than 20 cm tall, with some limited taller areas to provide accessible food during snow.

Heather can comprise 90% of the diet of grouse, although other plants are also utilised. Cotton-grass is of great value for grouse, particularly the flowers in the spring when food is a limiting factor. This food source is also eaten by sheep. Invertebrates also form an important part of the diet of grouse, especially the chicks, and are particularly numerous in wetter areas.

Further information: Hudson & Newborn 1995.

Other birds

Moorland management for grouse has an important role to play in maintaining the extent of open heather (RSPB 1998). Grouse moors provide extensive areas of heath and have the potential to support breeding populations of characteristic species, such as hen harrier, merlin, golden plover, black grouse and twite.

However, moorlands managed for grouse are not necessarily of high nature conservation interest for bird species other than red grouse (Brown & Bainbridge 1995). No other birds appear to share the same habitat preferences and aversions as do red grouse, and other moorland may be of equal or even higher value. Moorland bird species show a range of habitat associations and a higher species diversity would be expected in areas with a mosaic of different habitat types than in areas of pure heather moorland (Stillman 1995).

The distribution of breeding birds suggest that they are particularly affected by changes in the vegetation structure and composition, which affect the breeding, roosting and feeding potential. See the habitat and management requirements for moorland birds in Table 6.6.

The effect of burning on other moorland animals

A fire sweeping through the vegetation will kill all of the less mobile animals living above ground, and depending on the severity, many of those inhabiting the surface layers of the soil (Rowell 1988). Well controlled, winter burning is least damaging and burning small patches of habitat in rotation, as in management for grouse, will help to prevent whole populations from being destroyed.

Invertebrates

Different groups of invertebrate species are affected differently by burning, some increasing in burnt areas while others decline (Shaw *et al* 1996). Burning affects invertebrates both directly, by destroying individuals and their prey, and indirectly through changing the physical habitat characteristics and plant species composition. The latter affects both the vegetation structure and food sources for invertebrates.

The type and scale of burn determines the severity of the impact. Rapid, light winter burning allows many invertebrates to survive in the surface layer of soil, in damp litter, mosses and tussocks, and some species are in resting stages at this time. Hotter fires kill many more invertebrates. Large burns may prevent recolonisation.

The maintenance of a mosaic of different aged *Calluna* stands, including some areas which are never burnt, is the best conservation strategy, for example, for lepidoptera on northern heaths, because it maintains species diversity. The mobility of most invertebrates and the relatively small plots which are burned at any one time enable recolonisation by many invertebrate species. Individual species, however, may benefit or be harmed by burning, and where rarities are known to be present on a moor, their particular habitat requirements should be considered.

As with some plant species, stable, layering stands of heather which have had prolonged periods with no major disturbance can support certain invertebrates which need high humidity and shelter (MacDonald 1996a). Many of these species are uncommon and/or have poor powers of dispersal and recolonisation.

Burning of grassland can be detrimental to invertebrates. If virtually all the above ground vegetation is destroyed, entire populations at a site may be eliminated. It is particularly damaging to relatively immobile groups such as molluscs, which can be very slow to recolonise even small burnt sites (Kirby 1992).

Mammals

For mountain hares, traditional grouse moor management can be beneficial. Regular (eg 12-year rotation) burning will ensure a continued flush of young heather, which provides the primary food of this species. However, burning should be in a mosaic, so that hares have mature vegetation for cover and young heather for feeding within their home ranges. They also like large patches of short vegetation so that they can see predators and easily escape. Typically these habitats need to be provided within the 1-km range. Highest densities are found in heather moors overlying base-rich rocks, with fewer being found in areas over poor acidic rocks.

Amphibians and reptiles

Burning is not necessary to maintain amphibian and reptile populations. Where burning is conducted, to minimise the effects on these groups it should only be done during the winter and on as small an area as possible. It should be no more intense than to produce a light impact on the vegetation. Large burns are particularly detrimental to these animals, although mosaics of smaller burns and mature heather should be less problematic to reptiles.

Moorland burning and the law

Burning is restricted by law to a certain period of the year and all burning must follow the legal requirements and management guidelines detailed in the MAFF (1992a) Heather and Grass Burning Code and Scottish Natural Heritage Muirburn booklet (Scottish Natural Heritage 1993). See Box 6.6 for the legal requirements concerning burning and the following boxes for recommendations concerning burning of different habitat types.

Box 6.6 Legal requirements for moorland burning

Legal requirements for burning

Burning of heather, grass, gorse, bracken and bilberry is governed in England and Wales by The Heather and Grass etc. (Burning) Regulations 1986 (SI 1986 No. 428), as amended by The Heather and Grass etc. (Burning) (Amendment) Regulations 1987 (SI 1987 No. 1208).

See the MAFF leaflet *The heather and grass burning code* (1992a) and the Scottish Natural Heritage leaflet *A muirburn code* (1993).

By law, burning is only allowed between:

- 1 October-15 April in the uplands (ie Severely Disadvantaged Less Favoured Areas).
- 1 November-31 March in the lowlands.
- At other times under a licence which can be obtained only in very specific circumstances.

Licence applications must be made to the local office of the Ministry of Agriculture, Fisheries and Food (MAFF) 28 days in advance and no more than 56 days before burning is to finish.

Those undertaking burning must:

- Give not less than 1 day nor more than 7 days written notice of intent to burn to neighbours and owners and occupiers of the land, with details of dates, time, place and extent of the burn.
- Ensure that sufficient people and equipment are on hand to control the burn.
- Take all reasonable precautions to prevent injury or damage to people and animals.
- Follow special arrangements and plan well in advance if burning on a Site of Special Scientific Interest (SSSI). Burn according to a burning plan agreed and consented by English Nature.

Those undertaking burning must NOT:

- Start burning between sunset and sunrise.
- Cause a nuisance through the creation of smoke.
- Create dark smoke.
- Start a fire which is likely to injure, interrupt or endanger road users.
- Damage scheduled ancient monuments.

Burning dry heath for nature conservation

If not carried out appropriately, burning dwarf shrub heaths can be counter productive for grouse moors, agriculture and nature conservation alike, altering or destroying plant communities along with their associated invertebrate and bird populations. Developing burning programmes, utilising existing expertise and acquiring the necessary labour are all important in establishing appropriate burning management of moorland areas. A variety of burning management regimes, across one area of land as well as across the country, from more regular burning management to a total absence of burning in some areas, will best serve the needs of nature conservation.

In the absence of burning and the presence of nearby seed sources, heather-dominated areas may be colonised by shrubs and trees. These can regenerate in heather stands in gaps that are formed when plants age and begin to die back, opening up the bushes from the centre. Where the main objective is to maintain the dwarf shrub heath, control of some scrub invasion by burning may be appropriate. However, where the heath is sufficiently large for some loss of habitat to be acceptable, establishing scattered mosaics of native scrub and woodland, for example of hawthorn *Crataegus monogyna*, rowan *Sorbus aucuparia* and birch *Betula* spp, may be desirable.

Timing

Where burning is desirable for the objectives of the area, it should allow sufficient time for heather to regain dominance but prevent it from accumulating too much woody material. Heather is best burnt when it has reached the end of its building stage or the early mature phase. The time taken to reach this stage will depend on the climatic and edaphic conditions prevailing locally, but usual rotations are around 10-15 years (Coulson, Fielding & Goodyear 1992). A practical way to adjust the burning regime to take account of local productivity is to burn when the heather is 20-30 cm tall.

Generally, the older the heather stand at the time of burning, the longer the time taken for regeneration. From a wildlife point of view, this is not necessarily a disadvantage, because slower regeneration tends to encourage a more unevenly structured sward and a wider range of plant species to establish. For conservation purposes, some longer burning regimes will be desirable to favour certain plant and animal species, eg merlin *Falco columbarius* (to provide taller nesting cover), lichens (intolerant of frequent burns).

In practice moors are usually burnt in spring, often because this is the only time when the weather conditions are favourable. Some research suggests that heather regenerates more successfully after autumn fires (Mowforth & Sydes 1989). However, frost-heaving of seedlings over the winter may reduce successful regeneration, even if more seedlings appear. Spring burning can be preferable if it is conducted on cold, frosty days when the fire travels swiftly across the vegetation because it is less likely to damage species such as *Sphagnum* mosses.

Temperature

The temperature of the burn is very important if regeneration of heather is to be successful. A good burn clears away all the above-ground parts of the plants but leaves the stem bases from which, beneath the soil surface, new shoots are produced that can draw on the fully developed root system. A second means of regeneration is from the germination of seed and establishment of seedlings, which usually requires hotter, more intense fires to clear the litter and produce a good, consolidated seed bed. The actual temperature produced is determined by a number of factors including:

- wind speed;
- rate of passage;
- the amount of moisture in the vegetation;
- the amount and nature of the combustible material.

Old heather consists of a greater proportion of woody stems and can burn hotter and for longer than younger heather (Mowforth & Sydes 1989). However, old, degenerate stands tend to burn very irregularly and are not necessarily hotter. The most important factors are the amount of foliage and other combustible material, and the height of this above the ground, because of the effects of wind and air supply. Tall heather with a large amount of canopy material forming a continuous, finely divided, well aerated fuel source can be very intense and almost impossible or dangerous to control.

Some of the highest temperatures and longest durations of high temperatures have been found in building and mature heather stands (Hobbs & Gimingham 1984). As with older heather, the structure and especially the height of these stands is the important factor. Particularly severe burns can alter the physical structure, the chemical composition and even the hydrology of the soil, which influences the resulting vegetation and the appearance and character of the landscape.

Traditional grouse moor management does not favour low intensity fires because they leave large amounts of debris on the surface, which can retard regeneration (Whittaker & Gimingham 1962). However, this type of burn may favour a range of species other than grouse and be most appropriate for certain sites, eg those with reptile interest. If heather stems are thin and young (eg 1-4 mm diameter), they will resprout quite readily and the remaining litter is less of a problem.

Frequency

Bell heather, bilberry and cowberry may be temporarily abundant or dominant after fire, but are gradually suppressed by the regrowth of heather (Gimingham 1972). Where frequent burning suppresses heather regrowth these species can attain lasting dominance. Where burning is relaxed, the heather stands can become degenerate and less suitable for grouse and sheep grazing. They may also be open to invasion by grasses or bracken or, if seed parents are present, shrubs and trees (although this may be desirable for the nature conservation objectives of an area of heath).

Burning *Calluna*-dominated stands on mineral soils at about 3-6 year intervals shifts the dominance to grasses, especially wavy hair-grass on well drained soils and purple moor-grass on poorly drained soils (Miles 1988). This is because dwarf shrubs need sufficient time to grow tall enough to begin to shade out the graminoids, which regrow much more rapidly after disturbance.

Recommendations concerning burning of dry heath are contained in the following boxes.

Box 6.7 General recommendations concerning burning of dry heath

- Follow the legal requirements contained in Box 6.6.
- Plan a long-term programme of burning for the area concerned.
- Identify areas where burning would be harmful (see Box 6.8), mark them on a map and exclude these from the burning programme.
- Identify areas where burning is not necessary, because the heather is already regenerating vegetatively by layering, and exclude them from the burning programme.
- Identify areas where burning is desirable to promote diversity and mark them in a map for inclusion in the burning programme.
- Where burning is appropriate, it should be continued on a regular rotation basis, because this keeps stock moving around the moor and prevents recently burnt areas suffering excessive grazing.
- Use a variety of burning cycles and patch sizes across an area, to improve habitat complexity (see Boxes 6.9 and 6.10). Aim for patches as small as possible but occasional larger fires may suit some species.
- Burn some heathland areas and margins less intensively to encourage habitat diversity, particularly abutting onto other habitats.
- Consider cutting some areas instead of burning them (see section on cutting below).
- Ensure herbivore levels are appropriate to retain heather (see section on grazing above), and preferably stock should be shepherded to spread grazing evenly across the hill.
- Ensure that a sufficient total area is burnt at any one time to prevent concentration of livestock on recently burnt patches, to the extent that they severely poach the ground or retard or obliterate dwarf shrub regeneration.
- Follow the recommendations in the following boxes, including the safe burning guidelines in Box 6.10.

Box 6.8 Areas to be avoided when burning dry heath

To benefit wildlife, do not burn in the following situations:

Vegetation types:

- Dwarf shrub stands which have not been burnt for long periods (more than 40 years), where known, and which have well developed layering.
- Flushes and valley mires, because these important habitats can be damaged.
- Grass-heath mosaics, because the grassland may spread at the expense of the heathland, although this depends on the frequency of fire and the grazing pressure.
- Areas of bracken, and dwarf shrubs into areas of bracken. It may be advisable to leave or cut a strip of 5 m from the bracken edge, or burn narrow strips '30 m wide' at right angles to the bracken edge. Vigorous heather regeneration may be able to hold its own against bracken.
- Areas where the grazing pressure exceeds 1.5 ewes per hectare (or equivalents for other animals), because the regrowth is likely to be eaten out by stock, although this depends on the total area burnt.
- Areas where stock tend to congregate, as again the regrowth is likely to be eaten out.
- Large blocks of vegetation, because burning in smaller patches benefits all land uses (see Box 6.10), although the total area burnt is again important in preventing livestock from accumulating on burnt areas and grazing off the regeneration.

Physical conditions:

- Wet, shaded or humid situations (eg steep northerly slopes, bogs) where layering is likely and species sensitive to burning are likely to be found.
- Steep, rocky or scree slopes, rocky outcrops, gills and cloughs, because of the risk of erosion and the wildlife value of these habitats.
- Exposed summits, ridges, areas above the natural tree line (about 600 m), and where heather is already prostrate through natural causes, because vegetation cover here is often patchy and growth very slow.

For birds:

- Known merlin and hen harrier nesting sites, and also leave some areas of long heather elsewhere for new breeding birds.
- Wet flushes and small areas of cotton-grass, because cotton-grass flowers are an important food source in their own right and these areas are important sources of invertebrate food for birds.

For woodland and scrub:

- Some heathland margins, particularly adjacent to native shrubs and trees such as hawthorn, rowan and birch, so that mature dwarf shrub and scrubby vegetation can develop and diversify the habitat.
- Next to forests, woodlands, scrub and hedges, because of the danger to these features. Cutting here may be useful to create fire breaks.
- Juniper scrub, because of its wildlife value and slow regeneration (but see 6.7.4)

Box 6.9 Length of burning rotation for dry heath

- Take account of local productivity; grouse moor managers burn when the heather is 20-30 cm tall.

- For nature conservation objectives heather may be allowed to grow taller than 20-30 cm before burning, although the possible affects of this on the regeneration of dwarf shrubs and plant species diversity must be considered.

- Burning rotations can be from 6-10 years on Exmoor in southern England to 10-15 years in Scotland (Hester & Sydes 1992; Mowforth & Sydes 1989). In reality, particularly in the north of England and in Scotland, they are often much longer. They tend to be shortest towards the south and east and at lower altitudes.

- A longer rotation of 12-20 years may be preferable for nature conservation interests, because stands of dry heath in favourable condition (see Information note 1) can be 15-20 years old.

- Lengthen the burning rotation to say 20 years in the south west of England and 15 years in the Pennines, at least in some areas, and have other areas which are never burnt.

- Long burning rotations are particularly relevant on slopes, above gullies and cloughs, and at the moorland edge. This allows the heather to grow taller to provide nest sites for birds such as merlin, hen harrier, twite and ring ouzel.

- Use a shorter burning rotation on some flat or gently sloping (<15°C) ground to keep a short sward for nesting waders.

- A variety of burning rotations across a moor may be desirable.

- Once it is determined how many years it takes for the heather to reach the desired height, divide the total area in the burning programme by this number to obtain an average figure for the area to be burnt each year.

- Where heather is the dominant species but grows in mixtures with grasses, lengthen the burning cycle until the plants are taller than the height recommended above, and at least taller than the grasses (excluding flowering stems of grasses).

Box 6.10 Guidelines for safe moorland burning

Public safety

- Plan and be prepared well in advance.
- Inform the fire service when burning commences and when it is finished for the day.
- Have a mobile telephone or radio system available for calling up extra assistance or the fire service.
- Erect warning signs.
- Ensure fires do not put neighbouring areas at risk.

Weather conditions

- Burn when the weather is dry enough to allow a controlled burn but not so dry that the burn will be too hot.
- Choose a day with a steady but gentle breeze (Force 3, 7-10 knots or 8-12 miles per hour), which would move leaves and small twigs constantly but not blow dust about or move small branches of trees.
- Burning after frost or when the ground is wet helps to avoid damaging fires.

Equipment and people

- Use sufficient people who understand the work and know the ground well.
- Wear appropriate protective clothing; use fire resistant clothes and helmets with tinted, heat resistant visors, and avoid gloves because this allows the temperature of the fire to be assessed.
- Have sufficient, appropriate equipment on hand; the following can help:
    - ❑ knapsack sprayers with diesel are effective for initiating fire fronts;
    - ❑ water-sprayers should be used to control the fire, either knapsack ones for putting out small fires and hot spots, or vehicle mounted sprayers for larger areas, preferably on vehicles with a low ground pressure;
    - ❑ plenty of beaters and scrapers should be available;
    - ❑ foam additives increase the volume of water and are simple and easy to use;
    - ❑ fire-retardant foam is another option.
- Be realistic about the area of heather you intend to burn; estimates vary, but a guide for England is about 2 ha per person per day, which is calculated using a speed of fire advance of about 2 m per minute, a fire width restricted to 30 m and 6 hours of actual burning time in a day.

Box 6.10 Guidelines for safe moorland burning (cont.)

Fire breaks

- Choose natural boundaries for the burn wherever possible, or create fire breaks as soon as possible in the season.

- Fire breaks need to be at least 6 m wide and preferably more than 10 m long.

- Break up large areas of tall heather initially with a lattice pattern of long fire-breaks (Phillips & Watson 1995). These can be created by careful, small scale burning or cutting (see section on cutting below).

Direction of burns

- Always burn away from woodland, forests, scrub, mires, steep slopes, ancient monuments, and other areas of conservation value.

- Burn with the wind, preferably downhill and towards a fire break. Burning against the wind, or 'back burning', can be used to create fire breaks. It produces a hotter fire than burning with the wind, and is more difficult and will require greater expertise and man power.

- Control both flanks of the fire at a desired width, leaving the fire front to move in the predetermined direction, or have at least one flank defined by a natural or prepared fire break.

Size of burns

- Burn a patchwork of widely scattered, small areas across the moor, for example, long narrow strips up to 30 m wide and covering about 0.5-1.0 ha. Smaller burns are less likely to produce intense fires and are easier to control. They also provide structural diversity for birds and other animals, and help to spread the grazing pressure of sheep across the moor.

- On slopes, relatively shorter burns should be used down hill and longer burns along the contour of the slope

Severity of burns

- Burn so as to leave the bases of the stems, from which heather will regenerate vegetatively.

Burning of blanket mire and wet heath for nature conservation

The question often raised in relation to blanket mire and wet heath is whether or not it should be burnt. Fire cycles on mires are not fully understood (Lindsay 1995), but burning these habitats in the same manner as dry heaths is thought to reduce their conservation value (Usher & Thompson 1993). Burning on blanket mire and wet heath is not required to maintain their nature conservation interest (Mowforth & Sydes 1989; Rawes & Hobbs 1979) and for this reason it should be minimised and where possible eliminated.

Burning has a marked effect both on the floristic composition and production of blanket mire and wet heath vegetation (Heal & Perkins 1978). For example:

- unburnt bog can have greater species diversity than burned bog (Hobbs 1984);
- some plants, notably *Sphagnum* mosses, can be eliminated by burning;
- hare's-tail cotton-grass recovers quickly after burning and can become dominant;
- hare's-tail cotton-grass above ground standing crop after five years can be about 65% of the total vascular plant community (Gore & Olson 1967), and can assume permanent dominance if the community is burnt frequently (Rawes & Hobbs 1979);
- a short burning rotation (every 10 years) can result in increased dominance by *Eriophorum* spp, while a long burning rotation can lead to greater abundance of heather after fire;
- crowberry, bilberry and grasses can be encouraged if burning rotations are short;
- heather regenerates more slowly, taking about 20 years to regain its full dominance, when it can contribute 70% to the above-ground standing crop (Forrest 1971);
- heather on blanket bog may eventually be eliminated by a 10-year burning cycle;
- cloudberry and cross-leaved heath may dominate initially after fire, but are likely to be succeeded by heather during long intervals between fires (Mowforth & Sydes 1989).

The actual effects of burning on any particular area will depend on a number of factors, as discussed earlier. Recommendations concerning burning of blanket mire and wet heaths are contained in Box 6.11.

Box 6.11 Recommendations concerning burning of blanket mire and wet heath

- As a general rule when managing mires for nature conservation, if in doubt, do not burn (Brooks & Stoneman 1997).
- Where blanket bog and wet heath is in favourable condition (see Information Note 1), the ideal option for nature conservation purposes is not to burn at all.
- A 20-year burning regime is the recommended minimum rotation for blanket mires (Mowforth & Sydes 1989) and a burning rotation of 20-30 years may be preferable.
- Where burning is conducted, for conservation purposes it is desirable to convert some areas (wetter, steeper, higher altitude locations) to no burning areas.
- When conducting any burning on blanket mire or wet heath, follow all the legal requirements, areas to be avoided and other recommendations contained in the previous boxes.
- Large areas of old, tall heather on wet substrates are ideally left unburnt, because of the risk of very hot fires and little regeneration.
- Large areas dominated by cotton-grass *Eriophorum* spp. are best avoided because this will encourage these species, unless accompanied by stock reduction as part of a restoration phase.
- Areas which contain pools or peat hagging, and close to eroding runnels, should also not be burnt.
- Where accidental fires are likely and extensive areas of old, woody heather exist, burn fire breaks as a precaution (Mowforth & Sydes 1989) or consider cutting fire breaks (see below), but consider the possibly damaging effects of the use of machinery.
- Areas where *Molinia* is present at more than 20-30% cover, are best not burnt, because this will encourage this grass, but see Box 6.12 on burning of grassland.

Burning of upland unenclosed grassland for nature conservation

Burning of grassland favours plant species best able to withstand the effects of the burn, notably those with perennating structures protected at or below the surface of the ground (eg purple moor-grass and mat-grass). On wetter upland soils purple moor-grass and rushes *Juncus* spp. are sometimes burnt to prevent tussock formation and promote succulent new herbage for livestock (Crofts & Jefferson 1994).

As a rule, burning alone should not be used to manage grasslands. It can encourage purple moor-grass to dominate, and the nutrients released during burning can also encourage other undesirable plant species to invade. The aftermath needs to be grazed, and in conjunction with grazing, burning can be an effective reclamation technique.

Recommendations concerning burning of grassland are contained in Box 6.12 (and see 7.7.6).

Molinia *grassland*

Burning has traditionally been used in upland areas to burn off dead and unpalatable parts of purple moor-grass to provide an earlier, more nutritious and more accessible flush of young, palatable grass for grazing. Summer grazing on *Molinia* grasslands is only readily available if the leaf litter is burnt every year (Miles 1971), or if the tussocks are grazed intensively in the spring, usually with cattle (Grant, Hunter & Cross 1963).

Yearly burning perpetuates *Molinia* and debilitates heather (Miles 1971). *Molinia* is liable to dominate after burning on suitable damp substrates because most of its buds are protected from the fire by its dense tussocks (Mowforth & Sydes 1989). If it is not burned or grazed regularly, *Molinia* litter builds up, quickly smothering other vegetation and increasing its dominance. It can form large tussocks which may be very difficult to use or remove.

In certain areas, burning *Molinia* is beneficial for birds. In the South Peninnes, for example, burning removes the *Molinia* litter and exposes a rich source of seeds for twite and other finches in early spring. It also encourages flowering and seed production in grasses.

The major aims in management of *Molinia*-dominated areas for wildlife are to reduce the dominance of this species to allow more diverse communities to develop, and to produce habitats which are suitable for invertebrates and birds such as breeding waders. Recommendations for burning *Molinia* grassland are contained in Box 6.12. See also Boxes 6.2 and 6.3 on grazing of grasslands.

Lesser clubmoss

Box 6.12 Recommendations for burning upland unenclosed grassland
(For information on burning of meadows and enclosed pasture, see Chapter 7)

Do:

- Follow the legal requirements and general recommendations contained in the previous boxes.
- Burn in January, February or March to reduce the adverse effects of fire on flora and fauna.
- Burn small portions of the site on rotation, to decrease the likelihood of eliminating entire populations of plants or animals, and to increase the rate of recolonisation from the surrounding unburnt areas.
- Burn in small patches to provide a variety of conditions for wildlife.
- Burn on dry winter days when the ground is cold or wet, and there is a steady, gentle breeze (about 7-10 knots or 8-12 miles per hour).
- Burn with the wind, because it is less damaging to invertebrates as the fire travels faster and is cooler.
- Leave areas of tall, dense or tussocky vegetation to provide cover for small mammals and invertebrates.
- Identify natural fire breaks, or create them by rotovating or 'backburning' strips of land at least 5 m wide.
- Graze the aftermath.
- Leave some areas out of the burning cycle for a couple of cycles, to mature and develop a tussocky structure with a build up of litter, for invertebrates which require these conditions.
- Ensure there are always some areas in the mature, tussocky state, and that when they are eventually burnt there has been a period of overlap in condition with other areas that are allowed to retain this condition.

Do not:

- Introduce burning on un-burnt sites until the implications for the communities and species present are understood.
- Burn unless some sort of management regime, such as grazing, mowing or increasing the stocking density, is to be introduced after the burn (unless grazing at appropriate levels and times is not possible).
- Burn an entire site.
- Burn the same area every year.
- Burn where *Molinia* is present as part of a mixed plant community because it will increase rapidly at the expense of other species.

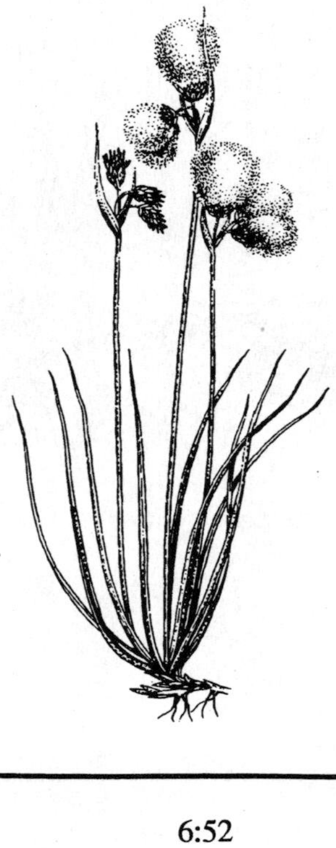

6.6.3 Burning and grazing combined

Burning and grazing of dry heath

To maintain dwarf shrub cover on dry heaths where grazing and burning occur together, the right balance needs to be attained. Limited grazing with appropriate burning can be compatible with maintaining dry heath. Heavy grazing causes the loss of heather whatever the burning practice.

Carefully burnt areas may be better able to withstand grazing than unburnt areas, because it promotes vigorous heather growth, which is more able to tolerate grazing. The mosaic of heather stands that results from patchwork burning also helps to spread the grazing pressure across an area. On a moor well managed by burning, moderate levels of sheep grazing can benefit both sheep and grouse, by maintaining the heather in the pioneer and building phases. This has the added benefit of increasing the interval needed between fires, with a concomitant reduction in the adverse impacts of burning (Shaw *et al* 1996).

The effect of grazing depends on the area burnt at any one time, as well as the relative attractiveness of recently burnt and less recently burnt areas. For example, small patch burning can lead to overgrazing of regeneration if labour is too limited to burn a sufficiently large number of patches to spread out the grazing impact. A large number of small burns or a few larger burns can actually reduce the tendency for regenerating heather to be overgrazed, provided the stocking rate is sufficiently low.

Burning and grazing of blanket mire and wet heath

In many upland areas of Britain, unfavourable burning and grazing regimes on wet moorlands can lead to a decline in the cover of heather, and its replacement by grass, sedge and moss species (Birse 1980).

Grazing of blanket bog at an intensity of less than 0.1 sheep per hectare can have a detectable effect on *Calluna* production during development after burning. The shoot weight can be reduced by 30-40% compared with growth in exclosures (Rawes & Williams 1973). Cloudberry can also be significantly affected by burning and grazing (Taylor & Marks 1971). A sheep density as low as one individual per 40 ha affects this plant because sheep preferentially graze its leaves and shoots. Burning increases the number and size of shoots produced and the period of peak grazing intensity on blanket bog corresponds with the time of maximum vegetative growth and flowering of cloudberry. Hence burning and grazing combined lead to virtually no flowers or fruits developing on this species.

After burning, grazing can allow hare's tail cotton-grass to gain dominance at the expense of dwarf shrubs, and considerably reduce the lichen cover (Rawes & Hobbs 1979).

Burning and grazing of *Molinia* grassland

Burning of *Molinia* has traditionally been used, particularly in the south west of England, to burn off dead and unpalatable plant matter and so provide a flush of young, palatable grass for grazing. Heavy grazing on infertile wet soils replaces heather swards with indigestible and unpalatable highly acidic grassland dominated by purple moor-grass or other species (Hester 1996; Miles 1988). Burning alone also encourages this species. However, burning and then grazing relatively intensively during the period of maximum growth and palatability of *Molinia*, ie mid-May to mid-July, can help to reduce the dominance of this species. See Box 6.4 regarding grazing of *Molinia*, Box 6.11 on burning of *Molinia* and also management of *Molinia* grasslands in Chapter 7 Meadows and enclosed pasture.

Further information: Todd 1997.

6.6.4 Cutting

In some circumstances moor burning may not be an appropriate management practice to use to encourage the regeneration of heather and introduce structural diversity in the vegetation. For example, burning may not be possible or desirable owing to:

- unsuitable weather conditions during the legally permitted time period;
- the proximity of other land uses, which would be damaged if fires ran out of control (eg forestry);
- high recreational use of an area;
- the presence of important, fire-sensitive animal or plant species, such as certain bryophytes and lichens;
- the lack of appropriate expertise or manpower.

In such situations, cutting can offer a potential solution (Ward, MacDonald & Matthew 1995) and has become increasingly important as a substitute for burning. It is also used as an additional tool to assist moorland burning practices, for example:

- in the cutting of fire breaks;
- in breaking up large areas of old, leggy heather and allowing the re-establishment of a burning programme;
- in providing a practical alternative to burning where this is not possible or desirable (see above);
- in cutting of drain sides to maintain visibility for safety;
- in fitting into the other demands of the farm when convenient and when labour is least in demand elsewhere, eg in January or February;
- in helping to control purple moor-grass where burning would be unsafe.

On the negative side, cutting, like burning, is a drastic and catastrophic event for the vegetation and its associated fauna (unlike the incremental effects of grazing, for example). The machinery used in cutting can damage fragile peaty ground and is restricted to areas with suitable topography. Cutting is also more expensive than burning, although the sale of cut heather for commercial purposes can reduce the cost (North York Moors National Park 1991).

Cutting appears to promote shoot regeneration, and for young heather stands on drier substrates little difference may be found in the rate of regeneration after burning or cutting (Gardner, Liepert & Rees 1993). However, in old stands of heather, cut areas may take longer to regenerate than burnt areas, and sometimes may not regenerate at all. The pulse of high temperature experienced during burning is thought to stimulate seed germination and vegetative growth of heather and a number of other species (Whittaker & Gimingham 1962). In addition burning removes the old stems and accumulated litter, which may prevent or slow down seedling germination and growth if the litter is not removed after cutting.

Cutting is probably best regarded as a complementary method to burning, being used where and when burning is not possible or desirable, and for creating fire breaks to improve fire control (Ward, MacDonald & Matthew 1995). It may also be an effective alternative to burning in vegetation containing a high proportion of purple moor-grass. Here mowing, removing the litter and grazing the aftermath can lead to increased species-richness. Recommendations concerning cutting of heather are contained in Box 6.13.

Further information: MacDonald 1996b; North York Moors National Park 1996; Snow & Marrs 1997.

The effect of cutting on moorland birds

Following the recommendations in Box 6.13 regarding cutting times should avoid any problems this method may cause to moorland birds.

The effect of cutting on moorland invertebrates

As with burning, the sudden and uniform effects of cutting can have an adverse impact on invertebrate populations, particularly those of specialist, monophagous species feeding on the aerial parts of plants. However, cutting may be less harmful to invertebrates than burning because it allows mobile and litter species to escape or avoid destruction. If an area is cut once a year, then it will be least damaging to invertebrate populations if this is done in late autumn or early spring.

Box 6.13 Recommendations concerning heather cutting

Time of heather cutting

Unlike heather burning, cutting is not restricted by law to any particular time. However, it is important to consider the following points:

- Avoid cutting during the main bird-nesting season from mid-April to the end of July.
- If possible, cut during the burning season, from 1 October to 15 April.
  Regeneration is generally better after spring rather than autumn cutting.
- Avoid cutting near popular areas if it is carried out during the flowering season because complaints from the public are likely to result.
- Avoid cutting when the ground is saturated, as this can damage the peat surface.
- Cut when appropriate for the vegetation concerned, eg every 10-20 years for heather growing alone or in mixtures with grass, but more frequently for fire breaks alongside forestry.

Areas to avoid when cutting heather

- Avoid wet areas and bogs, which are sensitive to disturbance and important for wildlife.
- Avoid cutting large areas of old heather because regeneration is unlikely to be very successful.
- Retain some areas of old heather for the benefit of nesting birds.
- Avoid archaeological sites, which can be easily damaged by cutting and vehicles.
  Records of known sites are held by Local Authorities and National Parks.
- Avoid steep and rocky ground, and check the area for large stones as these can damage cutting equipment.
- Leave a bank of old heather adjacent to roads because this will reduce the visual impact of the cut areas.

Box 6.13 Recommendations concerning heather cutting (cont.)

Method of heather cutting

- Plan a programme of cutting.

- Plan the size of the cuts.
  - ❑ Short cuts should be no more than 1 ha in size and preferably smaller if habitat diversity is to be increased.
  - ❑ If long cuts are made, the edges should be wavy to blend in with the landscape and contours.
  - ❑ The cut should not exceed 30 m in width.

- Leave a 10 cm heather stem above the ground.

- Use a 4-wheel drive tractor and on softer ground fit double wheels, to reduce compaction of the peat and the risk of bogging down.
  A Turner flail is extremely effective on both young and old heather (North York Moors National Park 1986).

What to do with the cut heather

- Do not leave material on the cut area as this prevents regeneration.
  - ❑ However, this depends on the density and nature of the cut material and the prevailing climate. Brash will break down more rapidly in western locations which experience frequent wetting and drying, and if the cut material is finely divided and thinly spread.
  - ❑ The brash can be rowed up on one side of the cut using equipment such as a helipede rotary win rower or a Vicon aerobat.
  - ❑ The rows can then be gathered and removed.
  - ❑ Alternatively, a double-chop forage harvester can be used, which chops the material finely and allows it to be incorporated into the soil quite rapidly.

- Do not store bales or heaps of cut heather on the moorland, as this kills the underlying vegetation and looks unsightly.

Uses of cut heather

- If the heather is cut after the flowering season it can be used as a seed source for restoration work on eroding or fire-damaged moorland. Alternatively, there are a number of commercial uses for cut heather.

Source: North York Moors National Park 1993a.

6.7 Other techniques for managing moorland

6.7.1 Controlling predators

Predator control is practised over substantial parts of the English uplands and has many potential effects on bird and mammal populations. As a result, common generalist predators such as crows and foxes are scarce over large areas of the uplands.

Foxes, stoats, weasels and carrion crows are the main predators of grouse on moorland and may be controlled by legal means. Legal predator control may also benefit other upland breeding birds (Brown & Bainbridge 1995), because it reduces predation on eggs and chicks. Such predation has been found to be a major direct cause of breeding failure in curlews, for example (Grant 1997). Nest predation is widely believed to be the most important cause of reproductive failure in birds in general (Cote & Sutherland 1995).

Predation may contribute to bird population declines by exacerbating problems caused by other factors such as cold weather, changing agricultural practices and the use of pesticides (Cote & Sutherland 1995). However, the role of predation in causing long-term declines of bird populations is far from clear. Some studies of predator removal programmes have resulted in increased breeding success or increased brood size of the target species, but evidence for longer-term benefits is more limited. Predator control may also allow higher densities of red grouse and other ground-nesting birds to exist than would otherwise be the case, although this has not been proven.

Where predator control is conducted it is particularly important in the late winter and early spring, although controls are needed all year, because if a hen bird is lost early in the season the chicks which she may have produced are also lost. Good farming hygiene is also important, because sheep carcasses and other edible waste encourages predators, particularly crows and foxes (although carrion is a useful food source for other birds such as buzzards). Crow numbers can be controlled using Larsen traps, and foxes are controlled by a variety of legal methods. The number of game keepers employed in grouse moor management has declined over the years. Therefore, where predator control is no longer practised, the breeding success of birds such as golden plover may decline (Parr 1992, 1993).

Certain birds of prey, hen harriers in particular, are considered by some moorland managers to be significant predators of grouse. Their persecution has led to conflict between conservation and grouse shooting interests (Redpath & Thirgood 1997). Illegal persecution on moors with a grouse shooting interest is suspected as a major factor in the serious decline of the hen harrier population in Britain (Clarke & Watson 1997). The number and distribution of hen harriers in England is believed to be limited by persecution (Etheridge, Summers & Green 1997). The distribution of grouse moors strongly limits that of buzzards and ravens, although it has not been proven whether this is because of persecution or several other factors such as moor management, and food and nest-site availability (Gibbons *et al* 1994). The killing of such birds is strictly illegal.

Further information: Hudson & Newborn 1995; Redpath & Thirgood 1997.

6.7.2 Managing the hydrology of moorland areas

The effects of moorland drainage

Artificial drainage damages moorland communities. It can lead to changes in the hydrology, morphology and ecology of blanket and other mires. It produces very few benefits and can lead to a variety of adverse effects (Burt, Heathwaite & Labadz 1990; Coulson, Butterfield & Henderson 1990; Heathwaite & Gottlich 1993; Hobbs 1986; Lindsay *et al* 1988; Stewart & Lance 1983, 1991; Thompson, MacDonald & Hudson 1995). These effects include:

- a lowering of the water table, especially in summer;
- a change in the pattern of water retention and movement in the peat body, the effect varying from a metre or so either side of the drainage ditch to far wider impacts and being influenced by the hydraulic conductivity (density) of the peat;
- drying the peat, resulting in a decrease in the permeability and bulk of the peat, and the processes of primary consolidation, shrinkage, secondary compression and wastage or subsidence of the mire surface;
- aeration of the peat, leading to chemical and biological changes which result in solute release;
- an accelerated rate of decomposition and erosion of the peat;
- changes in the water quality of the run-off and receiving water bodies, because of changes in the chemical characteristics and sediment loading;
- changes in both the magnitude and spatial distribution of run-off;
- an increased incidence of flooding;
- an increase in the silting-up of streams;
- a loss of wetland plants;
- a reduced number of invertebrates, which are used by grouse and other upland birds as a protein-rich food source for their chicks;
- a reduced invertebrate diversity, particularly of the scarcer species which tend to be associated with wetter areas;
- young birds, sheep and lambs becoming trapped in the open drains or 'grips';

Moorland drainage used to be subsidised and widely practised, with the intention of improving the vegetation for grouse or grazing stock. Now the grants are no longer available and it is generally discouraged and has declined.

Hydrological management of upland mires

Water supply is the key environmental factor that underpins the existence of all peat-forming systems or mires. Management of the hydrology of mires is of prime importance; management of the vegetation is a secondary factor, only possible once the water balance is under control (Rowell 1988).

Mire characteristics vary according to the mean position of the water table and its seasonal and climatic fluctuations, but the decisive prerequisite for mire growth is a water table that reaches almost to its surface. Peat in its natural state contains by volume 88-97% water, 2-10% dry matter and 1-7% gas (Ivanov 1981).

It is important to understand the following factors when attempting to conserve and restore mires:

- water status;
- water source;
- nutrient status;
- water chemistry.

Restoration work is possible in some areas, where ditches can be blocked with impermeable barriers (dams), sluices and weirs, to raise the water levels back to the surface. Much can be learnt from the experience gained on restoring lowland raised mires. See Box 6.14 for further details.

Further information: Brooks & Stoneman 1997; Rowell 1998; Information Note 9 Moorland grip blocking.

Box 6.14 Recommendations concerning hydrological management of moorland habitats

- No new drainage should be undertaken on any upland mires or heaths, especially around bog pools and wet flushed areas.
  - ❑ Drainage achieves little in terms of heather or grouse production and any drying is detrimental to feeding waders and grouse chicks (Brown & Bainbridge 1995).
- Leave undisturbed blanket and raised mires completely alone as far as possible.
  - ❑ However, disturbed sites may require considerable management effort to restore their hydrology and vegetation type (Burgess *et al* 1995).
- Maintain the complete hydrological unit of special mire sites.
- Prevent further physical disturbance to upland heaths and mires as far as possible.
- Seek to maintain the water table at or just above the surface of mires during the winter, and not more than 10 cm below the surface during the summer and preferably close to the surface.
- Avoid nutrient enrichment via water courses on upland heaths and mires.
  - ❑ Any water inputs should be acidic and nutrient poor.
- Block existing drains and seal any cracks in the peat to prevent further drainage.
  - ❑ See Information Note 9 for grip blocking specifications.
- Remove trees and shrubs from mires where they are considered to be threatening the interest of the habitat, while minimising disturbance and perhaps allowing some to develop into native scrub and woodland where appropriate (see Brooks & Stoneman 1997).
  - ❑ Note that birch, willow and bog myrtle scrub on upland mires can provide valuable invertebrate habitats, especially the younger trees and shrubs.
  - ❑ Several years of follow-up work such as hand-pulling of seedlings to control trees and shrubs may be necessary where removal is considered appropriate.
- Dig pools into the peat on already disturbed sites to provide a location where *Sphagnum* species can colonise and start to reclaim drier areas of peat.

6.7.3 Applying surface treatments to moorland areas

Applications include artificial fertilisers, animal slurry, farm yard manure (FYM), lime, pesticides and herbicides. There have also been instances of industrial waste being spread on moorland areas (eg paper pulp, sludge). These substances alter the nutrient status of the area and in addition can smother the vegetation. Ideally, none of these substances should be added to any moorland areas (but there are some exceptions, as discussed below).

Heaths and blanket mires have a low nutrient status. Grazing and burning tend to prevent the accumulation of nutrients in the system and so inhibit the natural trend towards replacement of dwarf-shrubs by grasses, trees or bracken (Gimingham 1995). Adding fertilisers alters the pH and nutrient status of the system, which gives grasses a competitive advantage over dwarf shrubs because they are better able to capitalise on the increased nutrients. This in turn may encourage a greater intensity of sheep grazing on the grass and dwarf shrubs alike. In this way, additions of nutrients may lead to a change in moorland habitats, such as the replacement of dwarf shrubs by grasses.

Grasslands that are unenclosed should not receive fertilisers. This is because adjacent habitats such as dwarf shrub heath can be adversely affected by increased nutrient levels, as well as increased sheep dunging where animals are attracted by the greater grass growth.

Botanically rich grasslands, in particular, should never have fertilisers applied if the nature conservation interest is to remain. Most species-rich swards of high botanical interest have developed in nutrient-poor conditions which have reduced growth rates and have allowed a rich variety of slow-growing stress-tolerant plants to coexist. Increasing nutrient levels by the addition of fertilisers, particularly nitrogenous ones, will favour more vigorous species, especially certain grasses, to the detriment of other plants. It is also likely to result in greater litter production, which smothers smaller plants and reduces the availability of gaps in the sward for germination. Corresponding changes in the composition and structure of the sward will also adversely affect the existing invertebrate fauna (Ausden & Treweek 1995).

The addition of lime or marl to acidic soils will affect the availability of nutrients by changing the exchange balance of soils. They should never be added to areas of botanical interest, or to areas from where they may wash into water courses and affect their fauna and flora, unless lime or marl have traditionally been applied to a site over a long period and no adverse aquatic effects will occur.

Herbicides may be acceptable applications for nature conservation purposes where, for example, physical or mechanical control methods are impractical. For example, weed-wiping to control creeping thistle and ragwort may be desirable on unenclosed limestone grassland, and asulam control of bracken may form part of moorland restoration programmes. Fertilisers and lime may also be appropriate on grassland areas as part of restoration programmes, for example after bracken control or severe erosion.

6.7.4 Managing moorland shrubs

Moorlands commonly contain areas of native shrubs and scattered trees, including hawthorn, rowan, birch, gorse and juniper *Juniperus communis*. These provide a valuable habitat for wildlife, particularly where they occur as a mosaic with other habitats, as well as being landscape features. Some areas of scrub may be of value for the woody species present, such as juniper and western gorse which have a limited distribution. Even where common species make up the scrub, the habitat is likely to be important for breeding, feeding and sheltering birds, mammals and invertebrates. Rare or local animal and plant species also occur in the vegetation of woodland-scrub-grassland margins, particularly where this is associated with ancient woodland and grassland.

In many situations it is desirable to protect and increase the scrub habitat, for example on extensive areas of moorland where shrub and woodland cover has declined. In other circumstances, control or removal may be more appropriate, such as where shrubs are regenerating into heathlands of limited extent or species-rich grassland.

Retaining and developing the cover of shrubs, scattered trees and light woodland on moorland is particularly beneficial for upland breeding birds and invertebrates. Light cover provides nest sites, song posts, foraging areas and sheltered roosts for birds such as black grouse, whinchat, stonechat, tree pipit *Anthus trivialis*, ring ouzel and, where old crow nests are available, nest sites for merlin. The gradation of grassland through scrub to woodland is also rich in invertebrate life. Upland woodland supports breeding birds including pied flycatcher *Ficedula hypoleuca*, redstart *Phoenicurus phoenicurus*, wood warbler *Phylloscopus sibilatrix*, siskin *Carduelis spinus* and redpoll *Acanthus flammea*, as well as a diversity of invertebrates.

Appropriate areas could be fenced in some situations to encourage natural regeneration by excluding grazing sheep and deer. Examples may include steep slopes, gullies, narrow cloughs and areas at the moorland edge. Other suitable areas are bracken beds or botanically poor grasslands such as those dominated by mat-grass *Nardus stricta* and rushes *Juncus* species. Areas of existing or developing shrubs are another obvious location for protection from grazing.

On less steep areas, the shrubs could be grazed or cut in rotation in order to retain a mosaic of age classes. Cutting could be carried out when the shrubs are about 5-15 years old, on about 10 % in any one year. Below old stands of shrubs where regeneration is poor the ground could be scarified to encouraged seedling establishment, but only if the stocking levels are suitably low to allow seedlings to survive.

The total area of shrubs and scattered trees could be increased by targeted planting of native species in areas of low existing wildlife interest, provided only species typical to the location and of local provenance are used (Rodwell & Patterson 1994). Such species might include hawthorn, rowan , birch and oak *Quercus* spp, with willow and alder *Alnus glutinosa* along water courses. Normally fencing would be needed to protect planted shrubs, but where this is not possible tubes and stakes could be considered without fencing. A disadvantage of this method is that tubes and stakes are likely to be damaged by wind and snow and may also be used as rubbing posts by stock.

Further information: Hopkins 1996; Rodwell & Patterson 1994; Chapter 8 Woodland and scrub.

Juniper

Juniper scrub is of considerable nature conservation importance because of its limited distribution and extent, and this is recognised by its inclusion in the Habitats Directive. It is particularly valuable for invertebrates. It was once widespread in the English upland fringes but is now thought to be declining at numerous locations and many populations show few signs of regenerating naturally (Barrett 1997). Remaining stands tend to be even-aged and dominated by mature and old bushes.

Disturbance of some kind, including burning, may be beneficial to juniper, because it encourages seedling establishment. However, adult plants are likely to be killed by burning, and where grazing animals are present their grazing and browsing is likely to destroy any successful seedling establishment. If it is possible to exclude grazing animals, including rabbits, then burning adjacent to fruiting, mature stands may be beneficial and encourage regeneration (A. MacDonald, pers comm). If burning is used as a tool then the rotation should be very long, eg 40 - 50 years at least, and mature bushes themselves should not be burnt, because the control of the spread of the fire would be very difficult. If restructuring of stands of mature juniper is felt desirable to diversify the ages present then cutting would be preferable to burning.

Juniper plants may establish where heather is tall, unburnt and only lightly grazed, because the heather tends to become more open in these circumstances and the juniper plants are partially protected from browsing, at least by sheep.

Further information: Barrett 1997; Clifton, Ranner & Ward 1995.

Gorse

European gorse *Ulex europeus* provides a wildlife habitat in itself, particularly for invertebrates and birds. However, it can invade areas of heath or grassland, thereby reducing the amount of valuable wildlife habitat or grazing land. It also poses problems for farmers because stock can become tangled in it.

Gorse scrub is often burnt or cut to control it. Burning gorse alone is of little benefit for long-term control of this species (MAFF 1992a). Its effect is to bring about a break in seed dormancy, resulting in the appearance of young seedlings as a carpet to re-invade the burned area. These may be controlled by light grazing, but this is unlikely to reduce the area of gorse in the long term, unless the stumps and regrowth are treated with herbicides, which is rarely acceptable in semi-natural habitats. Rotational burning can be useful for breaking up stands of gorse, allowing stock to move around the area, promoting a flush of grass for grazing and diversifying the age structure of the scrub.

The effect of cutting is similar to burning because it can increase the vigour and stimulate growth of gorse. As with burning, rotational cutting can be useful to agricultural and wildlife interests.

Western gorse can form part of the heathland community, especially in south west England, and is an important species in its own right because of its limited distribution. For wildlife interests, it is not appropriate to target control at this species, but it may be perceived as a problem by farmers because such heaths are relatively unproductive.

Rhododendron

Rhododendron *Rhododendron ponticum* is a problem on some moorlands, particularly in south west England and locally elsewhere. Preventing invasion should be the top priority where it is a threat, because this is better than trying to cure the problem once it has taken hold. However, it can be successfully removed by spraying the plants with glyphosate and a suitable wetting agent, although very thorough spraying is needed, and usually more than one application is required. This should be followed by treating the cut stumps with triclopyr and hand-pulling of seedlings in subsequent years. Rhododendron has a short-lived seed bank and the important factor is to remove the seed source.

Controlling tree and shrub invasion on mires

Active peat-forming *Sphagnum* vegetation is not generally invaded by trees, but a reduction in the water balance of a bog can lead to tree invasion (Burgess *et al* 1995). The main tree and shrub species which invade mires are birch, willow, rhododendron and Scots pine *Pinus sylvestris* (RSPB 1995). Some potential actions are given below.

- Assess whether the mire and its hydrology can be restored, or whether the area is too dry for restoration to be feasible.
- If the mire can be restored, identify a hydrological management programme to restore the hydrological integrity and make the area wetter.
- Remove seedlings and saplings by hand pulling.
- Remove older specimens by bow saws, brush cutters, or chain saws.
- Dispose of the material by various means dependent on the situation and conditions (see below).
- Some species, particularly birch and rhododendron, will coppice if cut and require secondary treatment. This may involve chemical applications (spray or weed wipe new growth or treat cut stumps), grinding or careful extraction of cut stumps, annual cutting of regrowth, grazing or flooding.

However, if a site is still relatively wet, disturbance resulting from trampling or the use of vehicles can cause long-term damage. Chemical applications also have the potential to harm bryophytes and aquatic systems.

There are various means of disposing of cut material on larger mires.

- Leaving on site stacked, unstacked or in ditches.
- Dragging or carrying off site, with or without the use of low ground pressure vehicles, with or without the use of brash or other temporary roads which are subsequently removed.
- Burning on site on sheets of corrugated iron raised above the bog surface by bricks, and removing the ash to prevent nutrient enrichment.
- Chipping on site, and leaving the remains in ditches or removing them.
- Winching off site.
- Removing material by sky-line logging systems.
- Removing material by helicopter.

6.7.5 Moorland management and the archaeological and historical interest

The moorlands of England contain a legacy of structures and systems related to over 6,000 years of agricultural and industrial activity (Wood-Gee 1996). Together with the geology, land form and vegetation, these remains reveal the history of the English uplands.

Management sympathetic to wildlife, as outlined in this chapter, is usually beneficial to archaeological interests. However, many aspects of farm work inadvertently result in damage. The implications for archaeology should be carefully considered before starting any work near archaeological sites and features. The following guidance for their protection should be adhered to (Wood-Gee 1996).

- Remember that sites can extend beyond visible remains. For example, complex prehistoric and medieval agricultural systems, extending to several hectares, may lie around a fort or homestead.
- A minimum 10 m margin should be allowed around identified sites or areas (more if the site is scheduled), and 20 m if planting trees or encouraging woodland regeneration.
- Adequate stocking of archaeological sites should be included in a grazing plan, to keep sites free of scrub and bracken, but without stocking so heavily that erosion or other physical damage results. Sheep may be preferable to cattle.
- Archaeological sites or features should never be used as stances for feed rings or shelter for stock. Supplementary feed should never be offered on or in the immediate vicinity of archaeological features.

- When re-seeding, ploughing or other soil disturbance should be avoided as it can destroy features in and around archaeological sites. Deeper ploughing of sites which are already cultivated should be avoided.

- Archaeological sites such as burial cairns or deserted settlements should not be used as dumping grounds. Consideration should be given to removing earlier dumped material.

- Use of metal detectors should not be allowed on ancient monuments, nor should any archaeological finds be removed.

- Any finds or new features should be reported to English Heritage, the Regional Archaeologist or local museum.

- Where sites have suffered erosion and the protective cover of turf or soil has been broken, sheep often congregate using the bare patches as social gathering areas. The initial erosion problems can soon worsen, leading to disappearance of earthen monuments or archaeological deposits. Prompt filling-in of scrapes or natural erosion hollows will protect such sites for the future. Stock proof (and where necessary rabbit proof) fencing may be necessary to reduce damage but details of measures to allow for continued grazing within the fenced areas should be included in a grazing plan.

- Consideration should be given to removing trees, scrub, gorse, bracken and woody plants to protect sites from damage. Disturbance of the ground surface should be minimised by cutting trees at ground level and spot treating stumps to prevent regrowth. If possible, the trunks of wind-thrown trees should be cut and the root plate replaced.

- New drainage should not be carried out on or near an ancient monument. Particular care is required when maintaining existing drains. Consideration should be given to resiting drains directly affecting archaeological sites.

- Ground disturbance should be avoided where rabbit control is carried out.

- Peat cutting or quarrying on the site of ancient monuments should not be permitted.

Further advice on protecting archaeological features, eg when burning or grazing land, is contained within the preceding sections.

Further information: Historic Scotland 1996.

6.8 Techniques to re-create moorland habitats

The term re-creation is generally used when the vegetation concerned is no longer present. Restoring or improving the condition of moorland habitats has already been covered in earlier sections of this chapter. Information has recently been published particularly about upland and lowland heathland and peatland re-creation and restoration, and much research is currently under way. It is not intended to reproduce the re-creation information here, but some general principles are included below.

6.8.1 Re-creation of heathland areas

Generally, it is most cost-effective and a higher nature conservation priority to concentrate effort on restoration by improving the condition of heavily grazed heathland, rather than trying to re-create it where it has completely disappeared (Thompson, MacDonald & Hudson 1995b). The problems of restoring heather and other dwarf shrubs to former heaths and moorland which have lost all such cover are naturally greater than repairing damage to existing heathland areas and preventing their loss in the first place (Ward, MacDonald & Matthew 1995).

The important factor in heathland re-creation is to reduce or remove the grazing pressure. It is best to target areas where heather and other dwarf shrubs are already frequent, if suppressed, to prevent further decline. Alternatively, target areas where dwarf shrubs are less abundant but have not yet disappeared, to enhance their status (Marrs & Welch 1991). If heather plants occur at more than four plants per square metre then a dramatic increase in heather cover can occur within five years when grazing is substantially or completely removed. Even at dwarf shrub frequencies lower than this, the approach is valuable and can provide good dwarf shrub cover over the longer term.

Survey data suggest that recovery from grassland is occurring on some sites, albeit at a slower rate than the loss (Hester 1996). The soil under heather contains a large seed bank which can remain viable for many years, even after heather has disappeared above ground. However, it needs exposure to light and, therefore, disturbance to germinate (Thompson, MacDonald & Hudson 1995b). Hence successful growth to adult plants is difficult to achieve in swards heavily dominated by grasses. Where no seed bank remains import of dwarf shrub seed will be necessary to re-create heathland. Techniques of scarifying, seeding and grazing control have been developed and widely employed now, to re-create heather and grass mixtures on areas of highly acidic grassland, and on bare peat created by bad burns or erosion (Anderson 1997; North York Moors National Park 1986, 1991; Philips 1993). Further development of seed collection, seed treatment, site preparation and application techniques is currently underway.

Heather and other dwarf shrub seed can be obtained by cutting seed-bearing plants from October to January. A forage harvester or flail mower and baler can be used where conditions are suitable (eg. flat, no boulders) and this material is normally applied at about 600 g per m^2. An alternative source of seed can be obtained by collecting the remaining litter and soil surface from recently burnt areas of vigorous heather, either by hand or an industrial vacuum cleaner run from a portable generator. This material is usually spread at the lower rate of about 200 g per m^2. If storage of either type of material is required, it should be dried first.

To prevent loss of the seed-bearing material from the application site, the application of an open covering of forestry brashings is employed. Alternatively, and particularly to avoid soil erosion, an acid soil tolerant, short-lived, nurse grass can be sown, such as rye-grass *Lolium perenne* or red fescue *Festuca rubra*. Common bent, wavy hair-grass or sheep's fescue have also been used, but these species may not necessarily be short-lived and so should be used with caution. Seed can be sown at a rate of about 2 g per m^2. On very infertile mineral or peat substrates, a light fertiliser dressing of NPK fertiliser at 50-100 kg/ha may be considered to assist heather and nurse grass establishment. For heather to establish under any of these techniques, there must be initial protection from grazing animals in some cases for up to five years.

Attempts have also been made to revegetate eroded peat surfaces, although this is very difficult to achieve, particularly over large areas. In the northern Pennines, as long as adequate NPK fertiliser was provided and sheep grazing prevented, a continuous cover of *Deschampsia flexuosa* could be achieved as a primary cover (Gore & Godfrey 1981).

Heather restoration on *Molinia*-dominated areas is unlikely to succeed unless *Molinia* is first controlled by herbicide or removed by turf stripping, and heather seed introduced into the denuded areas created. Grazing would then have to be excluded to enable establishment of heather plants. Attempts to establish heathland or even increase heather abundance in areas dominated by *Molinia* by simply excluding grazing are unlikely to be successful, although this will depend on the initial percentage of heather present. Ungrazed *Molinia* is likely to form a dense litter layer which prevents heather or other dwarf shrub seedlings developing. For further information on this subject see Todd 1997.

The slow attainment of mature bush size and the difficulties of transplanting make bilberry unsuitable for use as a main species in schemes to recreate moorland. Heather is easier to establish, either from transplants or seeding (Welch *et al* 1994).

Further information: Anderson, Tallis & Yalden 1997; Anderson & Gilbert 1998; Andrews & MacDonald 1996a; Bacon 1996; Dryden, Horton & Hall 1997; Gimingham 1992; Hudson & Newborn 1995; North York Moors National Park 1986, 1991; Parker 1995; Phillips 1997a; Pywell, Webb & Putwain 1996.

6.8.2 Re-creation of blanket mire after afforestation

If restoration of the blanket mire is the desired objective, the actions to be undertaken include damming ditches and felling trees where these are present. Cut trees can be either removed, left on the surface whole or chipped, or packed into ditches. If the mire has previously been fertilised, the area should be left for one to two years for nutrient levels to fall before the water levels are raised by ditch damming work (RSPB 1995).

Further information: Bacon & Lord 1996; Brooks & Stoneman 1997.

6.9 Pests and diseases affecting moorland

6.9.1 Fungal attack

Heather shoots may be damaged by snow mould *Fusarium* spp. or heather rhizomorph fungus *Marasmius androsaceus*, but these do not usually affect extensive areas of heather (Thompson, MacDonald & Hudson 1995b). These types of damage can be distinguished quite easily from the effects of heavy grazing because the heather shoots and leaves remain intact. Management can do little to alleviate the effects of fungal attack, but burning and reducing grazing pressure may encourage better heather growth.

6.9.2 Invertebrate pests

Heather beetle *Lochmaea suturalis* is a brown beetle about 6 mm in length. Both adults and larvae feed principally on heather, although, rarely, *Erica* spp. are also eaten. Heather beetle has caused extensive damage to heather moors across England between 1998 and 2000, and this current outbreak is thought to be one of the most serious in recent times. The impacts of this damage can last for many years, and there is, not surprisingly, a strong temptation to undertake dramatic control measures to counter any future outbreaks. However, no additional specific management is to be recommended or likely to be successful. Traditional heather management practices should continue to be followed (English Nature 1994e; Joint Nature Conservation Committee 2000).

Magpie moth *Abraxus grossulariata* larvae can damage heather and bilberry, and occasionally cause defoliation over fairly large areas, most often in Scotland.

Winter moth *Operophtera brumata* larvae can also damage heather and bilberry, but are usually a relatively minor problem.

Vapourer moth *Orygia antiqua* larvae, like those of the winter moth, feed on heather and bilberry but are a relatively minor problem.

Willow beetle *Lochmaea caprea* can cause extensive defoliation of crowberry *Empetrum nigrum* moorland.

Parasitic worms and **ticks** are pests of grouse, and both require control if populations of grouse are to thrive. The control of ticks, usually by treating the other main carrier, the sheep, help to reduce tick burdens on a moor and the incidence of 'louping ill', a disease carried by ticks which affects both sheep and grouse. Bracken harbours ticks and it is often controlled to reduce tick populations. Studies on moorland are being carried out by the Heather Trust, centred around reducing host potentials for ticks by manipulating wild mammal numbers, particularly in summer (Guthrie 1997).

Further information: English Nature 1994e; Hudson & Newborn 1995; MacDonald 1993; Thompson, MacDonald & Hudson 1995b.

Table 6.1 Mire types in the English uplands

Soligenous mires
• Associated with moving water, flushes or springs. • Slow rates of peat formation, as a result of an oxygenated, moving water supply. • Plant communities containing *Sphagnum recurvum, Molinia,* sedges, rushes and pleurocarpus mosses. • NVC communities include the small sedge and bryophtye fens M6 *Carex echinata-Sphagnum recurvum/auriculatum* mire, M10 *Carex dioica-Pinguicula vulgaris* mire and M11 *Carex demissa-Saxifraga aizoides* mire (Rodwell 1991b).
Basin mires
• Often associated with glacially deepened hollows. • Deep peat formation is possible, and the vegetation surface may be floating. • Generally no outflow of water and minimal ground water oscillation. • Encompass a wide range of NVC communities including small sedge and bryophyte fens, *Molinia* and *Juncus* fens, swamp and carr (Rodwell 1991b).
Valley mires
• Occur along the direction of the water flow, which is usually along the valley axis. • Exhibit a wide base-status range. • Encompass a wide range of NVC communities, including small sedge and bryophyte fens, *Molinia* and *Juncus* fens, swamp and carr (Rodwell 1991b).
Floodplain mires
• Develop on alluvium which is susceptible to flooding. • Common in base-rich areas and often follow the sequence: open water to swamp to carr. • Vegetation communities include *Sphagnum* where the nutrient status is low, and extend to reed and sedge communities where the nutrient supply is high. • Typical NVC types include various swamp communities.
Raised mires or bogs
• Usually confined and limited in extent, having a recognisable boundary called the rand. • Mire surface is isolated from the surrounding ground water table, resulting in an ombrotrophic plant community dependent on water and nutrients derived from atmospheric precipitation. • May have a characteristic domed shape, although this may be obscured by past peat cutting. • The typical NVC community is M18 *Erica tetralix-Sphagnum papillosum* raised and blanket mire (Rodwell 1991b).

Table 6.1	Mire types in the English uplands (continued)
Blanket bogs or mires	
•	Generally require high rainfall, high atmospheric humidity, a low temperature range and mean temperature, a low slope angle, low substrate permeability and low water aeration for formation.
•	Usually develop over impermeable soils or bedrock, although podsolisation, and the resultant formation of impermeable horizons within the mineral soil, may result in blanket mire development.
•	Depending on their location, they are known as plateau or saddle mires.
•	Often form on the watershed between water catchments.
•	Generally have frequent or abundant *Sphagnum*, although this is not always the case in English blanket mires (despite stratigraphic records indicating they once were), because of past management such as burning, draining and grazing.
•	NVC communities include M17 *Scirpus cespitosus-Eriophorum vaginatum*, M19 *Calluna vulgaris-Eriophorum vaginatum* and M20 *Eriophoroum vaginatum* blanket mires (Rodwell 1991b).

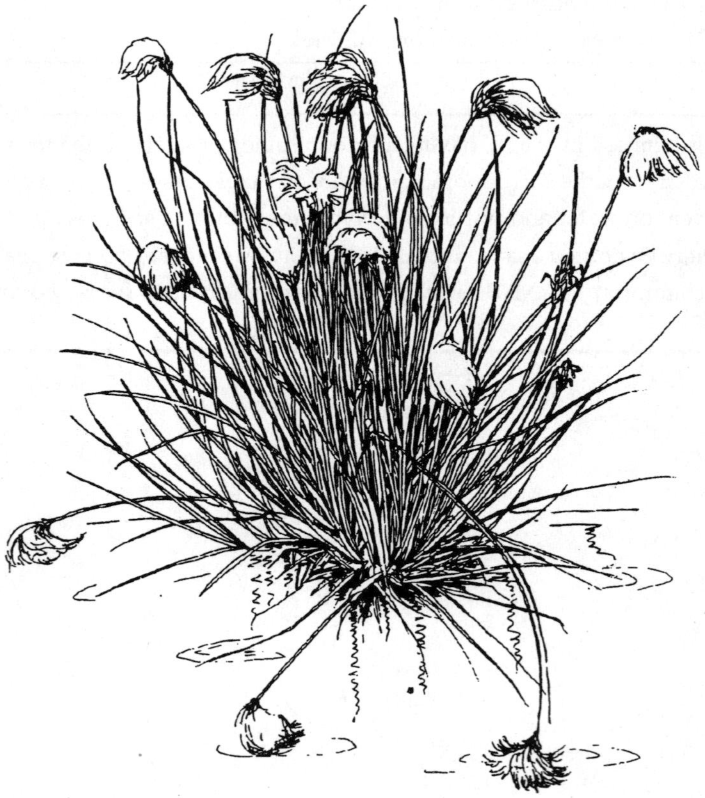

Table 6.2 Nationally rare and scarce vascular plants associated with moorland in England

Plant species	Status	Habitat requirements	Management requirements	Distribution by upland Natural Area
Ajuga pyramidalis pyramidal bugle	LR-ns	Dry heathland or grassland on free-draining, steep, sunny slopes with incomplete vegetation cover, usually on soils with medium base-status.	• Protect sites from destruction.	Cumbria Fells & Dales
Alchemilla glaucescens	LR-nt	Limestone grassland, usually on Carboniferous limestone, maintained by sheep-grazing.	• Protect sites from the application of fertilisers or pesticides. • Maintain moderate levels of sheep-grazing.	Cumbria Fells & Dales Forest of Bowland Pennine Dales Fringe Yorkshire Dales
Alchemilla minima	VU, EE Priority	Very short turf of base-rich *Festuca ovina* grassland. Generally in moist places at lower altitudes near flushed areas; at higher altitudes amongst limestone boulders and debris. It is well adapted to sheep-grazing. Its requirements are poorly understood.	• Maintain moderate grazing. • Protect sites from habitat destruction and the application of fertilisers or pesticides. • See Species Action Plan (UK Biodiversity Group 1998).	North Pennines Yorkshire Dales
Alchemilla wichurae	LR-ns	On damp basic soils. On herb-rich ledges and in upland grassland where grazing or mowing keep the vegetation short. Common by waterfalls or seepages on cliffs. Sometimes on bare rocks and scree and also track sides in the Yorkshire Dales.	• Where it grows on track sides, it needs protection from trampling by walkers and off-road vehicles. • Roadside populations need to be protected from agricultural enrichment which promotes the growth of coarse grasses.	Cumbria Fells & Dales North Pennines Yorkshire Dales

Plant species	Status	Habitat requirements	Management requirements	Distribution by upland Natural Area
Arenaria norvegica ssp. anglica English sandwort	Sched. 8 of WCA VU, EE	A stress-tolerant species of bare substrates, either on shallow, dry soils near to or amongst Carboniferous limestone pavement or on frequently flushed slopes around the edges of flushes and mires. Always on sparsely vegetated ground. Two colonies are in wet bryophyte-rich tufaceous flushes.	• Where necessary, protect the sites from recreational damage by walkers and off-road vehicles. • Control grazing at the sites to moderate levels. Levels of less than 1.5 ewes per hectare during the growing season have allowed populations to thrive. Moderate grazing is preferable to no grazing.	Yorkshire Dales
Asplenium septentrionale forked spleenwort	LR-ns	Steep or vertical faces of hard, base-poor, dark-coloured volcanic and metamorphic rocks, on dry, south-facing, unshaded slopes. Also occasionally on spoil heaps of metalliferous mines and old earthy, unmortared walls. It is intolerant of shade, waterlogging and competition from gorse and other shrubs.	• Landscaping or reclamation should avoid damage to the habitat. • Where necessary, shrubs should be cleared away.	Cumbria Fells & Dales Dartmoor North Pennines
Calamagrostis stricta narrow small-reed	LR-nt	Near-neutral bogs and marshes.	• Prevent drainage of sites.	Southern Pennines Yorkshire Dales
Carex ericetorum rare spring-sedge	LR-ns	Short limestone grassland.	• Protect sites from habitat destruction and the application of fertilisers or pesticides. • Maintain light or moderate levels of grazing.	Cumbria Fells & Dales North Pennines
Carex magellanica tall bog-sedge	LR-ns	Upland blanket bogs and valley mires, in *Sphagnum* lawns and in-filled hollows in wet, level moorlands and clearings in swampy woods.	• Prevent drainage of sites.	Border Uplands Cumbria Fells & Dales North Pennines

Plant species	Status	Habitat requirements	Management requirements	Distribution by upland Natural Area
Carex ornithopoda bird's-foot sedge	LR-nt	Open, calcareous grassland on Carboniferous limestone, often on thin, parched soils, which require light grazing to maintain the open character of the vegetation. Also close to exposed rocks on south-facing slopes, in full sun, and in shattered limestone pavement.	• Maintain light or moderate levels of grazing.	Cumbria Fells & Dales North Pennines White Peak Yorkshire Dales
Dactylorhiza traunsteineri narrow-leaved marsh-orchid	LR-ns	Wet, base rich habitats such as fens and flushes.	• Prevent drainage of sites and general lowering of the water table. • Maintain light or moderate levels of grazing.	Forest of Bowland North York Moors and Hills Yorkshire Dales
Dianthus deltoides maiden pink	LR-ns	In sandy grassland or heath, usually growing where the sward is broken by bare rock or soil. See Table 10.1.	• Control levels of grazing and other disturbance to moderate levels. • See Species Action Plan (UK Biodiversity Group 1998).	Border Uplands Clun & North West Herefordshire Hills Dark Peak North Pennines North York Moors and Hills White Peak Shropshire Hills
Equisetum pratense shade horsetail	LR-ns	Typically on river banks, on damp, base-flushed soils. Thriving best on deep, moist, freely-draining banks of essentially sandy soils or alluvial silt, flushed with base-rich water where there is light shade.	• Where sites are developing denser shade as woodland develops, it may be necessary to thin the canopy to provide the light shade which is most beneficial to this species.	North Pennines

Plant species	Status	Habitat requirements	Management requirements	Distribution by upland Natural Area
Equisetum variegatum variegated horsetail	LR-ns	A wide variety of open habitats. See Table 7.10.	• Maintain the site's hydrology, including water quality and patterns of water levels and flow.	Border Uplands Cumbria Fells & Dales Exmoor and the Quantocks North Pennines Yorkshire Dales
Euphrasia rivularis	LR-nt, E Priority	In bryophyte-rich flushes by streams, on wet, flushed slopes and on wet ledges and seepage areas on cliffs in montane areas.	• The conservation needs of this and other eyebrights are under review. Meanwhile, sites should be protected from habitat destruction. • See Species Action Plan (UK Steering Group 1995).	Cumbria Fells & Dales
Euphrasia vigursii	VU, EE Priority	Damp, grassy heathland. There has been a substantial and continuing loss of inland populations through habitat dereliction, especially the abandonment of grazing	• Many sites are likely to require grazing to maintain open vegetation, for example light grazing by ponies. • The conservation needs of this and other eyebrights are under review. • See Species Action Plan (UK Steering Group 1995).	Bodmin Moor Dartmoor
Gentiana pneumonanthe marsh gentian	LR-ns	Damp acid grassland or heathland. It is vulnerable to agricultural improvements such as ploughing and draining but also to agricultural neglect when grazing is reduced or stopped, and to excessive, uncontrolled burning. However, there is evidence from lowland heathland sites that burning can encourage regeneration and population increase.	• Protect sites from agricultural improvement. • Maintain moderate levels of grazing.	Cumbria Fells & Dales Forest of Bowland Shropshire Hills

Plant species	Status	Habitat requirements	Management requirements	Distribution by upland Natural Area
Hammarbya paludosa bog orchid	LR-ns	In boggy areas where the drainage water is moderately acid, frequently in *Sphagnum* and also on peaty mud and among grasses on the edge of runnels. Usually associated with some movement of water. Occurs on lightly grazed open mires.	• Protect sites from drainage and destruction.	Border Uplands Cumbria Fells & Dales Dartmoor Bodmin Moor North Pennines Yorkshire Dales
Illecebrum verticillatum coral-necklace	LR-ns	Neutral to acid soil in seasonally wet sandy or gravelly tracks and on shallow stream edges and flooded ditches. It requires open ground and some trampling is likely to be beneficial.	• Prevent interference with the water regime. • Some sites may require management to keep the vegetation open.	Bodmin Moor
Juncus alpino-articulatus alpine rush	LR-ns	Open, base-rich flushes, lake margins and mossy marshes on shallow soils. See Table 9.2.	• Protect sites from drainage and destruction.	North Pennines Yorkshire Dales
Juncus filiformis thread rush	LR-ns	Edges of lakes and reservoirs. See Table 7.10.	• Protect sites from changes in water regime which would prevent fluctuation levels. • Maintain the marshy or open, disturbed character of lake shores.	Cumbria Fells & Dales Forest of Bowland North Pennines Pennine Dales Fringe Yorkshire Dales
Limosella aquatica mudwort	LR-ns	On exposed mud at the edges of rivers, lakes, reservoirs, pools, ditches and winter-flooded ruts. Often on acidic soil and possibly favoured by nutrient enrichment by droppings. Many sites have been lost to drainage or to ponds becoming overgrown. See Table 9.2.	• Prevent drainage of sites. • Prevent the encroachment of scrub or other coarse vegetation.	Pennine Dales Fringe South West Peak Yorkshire Dales

Plant species	Status	Habitat requirements	Management requirements	Distribution by upland Natural Area
Linum perenne perennial flax	LR-ns	Base-rich grassland over limestone. See Table 7.10.	• Mow late in the year to 10-15 cm height, or light grazing by cattle or sheep all year or, preferably, during the winter only leaving a reasonably long sward. • It can persist for a number of years without management or, at least for a few years, moderate grazing throughout the year.	Cumbria Fells & Dales Yorkshire Dales
Lotus angustissimus slender bird's-foot trefoil	LR-ns	In grassland amongst scrub, around rocky outcrops and on grassy banks, usually by the sea. See Table 7.10.	• Protect sites from destruction.	Dartmoor Exmoor and the Quantocks
Lycopodium annotinum interrupted clubmoss	LR-ns	Upland heaths, flushes, grassland and open woods. Typically found in hollows and on steep slopes with late snow-lie in various sorts of heaths. On base-poor substrates, usually well drained.	• Protect sites from frequent moor burning and other forms of destruction.	Cumbria Fells & Dales
Lycopodiella inundata marsh clubmoss	LR-ns Priority	Bare, moist peaty, silty, sandy or sometimes muddy sites which are almost free of competition from other plants. On mires, heaths, lake margins and sand and clay pits, normally submerged in winter and spring and wet in summer. Most sites are highly acidic and deficient in bases and minerals. It may be particularly sensitive to pollution of rain and surface waters. At some sites to provide bare substrate, disturbance is required, for example poaching by livestock, peat-cutting or disturbance by vehicles.	• Protect the site from air- or water-borne pollution, and drainage. • Ensure that levels of disturbance are sufficient to provide bare substrate without damaging existing colonies. • Prevent the site becoming overgrown by coarse vegetation. • See Species Action Plan (UK Biodiversity Group 1998).	Cumbria Fells & Dales Dartmoor

Plant species	Status	Habitat requirements	Management requirements	Distribution by upland Natural Area
Lysimachia thyrsiflora tufted loosestrife	LR-ns	Fens and swamps among open, tall vegetation.	• All sites should be protected from drainage and lowering of ground waters.	North York Moors and Hills
Minuartia verna spring sandwort	LR-ns	Open or semi-open short grassland over calcareous rocks, among limestone rocks and scree or on old lead and zinc mine spoil, often associated with sites liable to soil erosion. Also on base-rich rock ledges and gullies, often at high altitude. The distribution is mainly restricted to sites with an annual rainfall of at least 100 cm and the species is susceptible to summer drought. It is threatened by insufficient grazing, which allows the sward to become too closed for the species.	• Protect sites from destruction. • Where possible, sites should be heavily grazed. Other forms of disturbance may be required where heavy grazing cannot be arranged.	Cumbria Fells & Dales Dark Peak North Pennines Pennine Dales Fringe South West Peak White Peak Yorkshire Dales
Myosotis stolonifera pale forget-me-not	LR-ns	Somewhat base-poor springs and seepage areas, soakways and flushes on hillsides and in valleys by pools, in ditches and in the backwaters of streams.	• Protect sites from destruction and drainage.	Border Uplands Cumbria Fells & Dales Dark Peak Forest of Bowland North York Moors and Hills Southern Pennines Yorkshire Dales
Persicaria mitis tasteless water-pepper	LR-ns	On wet or damp mud or peat banks, left exposed in summer. See Tables 7.10 and 9.2.	• Protect sites from drying out, filling in of ponds and fencing of ditches.	Border Uplands Shropshire Hills Yorkshire Dales

Plant species	Status	Habitat requirements	Management requirements	Distribution by upland Natural Area
Pilularia globulifera pillwort	LR-ns Priority	Bare wet substrates at the edges of slightly acid to neutral water bodies, usually on soft clays and silts. Unable to compete with larger plants such as reeds or other fen species nor survive under the shade of overhanging trees, it relies on fluctuations in the water level to control the spread of larger plants. In some sites the species relies on disturbance by cattle or horses to uncover bare substrate which it can colonise; at such sites it seems to disappear if grazing ceases. In Scotland it is also known to grow in water up to 2 m deep or as floating mats; it may be found in similar sites in England. See Tables 7.10 and 9.2.	• In sites where the species relies on a fluctuating water level, the pattern of fluctuating levels should be maintained. • In sites where the species relies on disturbance, then the site should be kept accessible to large livestock. In small sites, care should be taken that poaching is not accompanied by excessive manuring. In the absence of grazing animals, mechanical or manual means could be used to control the spread of swamp and fen and provide bare substrate for pillwort. • All sites should be protected from drainage or habitat destruction. • Protect the sites from water pollution, especially by agricultural fertilisers. • See Species Action Plan (UK Biodiversity Group 1998).	Black Mountains and Golden Valley Cumbria Fells & Dales Dartmoor Pennine Dales Fringe
Polygala amarella dwarf milkwort	VU	Open sites in short turf over calcareous rocks in well-drained sites. See Table 5.1.	• Protect sites from habitat destruction. • Where heavy grazing is thought to be restricting the populations, this should be controlled.	North Pennines Yorkshire Dales Cumbria Fells & Dales
Potentilla neumanniana spring cinquefoil	LR-ns	Open ground and seasonally parched, skeletal soils on limestone crags and screes. See Table 10.1.	• Some sites may require control of rank grasses or scrub, by cutting or grazing.	Cumbria Fells & Dales Oswestry Uplands White Peak Yorkshire Dales

Plant species	Status	Habitat requirements	Management requirements	Distribution by upland Natural Area
Primula farinosa bird's-eye primrose	LR-ns	Calcareous mires. See Table 7.10.	• Control grazing to moderate levels wherever possible. • Protect sites from agricultural intensification.	Cumbria Fells & Dales Forest of Bowland North Pennines North York Moors and Hills Pennine Dales Fringe White Peak Yorkshire Dales
Pyrola media intermediate wintergreen	LR-ns	Damp mossy habitats in woods and heaths. See Table 8.1.	• Sites which are grazed should be grazed only lightly. • Sites should not be planted with non-native trees.	North Pennines North York Moors and Hills
Sibthorpia europaea Cornish moneywort	LR-ns	In humid microclimates in sheltered sites on acidic soils and rocks. See Table 10.1.	• Protect sites from changes in hydrology and water regime.	Bodmin Moor Dartmoor Exmoor and the Quantocks
Silene nutans Nottingham catchfly	LR-ns	Open grassland on limestone, usually rough ungrazed grassland on shallow, well drained soils on steep slopes, ledges, etc. Populations can be lost where scrub is allowed to succeed the rough grassland.	• Sites should not be grazed. • Where necessary, occasional removal of woody species may be necessary.	White Peak
Spiranthes romanzoffiana Irish lady's-tresses	LR-ns Priority	In a carpet of *Molinia caerulea* on damp soil grazed by cattle, seasonally inundated or flushed.	• Ideally, it should be grazed when the plants are dormant.	Dartmoor

Plant species	Status	Habitat requirements	Management requirements	Distribution by upland Natural Area
Thlaspi caerulescens Alpine penny-cress	LR-ns	A pioneer colonist of metalliferous mine wastes and river gravels contaminated with lead, zinc and cadmium, often in limestone areas but also on shales. Usually in open vegetation but able to persist in a more closed turf. It is threatened by insufficient grazing, which allows the sward to become too closed for the species. See Table 5.1 & 10.1.	• Protect sites from destruction. • Where possible, sites should be heavily grazed. Other forms of disturbance may be required where heavy grazing cannot be arranged.	Border Uplands North Pennines White Peak Yorkshire Dales
Vaccinium microcarpum small cranberry	LR-ns	*Sphagnum* mires, often on small hummocks of glacial origin within blanket mires, also on *Sphagnum* hummocks.	• Protect sites from destruction.	Border Uplands
Viola lactea pale dog-violet	LR-ns	Patchy or open heaths or moors on level to gently sloping sites, with soil which is dry or water-logged in winter and where soil pH varies from 4.7-6.5. It cannot compete with taller vegetation and is vulnerable to agricultural neglect as well as modernisation.	• Tactics which control tall vegetation and create open soil will favour this plant. These could include grazing, general disturbance of soil along roads and paths, regular mowing and short winter burning rotations.	Bodmin Moor
Viola rupestris Teesdale violet	LR-nt	In open turf on base-rich sites, which are likely to have remained relatively open and treeless through out history. On the cold high limestone areas in heavily grazed swards. One site is at lower altitude on a warm south facing slope. At light levels of grazing the sward, typically dominated by *Sesleria caerulea*, can become overgrown, leading to a decline in the violet.	• Ensure sufficient grazing to keep a short, open turf.	Cumbria Fells & Dales North Pennines Yorkshire Dales

Key to Table 6.2

Status

Annex IIb	- listed on Annex IIb of the EC Habitats and Species Directive
Sched. 8 of WCA	- listed on schedule 8 of the Wildlife & Countryside Act.

Red list categories

CR	- critically endangered
EN	- endangered
VU	- vulnerable
DD	- data deficient
LR -nt	- Lower risk - near threatened
LR-ns	- Lower risk - nationally scarce
E	- endemic to Great Britain
EE	- endemic to England.

Biodiversity Action Plan (BAP)

Priority	- Priority species from UK Steering Group 1995 and UK Biodiversity Group 1998.
SCC	- Species of conservation concern from UK Steering Group 1995 and UK Biodiversity Group 1998.

Sources

Most information from Foley 1987; Grime, Hodgson & Hunt 1990; Hodgetts, Palmer & Wigginton 1996; I. Taylor pers comm; Page 1982; Porley & McDonnell 1997; R. Cooke pers comm; Rich 1997; Stewart, Pearman & Preston 1994; Wigginton 1999.

Table 6.3 Nationally rare and scarce bryophytes associated with moorland in England

Plant species	Status	Typical habitat	Distribution by upland Natural Area
Aloina ambigua	LR-ns	Rocks, banks, soil and walls. See Table 10.2	Bodmin Moor Cumbria Fells & Dales
Amblyodon dealbatus	LR-ns	A calcicole of wet, open ground such as tussocks in tufa-springs and on stream banks, cliffs and gravel where flushed by calcareous water.	Border Uplands Cumbria Fells & Dales North Pennines Yorkshire Dales
Barbilophozia kunzeana	LR-nt	Most habitats are damp or waterlogged, including mountain stream sides, basin mires, wet moorland hollows and valley bogs, in acidic to mildly basic conditions.	Border Uplands Yorkshire Dales
Brachythecium mildeanum	LR-ns	Wet, open grassland and stony ground overlying calcareous rocks.	Yorkshire Dales
Bryum intermedium	LR-ns	A calcicole on bare damp soil. See Table 10.2.	Border Uplands Cumbria Fells & Dales This species is widely overlooked and probably occurs in other upland natural areas.
Bryum riparium	LR-ns	In a range of intermittently wet non-calcareous habitats, including crevices in rocks in stream-beds and beside streams where kept moist by seepage from *Sphagnum*, on bare peat, on the sides of ditches and in arable fields within the flood zone of streams. It appears to be a poor competitor with other plants, but takes advantage of any open acid habitat to which the rhizoidal tubers happen to be washed.	Cumbria Fells & Dales Forest of Bowland
Bryum tenuisetum	LR-ns	On acid sandy or peaty soils, often on heathland or at the margin of upland reservoirs, very rarely in acid arable fields.	Pennine Dales Fringe

Plant species	Status	Typical habitat	Distribution by upland Natural Area
Calypogeia azurea	LR-ns	A calcifuge plant of peat, peaty or sandy soil, in blanket bog, on heaths, moorland and rocky banks. Rarely and possibly as an adventive, in woodland.	Cumbria Fells & Dales Yorkshire Dales
Campylopus schwarzii	LR-ns	Flushes or steep, acid, humus-rich banks among rocks, especially where there is some seepage of water, also on flushed rock-slabs, often in exposed moorland sites. Other habitats are dripping vertical rock-faces in open ravines, mountain cliffs, in bogs, on the edge of peaty pools and in turf in areas of late snow.	Cumbria Fells & Dales
Campylopus setifolius	LR-ns Priority	An oceanic species found in a variety of acid habitats, always with a humid microclimate. Often amongst tall *Calluna* on north to easterly aspects in steeply sloping turf; also on rock ledges with water dripping from above, in the spray zone of waterfalls, in block-screes and at the edge of streams and flushes. It is sometimes found in bogs.	Cumbria Fells & Dales
Campylopus subulatus	LR-ns	Unshaded, acid, gravelly and sandy places, including tracks, paths, lay-bys, old tarmac on roadsides and stony or gravelly river-margins.	Forest of Bowland Cumbria Fells & Dales Bodmin Moor
Catoscopium nigritum	LR-ns	Semi-open, rocky ground, in calcareous springs and flushes	North Pennines
Cephalozia catenulata	LR-ns	In woods and on peaty soil and banks. See Table 8.2.	Border Uplands Cumbria Fells & Dales Dartmoor North Yorkshire Moors & Hills Southern Pennines Yorkshire Dales Bodmin Moor
Cephalozia loitlesbergeri	LR-ns	On raised bogs, blanket mires, valley bogs and wet moors and also occasionally in damp heathland.	Cumbria Fells & Dales

Plant species	Status	Typical habitat	Distribution by upland Natural Area
Cephalozia macrostachya var. *macrostachya*	LR-ns	Largely confined to saturated micro-habitats on ombrogenous mires, valley bogs, acid basin-mires and very wet heaths. It generally grows amongst *Sphagnum*.	Exmoor and the Quantocks
Cephalozia pleniceps	LR-ns	In peat bogs, acid flushes and wet heathland as well as by streams, typically growing amongst *Sphagnum*.	Bodmin Moor
Cephaloziella elachista	LR-ns	Generally amongst larger bryophytes, especially *Sphagnum*, in raised and valley bogs. On wet heathland it has been found on the sides of decaying *Molinia* tussocks.	Cumbria Fells & Dales Shropshire Hills
Cephaloziella integerrima	EN	In lowland *Calluna* heath on damp clay soil or sand, especially where compacted by rabbits; also on mine waste and slatey soil in a quarry.	Bodmin Moor
Cephaloziella stellulifera	LR-ns	Mine-waste, coastal sites and on heathy tracks or sandy ditch-banks inland. See Table 10.2.	Bodmin Moor Exmoor and the Quantocks North Pennines Pennine Dales Fringe
Cinclidium stygium	LR-ns	Forming green or reddish tufts or patches in calcareous fens and marshes and in basic springs and flushes.	Cumbria Fells & Dales Yorkshire Dales
Cladopodiella francisci	LR-ns	Damp lowland heaths in southern England. Further north also in bogs, moorland and on lake sides, banks and ditch-edges.	Bodmin Moor Dartmoor
Dicranella crispa	LR-ns	In a wide variety of habitats but apparently absent from markedly acid or basic substrates. Most typical on disturbed open soil on banks of gravel, clay, loam or sand by roads, rivers and streams. Also on rocks, especially vertical sandstone.	Yorkshire Dales
Dicranum bergeri	VU	Raised bogs.	Border Uplands
Diplophyllum obtusifolium	LR-ns	A calcifuge pioneer of disturbed soil.	Bodmin Moor Cumbria Fells & Dales Exmoor and the Quantocks

Plant species	Status	Typical habitat	Distribution by upland Natural Area
Fossombronia fimbriata	LR-nt	Damp gravelly, sandy or schistose soil on stream sides, lake margins, roadsides and paths.	Border Uplands
Funaria muhlenbergii	LR-ns	A calcicole on bare soil among rocks, in turf, on anthills or on thinly earth-covered rocks. See Table 10.2.	Cumbria Fells & Dales Oswestry Uplands White Peak Yorkshire Dales
Hamatocaulis vernicosus slender green feather-moss	Annex IIb DD	Somewhat base-rich springs in upland districts. In the lowlands it is rare and generally occurs in spring-influenced sites in mildly basic small-sedge fens.	Cumbria Fells & Dales Shropshire Hills
Hennediella stanfordensis	LR-ns	On shaded, trampled ground by footpaths and under trees.	Shropshire Hills
Hypnum imponens	LR-ns	Wet heaths and raised valley- and blanket-bogs.	
Jamesoniella undulifolia marsh earwort	Sched. 8 of WCA EN Priority	In small quantity in wet minerotrophic *Sphagnum* mires.	Bodmin Moor Cumbria Fells & Dales
Jungermannia caespiticia	LR-nt	A pioneer species of moist base-poor soils in a variety of habitats including moorland edges, stream banks, reservoir margins and mine workings. In the Pennines it favours clay soil overlying Millstone Grit and more rarely, decaying shale. It occurs in pure patches or in association with other bryophytes and is somewhat erratic and seasonal in occurrence. The main growing season is in the autumn.	Dark Peak Southern Pennines Yorkshire Dales
Kurzia sylvatica	LR-ns	Steep peat-banks and moist organic soil in moorland and damp heaths, less often in bogs and occasionally in woodland. Sometimes also on damp, sheltered rock outcrops.	Cumbria Fells & Dales Border Uplands South West Peak
Lophozia obtusa	LR-ns	At higher altitudes it grows in mossy, often basic turf on sheltered north- or east-facing slopes or basic flushes. On lower ground it grows in woodland of birch and under *Calluna*.	North Pennines

Plant species	Status	Typical habitat	Distribution by upland Natural Area
Meesia uliginosa	LR-ns	Calcicole of wet, open ground on seeping rocks, tufa and gravel.	Cumbria Fells & Dales Border Uplands North Pennines
Moerckia hibernica	LR-ns	Damp, base-rich ground. See Table 7.11.	Cumbria Fells & Dales Yorkshire Dales
Nardia geoscyphus	LR-ns	On moist basic soil and rocks. See Table 10.2.	Border Uplands Dark Peak Dartmoor Forest of Bowland North Pennines Oswestry Uplands Southern Pennines South West Peak
Oncophorus virens	LR-ns	In damp calcareous turf. See Table 7.11.	Cumbria Fells & Dales North Pennines
Philonotis caespitosa	LR-ns	On moist or wet non-calcareous soil and rocks, where flushed or flooded by slightly basic mineral-rich water. See Table 10.2.	Bodmin Moor Border Uplands Cumbria Fells & Dales Dark Peak Exmoor and the Quantocks Forest of Bowland Pennine Dales Fringe Southern Pennines Yorkshire Dales
Physcomitrium sphaericum	LR-nt	As green patches or scattered shoots on mud exposed on the margins of lakes and reservoirs and on the beds of dried-up ponds.	Dark Peak Forest of Bowland South West Peak Pennine Dales Fringe

Plant species	Status	Typical habitat	Distribution by upland Natural Area
Pohlia andalusica	LR-nt	Damp sandy acidic soils, on heathy gravelly tracks, and on china clay and metalliferous mine-waste.	Bodmin Moor
Pohlia lescuriana	LR-ns	Preferring moisture-retentive soils, usually clay, although not those that are strongly basic. See Table 7.11.	Dark Peak Dartmoor Forest of Bowland Shropshire Hills Southern Pennines
Pseudobryum cinclidioides	LR-ns	In marshes and wet woodland. See Table 8.2.	North Pennines
Racomitrium elongatum	LR-ns	On sandy or gritty soils from near sea-level to high altitudes.	Cumbria Fells & Dales Border Uplands
Rhytidium rugosum	LR-ns	A calcicolous species of dry, short and often rather open grassland and turf on well drained shallow rendzina soils developed over a range of substrates including limestone. Also on dry south- to southwest-facing rock-ledges of inland cliffs and in limestone quarries.	Cumbria Fells & Dales North Pennines White Peak Yorkshire Dales
Scapania paludicola	EN	Lowland and subalpine bogs, acid mires and wet heaths, growing among *Sphagnum*.	Bodmin Moor Pennine Dales Fringe
Sphagnum affine	LR-ns	In a variety of weakly minerotrophic mires, including slightly basic flush-bogs, as well as on more swampy ground, in ditches and on flushed stream-banks.	Cumbria Fells & Dales
Sphagnum austinii	LR-ns	Raised and blanket bogs where the peat is deep and wet, frequently forming large hummocks among *Calluna vulgaris, Eriophorum vaginatum, Trichophorum cespitosum* and other bog species of *Sphagnum*.	Cumbria Fells & Dales Border Uplands Dartmoor

Plant species	Status	Typical habitat	Distribution by upland Natural Area
Sphagnum balticum Baltic bog-moss	Sched. 8 of WCA EN Priority	In wet hollows of raised and valley bogs.	Border Uplands
Sphagnum flexuosum	LR-ns	In marshes, woodland and on flushed rock-ledges. This species is thought to be under-recorded.	Cumbria Fells & Dales
Sphagnum majus	LR-nt	With *S. balticum* and *S. recurvum* in wet depressions in the marginal zone of a large valley bog.	Border Uplands
Sphagnum pulchrum	LR-ns	Forming carpets in depressions (including old peat-diggings) on ombrotrophic bogs, normally in very acid water.	Border Uplands
Tomentypnum nitens	LR-ns	Open, calcareous mires and flushes with gently flowing water, often on gentle slopes flushed by water from steeper ones.	Border Uplands North Pennines Yorkshire Dales Cumbria Fells & Dales South West Peak
Tortella densa	LR-ns	On limestone rocks and in grassy flushes. See Table 10.2.	Cumbria Fells & Dales North Pennines Yorkshire Dales
Tortula subulata var. *subinermis*	LR-ns	On soil and about tree-bases by streams and rivers.	Forest of Bowland White Peak
Trichostomopsis umbrosa	LR-ns	Damp, shady, calcareous places. See Table 10.2.	White Peak
Weissia microstoma var. *brachycarpa*	LR-ns	On wet non-calcareous clay, loam or marl. See Table 7.11.	Dark Peak Forest of Bowland

Plant species	Status	Typical habitat	Distribution by upland Natural Area
Weissia rostellata	LR-nt Priority	An ephemeral species colonising moist bare ground. Most frequent on gravelly ground and mud exposed in late summer and autumn on the margins of reservoirs and occasionally rivers, but also in a number of other situations including the banks of ditches, woodland rides and bare patches and turfy hollows in fields and pastures. Usually on clay or rich organic soil which is water-retentive or kept moist by its physical situation.	Border Uplands Forest of Bowland Southern Pennines

Key to Table 6.3

Status

Annex IIb - listed on Annex IIb of the EC Habitats and Species Directive

Sched. 8 of WCA - listed on schedule 8 of the Wildlife & Countryside Act.

Red list categories

CR - critically endangered

EN - endangered

VU - vulnerable

DD - data deficient

LR -nt - Lower risk - near threatened

LR-ns - Lower risk - nationally scarce

E - endemic to Great Britain

EE - endemic to England.

Biodiversity Action Plan (BAP)

Priority - Priority species from UK Steering Group 1995 and UK Biodiversity Group 1998.

SCC - Species of conservation concern from UK Steering Group 1995 and UK Biodiversity Group 1998.

Sources

Most information from Hill, Evans & Bell 1992; Hill, Preston & Smith 1992, 1994; Hodgetts, Palmer & Wigginton 1996 and Porley & McDonnell 1997.

Table 6.4 Plant communities associated with moorland areas in England

NVC code	NVC name	Inclusion in Annex 1 of Habitats Directive[1]	Significance in England[2]	Upland Natural Areas of England where community occurs[2] (see Figure 1.1)
HEATHS				
Dry heath				
H4	*Ulex gallii-Agrostis curtisii* heath.	Dry heaths	I	87, 92, 94
H8	*Calluna vulgaris-Ulex gallii* heath.	Dry heaths	I	4, 10, 25, 29, 30, 42, 58, 60, 87, 92, 94
H9	*Calluna vulgaris-Deschampsia flexuosa* heath.	Dry heaths	UK	2, 4, 8/15, 10, 12, 14, 17, 25, 29, 30, 42, 58
H10	*Calluna vulgaris-Erica cinerea* heath.	Alpine and sub-alpine heaths Dry heaths	UK	2, 4, 10, 12, 17, 42, 87, 92
H12	*Calluna vulgaris-Vaccinium myrtillus* heath.	Alpine and sub-alpine heaths Dry heaths	UK	2, 4, 8/15, 10, 12, 14, 17, 25, 29, 30, 42, 58, 60, 87, 92, 94
H13	See Chapter 5 Montane areas.			
H16	*Calluna vulgaris-Arctostaphylos uva-ursi* heath.	Alpine and sub-alpine heaths Dry heaths	L	10
H18	*Vaccinium myrtillus-Deschampsia flexuosa* moss-heath. See also Chapter 5 Montane areas.	Alpine and sub-alpine heaths Dry heaths	L	2, 4, 8/15, 10, 12, 14, 17, 25, 29, 42, 58, 60, 87, 92, 94
H19	See Chapter 5 Montane areas.			
H21	*Calluna vulgaris-Vaccinium myrtillus-Sphagnum capillifolium* heath	Alpine and sub-alpine heaths Dry heaths	I	2, 4, 10, 12, 17, 42, 87
H22	See Chapter 5 Montane areas.			

NVC code	NVC name	Inclusion in Annex 1 of Habitats Directive[1]	Significance in England[2]	Upland Natural Areas of England where community occurs[2] (see Figure 1.1)
MIRES				
Bog pools				
M1	*Sphagnum auriculatum* bog pool community	-	L	10, 87, 92
M2	*Sphagnum cuspidatum/recurvum* bog pool community	-	L	2, 4, 10, 12, 14, 25, 29, 87, 92
M3	*Eriophorum angustifolium* bog pool community	-	L	2, 4, 8/15, 10, 14, 25, 29, 87, 92
Small sedge bryophyte fens				
M4	*Carex rostrata-Sphagnum recurvum* mire.	Transition mires and quaking bogs	L	2, 4, 8/15, 10, 12, 25, 29, 58, 87, 92, 94
M5	*Carex rostrata-Sphagnum squarrosum* mire.	Transition mires and quaking bogs	L	10
M6	*Carex echinata-Sphagnum auriculatum/recurvum* mire.	-	I	2, 4, 8/15, 10, 12, 14, 17, 25, 29, 42, 58, 60, 87, 92, 94
M7, M8	See Ch 5 Montane areas.			
M9	*Carex rostrata-Calliergon cuspidatum* mire.	Transition mires and quaking bogs Alkaline fens	L	2, 4, 8/15, 10, 29, 41, 87
M10	*Carex dioica-Pinguicula vulgaris* mire.	Alpine pioneer formations of *Caricion bicoloris-atrofuscae** Alkaline fens	UK	2, 4, 8/15, 10, 12, 14, 17, 25, 29, 42, 60, 87
M11	*Carex demissa-Saxifraga aizoides* mire.	Alpine pioneer formations of *Caricion bicoloris-atrofuscae**	UK	4, 10, 42
M13	*Schoenus nigricans-Juncus subnodulosus* mire.	Alkaline fens	Not specified	17

NVC code	NVC name	Inclusion in Annex 1 of Habitats Directive[1]	Significance in England[2]	Upland Natural Areas of England where community occurs[2] (see Figure 1.1)
Wet heath				
M15	*Scirpus cespitosus-Erica tetralix* wet heath.	-	UK	2, 4, 10, 12, 17, 29, 60, 87, 92, 94
M16	*Erica tetralix-Sphagnum compactum* wet heath.	-	I	2, 4, 10, 17, 25, 29, 87, 92, 94
Blanket mires				
M17	*Scirpus cespitosus-Eriophorum vaginatum* blanket mire.	Blanket bog (active only*)	I	2, 4, 8/15, 10, 87, 92
M18	*Erica tetralix-Sphagnum papillosum* raised and blanket mire.	Blanket bog (active only*)	UK	2, 4, 8/15, 10, 12
M19	*Calluna vulgaris-Eriophorum vaginatum* blanket mire.	Blanket bog (active only*)	UK	2, 4, 8/15, 10, 12, 14, 25, 29, 42, 58, 60
M20	*Eriophorum vaginatum* blanket and raised mire.	-	UK	2, 4, 8/15, 10, 12, 14, 25, 29, 42, 60
Valley mires				
M21	*Narthecium ossifragum-Sphagnum papillosum* valley mire. See also Chapter 7 Meadows and enclosed pasture.	-	L	10, 17, 25, 29, 58, 92, 94
***Molinia* and *Juncus* fens**				
M22 - M24	See Chapter 7 Meadows and enclosed pasture.			
M25	*Molinia caerulea-Potentilla erecta* mire. See also Chapter 7 Meadows and enclosed pasture.	-	I	2, 4, 8/15, 10, 12, 14, 17, 25, 29, 42, 58, 87, 92, 94
M26	See Chapter 7 Meadows and enclosed pasture.			
Tall-herb fen				

NVC code	NVC name	Inclusion in Annex 1 of Habitats Directive[1]	Significance in England[2]	Upland Natural Areas of England where community occurs[2] (see Figure 1.1)
M27	See Chapter 9 Freshwater habitats.			
Springs				
M29 - M38	See Chapter 7 Meadows and enclosed pasture (M29, M35, M36, M37, M38) and Chapter 5 Montane areas (M31, M32).			
GRASSLAND				
Neutral (mesotrophic) grasslands				
MG2 - MG13	See Chapter 7 Meadows and enclosed pasture.			
Calcareous grasslands				
CG2	*Festuca ovina - Avenula pratensis* grassland. (See also Chapter 7 Meadows and enclosed pasture)	Semi-natural dry grasslands and scrubland facies on calcareous substrate (*Festuco brometalia*) (important orchid sites*)	Not specified	30, 41
CG3, CG6, CG7	See Chapter 7 Meadows and enclosed pasture.			
CG9	*Sesleria albicans-Galium sterneri* grassland. (See also Chapter 7 Meadows and enclosed pasture)	Semi-natural dry grasslands and scrubland facies on calcareous substrate (*Festuco brometalia*) (important orchid sites*)	I	2, 4, 8/15, 10, 14
CG10	*Festuca ovina-Agrostis capillaris - Thymus praecox* grassland. (See also Chapter 7 Meadows and enclosed pasture)	Species-rich *Nardus* grasslands, on siliceous substrates in mountain areas (and sub-mountain areas in continental Europe)*	UK	2, 4, 8/15, 10, 30, 42, 60
CG11	See Chapter 5 Montane areas.			

NVC code	NVC name	Inclusion in Annex 1 of Habitats Directive[1]	Significance in England[2]	Upland Natural Areas of England where community occurs[2] (see Figure 1.1)
Acid (calcifugous) grasslands				
U1	*Festuca ovina-Agrostis capillaris-Rumex acetosella* grassland.	-	L	4, 10, 42
U2	*Deschampsia flexuosa* grassland.	-	L	2, 4, 8/15, 10, 12, 14, 25, 29, 92
U3	*Agrostis curtisii* grassland.	-	I	87, 92, 94
U4	*Festuca ovina-Agrostis capillaris-Galium saxatile* grassland.	-	L	2, 4, 8/15, 10, 12, 14, 17, 25, 29, 30, 42, 58, 60, 87, 92, 94
U5	*Nardus stricta-Galium saxatile* grassland.	-	L	2, 4, 8/15, 10, 12, 14, 17, 25, 29, 30, 42, 58, 60, 87, 92, 94
U6	*Juncus squarrosus-Festuca ovina* grassland.	-	I	2, 4, 8/15, 10, 12, 14, 17, 25, 29, 42, 58, 60, 92, 94
U7, U10, U13	See Chapter 5 Montane areas.			
Tall-herb communities				
U15, U16, U17	See Chapter 10 Crags, scree and limestone pavement.			
Fern communities				
U19	See Chapter 10 Crags, scree and limestone pavement.			
U20	*Pteridium aquilinum-Galium saxatile* community.	-	-	2, 4, 8/15, 10, 12, 14, 17, 25, 29, 42, 58, 60, 87, 92, 94
U21	See Chapter 10 Crags, scree and limestone pavement.			

NVC code	NVC name	Inclusion in Annex 1 of Habitats Directive[1]	Significance in England[2]	Upland Natural Areas of England where community occurs[2] (see Figure 1.1)
Open vegetation				
OV37	*Festuca ovina-Minuartia verna* metalliferous grassland.	-	Not specified	4, 8/15, 30
OV38 - OV40	See Chapter 10 Crags, scree and limestone pavement.			
Woodland and scrub				
Various	See Chapter 8 Woodland and scrub.			

Key to Table 6.4

1 From Brown *et al* 1997.
* Priority habitat

2 From Drewitt & Manley 1997:
I Internationally scarce with UK representation;
UK Well developed in the UK but represented elsewhere;
L Widely developed in Europe.

NVC - National Vegetation Classification (Rodwell 1991, 1992 & 2000)

Table 6.5 **Breeding birds associated with moorland in England**

Bird species[1]	Birds of conservation concern in the UK[2]	Listed on Schedule 1 of the 1981 Wildlife & Countryside Act	Listed on Annex 1 of the EC Birds Directive	No. of British 10 km squares with breeding records 1988-90	% of breeding records in upland ITE squares[3]	Main upland habitat association	Principal Natural Areas supporting the species * = major/important areas[4]
Wigeon *Anas penelope*	Amber list	-	-	128	74.2	Moorland and fresh waters	2, 4*, 8*, 14
Teal *Anas crecca*	Amber list	-	-	571	52.5	Moorland and fresh waters	2*, 4*, 8*, 12*, 14, 25
Hen harrier *Circus cyaneus*	Red list	●	●	286	82.5	Moorland	2, 4, 8, 12* Extinct elsewhere/continuous persecution
Golden eagle *Aquila chrysaetos*	Amber list	●	●	216	88.9	Moorland and montane areas	10*, extinct elsewhere
Merlin *Falco columbarius*	Red list	●	●	386	87.3	Moorland and enclosed land	2, 4*, 8*, 10*, 12*, 14*, 15, 17*, 25*, 29, 42, 58, 87
Peregrine *Falco peregrinus*	Amber list	●	●	719	61.6	Moorland and montane areas	4, 8, 10*, 12, 14, 15, 25, 87*, 94
Red grouse *Lagopus lagopus scoticus*	-	-	-	749	78.6	Moorland	2*, 4*, 8*, 10, 12*, 14*, 15*, 17*, 25*, 29, 41, 42, 58(?), 87, 92
Black grouse *Tetra tetrix*	Red list Priority BAP species	-	-	278	86	Moorland and enclosed land	2, 4*, 8, 29, extinct elsewhere
Golden plover *Pluvialis apricaria*	Amber list	-	●	630	84.1	Moorland and enclosed land	2*, 4*, 8*, 10, 12*, 14*, 15, 17*, 25*, 29, 92
Dunlin *Calidris alpina*	Amber list	-	-	353	78.8	Moorland	2, 4*, 8*, 12, 14*, 25*

Bird species[1]	Birds of conservation concern in the UK[2]	Listed on Schedule 1 of the 1981 Wildlife & Countryside Act	Listed on Annex 1 of the EC Birds Directive	No. of British 10 km squares with breeding records 1988-90	% of breeding records in upland ITE squares[3]	Main upland habitat association	Principal Natural Areas supporting the species * = major/important areas[4]
Snipe *Gallinago gallinago*	Amber list	-	-	1,307	49.8	Enclosed land and moorland	All upland Natural Areas but 87, but note in particular 2*, 4*, 8*, 12*, 14*, 15*, 25*,29*
Curlew *Numenius arquata*	Amber list	-	-	1,354	48.1	Moorland and enclosed land	2*, 4*, 8*, 10, 12*, 14*, 15*, 17*, 25*, 29*, 30, 41, 42, 58, 60, 87, 92, 94
Redshank *Tringa totanus*	Amber list	-	-	1,046	36.8	Enclosed land and moorland	2*, 4*, 8*, 12*, 14*, 15, 25
Black-headed gull *Larus ridibundus*	-	-	-	671	46.2	Moorland and fresh waters.	2*, 4*, 8*, 10*, 12*, 14, 17
Common gull *Larus canus*	Amber list	-	-	575	62.6	Moorland and fresh waters	2*, 4
Short-eared owl *Asio flammeus*	Amber list	-	•	381	70.9	Moorland	2*, 4*, 8*, 12*, 14*, 15, 17*, 25*, 29
Meadow pipit *Anthus pratensis*	-	-	-	2,257	38.1	Moorland and enclosed land	All areas
Whinchat *Saxicola rubetra*	-	-	-	1,062	59.9	Moorland and scrub	2*, 4*, 8*, 10*, 12*, 14*, 15*, 17*, 25, 29*, 30, 41, 42, 60, 87*, 92*, 94*
Stonechat *Saxicola torquata*	Amber list	-	-	847	47.7	Moorland and scrub	10*, 42, 58, 87*, 92*, 94
Wheatear *Oenanthe oenanthe*	-	-	-	1,339	60.6	Montane areas, moorland and enclosed land	2*, 4*, 8*, 10*, 12, 14, 15, 17, 25, 29, 30*, 41, 42, 58, 60, 87, 92*, 94

Bird species[1]	Birds of conservation concern in the UK[2]	Listed on Schedule 1 of the 1981 Wildlife & Countryside Act	Listed on Annex 1 of the EC Birds Directive	No. of British 10 km squares with breeding records 1988-90	% of breeding records in upland ITE squares[3]	Main upland habitat association	Principal Natural Areas supporting the species * = major/important areas[4]
Ring ouzel *Turdus torquatus*	Amber list	-	-	401	93.5	Moorland and scrub	2, 4*, 8*, 10*, 12, 14*, 15(?), 17, 25, 29, 30, 42, 87, 92*
Raven *Corvus corax*	-	-	-	783	52	Moorland and montane areas	4*, 10*, 41*, 42*, 58*, 60*, 87*, 92*, 94*, extinct elsewhere but recolonising
Twite *Carduelis flavirostris*	Red list	-	-	420	70.2	Moorland and enclosed land	4, 8, 14*, 25*, 29*

Key to Table 6.5

1. Upland breeding bird species as identified in Stillman & Brown 1994.
2. Birds of conservation concern from RSPB 1996.
   BAP relates to the UK Biodiversity Action Plan and those species which are considered to be priority species (UK Biodiversity Group 1998; UK Steering Group 1995).
3. From Bunce & Barr 1988, using the 13 ITE land classes which were regarded as upland (information not available on an English basis).
4. The following 18 Natural Areas are classed as upland by English Nature:

No.	Natural Area name
2	Border Uplands
4	North Pennines
8	Yorkshire Dales
10	Cumbria Fells & Dales
12	Forest of Bowland
14	Southern Pennines
15	Pennine Dales Fringe
17	North York Moors and Hills
25	Dark Peak
29	South West Peak
30	White Peak
41	Oswestry Uplands
42	Shropshire Hills
58	Clun & North West Herefordshire Hills
60	Black Mountains and Golden Valley
87	Exmoor and the Quantocks
92	Dartmoor
94	Bodmin Moor

Table 6.6 Habitat and management requirements of birds associated with moorland in England

Moorland birds	Habitat requirements	Moorland habitat management
Wigeon	• Weak association with open moorland. • Nest on ground in amongst heather or bracken on bank or on wet moors and along stream sides. • Adult feeding areas likely to be nearby improved grasslands, perhaps adjacent to fresh waters - riparian grassland. • Chicks taken to feed on pools or in very wet areas. • Present April to July.	• Maintain natural drainage and all wetland features such as pools, flushes and boggy areas. • Create small, wet areas by blocking existing drains and grips.
Teal	• Weak association with moorland fringe, and diversity of damp to wet upland habitats. • Nest placed beneath tussocks or clumps of heather or grass adjacent to water or on wet bogs. • Adults and young forage in pools, bogs, wet heath, waterlogged grassland and nearby rivers and lakes. • Present March-July.	• Maintain natural drainage and all wetland features such as pools, flushes and boggy areas. • Create small, wet areas by blocking existing drains and grips. • Do not burn wet heath or blanket bog as these areas are rich in plant and insect food and very sensitive to drying out.
Hen harrier	• Strong association with heather moors. • Heather moors with a high grass component may be the most suitable for hen harriers: prey such as meadow pipits and voles are more abundant on such moors. • Nest placed on ground in areas of tall heather, on slope with good visibility. • Adults forage for small birds such as meadow pipits and red grouse (mainly chicks) and small mammals such as field voles, on heather and grass moors and over enclosed fields. • Food brought to dependent young in nest by adults. • Present all year, but most leave for lowland coastal areas outside breeding season April-end July.	• Retain existing scrub such as gorse and juniper and scattered trees such as hawthorn and rowan. • Where burning is desirable use a rotation of at least 20 years in some areas, for example on steep slopes and in gullies and cloughs, so that the heather can grow tall. • Do not burn areas of taller heather which have been used for nesting in the recent past.

Moorland birds	Habitat requirements	Moorland habitat management
Golden eagle	• Associated with remote, open country with cliffs or widely scattered woodland. • Nest placed on rock ledge on tall cliff or in large forest tree. • Adults forage on grouse, rabbits, mountain hares and carrion found mainly on moorland but also over enclosed land, particularly in winter. • Adults bring food to dependent young in nest. • Birds present throughout the year, nesting February to July.	• Manage to encourage grouse, rabbit abundance, and to increase the amount of carrion available. • Maintain large areas of open ground.
Merlin	• Strong association with heather moorlands. • Nest placed on ground in tall heather, or occasionally in bracken, on moderate to steep slopes. • Also nest occasionally in trees on moorland and at the edge of plantations. • Adults forage for a wide diversity of small bird prey (especially meadow pipit) over both moorland and enclosed grassland. • Food brought to nest for dependent young by adults. • Some birds present throughout the year, but many more present in breeding season, April-July, and most leave for lowland coastal areas in winter.	• Manage grazing to maintain or enhance the heath and mire communities. • Where burning is desirable use a rotation of at least 20 years in some areas, for example on steep slopes and in gullies and cloughs, so that the heather can grow tall. • Do not burn areas of taller heather which have been used for nesting in the recent past. • Leave some areas unburnt to allow scrub and scattered trees to grow as in some areas, eg Exmoor, merlins nest in such habitats. • Where bracken is controlled, cut or spray after the breeding season in late July/early August and leave a buffer zone near streams and gullies. • Leave areas of bracken on steep slopes or gullies. Only spray areas where the underlying sward is still intact and likely to recover, and target the invading edge for control.
Peregrine	• Nest placed on undisturbed steep crags, cliff ledge, chimney or ledge on tall building. • Adults forage on waders, grouse and pigeons caught over moorland, enclosed grasslands and urban areas. • Adults bring food to dependent young in nest. • Present throughout the year.	• Limit recreational disturbance during February-June to nest sites and potential nest sites.

Moorland birds	Habitat requirements	Moorland habitat management
Red grouse	• Nests on ground on heather moorland. • Strongly associated with heather moorland managed for grouse. • Adults feed particularly on young heather shoots, also bilberry shoots, cotton-grass flowers and invertebrates. • Chicks forage for invertebrates in wet and grassy patches on heather moors. • Present throughout the year.	• Manage grazing to maintain or enhance the heath and mire communities. • Shepherd stock to avoid localised heavy grazing. • Maintain natural drainage and all wetland features such as pools, flushes and boggy areas. • Create small, wet areas by blocking existing drains and grips. • Where burning is desirable use a rotation of at least 20 years in some areas, for example on steep slopes and in gullies and cloughs, so that the heather can grow tall. • Burn heather on rotation on flatter ground to provide a mosaic of different aged stands and burn patches of about a half to one hectare at a time. • Do not burn in areas where the heather is already prostrate through natural causes as regrowth will be slow. • Keep stock feeding to a minimum and away from heather or rotate feeding sites to reduce damage. • Avoid the use of fertilisers on moorland as this leads to the replacement of heather with grasses.

Moorland birds	Habitat requirements	Moorland habitat management
Black grouse	• Nests on ground in tall heather moorland or in rushy pastures. • Adults associate strongly with mixed moorland areas, with heather moors, *Vaccinium* heaths, *Eriophorum* bog and scrub and light woodland. • Chicks forage in wet flushes for invertebrates, particularly moth and sawfly larvae. • In winter, birds forage on heather moorland and amongst birch, rowan, hawthorn, alder and willow scrub. • Present in uplands throughout the year.	• Manage grazing to maintain or enhance the heath and mire communities. • Shepherd stock to avoid localised heavy grazing. • Maintain natural drainage and all wetland features such as pools, flushes and boggy areas. • Do not control rushes where bog mosses are also abundant. • Create small, wet areas by blocking existing drains and grips. • Retain existing scrub such as gorse and juniper and scattered trees such as hawthorn and rowan. • On gentler slopes graze or cut existing scrub on a rotation. Provide a range of habitats by clearing about 10% of scrub each year when it is about 10 years old. • Fence off areas of existing scrub to allow natural regeneration. Only fence off areas where grazing makes this essential by preventing natural regeneration. Ensure fencing is clearly marked to reduce the possibility of birds striking the fence. • Scarify the ground around old stands of scrub where regeneration is poor to encourage its spread. • Plant additional native trees and shrubs typical of the location on areas of low wildlife interest, targeting sheltered ghylls and cloughs. Suitable species may include native birch, alder, willow, rowan and hawthorn. Some aspen *Populus tremula*, juniper and Scots pine may be acceptable where locally present. • Do not burn wet heath or blanket bog as these areas are rich in plant and insect food and very sensitive to drying out. • Leave some areas unburnt to allow scrub and scattered trees to grow. • Avoid the use of fertilisers on moorland as this leads to the replacement of heather and grasses. • Where bracken is controlled, cut or spray after the breeding season in late July/early August and leave a buffer zone near streams and gullies. • Leave areas of bracken on steep slopes or gullies. Only spray areas where the underlying sward is still intact and likely to recover and target the invading edge for control.

Moorland birds	Habitat requirements	Moorland habitat management
Golden plover	• Strong association with flat or gently sloping ground, on unenclosed blanket bog and heather moors managed for grouse or sheep for nesting and enclosed pastures for feeding. • Nests on ground in short vegetation, created by burning, grazing or stunting on bogs or on ridge summits. • Chicks feed on grass patches on heather moor or in wet flushes - chicks may be led over a kilometre to feed in invertebrate rich areas by their parents. • When not incubating and before and following the breeding season, adults forage in enclosed, earthworm-rich, improved and semi-improved grassland up to at least 7 km away from nests. • Presence in uplands very weather dependent: in mild years or areas, birds may be present throughout the year, but more usually present between late February and end June.	• Maintain natural drainage and all wetland features such as pools, flushes and boggy areas. • Create small, wet areas by blocking existing drain and grips. • Use a shorter heather burning rotation on flatter ground. • Do not burn in areas where the heather is already prostrate through natural causes as regrowth will be slow. • Do not burn areas of undamaged blanket mire. • Graze so as to create areas of short turf on flat or gently sloping ground.
Dunlin	• Strong association with flat to gently sloping, waterlogged plateaux, particularly with wet blanket bog and pool complexes, although exact requirements poorly understood. • Nest in grass or *Eriophorum* tussock on blanket bog. • Chick and adult feeding areas not well known but include the edge of wet pools, and gullies on bog. • Present during breeding season only, late April-end June.	• Maintain natural drainage and all wetland features such as pools, flushes and boggy areas. • Create small, wet areas by blocking existing drains and grips.

Moorland birds	Habitat requirements	Moorland habitat management
Snipe	• Strong association with damp to wet unenclosed and enclosed land. • Nest placed on ground concealed in tussock in tall vegetation especially rushes in enclosed fields, wet moorland, grassland and wet flushes. • Adults forage for invertebrates in soft soil where water table near (< 20 cm) surface, in damp rushy flushes, pools, stream sides on moors and on enclosed land. • Chicks forage for invertebrates in damp, rushy flushes, pools on moor or in enclosed fields. • Present mainly late February-end June.	• Maintain natural drainage and all wetland features such as pools, flushes and boggy areas. • Create small, wet areas by blocking existing drains and grips. • Do not burn wet heath or blanket bog as these areas provide cover and are rich in plant and insect food. • Do not control rushes where bog mosses are also abundant.
Curlew	• Broad habitat association with flat or gently sloping ground, on low to moderate altitude moorlands and enclosed grasslands. • Nest in a wide range of sites, on the ground in both enclosed fields and on open moorland, in rough and wet grassland and in tall and short vegetation. For example, in *Eriophorum* and large grass tussocks, in tall rushes and amongst the dead stems of sharp-flowered rush, in short or prostrate heather, in fresh burnt patches, and amongst bracken litter. • On heavily grazed moors with short grassland, nesting birds undertake much feeding on these moors. Occasionally breeding adults will also feed in enclosed fields some distance (3-4 km) from nest sites, rather than using fields immediately adjacent to the moor. Prior to laying and during incubating, adults feed on improved and semi-improved pastures rich in invertebrates because they are feeding mainly on earthworms and leatherjackets. After hatching, adults feed in the same areas as the chicks. • Chicks feed particularly in areas of wet rushy grassland and flushes, and moorland nesting birds will often take chicks into neighbouring enclosed fields. Also feed on the ground beneath tall heather and on short burnt heather. • Present late February-end June.	• Maintain natural drainage and all wetland features such as pools, flushes and boggy areas. • Create small, wet areas by blocking existing drains and grips. • Use a shorter heather burning rotation on flatter ground and burn patches of about a half to one hectare at a time. • Do not burn wet heath or blanket bog as these areas are rich in plant and insect food and very sensitive to drying out.

Moorland birds	Habitat requirements	Moorland habitat management
Redshank	• Associated with riparian grasslands, unimproved and semi-improved pastures and, much less frequently, with damp moorland. • Nest is placed on ground in tussock in unimproved and semi-improved fields and allotments, in wet hollows or riparian grasslands. • Adults and chicks forage for invertebrates in wet riparian grasslands, stream sides and lake sides, enclosed improved land and wet, rushy patches in fields. • Present mid-April - end June.	• Maintain natural drainage and all wetland features such as pools, flushes and boggy areas. • Create small, wet areas by blocking existing drains and grips.
Black-headed gull	• Nest on ground in colonies on heather moors, blanket bogs or in riparian grasslands in river valleys, around reservoirs or on islands. • Adults forage widely for multitude of food items (invertebrates, carrion, waste) from fresh waters, improved, earthworm-rich pastures, tilled farmland, roadsides, etc. May take eggs and young of ground-nesting birds. • Food brought to dependent young by adults. • Present during April to June breeding season.	• Maintain natural drainage and all wetland features such as pools, flushes and boggy areas. • Create small, wet areas by blocking existing drains and grips. • Do not burn wet heath or blanket bog as these areas are rich in plant and insect food and very sensitive to drying out.
Common gull	• Nest on ground in colonies on heather moors, blanket bogs or riparian grasslands in river valleys, around reservoirs or on islands. • Adults forage widely for multitude of food items (invertebrates, carrion, waste) from fresh waters, improved, earthworm-rich pastures, tilled farmland, roadsides, etc. May also take the eggs and chicks of ground-nesting birds. • Food brought to dependent young by adults. • Present during April to June breeding season.	• Do not burn wet heath or blanket bog as these areas are rich in plant and insect food and very sensitive to drying out.

Moorland birds	Habitat requirements	Moorland habitat management
Short-eared owl	• Strong association with unenclosed moorland, particularly on moderate to steep slopes towards moorland edge, and with young forestry. • Nest on ground within patches of tall heather, amongst bracken litter or in tall grassland, usually with good visibility. • Adults forage over all open moorland and enclosed unimproved grasslands for small mammals. • Food brought to nest by adults. • Small, numbers present throughout year but most present during breeding season April-August.	• Where burning is desirable use a rotation of at least 20 years in some areas, for example on steep slopes and in gullies and cloughs, so that the heather can grow tall.
Meadow pipit	• Found in association with nearly all types of upland habitat . • Nest placed on ground in tussock or depression in heath, grass or bracken. • Birds forage for invertebrates in short or moderately tall vegetation. Densities appear to be greatest on heather moors with a higher grass component. • Food brought by adults to dependent young in nest . • Present mainly March-late July. Not usually present outside breeding season.	• Where burning is desirable use a rotation of at least 20 years in some areas, for example on steep slopes and in gullies and cloughs, so that the heather can grow tall. • Use a shorter heather burning rotation on flatter ground and burn patches of about a half to one hectare at a time.

Moorland birds	Habitat requirements	Moorland habitat management
Whinchat	• Strong association with tall vegetation, notably scrub, bracken and very tall grass and heather. • Adults sally for invertebrates from tall vegetation, fence posts and fencing wire or feed off ground on grassy patches amongst heather adjacent to bracken or on improved/semi-improved pastures. • Adults bring food to dependent young in nest. • Birds present end April-July.	• Maintain natural drainage and all wetland features such as pools, flushes and boggy areas. • Create small, wet areas by blocking existing drains and grips. • Retain existing scrub such as gorse and juniper and scattered trees such as hawthorn and rowan. • On gentler slopes graze or cut scrub on a rotation. Provide a range of habitats by clearing about 10% of scrub each year when it is about 10 years old. • Scarify the ground around old stands of scrub where regeneration is poor to encourage its spread. • Where burning is desirable use a rotation of at least 20 years in some areas, for example on steep slopes and in gullies and cloughs, so that the heather can grow tall. • Do not burn wet heath or blanket bog as these areas are rich in plant and insect food and very sensitive to drying out. • Leave some areas unburnt to allow scrub and scattered trees to grow. • Where bracken is controlled, cut or spray after the breeding season in late July/early August and leave a buffer zone near streams and gullies. • Leave areas of bracken on steep slopes or gullies. Only spray areas where the underlying sward is still intact and likely to recover and target the invading edge for control. • Do not control rushes where bog mosses are also abundant.

Moorland birds	Habitat requirements	Moorland habitat management
Stonechat	• Strong association with scrub, tall heather or bracken. • Nest placed low in bracken, gorse and other tall, thick scrub, trees or heather. • Adults feed on open grassy areas, within otherwise shrub-dominated habitat or amongst patches of bracken, so long as perches are available on tall vegetation. • Adults bring food to dependent young in nest. • Found throughout year on scrub areas on enclosed farmland and on open moorland.	• Maintain natural drainage and all wetland features such as pools, flushes and boggy areas. • Create small, wet areas by blocking existing drains and grips. • Retain existing scrub such as gorse and juniper and scattered trees such as hawthorn and rowan. • Where burning is desirable use a rotation of at least 20 years in some areas, for example on steep slopes and in gullies and cloughs, so that the heather can grow tall. • Leave some areas unburnt to allow scrub and scattered trees to grow. • Where bracken is controlled, cut or spray after the breeding season in late July/early August and leave a buffer zone near streams and gullies. • Leave areas of bracken on steep slopes or gullies. Only spray areas where the underlying sward is till intact and likely to recover and target the invading edge for control. • Do not control rushes where bog mosses are also abundant.
Wheatear	• Nest in hole in ground or wall, in bracken clump, beneath stones, on enclosed farmland, moorland or scree. • Adults forage for invertebrates over bare ground or short swards on heather and grass moors, stream sides, lake shores and enclosed farmland. • Adults bring food to dependent young in nest. • Birds usually present during extended breeding season, March-September.	• Maintain natural drainage and all wetland features such as pools, flushes and boggy areas. • Where bracken is controlled, cut or spray after the breeding season in late July/early August and leave a buffer zone near streams and gullies. • Leave areas of bracken on steep slopes or gullies. Only spray areas where the underlying sward is still intact and likely to recover and target the invading edge for control.

Moorland birds	Habitat requirements	Moorland habitat management
Ring ouzel	• Preference for nesting in areas of sloping land, particularly ghylls and stream sides and, rarely, trees. • Nest on ground in tall heather or bracken litter or in hole in wall or rock crevice. • Adults forage in short swards in enclosed fields, unenclosed moors, especially *Vaccinium* when fruiting. • Adults bring mainly invertebrate food to the nest for the chicks. • Relatively heavily grazed areas near to nest sites, with damp, short, earthworm-rich swards for feeding, may be important but key feeding habitats and foods require further study. • Birds present early April-end Sept. Absent from uplands in non-breeding season.	• Retain existing scrub such as gorse and juniper and scattered trees such as hawthorn and rowan. • Fence off areas where there is some scrub to allow natural regeneration. • Where burning is desirable use a rotation of at least 20 years in some areas, for example on steep slopes and in gullies and cloughs, so that the heather can grow tall. • Leave some areas unburnt to allow scrub and scattered trees to grow. • Where bracken is controlled, cut or spray after the breeding season in late July/early August and leave a buffer zone near streams and gullies. • Leave areas of bracken on steep slopes or gullies. Only spray areas where the underlying sward is still intact and likely to recovery and target the invading edge for control.
Raven	• In the uplands, nest on ledges on cliff or quarry faces, and less frequently in trees (preferably conifers) which are isolated, in small woods or at the edges of plantations (not deep in large forests), and on buildings. • Adults forage over open country for a variety of food, particularly carrion but also living animals, on moorland, enclosed and cultivated land, and roadsides. • Opportunist feeders, scavenging carrion such as sheep, rabbit, hare, other small mammals and birds. Also take live animal prey such as small rabbits and other small mammals, reptiles, amphibians and invertebrates. Can be major predators of eggs and chicks of other birds. Some vegetable material, such as seeds, buds, berries and cereal grains, is also eaten. • Food brought to dependent young in nest by adults. • Early nesters and disturbance to nests when young present can affect growth. • Present throughout the year.	• Maintain moorland trees and undisturbed cliffs for nesting. • Manage to encourage rabbit and carrion availability.

Moorland birds	Habitat requirements	Moorland habitat management
Twite	• Strong association with tall vegetation at moorland edge, often in close proximity to water and to flower-rich meadows. • Nest placed on ground or low down in tall heather, bracken litter or, more rarely, in grass, *Eriophorum* or small crevice, always on unenclosed land. • Adults forage for flower seeds collected in burnt *Molinia* patches and from farmyards, haystacks, etc in April and early May, from flower-rich meadows and pastures in May and June and from roadside verges and any remaining uncut meadows thereafter. Birds will forage up to at least 2 km from moorland nest site. • Food brought to dependent young in nest by adults. • Birds usually present during extended breeding season, April-September.	• Maintain natural drainage and all wetland features such as pools, flushes and boggy areas. • Create small, wet areas by blocking existing drains and grips to provide drinking areas. • Retain existing scrub such as gorse and juniper and scattered trees such as hawthorn and rowan. • Where burning is desirable use a rotation of at least 20 years in some areas, for example on steep slopes and in gullies and cloughs, so that the heather can grow tall. • Leave some areas unburnt to allow scrub and scattered trees to grow. • Where purple moor-grass is present as a uniform stand burn patches (ie not the whole area) annually. • Where bracken is controlled, cut or spray after the breeding season in late July/early August and leave a buffer zone near streams and gullies. • Leave areas of bracken on steep slopes or gullies. Only spray areas where the underlying sward is still intact and likely to recover and target the invading edge for control.

Table 6.7 Nationally rare and scarce invertebrates associated with moorland in England

Invertebrate species		Nature conservation status	Typical habitat	Distribution in upland England (not currently available in terms of Natural Areas)
Scientific Name	**English Name**			
Moths				
Anarta melanopa	Broad-bordered white underwing	RDB3 SCC	Moorland. Larvae feed on bilberry *Vaccinium myrtilus* and crowberry *Empetrum nigrum*. In mainland Britain this species is restricted to altitudes above 650 m.	Cheviot and West Cumbria only locations in England.
Aphelia unitana	–	RDB2	Moorland and limestone dales. Wide range of larval food plants.	Known locations at Malham Tarn, Yorkshire, Dovedale, Derbyshire, Mainfold Valley, Staffordshire and Heddon's Mouth, Exmoor.
Crambus ericella	Heath grass veneer	Nationally Scarce B	Ecology unknown - caterpillar likely to be on moorland grasses.	Cumbria and Yorks Dales. Widespread in Scotland
Carsia sororiata	Manchester treble bar	Nationally Scarce B	Caterpillar on bilberry, cowberry *Vaccinium vitis-idaea* and crowberry.	Northern and western moorland.
Dyscia fagaria	Grey scalloped bar	Nationally Scarce B	Caterpillar on heather *Calluna vulgaris*, bell-heather *Erica cinerea* and cross-leaved heath *Erica tetralix*.	Northern and western moorlands.
Epione paralellaria	Dark bordered beauty	RDB2/3 Priority	Lightly wooded upland heaths and lowland bogs. Feeds on willow *Salix* spp. and aspen *Populus tremula*.	Northumberland, Yorkshire.
Epirrita filigrammaria	Small autumnal moth	Nationally Scarce B	Caterpillar on heather and bilberry.	Northern and western moorlands.
Hypenodes humidalis	Marsh oblique-barred	Nationally Scarce B	Larva probably on cross-leaved heath.	Western moorlands - Somerset, Shropshire and Cumbria. Also southern lowland heaths.
Hyppa rectilinea	The saxon	Nationally Scarce A	Moorland and northern woods. Larva polyphagous.	Northumberland and Cumbria only in England.

Invertebrate species		Nature conservation status	Typical habitat	Distribution in upland England (not currently available in terms of Natural Areas)
Scientific Name	**English Name**			
Lithomoia solidaginis	Golden-rod brindle	Nationally Scarce B	Moorland and open woodland. Larva on goldenrod *Solidago virgaurea*.	Northern moorlands, south to Staffordshire. Regular migrant and turns up south of this as non-resident.
Perizoma minorata	Heath rivulet	Nationally Scarce B	On flowers/seeds of eyebrights *Euphrasia* spp in upland pasture/moorland.	Cumbria and Yorkshire in England.
Perizoma blandiata	Pretty pinion	Nationally Scarce B	On flowers/seeds of eyebrights in upland pasture/moorland.	Cumbria and Yorkshire in England.
Syngrapha interrogationis	Scarce silver Y	Nationally Scarce B	Moorland. Larvae on heather and bilberry.	Northern England, south to Staffordshire. Regular migrant elsewhere.
Xestia alpicola alpina	Northern dart	Nationally Scarce A. Priority	Moorland and high mountain tops. Larvae feed on crowberry and probably other dwarf shrubs.	Moorhouse, Pennines, Cumbria and the Cheviot.
Xestia ashworthii	Ashworth's rustic moth	Nationally Scarce A Priority	On heather and other upland plants (including foxglove *Digitalis purpurea*) in montane and moorland areas.	Northumberland.
Xylena exsoleta	Sword grass	Nationally Scarce B Priority	Moorland and open woodland. Larva polyphagous.	Northern England.
Butterflies				
Coenonympha tullia	Large heath	SCC	Fringes of blanket bogs and lowland raised mires. Larval food plant is hare's-tail cotton-grass *Eriophorum vaginatum*, adult nectar plant is cross-leaved heath.	In England, confined to the north.

Invertebrate species		Nature conservation status	Typical habitat	Distribution in upland England (not currently available in terms of Natural Areas)
Scientific Name	**English Name**			
Erebia aethiops	Scotch argus	England priority species	In England on sheltered calcareous/neutral grassland (*Sesleria* and *Molinia*) rather than moorland.	A few English colonies occur in Cumbria, mainly in carboniferous limestone regions north of Morecambe Bay, and the Cumbria/Yorkshire border on the Craven limestone.
Erebia epiphron	Small mountain ringlet	Nationally scarce B SCC	*Nardus* grassland, from around 400 m upwards.	In England it is restricted to the Lake District only occurring at high altitudes.
Mellicta athalia	Heath fritillary	RDB2 Priority	Moorland fringes between the open moor and usually, but not always, woodland. Larval food plant is primarily common cow-wheat *Melampyrum pratense*, although larger larvae can also use foxglove.	Exmoor.
Bugs				
Cixius cambricus	A lacehopper	Nationally Scarce B	Lacehopper feeding on roots of sedges, sometimes under stones. Upland grassland.	Largely Scotland and Wales but also Yorkshire Dales and Vale of York heaths.
Macrosteles alpinus	A planthopper	Nationally Scarce B	Planthopper on heath rush *Juncus squarrosus*. Moorland blanket bog and upland moist grassland.	Cumbria and Durham in England. More widespread in Scotland.
Flies				
Limonia stylifera	Cranefly	RDB2	Base-rich flushes in association with calcareous outcrops.	Moorhouse NNR, Cumbria and several Scottish sites.
Melanostoma dubium	Hoverfly	Nationally Scarce B	Hoverfly of upland boggy ground. Needs an abundance of nectar flowers, especially tormentil *Potentilla erecta*.	Craven Pennines and Lake District. More widespread in Scotland and Wales.

Invertebrate species		Nature conservation status	Typical habitat	Distribution in upland England (not currently available in terms of Natural Areas)
Scientific Name	**English Name**			
Tipula limbata	Cranefly	RDB3	Waterlogged soil on high moorland in England (and boggy woodland flushes in Scotland).	North Yorks Moors, Cumbrian and Durham Pennines.
Tipula serrulifera	Cranefly	RDB1	Waterlogged soil on high moorland in England.	Only recent site is high heather moorland in North Yorks Moors.
Beetles				
Aphodius fasciatus	Dung beetle	Nationally Scarce B	Moorland and montane dung beetle. Sheep and cattle dung.	North York Moors, Lake District and Pennines
Byrrhus arietinus.	Northern pill beetle	Nationally Scarce B	Feeds on moss - especially *Racomitrium* - on moors and mountain tops.	Pennines, Derbyshire Peaks, North York Moors and Lake District
Carabus nitens	Ground beetle	Nationally Scarce B	Moorland and wet heathland, boggy areas on moorland.	Not Scotland or Wales. Southern heathland species, getting onto high moorland in Pennines and North York Moors.
Geotrupes vernalis	Spring dor beetle	Nationally Scarce B	Moorland and heathland dor beetle. Sheep and cattle dung, usually early in the year.	Cumbria. Old records from Exmoor and North York Moors, also from lowland heaths in the Midlands and SE England. Possibly extinct in lowlands.
Miscodera arctica.	Ground beetle	Nationally Scarce B	Under stones and among moss and heather litter. Also mountain tops among *Racomitrium* and under stones.	Northern and western moorland, south to Exmoor. Also Vale of York heaths.
Olophrum consimile	Rove beetle	Nationally scarce A	Stream sides, wet moss and litter in fens at high altitude.	North York Moors only in England.
Patrobus sepentrionis	Ground beetle	Nationally Scarce B.	Under stones and among moss, usually where wet. Moorland and beside mountain streams.	Mainly Scotland but also Cumbria, Yorkshire Pennines and Humberhead Mires.
Pterostichus aethiops	Ground beetle.	Nationally Scarce B	Moorland species that may migrate to woodland in winter.	Northern upland moorland and bog.

Invertebrate species		Nature conservation status	Typical habitat	Distribution in upland England (not currently available in terms of Natural Areas)
Scientific Name	**English Name**			
Trechus rivularis	Ground beetle	RDB3 (over-rated)	Blanket bog and moorland.	North Yorkshire Moors, Northumberland and Wales (probably elsewhere but mistaken identity). Declining relict populations in eastern England fens.
Bees, wasps and ants				
Bombus distinguendus	Great yellow bumble-bee	Nationally Scarce B	Formerly fairly widespread bumble bee of various habitats. Has declined in most areas other than extreme northern and western parts of range.	North Yorks Moors.
Spiders				
Clubiona norvegica	A foliage spider	Nationally Scarce B	Spider among moss (especially *Sphagnum*) on high moorland.	Northern and western England - Cumbria, Yorkshire and Cheshire.
Diplocephalus protuberans	A money spider	Nationally Scarce B	Small spider living among moss , grass or rushes. Wet places in upland grassland and moorland, often by streams.	Northumberland, Cumbrian Pennines and North York Moors.
Hilaira nubigena	A money spider	Nationally Scarce A	Small spider of wet areas on moorland, usually in *Sphagnum* or at base of rushes.	Apart from single record in Sutherland, all records are from Yorks, Durham, Northumbrian/ Cumbrian Pennines.
Hilaira pervicax	A money spider	Nationally Scarce B	Small spider of wet areas on moorland, usually in *Sphagnum* or at base of rushes. Adult mainly in winter.	Northern and western moorland. Yorks/Cumbria/Northumberland in England.
Macrargus carpenteri	A money spider	Nationally Scarce A	Small spider of short heather or grass on high moorland.	Northern. Small areas of Scotland and Cumbria/Northumberland.
Semiljicola caliginosa	A money spider	Nationally Scarce B	Small spider of wet places on moorland. Among *Sphagnum* and other mosses and among rushes.	Northern species, south to Yorkshire Pennines.
Snails				

Invertebrate species		Nature conservation status	Typical habitat	Distribution in upland England (not currently available in terms of Natural Areas)
Scientific Name	English Name			
Vertigo genesii	Round-mouthed whorl snail	Annex II, RDB1 Priority	In moss and sedges in spring-fed alkaline flush at 495 m.	Widdybank Fell, Co Durham. Only known site in Britain.
Vertigo geyeri	A whorl snail	Annex II, RDB1 Priority	Tufa-depositing springs and calcareous upland fens and flushes.	Cumbria.

Key to Table 6.7

Status

Annex II	Listed on Annex II of the Habitats Directive
RDB1	Red Data Book category 1 Endangered
RDB2	Red Data Book category 2 Vulnerable
RDB3	Red Data Book category 3 Rare
RDB4	Red Data Book category 4 Out of danger
RDB5	Red Data Book category 5 Endemic
Nationally Scarce A	15-30 10 km squares of national grid
Nationally Scarce B	30-100 10 km squares of national grid
Priority	Priority species in the UK Biodiversity Action Plan (UK Biodiversity Group 1998; UK Steering Group 1995).
SCC	Species of conservation concern in the UK Biodiversity Action Plan (UK Biodiversity Group 1998; UK Steering Group 1995).

Table 6.8 Habitat and management requirements of moorland invertebrates

Moorland invertebrates	Habitat requirements	Management requirements
Ground-dwelling species	A variety of bare substrates, including bare peat, mineral soil, sand and rock. They are used by carnivorous species to hunt over and burrowing species to burrow in. Wet and dry bare substrates have different faunas but both are of value. Firm, rather than churned substrates are of most value. Moss, plant litter (including heather) and stones provide cover and over-wintering sites.	• Maintain a varied vegetation structure and succession including bare ground. • Value and retain eroded but firm substrate along paths and tracks, although this may be difficult on peaty soils and easier on mineral soil. (Peat hags can also be valuable and persist for long periods of time.) • Prevent substrate churning by too heavy use, especially by horses/motorbikes. • Allow some vegetation to escape the burning cycle and go into post maturity. • Do not be too fastidious in tidying up stones and rubble, collapsed stone walls, etc.
Pollen and nectar feeding species	A range and abundance of flowering plants throughout the year, especially species with early flowers or a long flowering period, are valuable to invertebrates as pollen and nectar sources. Heather flowers can be very abundant and are used particularly by bees, as well as some moth caterpillars which eat the flowers. Bilberry, tormentil and heath bedstraw are particularly valuable, as are common daisy, yarrow, ragwort, various thistle species and any umbellifers growing on marginal grassland, at the base of walls and along road verges. The extra-floral nectaries of bracken may be a useful nectar source for some small species early in the year.	• Adjust grazing levels to achieve maximum flowering. • Include ruderal/verge habitats in management regimes.
Ants	Tussocks, stones, stones and boulders, pieces of semi-decayed timber (including old fence-posts, etc.). The yellow meadow ant sometimes makes its domed nests on mineral soils on moorland grassland and supports a range of other species. The warm south-facing slopes of such nests may be important basking sites.	Retain such features for cover/nesting sites. • Avoid ploughing or cutting where there are large meadow ant nests.

Moorland invertebrates	Habitat requirements	Management requirements
Solitary bees and wasps	A variety of bare substrates to burrow into, in particular with southern/SE/SW orientation. Pollen and nectar sources.	• Varied vegetation structure and succession including bare ground. • See above re: nectar sources.
Web spinning spiders	Varied vegetation structure, including grasses, dwarf shrub heath (including mature heather) and scrub. Specialised upland spiders make their webs in screes and other accumulations of stones, especially in limestone districts.	• Adjust grazing and burning to maintain optimum mosaic, including allowing some areas to escape management into post maturity. • No management necessary. Do not disturb.
Molluscs	Moist, sheltered places such as amongst moss or rock crevices. Limestone substrates are important for molluscs and provide a source of calcium (see Chapter 10).	• Maintain light or no grazing. • Prevent disturbance or removal of rock habitats.
Phytophagous species	Taller, older heather supports the greatest abundance and number of species of phytophagous lepidoptera caterpillars. A diversity of appropriate moorland species, growing in a diversity of structural conditions and aspects, and with a range of young to mature growth phases, is desirable for phytophagous species on herbs. Limestone areas usually support a greater diversity of forbs for phytophagous species, including plants protected from grazing and calcicole food plant species.	• Adjust grazing to achieve maximum appropriate diversity of moorland herbs. • Restrict/prevent access of grazing stock to rock outcrops and wet seepages with richer floras.
Dung feeders	A supply of pesticide free sheep, cow, horse and/or deer dung.	• Consider using alternatives to avermectin helminthicides.
Species that live under stones (lapidicolous)	Rock outcrops, scree, dry stone walls and buildings, their remains, old mineral spoil heaps as well as naturally occurring rocks and stones. These are frequently used as cover for ground-dwelling species, as well as basking sites and territorial perches (see also Chapter 10).	• Prevent disturbance or removal of rock habitats. • Maintain light or no grazing. • Encourage non-intervention areas.

Moorland invertebrates	Habitat requirements	Management requirements
Moss-inhabiting species	Areas with significant moss cover, other than post-burn moss species such as *Funaria* spp. Moss cover may occur, for example, under heather, between stones, at the base of and on walls, shrubs and trees, around flushes and beside streams. This provides cover for a diversity of ground-dwelling species, and food and habitat for pill beetles and snow fleas.	• Maintain light or no grazing. • Encourage non-intervention areas.
Semi-aquatic species	Small hydrological features, such as peat pools, *Sphagnum* pools, flushes, seepages and trickles, and stream headwaters. Calcareous flushing adds considerably to species richness and also supports rarities among the Diptera. Varied margins of water bodies, including waterlogged moss, bare wet peat and bare mineral substrates are also of value. Often a need for nectar sources as adults.	• Prevent drainage and heavy grazing. Unlikely to benefit from other management unless scrubbing over. • Access by grazing animals may keep bare ground open. • See above re nectar sources.

Table 6.9 Mammals, amphibians and reptiles associated with moorland in England

Scientific name	Common name	Nature conservation status	Typical habitat	Distribution by upland Natural Area
Mammals				
Cervidae, eg *Capreolus capreolus*, *Cervus elaphus*	Deer, eg roe deer, red deer	Common and widespread; increasing. Important effects on vegetation structure.	Woodlands with open rides; open moorland, grassland adjacent to woodlands.	All have one or more species
Lepus timidus	Mountain hare	Introduced to the Peak District in the nineteenth century. Native to Britain. Locally common.	Open heathland and mountain grasslands.	Peak District
Martes martes	Pine marten	Very rare, vulnerable. Fully protected by Schedule 5 of the Wildlife and Countryside Act 1981 (as amended 1988).	Extensive conifer and deciduous woodland, often near open moorland.	Extremely rare
Microtus agrestis	Field vole	Widespread and common; important component in food chain.	Rough grass pasture, grass moorland, open woodland and rides and young 'pre-thicket' plantations.	All
Sciurus vulgaris	Red squirrel	Local, vulnerable. Fully protected by Schedule 5 of the Wildlife and Countryside Act 1991. Biodiversity Action Plan Priority species (UK Steering Group 1995).	Broadleaved and coniferous woodland.	Border Uplands North Pennines Cumbria Fells and Dales
Sorex spp	Shrews	Widespread; most species common.	Grass pasture, grass and heather moorland, open woodland and rides.	All

Scientific name	Common name	Nature conservation status	Typical habitat	Distribution by upland Natural Area
Amphibians				
Bufo bufo	Common toad	Widespread, locally common, but probably declining.	Uneven structured vegetation, eg grassland, woodland margins, near or connected to ponds or other water bodies with roughly neutral pH. Ponds may be deeper and presence of fish less a problem than for other amphibians. Will travel long distances to breeding ponds.	All
Rana temporaria	Common frog	Widespread, locally common.	Uneven structured vegetation, eg grassland, woodland margins, near or connected to ponds (can be small, must have shallow areas) or other water bodies with roughly neutral pH.	All
T. cristatus	Great crested newt	Widespread, declining but may be locally abundant and more often found in lowland habitats. Fully protected by Schedule 5 of the Wildlife and Countryside Act 1981. Biodiversity Action Plan Priority species (UK Steering Group 1995).	Breeding ponds of approximately neutral pH and free of fish with contiguous terrestrial habitat (usually in excess of 0.4 ha to sustain a viable population). Terrestrial habitat needs to contain a diversity of vegetation or physical structure. Tend to use larger ponds or rely more on clusters of nearby ponds than other newt species.	All except Exmoor and the Quantocks, Dartmoor and Bodmin Moor.
Triturus vulgaris *T. helveticus*	Smooth newt Palmate newt	Widespread, locally common. Palmate generally more tolerant of upland or more acid waters while smooth newts common and more abundant in lowland habitats.	Structurally varied habitats, eg grasslands, woodland edges, quarries, with nearby or integral ponds. Ponds can be small to fairly large.	All

Scientific name	Common name	Nature conservation status	Typical habitat	Distribution by upland Natural Area
Reptiles				
Lacerta vivipara *Anguis fragilis*	Common lizard Slow-worm	Widespread, can be locally common, but nationally probably declining. Partially protected by Schedule 5 of the Wildlife and Countryside Act 1981.	Structurally varied, open habitats; often providing basking areas. Banks, woodland margins, open moorland, tussocky grasslands and bogs. Areas should not be too wet. Limited dispersion potential means adults fairly sedentary and reflects importance of connected habitats for long-term survival of populations. Slow-worms tend to be found more in grassland habitats, especially where slugs and snails are present (major food item).	All
Natrix natrix	Grass snake	Widespread, locally common, but more associated with lowland habitats. Partially protected by Schedule 5 of the Wildlife and Countryside Act 1981.	Structurally varied habitats. Very mobile species; often associated with water (amphibians and fish are major prey items) and needs rotting vegetation for egg laying. Therefore more often associated with farmed areas than other snake species.	Most Natural Areas although records sparse in northern England
Vipera berus	Adder	Widespread, locally common, but declining. Partially protected by Schedule 5 of the Wildlife and Countryside Act 1981.	Structurally varied habitats, such as moors, woodland edges, ungrazed (or low intensity grazed) grassland. Especially in areas with low levels of disturbance, and in areas with several habitat types (eg woodland and moorland) in close proximity.	All

Source

Mitchell-Jones 1996.
Mitchell-Jones & Gent 1997.

Table 6.10 Habitat and management requirements of moorland mammals, amphibians and reptiles

Species	Habitat requirements	Management requirements
Mountain hare	Feed predominantly on heather, preferring younger shoots, and almost exclusively on it during the winter. Also eat cotton-grass species and grasses.	• Manage, via burning or cutting, to provide a good supply of young heather stems, in a mosaic with areas of cover, particularly mature heather, within the typical 1 km range.
Pine marten	Feed on small mammals, birds, berries and fruits in well-wooded habitats.	• Retain extensive woodland where the species may still be present.
Red squirrel	As a specialist pine-seed feeder they are best adapted to coniferous woodland. In broadleaved woodland they are at a serious disadvantage to the grey squirrel.	• Retain large areas of conifers (more than 2,000 ha) where populations persist. • Retain, and expand where possible, islands of conifers where populations remain. • Actively manage grey squirrel populations.
Small mammals	Require a structurally varied and botanically diverse vegetation, with a deep litter layer. This provides a good range of food plants (especially grasses and seed bearing plants) for the herbivorous species. It also supports the invertebrate prey of insectivores and provides suitable cover.	• Manage to promote a good ground cover and structural diversity of vegetation, with a litter understorey. • Retain stones and stable scree slopes as cover for the common shrew.
Deer	Use open moorlands for foraging. A mixed and diverse structure to the moor, especially with different vegetation types in close proximity, provides a variety of grazing and browsing. Woodlands are also valuable for shelter and feeding.	• Manage deer populations to ensure they remain healthy, of an appropriate age and sex structure. • Ensure they are not causing damage to important habitats through grazing and browsing.

Species	Habitat requirements	Management requirements
Reptiles	Favour large areas of natural and semi-natural vegetation with low levels of disturbance. Optimal habitats are warm, southerly aspects with a diverse vegetation. Require open areas for basking, with adjacent vegetation to provide cover from predators and over-heating. Thick tussocks of grasses, eg purple moor-grass *Molinia caerulea*, provide excellent habitats; each tussock can offer good basking sites as well as thick cover. Require areas for retreating from cold weather; hibernation occurs in vegetation (eg in a *Molinia* tussock or inside a dense bush of *Calluna*), underground (eg small mammal or rabbit burrows), next to tree or bush roots, below stones or in thick vegetation litter. Often a continuum from wet to dry vegetation is valuable, and snakes in particular move into wetter habitats during the summer months and drier areas for winter. A varied structure also provides habitats for the food species taken, including invertebrates, small mammals, amphibians and other reptiles.	• Manage to provide a mosaic of open areas and low vegetation amongst taller, bushier vegetation, particularly on southerly slopes. For example, uneven aged heather, tall grasses or other low shrub species. • Ensure suitable egg laying areas remain.
Amphibians	Require suitable breeding pools. Generally water of approximately neutral pH is preferred, although there are varying degrees of acid tolerance. Increasing acidity (ie decreasing pH) affects embryo development and survival and therefore breeding water with a pH of 4 or higher is required. Presence of other species can affect breeding success. For example, large numbers of predatory invertebrates, such as dragonfly larvae and water beetles, predate tadpoles. Fish also prey on frog and newt tadpoles. Require extensive areas of appropriate terrestrial habitat for feeding and hibernating. Terrestrial habitats need to offer structural variation, to provide the invertebrate foods eaten, to offer cover from extremes of temperature and to provide hibernation sites. Examples include hedgerows, the margins of deciduous woodland, dry stone walls, rocky ground and even man-made rubbish.	• Manage to ensure a mosaic of uneven vegetation structure, typically ranging from open ground to 1 m in height. • Ensure continuous habitats that take account of the needs for foraging and over-wintering (hibernation) sites. Large expanses of habitat are preferable. • Ensure suitable ponds, usually of approximately neutral, or only slightly acidic, pH, remain for breeding. • Seek to minimise disturbance; especially in sensitive areas.

Table 6.11 **Advantages and disadvantages of burning moorland habitats for various land uses**

This is a generalised summary of potential impacts, and actual effects will vary according to the characteristics of the area being considered. Further details, particularly of species-specific reactions, should be sought in the appropriate references (Gimingham 1972; MacDonald *et al* 1998; Miles 1987; Mowforth & Sydes 1989; Rowell 1988; RSPB 1995; Shaw *et al* 1996; Thompson *et al* 1995). Note that the land uses described regularly occur together on the same area of land.

Land use	Habitat	Potential advantages	Potential disadvantages
Nature conservation	Dwarf-shrub heath and blanket bog	Direct benefits (most apply to dwarf shrub heath): • Stimulates young heather growth and seedling regeneration, which is beneficial where the heath is in danger of being lost. • Encourages certain important animal and plant species, eg red grouse, golden plover, bog rosemary and cloudberry. • Creates a mosaic of stands of different ages and vegetation heights, so enhancing the structural variation of the vegetation and the diversity of invertebrates. • Creates bare ground which is required by some invertebrates. • May prevent trees and shrubs establishing, which is desirable is some situations, eg where birch is encroaching into south-western heaths (although burnt areas may provide effective seedbeds for tree species). • May rejuvenate heather so that it out competes bracken, although this is likely to be dependent on various factors, eg. grazing pressure, soil depth, heather age.	• May encourage the predominance of heather to the exclusion of other species. • Impoverishes the bryophyte and lichen flora. • May encourage the predominance of hare's-tail cotton-grass on some blanket bogs if inappropriate rotations used. • Encourages purple moor-grass on blanket bog and wet heath where it occurs, to the exclusion of other species. • May change vegetation communities from ones of wildlife interest to those of less interest (particularly in combination with other management practices such as heavy grazing or drainage), eg blanket mire to wet heath, wet or dry heath to grassland. • Reduces the likelihood of layering by dwarf-shrubs. • May discourage certain animal and plant species, such as less mobile animals (eg molluscs), some insects (eg springtails and mites) and plants which cannot tolerate fire (eg lesser twayblade, some mosses), although many survive in damp litter, mosses and tussocks with properly controlled winter burning.

Land use	Habitat	Potential advantages	Potential disadvantages
	Dwarf-shrub heath and blanket bog (cont.)	Indirect benefits: • Increases the tolerance of dwarf-shrubs to grazing. • Patch burning helps to spread the grazing pressure across an area. • Reduces the risk of uncontrolled and uncontrollable fires, which can destroy large areas of wildlife habitat.	• May prevent the establishment of native trees and shrubs, which are often desirable because they diversify the habitat and enhance the biodiversity. • May lead to erosion and loss of habitat when burns do not regenerate well, especially if the peat itself catches fire. • May remove habitats, damage populations and create even-aged stands when large areas are burnt instead of a mosaic of small patch burns, although if the fire burns unevenly this is not necessarily the case. • May encourage the spread of bracken in some circumstances.
	Purple moor-grass dominated areas	• Reduces the dominance of purple moor-grass, when conducted in combination with the appropriate grazing regime. • Reduces the risk of uncontrolled fires, which can destroy large areas of wildlife habitat. • Removes *Molinia* litter and exposes seed which is a vital food source for twite and other finches in early spring.	• Encourages purple moor-grass to the exclusion of other species, if not conducted in combination with the appropriate grazing regime. • May remove habitats, damage populations and create even-aged stands when large areas are burnt instead of a mosaic of small patch burns, although if the fire burns unevenly this is not necessarily the case.
	Enclosed grassland	• See Chapter 7 Meadows and enclosed pasture.	

Land use	Habitat	Potential advantages	Potential disadvantages
Grouse moors	Dwarf-shrub heath and blanket bog	• Encourages the growth of young heather, which increases the carrying capacity for red grouse. • Improves the nutritional quality of heather and other moorland plants, although the enhanced nutrient content of shoots falls off rapidly over the first five years after fire. • Leads to the predominance of dwarf-shrub vegetation (where grazing levels are appropriate). • Creates a mosaic of stands of different ages and heights, which is required by nesting and feeding grouse.	• May lead to homogenous stands of even-aged heather which reduces the diversity of plant and animal life. • Leads to erosion and reduced carrying capacity for grouse when burns do not regenerate well, especially if the peat itself catches fire. • May prevent the establishment of trees and shrubs, which are important for black grouse. • Prevents development of older heather important for some species of conservation interest. • Removes areas of taller heather used as nesting sites for merlin and hen harrier.
Agriculture	Dwarf-shrub heath and blanket bog	• Encourages the growth of young heather, which increases the carrying capacity of the area for stock. • Improves the nutritional quality of heather and other moorland plants, although the enhanced nutrient content of shoots falls off rapidly over the first five years after fire. • Enables and encourages stock to move around the land, thereby spreading the grazing pressure.	• May cause livestock to concentrate their grazing on burnt areas and prevent the regeneration of dwarf shrubs if the total area burnt is very small. • May lead to erosion and reduced carrying capacity for stock when burns do not regenerate well, especially if the peat itself catches fire. • May encourage the predominance of purple moor-grass and hare's-tail cotton-grass, where these occur and inappropriate burning rotations are used, thus reducing the stocking capacity when they replace heather.
	Purple moor-grass dominated areas	• Promotes the growth of young grass in spring which is then available earlier and more accessible and nutritious for stock grazing. • Prevents the accumulation of dead leaves and surface litter.	• Encourages the spread of purple moor-grass to the exclusion of all other species.
	Enclosed grassland	• See Chapter 7 Meadows and enclosed pasture.	

Land use	Habitat	Potential advantages	Potential disadvantages
Agriculture (cont)	Gorse	• Helps stock to move around the land and encourages an initial flush of grass growth. • Regenerating gorse will be more readily browsed.	• Regenerates and encourages the spread of gorse.
Other	Any habitat	• Reduces the likelihood of undesirable, uncontrolled fires by: ❑ reducing the amount of material available to burn; ❑ creating fire breaks. • Is a form of disturbance which can be important for maintaining some aspects of biological diversity and for some characteristic species.	• May destroy areas of valuable wildlife habitat, threaten public safety and property, tie up the emergencies services, cause erosion and scar the landscape when not adequately controlled. • May burn into the peat itself, if the peat surface is dry and the burning is not undertaken responsibly, leading to drying, oxidation, bare areas and erosion, which adversely affect all land uses, as well as water quality, flow rates and water courses.

& pasture

Meadows and enclosed pasture 7

Tables

Definition and location of meadows and enclosed pasture

7.1 Definition of meadows and enclosed pasture

This chapter covers the meadows and pastures found within the enclosed land of the English uplands. Pastures are grazed but not cut, while meadows are cut for either hay or silage and may or may not be grazed. While these areas are generally referred to as grasslands, they frequently contain a range of wetland plant communities (mires) which are also covered in this chapter. They may also be described in agricultural terms as in-bye, which is enclosed land in by the farm buildings, or allotment or intake, which is land taken in or enclosed from the hill.

Although grasslands can be composed of a rich mixture of plant species, grasses are typically dominant. Three broad types of dry grassland occur in Britain. These are defined by the type of substrate on which they occur (Crofts & Jefferson 1994, 1999). Neutral grasslands are found mostly within enclosed field systems on moist mineral soils with a pH of between 5 and 6.5. Calcareous grasslands occur on both enclosed and unenclosed land, largely on pervious calcareous bed rocks. The soils here tend to be shallow and typically have a pH range of between 6.5 and 8.5. Acid grasslands normally occur on acid soils, which have a pH below 5. Much grassland has been agriculturally 'improved', by the application of fertilisers or herbicides, drainage or ploughing and reseeding. Where these activities have not taken place they are termed 'semi-natural' or 'unimproved'. The National Vegetation Classification (NVC, Rodwell 1992) describes the grassland communities of England and those which occur in the enclosed uplands are listed in Table 7.12.

The majority of the wet grassland communities found in the enclosed uplands are technically mires, that is they are permanently or periodically waterlogged. Many of these communities, however, resemble grassland in structure and are managed in similar ways to grasslands, though in many cases grasses are replaced as the dominant species by small sedges *Carex* spp. or rushes *Juncus* spp. Depending on the species composition and structure of these communities they are varyingly referred to as wet, flushed or marshy grasslands, fen meadows, mires, flushes or bogs. These communities are listed in Table 7.12 and described in Rodwell (1991 and 1992). For the sake of simplicity these communities are referred to as wet grasslands hereafter.

The emphasis in this chapter is on semi-natural and 'semi-improved' grasslands, as these have a far greater wildlife value than agriculturally 'improved' grasslands. However, where agricultural grasslands are of wildlife interest, this has generally been derived from a long history of management, either as pasture or meadow.

7.2 Location and extent of meadows and enclosed pasture

Enclosed grasslands occur throughout the English uplands, predominantly along valley floors and on the lower valley sides. Some enclosures, however, occur on higher ground and can even extend to the hill tops. In the latter situations, the nature of the enclosed land is often very similar to the open fell or moor.

The extent of the grassland and mire communities found in the enclosed uplands of England varies with the grassland type. Agriculturally improved grasslands are extensive throughout, while unimproved grasslands and their associated mires are often restricted in their distribution. Semi-natural neutral grasslands in particular have become a scarce resource because they usually occur on relatively dry, even terrain which is easily improved (Jefferson *et al* 1994). Calcareous grasslands are more extensive, but again many have received applications of herbicides or fertilisers where full cultivation is not possible (Hillier, Walton & Wells 1990). Acid grasslands are the most extensive of the unimproved types, occurring on the poorest soils. Many acid grassland stands have been derived from dwarf-shrub heath via overgrazing.

At present it is not possible to provide a comprehensive account of the distribution and extent of enclosed dry grassland communities in England. Many of the communities which occur within the upland areas, as defined in this handbook, are more extensive in the lowlands of England. At least two grassland communities, however, MG3 *Anthoxanthum odoratum-Geranium sylvaticum* hay meadows and CG9 *Sesleria caerulea-Galium sterneri* grassland are only found in upland England. Recent estimates indicate that there are less than 1,000 ha of the upland hay meadow (NVC type MG3) in England, located for the most part in upland valleys in the north of England. Upland calcareous grassland has been estimated to cover around 10,000 ha in England, with the largest concentrations occurring in the north Pennines and Cumbria. Further information on the extent and location of lowland grassland types is detailed in Jefferson (1996), Jefferson & Robertson (1996a & b), UK Steering Group (1995) and 7.4.3 below.

Hopkins & Hopkins (1993) reviewed grassland in Britain. Although 50% of swards are over 20 years of age, most have been modified by intensive management. Inorganic fertiliser nitrogen is applied to 80% of these grasslands and only a small proportion are now of high conservation value, over 95% having been lost since 1930.

Wet grasslands occur throughout the enclosed uplands of England, wherever the ground is kept permanently or periodically wet through high annual rainfall, humidity or water table, or by the impervious nature of the underlying rock leading to springs and seepages. Enclosed wet grasslands have been subject to agricultural drainage, as well as other agricultural improvement techniques, and their extent has declined as a result. Again, the extent of these communities in the enclosed uplands of England has not been fully quantified but in Devon and Cornwall only 8% of the purple moor-grass *Molinia caerulea* and rush *Juncus* sp. pastures (known as Culm grassland) present in 1900 remains today (UK Steering Group 1995).

Habitats and species of meadows and enclosed pasture in the uplands

7.3 Why meadows and enclosed pasture are important

Meadows and enclosed pasture in upland England support a rich variety of wild plants and animals, including many rare and scarce species of plants, birds and invertebrates. They contain some semi-natural grassland communities which are now scarce in the UK as well as in Europe (Jefferson & Robertson 1996; Jefferson *et al* 1994; Willems 1990;). These grassland types include neutral grasslands such as northern hay meadows, calcareous grasslands, and certain wet grasslands with purple moor-grass. Certain types of acid grassland of the enclosed uplands are similarly limited in their distribution, occurring only in Britain and Ireland (NCC 1989; Ratcliffe & Thompson 1988). A range of internationally scarce mire communities are also found in the enclosed uplands, including calcareous flushes and alkaline fens. The international significance of the plant communities of meadows and pastures is recognised by their inclusion in the Habitats and Species Directive (see 7.4.3 and Table 7.13) and the UK Biodiversity Action Plan (UK Steering Group 1995).

Semi-natural meadows and pastures may contain a large number of plant species, that is they are species-rich. These include a range of nationally rare and scarce plants which are often restricted to these habitats (Tables 7.9 and 7.10). Semi-natural, as well as agriculturally semi-improved or improved grasslands, can provide feeding, breeding and sheltering habitats for nationally rare and scarce invertebrates, birds, bats and amphibians which are of conservation concern, for example because they are globally threatened or their numbers are declining (Tables 7.13, 7,16, and 7.17). Where such grasslands occur next to moorland they provide particularly valuable feeding areas for birds which nest on the unenclosed land. The international significance of certain plant and animal species of meadows and pastures is recognised by their inclusion in the Habitats and Species Directive (see 7.4) and the UK Biodiversity Action Plan (UK Steering Group 1995).

7.4 Habitats and species of meadows and enclosed pasture, their nature conservation status and distribution

7.4.1 Vascular plants

A wide range of plant species are associated with upland meadows and enclosed pastures, many of which are nationally rare and scarce (Table 7.9). Traditionally managed hay meadows can contain a striking variety and abundance of herbs such as wood crane's bill *Geranium sylvaticum*, great burnet *Sanguisorba officinalis*, pignut *Conopodium majus* and lady's mantles *Alchemilla* spp. Calcareous upland pastures can also be very species-rich, supporting plants such as blue moor-grass *Sesleria caerulea*, common rock rose *Helianthemum nummularia*, wild thyme *Thymus polytrichus*, carline thistle *Carlina vulgaris* and bird's-eye primrose *Primula farinosa*.

More acidic pastures tend to be less diverse in terms of plant species and can be dominated by grasses such as mat-grass *Nardus stricta* with heath bedstraw *Galium saxatile* and tormentil *Potentilla erecta*. Some acidic pastures are richer, particularly where mires are present or where there is a calcareous influence on the grassland, when common dog-violet *Viola riviniana* and common mouse-ear *Cerastium fontanum* may occur.

Marshy grasslands in the enclosed uplands may be dominated by purple moor-grass and rushes *Juncus* spp., but can also support a variety of other plants, including sedges *Carex* spp., meadowsweet *Filipendula ulmaria*, wild angelica *Angelica sylvestris*, ragged robin *Lychnis flos-cuculi* and marsh hawk's-beard *Crepis paludosa*.

Some of the species associated with enclosed grasslands are included in the UK Biodiversity Action Plan and Species Action Plans have been prepared for them (Table 7.9; UK Biodiversity Group 1998; UK Steering Group 1995).

7.4.2 Bryophytes

Dry grasslands are generally species-poor in relation to bryophytes and there are few specifically associated with meadows and enclosed pastures in upland or lowland Britain. Bryophytes are often very specialised in their niche requirements, and can occupy very restricted small niches. Thus some species may occur in small wetland features, areas of disturbed ground or on stream banks within enclosed grasslands. Some of these are nationally rare and scarce and are shown in Table 7.10.

7.4.3 Plant communities

The plant communities found in the enclosed pastures and meadows of upland England are shown in Tables 7.1 and 7.2 respectively. Table 7.12 shows the nature conservation status and distribution of these communities. Full descriptions and other information on these communities is given in Rodwell (1991 and 1992).

Of particular nature conservation significance are calcareous grasslands (NVC communities: CG2-CG10), examples of purple moor-grass wet grasslands with a calcareous influence (NVC: M24 and M26) and northern hay meadows (NVC: MG3). All these grassland types are of European nature conservation significance and merit the designation of Special Areas of Conservation under the EC Habitats and Species Directive.

The meadows and enclosed pastures of the English uplands are particularly important for several vegetation types which are scarce or absent in lowland England. In particular MG3 *Anthoxanthum odoratum-Geranium sylvaticum* northern hay meadows, with their characteristic sward of bulky tall herbs, are only found in the higher valleys of the Pennines and the Lake District. The MG5 *Cynosurus cristatus-Centaurea nigra* grassland is generally considered to be a lowland hay meadow and pasture grassland, but it also occurs on the upland margins, often as remnants within otherwise agriculturally improved fields. The CG9 *Sesleria caerulea-Galium sterneri* grassland is confined to the Carboniferous limestone of the Pennines, Cumbria and northern Lancashire. Similarly the species-rich M26 *Molinia caerulea-Crepis paludosa* mire community of base-rich and calcareous peats is only found in upland England and is largely restricted to the Pennines and the Lake District.

Enclosed grasslands also provide an important locus for wet grasslands dominated by either rush *Juncus* spp or purple moor-grass *Molinia caerulea* M23 *Juncus effusus/acutiflorus-Galium palustre* rush pasture, M24 *Molinia caerulea-Cirsium dissectum* fen meadow, M25 *Molinia caerulea-Potentilla erecta* mire and M26 *Molinia caerulea-Crepis paludosa* mire). These wet grassland and mire types are found on enclosed land throughout upland England, and in Devon and Cornwall. Wet grasslands are often associated with M16 *Erica tetralix-Sphagnum compactum* wet heath, and a variety of other mire and heath communities, including the uncommon M29 *Hypericum elodes-Potamogeton polygonifolius* and M21 *Narthecium ossifragum-Sphagnum papillosum* mires (Wolton 1994).

Floodplain grasslands are not a major feature of upland England, although they may occasionally be encountered. The principal communities involved are MG8 *Cynosurus cristatus-Caltha palustris* flood pasture (which can occur in association with MG3) and MG13 *Agrostis stolonifera-Alopecurus geniculatus* inundation grassland. MG4 *Alopecurus pratensis-Sanguisorba officinalis* flood meadow and MG11 *Festuca rubra-Agrostis stolonifera-Potentilla anserina* inundation grassland are also found in this habitat but they are almost, if not entirely, confined to lowland England.

Table 7.1 Plant communities associated with management as pasture

MG5	*Cynosurus cristatus-Centaurea nigra* grassland
MG6	*Lolium perenne-Cynosurus cristatus* grassland
MG7	*Lolium perenne* leys
MG8	*Cynosurus cristatus-Caltha palustris* grassland
MG9	*Holcus lanatus-Deschampsia cespitosa* grassland
MG10	*Holcus lanatus-Juncus effusus* rush pasture
MG11	*Festuca rubra-Agrostis stolonifera-Potentilla anserina* grassland
MG13	*Agrostis stolonifera-Alopecurus geniculatus* inundation grassland
CG2	*Festuca ovina-Avenula pratensis* grassland
CG3	*Bromopsis erectus* grassland
CG6	*Avenula pubescens* grassland
CG7	*Festuca ovina-Pilosella officinarum-Thymus polytrichus* grassland
CG9	*Sesleria caerulea-Galium sterneri* grassland
CG10	*Festuca ovina-Agrostis capillaris-Thymus polytrichus* grassland
U1	*Festuca ovina-Agrostis capillaris-Rumex acetosella* grassland
U2	*Deschampsia flexuosa* grassland
U3	*Agrostis curtisii* grassland
U4	*Festuca ovina-Agrostis capillaris-Galium saxatile* grassland
U5	*Nardus stricta-Galium saxatile* grassland
M15	*Trichophorum cespitosus-Erica tetralix* wet heath
M16	*Erica tetralix-Sphagnum compactum* wet heath
M22	*Juncus subnodulosus-Cirsium palustre* fen meadow
M23	*Juncus effusus/acutiflorus-Galium palustre* rush pasture
M24	*Molinia caerulea-Cirsium dissectum* fen meadow
M25	*Molinia caerulea-Potentilla erecta* mire
M26	*Molinia caerulea-Crepis paludosa* mire

Table 7.2 Plant communities associated with hay meadow management

Principal hay meadow communities	
MG3	*Anthoxanthum odoratum-Geranium sylvaticum* grassland
MG4	*Alopecurus pratensis-Sanguisorba officinalis* grassland
MG5	*Cynosurus cristatus-Centaurea nigra* grassland
Communities which may occasionally be mown for hay	
MG8	*Cynosurus cristatus-Caltha palustris* grassland
MG13	*Agrostis stolonifera-Alopecurus geniculatus* inundation grassland
M22	*Juncus subnodulosus-Cirsium palustre* fen meadow
M23	*Juncus effusus/acutiflorus-Galium palustre* rush pasture
M24	*Molinia caerulea-Cirsium dissectum* fen meadow
M25	*Molinia caerulea-Potentilla erecta* mire
M26	*Molinia caerulea-Crepis paludosa* mire
M27	*Filipendula ulmaria-Angelica sylvestris* mire

7.4.4 Birds

Enclosed upland pastures and meadows are of outstanding importance for birds. Not only can they support very high densities of breeding waders, such as curlew *Numenius arquata*, redshank *Tringa totanus*, lapwing *Vanellus vanellus* and snipe *Gallinago gallinago*, but they are also used for feeding before, during and after the breeding season by many of the birds which nest on adjacent moors, including merlin *Falco columbarius*.

Upland enclosed pastures are of considerable importance for a number of small passerines, including the skylark *Alauda arvensis*, which has suffered a major decline in its UK population during the last 25 years. Another increasingly rare bird, the black grouse *Tetrao tetrix*, uses upland grassland for feeding and breeding purposes. The corncrake *Crex crex* was once characteristic of meadows throughout Britain, but changes in grassland management, particularly the move from hay to silage with its earlier cutting dates, has caused its widespread loss from the English uplands. These three species - skylark, black grouse and corncrake - are all included in the UK Biodiversity Action Plan and Species Action Plans have been prepared for them (UK Biodiversity Group 1998; UK Steering Group 1995).

Breeding bird species which are positively associated with the uplands (as defined in Stillman & Brown 1998) and also with enclosed grasslands in England are shown in Table 7.14. Additional birds of conservation concern (RSPB 1996), for example skylark and lapwing, occur in these areas but are not positively associated with the uplands. Significant portions of the English populations of these birds nevertheless breed in the uplands and further details of these species can be found in the relevant Species Action Plans which have or will soon be completed as part of the UK Biodiversity Action Plan (UK Biodiversity Group 1998; UK Steering Group 1995).

7.4.5 Invertebrates

Most types of semi-natural grasslands are of considerable interest for invertebrates, with each grassland type supporting its own suite of species. Upland calcareous grasslands, including some enclosed pastures, are of particular importance for a number of nationally rare, scarce and uncommon butterfly species including the northern brown argus *Aricia artaxerxes* which feeds on common rock-rose, and the small blue *Cupido minimus* which feeds on kidney vetch *Anthyllis vulneraria*. Where there is some scrub or bracken such grassland may be important for the high brown fritillary *Argynnis adippe*, pearl-bordered fritillary *Boloria euphrosyne* and dark green fritillary *Argynnis aglaia*, which feed on violets *Viola* spp., particularly growing under fairly sparse bracken *Pteridium aquilinum*, as well as the Duke of Burgundy *Hemearis lucina*, which feeds on cowslip *Primula veris* and primrose *Primula vulgaris*.

The marsh fritillary *Eurodryas aurinia* and narrow-bordered bee hawk *Hemaris tityus* are species of wet grassland with devil's-bit scabious *Succisa pratensis* in south western and north western England. The heath fritillary *Mellicta athalia* feeds on a number of weedy species, notably ribwort plantain *Plantago lanceolata*, foxglove *Digitalis purpurea* and cow-wheat *Melampyrum pratense*, in sheltered upland grassland in the south west. Some root-feeding invertebrates favour upland grasslands, such as the click beetle *Anostirus castaneus*, which occurs at a single site in scrubby acid grassland in North Yorkshire in addition to the Isle of Wight.

Hay meadows support a very different, and usually depauperate invertebrate fauna compared to pastures. This is because the annual cutting of the sward interrupts the life-cycle of many species so that they are unable to survive under this management regime. However, the root-feeding click beetle, *Selatosomus pectinicornis*, favours old hay meadows, mainly in the north and west. Hay meadows and their surrounding hedgerows also provide an important food source for nectar feeding species during the period before they are cut.

Many of the species mentioned above are included in the UK Biodiversity Action Plan and Species Action Plans have been prepared for them (UK Steering Group 1995; UK Biodiversity Group 1998).

Further information: Barnett & Warren 1995a-e; Bourn & Warren 1998; Drake *et al* 1998; Kirby 1992; Ravenscroft & Warren 1996.

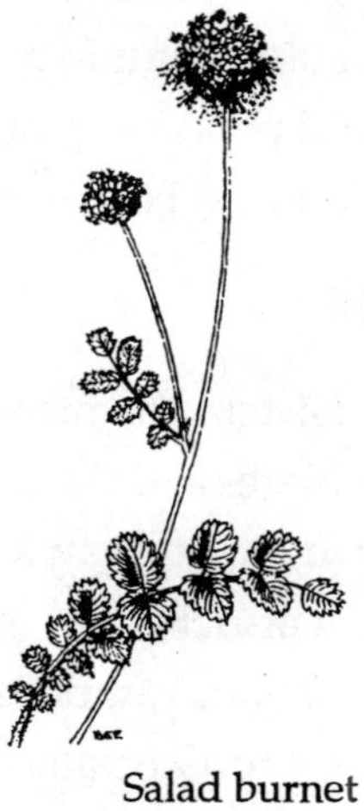

Salad burnet

7.4.6 Mammals

The value of enclosed upland grasslands for mammals depends upon the location, extent and management of the grassland (Table 7.16). In general, cut or heavily grazed grassland is of limited use to native mammals.

Upland meadows and enclosed pastures can support several mammal species, particularly field voles *Microtus agrestis* and shrews *Sorex* spp. where the grassland is structurally diverse. While these species are widespread and generally abundant, small mammals are an important component of the food chain, being important prey items for birds of prey, reptiles and carnivorous mammals. Areas rich with dung from domestic animals support many invertebrates, notably dung beetles and dung flies, which provide food for bats. Bats tend to favour field margins and woodland edges when foraging, and these features also provide food and shelter for other small mammals. Larger mammals such as foxes *Vulpes vulpes*, badgers *Meles meles* and roe deer *Capreolus capreolus* tend to breed in woodland but forage in pastures and meadows.

7.4.7 Amphibians and reptiles

Upland enclosed grassland may be of great importance for reptiles and amphibians and supports several species, including the common lizard *Lacerta vivipara*, common frog *Rana temporaria* and common toad *Bufo bufo* (Table 7.17). It is of value for both groups of animals where it is managed to provide an uneven structure to the vegetation. It is also important where it provides connections between other habitats, such as fragmented woodland or moorland areas, because these animals tend to be relatively poor dispersers. Field margins, such as dry stone walls and boundary banks, often provide habitats of value to reptiles and amphibians.

7.5 Habitat and management requirements of meadow and enclosed pasture species

Typical plant species of these habitats generally require the existing management to be continued, without intensification by reseeding, nutrient inputs or increased grazing pressures.

In general, structurally diverse grasslands are the most valuable, providing both food and cover for a variety of animals. Light grazing is beneficial where it creates a varied structure and prevents scrub encroachment, but heavy grazing (and cutting) results in a short and even sward which is less valuable for wildlife. Light grazing around ponds and other wetland features can favour wildlife by keeping them open, but heavy grazing damages both terrestrial and aquatic vegetation which is required by invertebrates and amphibians.

Where stock are treated with persistent chemicals to remove gut parasites (eg avermectins, see 7.7.5) the dung remains toxic to invertebrates and this in turn removes the food source of many other animals. While some dunging can improve the nutrient status of very nutrient-poor sites, too much can make grasslands and wetlands too nutrient-rich. This may lead, for example, to algal growth and poor water quality in ponds where invertebrates and amphibians breed. However, a very small number of species of specialised scarce invertebrates are associated with high nutrient levels in dung-rich water.

To encourage a diversity of wildlife, management should provide areas of grassland with varied heights and a supply of dung from animals untreated by persistent vermicides. Breeding, feeding and over-wintering areas, such as ponds and other wetlands and woods, should be retained. Manure and compost heaps can also add to biodiversity. Field boundaries such as hedges, dry stone walls and banks should be retained and appropriately managed, both for themselves and to provide connections between other habitats.

Brief habitat and management requirements of key plants, birds, mammals, amphibians and reptiles associated with meadows and enclosed pasture are shown in Tables 7.9, 7.11 and 7.14-7.17. Habitat management for invertebrates of enclosed grasslands is not covered in any further detail because this subject is considered to be adequately addressed in Kirby 1992.

Management of upland meadows and enclosed pasture

7.6 Managing upland meadows and enclosed pasture

This section, together with section 7.7, provides a basic guide to the management of wet and dry grasslands with wildlife interest in the enclosed land below the fell wall. Further information can be found in the *Lowland Grassland Management Handbook* (Crofts & Jefferson 1994, 1999) , *The Wet Grassland Guide: Managing floodplain and coastal wet grasslands for wildlife* (Treweek *et al* 1997) and *European wet grasslands: biodiversity, management and restoration* (Joyce & Wade 1998).

The following sections (7.6.2 to 7.7.7) are particularly relevant for land where some wildlife interest is present, that is semi-natural grasslands, 'wet grasslands' and semi-improved grasslands. Improved grasslands are not considered, although they can be of importance for some breeding and feeding birds. Section 7.6.1 provides a brief introduction to the formulation of an appropriate grassland management regime. The restoration of neglected grasslands and the re-creation of grassland on sites with limited nature conservation interest is considered in section 7.9.

The main agricultural practices which maintain grasslands include grazing, cutting, burning and cultivation; all are discussed in this section of the handbook. Other management practices, including rolling and chain harrowing, and managing pests, weeds, drainage and scrub are covered in the following section (7.7). Changing or stopping management practices can shift grasslands from one type to another. In the absence of some form of management, most types of enclosed grassland would be invaded by woody shrubs and develop into scrub and woodland (Ausden & Treweek 1995; Crofts & Jefferson 1994, 1999).

Most grasslands are used to provide food for livestock. The species composition and vegetation structure (both spatial and temporal) of a grassland is highly dependent on whether it is managed to provide food directly for livestock in the form of grazing, or as conserved fodder in the form of hay and silage. Pastures are grazed but not cut, and meadows are cut for either hay or silage and may or may not be grazed. This fundamental management distinction applies to all grassland types, wet or dry, regardless of substrate. It is uncommon, however, for acid or calcareous grasslands to be managed as meadows, as the most productive land on a farm is usually allocated to hay or silage production; this is invariably the land with deeper, mesotrophic soils and these soils tend to support neutral grasslands.

Table 7.3 shows the 'traditional' management treatments associated with the grassland communities found below the fell wall.

If the nature conservation interest of a grassland is to be maintained or enhanced the basic management practice which has given rise to the plant and animal communities of that field must be continued or, where that management practice has lapsed, reinstated. Unless the management practice of a field is known to have changed in the recent past, switching from meadow management to pasture only, or vice versa, will almost certainly result in a major decline in the wildlife interest of that grassland. It may well result in the loss of any rare or scarce species present in that field.

7.6.1 Establishing management objectives and options

When considering the most appropriate management regime for a particular grassland, information needs to be collected on a number of topics to facilitate the decision making process (see Table 7.4).

As a general principle the management regime of a grassland with known wildlife interest should only be altered where there is clear evidence that the interest is in decline. The most likely cause of such a decline is a change in the management at some point in the relatively recent past. Where this is thought to have occurred then the objective should be to return the management regime to one similar to that which supported the nature conservation interest originally present. Depending on the extent of the decline in the wildlife interest, this may, or may not, require some form of restoration management (see Sections 7.7.6 and 7.9) prior to reintroducing the original management regime.

Where a grassland is of limited nature conservation interest (and this situation is not the result of the degradation of a site previously considered to be of interest) then the site manager will have a greater range of management options. The manager will need to decide which options will result in the greatest increase in nature conservation interest on the site.

Buttercup

Table 7.3 'Traditional' management treatments of semi-natural grassland communities (Adapted from Crofts & Jefferson 1994).

NVC grassland community	Livestock grazing	Mowing & aftermath grazing	Spring grazing, mowing & aftermath grazing	Burning & grazing	Unmanaged/ sporadic management by grazing &/or mowing	Sporadic cultivation/ ploughing/ disturbance	Periodic flooding/ inundation
MG1					✔		
MG2					✔		
MG3			✔				
MG5	✔	✔	✔				
MG8	✔	✔	✔				✔
MG9	✔						
MG10	✔						
MG11	✔	✔					✔
MG13	✔	(✔)					✔
CG2	✔						
CG3	✔				✔		
CG6	✔				✔		
CG7	✔				✔	✔	
CG9	✔						
CG10	✔						
U1	✔					✔	
U2	✔						
U3	✔			✔			
U4	✔						
U5	✔						
M15	✔			✔			
M16	✔			✔			
M22	✔	✔					
M23	✔	✔					
M24	✔	✔					
M25	✔			✔			
M26	✔		✔				
M27					✔		
OV37					✔		

Table 7.4 Information required prior to establishing management objectives and options
(Adapted from Andrews & Rebane 1994)

Information required		Reason for information
Conservation status and interest	Information may already be available - see next column.	Organisations such as county wildlife trusts, English Nature or county/district councils may have already collected information which will assist the decision making process. The majority of unimproved enclosed grasslands will be designated as SSSIs or as Sites of Importance for Nature Conservation (SINCs).
Past management	Grazing regime, mowing practice, surface applications, etc (see current management below) from farm records and other historical information, including aerial photographs and old maps. (The plant species present may give an indication of this where management has lapsed and no other sources of information are available. A number of species are indicative of certain management practices, eg wood crane's-bill *Geranium sylvaticum* is unlikely to be found in permanent pasture.)	Past management practices will have played an important part in the development of a grassland's nature conservation interest. Where the interest is thought to be in decline it is likely that this is due to a change in management practices. Knowledge of how current management differs from previous practices may help formulate an action plan to stem any such decline and may provide a template for the new management regime.
Current management	Grazing regime: including livestock types, stocking rates, timing of grazing, use of supplementary feeding.	It is essential to know what the current grazing regime is. This will form the basis of the future regime, with adjustments, where required, based on the other information collected, particularly indicators of over or under-grazing.
	Mowing practice: including cutting dates and methods and details of grazing.	Again essential information needed if the nature conservation value is to be maintained or enhanced. This should be used in conjunction with the other information collected and adjusted where necessary.
	Use of surface applications such as lime, compound fertilisers and farm yard manure, including application rates.	The application of these surface treatments can have deleterious affects on the species composition of grasslands. The nature conservation interest of many grasslands has declined due to changes (almost invariably increases) in the use of surface treatments, particularly compound fertilisers. Some 'traditional' hay meadow regimes do, however, include use of farm yard manure or lime.
	Other management practices such as chain harrowing, rolling, burning etc.	Such practices can be harmful to the nature conservation interest of sites, or may be the key to any unusual features present.
	Weed control measures.	Weed control measures can be harmful to the nature conservation interest of grasslands.

	Information required	Reason for information
Stock boundaries	The condition of fences, hedges, walls and ditches needs to be known.	Boundaries need to be stock proof where grazing is to be a feature of the management regime.
Hydrology	Map those areas which flood (and record the season when flooded), or are flushed, and the presence of mires, ponds, water courses and the location of drains/dikes.	The hydrology of the site may have important implications for site management, including type of stock used and use of machinery.
Grassland structure and composition	Species composition, including species abundance.	Species composition will tend to indicate past management.
	Map the location and extent of tall coarse grassland, tussocks and areas with a deep litter layer.	These features can be indicative of under-grazing.
	Map the location and extent of bare ground, gappy swards, very closely grazed swards and the presence of 'injurious weeds'.	These features can be indicative of overgrazing.
	Map the location of trees, scrub and bracken.	Invasion by these features may indicate a lapse in management practices, though this could be historical rather than current. On larger sites these can enhance the nature conservation interest, but on smaller sites where the interest is primarily grassland then they may be deleterious to the nature conservation interest.
	Map the location of rare or scarce species present, including plants, breeding birds and butterflies.	The specific habitat requirements of any uncommon species present may need to be accommodated in the management regime.
Other features	Record features such as anthills, earth banks and ridge and furrow systems.	Anthills are indicative of old pasture and will be destroyed by the rolling and harrowing. Other features may be of historical/archeological interest.

7.6.2 Managing pastures

The majority of enclosed grassland in the uplands is managed as pasture, as are most, if not all, of the wet grasslands and mire communities that are found here. Pastures are managed principally by grazing and are normally not cut. Exceptions include, for example, methods of controlling rushes by topping.

Stock type

The type of stock used to graze a grassland is a significant determinant of the vegetation structure and species composition of a grassland sward. The three main livestock animals used in England, sheep, cattle and horses, all have different grazing attributes, and these are summarised in Table 7.5. In general, sheep are the most widely used stock, largely due to their cheapness and relative ease of handling. In a number of situations, however, cattle are preferable for conservation management, particularly where the ground is marshy or a tussocky sward structure is required. Ponies are relatively uncommon in the uplands, but they can be invaluable for nature conservation management where other stock are unavailable. Goats are not generally favoured by land managers, but in specific circumstances they can be useful, particularly for restoration management (section 7.9).

Table 7.5 Grazing attributes of sheep, cattle, horses and goats

Livestock type	Positive attributes	Negative attributes
Sheep	Readily available and cheap, relatively easy to handle.	Most breeds will not eat long or coarse grass and unsuitable for scrub control or restoration grazing.
	Produce uniform, tightly grazed sward, especially at high stocking densities.	Produce uniform, tightly grazed sward, especially at high stocking densities - poor for invertebrates.
	Light so do not cause trampling damage.	Unsuitable for particularly wet situations as susceptible to disease.
Cattle	Create a less uniform sward than sheep at lower stocking densities - greater structural diversity for invertebrates and tussocks are a requirement for many waders to breed.	Expensive to buy and valuable - farmers maybe less willing to graze cattle on semi-natural grassland due to its low productivity.
	Will maintain a short sward at higher stocking densities.	Harder to transport and handle than sheep. More likely to be treated with avermectins than sheep or goats.
	Trample and eat coarse grasses and will browse scrub - can be used for restoration grazing.	Require large amounts of water.
	Low level trampling damage and light poaching can be beneficial in providing niches for both invertebrates and short-lived plants, especially in upland calcareous or dry acid grassland.	Can cause trampling damage at higher stocking rates, particularly in winter, leading to weed infestations and erosion.
Ponies	Produce patchily grazed sward which can support diverse invertebrate communities.	Graze more palatable species, selectively - can result in overgrazed areas and uneaten coarse stands if stocking rate is too high.
	Native breeds of ponies are relatively cheap, require minimal handling and will eat coarse grasses and scrub-making them useful for restoration grazing.	Tend to have specific latrine areas which they do not graze - also result in localised nutrient enrichment and can lead to stands of nutrient demanding weeds. More likely to be treated with avermectins than sheep or goats.
	Low level trampling damage can be beneficial in providing niches for both invertebrates and short-lived plants.	Can cause trampling damage at higher stocking rates, particularly in winter, leading to weed infestations and erosion.
Goats	Preferential browsers so useful for dealing with scrub (but not birch or conifers).	Will tend to browse rather than graze so may be of limited use where grazing is the main requirement.
	Will eat and hence help to control rushes, tufted hair-grass and mat-grass at high stocking densities.	Handling and containment can be problematic and all goats require shelter.

The grazing attributes of livestock also vary between breeds. As a general rule upland and older breeds are most suitable for nature conservation and sustainable grazing. These tend to have originated in the north and west of Britain. These hardy breeds are able to utilise vegetation of low nutritional quality, require less husbandry and are more 'hard mouthed' than more modern or lowland breeds. 'Hard mouthed' breeds are less selective grazers than 'soft mouthed' breeds and will also browse scrub. Information Notes 3 and 5 provide more information on sheep and cattle breeds, as do Crofts & Jefferson (1994, 1999).

The grazing habits of stock also vary with age. With cattle, store animals, fattening beef animals and sucklers are the most suitable for environmentally sustainable management. With sheep, ewe or wether lambs (store lambs), barren or dry ewes and mature wethers are most likely to be suitable. It is important to note, however, that young and old stock are more 'soft mouthed' than 'middle aged' animals and so may not be suitable where coarse vegetation is to be grazed.

Stocking levels

The establishment of an appropriate stocking regime is vital if the wildlife value of a grassland is to be maintained or enhanced. Both too much and too little grazing can lead to a decline in the biodiversity of a sward. A wide variety of factors play a part in determining what the appropriate level will be and it is not possible to provide a precise guide here. The following general principles, however, should enable a land manager to draw up an appropriate regime to achieve both biodiversity and sustainable agriculture objectives once local factors have been taken into consideration. Where breeding waders are present the factors discussed in Section 7.8.1 should also be taken into account.

An example of management for wildlife on limestone grassland is given in Box 7.1.

Table 7.6 A guide to stocking rates for lowland grassland (animals per hectare)

No of grazing weeks per year	Calcareous grassland		Neutral grassland		Acidic grassland		Wet/marshy grassland	
	Sheep	Cattle	Sheep	Cattle	Sheep	Cattle	Sheep	Cattle
2	60	15	100	25	50	12	50	12
4	30	8	50	12.5	25	6	25	6
6	20	5	33	8	16	4	16	4
8	15	4	25	6	12	3	12	3
10	12	3	20	5	10	2.5	10	2.5
12	10	2.5	17	4	8	2	8	2
14	8.5	2	14	3.5	7	1.5	7	2
16	7.5	2	12.5	3	6	1.5	6	1.5
20	6	1.5	10	2.5	5	1	5	1
24	5	1	8	2	4	1	4	1
36	3.5	1	5.5	1.5	3	0.5	3	0.5
52	2.5	0.5	4	1	2	0.4	2	0.4
Annual stocking rate LU/ha/yr	0.25	0.25	0.5	0.5	0.2	0.2	0.2	0.2

Source: Nature Conservancy Council 1986b and Crofts & Jefferson 1999

The best guides to establishing an appropriate grazing regime are the vegetation composition, structure and sward height (Andrews & Rebane 1994). Management objectives will vary, but in general a sward height of 5-10 cm at the end of any particular grazing period should be the aim (unless tall grass is required for other conservation reasons; Crofts & Jefferson 1994, 1999). Reliable historical records of stocking levels can provide a useful starting point, but, where these are not available, the figures in Table 7.6 may provide a useful guide in more lowland situations. Table 7.7 gives examples of the stocking regimes required by various environmental land management schemes. They are, however, only a guide but may also help to provide a starting point.

Whatever the basis for the stocking rate used, regular assessment of the sward should be undertaken and the stocking rate adjusted as appropriate. Note, however, that stock may not be able to keep up with sward growth during the peak growing season, but they will generally be able to 'catch up' as productivity declines, to produce the desired sward height by the beginning of the next growing season.

Table 7.7 Examples of stocking rates for different vegetation types as specified by various environmental land management schemes

Scheme	Vegetation type	Stocking rate
Tir Gofal (Welsh Office *et al* 1999)	Whole farm.	Overall stocking rates should not exceed 2.4 LU/ha. Should not exceed levels carried in 1998.
	High mountain heath-moss and lichen heath + low-mat dwarf shrubs.	Not more than 0.05 LU/ha/yr. Remove all animals between October and March.
	Upland heath - >25% cover heathers, bilberry and other dwarf shrubs with variable amounts of coarse grasses.	Not more than 0.225 LU/ha/yr (dry heath) OR 0.1 LU/ha/yr (wet heath). At least 25% of stock removed between October and March.
	Unimproved acid grassland - dominated by sheep's fescue, bents, wavy hair-grass and mat-grass or heath rush.	Not more than 0.4 LU/ha/yr (can be increased up to 0.75 LU/ha/yr where dominated by bents and fescues).
	Unimproved neutral grassland - includes flower-rich and pastures below mountain wall.	Not more than 0.75 LU/ha/yr.
	Unimproved limestone grassland.	Not more than 0.4 LU/ha/yr. On limestone pavements not more than 0.15 LU/ha/yr.
	Semi-improved grasslands/hay meadows.	Not more than 1 LU/ha/yr (neutral) or 0.75/LU/ha/yr (acid or limestone).
	Marshy grassland.	Not more than 0.4 LU/ha/yr.
	Acid peatlands - blanket bog/lowland raised bog.	Not more than 0.05 LU/ha/yr. Avoid grazing between October and March.

Scheme	Vegetation type	Stocking rate
Countryside Stewardship Scheme (MAFF 1999)	Hay meadows.	Cut sward should be lightly grazed to achieve an average sward height of 20-50 mm through the winter period.
	Grazed pastures (lowland pasture & upland in-bye pasture).	April-December: at least 10 weeks light grazing, aiming to produce a sward height of 20-50 mm at end of grazing period (no stocking figures given). March-August: light grazing 'for a number of months' at 0.6 LU/ha may be required.
	Upland rough grazing pastures.	As for pastures but stocking should not exceed 0.25LU/ha.
	Culm grassland.	As for pastures except that grazing should be at a low level over a period of time and aim for a sward that is less than 15 cm for at least part of grazing season. Autumn or winter grazing is acceptable where there is no risk of poaching.
	Chalk and limestone grassland.	Graze lightly with sheep and/or cattle for at least 10 weeks in each year. Aim to produce an average sward height of 75 mm by end of summer. Stocking should not normally exceed 0.75 LU/ha.
	Upland limestone grasslands.	As for chalk & limestone but "rest the pasture" by limiting sheep grazing to 0.1 LU/ha and remove all cattle for a period of at least eight weeks between May and August.
	Regenerating suppressed heather moor: Heather comprises less than 25% of sward - aim to achieve 40-50% heather cover in years 1-5.	First year lightly graze summer grass growth between June and July, and between April and July in subsequent years. Stocking should not exceed 1 sheep/ha and livestock should be excluded at all other times. After achieving 40-50% heather cover, light winter grazing may be reintroduced with the aim of achieving 50-70% heather cover by year 10. Summer sheep grazing can be increased progressively to a maximum of 1.5 sheep/ha between lambing and tupping. Winter grazing not to exceed 0.75 sheep/ha between tupping and lambing.

Scheme	Vegetation type	Stocking rate
	Enhancing heather moorland: Heather comprises 25-50% of the sward.	Summer and winter stocking levels are set in accordance with the type and condition of vegetation on the moor subject to general maxima: • maximum summer stocking (lambing to tupping) 1.5 sheep/ha; • maximum winter stocking (tupping to lambing) 0.75 sheep/ha; • where appropriate, light summer cattle grazing; • no cattle on moor (1 October-31 March).
	Management of heather moorland habitat.	Heather in good condition. Additional stock reductions may be agreed to speed up regeneration or to accommodate rare or unusual species.
Clun Environmentally Sensitive Area (ESA) (MAFF 1998a)	Wet areas. [Applicable to wet pasture.]	Exclude stock between 1 April and 30 June. Graze so as not to cause poaching, over grazing or under-grazing at other times.
Dartmoor ESA (MAFF 1998b)	Dry grass moorland (Tier 1 - maintenance). [Applicable to acid grassland.]	Do not exceed 0.36 LU/ha (excluding ponies) between 16 April and 31 October. Do not exceed 0.235 LU/ha (excluding ponies) between 1 November and 15 April. Do not exceed 0.04 LU/ha for ponies.
	Moorland (Tier 1 - maintenance). [Applicable to other moorland including heath and blanket bog.]	Do not exceed 0.225 LU/ha (excluding ponies) between 16 April and 31 October. Do not exceed 0.17 LU/ha (excluding ponies) between 1 November and 15 April. Do not exceed 0.04 LU/ha for ponies.
	Heather moorland (Tier 2). [Applicable to acid grassland, heath and blanket bog. Designed to increase the area and improve the condition of heather moorland.]	Do not exceed 0.17 LU/ha (excluding ponies) between 16 April and 31 August. Do not exceed 0.08 LU/ha (excluding ponies) between 1 September and 15 April. Do not exceed 0.04 LU/ha for ponies.
Exmoor ESA (MAFF 1998c)	Heather moorland and coastal heath (Tier 1 - maintenance). [Applicable to dry heath.]	Do not exceed 0.225 LU/ha throughout the year. Between 1 November and 15 April: • remove all cattle; • graze with sheep at no more than 1 ewe/ha; • pony grazing only with written approval.

Scheme	Vegetation type	Stocking rate
	Heather moorland and coastal heath (Tier 2). [Applicable to dry heath. Designed to increase the area and improve the condition of heather moorland.]	Do not exceed 0.1 LU/ha between 16 April and 31 October. Remove all livestock other than pure-bred Exmoor ponies between 1 November and 15 April.
Lake District ESA (MAFF 1998d)	Fell without heather. [Applicable to areas of acid grassland].	Do not exceed 0.3 LU/ha.
	Intermediate heather fell. [Applicable to areas with a mosaic of dry heath and acid grassland. Designed to increase the extent of heath and improve its quality.]	Do not exceed 0.15 LU/ha. Between 1 December and 28 February remove: • all cattle; • all replacement hoggs; • 25% of remaining livestock units (ie 25% of overwintering ewes).
	Heather fell (Tier 1 - maintenance). [Applicable to areas of dry heath.]	Do not exceed 0.225 LU/ha throughout the year. Between 1 October and 28 February remove: • all cattle; • all replacement hoggs; • 25% of remaining livestock units (ie 25% of overwintering ewes).
	Heather fell (Tier 2). [Applicable to areas of dry heath. Designed to increase the extent of heath and improve its quality.]	Do not exceed 0.1 LU/ha throughout the year. Between 1 October and 28 February remove: • all cattle; • all replacement hoggs; • 25% of remaining livestock units (ie 25% of overwintering ewes).
Shropshire Hills ESA (MAFF 1998e)	Moorland (Tier 1 - maintenance). [Applicable to heather and other semi-natural upland vegetation.]	Do not exceed 0.225 LU/ha. Between 1 November and 28 February remove: • all cattle; • 25% of remaining livestock units (ie 25% of overwintering ewes).
	Heather moorland (Tier 2). [Applicable to heather and other semi-natural upland vegetation. Designed to increase the area and improve the condition of heather moorland.]	Do not exceed 0.1 LU/ha between 1 March and 31 October. Remove all livestock between 1 November and 28 February.

Scheme	Vegetation type	Stocking rate
South West Peak ESA (MAFF 1998f)	Extensive pastures.	Limit stock numbers between 1 April and 30 June to no more than 0.6 LU/ha. Graze so as not to cause poaching, overgrazing or under-grazing at other times.
	Wet areas. [Applicable to wet pasture.]	Exclude stock between 1 April and 30 June. Graze so as not to cause poaching, overgrazing or under-grazing at other times.
	Moorland (Tier 1 - maintenance). [Applicable to dry heath, acid grassland and blanket bog.]	Do not exceed 0.225 LU/ha throughout the year. Between 1 November and 28 February remove: • all cattle & horses; • all sheep replacements; • 25% of remaining livestock units (ie 25% of overwintering ewes).
	Moorland (Tier 2). [Designed to enhance the wildlife value of moorland.]	Do not exceed 0.1 LU/ha between 1 March and 30 September. Remove all livestock between 1 October and 28 February.
ESAs general (MAFF 1998 a, b, c, d, e & f)	Low-input permanent grassland, unimproved pasture, enclosed rough land/grazing, intake and in-bye (except where other regimes are specified above).	Do not graze so as to cause poaching, overgrazing or under-grazing. Additional grazing supplements (eg for off-wintering) are normally available.

Table 7.8 The effects of grazing at different times of year
(Adapted from Crofts & Jefferson 1994)

Timing	Advantages	Disadvantages
Spring (April/May)	Useful where the dominant species is particularly unpalatable, eg mat-grass, rushes, tor-grass etc. Checks growth of scrub seedlings and in some cases can be used to check growth of ragwort. Can be beneficial for invertebrates in creating bare ground.	Continual spring grazing on sites with early flowering plants such as early purple orchid *Orchis mascula* and green-winged orchid *O. morio* can cause local extinctions. Continual heavy grazing at this time can prevent development of structural diversity in the sward and considerably reduce the diversity of invertebrates present. Trampling of eggs and chicks can be a problem where waders breed.
Summer (May-September)	Can help control tall herb species such as meadowsweet *Filipendula ulmaria*. Less nutrient build up from animal dung due to greater micro-bacterial processes.	At high stocking rates grazing removes flowers, reducing nectar sources for invertebrates and lessens aesthetic appeal for visitors. Also reduces structural variability of sward, which is important for tussock-dwelling invertebrates, web-spinning spiders, and flower- and seed-feeding species. Heavy grazing pressure can prevent flowers from setting seed. Although perennials will be able to persist in a vegetative form, continual summer grazing will affect the abundance of annual species.
Autumn (September/ October)	Least damaging time for sensitive invertebrates. Has little effect on most species which finish flowering and set seed before this time. May help seeds to establish through trampling.	Removes flowers of late flowering species such as devil's-bit scabious *Succisa pratensis*. This can have a knock-on effect for the marsh fritillary butterfly *Euphydryas aurinia* which depends on this species for food. Also reduces/eliminates seed heads, which are important for species such as picture-winged flies, which use seed heads of composites (as does winter grazing).
Winter (October-April)	Most grassland herbs are not directly affected by winter grazing as they are generally dormant (depending on weather to some extent). May encourage tillering of some grass species. Less damaging to invertebrates which are usually over-wintering in the base of tussocks. Moderate trampling breaks up the litter layer exposing ground for colonising by annuals the next spring.	Heavy trampling can lead to poaching and infestation by weed species. Does not remove as many nutrients by grazing. More nutrients from dung absorbed by soil as lower levels of micro-bacterial activity. Stock may lose condition. Hard winter grazing which removes all plant litter and tussock structure can destroy the habitat of many over-wintering invertebrates.

Duration and timing of grazing

As Table 7.7 suggests, it is not simply the number of stock that is important; the length of time and season they graze a field is important as well. The same grazing level (but not necessarily outcome) can be achieved both by grazing throughout the year and by grazing with a larger number of animals for only part of the year. Short periods of intense grazing can be useful in problem situations, but the rapid defoliation which results can be catastrophic for many invertebrates, so careful consideration is required before such action is implemented. In many situations the duration of grazing is dictated by when stock are available, and this is particularly so when the land manager is relying on a third party to supply the stock.

The timing of the grazing period can greatly affect the nature conservation interest of a grassland sward. It is not just the vegetation that is affected; bird and invertebrate populations that utilise the grassland will also be affected by the time of year at which grazing occurs. Table 7.8 summarises the effects of grazing at different times of year.

The duration and timing of grazing are also affected by the way stock utilise the ground. They do not always graze an area evenly, because some vegetation is more palatable than others and some areas are closer to the farm, water or feeding points, or are more sheltered. Shepherding will also affect the distribution and hence the impact of the stock across the land (see Chapter 6).

Surface treatments

Unimproved pasture

Application of artificial and organic fertilisers 'straight' N (nitrogen) and compound NPK (nitrogen, phosphorous and potassium), hoof and horn meal, dried blood and liquid seaweed rapidly reduces the species richness and diversity of semi-natural swards, even at low application rates such as 25 kg/ha/year of inorganic N. The use of such fertilisers is generally unacceptable on any type of semi-natural unimproved grassland if the nature conservation interest is to be maintained (Crofts & Jefferson 1994, 1999). Likewise, slurry and sewage sludge provide an immediate source of N, P and K and their application seriously damages the nature conservation interest of semi-natural grasslands. Therefore, they should not be applied.

Well rotted farm yard manure should not be applied to semi-natural grassland managed solely as pasture.

Lime should not be applied to semi-natural acidic grasslands (NVC communities U1 to U5) or calcium deficient neutral grassland (NVC MG5c *Danthonia decumbens* sub-community). Application of lime to other neutral and calcareous grasslands is acceptable where this is a proven long-established practice. It should not, however, be used where there is an intimate mosaic of calcareous and acidic grasslands or heath communities. Lime should be applied no more frequently than once every five to 10 years and at no more than three tonnes per hectare of calcium oxide (CaO) equivalent in any one dressing (Crofts & Jefferson 1994, 1999).

'Semi-improved' pasture

There are extensive areas of 'semi-improved' pasture in the enclosed uplands. Much of this land will have received low levels of nutrient input for many decades and some will be formerly improved pasture which is reverting to unimproved grassland because the nutrient inputs have stopped and the drainage changed. While this grassland is of lower nature conservation interest than unimproved pasture it can still be of considerable importance, particularly in areas where there is little or no unimproved grassland. Without surface treatments these grasslands may, in the medium to long term, revert to unimproved grassland.

Two management options are available for this type of pasture:

1. Initiate the reversion of the sward to unimproved semi-natural grassland by ceasing all applications of fertilisers, farm yard manure, slurry or lime.

2. Maintain the sward in its semi-improved state by continuing light applications of fertilisers and/or lime at low levels. Application rates should not, in general, exceed 50-100 kg/ha of artificial fertilisers or 12-20 tonnes/ha of well rotted farm yard manure per year. Lime should be applied no more frequently than once every five to 10 years and at no more than three tonnes per hectare of calcium oxide (CaO) equivalent in any one dressing.

Which option is taken will depend on the management objectives for (and particular nature conservation interest) of the pasture in question.

Allotments

Many allotments which lie adjacent to unenclosed moorland support identical vegetation to that of the unenclosed moorland. Where this is so they should be managed in a similar manner to the moorland. The management of dry heath, blanket mire, bracken and unenclosed grasslands is covered in Chapter 6, but see also Table 7.7.

Where allotments have been agriculturally improved or have a low wildlife value, they can benefit nature conservation by being used in a two pasture system (Mowforth & Sydes 1989). This involves using them for grazing only when herbage quality is most important to the stock. For sheep this is in the autumn prior to tupping and in the spring immediately before lambing and during lactation. In this way, lamb production can be maintained while effects on adjacent moorland are reduced. It enables the fell vegetation to achieve a higher nature conservation quality than would otherwise be agriculturally feasible.

Box 7.1 Example of limestone grassland management for wildlife

English Nature Craven Limestone Grassland Wildlife Enhancement Scheme (WES)

The Craven limestone grassland WES operates within the Craven District of North Yorkshire and applies to a series of Sites of Special Scientific Interest (SSSI) in the Yorkshire Dales. These SSSIs contain species-rich limestone grassland and the scheme aims to maintain and enhance the wildlife interest of the land.

The scheme allows for a variety of management regimes to increase the nature conservation condition of limestone grassland. The standard prescription (Tier 1) is as follows (Mercer & Evans 1997):

- Graze stock at no more than 1 ewe/ha (or equivalent) for any continuous period of eight weeks between 1 May and 31 August.
- At any other time graze stock at no more than 2 ewes/ha (or equivalent). Grazing rates may be higher when gathering stock on up to five separate days per year.
- Ideally, in summer cattle should be grazed, rather than sheep.
- Livestock equivalents are calculated on the basis of 5 ewes = 1 adult cow/bull/bullock.
- Milking dairy cows may not be grazed.
- Lambs (up to 1 October) and calves at foot are included in stocking rates for adult stock.
- Any control of thistles should be by mechanical means or chemical spot treatment.
- Any winter stock feeding must be carried out in specified areas without causing poaching and any waste must be cleaned away.
- No application of farmyard manure, slurry, artificial fertiliser or lime.
- All wet areas must be retained.
- Rabbits must be controlled.

Two examples of the effects of this regime are summarised below (Mercer & Evans 1997).

A different set of prescriptions apply to areas of limestone pavement and woodland.

Malham-Arncliffe SSSI (The Gill)

The effect of five years under this management regime following 10 years of heavy stocking (5-6ewes/ha, with stock removed in late summer) on two key limestone grassland plant species has been beneficial. Results from the Malham-Arncliffe (The Gill) monitoring programme show the following:

	1991 (start of management agreement)	1996
Mountain avens *Dryas octopetala*	9 (no flowers)	21 (4 flowers)
Rock rose *Helianthemum nummularium*	129	147

Lords Wood Pasture SSSI

The reintroduction of light autumn grazing in accordance with Tier 1 stocking rates following a period where grazing was absent, resulted in new site records for northern brown argus *Aricia artaxeres* and small skipper *Thymelius flavus* butterflies. Autumn grazing removed the coarse vegetation that had built up when there was no grazing, resulting in abundant flowering of species such as rock rose *Helianthemum nummularium*, ladies bedstraw *Galium verum* and bird's-foot trefoil *Lotus corniculatus* in the slightly calcareous grassland.

7.6.3 Managing meadows

A meadow is any grassland mown to produce a conserved forage crop. Two basic systems of meadow management are practised in the UK today: hay production and silage production. The principal difference between the two systems is that hay is allowed to dry in the field after it is cut, so that its moisture content is reduced to around 20-25%. This usually takes about three rain-free days, after which the hay is stored as unwrapped bales. In silage production, the cut grass is kept in a relatively moist state (moisture content is reduced from 80% in the uncut grass to 70-75%) and stored in anaerobic conditions, either in clamps or in big bales wrapped in polythene.

Hay making tends to be practised in less intensive farming systems. Fertiliser inputs tend to be lower and reseeding with high yield grasses is less common. In some cases swards may have been in existence for centuries. In hay making systems only one crop is harvested in the year, usually in July, which is generally after ground-nesting birds have left the nest.

Silage production is a more capital intensive system than hay making, so it tends to be used on larger, more intensive farms. Because of the high initial capital investment (for equipment and machinery) there is a requirement to maximise returns and consequently silage systems tend to use high inputs of fertilisers to maximise production. This allows several grass crops to be harvested each year, starting in late April/mid-May, although in some cases only one cut is taken per season (big-bale silage). An early cutting date has a detrimental effect on ground-nesting birds, for example corncrake, which will still be on the nest at this time. To maximise yields, most fields in silage production are sown with high yielding varieties of perennial rye-grass *Lolium perenne*.

Fields managed for silage tend to be of limited nature conservation interest, owing to the species-poor swards and the early cutting date, although they may support ground-nesting and wintering birds and provide feeding grounds for breeding waders. Big-bale silage fields may contain more wildlife value because they are cut only once and can be composed of less agriculturally improved swards. Hay meadows where 'traditional' low input management has continued to the present day can be of considerable importance for biodiversity.

This section is largely concerned with those hay meadows where the continuance of 'traditional' management practices has resulted in species-rich swards. The main meadow management system encountered in the uplands is the northern hay meadow type, which has produced a characteristic plant community (NVC community MG3). However, other systems and communities may also be encountered (see Table 7.2). In Britain calcareous and acidic grasslands are rarely managed for hay production.

Cutting/mowing

Mowing differs from grazing in its effect on the sward in several ways. It is non-selective, results in a sudden removal of biomass, does not produce patchiness in the vegetation and does not create open ground and gaps in the sward. Bare patches are important for invertebrates and the establishment of new plants. As a result cutting can produce a very different species composition compared with that produced through grazing.

Hay meadows are frequently of limited value for invertebrates except as a nectar source, and so are not generally the primary objective of hay meadow management for conservation. This is because cutting alone is poor for invertebrates; it results in a sudden defoliation and low structural diversity. It can be used for invertebrate conservation, however, preferably on a rotational basis, where grazing is not possible (see 7.8.2).

Timing of cutting

The timing of the cut is greatly influenced by environmental factors such as climate, altitude and aspect. Summer weather can be very unsettled in the uplands and a certain amount of flexibility is required. Generally speaking northern (Pennine and Lake District) hay meadows are normally cut in mid- to late-July, while farther south cutting may take place between mid-June to early July. As the species-richness of meadows has been created and maintained by traditional meadow management, continuing traditional cutting times is recommended to maintain this interest. Cutting should not take place during the bird breeding season, which is defined as 15 March to 15 July, to prevent eggs and young being destroyed. Where reliable historical information is not available, the dates above can be used as a guide. Repeated early cutting has been shown to reduce species-richness (Smith 1994), and for nature conservation purposes an occasional late cut (in August or September, once every five years) is thought to be beneficial for late flowering species (Andrews & Rebane 1994; Crofts & Jefferson 1994, 1999).

Methods

Hay is usually cut using drum or disc mowers driven by the power take-off (PTO) on the back of the tractor. Cutting should be straight forward, though several factors should be taken into account:

- Avoid low cutting heights as this can scalp the ground, producing areas suitable for weed invasion.

- Mowing from the centre of the field outwards or from side to side will allow breeding birds and mammals to escape.

- The use of machinery in damp conditions can result in rutting which can produce bare ground suitable for weed invasion.

- On ridge and furrow fields modern cutters tend to scalp ridges and leave tall vegetation in furrows. Finger bar cutters are more suitable in these circumstances.

Removing the hay crop is the key to retaining the wildlife interest of the meadow. Firstly, it removes nutrients from the system; secondly, the mechanical action of collecting the grass creates small areas of bare ground which allows annual species to re-establish in the sward. Bales should be removed from the field within three to four weeks.

While failing to mow, bale and remove a crop for a single year is unlikely to have any long-term consequences for the botanical richness of a field, it can make management more difficult in the following year. When harvesting is not completed it is advisable to graze the sward with either sheep or cattle then top it with a flail mower or chain harrow it in the autumn. Alternatively, a forage harvester can be used to remove the crop for disposal off the field.

Grazing in meadows

Grazing in some form is an integral part of most, if not all, meadow management systems. There are two main meadow grazing regimes in the UK. Northern hay meadows (MG3) are traditionally grazed in spring (April and May) and stock removed, or 'shut up', in late May prior to cutting in July. The late summer and autumn growth (aftermath) is grazed from late summer (August) onwards. From then on grazing usually occurs, at least sporadically, through the winter, depending on stock movements on the farm. Although on many farms sheep are grazed on the unenclosed moor from late December/January through to the beginning of April. More lowland and southern meadows are not usually grazed in spring, but late summer/autumn aftermath grazing almost always occurs.

Grazing, particularly aftermath grazing, is essential for the maintenance of the botanical diversity of hay meadows. Kirkham, Mounford & Wilkins (1996) and Smith (1997) have both shown that cessation of aftermath grazing results in decreases in species-richness and changes in species composition in meadow swards.

At the end of the autumn/winter grazing period the sward height should not generally exceed 10 cm, depending on the nature conservation objectives. Where wintering wildfowl or spring-nesting waders are present then the sward height should be around 3 cm (Crofts & Jefferson 1994, 1999).

Changes in long-established traditional meadow management regimes, including the grazing regime, should not be made where that regime is already fulfilling the objectives. Where available, reliable historical information should be used as a guide for establishing grazing regimes in hay meadows. Where such information is not available the timings given above, together with the advice on stock type and stocking levels given in Section 7.6.2 should be used as a guide, with adjustments made for local conditions as necessary.

Both cattle and sheep are suitable for grazing meadows. Horses can also be used; however, special care must be taken to prevent overgrazing. Poaching and the creation of bare ground in general is undesirable as it allows weeds to become established in the sward.

Surface treatments in meadows

As for pastures the application of artificial and organic fertilisers ('straight' N and compound NPK, hoof and horn meal, dried blood, liquid seaweed) rapidly reduces the species richness and diversity of hay meadow swards. The use of such fertilisers is generally unacceptable on any type of semi-natural unimproved grassland. Likewise slurry and sewage sludge provide an immediate source of N, P and K and their application seriously damages the nature conservation interest of semi-natural grasslands. Therefore they should not be applied.

Well rotted farm yard manure (manure that has been stored for at least four months) should only be applied to hay meadows on neutral soils where there is a proven history of use and no evidence of loss of nature conservation interest of the sward. On meadows supporting breeding waders and wildfowl farm yard manure should only be spread outside the breeding season, which is defined as 15 March to 15 July. Application rates should not normally exceed 20 tonnes/ha every three to five years and should only be applied in a single dressing (Crofts & Jefferson 1994, 1999). Further research is required on the effects of different application rates of farm yard manure and it may be that higher rates are acceptable, but at present a precautionary approach is advised.

Lime should not be applied to calcium deficient meadows (NVC MG5c *Danthonia decumbens* sub-community). Application of lime to other hay meadows is acceptable where this is a proven long-established practice. Lime should be applied no more frequently than once every five to 10 years and at no more than three tonnes per hectare of calcium oxide (CaO) equivalent in any one dressing (Crofts & Jefferson 1994, 1999).

Cow parsley

Frequent or abundant cow parsley *Anthriscus sylvestris* in hay meadows normally indicates inappropriate management for biodivesity. It increases in abundance when aftermath grazing lapses and/or where inputs of nitrogen, particularly inorganic forms, are inappropriately high. Its control may be necessary where it is out-competing other desired vegetation.

To control or prevent its spread (R Jefferson, pers comm):

- maintain or re-establish aftermath grazing, but avoid poaching, which creates niches for new plants;
- prevent inputs of artificial fertilisers or other nutrients (except farm yard manure where there is clear evidence of long-term historical use, see above);
- cut three or more times each year, where this species is dominant and cutting is not detrimental to other interests (eg outside the bird breeding season).

7.6.4 Flushed grassland and mires

Flushed (as opposed to floodplain) wet grasslands dominated by rushes *Juncus* spp and/or purple moor-grass are widespread in upland England below the fell wall. A number of reotrophic (ground water fed) mire communities in the form of flushes and valley mires can be found in association both with these wet grasslands and the drier pastures dealt with above. Flushes may also be found in meadows. Flushed grasslands and mires are very valuable for plants and animals, especially where there is a calcareous influence. They can contain rich invertebrate faunas, with crane flies, soldier flies, ground beetles and spiders. Where such grasslands support marsh violets *Viola palustris*, they can be the habitat of the small pearl-bordered fritillary.

To a large extent all these habitats can be managed in a similar manner and are treated together here. They are generally managed as pasture although some examples are managed as meadows (Table 7.2). Where the latter is the case section 7.6.3 should be referred to. Where managed as pasture, this type of vegetation should be lightly summer grazed, preferably with cattle, but hardy breeds of pony may also be acceptable. Sheep are not generally suited to wet conditions as they are prone to a number of diseases in these conditions, although many flushed grasslands are sheep grazed as they occur in mosaics with drier plant communities.

Suggested grazing times and stocking rates are as follows:

Grazing period:	late May to late September/mid-October. However, where breeding waders are present the stocking levels should be reduced to avoid losses of eggs or chicks through trampling.	
Stocking rate:	*Molinia* grassland and valley mires:	1 cow/ha (0.65 LU/ha)
	Rush pasture and fen meadow:	1-2 cows/ha (0.65-1.3 LU/ha)

These stocking rates are only approximate guides and sward height, structure and poaching should be assessed on a regular basis. As a general rule, the grazing regime should be adjusted so that the sward height over the majority of the area is less than 15 cm high for at least part of the year, excluding rush and *Molinia* tussocks. Where *Molinia* is present it can dominant the sward and in time create a very tussocky structure. The aim is usually to prevent the tussocks developing by grazing so as to achieve a smooth, even sward (see also Chapter 6 on *Molinia*). It should be noted, however, that many breeding waders prefer a tussocky sward so a uniform sward height is undesirable in areas important for birds (Ausden & Treweek 1995). An example of appropriate management prescriptions for species-rich *Molinia* grassland is given in Box 7.2.

Where these wet features are found within areas of drier grasslands, the most appropriate management regime will depend on the wildlife interest of the habitats present, as well as their extent. Flush and valley mire communities require no more than light grazing to prevent succession to woodland. This is especially true of the wetter communities, such as those dominated by bottle sedge *Carex rostrata*. Some flush communities, particularly M10 *Carex dioica-Pinguicula vulgaris* flushes, may require trampling, such as that associated with light grazing, to maintain species richness. However, repeated heavy trampling will lead to a loss of nature conservation interest in the long term.

Box 7.2 English Nature Culm Grassland Wildlife Enhancement Scheme

Culm grassland is a mosaic of wet acidic grassland, wet heath, fen and mire communities. It is largely confined to south west England, southern Wales and south west Scotland. Although English examples are largely found in lowland England this habitat does extend into upland areas in the Dartmoor Natural Area. Also the management recommendations given for this habitat in Wolton (1994) are considered to be relevant to other wet grasslands found in the uplands.

The ideal management of Culm grassland

Grazing

Sites should be grazed by cattle at times between late May and late September. Stocking levels should be adjusted so as to ensure that the sward over the majority of any field is less than 15 cm high for at least part of the year, excepting areas dominated by tussocks of rush or *Molinia*. However, the ground surface should never be heavily poached and no attempt should be made to graze the whole of a field closely.

Flexibility in the grazing regime is essential, to allow for vagaries of weather and stock availability and differences between sites in plant community composition. If cattle are not available, ponies or even hill sheep are permissible in the short term.

Stocking levels

Guidance stocking levels are: for *Molinia*-dominated fields, over a 20-week period, one suckler cow per 0.8 ha or two 12-24 month stock cattle per hectare. These figures may be increased by up to 50% for rush-dominated fields. Rather than shut stock into Culm Grassland fields it may often be more practical, particularly on small sites, to run the land in with adjoining improved pasture.

Topping and burning

Often adequate grazing cannot be achieved because the land is not stock-proof or without risking heavy poaching, particularly in wet summers. Under these circumstances autumn cutting or winter burning will be necessary. Rush-dominated fields should be topped after the beginning of August at a minimum height of 15 cm. Either a flail mower should be used or cut material removed from site. *Molinia*-dominated fields should if necessary be burnt, preferably during January to February, once every other winter. No more than half of a site, and preferably of each field, should be burnt in any one year and fires should be quick and cool, just taking off the leaf litter. No attempt should be made to burn boggy or peaty areas, or right up to the field edges.

Tree and shrub management

Areas of trees and shrubs should be managed so that they are in an optimal, stable balance with the open sward. The greater part of each field should be kept open, but with scattered bushes or clumps of bushes throughout, larger ones at about 40 m intervals and smaller ones more frequently. Willow *Salix* spp should be especially favoured (and not oak *Quercus* spp). Thick, overgrown hedges that grade down from mature trees through scrub and tall grassland to a short sward are to be encouraged.

Scrub clearance

Where it is necessary to clear trees and shrubs from abandoned sites to reach the optimal balance given above, this should be done between September and March, preferably using hand-held tools. The use of vehicles should be avoided if possible. Cut material should be stacked near field edges or in adjacent woodland, or burnt off site. Following scrub clearance from neglected sites it may be necessary to:

a. Burn off any accumulations of leaf litter during the winter. No more than one third of any field should be so burnt in any one year.

b. Fence the land and ensure drinking water is available.

7.6.5 Floodplain grasslands

Floodplain grasslands are uncommon in upland England, though they may occasionally be encountered. The management of these grasslands is covered in detail in *The Wet Grassland Guide: Managing floodplain and coastal wet grasslands for wildlife* (Treweek *et al* 1997) and land managers are advised to consult this document where major management decisions are concerned. Box 7.3, however, gives a brief summary of the management of floodplain grasslands.

Box 7.3 A summary of the management of floodplain grasslands for nature conservation (adapted from Andrews & Rebane 1994)

- Do not change the hydrological regimes of grasslands subject to winter flooding or with high spring and early summer water tables.
- Continue traditional mowing and grazing management.
- Do not improve the sward agriculturally.
- On peat maintain a high water table in spring and early summer by managing adjacent ditch water levels.
- On clay or silt soils use surface flooding to maintain wet conditions suitable for breeding waders.
- Where land drainage has lowered the water table, reinstate former conditions by 'reverse drainage' or surface re-wetting. (Re-wetting by surface flooding is inappropriate where the sward is plant-rich.)

7.7 Further management techniques for upland meadows and enclosed pasture

7.7.1 Drainage

Where long-standing drainage systems are present in fields with significant nature conservation interest, particularly in meadows, they should be retained. Maintenance works should not damage the sward. Semi-natural grasslands that are traditionally drained include some upland hay meadows (MG3 and fen meadow communities; Crofts & Jefferson 1994, 1999).

Drainage systems should not, however, be extended during maintenance into areas of mire or other wet areas which have not been previously drained. Where drainage systems have been recently installed in mires or other wet grasslands of nature conservation interest they should be blocked as otherwise the interest of the habitat is likely to be lost.

7.7.2 Stock feeding

Stock feeding in areas of wildlife interest can lead to nutrient enrichment and poaching of the ground, resulting in the loss of characteristic plants and animals. However, stock feeding during severe weather is a standard agricultural practice. The following practices are recommended:

- Seek to avoid stock feeding wherever possible but if unavoidable keep it to a minimum.
- Where stock feeding is unavoidable, do not undertake it on areas of wildlife value.
- The exception is in hay meadows, where hay made from the specific meadow should be used rather than imported hay or silage. The hay should also be spread widely and thinly over the field rather than placed in one area.
- Feed in small quantities at widely scattered sites, avoiding using the same sites and making sure that all the food is eaten (this is more appropriate for sheep).
- Or, rotate the feeding sites to avoid excessive pressure on any one area.
- Alternatively, locate a permanent feeder in a place with the least or no wildlife value and treat this as a sacrificial 'write-off' area.

7.7.3 Rolling and chain harrowing

Rolling is usually undertaken in spring and involves rollers towed by a tractor for levelling grassland, pressing in stones, encouraging the tillering of grasses and flattening mole hills. The aim is to prepare the ground for hay or silage harvesting later in the season. Rollers consist of two or three smooth-surfaced, hollow, rotating cylinders to which ballast can be added for weight (Crofts & Jefferson 1994, 1999). A chain harrow consists of a large number of small spikes carried on a flexible chain frame usually trailed by a tractor. They are used on grassland to break up matted swards, to spread dung after grazing and to spread molehills.

Rolling and chain harrowing are generally compatible with maintaining wildlife interests when conducted in spring, but the timing and wetness of the site are important. Advisable restrictions are shown in Box 7.4 (Crofts & Jefferson 1994, 1999).

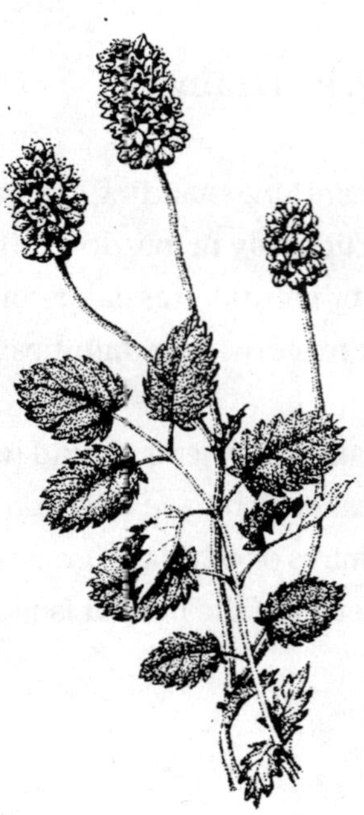

Great burnet

Box 7.4 Recommendations concerning rolling and chain harrowing of enclosed grasslands

- Where grassland is important for ground-nesting birds, neither rolling nor harrowing should take place between 15 March and 15 July because these activities crush eggs and chicks.
- Where grassland supports early flowering species which may be vulnerable to damage by rolling, it should take place about six to eight weeks before flowering (ie not after 15 March).
- Sites with ant hills should not be rolled or harrowed.
- Wet sites should not be rolled because compaction and rutting by wheels may cause damage. Harrowing may be a more acceptable alternative or all terrain vehicles (ATVs) towing the equipment may avoid damage.

7.7.4 Managing problem species

Bracken

Bracken is commonly viewed as an invasive plant of grassland that reduces the area of grass available for stock grazing and, where severe, reduces the overall wildlife interest. However, it also provides essential habitat for the whinchat *Saxicola rubetra* and a variety of invertebrates, such as the high brown fritillary butterfly. The problems this species causes for farmers and the potential value of bracken to wildlife are covered in detail in Information Note 6, along with guidelines on its management.

Rushes

There are several types of rush *Juncus* spp. found in the enclosed grasslands of the uplands but the two most commonly occurring species are soft rush *Juncus effusus* and compact rush *Juncus conglomeratus*. Both are associated with damp fields. Rush infestation can be caused by a number of factors, including under-soil drainage systems falling into disrepair and poaching. Severe trampling can also lead to rushes becoming dominant in wet grasslands and they can remain dominant in a sward for long periods. They produce very large amounts of seed, which can persist in a dormant state in the soil until activated by further soil disturbance.

While rushes can invade pastures they are also an integral component of many semi-natural vegetation types of high nature conservation interest, including acid and mesotrophic flushes, rush pastures and fen meadows. Rush tussocks provide nest sites and cover for snipe, redshank and curlew and their chicks. Stands of rushes support various invertebrate species, which in turn are a food source for young birds, including black grouse.

Despite these positive attributes there are occasions where rushes may need to be controlled (Crofts & Jefferson 1994, 1999):

- where rush infestations reduce the species and structural diversity of swards of wildlife interest;

- in semi-natural swards where rushes are not generally a major component and they reduce the amount of grazing available;

- where the spread of rushes reduces the extent of short turf between tussocks which is required by breeding waders.

The most widely used and generally recommended method of controlling rushes is topping (cutting at a height of around 15 cm) in early August (after the bird breeding season). This will usually reduce the vigour of rushes to a level where they are controlled by normal grazing if carried out two years in succession. Herbicides can be used, if target methods such as spot-spraying or weed wiping are employed. However, whenever possible, herbicide use should be avoided in sensitive areas and near water courses. Good practice codes for herbicide use should always be followed (MAFF & HSC 1990; MAFF 1998g & h).

Docks, thistles and ragwort

Curled dock *Rumex crispus* and broad-leaved dock *R. conglomeratus*, spear thistle *Cirsium vulgare* and creeping thistle *C. arvense* and common ragwort *Senecio jacobaea* can become injurious agricultural 'weeds' when they become extensive in grassland swards. They can be controlled by topping prior to flowering (but not ragwort), spot control with herbicide, weed wiping on larger areas and hand control techniques such as pulling or cutting (not ragwort) at ground level prior to flowering. Cut or pulled plants should be removed from the site, particularly ragwort as it remains toxic and palatable to stock after wilting. As with rushes, the use of herbicides should be avoided, whenever possible, where nature conservation is the primary objective. Where injurious weeds pose a serious threat to agriculture or agricultural production, MAFF may require control action to be taken. It may be an offence under the Weeds Act 1959 to fail to control injurious weeds when under notice by MAFF to do so. Further information on weed control methods is contained in Crofts & Jefferson (1994, 1999).

Rabbits

Rabbits *Oryctolagus cuniculus* are the most significant non-domestic grazers and continuous heavy rabbit grazing can be damaging to the nature conservation interest of semi-natural grasslands, particularly those on shallow soils. Rabbit grazing has, however, maintained grassland on sites that would otherwise have developed into coarse grassland or scrub and also provide important niches for invertebrates. Where rabbit grazing is a problem, see Information Note 8 on methods of rabbit control.

7.7.5 Use of avermectin anthelmintics

Avermectins are a group of chemicals, several of which are used as veterinary medicines to control internal and external parasites in livestock. They are used in a range of animals, including cattle, sheep, horses and pigs. They are administered to stock by injection, oral drench or pour-on, or as a slow-release bolus. These chemicals are excreted in the dung of treated stock and remain active against invertebrates that colonise dung. They can have a significant effect on the invertebrate fauna of grassland, particularly dung flies and dung beetles. Invertebrates form an important food source for other animals, particularly bats and birds, and rare invertebrates associated with dung in grassland may be adversely affected.

The length of time the dung remains toxic varies according to the application method. This ranges from one to two weeks following the use of an oral drench in sheep, to several weeks following a single injection in sheep and cattle, and five to six months for the Ivermectin bolus in cattle.

The use of avermectins, particularly the original active form, Ivermectin, is not generally recommended on pastures and meadows with wildlife interest, especially where rare or scarce invertebrates, including aquatic species, might be affected. Crofts & Jefferson (1999) give alternatives for the treatment of internal and external parasites. See also Cooke 1997 on avermectin use in livestock.

7.7.6 Burning

Burning is not a management technique which is widely used in the enclosed grasslands of upland England. In general it is not recommended as a management practice for meadows and pastures with wildlife interest.

Grassland burning has traditionally been used in upland areas to burn off dead and unpalatable grasses, especially purple moor-grass, to provide a flush of young, palatable grass for grazing (Ausden & Treweek 1995). It favours plant species which are able to withstand the effects of the burn, for example, those with growing points protected at or below the surface of the ground, such as purple moor-grass and mat-grass. These species can become dominant with repeated burning, to the exclusion of other valued plant species and their associated animals.

Crofts & Jefferson (1994, 1999) discuss burning in greater detail, including situations where it can be a useful tool. Wolton (1994) discusses burning on Culm grasslands of Devon and Cornwall. See also Chapter 6 Moorland.

7.7.7 Managing scrub

Scrub usually develops where management such as grazing, burning or mowing is reduced or ceases altogether. It develops most easily in the more open conditions of shallow soils, such as on limestone and on rocky ground, and is slow to invade grasslands on deep, fertile soils because of the dense cover of grasses or herbs (Hopkins 1996).

In enclosed grasslands scrub is often viewed as an undesirable development. This is particularly true where it is invading an area of existing high nature conservation interest, such as species-rich hay meadows or limestone grassland. However, scrub can have considerable nature conservation value in its own right and the positive aspects of scrub are now being given greater emphasis (Hopkins 1996, Mortimer *et al* 2000).

Nature conservation interest of scrub

Scrub, scattered trees and open woodland is of great value to birds. Light scrub cover provides nest sites, song posts, foraging areas and sheltered roosts for birds such as black grouse, whinchat, stonechat *S. torquata*, tree pipit *Antacus trivialis* and ring ouzel *Turdus torquatus*. Scrub is also very important for invertebrates, providing food and shelter and a range of vegetation structures which lead to a diverse invertebrate fauna. Many species occur at the margin of scrub and grassland, eg the northern brown argus butterfly and the Duke of Burgundy butterfly. Additionally, a number of uncommon plant species are characteristic of scrub margins, including globe flower *Trollius europaeus* and dark-red helleborine *Epipactis atrorubens* (Crofts & Jefferson 1994, 1999). Scattered trees such as rowan *Sorbus aucuparia*, and shrubs like hawthorn *Crataegus monogyna*, gorse *Ulex europaeus* and juniper *Juniperus communis*, are particularly beneficial on steep banks where bird and invertebrate interest might otherwise be limited.

Juniper scrub is a nationally rare habitat type and all examples should be maintained and, where appropriate, extended.

Where scrub grades into upland native woodland it provides a diversity of habitats beneficial to animals and plants alike. Upland woodland itself supports its own particular flora and fauna, covered in greater detail in Chapter 8. For further details of the ecology and conservation of scrub in general see Chapter 8, Hopkins (1996) and Mortimer *et al* (2000)

Managing scrub in enclosed pastures

Scrub should be retained and developed amongst enclosed upland farmland, to encourage breeding bird and invertebrate populations, provided its development does not threaten another habitat of wildlife value.

Scrub-grassland interfaces can be managed and maintained by rotational cutting on a five to 10 year cycle. Areas of scrub should be cut back to create scalloped edges to increase the length of interface. Where grazing levels are adequate, this can generally be done without using herbicide stump treatments to prevent re-growth. However, where grazing is absent or inadequate and species capable of rapid underground vegetative spread are present, eg blackthorn *Prunus spinosa*, then some herbicide control may be required to prevent such species dominating. Where scrub regeneration is desirable, but poor, it can be encouraged by scarification of the soil. Grazing may also be beneficial in these circumstances.

Grazing can be used to create a range of growth stages, using temporary fencing to exclude and include areas of scrub from grazing. If grazing is reintroduced to sites where it has been relaxed or abandoned, care must be taken to ensure that any intensive restoration grazing does not result in major damage to the floristic and entomological interest of the scrub boundary.

Open scrub is generally of greater wildlife value than dense scrub. Where closed canopies have developed, the grassland that would result from scrub clearance is likely to be of less wildlife interest than the woodland that would develop. Ward (1990) suggests that where scrub has developed a closed canopy with little or no field layer it can be managed on a 30-year rotation, clear-felling sections and allowing them to develop back into scrub. Ward (1990) found that scrub stands originating from dense scrub with bare ground produced a more species-rich community than stands originating from scrub clearance in earlier successional stages where tall grassland was present.

Reversing scrub invasion

Scrub can be removed either by hand- or machine-cutting or by grazing with goats. Cutting is the technique most commonly used. Sheep are generally unsuitable for grazing sites with scrub as they are prone to becoming entangled in branches. Cattle or horses of hardy breeds may be used to reduce minor encroachment by scrub if stocked at high densities in spring, but are unlikely to be capable of eradicating scrub from a site.

The clearance of closed canopy scrub does not normally result in its replacement by species-rich grassland because soil conditions alter under scrub and nutrient enrichment occurs. When such scrub is cleared there is often a rapid growth of nutrient-loving plants which smother slower growing grassland species. Grazing and cutting may reduce the vigour of the undesirable species but this may take a considerable time as the build-up of nutrients in the soil, especially phosphorus, is an extremely slow and difficult process to reverse. The best option, therefore, is to act before the canopy becomes dense, when some of the original grassland vegetation remains beneath the shrubs and the accumulation of leaf litter and other organic material has not significantly changed the soil nutrient status.

Where eradicating or reducing scrub will be of benefit, for example where there is scrub invasion of species-rich swards, then clearance should be carried out in winter, either by hand (mattocks, chain saws and axes) or using machinery (tractor-mounted flails, sickle-bar mowers, forage harvesters and excavators with root forks). The most appropriate method will depend on the resources available, the size of the area to be cleared, the terrain, stem size, scrub species and the nature conservation interest of the sward. Heavy machinery is generally unsuitable for species-rich or wet grassland, because it disturbs the ground, and for steep and rocky terrain. Stumps should be treated with suitable herbicides to prevent regrowth. Any regrowth present the following summer should be retreated with herbicide. Herbicides should not be applied by spraying where the ground flora is of nature conservation interest.

Grazing, other than by goats, is not normally an effective method of reducing or eradicating scrub. Goats, however, are preferential browsers and have been used to eradicate large areas of scrub (Crofts & Jefferson 1994, 1999).

Managing juniper scrub

Juniper does not reproduce vegetatively and a closed grass sward prevents its establishment from seeding. Because of this, reduction or removal of grazing alone is unlikely to be successful in promoting significant regeneration of juniper beyond an initial spurt. Bare ground is required if significant regeneration is to occur. This can be created by scarification or burning, although the latter should only be used where there is no danger of damaging existing juniper bushes. Juniper tends to establish best on the edges of existing stands rather than within them due to the shading effect of mature bushes.

Further information: Barrett 1997.

7.7.8 Archaeological and historical interests and management in enclosed grasslands

Archaeological sites and features are often preserved in unimproved grassland. Those which survive today are only a small proportion of the original number. These fragile and fragmentary remains are easily destroyed by changes in land use and management. Once gone, this unique record of the evolution of the countryside and how people once lived is lost for ever.

Management which is sympathetic to wildlife, as outlined in this chapter, is usually beneficial to archaeological interests. However, many aspects of farm work inadvertently result in damage. The implications for archaeology should be carefully considered before starting any work near archaeological sites and features.

Further information: Chapter 3 Decision making; Wood-Gee 1996.

7.8 Specific management for fauna

On many enclosed unimproved semi-natural grassland sites management is likely to be aimed principally at the vegetation. However, many of these sites may also have considerable entomological and/or ornithological interest, as may semi-improved grasslands. Additionally, improved pastures can be important in providing rich feeding for lapwing, golden plover *Pluvialis apricaria*, curlew and ring ouzel when they are not incubating eggs or tending chicks. Birds may fly several kilometres from the moors to feed in such areas. The following sections provide a brief overview of how management practices can be modified to enhance the value of grasslands for these groups.

7.8.1 Managing for birds

Unimproved permanent pastures and traditionally managed hay meadows are generally of greater benefit to birds than improved grasslands. Agricultural improvement, including drainage, applying inorganic fertilisers and reseeding, has been shown to result in the virtual disappearance of snipe and marked reductions in the density of, and proportion of fields used by redshank, curlew and lapwing (Baines 1988). In contrast, oystercatchers were found to nest on improved grasslands. Thus, the species composition on unimproved grasslands changes following improvement and within large areas containing many fields, the overall density of waders declines as the percentage of improved fields increases.

Sward structure

There is a pronounced dichotomy in the habitat preferences of bird species breeding in grassland. Species such as lapwing and wheatear *Oenanthe oenanthe* favour short, closely cropped swards (<2 cm), while species such as redshank, snipe, meadow pipit *Anthus pratensis*, skylark, whinchat and curlew prefer more lightly grazed, tussocky vegetation. Lightly grazed swards also support large vole populations which are preyed upon by raptors and owls.

- Short swards can be produced by sheep grazing, cattle, if stocked at moderately high densities, or rabbits.

- More tussocky swards with a high degree of structural diversity, particularly for breeding waders, are best produced by cattle, or sheep and cattle, at low stocking densities.

Additionally, the tall swards of hay meadows can support breeding birds, including corncrake.

Stocking levels/timing

Stocking levels also play a vital role in determining the breeding success of waders owing to stock trampling eggs and young. Grazing during the breeding season (15 March-15 July) reduce breeding success and this effect is increased with increased stocking density. Green (1986) has shown that at a stocking density of 1 cow/ha 18% of lapwing nests, 34% of snipe nests and 43% of redshank nests are trampled. At 2 cows/ha this increases to 33%, 57% and 67% respectively. With sheep grazing similar patterns are found, though at higher stocking densities.

If compatible with other nature conservation objectives, grazing during the wader breeding season should be avoided where breeding waders are present. Where grazing is required during this period then stocking densities below 0.5 cattle, or 1 sheep, per hectare should be used, to keep trampling levels below 25% for the above species.

Timing of cutting and other mechanical management practices

Cutting of meadows, rolling, chain harrowing and similar practices should only be carried out outside the breeding season (as above).

Water levels

Wetland features such as flushes, pools, damp grassland and patches of rushes are essential habitat requirements for breeding waders, as they provide both sources of food and nest sites. Poorly drained land, especially where *Sphagnum* and/or rushes have developed, supports a rich invertebrate fauna and is a major feeding ground for chicks of grouse and waders. These birds may travel considerable distances from their nest sites to reach such areas. Birds such as snipe also rely on wet grasslands for breeding and feeding, and require the upper soil to be moist to allow them to probe for food (Ausden & Treweek 1995). The pricipal requirement is water levels high enough during summer to keep the surface moist. Natural water levels should be maintained and such features as pools and flushes retained. No new drainage should be undertaken in such areas and existing drains should be blocked, using techniques which minimise hazards to livestock and create small wetland features.

More complex control of water levels is not a feature of management in upland England. Land managers requiring information on managing water levels in floodplain grasslands should refer to Treweek *et al* (1997) or Crofts & Jefferson (1994, 1999).

Figure 7.1 shows a range of stylised, ideal, enclosed grasslands for birds.

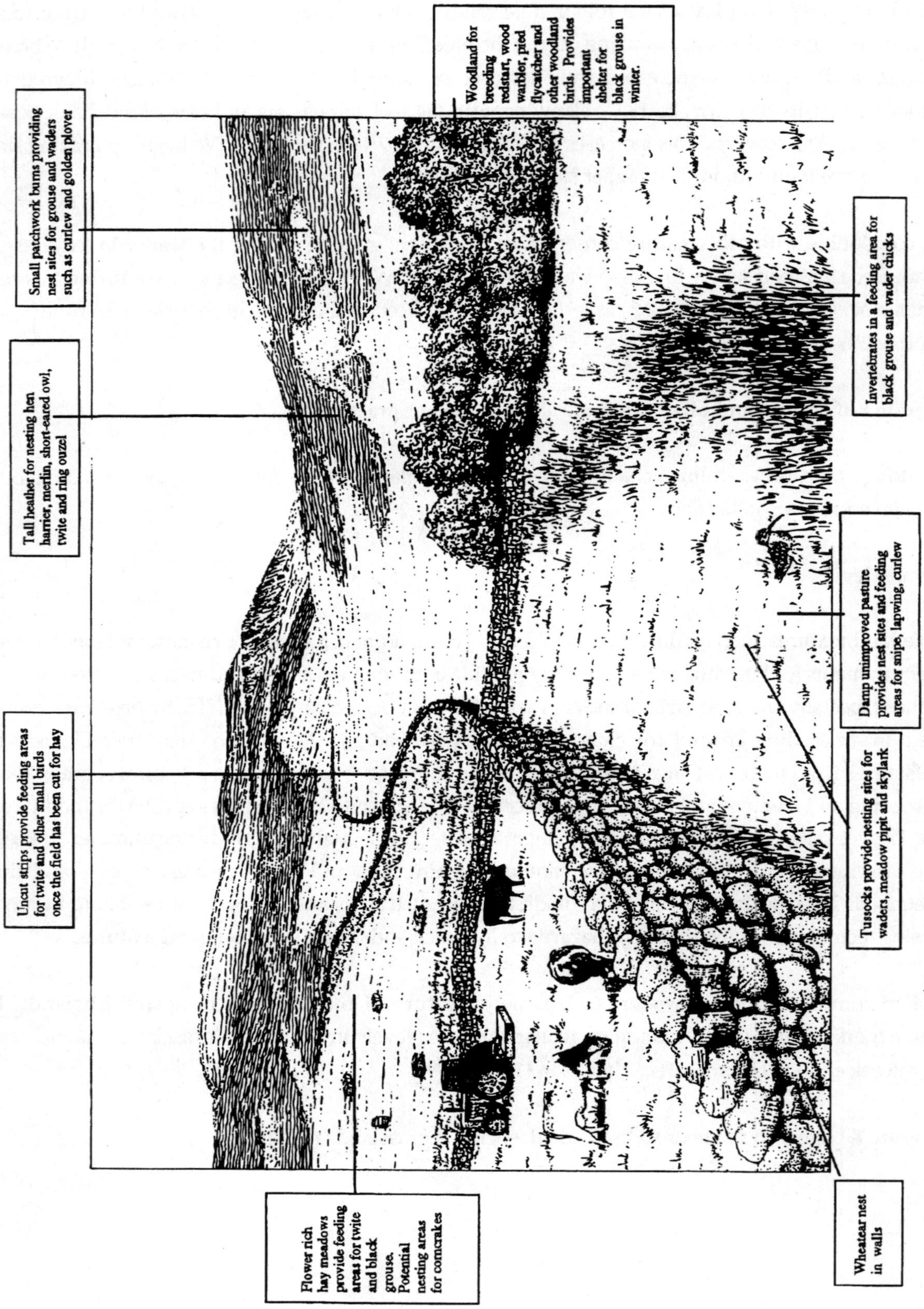

Figure 7.1. Stylised, ideal enclosed grassland and adjacent habitats for birds in the English uplands

7.8.2 Managing for invertebrates

The following are some general principles which should enhance general invertebrate diversity (Kirby 1992). Where specific rare or scarce species are known to be present specialist advice should be sought from appropriate sources.

- Continuity of management through time, ie consistency, is highly important in maintaining invertebrate diversity.
- Invertebrate diversity is heavily dependent on the structural diversity of the vegetation. Ideally the sward should contain areas of both short turf and stands of taller grass and tussocks.
- Short turf is especially valuable on south-facing slopes.
- Areas of bare ground are important for many invertebrate species, although too much can cause problems such as weed invasion.
- Grazing is the best management option for maintaining invertebrate diversity (but hay meadow management should not be compromised or changed to pasture).
- Cattle are better than sheep as they can produce a more structurally diverse sward. They also produce more bare ground, although heavy poaching is detrimental to wildlife interests.
- Winter grazing should allow at least some tussocks to remain.
- Where grazing is carried out throughout the year it should be at a low stocking density.
- Overgrazing, ie reducing the physical structure of the vegetation to a uniformly short sward, reduces invertebrate diversity because some areas of taller vegetation can be important for invertebrates.
- Cutting alone is poor for invertebrates (although hay meadow management should not be compromised or changed to pasture). It results in a sudden defoliation and low structural diversity. It can, however, be used, preferably on a rotational basis, where grazing is not possible.
- Scrub-grassland interfaces should be maximised: scalloped edges and long narrow bands of scrub are better than dense blocks. Rotational cutting can be used to maintain the structural diversity of scrub.
- Burning is not generally recommended as a management technique unless there has been a long history of such management.

7.9 Techniques to restore species-rich meadows and enclosed pasture

In the absence of management grassland will tend to become dominated by coarse grasses, tall herbs and scrub. This generally results in a reduction of botanical interest, although it should be noted that rank grassland does provide habitat for invertebrates, small mammals and reptiles.

Under-grazing can also lead to grasslands becoming rank. Stock are able to selectively graze the more palatable species present and avoid coarser grasses, herbs and shrubs when sward production is greater than that which the stock present are capable of utilising.

Prior to implementing any form of restoration management it is important to assess the current nature conservation value of the site; research its ecological and management history; assess the type of grassland the land could support and whether it is feasible to recreate it via management; and decide whether the management anticipated would improve or reduce the current wildlife value of the site.

There will be instances where restoration to grassland will achieve little for nature conservation, such as when a dense canopy of scrub has developed and there is little ground flora. In this situation it is likely to be difficult to restore species-rich grassland owing to the increased nutrient status of the soil following the build-up of leaf litter. Where this is the case other management objectives may need to be considered, such as rotational cutting to maintain scrub or management to promote the development of woodland (see Section 7.7.7 and Chapter 8). In some cases it may be possible to remove the nutrient-rich surface layer through scraping. In any grassland, testing the seed bank can reveal whether the desired plant species are still present and viable.

Some area may be much easier to restore than others. For example, semi-improved grasslands containing remnants of species-rich communities or a variety of plant species reminiscent of more valued grassland types, are likely to be easier to restore than grass leys (see Crofts & Jefferson 1999).

Before implementing any restoration management clear management objectives should be drawn up, against which the effects of the implemented management can be assessed.

Environmental land management schemes, such as the Countryside Stewardship and Environmentally Sensitive Area schemes, include provision for the restoration, and in some cases the re-creation, of species-rich grasslands.

7.9.1 Restoration management

Cattle, particularly the hardier breeds, or hardy breeds of pony (or goats) are capable of tackling coarse, rank grassland. Sheep tend to be less suited to restoration grazing as they tend to prefer short swards and fine grasses. They are, however, useful on steep slopes where heavier stock are likely to cause significant trampling damage, or where the sward has been pre-treated by prior grazing with cattle or mowing to remove the coarser herbage (Crofts & Jefferson 1994, 1999).

Although timing of grazing is not critical, where particularly unpalatable species, such as purple moor-grass, mat-grass or, occasionally in the uplands, tor-grass *Brachypodium pinnatum* are present, it is best to graze in spring when fresh growth is being produced. Spring grazing will also help to control scrub where this is desirable. Note, however, that this option may not be ideal where certain ground-nesting birds are present.

Grazing at high stocking densities for short periods or at lower densities for a longer time can reclaim rank grassland. High stocking rates may be necessary in some instances to force animals to eat relatively unpalatable vegetation. However, care is needed when reintroducing high grazing pressures because it can have a damaging effect on invertebrate populations. For example, reductions in marsh fritillary numbers in specific locations was attributed to the introduction of high stocking rates to control scrub and coarse grassland (Warren & Bourn 1997). The increased stocking rate reduced the sward height to below that required by this butterfly. Often invertebrates associated with taller swards require the grassland to be grazed at particular stocking levels or certain times of year. Therefore, where rare or scarce invertebrates associated with taller swards are present it may be prudent to exclude some areas from grazing, at least temporarily during the restoration process, possibly on a rotational basis, to allow populations to be maintained (Kirby 1992)

Mowing can be used to aid restoration management, particularly to remove taller vegetation if sheep are to be used. It is not, however, as effective a restoration method as grazing as it does not break up the litter layer unless it is followed by chain harrowing.

Burning, followed by grazing, can also be used to clear coarse vegetation. Burning should only be carried out in January, February and early March as this reduces the adverse effects of fire on flora and fauna. Burning codes and regulations must be followed at all times (see Chapter 6 Moorland). Prior to using burning as a restoration tool, consideration should be given to the potential adverse effects it can have on invertebrates over-wintering in the litter layer.

If grazing is not an option for restoration management owing to lack of availability of livestock then serious consideration should be given as to whether restoration is appropriate in the first place as grazing will be required to maintain any restored sward.

7.9.2 Grassland re-creation

Those seeking to establish grassland swards of nature conservation interest on land with little or no nature conservation interest, such as arable fields, industrial sites or quarry/mining spoil, should consult *The lowland grassland handbook* (Crofts & Jefferson 1999), *Reclamation of Damaged Land for Nature Conservation* (Department of the Environment 1996b), *The establishment and management of wildflower meadows* (Wells, Cox & Frost 1989) and *Habitat restoration project: factsheets and bibliographies* (Dryden, Horton & Hall 1997).

Table 7.9 Nationally rare and scarce vascular plants associated with meadows and enclosed pastures in England

Plant species	Status	Habitat requirements	Management requirements	Distribution by upland Natural Area
Alchemilla acutiloba an alchemilla	LR-nt	Hay meadows or roadside verges. The species will not survive in intensively managed grass fields especially those cut early for silage.	• Traditional hay meadow management without reseeding or heavy use of fertilisers. • Populations in roadside verges may benefit from occasional cutting of the vegetation, but not before ripe seed has been set.	North Pennines
Alchemilla glaucescens an alchemilla	LR-nt	Limestone grassland maintained by sheep-grazing.	• Protect sites from the application of fertilisers or pesticides. • Maintain moderate levels of sheep grazing.	Cumbria Fells & Dales Forest of Bowland Pennine Dales Fringe Yorkshire Dales
Alchemilla glomerulans an alchemilla	LR-ns	Ungrazed or lightly grazed habitats on base-poor rocks. In Teesdale, also in species-rich hay meadows and roadsides. See Table 10.1.	• Prevent heavy grazing.	Border Uplands North Pennines Yorkshire Dales
Alchemilla gracilis an alchemilla	VU	More or less closed grassland over Carboniferous limestone. A few plants are also known from rough pasture, a hay meadow and a grassy roadside verge. It is thought to rely on grassland remaining unimproved and, at some sites, on continued grazing.	• Traditional methods of managing hay meadows and pasture, with no reseeding or heavy use of fertilisers. • Grazed sites should continue to be grazed. • Consideration should be given to cutting of roadside verges, following the setting of seed.	Border Uplands
Alchemilla minima an alchemilla	VU, EE	Very short, moist, calcareous, *Festuca ovina* grassland or amongst limestone boulders and debris. It is well adapted to sheep grazing. Its requirements are poorly understood. See Table 6.1.	• Maintain moderate grazing. • Protect sites from habitat destruction and the application of fertilisers or pesticides. • See Species Action Plan (UK Biodiversity Group 1998).	North Pennines Yorkshire Dales
Alchemilla monticola an alchemilla	LR-nt	Traditionally managed hay meadows or roadside verges. It depends on the continuation of traditional farming. Populations on road verges may be threatened by mowing where this is done too early in the year, before the setting of seed.	• Traditional hay meadow management without reseeding or heavy use of fertilisers. • Populations in roadside verges may benefit from occasional cutting of the vegetation, but not before ripe seed has been set.	North Pennines Pennine Dales Fringe

Plant species	Status	Habitat requirements	Management requirements	Distribution by upland Natural Area
Alchemilla subcrenata an alchemilla	EN	Species-rich hay meadows or pastures. It requires traditional methods of hay cropping and is damaged by early cutting before seed has been set.	• Traditional management of hay meadows and pastures, without reseeding or heavy use of fertilisers, or early cutting. • Populations in roadside verges may benefit from occasional cutting of the vegetation, but not before ripe seed has been set.	North Pennines
Arabis glabra tower mustard	VU	Light sandy soils over limestone, on disturbed, free-draining ground. It does not survive long where a dense cover of grasses develops or under trees.	• Protect sites from destruction and habitat degradation. • See Species Action Plan (UK Biodiversity Group 1998).	Pennine Dales Fringe White Peak
Bartsia alpina Alpine bartsia	LR-nt	A perennial hemiparasite of moist, basic soils in upland meadows and pastures. Also on the drier hummocks within base-rich flushes and on species-rich flushed banks. Light grazing and trampling by cattle and/or sheep is necessary in the sites with hummocky flush-pasture; prevention of sheep-grazing in summer allows the plants to flower. Heavy poaching by cattle is detrimental. Some colonies by paths have been damaged by trampling.	• Protect sites from drainage. • Where relevant, prevent trampling of populations. • If possible, exclude sheep in summer and control grazing in the rest of the year to moderate levels, high enough to keep the vegetation low and open, while allowing the plants to grow and flower.	Cumbria Fells & Dales North Pennines Yorkshire Dales
Carex ericetorum rare spring-sedge	LR-ns	Short grassland on limestone.	• Protect sites from destruction.	Cumbria Fells & Dales North Pennines
Carex ornithopoda bird's-foot sedge	LR-nt	Open, calcareous grassland on Carboniferous limestone, often on thin, parched soils, which require light grazing to maintain the open character of the vegetation. Also close to exposed rocks on south-facing slopes, in full sun, and in shattered limestone pavement.	• Maintain light or moderate levels of grazing.	Cumbria Fells & Dales North Pennines White Peak Yorkshire Dales

Plant species	Status	Habitat requirements	Management requirements	Distribution by upland Natural Area
Chamaemelum nobile chamomile	LR-ns	Herb-rich, closely grazed or mown, moderately acidic grassland which has not been heavily sprayed or fertilised, often wet in winter. It cannot compete with the tall herbs or scrub which develop when grazing stops. It has also been lost when sites are drained.	• Maintain grazing by ponies and cattle in sites which are currently grazed. • Prevent the use of fertilisers and pesticides. • Prevent roadside sites being unnecessarily fenced.	Bodmin Moor Dartmoor Exmoor and the Quantocks
Crepis mollis northern hawk's-beard	LR-ns	Herb-rich grassland or wood pasture on shallow, slightly flushed, base-rich soils, often on north-facing slopes.	• Not currently understood.	Border Uplands Cumbria Fells & Dales North Pennines Yorkshire Dales
Crepis praemorsa leafless hawk's-beard	EN	Grazed calcareous pasture.	• Not currently understood.	Cumbria Fells and Dales
Dactylorhiza traunsteineri narrow-leaved marsh-orchid	LR-ns	Wet, base-rich habitats, especially fens or flushes. A reduction of grazing places the species at a competitive disadvantage.	• Maintain moderate levels of grazing where possible. • Protect sites from drainage or other activities which lower levels of ground or surface waters, including the planting of conifers nearby.	Forest of Bowland North York Moors and Hills Yorkshire Dales
Dianthus armeria Deptford pink	VU Sched 8 priority	Dry pastures, field margins and hedgerows on light, sandy, often rather basic soil, preferring short grassland with some open ground maintained by grazing or some other form of disturbance. It dies out when shaded by coarse grasses or scrub.	• Where possible, sites should be grazed. • Some populations may benefit from disturbance of the soil to expose buried seed. • See Species Action Plan (UK Biodiversity Group 1998).	Exmoor and the Quantocks

Plant species	Status	Habitat requirements	Management requirements	Distribution by upland Natural Area
Dianthus deltoides maiden pink	LR-ns	In sandy grassland or heath, on sunny slopes on soils with some base-content, often where the sward is broken by bare soil or rocks. Although susceptible to heavy grazing, at many sites it requires some grazing to maintain an open sward. See Table 10.1.	• Control levels of grazing and other disturbance to moderate levels.	Border Uplands Clun & North West Herefordshire Hills Dark Peak North Pennines North York Moors and Hills White Peak Shropshire Hills
Equisetum variegatum variegated horsetail	LR-ns	A wide variety of open habitats including river gravels, upland flushes and calcareous springs, usually on fairly basic, moist sandy or gravelly substrates, with a pH of 6.5-7.3 or higher, where competition from other plants is reduced by winter-flooding or the mobility of the substrate.	• Maintain the site's hydrology, including water quality and patterns of water levels and flow.	Border Uplands Cumbria Fells & Dales Exmoor and the Quantocks North Pennines Yorkshire Dales
Eryngium campestre field eryngo	Sched. 8 of WCA VU	Neutral or calcareous semi-natural grassland on light soils. Open ground is necessary for germination and establishment of seedlings, and light disturbance of the soil is beneficial.	• Artificial fertilisers should not be used. • Where possible sites should be grazed by cattle or sheep; mowing with occasional disturbance of the soil is an acceptable alternative. • Rough grassland and scrub should be controlled.	Exmoor and the Quantocks
Euphrasia rostkoviana subsp. *montana* a euphrasia	LR-ns	Upland hay meadows, mainly in relatively dry sites but also in wet meadows and upland fens. It appears to be adapted to mature much of its seed before the hay is cut. It rarely if ever colonises improved grasslands.	• Traditional management of hay meadows, without reseeding or artificial fertilisers.	Border Uplands Cumbria Fells & Dales Yorkshire Dales

Plant species	Status	Habitat requirements	Management requirements	Distribution by upland Natural Area
Euphrasia rostkoviana subsp. *rostkoviana* a euphrasia	LR-ns	Fertile soils in damp, herb-rich hay meadows, riverside grassland, lightly grazed pasture or grassy roadsides. It is a hemiparasitic annual which requires a cold period before germination. In hay meadows, much of the seed is thought to be produced after the first cutting of hay.	• Traditional management of hay meadows and pastures, without reseeding or artificial fertilisers.	Black Mountains and Golden Valley Cumbria Fells & Dales Forest of Bowland Shropshire Hills
Fumaria purpurea purple ramping-fumitory	LR-ns Priority	Hedge-banks, earthy walls or cliffs, cultivated fields or waste ground. It is usually most abundant where there is disturbance or where habitats are opened up by summer drought.	• Not currently understood. • See Species Action Plan (UK Biodiversity Group 1998).	Shropshire Hills
Galeopsis angustifolia red hemp-nettle	LR-ns Priority	Usually on well drained, warm soils, often where competition is not great, especially arable fields on calcareous soils. It is most frequent in spring-sown crops and competes poorly with dense, heavily fertilised crops. Early ploughing of stubble may also reduce populations.	• Important populations should be managed by traditional arable methods, with modest use of fertilisers. • See Species Action Plan (UK Biodiversity Group 1998).	Cumbria Fells & Dales Oswestry Uplands Pennine Dales Fringe White Peak
Juncus filiformis thread rush	LR-ns	Periodically flooded wet marshy pasture or open communities on lake-shore sand and gravel. Some lake sites have been damaged by misguided 'erosion protection'.	• Protect sites from changes in the water regime which would prevent the fluctuation of levels. • Maintain the marshy or open, disturbed character of lake shores.	Cumbria Fells & Dales Forest of Bowland North Pennines Pennine Dales Fringe Yorkshire Dales
Linum perenne perennial flax	LR-ns, sub-species E	Base-rich grassland over limestone. In open, sunny, well drained situations on road verges, dry banks, lightly grazed grassland and similar habitats. It is slow-growing and a poor competitor which is readily shaded out by scrub and tall plants; it reproduces solely by seed. Heavy grazing and repeated close mowing will also eliminate the species.	• Mowing late in the year to 10-15 cm height, or light grazing by cattle or sheep all year or, preferably, during the winter only leaving a reasonably long sward. • It can persist for a number of years without management or, at least for a few years, moderate grazing throughout the year.[1]	Cumbria Fells & Dales Yorkshire Dales

Plant species	**Status**	**Habitat requirements**	**Management requirements**	**Distribution by upland Natural Area**
Lotus angustissimus slender bird's-foot trefoil	LR-ns	Short open-textured grassland swards over thin drought-prone soils, amongst scrub, around rocky outcrops and on grassy banks, most typically near the sea. Patches of bare soil are essential for germination of seed and cutting of scrub, trampling, fire and especially drought may all be useful in creating bare patches.	• Where the vegetation has become dense or closed, some disturbance should be carried out to provide patches of open ground.	Dartmoor Exmoor and the Quantocks
Lysimachia thyrsiflora tufted loose strife	LR-ns	Fens and swamps, usually among open, tall vegetation.	• All sites should be protected from drainage and lowering of ground waters.	North York Moors and Hills
Mentha pulegium penny royal	Sched. 8 of WCA VU	Short, seasonally inundated grassland over clay and silt, subjected to intense all year round grazing, trampling, dunging or disturbance by livestock or vehicles, causing poaching or ruts. It relies on the traditional management of commons and village greens.	• Traditional pastoral management, with, for example, grazing by cattle or horses. • Resist proposals to 'tidy up' sites for this species. • Maintain the seasonal pattern of water levels. • See Species Action Plan (UK Biodiversity Group 1998).	Exmoor and the Quantocks
Meum athamanticum spignel	LR-ns	Dry neutral or acidic grassland in unimproved pastures, hay meadows and roadside banks, typically over slightly acid soils. It is unpopular with farmers as it can taint cow's milk.	• Where possible, continue with traditional grassland husbandry, without pesticides, reseeding or artificial fertilisers.	Border Uplands Cumbria Fells & Dales Pennine Dales Fringe
Myosotis stolonifera pale forget-me-not	LR-ns	Wet, somewhat base-poor, springs and seepage areas, soakways and flushes on hillsides and in valleys by pools, in ditches and in backwaters of streams.	• Protect major sites from destruction and drainage.	Border Uplands Cumbria Fells & Dales Dark Peak Forest of Bowland North York Moors and Hills Southern Pennines Yorkshire Dales

Plant species	Status	Habitat requirements	Management requirements	Distribution by upland Natural Area
Oenanthe silaifolia narrow-leaved water dropwort	LR-ns	Unimproved, damp meadows, primarily hay meadows on riverside alluvium, which receive calcareous flood water in winter. The plants have tubers and are long-lived; most are mown each year before seed is set. Even quite modest agricultural intensification will eliminate the species.	• Continue traditional grassland management, with no ploughing, reseeding or use of artificial fertilisers or pesticides.	White Peak
Orchis ustulata burnt orchid	LR-ns	Short, well drained, open limestone grassland mainly in the lowlands. It is not a strong competitor and may be shaded out if the vegetation is left ungrazed; heavy grazing is also considered to be detrimental. Ploughing and the application of inorganic fertilisers appear to be fatal.[2] There are two varieties of this species: var. *ustulata* mainly flowers in May, var. *aestivalis* in July.	• Grazing should be light and preferably by sheep or sheep and cattle. • Pasture can be grazed from early spring until April and again from July (from late August for var. *aestivalis*). • Hay meadows can be traditionally managed, with no grazing between May and the end of July, followed by light grazing through the winter.[1] • Prevent ploughing or the use of inorganic fertilisers.	North York Moors and Hills Pennine Dales Fringe White Peak Yorkshire Dales
Persicaria mitis tasteless water-pepper	LR-ns	Wet mud or peat banks left exposed in late summer as the water level drops. By ditches, in wet hollows, by cattle-trampled patches in pastures, by ponds, near former middens and in abandoned peat-cuttings.	• Protect major sites from drying out, filling in of ponds and fencing of ditches.	Border Uplands Shropshire Hills Yorkshire Dales

Plant species	**Status**	**Habitat requirements**	**Management requirements**	**Distribution by upland Natural Area**
Pilularia globulifera pillwort	LR-ns	Bare wet substrates at the edges of slightly acid to neutral water bodies. Unable to compete with larger plants such as reeds or other fen species nor survive under the shade of overhanging trees, it relies on fluctuations in the water level to control the spread of larger plants. In some sites the species relies on disturbance by cattle or horses to uncover bare substrate which it can colonise; at such sites it seems to disappear if grazing ceases.[3]	• In sites where the species relies on a fluctuating water level, the pattern of fluctuating levels should be maintained. • In sites where the species relies on disturbance, then the site should be kept accessible to large livestock. In small sites, care should be taken that poaching is not accompanied by excessive manuring. In the absence of grazing animals, mechanical or manual means could be used to control the spread of swamp and fen and provide bare substrate for pillwort. • All sites should be protected from drainage or habitat destruction. • Protect the sites from water pollution, especially by agricultural fertilisers. • See Species Action Plan (UK Biodiversity Group 1998).	Black Mountains and Golden Valley Cumbria Fells & Dales Dartmoor Pennine Dales Fringe
Primula farinosa bird's-eye primrose	LR-ns	Calcareous flushes, marshes and mires, most typically amongst grasses and sedges on low hummocks of calcareous gravelly clay around eroded springs and stream banks. Also on steeply sloping banks of streams and rivers and in closely grazed moist pasture. It is vulnerable to agricultural intensification, including draining, manuring, use of inorganic fertilisers, reseeding and heavy grazing. Some grazing can be beneficial in creating open ground and restricting competition from taller plants.	• Control grazing to moderate levels wherever possible. • Protect sites from agricultural intensification.	Cumbria Fells & Dales Forest of Bowland North Pennines North York Moors and Hills Pennine Dales Fringe White Peak Yorkshire Dales

Plant species	Status	Habitat requirements	Management requirements	Distribution by upland Natural Area
Scandix pecten-veneris shepherd's-needle	LR-ns Priority	Arable fields on soils which are dry in summer, often heavy, calcareous clays. It has declined sharply with the use of modern herbicides.	• Where possible, herbicide use should be controlled to low levels where this species grows. Reduced use can be carefully targeted to small areas such as field margins or even smaller areas. • See Species Action Plan (UK Biodiversity Group 1998).	Dartmoor Exmoor and the Quantocks Forest of Bowland
Senecio cambrensis Welsh groundsel	LR-nt E	An ephemeral species of disturbed sites such as roadsides and waste ground on dry soils.	• The habitats of this species are not really suitable for conservation management, but populations should occasionally be monitored. • Seed from a range of populations should be maintained in seed banks in case of widespread losses.	Oswestry Uplands
Silene gallica small-flowered catch fly	LR-ns Priority	Cultivated or disturbed ground, most frequently on sandy soils. The autumn germinating seedlings are killed at temperatures below minus10°C. The species is eradicated by the routine use of herbicides and inorganic fertilisers.	• Remaining sites should be protected from intensive use of herbicides and fertilisers. • See Species Action Plan (UK Biodiversity Group 1998).	Exmoor and the Quantocks
Verbascum lychnitis white mullein	LR-ns	Waste places, disturbed ground, open grassy places on roadsides and banks, usually on calcareous soils. Seed retain their viability for many years when buried in soil, for example in woodland, and large colonies can emerge following disturbance.	• Periodic disturbance of sites with current or recent populations.	Exmoor and the Quantocks
Verbascum virgatum twiggy mullein	LR-ns	Dry banks, old walls, waste places or pastures. It cannot survive much competition and often disappears when lack of management allows coarse grassland and scrub to grow up.	• Control the growth of scrub and tall vegetation by grazing or cutting as appropriate.	Exmoor and the Quantocks

Key to Table 7.9

Status

Annex IIb	- listed on Annex IIb of the EC Habitats and Species Directive
Sched. 8 of WCA	- listed on schedule 8 of the Wildlife & Countryside Act.

Red list categories

CR	- critically endangered
EN	- endangered
VU	- vulnerable
DD	- data deficient
LR -nt	- Lower risk-near threatened
LR-ns	- Lower risk-nationally scarce.
E	- endemic to Great Britain
EE	- endemic to England.

Biodiversity Action Plan (BAP)

Priority	- Priority species from UK Steering Group 1995 and UK Biodiversity Group 1998.
SCC	- Species of conservation concern from UK Steering Group 1995 and UK Biodiversity Group 1998.

Sources

Most information from Hodgetts, Palmer & Wigginton 1996; Porley & McDonnell 1997; Stewart, Pearman & Preston 1994; Wigginton 1999.

1. Rich 1997. 2. Foley 1987. 3. R Cooke, pers comm.

Table 7.10 Nationally rare and scarce bryophytes associated with upland meadows and enclosed pastures in England

Plant species	Status	Typical habitat	Distribution by upland Natural Area
Anthoceros agrestis	LR-ns	A summer annual on neutral or slightly alkaline, water-retentive disturbed clay and loam, especially in arable fields	Bodmin Moor
Hamatocaulis vernicosus slender green feather-moss	Annex IIb DD	Base-rich flushes. See Table 6.2.	Cumbria Fells & Dales Shropshire Hills
Moerckia hibernica	LR-ns	Base-rich flushes, fens, quarries, on ditch banks and on silty or marshy ground.	Cumbria Fells & Dales Yorkshire Dales
Oncophorus virens	LR-ns	In damp calcareous turf, especially in flushes and close to streams.	Cumbria Fells & Dales North Pennines
Philonotis caespitosa	LR-ns	On moist or wet non-calcareous soil and rocks, where flushed or flooded by slightly basic mineral-rich water.	Bodmin Moor Border Uplands Cumbria Fells & Dales Dark Peak Exmoor and the Quantocks Forest of Bowland Pennine Dales Fringe Southern Pennines Yorkshire Dales
Pohlia lescuriana	LR-ns	Preferring moisture-retentive soils, usually clay, although not those that are strongly basic. On banks of streams and ditches, at the margins of ponds and reservoirs, on bare soil in old fields, in ruts, on moist compacted soil by paths and on open clay soil in woodland rides.	Dark Peak Dartmoor Forest of Bowland Shropshire Hills Southern Pennines
Rhytidium rugosum	LR-ns	Open grassland on well-drained soils. See Table 6.2.	Cumbria Fells & Dales North Pennines White Peak Yorkshire Dales
Sphagnum affine	LR-ns	In a variety of weakly minerotrophic mires.	Cumbria Fells & Dales

Plant species	Status	Typical habitat	Distribution by upland Natural Area
Sphagnum angustifolium	LR-ns	On flushed ground beside streams, on banks, in marshes and in open woodland, confined to minerotrophic sites.	Border Uplands
Sphagnum flexuosum	LR-ns	In weakly minerotrophic marshes, in wet open woodland and on flushed rock-ledges.	Cumbria Fells & Dales This species is thought to be under-recorded.
Tomentypnum nitens	LR-ns	Wet fields and flushes with gently flowing water of pH 5.8 or more, often on gentle slopes.	Border Uplands Cumbria Fells & Dales North Pennines South West Peak Yorkshire Dales
Tortula subulata var. *subinermis*	LR-ns	On soil and about tree-bases by streams and rivers.	Forest of Bowland White Peak
Weissia microstoma var. *brachycarpa*	LR-ns	On wet non-calcareous clay, loam or marl. It is known from fields, woodland rides and glades, ditch-banks, pits and reservoir margins.	Dark Peak Forest of Bowland
Weissia rostellata	LR-nt Priority	An ephemeral species colonising moist bare ground. See Table 6.2.	Border Uplands Forest of Bowland Southern Pennines

Key to Table 7.10

Status

Annex IIb	- listed on Annex IIb of the EC Habitats and Species Directive
Sched. 8 of WCA	- listed on schedule 8 of the Wildlife & Countryside Act.

Red list categories

CR	- critically endangered
EN	- endangered
VU	- vulnerable
DD	- data deficient
LR -nt	- Lower risk-near threatened
LR-ns	- Lower risk-nationally scarce
E	- endemic to Great Britain
EE	- endemic to England.

Biodiversity Action Plan (BAP)

Priority	- Priority species from UK Steering Group 1995 and UK Biodiversity Group 1998.
SCC	- Species of conservation concern from UK Steering Group 1995 and UK Biodiversity Group 1998.

Sources

Most information from Hill, Evans & Bell 1992; Hill, Preston & Smith 1992 & 1994; Hodgetts, Palmer & Wigginton 1996 and Porley & McDonnell 1997.

Table 7.11 Habitat and management requirements of nationally rare and scarce bryophytes associated with meadows and enclosed pastures in England

Plants	Habitat requirements	Management requirements
Plants of arable fields, bare soil and mud.	Some of these species take about 18 months to complete their life-cycle and are damaged by autumn ploughing (N. Hodgetts pers comm).	• Some disturbance is required to provide patches of bare mud. • Ploughing should wherever possible be in spring.
Plants of fens and flushes	Adequate levels of unpolluted water. Some species benefit from disturbance to open the vegetation.	• Protect sites from artificial reduction of levels or flows of ground or surface water. • Where possible prevent contamination of ground and surface waters by agricultural and other chemicals.

Carline thistle

Table 7.12 Semi-natural plant communities associated with enclosed grassland in the uplands of England

NVC code	NVC name	Inclusion in Annex 1 of the Habitats Directive[1]	Significance in England[2]	Upland Natural Areas of England where community occurs[3]
Grassland				
Neutral (mesotrophic) grasslands				
MG1	*Arrhenatherum elatius* grassland.	--	Not specified	30
MG2	*Arrhenatherum elatius-Filipendula ulmaria* tall herb grassland.	--	Not specified	4, 8/15, 30
MG3	*Anthoxanthum odoratum-Geranium sylvaticum* northern hay meadow.	Mountain hay meadows (British types with *Geranium sylvaticum*)	Not specified	2, 4, 8/15, 10, 14
MG5	*Cynosurus cristatus-Centaurea nigra* lowland hay meadow and pasture.	--	Not specified	4, 8/15, 10, 12, 14, 17, 25, 29, 30, 41, 42, 58, 60, 87, 92, 94
MG8	*Cynosurus cristatus-Caltha palustris* flood pasture.	--	Not specified	4, 8/15, 10, 14, 29, 41
MG10	*Holcus lanatus-Juncus effusus* rush-pasture.	--	Not specified	2, 8/15
MG11	*Festuca rubra-Agrostis stolonifera - Potentilla anserina* inundation grassland.	--	Not specified	87
MG13	*Agrostis stolonifera-Alopecurus geniculatus* inundation grassland, silver meadows.	--	Not specified	87

NVC code	NVC name	Inclusion in Annex 1 of the Habitats Directive[1]	Significance in England[2]	Upland Natural Areas of England where community occurs[3]
Calcareous grassland				
CG2	*Festuca ovina-Avenula pratensis* grassland. (See also Ch 6 Moorland).	Semi-natural dry grasslands and scrubland facies on calcareous substrate (*Festuco brometalia*) (important orchid sites*)	Not specified	2, 8/15, 10, 12, 17, 30, 41
CG3	*Bromopsis erectus* grassland.	Semi-natural dry grasslands and scrubland facies on calcareous substrate (*Festuco brometalia*) (important orchid sites*)	Not specified	42
CG6	*Helictotrichon pubescens* grassland.	Semi-natural dry grasslands and scrubland facies on calcareous substrate (*Festuco brometalia*) (important orchid sites*)	Not specified	2
CG7	*Festuca ovina-Pilosella officinarum-Thymus polytrichus* grassland.	Semi-natural dry grasslands and scrubland facies on calcareous substrate (*Festuco brometalia*) (important orchid sites*)	Not specified	2, 30, 41
CG9	*Sesleria caerulea-Galium sterneri* grassland. (See also Ch 6 Moorland.)	Semi-natural dry grasslands and scrubland facies on calcareous substrate (*Festuco brometalia*) (important orchid sites*)	I	2, 4, 8/15, 10, 12 14
CG10	*Festuca ovina-Agrostis capillaris-Thymus praecox* grassland. (See also Ch 6 Moorland.)	Species-rich *Nardus* grasslands, on siliceous substrates in mountain areas (and sub-mountain areas in continental Europe)*	UK	2, 4, 8/15, 10, 12, 30, 42, 60
CG11	See Ch 5 Montane areas.			

NVC code	NVC name	Inclusion in Annex 1 of the Habitats Directive[1]	Significance in England[2]	Upland Natural Areas of England where community occurs[3]
Acid grassland				
U1 - U6	See Ch 6 Moorland.			
U7, U10, U13	See Ch 5 Montane areas.			
U15, U16, U17, U19, U21	See Ch 10 Crags, scree & limestone pavement.			
U20	See Ch 6 Moorland.			
Open vegetation				
OV37	See Ch 6 Moorland.			
OV38-OV40	See Ch 10 Crags, scree & limestone pavement.			
Mires				
Bog pools				
M1-M3	See Ch 6 Moorland.			
Small sedge bryophyte fens				
M4	*Carex rostrata-Sphagnum recurvum* mire.	Transition mires and quaking bogs	L	2, 4, 8/15, 10, 12, 25, 29, 58, 87, 92, 94
M5	*Carex rostrata-Sphagnum squarrosum* mire.	Transition mires and quaking bogs	L	10
M6	*Carex echinata-Sphagnum auriculatum/recurvum* mire.	--	I	2, 4, 8/15, 10, 12, 14, 17, 25, 29, 42, 58, 60, 87, 92, 94
M7, M8	See Ch 5 Montane areas.			
M9	*Carex rostrata-Calliergon cuspidatum* mire.	Transition mires and quaking bogs Alkaline fens	L	2, 4, 8/15, 10, 29, 41, 87
M10	*Carex dioica-Pinguicula vulgaris* mire.	Alpine pioneer formations of *Caricion bicoloris-atrofuscae** Alkaline fens	UK	2, 4, 8/15, 10, 12, 14, 17, 25, 29, 42, 60, 87
M11	*Carex demissa-Saxifraga aizoides* mire.	Alpine pioneer formations of *Caricion bicoloris-atrofuscae**	UK	4, 10, 42

NVC code	NVC name	Inclusion in Annex 1 of the Habitats Directive[1]	Significance in England[2]	Upland Natural Areas of England where community occurs[3]
M13	*Schoenus nigricans-Juncus subnodulosus* mire.	Alkaline fens	Not specified	17
Wet heath & blanket mire				
M15-M20	See CH 6 Moorland.			
Valley mire				
M21	*Narthecium ossifragum-Sphagnum papillosum* valley mire.	--	L	10, 17, 25, 29, 58, 92, 94
***Molinia* and *Juncus* fens**				
M22	*Juncus subnodulosus-Cirsium palustris* fen-meadow.	--	Not specified	17, 41
M23	*Juncus effusus/acutiflorus-Galium palustre* rush-meadow.	--	I	2, 4, 8/15, 10, 12, 14, 17, 25, 29, 41, 42, 58, 87, 92, 94
M24	*Molinia caerulea-Cirsium dissectum* fen-meadow.	*Molinia* meadows on chalk and clay (Eu-*Molinia*)	Not specified	29, 87, 92
M25	*Molinia caerulea-Potentilla erecta* mire.	--	I	2, 4, 8/15, 10, 12, 14, 17, 25, 29, 42, 58, 87, 92, 94
M26	*Molinia caerulea-Crepis paludosa* mire.	*Molinia* meadows on chalk and clay (Eu-*Molinia*)	I	4, 8/15, 10, 29, 58
Tall-herb fen				
M27	*Filipendula ulmaria-Angelica sylvestris* mire.	--	Not specified	8/15, 10, 17, 29, 41
Springs				
M29	*Hypericum elodes-Potamogeton polygonifolius* soakway.	--	I	10, 42, 87, 92
M31-M32	See Ch 5 Montane areas.			
M35	*Ranunculus omiophyllus-Montia fontana* rill.	--	L	4, 10, 25, 42, 87

NVC code	NVC name	Inclusion in Annex 1 of the Habitats Directive[1]	Significance in England[2]	Upland Natural Areas of England where community occurs[3]
M36	Lowland springs and stream banks of shaded situations.	--	L	42
M37	*Cratoneuron commutatum-Festuca rubra* spring.	Petrifying springs with tufa formation (*Cratoneurion*)*	L	4, 8/15, 10, 25
M38	*Cratoneuron commutatum-Carex nigra* spring.	Petrifying springs with tufa formation (*Cratoneurion*)*	L	4

Key to Table 7.12

1. Taken from Brown *et al* 1997
   * Priority habitat.
2. Taken from Drewitt & Manley 1997 and Jefferson 1996.
   - I Internationally scarce with UK representation.
   - UK Well developed in UK but represented elsewhere.
   - L Well developed in Europe.

3. The following 18 Natural Areas are classed as upland by English Nature:

No	Natural Area name
2	Border Uplands
4	North Pennines
8	Yorkshire Dales
10	Cumbria Fells & Dales
12	Forest of Bowland
14	Southern Pennines
15	Pennine Dales Fringe
17	North York Moors and Hills
25	Dark Peak
29	South West Peak
30	White Peak
41	Oswestry Uplands
42	Shropshire Hills
58	Clun & North West Herefordshire Hills
60	Black Mountains and Golden Valley
87	Exmoor and the Quantocks
92	Dartmoor
94	Bodmin Moor.

Table 7.13 Breeding birds associated with upland enclosed grasslands in England

Bird species[1]	Birds of conservation concern in the UK[2]	Listed on Schedule 1 of the 1981 Wildlife & Countryside Act	Listed on Annex 1 of the EC Birds Directive	No of British 10-km squares with breeding records 1988-90	% of breeding records in upland ITE squares[3]	Main upland habitat associations	Principal upland Natural Areas supporting the species *= major/important areas[4]
Red kite *Milvus milvus*	Red list	●	●	45	71.1	Woodland	Extinct in English uplands
Buzzard *Buteo buteo*	-	-	-	1,174	47.6	Woodland and enclosed land	2, 4*, 8, 10*, 41*, 42*, 58*, 60*, 87*, 92*, 94*
Merlin *Falco columbarius*	Red list	●	●	386	87.3	Moorland and enclosed land	2, 4*, 8*, 10*, 12*, 14*, 15, 17*, 25*, 29, 42, 58, 87
Black grouse *Tetrao tetrix*	Red list Priority BAP species	-	-	278	86	Moorland and enclosed land	2, 4*, 8, 29, extinct elsewhere
Corncrake *Crex crex*	Red list Priority BAP species	●	●	105	51.4	Enclosed land	Extinct in English uplands
Oystercatcher *Haematopus ostralegus*	Amber list	-	-	1,365	44	Enclosed land and fresh waters	2*, 4*, 8*, 10, 12*, 14*, 15
Golden plover *Pluvialis apricaria*	Amber list	-	●	630	84.1	Moorland and enclosed land	2*, 4*, 8*, 10, 12*, 14*, 15, 17*, 25*, 29, 92
Snipe *Gallinago gallinago*	Amber list	-	-	1,307	49.8	Enclosed land and moorland	All upland NAs but 87, but note in particular 2*, 4*, 8*, 12*, 14*, 15*, 25*, 29*
Curlew *Numenius arquata*	Amber list	-	-	1,354	48.1	Moorland and enclosed land	2*, 4*, 8*, 10, 12*, 14*, 15*, 17*, 25*, 29*, 30, 41, 42, 58, 60, 87, 92, 94
Redshank *Tringa totanus*	Amber list	-	-	1,046	36.8	Enclosed land and moorland	2*, 4*, 8*, 12*, 14*, 15, 25
Short-eared owl *Asio flammeus*	Amber list	-	●	381	70.9	Moorland	2*, 4*, 8*, 12*, 14*, 15, 17*, 25*, 29

Bird species[1]	**Birds of conservation concern in the UK[2]**	**Listed on Schedule 1 of the 1981 Wildlife & Countryside Act**	**Listed on Annex 1 of the EC Birds Directive**	**No of British 10-km squares with breeding records 1988-90**	**% of breeding records in upland ITE squares[3]**	**Main upland habitat associations**	**Principal upland Natural Areas supporting the species *= major/important areas[4]**
Meadow pipit *Anthus pratensis*	-	-	-	2,257	38.1	Moorland and enclosed land	All areas
Pied wagtail *Motacilla alba*	-	-	-	2,466	32.5	Ubiquitous	All areas
Whinchat *Saxicola rubetra*	-	-	-	1,062	59.9	Moorland and scrub	2*, 4*, 8*, 10*, 12*, 14*, 15*, 17*, 25, 29*, 30, 41, 42, 60, 87*, 92*, 94*
Stonechat *Saxicola torquata*	Amber list	-	-	847	47.7	Moorland and scrub	10*, 42, 58, 87*, 92*, 94
Wheatear *Oenanthe oenanthe*	-	-	-	1,339	60.6	Montane areas, moorland and enclosed land	2*, 4*, 8*, 10*, 12, 14, 15, 17, 25, 29, 30*, 41, 42, 58, 60, 87, 92*, 94
Twite *Carduelis flavirostris*	Red list	-	-	420	70.2	Moorland and enclosed land	4, 8, 14*, 25*, 29*

Key to Table 7.13

1. Upland breeding bird species as identified in Stillman & Brown 1998.
2. Birds of conservation concern from RSPB 1996.
   BAP relates to the UK Biodiversity Action Plan and those species which are considered to be priority species (UK Steering Group 1995; UK Biodiversity Group 1998).
3. From Bunce & Barr 1988, using the 13 ITE land classes which were regarded as upland (information not available on an English basis).
4. The following 18 Natural Areas are classed as upland by English Nature:

No	**Natural Area name**
2	Border Uplands
4	North Pennines
8	Yorkshire Dales
10	Cumbria Fells & Dales
12	Forest of Bowland
14	Southern Pennines
15	Pennine Dales Fringe
17	North York Moors and Hills
25	Dark Peak
29	South West Peak
30	White Peak
41	Oswestry Uplands
42	Shropshire Hills
58	Clun & North West Herefordshire Hills
60	Black Mountains and Golden Valley
87	Exmoor and the Quantocks
92	Dartmoor
94	Bodmin Moor

Table 7.14 Habitat requirements of birds associated with upland enclosed grasslands in England

Bird species	Habitat requirements
Red kite *Milvus milvus*	• Strong association with native woodland. • Nest placed high in native woodland tree. • Adults forage widely for carrion across roadsides and hillsides and for earthworms in improved and semi-improved pastures and tilled land. • Food brought to dependent young in nest by adults. • Present throughout year but extinct in English uplands.
Buzzard *Buteo buteo*	• Strong association with woodland and enclosed grassland at the moorland fringe. • Nest placed in isolated or woodland trees or occasionally on rock ledges, usually within woodland. • Adults feed over all types of open country - moors, acid grasslands, tilled land and pastures and meadows, taking earthworms from pastures and tilled land and small mammals, road kills and other carrion from hill and roadsides. • Adults bring food to dependent young in nest. • Present throughout the year.
Merlin *Falco columbarius*	• Strong association with heather moorlands. • Nest placed on ground in tall heather, or occasionally in bracken, on moderate to steep slopes. • Also nests occasionally in trees on moorland and at the edge of plantations. • Adults forage for a wide diversity of small bird prey (especially meadow pipit) over both moorland and enclosed grassland. • Food brought to nest for dependent young by adults. • Some birds present throughout the year, but many more present in breeding season, April-July.
Black grouse *Tetrao tetrix*	• Nests on ground in tall heather moorland or in rushy pastures. • Adults associate strongly with mixed moorland areas, with heather moors, *Vaccinium* heaths, *Eriophorum* bog and scrub and light woodland. • Chicks forage in wet flushes for invertebrates, particularly moth and sawfly larvae. • In winter, birds forage on heather moorland and amongst birch, rowan, hawthorn, alder and willow scrub. • Present in uplands throughout the year.
Corncrake *Crex crex*	• Strong association with traditionally managed hay meadows, particularly those with damp patches where sward height is tall enough to conceal birds on return in mid-April. • Nest placed on ground in meadow grasses. • Adults and young forage for invertebrates in hay fields - cutting dates must be sufficiently late to avoid destroying nests, eggs and young and cut should be from inside out to allow escape of remaining birds. • Extinct in English uplands, otherwise present mid-April to end August.
Oystercatcher *Haematopus ostralegus*	• Strong association with riparian grasslands. • Nest placed on sparsely vegetated ground in riparian gravels or other bare patches in improved/semi-improved fields and riparian grasslands, usually near lake or river. • Adults forage for earthworms and other invertebrates in improved, worm-rich pastures and riparian grasslands. • Chicks feed in damp flushes, pools and stream sides, and in semi-improved pastures. • Present late February to end June.

Bird species	Habitat requirements
Golden plover *Pluvialis apricaria*	• Strong association with flat or gently sloping ground, on unenclosed blanket bog and heather moors managed for grouse or sheep for nesting and enclosed pastures for feeding. • Nests on ground in short vegetation, created by burning, grazing or stunting on bogs or on ridge summits. • Chicks feed on grass patches on heather moor or in wet flushes - chicks may be led over a kilometre to feed in invertebrate rich areas by their parents. • When not incubating and before and following the breeding season, adults forage in enclosed, earthworm-rich, improved and semi-improved grassland up to at least 7 km from nests. • Presence in uplands very weather dependent: in mild years or areas, birds may be present throughout the year, but more usually present between late February and end June.
Snipe *Gallinago gallinago*	• Strong association with damp to wet unenclosed and enclosed land. • Nest placed on ground concealed in tussock in tall vegetation especially rushes in enclosed fields, wet moorland, grassland and wet flushes. • Adults forage for invertebrates in soft soil where water table near (<20 cm) surface, in damp rushy flushes, pools, stream sides on moors and on enclosed land. • Chicks forage for invertebrates in damp, rushy flushes, pools on moor or in enclosed fields. • Present mainly late February to end June.
Curlew *Numenius arquata*	Broad habitat association with flat or gently sloping ground, on low to moderate altitude moorlands and enclosed grasslands. • Nest in a wide range of sites, on the ground in both enclosed fields and on moorland, in tall and short vegetation. For example, in *Eriophorum* and large grass tussocks, in tall rushes and amongst the dead stems of sharp-flowered rush, in short or prostrate heather, in fresh burnt patches, and amongst bracken litter. • On heavily grazed moors with short grassland, nesting birds undertake much feeding on these moors. Occasionally breeding adults will also feed in enclosed fields some distance (3-4 km) from nest sites, rather than using fields immediately adjacent to the moor. Prior to laying and during incubating, adults feed on improved and semi-improved pastures rich in invertebrates because they are feeding mainly on earthworms and leatherjackets. After hatching, adults feed in the same areas as the chicks. • Chicks feed particularly in areas of wet rushy grassland and flushes, and moorland nesting birds will often take chicks into neighbouring enclosed fields. Also feed on the ground beneath tall heather, on short burnt heather, • Present late February to end June.
Redshank *Tringa totanus*	• Associated with riparian grasslands, unimproved and semi-improved pastures and, much less frequently, with damp moorland. • Nest is placed on ground in tussock in unimproved and semi-improved fields and allotments, in wet hollows or riparian grasslands. • Adults and chicks forage for invertebrates in wet riparian grasslands, stream sides and lake sides, enclosed improved land and wet, rushy patches in fields. • Present mid-April to end June.

Bird species	Habitat requirements
Short-eared owl *Asio flammeus*	• Strong association with unenclosed moorland, particularly on moderate to steep slopes towards moorland edge, and with young forestry. • Nests on ground within patches of tall heather, amongst bracken litter or in tall grassland, usually with good visibility. • Adults forage over all open moorland and enclosed unimproved grasslands for small mammals. • Food brought to nest by adults. • Small numbers present throughout year but most present during breeding season April to August.
Meadow pipit *Anthus pratensis*	• Found in association with nearly all types of upland habitat . • Nest placed on ground in tussock or depression in heath, grass or bracken. • Birds forage for invertebrates in short or moderately tall vegetation. Densities appear to be greatest on heather moors with a higher grass component. • Food brought by adults to dependent young in nest. • Present mainly March to late July. Not usually present outside breeding season.
Pied wagtail *Motacilla alba*	• Avoidance of open moorland but strong association with enclosed grasslands, farm buildings and stream sides in valleys. • Nest placed in hole in wall, outhouse, under stones, in open grassy places, screes. • Adults forage for invertebrate food in improved fields, farmyards, stream sides, lake shores and roadsides. • Food brought by adults to dependent young in nest. • Present throughout the year.
Whinchat *Saxicola rubetra*	• Strong association with tall vegetation, notably scrub, bracken and very tall grass and heather. • Adults sally for invertebrates from tall vegetation, fence posts and fencing wire or feed off ground on grassy patches amongst heather adjacent to bracken or on improved/semi-improved pastures. • Adults bring food to dependent young in nest. • Birds present end April to July.
Stonechat *Saxicola torquata*	• Strong association with scrub, tall heather or bracken. • Nest placed low in bracken, gorse and other tall, thick scrub, trees or heather. • Adults feed on open grassy areas, within otherwise shrub-dominated habitat or amongst patches of bracken, so long as perches are available on tall vegetation. • Adults bring food to dependent young in nest. • Found throughout year on scrub areas on enclosed farmland and on open moorland.
Wheatear *Oenanthe oenanthe*	• Nest in hole in ground or wall, in bracken clump, beneath stones, on enclosed farmland, moorland or scree. • Adults forage for invertebrates over bare ground or short swards on heather moors, stream sides, lake shores and enclosed farmland. • Adults bring food to dependent young in nest. • Birds usually present during extended breeding season, March to September.

Bird species	Habitat requirements
Twite *Carduelis flavirostris*	• Strong association with tall vegetation at moorland edge, often in close proximity to water and to flower-rich meadows. • Nest placed on ground or low down in tall heather, bracken litter or, more rarely, in grass, *Eriophorum* or small crevice, always on unenclosed land. • Adults forage for flower seeds collected in burnt *Molinia* patches and from farmyards and haystacks in April and early May, from flower-rich meadows and pastures in May and June and from roadside verges and any remaining uncut meadows thereafter. Birds will forage up to at least 2 km from moorland nest site. • Food brought to dependent young in nest by adults. • Birds usually present during extended breeding season, April to September.

Table 7.15 Management guidelines for birds associated with upland enclosed grasslands in England

Management of enclosed grassland for birds
• Maintain natural drainage and wetland features such as pools and flushes. • Create small wet areas by blocking existing drains and grips. • Do not reseed or plough permanent pastures. • Do not apply inorganic or organic fertiliser, slurry or lime to upland farmland unless this has been a traditional practice. • If rolling is necessary, roll immediately after drilling and before nesting season in April. • Graze over an extended period using a low density of stock. Cattle or horses will produce a tussocky sward favoured by breeding waders. • Turn stock out onto fields used by nesting waders after second week in June. • Cut hay meadows after mid-July to avoid harming nesting birds. • Leave an uncut strip at the edge of the meadow and allow wild flowers to colonise lanes and roadsides. • Control dense stands of rushes using a combination of cutting and grazing to achieve a scattered cover of 10-20% of the field.
Management of scrub in enclosed grassland for birds
• On steep slopes retain scrub such as gorse and juniper and scattered trees such as hawthorn and rowan. • On gentler slopes graze or cut scrub in rotation. Provide a range of habitats by clearing about 10% of scrub each year when it is about 10 years old.
Woodland and scrub creation in enclosed grassland for birds
• Fence off areas where there is some scrub to allow natural regeneration. • Scarify the ground where old stands of scrub have been removed and regeneration is poor. • Plant native tree species on areas of low wildlife interest.

Table 7.16 Mammals associated with upland meadows and enclosed pastures in England

Scientific name	Common name	Nature conservation status	Typical habitat	Distribution by upland Natural Area[1]
Cervidae eg *Capreolus capreolus, Cervus elaphus*	Deer, eg roe deer, red deer	Common and widespread; increasing. Important effects on vegetation structure.	Woodlands with open rides; open moorland, grassland adjacent to woodlands	All have one or more species
Vespertilionidae	Bats	Widespread; some species common. All bats are fully protected by Schedule 5 of the Wildlife and Countryside Act 1981, and some are Priority Biodiversity Action Plan species (UK Biodiversity Group 1998; UK Steering Group 1995).	Open pasture adjacent to woodlands, woodland rides	All, but more abundant in lowland river valleys
Microtus agrestis	Field vole	Widespread and common; important component in food chain.	Rough grass pasture, grass moorland, open woodland and rides and young 'pre-thicket' plantations	All
Sorex spp	Shrews	Widespread; most species common.	Grass pasture, grass and heather moorland, open woodland and rides	All

Source

Mitchell-Jones & Gent 1997.

[1] The following 18 Natural Areas are classed as upland by English Nature:

No	Natural Area name
2	Border Uplands
4	North Pennines
8	Yorkshire Dales
10	Cumbria Fells & Dales
12	Forest of Bowland
14	Southern Pennines
15	Pennine Dales Fringe
17	North York Moors and Hills
25	Dark Peak
29	South West Peak
30	White Peak
41	Oswestry Uplands
42	Shropshire Hills
58	Clun & North West Herefordshire Hills
60	Black Mountains and Golden Valley
87	Exmoor and the Quantocks
92	Dartmoor
94	Bodmin Moor.

Table 7.17 Amphibians and reptiles associated with upland meadows and enclosed pastures in England

Scientific name	English name	Nature conservation status	Typical habitat	Distribution by upland Natural Area[1]
Rana temporaria	Common frog	Widespread, locally common.	Uneven structured vegetation, eg grassland, woodland margins, near or connected to ponds (can be small, must have shallow areas) or other water bodies with roughly neutral pH.	All
Bufo bufo	Common toad	Widespread, locally common, but probably declining.	Uneven structured vegetation, eg grassland, woodland margins, near or connected to ponds or other water bodies with roughly neutral pH. Ponds may be deeper and presence of fish less a problem than for other amphibians. Will travel long distances to breeding ponds.	All
Triturus vulgaris *T. helveticus*	Smooth newt Palmate newt	Widespread, locally common. Palmate generally more associated with upland or more acid waters while smooth newt common, more abundant in lowland habitats.	Structurally varied habitats, eg grasslands, woodland edges, quarries, with nearby or integral ponds. Ponds can be small to fairly large.	All
T. cristatus	Great crested newt	Widespread, declining but may be locally abundant and more often found in lowland habitats. Fully protected by Schedule 5 of the Wildlife and Countryside Act 1981, and a Priority Biodiversity Action Plan species (UK Steering Group 1995).	As for other newt species (see above). Great crested newts tend to use larger ponds or rely more on clusters of nearby ponds than other newt species.	All

Scientific name	English name	Nature conservation status	Typical habitat	Distribution by upland Natural Area[1]
Lacerta vivipara *Anguis fragilis*	common lizard slow-worm	Widespread, can be locally common, but nationally probably declining. Partially protected by Schedule 5 of the Wildlife and Countryside Act 1981.	Structurally varied, open habitats; often providing basking areas. Banks, woodland margins, open moorland, tussocky grasslands and bogs. Areas should not be too wet. Limited dispersion potential means adults fairly sedentary and reflects importance of connected habitats for long term survival of populations. Slow-worms tend to be found more in grassland habitats, especially where slugs and snails are present (major food item).	All
Vipera berus	adder	Widespread, locally common, but declining. Partially protected by Schedule 5 of the Wildlife and Countryside Act 1981.	Structurally varied habitats, such as moors, woodland edges, ungrazed (or low intensity grazed) grassland. Especially in areas with low levels of disturbance, and in areas with several habitat types (eg. woodland and moorland) in close proximity.	All
Natrix natrix	grass snake	Widespread, locally common, but more associated with lowland habitats. Partially protected by Schedule 5 of the Wildlife and Countryside Act 1981.	Structurally varied habitats. Very mobile species; often associated with water (amphibians and fish are major prey items) and needs rotting vegetation for egg laying. Therefore more often associated with farmed areas than other snake species.	Most Natural Areas though records sparse in northern England

Source

Mitchell-Jones & Gent 1999

[1] The following 18 Natural Areas are classed as upland by English Nature:

No	Natural Area name
2	Border Uplands
4	North Pennines
8	Yorkshire Dales
10	Cumbria Fells & Dales
12	Forest of Bowland
14	Southern Pennines
15	Pennine Dales Fringe
17	North York Moors and Hills
25	Dark Peak
29	South West Peak
30	White Peak
41	Oswestry Uplands
42	Shropshire Hills
58	Clun & North West Herefordshire Hills
60	Black Mountains and Golden Valley
87	Exmoor and the Quantocks
92	Dartmoor
94	Bodmin Moor.

Woodland

Woodland and scrub 8

Tables

Definition and location of woodland and scrub in the uplands

8.1 Definition of woodland and scrub in the uplands

Woodland includes all areas where trees are abundant in the vegetation and strongly determine the nature of the lower-growing plant communities and the animals. Woodland may be split into 'semi-natural' stands which are composed largely of trees and shrubs native to the site that have grown up from natural regeneration, coppice or stump regrowth; and 'plantations' where the trees are largely planted. Plantations are most commonly of non-native species (such as Sitka spruce *Picea sitchensis* or lodgepole pine *Pinus contorta*) but may be of locally native species such as oak *Quercus* spp. Woods (or parts of woods) are described as 'ancient' where there appears to have been continuity of woodland cover on the site since 1600 AD and as 'recent' where there is evidence that the site was, for example, open moorland, bog or grassland at some time in the last 400 years and that therefore the woodland has originated after 1600 AD. The terms 'ancient' and 'recent' refer to the history of the site as woodland, whereas 'semi-natural' and 'plantation' refer to the composition of the current crop of trees on the site. Ancient sites may now carry plantations, recent woods may be semi-natural, eg where birch is regenerating on drying-out bogs.

Woods that are both ancient and semi-natural tend to be the most important for nature conservation. Most ancient semi-natural woodland in the English uplands was formerly managed as 'coppice' (or coppice-with-standards), particularly for the oak bark and charcoal industries. These woods often still show signs of such working in their structure with many even-aged, multiple stemmed trees, whereas under more natural conditions trees would mainly be present as single-stemmed individuals growing as 'high forest'. High forest is the usual structure in recent woodland and plantations. A third type of woodland structure is 'wood-pasture' where the trees are usually wide-spaced, very old (veterans), and may have been pollarded in the past. This is more commonly found in lowland parks but occurs in places on the upland fringes. Some of these structural differences have become blurred because, following abandonment of coppicing in the nineteenth century, many upland woods now consist of grazed high forest. This has a different conservation interest to that of lowland wood pastures.

Scrub refers to low-growing communities where the major woody components are bushes (eg hawthorn *Crataegus monogyna*, juniper *Juniperus communis*, blackthorn *Prunus spinosa*) or undershrubs such as bramble *Rubus* spp, gorse *Ulex europaeus*, or broom *Cytisus scoparius*. Stands of young trees or of sallows *Salix* spp are usually treated as woodland. In the past foresters have also used the term scrub to refer to unproductive woodland of oak and birch. That usage is not followed here.

The term forest is used generally to mean any large area of woodland; or, with a capital F, to refer to a former Royal Hunting Forest. These Hunting Forests (eg at Bowland or Pickering) were areas defined by medieval kings and queens (occasionally other nobles) to which applied specific laws on hunting, mainly of deer. They might or might not have contained much woodland.

Further information: Kirby 1996a; Kirby & Patterson 1993; Rackham 1980, 1986, 1990; Ratcliffe 1977. Discussion of terms 'ancient' and 'semi-natural', and significance of ancient semi-natural woodland: Peterken 1977, 1993, 1996; Spencer & Kirby 1992.

8.2 Location of woodland and scrub in the uplands

Most of the uplands below 600 m were probably covered by woodland 7,000 years ago but thereafter clearance occurred to varying degrees and at varying times. However, by a thousand years ago, the woodland cover in the uplands was probably less than 20% of the land area and it continued to shrink, except in periods when locally there was a downturn in agricultural incomes or there was a thriving market for wood products. Interest in management might lead to fields being converted to coppices; in 1803 it was noted that 'proprietors of Colton (S. Cumbria) had ceased to breed sheep, so far were they involved in the cultivation of coppices.' Over the last 100 years, however, interest in woodland management has generally waned and most of the broadleaved woods are now used only for sheltered grazing, with consequent effects on their regeneration.

Ancient woodland sites are scattered throughout the uplands, although they are usually less common than in the lowlands, (see relevant county Ancient Woodland Inventories, Table 8.10). Recent semi-natural woodland and scrub tend to show a similar distribution pattern. The woods are generally small (less than 20 ha). Commonly, upland woods occur along steep valley sides, although the woods rarely extend above 350 m. Scattered trees occur at higher altitudes along gills and restoration of tree line woodland could be based around such fragments. Some woodland communities typical of the uplands also occur at lower altitudes, even down to sea level, for example the oak woods along the Fal Estuary or in the Forest of Dean. Therefore, although this chapter concentrates on the conservation of these woodland communities within the defined upland Natural Areas (Fig. 1.1), this must not be seen as separate from what is happening to (or being proposed for) these same communities elsewhere.

Most woodland in the uplands is recent. Large areas of coniferous plantations have been established over the last 100 years in the uplands because land for planting has generally been cheaper than in the lowlands. Their establishment has often been controversial, because they replaced open ground of high conservation value; in some cases these open habitats are being restored as the plantations come up for felling. However, some of these stands have now become a nature conservation resource in their own right.

Habitats and species of woodland and scrub in the uplands

8.3 Why upland woodland and scrub are important

Upland woods and scrub contain natural and cultural landscape features of national and international importance. These include a wide range of species and communities not found in lowland English woods and the transition zones between species with a broadly southern-continental versus a more northerly distribution.

Some, but not all, of these features are better represented in Scotland or Wales. The oak woods in England, for example, tend to be smaller and more fragmented than those in Scotland; the distinctive bryophyte communities associated with the mild, moist conditions of the west are less well developed. On the other hand the upland ashwoods, which contain many rare vascular plants, are more extensive and varied in England than in Wales and Scotland.

This chapter is mainly concerned with the conservation value and management of the woodland. However, in the uplands many of the species, features and processes are closely linked to their surroundings. Some upland birds may use woodland for nesting, but forage over the adjacent open ground; conversely open-ground nesting birds may sometimes be at risk from predators living within adjacent new plantations. Fires may be desirable to maintain some dwarf-shrub communities, but are damaging if they spread into adjacent woodland. Airborne pollutants may be deposited on tree leaves and subsequently be washed off, leading to increased acidification of forest streams. More work is needed on the distribution of existing and new woodland that best meets both woodland and open-ground conservation objectives.

8.4 Habitats and species in upland woodland and scrub, their nature conservation status and distribution

8.4.1 Vascular plants

The woodland communities on acid soils in the uplands are characteristically poor in vascular plants, but the woods as a whole are often rich because they also contain base-rich flushes and wet areas. These flushed areas may include nationally rare and scarce plants such as touch-me-not *Impatiens noli-tangere*, tall fescue *Festuca altissima* and Irish spurge *Euphorbia hyberna*. Upland woods on limestone, particularly those associated with limestone pavement, have also long been noted for their richness and occurrence of rarities including lady's slipper orchid *Cypripedium calceolus*, baneberry *Actaea spicata* and mezereum *Daphne mezereum*. North-western species such as marsh hawkweed *Crepis paludosa*, globe flower *Trollius europaeus* and hay-scented fern *Dryopteris aemula* may share woods with southern continental ones such as herb paris *Paris quadrifolia*. Upland woods are thus nationally important for higher plants.

Nationally rare and scarce vascular plants associated with upland woodland and scrub are listed in Table 8.1. The assignment to Natural Areas is a first approximation and species that occur close to the boundary between two areas may have been assigned to both. In addition the distinction between woodland and non-woodland plants is less clear-cut than in the lowlands: some plants elsewhere associated with wood-edge may in the uplands occur in open tall-herb communities such as on cliff ledges and limestone pavement.

8.4.2 Bryophytes and lichens

The western oak woods are amongst the richest for bryophytes in England and are of national and international importance. Some of the rare species found in these woods are listed in Table 8.2. The bryophyte richness and abundance of the woods comes from the combination of high rainfall and a suppression of the shrub layer and field layer cover by grazing. The occurrence of many boulders and other microsites which remain moist but do not develop higher plant cover is also important. Finally the low level of felling in many of these woods over the last 100 years has helped to maintain humidity levels within the woods.

Many western woods and parkland also have a relatively high lichen diversity, despite the scarcity of very big trees in many of the woods. The relatively clean air and high light levels below the canopy are conducive to good lichen growth. Some nationally rare and scarce lichens associated with upland woodland and scrub are shown in Table 8.3.

Further information: Church *et al* 1996 ; Hodgetts 1996; Ratcliffe 1968.

8.4.3 Plant communities

In Table 8.4 the broad woodland groupings used in the Biodiversity Action Plans (BAP) are related to the main woodland National Vegetation Classification types along with their rough equivalents in other systems. The relationships are rarely one-to-one and so, while the most obvious links have been indicated, they are not exclusive in either direction. The listing of a Habitats Directive type against a set of NVC communities does not necessarily mean that all stands within these communities correspond to the Directive type, or, even if some do, that there are stands of sufficient quality to be considered for listing under the Directive.

Unlike in lowland woods the NVC types largely take account of most of the variations previously recognised in the Stand Type system. However, at the lowland/upland boundary and on base-rich soils special attention may need to be paid to the occurrence of wych elm (Stand Group 1), lime (Stand Groups 4, 5) and field maple (Stand Group 2). In addition, woods usually contain patches of open or wetland habitats which may be particularly important for various animal groups. Wood/scrub edges are, for example often particularly rich in higher plants and insects.

Virtually all woodland NVC types occur in the uplands, but some are at a much lower frequency than in the lowlands. For the purposes of this handbook the types of woodland most frequently encountered in the uplands have been grouped in the following way:

- upland oak woods;
- upland ash woodland;
- wet woodland;
- ancient wood pasture;
- scrub;
- replanted ancient sites;
- recent plantations.

The first four of these represent BAP priority habitats. Scrub is recognised as a separate Phase 1 category and, like the previous four, is contained within the Broadleaved and Yew BAP broad habitat type. The two plantation types have been highlighted because of their different management needs and priorities.

The assessment of the conservation significance of different classes of woodland has been done by these broad groups (Table 8.5).

The main woodland and scrub NVC communities occur in virtually all the upland Natural Areas, albeit sometimes in fragmentary form, because the majority of land in the sub-montane zone is only maintained in an open state through anthropogenic activity. Further information on the character of the ancient woodland in particular areas is given in the relevant profile reports and county ancient woodland inventories (Tables 8.8-8.10).

Further information on these communities and their significance in the uplands: Hall 1997; Kirby 1996a; Kirby & Reid 1997; Peterken 1993; Reid, Kirby & Cooke 1996; Rodwell 1991.

8.4.4 Birds

Upland oak woods have a distinctive bird assemblage which includes redstart *Phoenicurus phoenicurus*, wood warbler *Phylloscopus sibilatrix* and pied flycatcher *Ficedula hypoleuca*. Many of these woods are heavily grazed, usually by sheep, and hence lack dense undergrowth. Although this means that such woods lack many of the shrub-nesting species found in less heavily grazed lowland woods, some grazing appears to benefit the above three characteristic species of the oak woods. Reduction of grazing within these woods could generate a more complex vegetation structure that may lead to an increase in overall densities and numbers of breeding birds, but it is likely that these characteristic upland oak wood bird species would decline under such a regime.

Important bird populations, including goshawk *Accipiter gentilis*, crossbill *Loxia curvirostra* and siskin *Carduelis spinus*, are now found within some of the larger upland conifer plantations. These species have expanded their range and national populations largely in response to the creation of the new forests. Nightjar *Caprimulgus europaeus*, which have declined greatly in recent decades, have also colonised clear-fells and open areas in some upland plantations (although this species is not considered further because it is more associated the lowlands, Stillman & Brown 1998). Merlin *Falco columbarius* have also taken to nesting within the edges of some upland forests. There is considerable scope for integrating bird conservation into the management and design of these plantations.

Scrub is potentially important to species such as black grouse *Tetrao tetrix*, whitethroat *Sylvia communis*, grasshopper warbler *Locustella naevia*, whinchat *Saxicola rubetra* and stonechat *S. torquata*. Relaxation of grazing and burning in the uplands may be associated with scrub development which, depending on factors such as exposure and grazing patterns, may eventually develop into woodland or persist as some form of scrub. This vegetational change would trigger large changes in bird communities, although rather little is known about the current bird assemblages in scrub patches in the English uplands. In addition, by enhancing population densities of small songbirds it may serve to increase numbers of birds of prey such as merlin and hen harrier *Circus cyaneus*.

Birds associated with upland woodland and scrub are shown in Table 8.6, with their nature conservation status.

Further information: Currie & Elliot 1997; Fuller 1982, 1995, 1996; Petty & Avery 1990.

8.4.5 Invertebrates

Upland woods and scrub have been less well studied from an invertebrate point of view than lowland sites, so any overall assessment must be preliminary. Table 8.7 indicates those BAP priority species that are believed to be associated with upland oak and ash woodland, including for example the blue ground beetle *Carabus intricatus*, found in Britain only in two small woods on the edge of Dartmoor.

The oak woods are often notable for their wood ants and, as with other groups, northern *Formica lugubris* and southern *F. rufa* species meet in the English uplands. Woodland edges, very open glades and, in particular, broadleaved scrub are a very important habitat for a wide range of invertebrates in the uplands in that they can provide structural diversity and particularly warm microhabitats in the form of sheltered sun-traps and nectar sources. These habitats are particularly valuable for butterflies such as the heath fritillary *Mellicta athalia*, high brown fritillary *Argynnis adippe* and pearl-bordered fritillary *Boloria euphrosyne* in the south western peninsula uplands. The latter two species also use open scrub on calcareous grassland and coppice woodland on the carboniferous limestone around Morecambe Bay. The Duke of Burgundy butterfly *Hemearis lucina* uses cowslip and primrose plants in scrubby grassland in the same area and on the North Yorks Moors.

High brown fritillary

The netted carpet moth is another significant species which feeds on touch-me-not balsam in the woods of the Lake District; the orange underwing *Jodia croceago* is recorded from Dartmoor and the north Somerset coast and at least nine nationally scarce moths are associated with woodland in the south-west uplands. Upland juniper scrub supports a small number of upland species associated with this shrub, in particular the nationally scarce moths the juniper carpet *Thera juniperata* and chestnut coloured carpet *Thera cognata*. Both of these occur on juniper in the northern Pennines and Lake district, although the juniper carpet also occurs on the southern heathland juniper. Most other juniper feeding species of invertebrate occur only on juniper in the south of England. The nationally rare picture-winged fly *Platyparaea discoidea* is now almost entirely restricted to calcareous woodlands in the Craven Pennines where it feeds inside stems of giant bellflower *Campanula latifolia*, while the nationally rare fly *Pedicia robusta* occurs on Bodmin Moor.

Upland woods often support significant mollusc faunas. These include species restricted, in the lowlands, to top quality ancient woodland sites. Woodland molluscs are very prone to desiccation. The richness of uplands woods is mainly due to high rainfall, humidity and the cover of mosses. Snails include *Leiostyla anglica* (rare overall in Europe, with most of its range within Britain), *Zenobiella subrufescens*, *Spermodea lamellata* and *Ashfordia granulata* and the slugs *Limax tenellus* and *L. cinereoniger*. The same moist habitat supports the rare pill woodlouse *Armadillidium pictum* and local species *A. pulchellum*. Both occur in basic/calcareous woods in the uplands in the north and west. Abundant moss growing on trees can also support assemblages of local ground and rove beetles, false scorpions and craneflies while wet woodland soils, especially where calcareous, support rich cranefly and fungus-gnat communities.

Dead wood species are not well represented because the intensity of past coppice working has kept dead wood levels low. Dead wood levels are, however, now building up again because of the lack of recent management in many sites. Dead wood present within the old coppice stools can support a rich invertebrate fauna. One nationally scarce dead wood species that is more prevalent in the uplands, north and west, is *Hylecoetus dermestoides*, a beetle which bores into firm dead oak timber.

Further information: Kirby 1992.

8.4.6 Mammals, amphibians and reptiles

Upland woods are the last mainland refuge in England for the red squirrel *Sciurcus vulgaris* and efforts continue to try to prevent the establishment of grey squirrel *S. carolinensis* where not already present. Very large woods (in excess of 2000 ha) and composed mainly of coniferous species are likely to provide the best refuges for red squirrels because these provide the poorest habitat for grey squirrels. A diverse age structure is ideal with 50-60% of the trees being of cone bearing age. Young trees of 15-30 years provide good cover, and continuous belts of trees linking seed-bearing areas are desirable. In some areas coordinated control of grey squirrels by cage trapping may be desirable. Local squirrel projects should be contacted for details; Forestry Commission offices will have the relevant addresses.

In the south upland and upland fringe broadleaf woods with a good range of understorey shrubs can hold populations of dormice *Muscardinus avellanarius*. Young plantations are valuable habitats for small mammals, when there is a thick covering of ground vegetation. Later similar conditions may be provided along wide grassy rides. High populations of small mammals as well as being of value in their own right provide food for a wide range of predators.

Otters *Lutra lutra* may use riverside woodland strips and lines of trees. Native deer (roe *Capreolus capreolus* and red *Cervus elaphus*) occur in upland woods and both these and domestic stock (mainly sheep, ponies, cattle) can have very great impacts on the conservation management of the woods in both a positive and negative way. The main issue with deer is likely to be their control. Shooting and fencing combined with good forest design are the only generally effective methods.

Large upland woods in the north including conifer plantations, may become particularly important for pine marten *Martes martes*. Around 150 ha of woodland is needed for each territory, preferably with a range of ages and sizes of trees. Adjacent undisturbed rough moorland can provide places to which the animals retreat during forestry operations.

Newly planted forest can offer ideal habitats for reptiles. The early stages following digging of soils, especially where areas are ploughed, provide a wide range of topographical features and frequently a good flush of vegetation. The trees themselves, during the first five or so years, will ameliorate the climate at ground level (reducing wind chill). The large number of small mammals associated with these woods will also benefit snake populations. However, as the trees grow and the canopy begins to shade out ground vegetation, woodland especially coniferous plantations, become unsuitable for reptiles. Not only will the areas not sustain a population, but the forestry crop will create a barrier to dispersion. The value of woods for amphibians tends to be associated with the associated wetland areas, but they will disperse into and use woodland with a good ground cover and humid microclimate.

8.5 Habitat and management requirements of species of upland woodland and scrub

The habitat and management requirements of key upland woodland and scrub species are found in tables at the end of the chapter.

Further information: Fuller 1992, 1996; Fuller & Peterken 1995; Fuller & Warren 1993, 1995; Warren & Fuller 1993.

Management of upland woodland and scrub

8.6 Conservation objectives for habitats and species of upland woodland and scrub

8.6.1 Introduction

National government policies for forestry are aimed at:

- the sustainable management of our existing woods and forests;
- a steady expansion of tree cover to increase the many diverse benefits that forests provide.

These have been confirmed in the England Forestry Strategy which aims to encourage increases in:

- the role of forestry in the rural economy;
- the area of woodland created on derelict and former industrial land as well as a reduction in the cost of creating this woodland;
- the area of woodland available for access;
- the area of semi-natural and native woodland together with a reduction in the fragmentation of ancient semi-natural woodland;
- the resources available for forestry and woodland through new partnerships between public, private and voluntary sectors;
- integrated action across government to implement the strategy;
- people's involvement with England's woods and forests and a better understanding of the benefits they bring.

Sustainable forestry definitions based on the international forestry conferences held at Rio in 1992 and Helsinki in 1993 recognise that maintaining forest biodiversity is an essential part of the process and also that this must not be at the expense of important open ground habitats and species, whether associated with natural or cultural landscapes.

Further information: Forestry Commission 1998; HMSO 1994a; Kirby 1996b.

8.6.2 General objectives for upland woodland and scrub

General woodland conservation objectives are as follows:

- Maintain and expand (through restoration of replanted areas) the area of ancient semi-natural woodland with its distinctive plant and animal communities.
- Maintain and, if possible, enhance populations of rare woodland species.
- Maintain and enhance the populations of all native woodland species.
- Maintain the traditional range of native species and communities.

These are developed in the *Position statement on environmentally sustainable forestry and woodland management* produced by English Nature (1994b) (reconfirmed 1997):

- Ancient semi-natural woods are irreplaceable, and must be protected and managed so as to maintain and enhance their special character. The expansion of such woods on to adjacent land by natural regeneration should be encouraged.
- Many ancient woods have lost nature conservation value through being converted to plantations. Restoration of their native tree and shrub communities should be encouraged.
- More recent woods and plantations, especially semi-natural woodland, should also be managed so as to maintain and increase their value as wildlife habitat.
- Some woodland has grown up or been planted on important open ground habitats such as lowland heath, which is nationally and internationally scarce. Restoration of the former open habitat should be encouraged. An uplands example would be restoration of the Border Mires.
- New woodland should be created in appropriate locations, and the use of natural regeneration for this purpose should be encouraged. It is important that existing good wildlife habitat and features of geological and geomorphological interest are not damaged. New woodland in both uplands and lowlands should be targeted on land of low existing value for nature conservation and earth heritage features, such as arable farmland and intensive grassland, and located where it will do most to enhance the local habitat mosaic. More use should be made of locally native trees and shrubs, and woodland designs which favour wildlife. In the uplands bracken land and some acid grassland might also be suitable as sites for new woodland.

- In many woods management is necessary to maintain both timber production and nature conservation value. The use of management plans to coordinate economic, environmental and social objectives should be standard practice.

- There is also a case to allow some upland woods to develop naturally (ie minimum intervention) although often fencing would be required to exclude grazing.

The above apply across all upland Natural Areas.

Further information: English Nature 1994b; Good *et al* 1997; Kirby 1993; Kirby & Reid 1997.

8.6.3 Expansion of native woodland in the uplands

English Nature recognises that there is potential for some expansion in the uplands, and would welcome more new native woodland in most of the upland Natural Areas.

Within the uplands one of the reasons for wanting more woodland is to reduce the isolation of existing sites and to off-set the effects of past woodland fragmentation. New woodland can help to reduce such adverse effects by extending existing sites and by linking them up with others. New woodland formed next to existing woods or other features such as hedges and streams will also be richer than that created in isolated situations. However, the new woodland should avoid both the direct loss or increased isolation and fragmentation of other important habitats such as heather moorland. The following principles may help to judge the priority that should be attached to linking up existing woodland blocks.

- In areas that are rich in woodland and other semi-natural habitats, often with concentrations of SSSIs or other conservation areas, creating direct links between the woods is less critical than simply expanding the area of woodland and improving the management of what is there already. New woods, wherever they are put, are likely to be close enough to other semi-natural features for colonisation to be rapid, at least for the more mobile species.

- Where there are isolated patches of woodland, new woods should be added on to what exists. Existing woods and hedges should be encouraged to spread by natural regeneration on to suitable adjacent ground.

- In the long term there are parts of the country where widely separated blocks of woodland need to be linked to allow easier movement for species through the landscape. Initially this may be achieved more efficiently by creating a series of small stepping-stone woods through the gap rather than a single long thin corridor of woodland. A balance therefore needs to be struck between the advantages of linking up existing woodlands against the disadvantages of fragmenting other habitats.

- Some large new woods should be created as part of future forest expansion, but if they are in isolated locations they are unlikely to attract many of the specialist species that in theory would require large areas, because such species also tend to be poor colonists. Thus there may be a need to consider introduction or translocation of species in such circumstances.

Further information: Buckley & Fraser 1998; Good *et al* 1997.

8.6.4 Management objectives for woodland

No single management regime is correct for a given woodland type in all situations. Instead overall conservation objectives can only be met if a variety of treatments are applied to different woods, to provide the range of structures required by different groups of woodland species within the limited areas of woodland available. There is a need to bring together ideas on woodland expansion and the balance between different ways in which woods may be managed, with the needs of particular woodland types. The balance will also depend on how a wood has been treated in the past and its location. Boxes 8.1-8.3 indicate criteria for judging the likely value of restoring coppice or going for minimum intervention, two of the possible options.

Further information: Fuller & Peterken 1995; Fuller & Warren 1995.

8.6.5 Developing priorities for different woodland types

The various types of woodland feature are considered in turn below. Overall targets for maintenance and expansion of the four BAP priority types are set out in the relevant action plans and are being translated into indicative ones for different natural areas within the uplands.

Oakwoods. This was often managed as coppice in the past, but the future preferred management is likely to be high forest, either managed or minimum intervention, with only limited areas of coppice restoration. Most of the woods are grazed at present: some reduction in grazing is usually desirable, but complete and permanent exclusion of stock and deer is not always either possible or beneficial in conservation terms, particularly in the most oceanic woods. Rhododendron is a major threat to many sites and needs to be controlled/eliminated where possible (Tabbush & Williamson 1987).

Upland ashwoods. In the uplands the bulk of this is on the northern limestones, in the Dales and the southern Lake District (Morecambe Bay area). There is more scope and value in restoring coppice in some of these woods than in the oakwoods particularly as some have very good butterfly populations, but high forest (either managed and minimum intervention) is also likely to be beneficial. There is little benefit in keeping high levels of grazing in most of these woods.

Wet woodland. Alder *Alnus glutinosa,* willow and wet birch *Bertula* spp woodland is usually likely to benefit from minimum intervention with only light levels of grazing. Expansion of their area is desirable. In places there may be a case for clearing wet woodland, that has developed recently, to restore a more important open habitat. Such action needs to be well justified, since in the uplands all wet woodland is a scarce habitat and even recent examples may be very important for invertebrates.

Ancient wood pasture. Areas of veteran trees usually in a parkland setting tend to be less formal and less well-defined than in the lowlands. They are most likely to be found on the fringes of the uplands proper. Wherever it does occur the priority is to retain the existing old trees and to encourage a succession of younger ones which will eventually replace them. There is currently no national inventory of these wood pastures, but it is likely that the highest concentrations in the upland Natural Areas are in the south-west, Welsh Borders and the margins of the Peak District.

Replanted ancient sites. Ancient woodland of a variety of types has been replanted, usually with conifers, but more locally with plantations of introduced broadleaves such as beech (outside its native range) and sycamore *Acer pseudoplatanus*. Restoration work is in its infancy and there are few studies as to how quickly the ground flora and other elements of the system can be restored (Kirby & May 1989; Radford 1998). The Habitat Action Plan targets include restoration from conifers to semi-natural woodland and much of this is likely to be in the uplands. Efforts should be concentrated on those woods that are most likely to show a strong response, for example:

- those that have only recently been replanted (during the last 30 years);
- where some of the former broadleaved cover and/or the ground flora survives within the crop;
- those with a species-rich ride system or other open habitats present which may serve as source of colonising species.

Scrub. Juniper scrub should be maintained where it occurs. Where stock is present, rubbing damage by grazing cattle or sheep can lead to the death of branches and whole bushes. Small mammals, hares and rabbits can also have a significant effect through the removal of young shoots and bark. Grazing, and also fire, can both play a part in juniper regeneration by creating bare soil where young plants can establish (Clifton, Ranner & Ward 1995). Care is required as heavy grazing of young seedlings, once established, will cause heavy losses while burning around existing bushes must be avoided.

Other scrub should be encouraged as part of the overall habitat mosaic, where it is not replacing more important open vegetation with the general aim of increasing its total extent. Spatial patchiness is an extremely important habitat feature for many plants and animals. Edges are particularly important and intimate mixtures of grass, scrub and woodland can be advantageous to insects (Mortimer *et al* 2000). In some cases the scrub may be a temporary stage that develops later into woodland; in other cases it may become a more-or-less permanent feature. In the higher upland areas we should seek to recreate areas of sub-montane scrub.

Recent plantations. These can contain a wide range of native species and habitat patches even where they are largely composed of introduced conifers. Some should be restored to open vegetation types - some 15,000-20,000 ha might be identified for conversion over the next 50 years. However, English Nature recognises and wishes to build on the diversity that exists in this new element in the landscape, particularly as its extent is likely to increase. Some uncommon species, particularly birds such as the goshawk, now have their upland strongholds in these plantations (Currie & Elliott 1997). As the forests are felled and restocked, opportunities exist to increase their structural diversity (without altering their main species) and to reduce their impact on, for example, the acidification of streams. Methods of assessing biodiversity within these new forests and setting targets for what should be achieved are being developed by the Forest Commission, and further work will be needed on this.

8.7 Managing upland woodland and scrub

The techniques used in the management of upland woods are likely to be broadly determined by whether they are being treated primarily for nature conservation, as part of a forestry regime, or are considered part of the agricultural holding. Nature conservation objectives must be integrated with other concerns to provide the basis for the long-term sustainable management of the woodland resource.

Key aspects to be considered for each woodland are:

- the impact on the overall species composition of the wood;
- the effects on the vertical structure (number of vegetation layers, ie ground, field, shrub, canopy);
- the effects on horizontal structure (variation between stands across the wood);
- what will happen to the amount of open space in the wood;
- what will happen to wet areas in the wood;
- implications for dead wood and old trees;
- management of large herbivores (usually deer and sheep);
- what will the wood be like if this approach is followed for the next 50 years?

In the big upland conifer plantations the aspects above should still be considered, but usually at a bigger scale of working. Further encouragement is needed to increase the use of native broadleaves on appropriate soils, some stands left as long-term retentions, more open space and the restoration of key open habitats such as bogs. Forest design plans should be used to encourage the development of structural variety at a landscape scale. The emphasis in the rest of the section is therefore on broadleaved woodland.

8.7.1 Management using forestry techniques

Silvicultural techniques can be used to create the types of structures and conditions that are needed from a nature conservation viewpoint and to meet the owner's objectives. Active management may be proposed, with the woods managed as coppice/coppice-with-standards or as high forest; high levels of grazing may be present as part of an ancient wood-pasture system or more commonly as a recent addition to former coppice woods; or sites may be assigned to minimum intervention. The effects of different systems and operations depend on the scale at which they are applied both in time and space. Boxes 8.1 and 8.2 illustrate the factors that should be used to judge the appropriateness of different options for particular sites, for example criteria in choosing either minimum intervention or coppice options. Box 8.3 compares different options in terms of which elements of the woodland system are likely to benefit or be disadvantaged.

Further information: Evans 1984; Forestry Commission 1994; Kirby 1984; Watkins 1990.

Box 8.1 Desirable characteristics for woods that are to be put into minimum intervention

- Large area
- Compact shape
- Little recent treatment or unnatural disturbance
- Few introduced species and no highly invasive ones
- No major external deleterious factors operating, eg spray drift from neighbouring agricultural land
- Not noted for rare or unusual species that depend on management for their survival on site
- Stable ownership
- Diversity of age structure.

Source: Kirby & Rush 1994

Further information: Mountford 2000; Peterken 2000.

Box 8.2 Criteria for or against restoration of coppicing of stands in ancient woods
(Note: individual woods may contain both coppiced and non-coppiced stands)

For coppice restoration:

- Woods with a history of coppicing and which have been cut over since 1900, preferably during the last 40 years.
- Woods in regions where coppice management has been common until recently.
- Woods likely to produce a diverse ground flora and/or food plants for invertebrates requiring open glades or young scrubby stands. Woods on base-rich or poorly drained soils are more likely to produce a rich response to coppicing than species-poor woods on acid soils.
- Woods with a wide variety of trees and shrubs or distinct patterns in their distribution and abundance. In many cases this diversity is likely to be best maintained by restoring coppice, rather than by allowing high forest to develop.
- Woods with large old coppice stools - a feature of interest in their own right.
- Woods with elements of open grassland, scrub or heath communities that have been largely lost from the surrounding landscapes.
- Woods particularly noted for rare and unusual species that depended in the past on coppice regimes.
- Practical considerations: deer damage on regrowth can be kept within bounds; or the coppice cycle once started can be kept going.

Against coppice restoration:

- Woods with communities of epiphytic lichens and bryophytes that may not tolerate the sudden changes in light and humidity associated with coppicing.
- Long-neglected woods that have developed a mature high forest structure with much dead wood and many veteran trees.
- Woods with high levels of either domestic or wild grazing animals which cannot be controlled easily (see Fuller & Peterken 1995 and Fuller & Warren 1995).
- Practical considerations: regrowth cannot be protected; or cycle cannot be maintained.

Preliminary estimates are that a two- to three-fold increase in the area of ancient semi-natural woodland that is being worked as coppice, ie to about 60,000-70,000 ha, should be the target for 2010. However, most of this is likely to be in the lowlands.

Box 8.3 Likely impact on selected nature conservation features of different management systems (from notes prepared by Dr G F Peterken)

This box summarises in general terms the impact of different management approaches on different elements of the woodland system. o = neutral impact; + positive; - negative. Note that in all cases the appropriate scale of management, type of coppicing, level of grazing is needed for the benefits to be realised. The significance of the impacts will also vary from situation to situation: at times regeneration may be critical; in other circumstances the maintenance of open space may be more important.

Different management types can be complementary in conservation terms. Although each may have negative aspects identified it does not mean that a particular type is undesirable because each have complementary positive aspects (Fuller & Warren 1995).

Minimum intervention stands

+ accumulation of dead wood as dead wood in old stools and pollards replaced by dead wood from branches, suppressed trees and dying underwood
+ mature stands
+ natural processes operate producing increasingly natural structure
+ irregularity of structure
- no young growth in the short term
- composition unstable
- invasive species may spread
- negligible or low gap creation rate for decades
- rides shaded; often with no permanent open spaces

Grazed upland woodland

+ usually some large dead wood
+ bryophyte carpets
+ mosaic of woodland and pasture common, especially on margins
+ mature stands
+ open understorey suits birds such as pied flycatchers, wood warblers
+ less shade on the tree trunks so better opportunities for lichen growth
+ light grazing reduces dominance of species such as bramble, greater woodrush *Luzula sylvatica* and so promotes species diversity
- lack of low shrubby cover limits populations of small mammals and many birds
- shrub stratum thinned
- regeneration lacking, or biased to shade-bearing shrubs ground vegetation dominated by grasses; woodland herbs mainly in stream sides and other inaccessible places

Wood-pasture, parkland or unenclosed forest

o soils sometimes podzolised
+ numerous old trees
+ much dead wood, particularly within old trees
+ mosaic of trees and open areas
- lack of succession of main tree species
- composition simplified to mainly oak and shrubs
- structure artificial
- ground vegetation strongly modified by grazing
- lack of low shrubby cover limits populations of small mammals and many birds

High forest, even aged, moderate to large wood

o summer-growing species predominate
o natural age structure is unusual
o temporary open space formed in pulses separated by decades
o rides semi-shaded; often totally shaded at end of rotation
+ mature structure which may be relatively natural at end of rotation
+ ground flora of woodland species
- composition simplified by planting and competition
- abrupt changes in composition are usual
- dead wood mostly of small dimensions
- soil drainage often made more effective

Coppice/coppice-with-standards, moderate to large wood

o ground flora biased to spring-flowering species
o stand composition biased to oak, shrubs and shade intolerant woody species
+ much young growth
+ diverse, semi-natural stand composition
+ stable stand composition
+ diverse structure within stands
+ temporary open space permanently present
+ high rate of gap creation
+ permanently open rides
+ long internal edges
+ ground flora of woodland species
+ dead wood in old stools and boundary pollards
- no mature stands
- few old trees and little fallen dead wood
- artificial stand structure

Box 8.4 Possible approaches to grazing management in upland woods

Using woodland vegetation to assess grazing level

Heavy grazing or browsing, look for:

- an absence of shrubs
- 'topiary' effects on remaining shrubs
- a browse line on mature trees
- ground vegetation <10 cm tall, mostly grasses and mosses
- tree seedlings not above ground vegetation height
- abundant dung from grazing animals

Moderate grazing or browsing, look for:

- patchy shrubs showing evidence of pruning or a browse line
- ground vegetation up to 30 cm, as a mixture of grasses, herbs or heaths. Localised close-cropped lawns where there is a concentration of grazing
- tree saplings projecting above ground vegetation in a few areas

Light or no grazing or browsing, look for:

- well developed shrub layer, with no obvious browse line
- a lush ground vegetation, where shrub layer is not too dense (eg 30-50% cover), dominated by grazing-sensitive species eg bramble and honeysuckle or greater woodrush
- ground mosses uncommon
- tree seedlings/saplings common in gaps.

Management scenarios

Site/management objective	*Appropriate management*
Promote tree regeneration on wood margins where it is restricted by bracken.	Use cattle, if available, to trample bracken and achieve a good seed bed; remove stock to allow seedling to establish, then change to light sheep grazing.
Promote regeneration and develop ground flora and shrub layers in a heavily grazed oak coppice with a gappy canopy and little understorey.	Initially (first 10 years) try complete exclusion of stock or deer; aim to reduce surrounding deer populations when fencing is removed.
As above, but where bryophytes are an important feature (wetter areas in west).	Total exclusion is undesirable as strong ground flora and understorey growth might shade out bryophytes; try fencing small area under canopy gaps or individual tree protection; reducing the level of grazing by deer culling or stock reduction would also be useful.
Promote regeneration in heavily grazed woodland with a closed canopy.	Regeneration may be limited as much by shade as by grazing. Reducing grazing may be unhelpful as a grass mat will develop over the potential seed bed; some gaps will need to be created in addition to other grazing measures (above).

Box 8.4 Possible approaches to grazing management in upland woods (cont.)

The appropriateness of individual techniques will thus vary with the site and the grazing species which is having most effect. Fencing against deer will not solve a rabbit grazing problem. The manager will, therefore, require a flexible approach which may have to be coordinated with other land users.

Techniques used in grazing management

- **exclusion of grazing animals from the wood by fencing (seasonal, rotational, etc)**

(Further information on forestry fencing in Pepper 1992)

Permanent exclusion may not be ideal for nature conservation and restricts value as stock shelter; fencing off smaller areas for 10 (or 20) years then moving the fenced area after regeneration can be successful and will maintain the grazed structure required by some plants and animals.

- **individual tree protection**

Using plastic tubes to protect trees will be successful provided they are the correct height (taller for red deer and cattle) and are maintained; ground flora is not protected by this means.

- **reducing density of grazing animals by culling (deer) or herd/flock reduction (domestic)**

Deer culling may need to be coordinated across wide areas to achieve significant results (eg through local Deer Management Groups organised under the England Deer Initiative).

- **reducing use of a wood by animals**

By building a winter barn for stock shelter; moving supplementary feeding areas out of woods.

Hawthorn

8.7.2 Management through grazing control

Large herbivores are a natural part of woodland systems and have effects on them from the landscape level down to their effect on the balance between bryophytes and higher plants in the ground flora. Many upland woods, even where not historically treated as wood-pasture, have been heavily grazed by stock over the last 100 years, and deer pressures are also increasing. In most woods therefore some reduction in grazing pressure is likely to be desirable, if not immediately, then at least at some time in the next 20 years. In some cases it may be appropriate to exclude stock completely to promote regeneration and allow the ground flora to develop.

How and when this is achieved depends on the particular objectives of management and whether it is domestic stock or deer whose pressure needs to be regulated. Box 8.4 sets out a series of possible models for grazing management that may help people to decide on appropriate measures for any particular wood. Temporary fencing around gaps, for example, may be appropriate where the primary concern is with regeneration; wholesale reduction of grazing pressure may be needed where impacts on the ground vegetation are significant. Maintenance of walls around woods may reduce the pressure from stock sufficiently that damage from deer browsing is light enough to be acceptable.

Where fences are used care needs to be taken in their siting to ensure that they do not lead to deaths of grouse through collisions (Currie & Elliot 1997).

Further information: English Nature 1996b, 1997c; Kirby,Mitchell & Hester 1994; Hester, Mitchell & Kirby 1996; Hester *et al* 1998; Mitchell & Kirby 1990; Mitchell *et al* 1996; Pepper 1992; Putman 1996.

8.7.3 Recreation and game management in upland woods and scrub

In most sites disturbance and damage from recreational use of woods tends to be localised, for example around popular beauty spots or along major trails. There may be more significant disturbance to some breeding birds; colonial nesters and raptors may be particularly at risk. Guidance based on forestry operations can be applied to likely impact of disturbance to nest sites in such circumstances.

Intensive pheasant rearing and release pens tends to be more of a lowland activity, but can be locally important on the upland fringe woodland. Widespread damage to semi-natural vegetation can occur in pens, around feeding areas and along rides and tracks, especially if straw is put down. Therefore pens and feeding areas should be located away from areas of nature conservation interest. There should be no introduction of non-native shrubs or use of straw bales to provide cover or shelter for the pheasants. There has been concern about predation on butterfly larvae although this impact has not been proven.

Further information: Anderson & Radford 1992; Carroll & Robertson 1997; Currie & Elliot 1997.

8.7.4 Burning in upland woodland and scrub

Burning is commonly used on the open moor to manage grouse habitat and improve the grazing for sheep. This practice has prevented the natural spread of woodland over a long period. Burning has no place at all in the management of broadleaved woods and fires should not be allowed to run into them. If fires get into coniferous stands major commercial damage will be caused.

There may be some case for very small-scale controlled burning to promote the regeneration of juniper scrub: for example Tynron juniper wood in southern Scotland regenerated well after fire. This should not normally be considered, however, where the fire would affect existing juniper bushes. At one site regeneration was stimulated in a different way; the bushes were cut and dragged across the site.

Further information: Clifton, Ranner & Ward 1995

8.7.5 Techniques to re-create upland woodland and scrub

Ancient semi-natural woods cannot be re-created, but there is an increased interest in creating new species-rich and semi-natural woodland, to diversify upland plantations and as 'new native woods' in their own right. In the National Parks there is a specific programme to promote new native woodland run by both the Forestry Commission and the National Parks Authority. This is currently supported by a specific 'challenge fund' element to the forestry grants.

New woodland is best created or encouraged on sites which are adjacent to other woodland or semi-natural vegetation (stream sides, hedges, rock outcrops) from which species may colonise the new wood. Very nutrient-rich soils, for example on old arable, are unlikely to develop an interesting woodland flora quickly because of competition from tall grasses and weedy species. Occasionally there will be circumstances where stripping off the topsoil should be considered. This is, however, unlikely to be the case in the uplands. Variations in geology, topography or drainage on the site provide for potentially greater variation in the wood that develops.

Allowing a new wood to develop by natural regeneration often produces the most varied and species-rich result. It also helps to perpetuate the local genetic stock of native trees. The higher the altitude and the more exposed the site, the longer it may take for colonisation to occur, even in the absence of grazing. Some forms of dense vegetation such as deep bracken *Pteridium aquilinum* beds may also slow down colonisation.

If local seed sources of native trees and shrubs are lacking it may be necessary to plant them. The following planting procedures help to mimic the patterns that occur in semi-natural woodland.

- Use mixtures of native species rather than single species stands.
- Use groups (10-30 m across) rather than line mixtures.
- Include shrubs as well as trees.

- Leave 20% of the ground unplanted.

- Vary the planting density from blocks where 2 x 2 m spacing is used to others with 10 x 10 m or wider spacing. The wide spaces leave scope for future natural regeneration and the creation of an uneven aged stand while the denser plantings create shade conditions more rapidly in which a 'woodland' flora may develop.

Techniques for introducing other elements of the woodland system, such as ground flora, invertebrates and dead wood, are being explored, but are not sufficiently well established to be recommended. Creating woodland in this way is not a substitute for retaining existing semi-natural stands.

Further information: Good *et al* 1997; Rodwell & Patterson 1994; Thompson *et al* 1999; Watkins 1991.

Table 8.1 Some nationally rare and scarce vascular plants associated with upland woodland and scrub

Plant species	Status	Habitat requirements	Management requirements	Distribution by upland Natural Area
Aconitum napellus monk's-hood	LR-ns	Shady wet hazel *Corylus avellana*, alder and oak woodland, mostly near or along the banks of streams. Occasionally found where there are only scattered trees.	• Protect sites from drainage. • It is poisonous to stock.	Clun & North-West Herefordshire Hills Shropshire Hills
Actaea spicata baneberry	LR-ns	Woods, grikes and shaded ledges on limestone. It will tolerate dense shade, but not competition from more vigorous plants, for example bramble.	• Where populations seem to be threatened by more competitive species, these should be controlled. • It is reputed to be toxic to stock.	Yorkshire Dales Cumbria Fells and Dales North York Moors and Hills
Bromopsis benekenii lesser hairy-brome	LR-ns	Woods on shallow limestone or other calcareous soils in steep valleys, in deciduous woods, woodland margins and scrub, on moderate humus in light shade. This species is hard to identify and is thought to be under-recorded.	• Protect sites from habitat destruction.	Yorkshire Dales Shropshire Hills

Plant species	Status	Habitat requirements	Management requirements	Distribution by upland Natural Area
Campanula patula spreading bellflower	LR-ns	Open woodland, wood borders and rock outcrops. On disturbed ground on grassy banks by rivers or roads, in hedgerows, edges of fields, woodland and scrub and green lanes; on dry, sandy stony or loamy soils. It requires some warmth and favours dry, well-drained, sunny, mildly acidic to neutral sites with a low nutrient status. It can tolerate partial shade but not competition; any management which favours a closed sward is damaging (K. Hearn pers comm). It is intolerant of heavy grazing but may persist in lightly grazed places such as open horse-grazed swards and orchards. It is seldom found far from ancient woodland. The seed, which appears to be long-lived in the soil, may need disturbed and sunny ground to germinate; plants can reappear in old stations following disturbance of the soil. The increased use of agricultural fertilisers and herbicides and the cessation of traditional woodland management, including coppicing, have contributed to its decline.	• The use of chemical fertilisers or pesticides should be avoided. • Sites where woodland or tall vegetation have developed should be cleared by careful cutting, to open up the vegetation and provide bare soil for germination. • Sites where the species is known to have grown in the past would also benefit from this management. • Where sites are or have been grazed, light or moderate levels of grazing should be maintained.	Black Mountains and Golden Valley Clun and North West Herefordshire Hills Shropshire Hills

Plant species	Status	Habitat requirements	Management requirements	Distribution by upland Natural Area
Cardamine impatiens narrow-leaved bitter-cress	LR-ns	Shady woodland, rocks, grikes, screes, banks of rivers and streams, or damp roadsides, often on moist limestone soils. Dormant seed can retain their viability buried in the soil for many years and populations can be unpredictable in appearance. In woodland, it can appear in cleared sites after felling, thrive for two to three years, and then dwindle leaving no plants but a renewed seed bank.	• Where relevant, protect sites from drainage.	Yorkshire Dales Clun and North West Herefordshire Hills Shropshire Hills White Peak Cumbria Fells and Dales Dark Peak
Carex digitata fingered sedge	LR-ns	Open woods and on scree and the shaded ledges of limestone quarries.	• Protect sites from habitat destruction.	Cumbria Fells and Dales North York Moors and Hills Pennine Dales Fringe Shropshire Hills White Peak
Carex elongata elongated sedge	LR-ns	Usually in sites which flood in winter and dry out in summer.	• Protect sites from habitat destruction.	Cumbria Fells and Dales
Carex flava large yellow sedge	VU	One site along the transition between the base of a limestone slope supporting ash woodland and the edge of a raised mire supporting downy birch *Betula pubescens*-*Molinia* woodland. The peaty mineral soil is kept moist by seepage from neighbouring limestone outcrops. In light shade.	• Selective felling and thinning of the canopy have allowed the population to increase. • Protect the hydrological conditions at the site to maintain water levels and water quality.	Cumbria Fells and Dales

Plant species	Status	Habitat requirements	Management requirements	Distribution by upland Natural Area
Cephalanthera longifolia narrow-leaved helleborine	LR-ns SCC	Woods on hard limestone, often under ash, oak or beech *Fagus sylvatica*. Often on steep slopes where the canopy of trees is naturally thin and patchy, including limestone gorges and woodland on limestone ridges or outcrops. Also in woodland rides and margins. It is light-demanding, but not adapted to rapidly changing light intensities such as occur in coppicing regimes. The species is thought still to be vulnerable to damage by collecting, but most of its decline is attributed to natural, changes in woodland composition and changes in forestry which result in reduced levels of insolation.	• Research is needed into the best methods to manage sites of this species.	North Pennines
Circaea alpina Alpine enchanter's-nightshade	LR-ns	Open and usually shaded or north-facing seepage areas and stream sides. In the Lake District, it is characteristic of rocky, bryophyte-rich submontane sessile oak *Quercus petraea* woodland. The main method of reproduction is probably by rhizome but it does fruit freely. It may have declined due to competition with the closely related and much more vigorous hybrid, *C.* x *intermedia*.	• Protect sites from drainage.	North Pennines White Peak Yorkshire Dales Cumbria Fells and Dales
Corallorhiza trifida coralroot orchid	LR-ns	Amongst moss cushions and thick leaf mould in damp pine plantations and birch woods and in willow and alder carr. It seems to have exacting requirements for the water table. The plants are saprophytic and, except for a few weeks flowering, survive as underground rhizomes. Fluctuating numbers of flower spikes can make populations appear to vanish in some years.	• Protect sites from changes in surface or ground waters.	Border Uplands Yorkshire Dales Forest of Bowland

Plant species	Status	Habitat requirements	Management requirements	Distribution by upland Natural Area
Cypripedium calceolus lady's-slipper orchid	Annexes II + IV CR Priority Sched 8	On well drained soil in herb-rich limestone grassland on a fairly steep slope adjacent to woodland.	• Continue to protect the site from unauthorised interference and disturbance by gardeners and botanists. • Continue to control levels of grazing to avoid heavy grazing pressure. • The species is covered by the Species Action Plan (UK Steering Group 1995), the Lady's Slipper Orchid Advisory Committee and by a species recovery project, which is reviewed annually and includes the use of wardening and techniques of micropropagation.	Yorkshire Dales
Daphne mezereum mezereon	LR-ns	Woodland on calcareous soils. It probably requires open ground for germination; as a dense canopy develops, it may fail to flower. Native populations have declined, perhaps because of habitat destruction and collecting.	• Protect sites from destruction of the habitat. • Where the woodland canopy has become closed, selected thinning may be beneficial. • The plant is poisonous.	Yorkshire Dales Cumbria Fells and Dales White Peak
Epipactis atrorubens dark-red helleborine	LR-ns	Carboniferous and magnesian limestone woodland and grikes, also scree. Tends to be associated with open glades, wood-edge and scrub rather than closed-canopy woodland.	• Protect sites from habitat destruction.	Yorkshire Dales Cumbria Fells and Dales North Pennines White Peak
Epipactis leptochila var. *leptochila* narrow-lipped helleborine	LR-ns	Under birch on well drained stony substrates kept open through such influences as the presence of lead and zinc tailings, runways of old aerodromes and coal spoil. It is a perennial species which irregularly appears above ground; subterranean population sizes may be more stable and much greater. In the north, where most upland populations are found, it appears in temporarily disturbed sites but fails to flower and then disappears as shade increases with development of tall vegetation, scrub and woodland.	• Where populations are threatened by the growth of taller plants, these should be cleared.	Border Uplands North Pennines Pennine Dales Fringe Shropshire Hills

Plant species	Status	Habitat requirements	Management requirements	Distribution by upland Natural Area
Epipactis phyllanthes green-flowered helleborine	LR-ns	Bare, dry shaded sites under trees on well drained, usually somewhat acidic soils with relatively low humus content. It disappears from well known sites and appears in totally new areas in an unpredictable manner; site occupancy rarely exceeds 30 years.	• Protect sites from habitat destruction.	Border Uplands Pennine Dales Fringe Shropshire Hills
Epipactis youngiana Young's helleborine	Sched. 8 of WCA EN, EE Priority	Woodland on heavy, often heavy-metal-polluted soils, but the habitat requirements are not clearly understood.	• Protect the remaining populations from habitat loss and damage, such as clear-felling or extraction of spoil. • See Species Action Plan (UK Biodiversity Group 1998).	Border Uplands
Equisetum pratense shade horsetail	LR-ns	River banks.	• Protect sites from habitat destruction.	North Pennines
Euphorbia hyberna Irish spurge	VU	Ancient, formerly coppiced, oak woodland, in openings and other places which receive dappled sun. It grows and flowers early, before the trees are in full leaf; individual plants can live for at least 20 years.	• Protect sites from destruction of the habitat.	Exmoor and the Quantocks
Goodyera repens creeping lady's tresses	LR-ns	In a moist layer of moss and pine-needles in coniferous woodland, both semi-natural and planted, usually with Scot's pine *Pinus sylvestris* and some birch. Within colonies, vegetative reproduction seems to predominate, by stolons spreading just below the surface of the moss. It is vulnerable to clear-felling and replanting with different conifers and is also susceptible to shading by scrub and brambles.	• Protect sites from clear-felling and unsuitable replanting. • Where populations are threatened by encroachment of scrub or brambles, these should be controlled by cutting.	Border Uplands North Pennines

Plant species	Status	Habitat requirements	Management requirements	Distribution by upland Natural Area
Helleborus foetidus stinking hellebore	LR-ns	Shallow soil over calcareous clay. It grows in both exposed and partially shaded places but rarely in deep shade and it avoids dense competition. Where surrounding vegetation creates a humid atmosphere in winter, growth and reproduction are significantly reduced by fungal attack. Spread to new sites is limited. Many hedgerow sites have been lost to hedgerow removal, herbicide drift and damage by tractors during flailing of hedges.	• Hedgerows containing important populations of this species should be protected from destruction, from drift of agricultural chemicals and careless trimming of hedgerows. • Wherever possible sites should be protected from habitat destruction.	Oswestry Uplands
Hordelymus europaeus wood barley	LR-ns	On calcareous wood banks and hedgerows, often on or near mediaeval boundary banks. Typically under light shade such as high elm *Ulmus glabra* canopies or shrubs near the edge of a wood. It persists in woods that are managed by coppicing or periodic clear-felling	• Protect sites from habitat destruction.	Border Uplands Cumbria Fells & Dales Yorkshire Dales North Pennines North York Moors and Hills Pennine Dales Fringe Shropshire Hills White Peak
Impatiens noli-tangere touch-me-not balsam	LR-ns	In woods in damp, nutrient-rich soil in stream side silt, mainly under alder and oak, and valley seepage areas under oak and sometimes ash. The seeds probably have only a short viability and there is little evidence of a seed bank.	• All sites should be protected from habitat destruction and from changes in levels of surface and ground waters.	Border Uplands Clun and North West Herefordshire Hills? Cumbria Fells & Dales Shropshire Hills
Maianthemum bifolium May lily	VU SCC	In the ground layer of oak-birch woods on well drained acidic soils. It is tolerant of shade, and at one site management to create dappled rather than total shade has been successful in encouraging the vegetative spread of May lily. This was achieved by removing holly *Ilex aquifolium* from the site.	• Where the spread of plants is thought to be limited by heavy shade, consideration should be given to opening up but not completely removing the canopy.	North Pennines North York Moors and Hills

Plant species	Status	Habitat requirements	Management requirements	Distribution by upland Natural Area
Melittis melissophyllum bastard balm	LR-ns	Within and at the edges of woodland, on hedge banks in sheltered river-valleys and in scrub, on moisture-retentive, base-rich soils. It responds well to coppicing and can be abundant in cleared areas of woodland. It appears to benefit from high humidity and light shade. Populations can be large, especially in wooded areas, if the habitat is kept somewhat open.	• Protect sites from habitat destruction. • Sites which have become overgrown with dense trees or scrub may benefit from coppicing or clearing.	Bodmin Moor Dartmoor Exmoor and the Quantocks
Orobanche rapum-genistae greater broomrape	LR-ns SCC	A root parasite of leguminous shrubs, especially broom and gorse, in hedge banks and scrubby areas on rough hillsides. Its vigour is often increased after burning of the host plants. Colonisation of new sites is rare. The parasitic lifestyle of the broomrape can fatally reduce the vigour of its host, even leading to its own extinction from sites where its host is not abundant. Scrub clearance may have led to the species decline. The species can reappear when afforested areas are opened up, as for example in southern England following the great storms of 1987.	• Ensure that the population of the host plants is healthy, with plants of a range of ages. • Where sites have become overgrown by trees, selected clearing may restore the broomrape. • At some sites, controlled burning of the host plants may be beneficial.	Border Uplands Clun and North West Herefordshire Hills Cumbria Fells and Dales Dartmoor Exmoor and the Quantocks North Pennines Shropshire Hills
Orobanche reticulata thistle broomrape	Sched. 8 of WCA LR-nt SCC	Parasitic on thistles *Cirsium* and sometimes *Carduus* species in clearings in woodland and scrub on calcareous soil. Appears to avoid the most dense patches of thistles and may require high levels of light for germination. It is thought that rivers may be important to the species for dispersal of seed.	• The main host plant, *Cirsium arvense*, is a notifiable weed. Where control by herbicides is unavoidable, patches should be controlled in rotation so that there are always some expanding colonies of thistle. • Scrub and woodland should be controlled so that the thistles and broomrape have enough light. • Protect sites from damage by developments such as flood defence works and gravel extraction. • Continue the experimental management and monitoring at a woodland site.	Pennine Dales Fringe

Plant species	Status	Habitat requirements	Management requirements	Distribution by upland Natural Area
Physospermum cornubiense bladderseed	VU SCC	Open woodland, European gorse scrub on heaths, rough grassy slopes (often in stream valleys), scrubby *Molinia* heath and roadside banks where there is sheltering scrub or woodland. It does well in open habitats but fails to flower in dense shade and plants heavily overgrown with other vegetation may not even produce leaves. The rootstock, however, can be remarkably persistent and seed can remain viable in the soil for many years: after burning or clearance, hundreds of plants can appear. Factors contributing to its decline have been agricultural neglect, including the cessation of gorse-cutting, regular burning and grazing, as well as changes in woodland management such as lack of clearance, afforestation and tree-planting accompanied by heavy use of herbicides.	• The best management will be different at different sites, but in general should be such as to create and maintain open vegetation. • The creation of clearings on a five-year cycle has been found to benefit the species in one wood.	Bodmin Moor

Plant species	Status	Habitat requirements	Management requirements	Distribution by upland Natural Area
Polemonium caeruleum Jacob's-ladder	LR-nt SCC	Cool, moist, north-facing slopes of Carboniferous limestone, often with an open canopy of ash, also on clay soils along river banks. Grassland species in the Peak District. It is sensitive to drought and relies on a damp microclimate, often on damp north-facing slopes with a light canopy of trees or scrub, on thin organic soils. Grazing suppresses flowering and is thought generally to be undesirable, but on those sites prone to succession to woodland, very light and occasional grazing might be needed to maintain the appropriate structure of the vegetation. Cattle are thought to cause less damage than sheep.[1]	• The following management prescriptions are thought appropriate but are still experimental. • Where sites are part of grazing units, grazing by cattle between early September and the end of December for one in every three years; density of stock should be low enough to prevent poaching. • Occasional mowing or strimming, for example once every three years, may be a substitute where grazing is not practicable. • Where populations are confined by grazing to ledges, fencing off the adjacent vegetation and reducing grazing there may allow the population to expand. • Where plants grow in dense shade, thinning of the canopy may benefit the plants.	Border Uplands Yorkshire Dales White Peak
Polygonatum odoratum angular Solomon's-seal	LR-ns	Ancient woodland on limestone and limestone pavement, well drained steep slopes or small cliffs. Plants do not appear readily able to colonise new sites.	• Protect sites from quarrying of limestone and removal of limestone pavement.	Yorkshire Dales Cumbria Fells and Dales White Peak Border Uplands
Pyrola media intermediate wintergreen	LR-ns	Damp mossy habitats in old woods or plantations, also in heaths under *Calluna* and *Vaccinium myrtillus*. Mildly acidic to slightly basic, well drained soils. The species can recover successfully following moorland fires. Some colonies have been lost to afforestation. Grazing which is heavy enough to damage the dwarf shrub heath under which this species sometimes grows would be expected to damage it.	• Sites that are grazed should be grazed only lightly. • Sites should not be planted with non-native trees.	North Pennines North York Moors and Hills

Plant species	Status	Habitat requirements	Management requirements	Distribution by upland Natural Area
Pyrola rotundifolia subsp. *rotundifolia* round-leaved wintergreen	LR-ns	Damp, calcareous habitats, often under a canopy of willows or pine. It is reliant on mycorrhizal fungi for seedling growth and establishment.	• Maintain the water regime, including water quality and periodicity of water levels.	Shropshire Hills White Peak Yorkshire Dales
Ribes alpinum mountain currant	LR-ns SCC	An under-shrub of steeply sloping ash woodland on Carboniferous or, more rarely, magnesian limestone, which often forms trailing mats over the edges of vertical rocks and small cliffs and in ravines. Most colonies are in the sheltered, damper dale bottoms. It is a dioecious species which requires both species to be present for good seed to be set; it can spread vegetatively and by fruit dispersal. Seedlings thrive only where grazing and competition from other shrubs are removed.	• Where populations are thought to be threatened by grazing or larger shrubs, these should be removed.	Yorkshire Dales North York Moors and Hills Pennine Dales Fringe South West Peak White Peak Yorkshire Dales
Ribes spicatum downy currant	LR-ns	Rocky woods on basic soils, usually over Carboniferous limestone, in scrubby woodland and in the deeper grikes of limestone pavement. Also along streams and rivers in wooded ravines and where a thin strip of trees has been left along rocky river banks. The species is hard to identify except when in flower and is thought to be under-recorded.	• Protect sites from habitat destruction.	Border Uplands Yorkshire Dales North Pennines Pennine Dales Fringe Cumbria Fells and Dales
Sesleria caerulea blue moor-grass	LR-ns	Limestone ash woodland (but may also form extensive stands of open grassland).	• Protect sites from habitat destruction.	Border Uplands Cumbria Fells and Dales Pennine Dales Fringe North Pennines White Peak Yorkshire Dales
Sorbus anglica	E SCC VU	Scrub and woodland, mainly on Carboniferous limestone.	• Protect sites from habitat destruction and damage to individual trees.	Exmoor and the Quantocks Oswestry Uplands

Plant species	Status	Habitat requirements	Management requirements	Distribution by upland Natural Area
Sorbus devoniensis	LR-ns	Hedgerows on non-calcareous Devonian and Carboniferous shale, slates and grits, also in steep rocky oak scrub over Old Red Sandstone. Occasionally in scrubby heath and moorland. The species establishes readily from seed and young trees are frequent in suitable habitats.	• Protect sites from destruction of the habitat and of individual trees.	Dartmoor Exmoor and the Quantocks
Sorbus lancastriensis	LR-nt, EE	Rocky scrub and woodland on Carboniferous limestone.	• Protect sites from habitat destruction and damage to individual trees.	Cumbria Fells and Dales
Sorbus subcuneata	VU, EE	In open rocky woodland of sessile oak on Old Red Sandstone. It reproduces from seed, which are abundant in good years, and young trees are frequent.	• Protect sites from habitat destruction and damage to individual trees.	Exmoor and the Quantocks
Sorbus vexans	VU, EE	Open woodland of sessile oak on steep slopes of Old Red Sandstone or slate near the sea. Seed are abundant in good years, and small trees are frequent. It will also regrow from the base following damage.	• Protect sites from habitat destruction and damage to individual trees. • Where *Rhododendron ponticum* also grows at the site, its spread should be controlled.	Exmoor and the Quantocks
Thelypteris palustris marsh fern	LR-ns	Mesotrophic mires, fens and fen carr.	• Protect sites from habitat destruction.	Dark Peak Yorkshire Dales
Tilia platyphyllos large-leaved lime	LR-ns	Usually a large tree or coppice stool in old woodland with a mixed canopy, also on ledges of cliffs. Mostly on calcareous soils; more rarely on acid soils derived from volcanic rocks. It is very long-lived, probably reaching 500-700 years of age, and reproduces vegetatively by shoots from the base of the trunk or fallen branches. Fruits are usually fertile and seedlings are frequent, although saplings are rare. Saplings survive in deep shade but strong growth of young trees occurs mainly in gaps. It is tolerant of neglect and is lost only when woodland is grubbed out. Young coppice growth and seedlings are intolerant of grazing.[2]	• Protect sites from habitat destruction and damage to individual trees. • Young growth which is accessible to livestock should be protected from grazing.	Black Mountains and Golden Valley Clun and North West Herefordshire Hills North York Moors and Hills Pennine Dales Fringe Shropshire Hills White Peak

Key to status

Annex IIb	- listed on Annex IIb of the EC Habitats and Species Directive
Sched. 8 of WCA	- listed on schedule 8 of the Wildlife & Countryside Act.

Red list categories

CR	- critically endangered
EN	- endangered
VU	- vulnerable
DD	- data deficient
LR -nt	- lower risk - near threatened
LR-ns	- lower risk - nationally scarce
E	- endemic to Great Britain
EE	- endemic to England.

Biodiversity Action Plan (BAP)

Priority	- Priority species from UK Steering Group 1995 and UK Biodiversity Group 1998.
SCC	- Species of conservation concern from UK Steering Group 1995 and UK Biodiversity Group 1998.

Sources

Most information from Hodgetts, Palmer & wigginton 1996; Porley & McDonnell 1997; Stewart, Pearman & Preston 1994 and Wigginton 1999.

1. Rich 1997.
2. I. Taylor, pers comm.

Jacob's ladder

Table 8.2 Nationally rare and scarce bryophytes associated with upland woodland and scrub

Plant species	Status	Typical habitat	Distribution by upland Natural Area
Amblystegium jungermannioides	LR-ns	Damp basic rocks and rock crevices in shaded locations, often in moist woodlands or wooded ravines, but also on montane rocks. On limestone, calcareous sandstone and schist and occasionally on tufa or other basic rocks. Also on basic soil on rock surfaces or in crevices.	Yorkshire Dales White Peak
Anastrophyllum hellerianum	LR-ns	A dwarf and often inconspicuous species of damp rotting, usually decorticated logs and stumps in shady situations in subalpine woodlands and wooded ravines.	Cumbria Fells and Dales
Brachythecium appleyardiae	LR-nt, EE Priority	On shaded rocks of Carboniferous Limestone, on a thin layer of soil overlying rock-ledges in wooded valleys.	White Peak
Brachythecium salebrosum	LR-ns	On rotting wood in wet shady woodlands.	Southern Pennines
Buxbaumia aphylla	LR-ns	A calcifuge of sporadic and often ephemeral occurrence. See Table 6.2.	Shropshire Hills Southern Pennines
Calypogeia integristipula	LR-ns	Rocks in woodland and other shaded sites. See Table 10.2	Border Uplands North Pennines South West Peak Yorkshire Dales
Campylium calcareum	LR-ns	A strong calcicole, growing on limestone rocks, on flints, on roots and stumps and on hard basic earth in well drained situations, often in deep shade. Rarely on walls.	Border Uplands North Pennines North Yorkshire Moors & Hills White Peak Yorkshire Dales
Campylium elodes	LR-ns	Calcareous swamp woodland, sometimes on tree-bases.	Cumbria Fells and Dales Yorkshire Dales

Plant species	Status	Typical habitat	Distribution by upland Natural Area
Cephalozia catenulata	LR-ns	On damp, rotting tree-trunks in humid woodlands in the west. Also on peaty soil and banks, often in sheltered rocky ground.	Border Uplands Cumbria Fells and Dales Dartmoor North Yorkshire Moors & Hills Southern Pennines Yorkshire Dales Bodmin Moor
Cryptothallus mirabilis	LR-ns	A parasitic liverwort of wet acid peat, growing a few centimetres below the soil surface. Most commonly under *Sphagnum* in boggy birch woods, but also between the tussocks in wet *Molinia* communities and under *Pellia*.	Cumbria Fells and Dales Dartmoor Distribution not well known.
Dicranum flagellare	LR-ns	On decaying logs and stumps in woods.	Yorkshire Dales
Dicranum polysetum	LR-ns	A lowland species found principally on the ground in coniferous (especially *Pinus*) woods and plantations, but also in birch woodland, on heaths and in raised bogs. It appears to be spreading.	Cumbria Fells and Dales Pennine Dales Fringe
Dumortiera hirsuta	VU	Forming extensive patches on well shaded, continuously moist and often dripping rocks and steep banks of soil in wooded glens at low elevations. Tends to favour mildly basic substrates.	Exmoor and the Quantocks
Ephemerum sessile	LR-nt SCC	An ephemeral species of neutral and acid soils, mainly on woodland rides and on mud at the edge of reservoirs.	Border Uplands Dark Peak Exmoor and the Quantocks Forest of Bowland
Eurhynchium striatulum	LR-ns	A strict calcicole confined to chalk and limestone, where it grows on dry, shaded stones, rocks, walls and tree-roots.	Cumbria Fells and Dales White Peak Yorkshire Dales

Plant species	Status	Typical habitat	Distribution by upland Natural Area
Fissidens limbatus	LR-ns	On calcareous to slightly acid substrates in sheltered but not wet habitats, growing on compacted soil or on thin soil over rock. Most frequent on banks in woods and hedgerows or by streams and ditches, especially near the coast. Also on shaded boulders, on mortar in stone walls, on soil between limestone rocks and in rabbit-holes.	Cumbria Fells and Dales Exmoor and the Quantocks Forest of Bowland White Peak
Fissidens taxifolius subsp. *pallidicaulis*	LR-ns	On rocky stream-banks.	Cumbria Fells and Dales
Habrodon perpusillus	EN	A slender epiphyte, found in tightly appressed patches or occasionally creeping through other bryophytes on well illuminated trunks or branches of trees and shrubs, usually on basic bark, sycamore being the most frequent host with records also from ash, elm and more rarely aspen *Populus tremula*, birch, blackthorn *Prunus spinosa*, elder *Sambucus nigra*, hawthorn, lime *Tilia* sp, oak and willow.	Forest of Bowland
Hennediella macrophylla[1]	LR-ns	Shaded trampled ground, in cultivated flower beds and under trees on river banks.	Border Uplands
Hennediella stanfordensis	LR-ns	On shaded, trampled ground by footpaths and under trees on the banks of rivers.	Shropshire Hills
Homomallium incurvatum	EN	A calcicole on rocks, walls or sometimes soil-banks in sheltered and shaded situations in valley woodlands, particularly on limestone.	Yorkshire Dales
Jamesoniella autumnalis	LR-ns	Favours damp, decaying, decorticated logs and stumps in oak or birch woods on steep, block-strewn slopes with a range of aspects. Also occurs on damp, shaded acid or mildly basic blocks and low outcrops of rock that are periodically flushed in sheltered oak or mixed oak-birch woods, wooded valleys and on steep slopes.	Bodmin Moor Cumbria Fells and Dales Dartmoor

Plant species	Status	Typical habitat	Distribution by upland Natural Area
Jubula hutchinsiae	LR-ns	As pure, dark green patches in shady rock crevices in cascading streams. It sometimes occurs epiphytically on other bryophytes in dripping caves by waterfalls and in wooded ravines. It occurs on a wide range of rock types including limestone but is very rare on the most acidic rocks.	Cumbria Fells and Dales Dartmoor Southern Pennines
Jungermannia leiantha	EN	On wet rocks and flushes in woodland and other shaded habitats, most of the records being from sheltered valleys and ravines. The wide variety of rock types includes sandstones, shales and slates, but always with some base content.	Yorkshire Dales
Kurzia sylvatica	LR-ns	Occasional in woodland. See Table 6.2.	Border Uplands Cumbria Fells and Dales South West Peak
Leptodon smithii	LR-ns	An epiphyte of tree-boles in woods, parks, churchyards, on roadsides and in hedgerows, also occurring on branches of shrubs in laid hedges. It is most frequent on hosts with acid bark, commonest until recently on elm. It is also often found on ash and sycamore and sometimes recorded from beech, elder, field maple *Acer campestre*, hawthorn, lime, oak, poplar *Populus* sp, rhododendron *Rhododendron ponticum*, sallow and spindle *Euonymus europaeus*. It is notably tolerant of dry shade and can grow on the underside of leaning trees. Rarely on walls and calcareous rocks.	Cumbria Fells and Dales Exmoor and the Quantocks
Leucobryum juniperoideum	LR-ns	Most records are from acidic oak and beech woodland. It is sometimes locally abundant, forming dense cushions at soil level and extending onto rock outcrops, tree bases and occasionally stumps, trunks and branches. It has also been found in wooded ravines, sweet chestnut *Castanea sativa* coppice, conifer woodland and rarely in open habitats such as heathland. Poorly drained soils are generally avoided.	Bodmin Moor Forest of Bowland South West Peak Yorkshire Dales

Plant species	Status	Typical habitat	Distribution by upland Natural Area
Lophozia longidens	LR-ns	On the bark of living trees in sheltered situations, sometimes also on rocks.	North Pennines
Lophozia obtusa	LR-ns	Basic turf, flushes and woods. See Table 6.2.	North Pennines
Myrinia pulvinata	LR-nt	Confined to tree-boles and roots, often of alder, on banks in the middle and lower reaches of streams and rivers where there is a well defined flood zone. Usually embedded in silt or sand.	Shropshire Hills
Orthotrichum pallens	CR Priority	On the bark of ash, hazel, sycamore, willow and wych elm, often in rather open sites such as river sides.	Dark Peak
Orthotrichum sprucei	LR-ns Priority	Confined to the exposed roots, trunks and branches of trees and shrubs by streams and rivers, growing above the normal water-level in a zone which is usually dry but liable to occasional flooding. The lower parts of the plant are often embedded in fine silt. Usual hosts are alder, ash and willow; also recorded from wooden palings.	Border Uplands Clun and North West Herefordshire Hills Cumbria Fells and Dales Forest of Bowland North Yorkshire Moors & Hills Oswestry Uplands White Peak Yorkshire Dales
Philonotis arnellii	LR-ns	Sometimes in woodland rides. See Table 10.2.	Border Uplands Cumbria Fells and Dales Forest of Bowland Shropshire Hills
Plagiothecium laetum	LR-ns	Non-calcareous sites on tree-bases, stumps, rotten logs and soil in broad-leaved woodland; seldom under conifers. In the mountains also on banks and among boulders.	Cumbria Fells and Dales Border Uplands Clun and North West Herefordshire Hills North Yorkshire Moors & Hills Shropshire Hills South West Peak
Plagiothecium ruthei	LR-ns	Generally a calcifuge plant of wet shady places, especially in woodland.	Yorkshire Dales

Plant species	Status	Typical habitat	Distribution by upland Natural Area
Pohlia lescuriana	LR-ns	Preferring moisture-retentive soils, usually clay, although not those that are strongly basic.	Dark Peak Dartmoor Forest of Bowland Shropshire Hills Southern Pennines
Pseudobryum cinclidioides	LR-ns	Forming bright green patches or swards, green below, in marshes, carr and wet woodland by the shores of lakes, in flushes and springs and by peaty pools in the hills.	North Pennines
Pylaisia polyantha	LR-ns	Epiphytic on the trunks and branches of a range of broadleaved trees and shrubs in lowland hedgerows and open woodland, very rarely on stumps or logs. Most frequent on hawthorn, ash, elm and lime.	Border Uplands
Rhynchostegiella curviseta	LR-ns	Damp stones and tree-roots, especially on wooded stream-banks. Also in artificial habitats such as bridge supports and retaining walls by rivers, canals and lakes and on the banks of shaded lanes and cuttings. Natural substrates include sandstone and limestone; absent from very acid situations.	Exmoor and the Quantocks
Riccia subbifurca	LR-ns	On moist, thinly vegetated soil. See Table 10.2.	Bodmin Moor Yorkshire Dales
Schistostega pennata	LR-ns	A calcifuge species of deep shade on soft, often crumbling acid soil in dark recesses of shaded lanes and hedge banks, especially in southwest England, under overhanging banks in woodland and quarries, entrances to caves and mine shafts, disused rabbit burrows and deep crevices between granite blocks and in granite tors and sandstone cliffs.	Bodmin Moor Dartmoor Exmoor and the Quantocks Shropshire Hills Southern Pennines South West Peak Yorkshire Dales

Plant species	Status	Typical habitat	Distribution by upland Natural Area
Sematophyllum micans	LR-ns	As pure patches or mixed with other bryophytes on periodically irrigated, lightly to moderately shaded, acid or mildly basic, gently sloping slabs and boulders with incomplete bryophyte cover. Most usually in deciduous woodland (mainly oak or birch) on steep rocky slopes facing north to east, less often on intermittently flushed rocks in north- or east-facing wooded ravines and by waterfalls.	Cumbria Fells and Dales
Sphagnum angustifolium	LR-ns	On flushed ground in moorland and open woodland.	Border Uplands
Sphagnum flexuosum	LR-ns	In marshes, in wet open woodland and on rock-ledges. See Table 6.2.	Cumbria Fells and Dales This species is thought to be under-recorded.
Tortula subulata var. *graeffii*	LR-ns	Calcareous habitats on light soils and about tree-bases, growing on roadside and woodland banks, on ledges and crevices of rocks and on old walls. Also on tree-bases and roots in the flood zones of rivers and streams.	Yorkshire Dales
Tortula virescens	LR-ns	On the boles and bases of mature trees in open situation, less often on smaller trees such as elder.	Yorkshire Dales White Peak
Tritomaria exsecta	LR-ns	Woods, especially in sheltered ravines where it inhabits stumps and logs, more rarely mossy rocks and peaty banks.	Cumbria Fells and Dales
Weissia microstoma var. brachycarpa	LR-ns	On wet non-calcareous clay, loam or marl.	Dark Peak Forest of Bowland

Key to status

Annex IIb	- listed on Annex IIb of the EC Habitats and Species Directive
Sched. 8 of WCA	- listed on schedule 8 of the Wildlife & Countryside Act.
Red list categories	
CR	- critically endangered
EN	- endangered
VU	- vulnerable
DD	- data deficient
LR -nt	- lower risk - near threatened
LR-ns	- lower risk - nationally scarce.
E	- endemic to Great Britain
EE	- endemic to England.
Biodiversity Action Plan (BAP)	
Priority	- Priority species from UK Steering Group 1995 and UK Biodiversity Group 1998.
SCC	- Species of conservation concern from UK Steering Group 1995 and UK Biodiversity Group 1998.

Sources

Most information from Hill, Preston & Smith 1991, 1992 & 1994; Hodgetts, Palmer & Wigginton 1996 and Porley & McDonnell 1997.

[1] *Hennediella macrophylla* is thought to have been introduced from New Zealand.

Table 8.3 Selected red list lichens associated with upland woodland

Plant species	Status	Typical habitat	Distribution
Biatoridium monasteriense	EN	Sheltered ancient woodland, mostly on base-rich bark of elm, ash and elder.	Cumberland
Bryoria smithii	CR	Acid bark of oak and mossy boulders in fairly well-lit situations.	Dartmoor
Graphina pauciloculata	VU	Smooth bark of hazel, holly and young oak in moist open woodland and carr.	Dartmoor Bodmin Moor
Schismatomma graphidioides	VU	Slightly nutrient-enriched bark of old or mature deciduous trees, including ash, beech and oak; woodland edges and sheltered parkland.	Exmoor and Devon
Sclerophora nivea	VU	Sheltered sites in dry bark crevices.	Northumberland
Usnea madeirensis	VU	On deciduous trees, shrubs and rock outcrops in windy situations.	Bodmin Moor

Key to status

Red list categories

CR - critically endangered
EN - endangered
VU - vulnerable

The information in this table was supplied by P. Lambley, pers comm. See also Church *et al* 1996 and Purvis *et al* 1992.

Table 8.4 Relationships between the various different types of woodland (minor types in brackets)

BAP Priority Habitat (those enboldened are most likely to be of significance in the English uplands)	**Forestry Commission Guide Type**	**CORINE**	**Habitats Directive Annex 1 Type**	**NVC Type**	**Stand Types**
Lowland beech and yew woods	1. Lowland acid beech and oakwoods 2. Lowland beech-ash woods	42.A71 41.13 41.12 (41.16)	*Taxus baccata* woodland *Asperulo-Fagetum* beech forests Beech forests with *Ilex* and *Taxus*	W13 W12 W14, W15	No direct equivalent 8C 8A, 8B, 8D, 8E
Lowland oak and mixed deciduous woodland	1. Lowland acid beech and oakwoods 3. Lowland mixed broadleaved woods	41.23, 41.32 (41.24) (41.51) 41.52	(*Tilio-acerion*) (*Stellario-Carpinetum*) (Old oakwoods on sandy plains)	W8a-d (e-g) W10a-d (e), W16	1(A), B, 2, 3A, B, 4, 7C, 9, 10 5, 6C, D, 9, 12
Lowland wood-pasture and parkland	Referred to particularly in Lowland acid beech and oakwoods guide (1), but no real equivalent	84.5 (but not a good equivalent)	Includes examples of beech forests with *Ilex* and *Taxus*. Old oakwoods on sandy plains	W14, W15 W10, W16	Group 8 Group 6
Upland mixed ash	4. Upland mixed ashwoods	41.31, 41.32, 41.41, 42.A71 (62.3)	*Tilio-Acerion* *Taxus baccata* woodland limestone pavement	(W7c) W8(a-c) d-g , W9 W13	1A, C, D, 3C, D, 4C, 7D No direct equivalent
Upland oak woodland	5. Upland oakwoods	41.53, 41.52	Old oakwoods with *Ilex* and *Blechnum* in the British Isles	W10(a)e, W11, W16b, W17	6A, 6B (8A, 8B)
Northern birchwoods	6. Upland birchwoods	41.53, 41.52	Old oakwoods with *Ilex* and *Blechnum* in the British Isles	W10e, W11, W17 W4a, b	Mainly stand group 12

BAP Priority Habitat (those enboldened are most likely to be of significance in the English uplands)	Forestry Commission Guide Type	CORINE	Habitats Directive Annex 1 Type	NVC Type	Stand Types
Native pinewood	7. Native pinewoods	42.51 44.A2	Caledonian forest Bog woodland	W18, (W19) W4(a), b, c	11
Wet woods	8. Wet woodland	44.A1 44.31 44.13 44.92	Bog woodland Residual alluvial woodland	W4(a), b, c W5, W6, W7 W1, W2, W3	(12) 7A, B, D, E No equivalent
Scrub	No equivalent	31.883 31.81	Juniper formations on grasslands	W19 (acid soils), W21d W21, W22,W23, W24,W25	No equivalent

Notes

Lowland wood-pasture includes some non-woodland habitats as well as overlapping with various other Priority Habitats.

Upland birchwoods in England are usually best referred to the upland oakwood category rather than to the northern birchwoods which are mainly a Scottish type.

Table 8.5 Conservation significance of different broad groupings

Feature	Conservation priority (A high, B medium)	Description (W10, W11 etc = NVC types)	Significance (HSD = the EU Habitats and Species Directive)
1. Upland oak woodland		Predominantly acid oak-birch woodland (mainly W10e, W11, W16, W17), but with associated base-rich (W9) and wet communities (W4, W7). Usually ancient or at least with an ancient core.	Includes the HSD category (Old oakwoods with *Ilex* and *Blechnum* in the British Isles). Many species of non-vascular plants and ferns are best represented in England in these woods. Some of these appear to be very slow to colonise new sites. Distinctive woodland bird community. Their structure and to some extent their composition has been modified by past treatment often as coppice, and by heavy grazing but recent neglect (in most sites) is leading to a more natural state developing.
	A	All extensive (>20 ha) ancient stands and smaller areas (5-20 ha) where they are in good condition or in areas where extensive stands are scarce.	
	B	Smaller stands of the above, particularly those of predominantly recent origin.	
2. Upland ash woodland		Predominantly ash woodland with some elm, lime (mainly W8d-g W9), with locally yew (W13). Usually ancient or with an ancient core. Associated with and sometimes developed on limestone pavement.	Includes the HSD categories *Tilio-Acerion* and *Taxus baccata* woodland (both also occur in the lowlands) and the limestone pavement category. Can be extremely rich in higher plants including national rarities (eg *Daphne mezereum*). Structure heavily modified by past treatment (both silvicultural and grazing) but locally developing towards a more natural state.
	A	All extensive (>20 ha) ancient stands and smaller areas (5-20 ha) where they are in good condition or in areas where extensive stands are scarce.	
	B	Smaller stands of the above, particularly those of predominantly recent origin.	

Feature	Conservation priority (A high, B medium)	Description (W10, W11 etc = NVC types)	Significance (HSD = the EU Habitats and Species Directive)
3. Wet woodland		Woodland mainly composed of alder, willows and sometimes birch on wet soils (both mineral and organic substrates) (mainly W7, W4, W3, less often in the uplands W1, 2, 5, 6). Some stands are ancient and are usually found in association with other types (eg as part of upland oakwoods), many are, however, recent and in some cases may be invading important fen and bog habitats.	Residual alluvial woodland and bog woodland have been identified in the HSD and some upland stands show some of these characteristics. More generally wet woodland is a nationally scarce resource, usually present only as very small stands. The sites tend to be particularly rich is higher plants and insects.
	A	Ancient stands over 5 ha and recent stands over 20 ha where these are in good condition and not replacing important open wetland.	
	B	Other stands of this type.	
4. Ancient wood pasture	A	This does not include grazed western oakwoods (see 1 above). Rather it includes stands of large old trees, often widely spaced forming parkland, but sometimes with younger growth or plantations in between. They are more likely to occur on the upland fringes than in the uplands proper.	This is a rare habitat on a European scale and England has the bulk of the UK resource. The stands are notable for their epiphytic flora and for the saproxylic invertebrates, particularly those found in the rotting hearts of the trees.
5. Replanted ancient sites	B	Ancient woodland of a variety of types that has been replanted, usually by conifers, less often non-native broadleaves.	These sites usually still contain remnants of the former vegetation and some of the fauna. They have a high potential for restoration to native woodland communities. They have been given 'medium priority' not because the area of them needs to be maintained (the ideal is that it should be reduced as they are converted back to native broadleaves) but because the overall interest of plantation sites should not be reduced - ie by total clearance or by further replanting.

Feature	Conservation priority (A high, B medium)	Description (W10, W11 etc = NVC types)	Significance (HSD = the EU Habitats and Species Directive)
6. Scrub	A	Juniper scrub (W19) and other high altitude (>300 m) stands.	Juniper is a rare habitat type in England, although locally extensive stands exist as for example in Teesdale. Juniper scrub on heath or calcareous grassland has been identified in the HSD. High altitude stands are important because although there is no longer a natural tree line anywhere in England, these could form the nucleus for trying to re-create one. Dwarf montane willow stands (W20) are also a vegetation type that should be considered for restoration in appropriate places.
	B	Other scrub	Scrub is a natural component of upland vegetation which is rarely allowed to develop because of grazing pressure and burning. The development of scrub in the uplands would diversify invertebrate and bird populations, particularly where allowed to develop as a mosaic with grassland, moorland and woodland.
7. Recent plantations	B	Mainly composed of introduced conifers (particularly Sitka spruce), grown in large even-aged stands.	Some recent plantations in the uplands will be removed to restore open semi-natural habits or broadleaved woodland. Elsewhere there may be some expansion of plantations where these do not affect significant semi-natural habitats. In any new stands and in existing forests there is considerable scope for integrating nature conservation into their design and management.

Table 8.6 Birds associated with upland woodland and scrub in England

Bird species[1]	Birds of conservation concern in the UK[2]	Listed on Schedule 1 of the 1981 Wildlife & Countryside Act	Listed on Annex 1 of the EC Birds Directive	No of British 10 km squares with breeding records 1988-90	% of breeding records in upland ITE squares[3]	Main upland habitat association	Principal Natural Areas supporting the species *=major/important areas[4]
Red kite *Milvus milvus*	Red list	•	•	45	71.1	Woodland	Extinct in English uplands
Goshawk *Accipiter gentilis*	-	•	-	91	52.7	Woodland	2*, 4, 8, 14, 15, 17, 25, 29, 30, 41, spreading fast
Buzzard *Buteo buteo*	-	-	-	1,174	47.6	Woodland and moorland	2, 4*, 8, 10*, 41*, 42*, 58*, 60*, 87*, 92*, 94*
Merlin *Falco columbarius*	Red list	•	•	386	87.3	Moorland and enclosed land	2. 4*, 8*, 10*, 12*, 14*, 15, 17*, 25*, 29, 42, 58, 87
Black grouse *Tetrao tetrix*	Red list Priority BAP species	-	-	278	86.0	Moorland and enclosed land	2, 4*, 8, 29, extinct elsewhere
Short-eared owl *Asio flammeus*	Amber list	-	•	381	70.9	Moorland	2*, 4*, 8*, 12*, 14*, 15, 17*, 25*, 29
Tree pipit *Anthius trivialis*	-	-	-	1,215	46.0	Woodland and scrub	2, 4*, 8, 10*, 12, 14, 15, 17, 25*, 29, 30, 41, 42, 58, 60, 87*, 92*, 94
Redstart *Phoenicurus phoenicurus*	Amber	-	-	1,019	51.9	Woodland	All areas
Whinchat *Saxicola rubetra*	-	-	-	1,062	59.9	Moorland and scrub	2*, 4*, 8*, 10*, 12*, 14*, 15*, 17*, 25, 29*, 30, 41, 42, 60, 87*, 92*, 94*
Stonechat *Saxicola torquata*	Amber	-	-	847	47.7	Moorland and scrub	10*, 42, 58, 87*, 92*, 94
Ring ouzel *Turdus torquatus*	Amber	-	-	401	93.5	Moorland and scrub	2, 4*, 8*, 10*, 12, 14*, 15(?), 17, 25, 29, 30, 42, 87, 92*

Bird species[1]	Birds of conservation concern in the UK[2]	Listed on Schedule 1 of the 1981 Wildlife & Countryside Act	Listed on Annex 1 of the EC Birds Directive	No of British 10 km squares with breeding records 1988-90	% of breeding records in upland ITE squares[3]	Main upland habitat association	Principal Natural Areas supporting the species *=major/important areas[4]
Wood warbler *Phylloscopus sibilatrix*	-	-	-	859	46.7	Woodland	2, 4*, 8, 10*, 12, 14, 15, 17, 25, 29, 30, 41*, 42*, 58*, 60*, 87*, 92*, 94*
Pied flycatcher *Ficedula hypoleuca*	-	-	-	547	45.5	Woodland	2, 4*, 8, 10*, 12, 14, 15, 17, 25, 29, 30*, 41*, 42*, 58*, 60*, 87*, 92*, 94*
Siskin *Carduelis spinus*	-	-	-	728	65.7	Woodland	2*, 4*, 8, 10, 12, 17, 41, 42, 58, 60, 84, 92*
Redpoll *Carduelis flammea*	-	-	-	1,184	42.2	Woodland	2*, 4*, 8, 10, 12*, 14, 15, 17, 25, 42, 87*, 92
Crossbill *Loxia curvirostra*	-	•	-	364	57.7	Woodland	4, 8, 12, 14*, 25*, 29*

Key

1. Upland breeding bird species as identified in Stillman & Brown 1994.
2. From RSPB 1996.
3. From Bunce & Barr 1988, using the 13 ITE land classes which were regarded as upland (information not available on an English basis).
4. The following 18 Natural Areas are classed as upland by English Nature:

No	**Natural Area name**
2	Border Uplands
4	North Pennines
8	Yorkshire Dales
10	Cumbria Fells & Dales
12	Forest of Bowland
14	Southern Pennines
15	Pennine Dales Fringe
17	North York Moors and Hills
25	Dark Peak
29	South West Peak
30	White Peak
41	Oswestry Uplands
42	Shropshire Hills
58	Clun and North West Herefordshire Hills
60	Black Mountains and Golden Valley
87	Exmoor and the Quantocks
92	Dartmoor
94	Bodmin Moor

Table 8.7 Biodiversity Action Plan listed invertebrates associated with upland woodland or upland scrub in England (UK Steering Group 1995)

Scientific name	English name	Typical habitat	Importance of this habitat
Lipsothrix nervosa	a cranefly	Wet woodland	P
Lipsothrix ecucullata	a cranefly	Wet woodland	P
Lipsothrix errans	a cranefly	Wet woodland	P
Lipsothrix nigristigma	a cranefly	Wet woodland	P
Eustroma reticulata	netted carpet moth	Wet woodland	P
Formica lugubris	a wood ant	Upland oak woodland	S
Mellicta athalia	heath fritillary butterfly	Light scrub on grassy hillsides	S
Carterocephalus palaemon	checkered skipper butterfly	Upland oak woodland	x
Boloria euphrosyne	pearl-bordered fritillary butterfly	Scrub/coppice	P
Argynnis adippe	high brown fritillary butterfly	Scrub/coppice/bracken	P
Carabus intricatus	blue ground beetle	Upland oak woodland	P
Rheumaptera hastata	argent and sable moth	Upland oak woodland	x
Procas granulicollis	a weevil	Upland oak woodland	P

Key
P = primary habitat
S = significant habitat
x = also occurs in this habitat

Table 8.8 Significance of each Natural Area for different National Vegetation Classification (NVC) types

Natural Area		Types of national significance	Types of local significance	Other types believed to be present
2	Border Uplands	W19	W7, W9, W11, W16	W3, W4, W6, W10, W17
4	North Pennines	W7, W19	W5, W8, W9, W10, W11	W4, W6
8	Yorkshire Dales	W8	W7, 9, 11, 13, 17, 19	W6, 10
10	Cumbria Fells and Dales	W3, 7, 8, 9, 11, 13, 16, 17, 19	W5, 6	W1
12	Forest of Bowland	W11	W7, 9, 10, 17	W1, 6, 16
14	Southern Pennines	-	W4, 7, 8, 9, 10, 11, 16, 17	W6
15	Pennine Dales Fringe	-	W10, W8, W16	W2, W4, W5, W6, W7, W9, W11, W12, W13, W15
17	North York Moors	-	W7, 8, 10, 16	W3, 4, 6, 9
25	Dark Peak	-	W7, 10, 16	W1, 6, 8, 11
29	South West Peak	-	W4, 7, 11	W6, 8, 10, 16
30	White Peak	W8	W7, 9, 11	W6, 10
41	Oswestry Uplands	-	W8	W6, 10
42	Shropshire Hills	W16	W7, 8, 9, 10	W6
58	Clun and North West Herefordshire Hills.	W10, 16	W6, 7, 8, 9, 17	W1, 11
60	Black Mountains and Golden Valley	-	W7, 8, 9, 10, 11	W1, 6
87	Exmoor and the Quantocks	W11, 16, 17	W4, 7, 8, 10	W1, 6, 9
92	Dartmoor	W7, 11, 17	W1, 4, 9, 10	W6
94	Bodmin Moor	-	W1, 7, 8, 10, 16, 17	W4, 6, 11

Table 8.9 Upland Natural Areas which contain nationally significant areas of different woodland groupings

Upland Natural Area	Upland oakwoods	Upland mixed ash	Wet woodland	Lowland wood pastures	Replanted ancient sites	Scrub	Recent conifer plantations
2 Border Uplands						✓	✓
4 North Pennines			✓			✓	✓
8 Yorkshire Dales		✓					✓
10 Cumbria Fells and Dales	✓	✓	✓		✓	✓	✓
12 Forest of Bowland	✓						
17 North York Moors					✓		✓
30 White Peak		✓					
41 Oswestry Uplands				✓			
42 Shropshire Hills	✓			✓			
58 Clun & North West Herefordshire Hills	✓		✓	✓	✓		
60 Black Mountains/ Golden Valley				✓			
87 Exmoor and the Quantocks	✓			✓			
92 Dartmoor	✓		✓				✓
94 Bodmin Moor			✓				

Note

This table only considers the upland Natural Areas as defined in Figure 1.1. Equally important areas for most of these types occur elsewhere in the country.

Table 8.10 List of relevant county ancient woodland inventories (AWI)

Natural Area	County AWI	Date
Border Uplands	Northumberland	1988
North Pennines	Northumberland	1988
	Durham	1987
	Cumbria	1994
Cumbria Fells and Dales	Cumbria	1994
	Lancashire	1994
North York Moors	Cleveland	1987
	North Yorkshire	1994
Yorkshire Dales	Cumbria	1994
	North Yorkshire	1994
	Lancashire	1994
Forest of Bowland	North Yorkshire	1994
	Lancashire	1994
Southern Pennines	North Yorkshire	1994
	Lancashire	1994
	West Yorkshire	1994
	Greater Manchester	1988
Dark Peak	West Yorkshire	1994
	Greater Manchester	1988
	South Yorkshire	1986
	Derbyshire	1992
Pennine Dales Fringe	Durham	1987
	Richmondshire	1994
	Harrogate, Hambleton	1994
	West Yorkshire	1994
White Peak	Derbyshire	1992
	Staffordshire	1993
South West Peak	Derbyshire	1992
	Staffordshire	1993
	Cheshire	1988
Oswestry Uplands	Shropshire	1988
Shropshire Hills	Shropshire	1988
Clun and North West Hereford Hills	Herefordshire	1986
	Worcestershire	1986
	Shropshire	1988
Black Mountains and Golden Valley	Herefordshire	1986
	Worcestershire	1986
Exmoor and the Quantocks	Devon	1986
	Somerset	1986
Dartmoor	Devon	1986
Bodmin Moor	Cornwall	1986

Table 8.11 Habitat and management requirements of non-vascular plants associated with upland woodland and scrub

Plants	Habitat requirements	Management requirements
All woodland non-vascular plants	All species require an appropriate canopy and woodland structure, which will be site-specific. Most species need medium shade and reasonably constant, high humidity. Many rare lichens are restricted to single trees and are therefore vulnerable to extinctions from accidental events such as gales or fires; lichens may require higher levels of light than other groups.	• Avoid clear-felling. • Avoid coppicing, especially in those parts of a wood which are identified as containing good populations of bryophytes. These are often ravines or north-facing slopes. • Where invasive species, which may include beech, are a problem, these should be controlled. • At most sites, levels of grazing need to be high enough to control the growth of rank vegetation, but low enough to prevent damage to non-vascular plants and to allow regeneration of woodland trees. It may be advisable to fence parts of the wood to allow regeneration, or to protect individual saplings.
Plants of wet and dry rocks	Such species generally require some shade and may have retreated to the shade of rocky places during previous large-scale felling in a wood. Lichens on rocks are vulnerable to damage by fire (P. Lambley pers comm).	• Retain a canopy in these areas to encourage the spread of species back into other woodland habitats. • Protect important populations from damage by climbers and encourage walkers to keep to paths. • Prevent or control fires and the spread of fire.
Plants of rotting wood	Rotting stumps and branches, both standing and fallen, generally with a canopy providing some shade.	• Ensure that dead wood is allowed to rot on site where it falls and that dead trees are allowed to stand wherever possible. • Where trees are felled or thinned, at least some of the wood should be left on the ground.

Plants	Habitat requirements	Management requirements
Plants of living bark on branches, trunks and roots	Live trees of native species, including a range of ages. Different groups have requirements for different intensity of shade: generally lichens are likely to favour the lighter shade of woodland edges and clearings; bryophytes typically require higher levels of shade and humidity.	• Protect trees with a rich epiphytic flora from felling, lopping or damage by drifting agricultural chemicals. • Ensure that such trees have an intensity of shading appropriate to their epiphytes. • In some circumstances, it may be of use to prolong by pollarding the life of ancient trees which carry a rich epiphytic flora. • Ensure that young trees are able to regenerate, by controlling grazing levels or protecting individual tree seedlings and saplings.
Plants of tree-boles and roots in the flood-zone of rivers	Live trees usually of native species and periodic flooding by unpolluted water.	• Maintain natural morphology and vegetation in the stream bed and river corridor. • Protect streams from upstream developments which would affect flows and water quality, including agricultural and forestry operations.
Plants of swampy woodland	Wet ground with appropriate water chemistry, live trees usually of native species and little or no disturbance.	• Non-vascular plants of wet woodland, including flushes and stream sides, are particularly vulnerable to damage by heavy livestock such as cattle, which should therefore be excluded. • Maintain the water table and surface waters in as natural a state as possible, with regard to water quality, levels and flows, and the annual pattern of levels and flows.

Plants	Habitat requirements	Management requirements
Pasture woodland and parkland	Usually very old trees which receive some direct sunlight. These populations are vulnerable to chance events such as wind-throw or fire, which can remove important trees. They are also sensitive to drift of agricultural fertilisers and pesticides.	• Prevent or reduce the use of agricultural chemicals around the site. • Attention needs to be given to providing the next generation of very old trees, preferably by allowing regeneration from seed produced on site, or by replanting with carefully selected saplings. Seedlings and saplings will need protection from grazing animals. • Prolong the life of existing host trees as long as possible, possibly by careful pollarding by workers who understand where all the important colonies of non-vascular plants are located.

Sources

Most information from *The conservation of lower plants in woodland* (Hodgetts 1996).

Table 8.12 Habitat requirements of birds associated with upland woodland and scrub

Woodland birds	Habitat requirements
Red kite	• Strong association with native woodland • Nests placed high in native woodland tree • Adults forage widely for carrion across road sides and hillsides and for earthworms in improved and semi-improved pastures and tilled land • Food brought to dependent young in nest by adults • Present throughout year but extinct in English upland
Goshawk	• Nest placed high in tree in native or plantation forest • Adults forage for small to medium-sized birds along woodland rides, clearings, in enclosed fields and across open moorland • Adults bring food to dependent young in nest • Present throughout the year
Buzzard	• Strong association with woodland and enclosed grassland at the moorland fringe • Nest placed in isolated or woodland trees or occasionally on rock ledges, usually within woodland • Adults feed over all types of open country - moors, acid grasslands, tilled land, pastures and meadows, taking earthworms from pastures and tilled land and small mammals, road kills and other carrion from hill and road sides • Adults bring food to dependent young in nest • Present throughout the year
Merlin	See Chapter 6
Black grouse	See Chapter 6
Short-eared owl	See Chapter 6
Tree pipit	• Strong association with scattered trees on moorland fringe, with light woodland and woodland clearings and isolate trees often over grass or bracken • Nest placed on ground in grass tussock or other herbage • Adults forage for invertebrates on sparsely vegetated ground in open areas near to light, open (often heavily grazed) woodland coppice and shrubby hillsides • Adults bring food to dependent young in nest • Present late April to end August
Redstart	• Strong association with native upland woodland (oakwood, birch and alder woods), upland copses, tall hedgerows and also isolated roadside or field corner trees or trees in lightly wooded ghylls or stream sides • Nest placed within tree holes and holes in walls • Adults forage for invertebrates on ground and amongst canopy of woodland and scattered trees at moorland edge • Food brought to dependent young in nest • Present late April to end August
Whinchat	See Chapter 7

Woodland birds	Habitat requirements
Stonechat	See Chapter 7
Ring ouzel	See Chapter 10
Wood warbler	• Strong association with closed canopy deciduous woods with little understorey, principally oakwood but also birch • Nest placed on ground amongst tall herbage and leaf litter • Birds forage for a wide diversity of invertebrate prey both on ground and in canopy of woods • Adults bring food to dependent young in nest • Present late April to end August
Pied flycatcher	• Strong association with grazed, native upland oak and ash woodland in valleys, ghylls and at moorland edge • Nest placed in tree hole in oak-dominated woodland. Birds also take readily to nesting in nest boxes • Adults forage amongst canopy and mid-levels of open, grazed woodland • Adults bring food to dependent young in nest • Present late April to end August
Siskin	• Strong association with upland woodland, both native and of introduced conifer • Adults feed on deciduous and coniferous tree seeds • Adults bring food to dependent young in nest • Present throughout the year
Redpoll	• Strong association with deciduous native woodland, particularly early birch and conifer growth • Adults forage for birch and other small tree seeds in upland woods • Adults bring food to dependent young in nest • Present throughout the year
Crossbill	• Strong association with introduced conifer plantations • Nest placed in outer branches of mature conifers • Adults forage for conifer seeds in forest, mainly pine but also larch and spruce • Adults bring food to dependent young in nest • Present throughout the year

Table 8.13 Management guidelines for birds associated with upland woodland and scrub

Woodland	Scrub
• Manage the wood according to the appropriate objectives (see 8.6) and management practices (see 8.8).	• Retain existing scrub, such as gorse and juniper, and scattered trees such as hawthorn and rowan.
• Maintain a mixture of tree and shrub age classes.	• Encourage the development of scrub wherever possible on areas of low wildlife interest, by:
• Manipulate grazing in wood pasture and grazed woodland to create a mosaic of grazed and ungrazed patches. This will allow regeneration and so maintain the wood, while benefiting species requiring open conditions, such as pied flycatchers, wood warblers, redstarts and some rare non-vascular plants.	Reducing grazing in areas where there is some scrub, to allow natural regeneration. Fencing off areas where there is some scrub, to allow natural regeneration. • Where grazing levels are low enough to allow regeneration, and slopes are gentle:
• Retain old trees and dead wood to provide nest sites and invertebrate food.	Graze existing scrub on rotation to create a range of growth stages.
• Maintain natural drainage and wetland features such as pools and flushes.	Or cut about 10% of scrub each year, when it is about 10 years old, to provide a range of habitats.
• Consider management or creation of woodland rides, glades and varied external edges, to increase the diversity of habitats present.	Scarify the ground where old stands of scrub have been removed and regeneration is poor.
• Plant native trees on areas of low wildlife interest.	Plant shrub species native to the area and preferably of local provenance, but only where no natural regeneration is likely.

Freshwater

Freshwater habitats 9

Tables

Definition and location of freshwater habitats in the uplands

9.1 Definition of freshwater habitats in the uplands

Fresh water has a salinity content of less than 0.5% (McLusky 1994). Freshwater habitats include truly aquatic habitats, ie areas of standing and running water, and the wetland areas associated with them, ie where water is near, at, or above the level of the land (Smith 1979), such as marginal and inundation areas, swamps and fens, bogs and mires, and wet woodland. These areas may be semi-natural in origin, heavily man-modified, or created as a result of man's activities.

This chapter will focus upon the true aquatic habitats as well as swamps and fens. This includes lakes, reservoirs, tarns, ponds, rivers and streams, and their surrounding wetlands. Marginal and inundation grassland communities are discussed in Chapter 7, bogs and mires are discussed in Chapter 6, and wet woodland habitats are discussed in Chapter 8.

Freshwater systems contain a range of habitats. For example, a lake contains sheltered bays, wave-washed shores, and depth zones from shallow areas to deep water. Rivers may contain mid-channel islands, side and point bars, and meanders.

Truly aquatic habitats can be classified according to water movement and nutrient content. In lotic (flowing water) systems, currents are induced by gravity, and tend to be constant in direction. By contrast, the current in lentic (standing water) systems results from wind action and may vary in direction and velocity (Ratcliffe 1977).

Nutrient levels, particularly the presence of nitrogen, phosphorus, and calcium carbonate (alkalinity), dictate the character of freshwater habitats. Five categories can be recognised defined broadly upon nitrogen and phosphorus levels, ranging from dystrophic and oligotrophic systems poor in nutrients, through mesotrophic, to eutrophic and hypertrophic systems high in nutrients (see Table 9.1 and 9.2). Sites with high concentrations of calcium carbonate (defined as greater than 100 mg/l) are called marl sites.

Many other factors also influence the distribution of aquatic organisms. For plants, substrate has an important role. This includes both the structure and nutrient status of the substrate. Where the nutrient status of the substrate differs from that of the water it is more likely that the over-riding influence on the floral community will be exerted by the soil chemistry (Holmes & Newbold 1984).

Water depth and permanency affect the type of vegetation communities found. Some plants characteristically grow in water which persists throughout the year and are true aquatic species (Preston & Croft 1997). The entire plant may be submerged or may float on the water surface, or the basal parts may be rooted in water but send out aerial leaves and inflorescences. Some aquatic plants are adapted to life in the boundary between the land and the water, where changes in water level are frequent.

Table 9.1 Classification of different freshwater types according to alkalinity

	Alkalinity		
	Milligrams per litre of calcium carbonate (mg l^{-1} Ca CO_3)	Milliequivalents per litre (meq l^{-1})	pH
Dystrophic	0-2	(0-0.04)	<6
Oligotrophic	0-10	(0-0.2)	6-7
Mesotrophic	10-30	(0.2-0.6)	*c.* 7
Eutrophic	>30	(>0.6)	>7
Marl	>100	(>2.0)	>7.4

Source: Ratcliffe 1977

Table 9.2 Classification of different standing freshwater types according to nitrogen (N) and phosphorous (P) content

	Total P	Inorganic N
	Milligrams per litre (mg l^{-1})	Milligrams per litre (mg l^{-1})
Ultra-oligotrophic	<0.005	<0.02
Oligo-mesotrophic	0.005-0.01	0.2-0.4
Meso-eutrophic	0.01-0.03	0.3-0.65
Eu-polytrophic	0.03-0.1	0.5-1.5
Polytrophic	>0.1	>1.5

Source: Vollenweider 1968

9.2 Location and extent of freshwater habitats in the uplands

Freshwater and wetland habitats are widely distributed throughout the uplands of England. Their occurrence reflects the topography and geology of the area as well as annual precipitation levels. For example in the Cumbrian Fells and Dales, standing waters account for around 2%of the total land area, while the mean area of standing waters ranges from 0.5 km^2 to >1 km^2 (Smith & Lyle 1979). The frequency of streams per 100 km^2 is highest in the south west of England with between 5-7.5 per 100 km^2 (Smith & Lyle 1979).

Habitats and species of fresh water in the uplands

9.3 Why upland freshwater habitats are important

Most natural lakes of glacial origin in Britain are classified as oligotrophic waters (Ratcliffe 1977). They are found in areas where the underlying rocks are resistant to weathering. Such areas are most often associated with upland and mountain areas. Scotland has some of the best examples of oligotrophic freshwater habitats in Britain as a whole, but England also contains examples. Due to their low nutrient status, oligotrophic systems are particularly vulnerable to change caused by nutrient enrichment and acidification. As many have been enriched, those remaining are valued as examples of this habitat type.

Oligotrophic waters support a characteristic suite of plant and animal communities, including several rare and scarce species. Most of these species are adapted to the low nutrient status of these systems and any change in this status is likely to lead to their loss.

Mesotrophic and eutrophic waters are less well represented in upland areas, mainly because the geology of these areas is predominantly nutrient poor. Where they are present they are often confined to the valley bottoms. Marl sites are scarce in the UK and in the uplands are confined to limestone areas. The most notable marl lake within England's upland Natural Areas is Malham Tarn, the highest marl lake in the UK. Mesotrophic, eutrophic and marl systems all support their own characteristic flora and fauna.

River systems and other wetland habitats in the uplands similarly support characteristic, rare and scarce plant and animal communities and species which are unable to survive in any other conditions.

9.4 Habitats and species of freshwater in the uplands, their nature conservation status and distribution

9.4.1 Vascular plants

Freshwater vascular plant species of nature conservation significance in upland Natural Areas of England are shown in Table 9.3, with their nature conservation status and distribution in upland Natural Areas (Preston & Croft 1997; Stewart, Pearman & Preston 1994). Two upland, freshwater, aquatic macrophytes, floating water plantain *Luronium natans* and slender naiad *Najas flexilis*, are recognised as threatened throughout their European range and in need of special protection. Pillwort *Pilularia globulifera* is an aquatic fern species which is more common in Britain than the rest of Europe. It is normally associated with water bodies at low altitude but is also found in upland Natural Areas.

Aquatic plant species have traditionally been overlooked by botanists and many species are under recorded. They often have specific habitat requirements and their distribution mirrors that of the distribution of suitable aquatic habitats. For example, true aquatic plants are restricted to open or running water and other important factors include water movement, alkalinity, nutrient levels, substrate and depth (Pearsall 1920). The ability to reach new aquatic systems is the main limiting factor.

Some plant species are very closely associated with particular nutrient levels. For example, quillwort *Isoetes lacustris* is only found associated with oligotrophic waters and consequently has a mainly north and west distribution. Other species are more catholic in their requirements and may be found in a range of aquatic habitats eg floating leaved pondweed *Potamogeton natans*.

As part of the UK Biodiversity Action Plan, Species Action Plans have been prepared for priority freshwater species to ensure their protection (Taylor 1994; UK Biodiversity Group 1998; UK Steering Group 1995).

9.4.2 Bryophytes and lichens

Mosses and liverworts make up the bulk of the vegetation of upland and rocky rivers, which do not tend to support the range or quantity of aquatic macrophytes found in more nutrient-rich, lowland situations. In addition, they can be abundant in the wet or damp conditions around freshwater habitats. Nationally rare and scarce freshwater bryophytes and lichens in the English uplands are identified in Table 9.4, along with their nature conservation status and distribution.

9.4.3 Plant communities

The vegetation of upland freshwater areas varies between different habitats. Truly aquatic habitats may be characterised by the presence of algae, floating vegetation, submerged vegetation, marginal or emergent vegetation. Swamp and fen habitats may be characterised by a range of grassland communities, and reed or rush dominated vegetation. The communities of wet grassland, mires, bogs and woodlands are described elsewhere in this handbook.

The National Vegetation Classification (NVC) has been designed as a mechanism to describe all vegetation communities, including the vegetation of true aquatic habitats and swamp and fen habitats (Rodwell 1995). There is some caution amongst aquatic botanists concerning the adequacy of the data set which was used as the basis for the aquatic chapter. Independently of the NVC project two systems were developed for the classification of the vegetation communities of standing and running waters (Holmes 1983; Holmes, Boon & Rowell 1998; Palmer 1989; Palmer, Bell & Butterfield 1992). These systems form the basis of SSSI selection and for this reason they are used here. The NVC is used to describe the vegetation of swamp and fen habitats.

The vegetation communities of lentic, lotic, and swamp and fen habitats present in upland areas of England are shown in Tables 9.5, 9.6 and 9.7. A range of these habitats are listed on Annex 1 of the Habitats Directive, including oligotrophic and marl lakes, and "floating vegetation of *Ranunculus* of plain and submountainous rivers" .

Standing waters

The classification for standing waters relies on the macrophyte vegetation and consists of 10 types, ranging from dystrophic, through oligotrophic, mesotrophic and brackish, to eutrophic (Palmer 1989; Palmer, Bell & Butterfield 1992). In general oligotrophic waters (Types 1-3) have a predominantly north and west distribution, and are found in areas where the underlying geology is base-poor. They are the commonest type to be found in the uplands of England. Type 2 communities are common in the upland tarns of the Lake District, whilst Type 3 and Type 5 are found in a number of the larger lakes in this region. Types 8, 9 and 10, ie those with high alkalinity and pH, have a more restricted distribution in the uplands and are more typical of lowland areas, eg the meres of Shropshire, Cheshire and Staffordshire. Type 9 communities within the uplands are restricted to the Cumbrian Fells and Dales.

Running waters

The classification system for British rivers is based on their aquatic plant communities (Holmes 1983; Holmes, Boon & Rowell 1998). There are four broad groups (A-D) representing an environmental gradient from lowland eutrophic rivers to those that are essentially upland, torrential and oligotrophic. These four groups are divided into 10 river community types. Those relevant to the uplands are described below and shown in Table 9.6.

Upland rivers are generally distributed towards the western side of the country, reflecting areas of higher rainfall and topography. The nature of vegetation communities changes along their length, reflecting changes in slope, geology and substrate. Thus a single river may be classified as several types along its length from source to mouth.

In the English uplands river types 6, 7, 8 and 10 are most frequent. The communities associated with Type 6 have variable characteristics but a close affinity with areas of sandstone and hard limestone. They occur predominantly in the north and west of the country, and tend to form the downstream reaches of rivers which rise at moderate to high altitudes. Type 7 rivers generally have a neutral or mesotrophic status and examples can be found in the north Pennines and in south west England on Exmoor. Like Type 6 rivers they tend to be found in areas which receive high rainfall. Type 8 communities are often associated with rivers that flow through upland bogs and fens. They occur most frequently in Scotland and Wales but examples can be found in the Lake District, the Pennines and south west England. The communities of Type 9 and 10 rivers are truly oligotrophic, occurring on neutral or slightly acidic geology. Most sites occur at high altitudes and generally they have a more northerly and westerly distribution. Type 2 rivers occur infrequently in upland areas, and are associated with clay substrates. An example occurs in the central Marches on the Welsh border.

Swamp and fen communities

The distribution of swamp and tall-herb fen communities in the upland Natural Areas of England are shown in Table 9.7. As with the standing water types, fen and swamp communities tend to be distributed according to trophic status. The *Carex rostrata* swamp (S9) and the *Carex rostrata-Potentilla palustris* fen (S27) communities are largely restricted to oligotrophic and mesotrophic waters, while the *Sparganium erectum* swamp (S14) and the *Phalaris arundinacea* fen is more commonly found in mesotrophic to eutrophic waters. Certain communities have specific habitat requirements, which are only met in a few localities. The *Cladium mariscus* swamp and sedge-beds (S2) are restricted to areas with a calcareous influence. Examples of this community in upland areas are restricted to the Carboniferous Limestone of the Cumbria Fells and Dales.

9.4.4 Birds

Birds use freshwater habitats for feeding, breeding and roosting. The species present and the activities occurring at any one location vary seasonally. For example, certain species are found along rivers during the breeding season, while others roost around lakes in the winter.

A variety of species are regularly associated with upland freshwater habitats in England, although only the dipper *Cinclus cinclus* is confined largely to the uplands. Other species include wigeon *Anas penelope*, teal *A. crecca*, goosander *Mergus merganser*, osprey *Pandion haliaetus*, common sandpiper *Actitis hypoleucos*, black-headed gull *Larus ridibundus*, common gull *Larus canus* and grey wagtail *Motacilla cinerea* (Table 9.8). The adults and young of some birds may forage at the water's edge if it occurs within their territory, eg waders such as oystercatcher *Haematopus ostralegus*, redshank *Tringa totanus* and snipe

Gallinago gallinago, but these are covered in more detail elsewhere in this handbook. Many more bird species occur on freshwater habitats in the uplands but most are more generally associated with lowland habitats and so are not covered here (see Stillman & Brown 1994 for the identification of breeding bird species associated with the uplands). Examples include kingfisher *Alcedo atthis*, sand martin *Riparia riparia*, yellow wagtail *Motatilla flava*, whooper swan *Cygnus cygnus*, geese and cormorant *Phalacrocorax carbo*.

Only three of the species considered here are regarded as being of nature conservation concern - teal, wigeon and osprey (RSPB 1996). For the former two species this is because of the international importance of their winter populations in Britain. As they winter in the lowlands, especially coastal wetlands, they should not be a particular concern for upland land managers. Ospreys are of concern due to their historical decline and their unfavourable conservation status in Europe. They currently use a few sites in northern England and may become established as a breeding species in due course.

The dipper is a useful indicator of river quality and condition, because it shows a strong correlation with the abundance or availability of large stream invertebrates, such as caddis larvae and mayfly nymphs, on which it feeds. These insects decline or disappear as water quality declines, for example in terms of increased nutrients or suspended solids. They also become less available to dippers as water depth increases. Any factors affecting the numbers, distribution and availability of these prey items are likely also to affect the number and distribution of breeding dippers (Marchant *et al* 1990).

Goosanders are of note because they have substantially increased and spread south from Scotland and into England over the last century (Marchant *et al* 1990). This has brought them into conflict with fishing interests in some areas because they feed on fish.

9.4.5 Invertebrates

A large and varied set of habitats is covered by this chapter and these support a great diversity of invertebrates. Invertebrates are found in all freshwater habitats and many are species of conservation concern because of their rarity or the restricted nature of their distribution.

Larger water bodies, such as pools, tarns and lakes, support aquatic invertebrates including dragonflies, water beetles and pea mussels. Rivers and streams can contain insects such as mayflies, caddis flies and stoneflies. The margins of freshwater habitats and surrounding wet areas support beetles, craneflies, spiders, snails and many other invertebrates. In the majority of water bodies, the margins are the most important parts for invertebrates, including the emergent plants, marginal mud or shallow water (Kirby 1992). Physical features in and around water courses, such as sand, silt and shingle shoals, bars and banks, are also particularly important for invertebrates such as beetles, flies and spiders. Away from water courses and bodies, a very small volume of water or area of wet habitat may provide a breeding site because invertebrates are small.

The greatest diversity of stoneflies and mayflies occurs in clean stony rivers and large streams, making the uplands particularly important for these groups. With the exception of stonefly *Rhabdiopteryx acuminata*, none of those characteristic of upland rivers and streams is nationally scarce.

In still water, caddis flies, some mayflies and water boatmen are often the most frequent species, and include several species restricted to upland locations, such as the boatmen *Callicorixa wollastoni* and *Arctocorisa carinata* and the water skater *Gerris costai* in peat pools, and the cased caddis *Apatania muliebris* on stony lakes shores.

Exposed gravels deposited by rivers, especially in their lower reaches where the beds can be large, support a large number of ground beetles and rove beetles rarely found in other situations. A smaller number of flies and spiders are also restricted to this apparently inhospitable habitats.

Invertebrates of freshwater habitats are more than adequately discussed by other publications and this will not be duplicated here (Kirby 1992; RSPB, NRA & RSNC 1994). However, important molluscs and crustaceans are particularly associated with fresh water in the English uplands and these will be covered here. They include the freshwater pearl mussel *Margaritifera margaritifera*, the bivalve *Psidium conventus*, the white-clawed crayfish *Austropotamobius pallipes* and opossum shrimp *Mysis relicta* (Table 9.9).

Unfortunately there has been a dramatic decline in many of the known populations of the freshwater pearl mussel in England to the point where the majority are now considered functionally extinct. However, there are a few populations within Cumbria, Shropshire, North Yorkshire and Northumberland, one or two of which are quite large, which are still considered to be viable. These populations will require special efforts if their long-term conservation is to be achieved.

The increased spread of non-native crayfish species and the associated crayfish plague disease, from the south to the north of England has led to major losses of the once widespread native crayfish due to both the disease itself and competition for food and shelter. Fortunately the upland areas of England remain relatively unaffected by non-natives or plague and are therefore an increasingly important area for the native crayfish. This has been recognised by the designation of a major part of upland England as a no-go area for non-native species under the MAFF Crayfish Order (MAFF 1996a). A number of rivers in Cumbria, the Yorkshire Dales, the North Yorkshire Moors and the Peak District, particularly those which run off limestone, hold strong healthy populations. There are also a number of lakes and reservoirs which contain good populations and these are potentially important refuge sites if plague were to advance farther north. Protection of all these sites is vital if long-term conservation of native crayfish is to be achieved.

9.4.6 Mammals

Mammals associated with upland freshwater habitats in England include otter *Lutra lutra*, water vole *Arvicola terrestris* and water shrew *Neomys fodiens*. Bats are also associated with these habitats because they use them as feeding areas. They include in particular Daubenton's bat *Myotis daubentonii*, but also the whiskered bat *Myotis mystacinus*, Natterer's bat *Myotis nattereri*, noctule *Nyctalus noctula* and pipistrelle *Pipistrellus* spp.

The otter has a localised distribution, and is extinct or endangered over much of mainland Britain and vulnerable elsewhere. However, the species is generally increasing following major losses between the late 1950s and the 1970s. It tends to be more common away from intensive agriculture or industrialised areas. The water vole is still moderately common but also declining. There has been a significant decline in the number of populations over the course of this century. It is widespread and generally more associated with lowlands (usually below an altitude of 50 m), but they have been recorded in head streams in the uplands (up to 660 m). The water shrew is widespread and locally common. The patchy distribution and ephemeral nature of the populations mean that population trends are uncertain but they are possibly declining. Bat populations generally are also declining.

Mink *Mustela vison* have become naturalised along many rivers of the British Isles since their escape from fur farms. They are predators of a wide variety of mammals, birds, fish and invertebrates and their effect on waterfowl and other wildlife is controversial.

9.4.7 Amphibians and reptiles

Amphibians and reptiles particularly associated with upland freshwater habitats include frogs, toads, newts and the grass snake *Natrix natrix*. Adder *Viper aberus* and slow worm *Anguis fragilis* also occur in the uplands, in a variety of habitats, and are covered elsewhere in this handbook.

- Common frog *Rana temporaria*: widespread, locally common.
- Common toad *Bufo bufo*: widespread, locally common.
- Natterjack toad *Bufo calamita*: localised, very limited distribution in uplands (one known fell site, Habitats & Species Directive Annex IV).
- Palmate newt *Triturus helveticus*: widespread, locally common.
- Smooth newt *Triturus vulgaris*: widespread, locally common.
- Great crested newt *Triturus cristatus*: widespread, declining but may be locally abundant, and more often found in lowland habitats (Habitats & Species Directive Annexes II and IV).
- Grass snake *Natrix natrix*: widespread, locally common but more associated with lowland habitats. This is the reptile species most associated with water on account of the notable occurrence of fish and amphibians in its diet.

9.4.8 Fish

Fish species important in nature conservation terms and associated with upland freshwater habitats are shown in Table 9.10. Species associated with upland rivers and streams include salmon *Salmo salar*, brown trout *Salmo trutta*, sea lamprey *Petromyzon marinus*, brook lamprey *Lampetra planeri*, river lamprey *L. fluviatilis* and bullhead *Cottus gobio*. All are widespread throughout the uplands. In addition, twaite *Alosa fallax* and allis shad *A. alosa* are restricted to a small number of estuaries and river systems, along the west coast. Grayling *Thymallus thymallus* are known from a number of locations. It is likely that the populations of grayling have been introduced, and in many cases will be maintained through stocking. In some areas they may be subject to culling where it is perceived that they compete with other salmonids.

Significant species associated with upland lakes and tarns include vendace *Coregonus albula*, schelly *C. lavaretus* and arctic char *Salvelinus alpinus*. Vendace are restricted to two lakes, Bassenthwaite and Derwent Water both within the Lake District. Schelly are restricted to four lakes, Brotherswater, Haweswater, Red Tarn and Ullswater all within the Lake District. Arctic char are also confined to the Lake District but their distribution is more widespread.

A number of the fish species listed above are migratory species. Adults of some species live out at sea and only migrate into freshwater to spawn (anadromous species). The juveniles spend varying amounts of time in freshwater before returning to the sea. Some species, eels *Anguilla anguilla* for example, return to the sea to spawn (catadromous). Other species simply migrate within the river system (non-anadromous). However, salmonids, shad and lampreys all have forms with differing migratory habits which utilise different parts of river systems.

Adult salmon migrate to fresh water between early spring and autumn. The early spring run fish tend to be older fish that have spent several winters at sea, while the late running fish tend to be young fish that have spent only one winter at sea. The extent of their migration through an individual catchment will depend on the location of obstructions as well as the flows at the time of the migration. Spawning occurs between November and January. Eggs are laid in gravel beds and emergent fry quickly develop into parr, which may redistribute themselves in the river. At one to two years old they smolt up and migrate back down to sea.

Brown trout were formerly commonplace in upland waters and are now becoming less common, probably due to the introduction of rainbow trout. There are two forms, migratory sea trout and the non-migratory brown trout. Both forms spawn in upland rivers and streams.

River lamprey migrate into fresh water in spring and if no obstructions occur, adults will migrate up into the headwaters of a river system. Juveniles will remain in fresh water for up to five years. Sea lamprey also migrate but they tend to move only a short way into the river system, and spawn in deep fast-flowing waters in the lower reaches of a river. Interestingly, brook lamprey do not migrate, but remain in fresh water all their life. The only migration which occurs involves the young (ammocoetes) moving downstream from spawning gravels to silt beds and the return movement of developed adults to the spawning gravels.

Little is known about the migration of the allis shad, but it would appear that adults move from the estuary into the lower reaches of rivers during April to August. In contrast twaite shad have been known to migrate long distances up main rivers, but rarely into tributaries.

Many fresh waters, both still and flowing, have been subject to fish introductions in the past and now support species not characteristic of these areas. Pike *Esox lucinus* for example have been introduced into waters where the species did not naturally occur. These 'alien' species can have major impacts on other fish species and/or the general lake or river ecology. This is well illustrated by the introduction of ruffe *Gymnocephalus cernuus* and roach *Rutilus rutilus* into Bassenthwaite. The ruffe, a small predatory fish, probably originally introduced through its use as a live bait, is now known to prey on vendace eggs. Competition and predation from pike, perch *Perca fluviatillis*, roach and other species is probably also very harmful to vendace populations (Maitland 1996).

Another fish problem in fresh waters has been the stocking of rainbow trout *Salmo gairdneri*. Native to the Pacific Coast of North America these have now been widely introduced for their sporting and food value. Within England there are now some rivers with self sustaining populations, ie R. Wye in the Peak District, while in other rivers small populations are maintained by the regular stocking of hatchery reared fish.

Inappropriate stocking is not confined to new species of native or non-native species. There are also many examples of indiscriminate stocking of salmon and brown trout to enhance natural stock. These have direct implications for the genetic integrity and local adaptation of native stocks, and are now generally not endorsed by the regulatory agency, the Environment Agency, except in extreme conditions where major mitigation schemes are necessary (see Environment Agency 1998b).

9.5 Habitat and management requirements of upland freshwater species

9.5.1 Vascular plants

The management requirements of upland freshwater plant species can be divided into those which relate to the growth form of the plant (eg emergent or submerged) and those which are more species specific. In the case of rare or scarce species, management is carried out to promote growth and encourage re-colonisation of new areas. For invasive species management aims to prevent the spread of new plants and destroy existing growth (see 9.10.7).

The general management requirements for promoting plant growth are (Gardiner 1996):

- maintenance of water quality;
- maintenance of appropriate water levels;
- control rates of sediment erosion and accretion.

Tables 9.14-9.16 provide the habitat and management requirements of selected freshwater plants.

Further information: Maitland & Morgan 1997; Newbold & Mountford 1997; RSPB, NRA & RSNC 1994.

9.5.2 Birds

A high degree of naturalness and good water quality are particularly important elements of freshwater habitats for the birds associated with them. The availability of nesting sites also influences whether birds can live in a particular area. Water levels, flow regimes, and the associated wetland, bank side and other surrounding habitats are also important. Many species feed on invertebrates while others feed on plants or fish. The invertebrates may be associated with the freshwater system or the surrounding habitats, such as grassland. A summary of these habitat and management requirements are shown in Tables 9.17 and 9.18.

9.5.3 Invertebrates

Guidance on the habitat and management requirements of invertebrates of freshwater wetlands are covered extensively in Kirby (1992) and RSPB, NRA & RSNC (1994) and for this reason are not repeated here. However, two invertebrates, the pearl mussel and white-clawed crayfish are of particular nature conservation concern in upland fresh waters and their requirements are discussed below.

In general terms, the habitat requirements of freshwater pearl mussels and the white-clawed crayfish are similar. They require unpolluted, well oxygenated water, clean gravels for reproducing and a mosaic of habitat features to provide food and shelter. The habitat and management requirements of these species are summarised in Table 9.19.

Pearl mussel

Pearl mussels are associated with clear, cool, fast-flowing unpolluted rivers with soft water, ie water low in calcium and nutrients. Nutrient enrichment (eutrophication) is believed to be the single most important factor to have caused their decline in England.

Mussels tend to favour gravel pockets behind emergent boulders in riffle areas. However, they can also be found in deep pools up to 2 m deep with slow flows. Although habitat preferences are varied, they do prefer stable areas and are also rarely found in fine sediments. Consequently they are often found in linear beds along the line of greatest flow and maximum stability. There also appears to be a preference for areas with shade from overhanging vegetation. The requirements of pearl mussel, and the implications of these for the management of rivers containing pearl mussel are thoroughly reviewed by Oliver & Killeen (1996).

White-clawed crayfish

Crayfish can be found in a variety of rivers and still waters. Their main requirement is for well oxygenated, calcium rich water. Although found in riffles or fast-flowing waters hiding under stones and cobbles, they are most abundant in slower flowing waters where they can also hide up within uncut banks and tree roots.

9.5.4 Mammals

Habitat and management requirements of certain mammals associated with fresh waters are shown in Table 9.20. The quality of the water and the surrounding habitat are particularly important for these species. For example, otters require a range of habitats along the river margin with a good vegetation structure providing cover up to the river edge. Diverse bank side vegetation and associated wetlands are also required by other mammals such as water vole and water shrew.

9.5.5 Amphibians and reptiles

Amphibians are obviously particularly associated with water systems and wetland habitats. The habitat and management requirements of the rarer amphibians, great crested newt and natterjack toad, are shown in Table 9.20. For these and the commoner species, pond, lake and reservoir management is very important. In upland systems, with generally nutrient-poor soils, exposed conditions, high water tables in bogs and grazing pressures, the need to manage water bodies may be less than in lowland situations.

Ideally for amphibians, ponds and the margins of larger water bodies should be unshaded by trees and bushes, at least to the southern side, and there needs to be sufficient open water for egg laying and courtship. There will be cases where water bodies need to be managed to remove invasive plants or accumulated silt and sediment. Plant removal can be by hand or through the use of herbicides, although clearly the impact of the latter on non-target species needs to be considered. Grazing can also be used to remove vegetation and open up water bodies. Silt removal usually requires digging, for example with a JCB. Where management of this nature is required, it is preferable to manage only part of the water body at any one time so that other interests present are not jeopardised.

In areas with amphibians but a shortage of breeding water, new ponds can be created or old ones restored. In some areas, especially those with high water tables, pond creation can be simple, perhaps by reducing water flow or seepage and in others by excavating a hole in the ground. Equally, in quarries where the ground is impermeable collected rain water can form very valuable ponds. Elsewhere, creation of standing water is more difficult and may have undesirable impacts on the hydrology elsewhere. In some cases, the creation of artificially lined ponds may be appropriate. Concrete, plastic or butyl lined and puddled clay ponds (dew ponds) have been used successfully in some areas.

For amphibians it is often better to create a series of small water bodies, each perhaps approximately 100-200 metres squared, rather than a single large pond. Generally these should not be too deep, usually less than one metre, and have shallower margins. This means that any individual pond is less likely to become unsuitable in any year (eg through fish incursion) and means that damage to surrounding areas will be minimised and more easily reversed if necessary. Emergency management, for example deepening ponds in dry years, should be avoided; ponds should not be deepened unless it appears that water tables will be lowered for more than just the occasional dry year. Over-zealous pond deepening has actually caused more problems for natterjack toads, for example, because the habitat subsequently became more suitable for the commoner species of amphibian.

In areas where amphibian populations are being threatened due to acidification, the addition of chalk or quick lime can be considered. The objective is to raise the pH above 5, and for amphibians ideally towards pH 7. Doses between 1 kg per 4 m^2 have been recommended, depending on depth (more for deeper ponds). Pond area is usually calculated on area during the winter months. Timing of application depends on the species being conserved: for the common five species application should be in January or February; for natterjacks lime should be applied in March or early April so that it does not benefit the commoner species. Care needs to be taken when applying lime to avoid damaging other acid-loving species found in these ponds, or in areas where the water may drain or leach. This may mean that in some cases the pH should be raised only a minimal amount or in others that this application is not appropriate. In the latter case, conservation of amphibians may require the creation of artificial ponds. Other features can also be created to enhance habitats for all amphibians, such as log piles on the surrounding land to create hibernation areas.

The common lizard, slow worm, adder and grass snake are often found in damp habitats associated with fresh waters. However, the grass snake is the most aquatic of the reptiles, often swimming and feeding on amphibians. As with most animals of fresh waters, good water quality, a diverse range of surrounding habitats and a plentiful supply of food are important. A summary of its habitat and management requirements is shown in Table 9.20.

Further information: Beebee & Denton 1996; Gent & Gibson 1998.

9.5.6 Fish

Fish require unpolluted, well oxygenated water, clean gravels for spawning and a mosaic of habitat features to provide food and shelter. The habitat and management requirements of fish species of conservation concern in upland freshwater habitats are summarised in Table 9.21.

Bullhead, although widespread throughout river catchments, appear to favour fast-flowing clear shallow water and are particularly abundant in the headwaters of upland streams where they will be found sheltering deep within the river gravels. However, they can also be found lower down the river sheltering in thick weed beds.

All species of lamprey need clean gravels for spawning. The sea and river lamprey, which tend to spawn lower down in a river system, can use large gravels. The smaller brook lamprey, which is found in the upper reaches, appears to prefer small sized gravels in areas where the current is not too strong. Once hatched, the ammocoete larvae of all three species drift downstream and burrow into beds of fine silt or sand, where they remain for five to six years until they mature into adults. Beds located within shaded margins are commonly used but if the amount of fine material is limited cobbles and small stones can be utilised. Although lampreys need silt, they cannot survive in silt with a high organic content since this also tends to have little or no oxygen.

Both salmon and trout require deposits of clean deep gravel in fast-flowing water for spawning. As young salmon and trout develop they require medium-fast riffles and runs where there is plenty of cover in the form of weeds or rocks and an increased supply of food. The water should be cool, clean and oxygenated. Adult salmon and trout need space in deeper water, with plenty of cover in the form of undercut banks, overhanging vegetation, weed or rocks.

Grayling occur mainly in clean, well oxygenated, fast-flowing streams and rivers, but can thrive at oxygen concentrations at which trout would begin to feel uncomfortable.

Allis and twaite shad occur in a small number of estuaries and river systems along the west coast. Little is known about the habitat requirements of shad in fresh water, although French research has shown that both twaite and allis shad can use the same areas for spawning. Twaite shad are known to spawn at night in shallow areas of water near to a deep pool where the fish congregate beforehand.

Vendace and schelly require deep, cool, well oxygenated water and in England occur only in lakes. Oxygen in particular is a key factor. Spawning takes place in littoral gravels and these need to be clean and unsilted. Recent sampling in 1996 and 1997 has shown that many of the areas known to have supported spawning in the past are now covered with fine organic silt rendering them unsuitable for spawning. Arctic char have a reputation of being found only in large, deep, oligotrophic lakes, lying in glaciated basins. Although this is often the case, there are also populations that spawn in shallow, biologically rich habitats in rivers.

Further information: Maitland & Morgan 1997; Newbold & Mountford 1997; RSPB, NRA & RSNC 1994.

Management of upland freshwater habitats

9.6 Conservation objectives for upland freshwater habitats and species

9.6.1 Vascular plants

Conservation objectives for the two internationally important plant species of upland fresh waters, floating water-plantain *Luronium natans* and slender naiad *Najas flexilis*, are given in their Species Action Plans (UK Steering Group 1995). Species Action Plans for other freshwater species have also been produced (UK Biodiversity Group 1998).

9.6.2 Plant communities

General conservation objectives for plant communities of standing waters, running waters and swamp and fen habitats are listed in Tables 9.11-9.13. In many cases the main focus should be to minimise the impacts of routine use and management, for example abstraction or channelisation, upon the conservation interest of a freshwater site. This generally relates to maintaining or restoring the appropriate water quality, water level and rate of sediment erosion and accretion. In cases where aquatic vegetation needs to be managed, it may be to control the dominance by floating leaved species, or to reduce the spread of marginal and emergent communities.

In general, aquatic plant communities require minimal management for nature conservation purposes. Traditionally, management has focused upon either the control of nuisance 'weed' species, and, to a lesser extent, the re-establishment of plant communities following major perturbations (eg eutrophication of the Norfolk Broads). Options to combat eutrophication in certain locations have also been proposed (English Nature 1998b).

Further information: English Nature 1997d; Gardiner 1996.

9.6.3 Wetland habitats

The following objectives have been identified by English Nature for freshwater wetlands in upland Natural Areas (Gardiner 1996):

- Maintain and enhance the current extent, diversity and condition of wetland habitats through appropriate management and subsequent monitoring.

- Meet all the requirements of international treaties relating to wetland conservation, namely the Ramsar convention, Birds Directive and Habitats and Species Directive.

- Restore and enhance the hydrology, water quality and management of wetland sites that are currently considered to be in an unfavourable condition.

- Seek opportunities for habitat creation of wetland habitats.

- Maintain and enhance important populations of wetland plants and animals and carry out appropriate monitoring to determine their status.

Further information: English Nature 1997d; Gardiner 1996.

9.6.4 Animals

Objectives are included below for native crayfish, the freshwater pearl mussel and freshwater fish, as examples of conservation objectives for animals in upland freshwater habitats in England. Those for the former two species have been identified by the UK Biodiversity Action Plan (UK Steering Group 1995) while the objectives for freshwater fish in upland areas have been identified by English Nature.

White-clawed crayfish

- Maintain existing populations through appropriate habitat and water quality management.

- Prevent further spread of non-native species into areas containing native species.

- Develop and apply tools and techniques for eradicating non-native crayfish populations, particularly where they threaten sensitive sites or important populations of native crayfish.

- Support, where feasible and appropriate reintroduction programmes of native crayfish.

Pearl mussel

- Maintain and where possible increase the size of existing populations through appropriate habitat, water quality and land use management.

- Seek to re-establish new populations of this species in at least 10 suitable former areas.

Fish

- Maintain and where appropriate enhance existing populations through appropriate monitoring and subsequent habitat and water quality management.

- Meet all the requirements of international commitments, namely the Ramsar Convention and Habitats and Species Directive.

- Seek opportunities for habitat creation.

- Support appropriate translocation programmes for rare and endangered species.

- Resist future stocking of fish unless appropriate to secure long-term conservation status.

9.7 Managing freshwater habitats

Char

For the majority of freshwater habitats, management is usually only required where human activities have caused a change in the natural conditions, or where particularly vigorous plants start to dominate the vegetation communities. In the following sections the impact of human activities upon freshwater systems is reviewed. Advice on ways to minimise or reverse adverse impacts through management is highlighted. These issues are considered under three headings:

- wider issues, ie those which occur outwith the catchment, but may affect fresh waters (9.8);
- activities which occur within the catchment (9.9);
- direct uses of water bodies and the resulting impacts (9.10).

When managing fresh waters it is essential that the many legal requirements affecting these areas are followed. These are too numerous to cover in this handbook and appropriate publications are available (eg Fry 1997; Gregory 1994; Howarth 1992; Lister 1996; Longworth 1992; Polden & Jackson 1994; Wolf & White 1997). The Environment Agency (formerly the National Rivers Authority) is responsible for the protection of the water environment in England and Wales. The organisation has statutory responsibilities for water resources, pollution control, flood defence, fisheries, conservation, recreation and navigation. It is advisable to contact them prior to initiating new management regimes.

Freshwater habitats are dynamic systems. The quantity and relative proportions of particular species within the communities may change annually depending upon, for example, spring light levels and rainfall. Little is currently known about natural fluctuations in systems making detection of long term trends difficult.

Land use in the uplands, however, has a significant effect on the geomorphological processes occurring in river systems. Increased grazing and deforestation, for example, particularly at the headwaters of a catchment, reduce the water-carrying capacity of the ground. Soil erosion, sediment transport and bank side erosion are then increased, and produce a higher sediment loading of the system. Many of the problems that are being tackled by river management are really only addressing symptoms of problems caused by land management practices in the headwaters of the catchment.

9.8 Wider issues affecting freshwater habitats

9.8.1 Acidification

Acid rain originates from oxides of sulphur and oxides of nitrogen released during the combustion of fossil fuels. Following oxidation and reaction with moisture in the atmosphere acid rain or snow is produced (wet deposition). In areas where there are insufficient base ions in the soil or the water to buffer the acid cations, these cause significant decreases in pH. This is particularly the case in upland areas across England, where the predominant underlying rocks are acidic or resistant to weathering, eg granite, and provide little buffering capacity in the soil or water. Certain vegetation types, in particular coniferous forestry, also tend to exacerbate the problems of acidification by accumulating the pollutants on their foliage.

The pH of freshwater habitats is critical to the plants and animals present. The preferred pH range of many aquatic plants, for example, is around neutral (Table 9.1). Acidification of fresh water is likely to alter plant and animal communities, and could lead to the loss of rare or scarce species where it is particularly severe.

The long-term solution lies in reducing emissions of pollutants to the atmosphere. Liming of adjacent land has been used to counter the impact of acidification, but has uncertain results and is rarely recommended.

Further information: Howells & Dalziel 1992; Ormerod & Buckton 1994.

9.8.2 Climate change

In addition to the predicted increases in temperature (see 2.13.3), climate models also forecast that precipitation will rise. The UK Climate Change Impacts Review Group study (CCIRG 1996) envisages a gradient of warming in the UK from south east to north west, with winter warming ranging from 2° C to 0.8° C by the 2050s and summer warming from 1.8° C to 1.2° C. The study also predicts that annual precipitation will rise by 5% by the 2020s and 10% by the 2050s. Winter precipitation is likely to increase everywhere, whereas summer rainfall is forecast to decrease in the south east and increase in the north west.

The Environment Agency has identified a number of issues relevant to climate change on freshwater systems. These include the reliability of ground water resources and ground water recharge, and changes in wetland and riverine environments, including flow patterns and flood risk, water resources and quality, fish habitats and the aesthetic quality of river corridors. Clearly these issues must be given consideration when developing strategies for managing freshwater habitats in the uplands, with due regard being given to adaptation, mitigation and determination of policy, particularly in relation to other key areas of nature conservation policy.

9.9 Catchment issues affecting freshwater habitats

9.9.1 Agriculture

Agriculture is the principal land use in most upland areas and is a major catchment issue affecting freshwater habitats.

Pastoral

In many upland areas natural water bodies such as streams or tarns are used as drinking water sites for stock. This can result in severe trampling of the banks, leading to erosion of river or stream margins, particularly where banks are steep and prone to collapse. It can lead to increased sedimentation in the water body, which may affect the aquatic flora and fauna. Many aquatic plants, for example, require clear water in order to photosynthesise, and many fish require clean gravels for spawning.

Stock access to riparian sand and shingle banks severely reduces their value in supporting significant invertebrate communities. Cattle may also graze aquatic vegetation (mainly emergent species) where they are able to wade into shallow streams and standing water bodies. Damage to the substratum and increased turbidity can be particularly acute in small ponds where cattle may have access to the entire water body.

Trampling of any water margin can lead to the loss of emergent and edge species. Some plant species, such as lesser water-plantain *Baldellia ranunculoides* and blinks *Montia fontana*, benefit from a low level of trampling and disturbance because it creates openings for colonisation. However, many marginal species will be lost if heavy trampling by cattle continues. This not only destroys the plant communities, but also the habitats used by invertebrates, for example dragonflies and damselflies, which require emergent vegetation. In addition, it removes the cover and food required by other animals such as water voles.

Methods for managing watering areas will vary according to the slope of the bank and surrounding land (Environment Agency 1998c; MAFF 1992a, 1997c & 1999b. Where the slope of the bank is shallow, stock can be allowed open access to the water's edge provided repeated trampling does not result in a 'cliff' rather than a slope. If stream banks are steep throughout the length of the stream, it may be best to fence the entire length, allowing the fence line to pass through the stream itself where there is a bend in its course. The unfenced area can then become the watering area, and although it will become eroded the remaining length of stream is protected. (See also 9.10.8 regarding pastoral land around small ponds and tarns)

The fertiliser and slurry spreading associated with pastoral management can lead to enrichment of water systems and subsequent changes in the flora and fauna. This is particularly so if it is spread on valley sides when run-off is likely (eg the ground is sodden or very dry). It can also occur via nutrients entering ground water in permeable areas. Nutrient run-off may be reduced by buffer strips which separate water courses from nearby farm land (see Box 9.1). For appropriate application rates for different substance on different grassland types see Chapter 7.

In general, the introduction of nitrogen and phosphorous into an oligotrophic upland water body will cause an increase in trophic status and thus a change in the associated plant and animal communities. Micro algae such as cyanobacteria and dinoflagellates, which multiply in response to increased nutrient levels, increase the turbidity of the water column and cause a decline in submerged macrophyte species (see also 9.10.3). The turbidity also affects the animals that the water course can support, particularly those requiring clear water and clean gravel beds.

In standing waters dissolved oxygen levels in the surface water layer (the epilimnion) will increase due to enhanced algal photosynthesis. However, increased sedimentation and decomposition will cause de-oxygenation of deeper water (the hypolimnion) and at the sediment surface. The result is a decrease in pH and an accompanying release of nutrients stored in the sediment. It is for this reason that measures to restore lakes which have undergone eutrophication often involve the removal of surface sediment.

Where livestock are allowed to enter a water course, direct defecation will lead to local enrichment, particularly in standing or slow moving waters. Oligotrophic plant and animal communities may then be replaced by those more characteristic of eutrophic conditions. In marginal habitats ruderal plant species such as nettle *Urtica dioica* may encroach into locally enriched areas.

An additional potential problem for freshwater habitats arising from livestock management is the toxic effect of sheep dip (see 9.10.3 and Box 9.6).

Arable

During the twentieth century, arable cultivation, particularly for cereals, has declined dramatically in the uplands with livestock production and associated grassland systems becoming virtually the sole activity. However, in the lower reaches of freshwater systems that originate at higher altitudes, arable farming becomes more widespread and significant to wildlife interests.

Excessive application of organic and inorganic fertiliser are considered to be the main source of pollution of fresh water from agricultural sources (Economic Commission for Europe 1993). The nitrate and phosphate within these fertilisers behave differently when they reach the soil. The nitrate ion is relatively soluble (because it is repelled by the negatively charged soil particles) and so moves into water courses relatively easily. The phosphate ion is readily precipitated as insoluble iron, calcium or aluminium phosphate and is therefore unavailable for uptake by plants. Inputs of phosphate into fresh water arises largely as a result of soil erosion, although it is now suspected that soils may be saturated and acting as a source rather than a sink.

For arable land, applications of fertilisers should not exceed the crop requirement and should also take account of the current levels of nutrients in the soil. The appropriate amount should be applied in one application. Fertilisers, agro-chemicals, lime or other soil improvers should not be applied within the river or lake margin and all fertilisers should be spread in accordance with the *Codes of good agricultural practice* (MAFF 1998g & h).

The leaching of nutrients from cultivated land varies according to the particular crop in question; lowest rates occur from unfertilised permanent grassland, whilst highest rates are associated with fields planted with vegetables. Soil type and nutrient content, climatic and meteorological conditions and crop rotation are also important factors (Economic Commission for Europe 1993).

Land left unvegetated during the winter months is a potential cause of soil erosion. Increased levels of suspended solids in a water body will lead to smothering of submerged plant species. A change in the turbidity of the water and the nature of the substrate, for example from stony to silty, will affect the animals present, particularly certain invertebrates and spawning fish.

Reducing nutrient and sediment run-off in the short term may be addressed by the development of buffer strips which separate water courses from nearby farm land. (See Box 9.1 for details on buffer strips.) However, in the long term changes in agricultural practice are also needed.

Further information: English Nature 1995a; Environment Agency 1998c; MAFF 1992a, 1997c, 1998g & h; MAFF and Welsh Office 1991.

Box 9.1 Establishing buffer areas

Buffer areas

This term is used to describe a strip or zone of vegetation which lies adjacent to a water course and does not receive the nutrients or chemicals applied to the adjacent land. It acts as a 'sink' for the substances derived from the adjacent land.

How buffer areas work

Buffer areas work in two ways. They distance the area concerned from the water course, so reducing the likelihood of spray drift or sediment entering the water. In addition, the water that passes through the soil in the buffer area can be chemically transformed to reduce its pollutant load.

Buffer areas can minimise direct contamination with manures, pesticides and fertilisers. In addition buffer areas are a useful tool in controlling soil erosion. For further details see Environment Agency 1996b.

Limitations of buffer areas

Buffer areas are ineffective where the underlying geology is permeable, eg on limestone, although they will still be effective in helping to minimise pesticide drift. The nature of drainage systems in limestone can cause pollution to enter a water course several miles from the source of the pollutant.

The majority of nutrient enrichment arises from nitrate or phosphorous moving through the soil and drains. Much agricultural land is drained and under-drainage will by-pass a buffer area, making it largely ineffective. The buffer area must also be correctly sited to ensure that it intercepts a good proportion of soil water or surface run-off. For example, buffer areas will not be effective where water directly infiltrates ground water or is channelled away from the buffer by site hydrology. The value of buffer areas will be maximised if inputs of nutrients are limited in the upstream catchment, because buffering all streams and ditches in the headwaters may be impractical.

Types of buffer areas

Wooded buffer strips are more effective than well vegetated grass strips at removing nitrogen, whilst vegetated strips are more effective at removing suspended solids (and therefore particulate phosphorous). A combination of both will be the most effective. Bare earth is of no use in controlling diffuse pollution, while a mown grass strip is of limited use.

In some cases pollutants coalesce into discrete areas owing to land form or hydrology. Buffer zones targeted at these areas could negate the need for buffer strips.

Pollution removal

About 80% of the suspended solids in run-off (which may contain phosphorous and pesticides) can be trapped on the surface or infiltrate the buffer area. Buffer areas can also remove nearly all the nitrate in water that passes through them at a depth of less than 30 cm. The soil surface must remain relatively dry for phosphorus to be retained, whilst optimum nitrate removal occurs when the subsoil is wet.. The potential of buffer strips to remove pesticides remains unproven, as the anaerobic conditions favouring the denitrification process (removal of nitrate) are likely to cause the release of pesticides.

Box 9.1 Establishing buffer areas cont.

Value of buffer strips for wildlife

The area at the edge of the buffer strip will be the most effective for diffuse pollution control, while the potential value for wildlife will increase closer to the river itself where nutrient and pesticide levels are low. Obviously the wider the buffer strip the more valuable it will be to wildlife. The wildlife of the water system being protected by the buffer strip, eg aquatic plants, invertebrates, and fish, will also benefit from the reduced inputs.

Buffer strip widths

The required width will vary according to whether the strip is required for wildlife value as well as pollution control.

- A strip of minimum 10 m for wildlife has been recommended by Petersen & La Coursiere (1992), but other studies have recommended 30 m or 90 m on rivers with a floodplain.
- For buffer strips required only for pollution control a width of 2-3 m is adequate provided it is well vegetated.

Further information: Environment Agency 1996b; Petersen, Petersen & La Coursiere 1992.

Water shrew

9.9.2 Forestry

The rate of afforestation of upland catchments in England has decreased significantly in the last 15 years. However, large conifer plantations in upland areas have significant effects upon the freshwater systems that drain them. These include altering the hydrology of surrounding areas, changing erosion and sedimentation rates, and affecting water quality.

Changes in hydrology

Deep ploughing of wet areas results in a lowering of the water table and a loss of wetland species. Drains that expose peat areas reduce their capacity to retain water and this can lead to a greater likelihood of flash flooding at some times of year. Conversely, reduced flows may result at other times owing to the reduced capacity of the land to hold water.

Erosion and sedimentation

Extensive drainage operations lead to increased rates of run-off from the ground and increased flows in receiving streams. Streams often lose their natural channels as they are converted into drainage runnels (Nature Conservancy Council 1986a). The increased spate of streams creates greater erosive power leading to sediment transport and re-distribution of sediment deposits. Studies carried out by Battarbee *et al* (1985) compared sediment transport in afforested and unafforested catchments. In lakes with 15-70% afforestation there was a marked increase in sedimentation resulting from soil erosion in the catchment.

Sedimentation resulting from soil erosion in the catchment may lead to changes in the aquatic flora of the receiving water body. Submerged plant communities in particular will suffer from blanketing of the substratum. They may have difficulty in rooting and therefore are more likely to be scoured out in flood conditions. Increased turbidity in the water column will decrease light penetration, thereby inhibiting photosynthesis. The result may be a change from a mixed community of submerged and floating leaved species to dominance by floating leaved species, and, eventually colonisation by marginal emergent species as siltation progresses.

As sedimentation progresses, the aquatic fauna will also change. For example, species requiring clear water and stony beds will be replaced by those adapted to turbid water and soft substratum. Fish spawning can also be affected by sedimentation.

Erosion may also lead to changes in the water chemistry, particularly where high levels of peat are entering the system. This in turn will alter the aquatic communities present to those which are adapted to the new conditions.

Nutrient enrichment

Fertiliser, in the form of rock phosphate, is added to the soil to increase the nutrient status of afforested areas. The result is an almost immediate enrichment of forest streams that drain the affected areas (Nature Conservancy Council 1986a). The effects of nutrient enrichment on plant communities and species have been dealt with in 9.9.1.

Acidification

Coniferous forestry is particularly important in accelerating the process of acidification. The large surface area offered by their leaves enables the trees to accumulate acidifying pollutants from the air in a particulate form (dry deposition) or from mists and fogs (occult deposition).

Waters that have become acidified have a combination of low pH and low concentration of calcium, coupled with a high concentration of aluminium leached from the soil. This combination has a damaging effect on flora and fauna. For example, acidified systems generally support a less diverse macrophyte flora. Tolerant species such as bulbous rush *Juncus bulbosus* and *Sphagnum* spp are likely to proliferate under acid conditions, as a result of reduced competition.

Increased alkalinity due to liming

Liming has been used as a means of ameliorating the effects of acid deposition on fresh water, particularly in relation to restoring declining fish stocks. Liming is either carried out through direct application to the water body or indirectly via the catchment. Direct liming is only effective if applied to a standing water body with a long residence time; in better flushed systems the buffering effect of the lime is rapidly lost. Rivers and streams are often dosed periodically in proportion to their flow, water level and pH.

Catchment liming involves dosing the hydrological source of the water body, usually springs and flushes. It mitigates the effects of acid surges and prevents harmful metals leaking into the water course. However, a number of concerns have been raised over the widespread use of liming as a means of ameliorating the effects of acid deposition.

- The addition of lime to acidified waters does not restore the water body to the pre-acidified state, but, in effect, hardens previously soft waters.
- In some cases liming can cause damage to the catchment comparable with acidification.
- Liming does not stop the input of aluminium to watercourses, although it does convert it to the less toxic non-labile form.
- Liming can cause the loss of nitrate to water courses; the impact of which is uncertain (Farmer 1992).

Liming is likely to affect the flora and fauna of the water body, especially if applied to springs and flushes. Species composition is likely to change because calcifuge species are discouraged. Unless lime-rich water bodies are present nearby, there is unlikely to be colonisation by calcicoles.

Liming of oligotrophic lakes tends to lead to an increase in species diversity, accompanied by changes in dominance. Acidophilic (acid loving) plant species such as the *Sphagnum* mosses tend to decline or disappear, whilst liverworts and filamentous green algae proliferate. Battarbee *et al* (1992) should be consulted for a detailed account of the effects of liming on the macrophyte flora of an oligotrophic system. In addition the increase in alkalinity of limed waters may lead to a transition from ultra-oligotrophic and oligotrophic state to a more species-rich, mesotrophic situation.

Shading

Loss of light on riparian margins can discourage or eliminate plant and animal species.

9.9.3 Mining and quarrying

Mines and quarries are often sited in upland areas, particularly those underlain by limestone. Mining poses a number of environmental problems with relation to fresh waters, in particular the leaching of mine wastes into running or standing waters. The result may be direct pollution of water courses, with the consequent effects on wildlife.

9.10 Direct management issues affecting freshwater habitats

9.10.1 Direct abstraction

Many upland stream, rivers and water bodies have been developed as a source of drinking water for private and public supply. Water is abstracted directly from surface or ground waters, thereby posing a threat to water levels and flow regimes downstream of the abstraction point. Water may also be abstracted for non-consumptive use, for example by hydro-electric power stations or by fish farms. In these cases river flows may be reduced between abstraction and discharge points.

Reducing the flows in rivers can lead to grasses and other vegetation taking over the river bed, making it very difficult for characteristic water plants to return. Low flows also exacerbate the effects of pollution and enrichment. Reduced flushing rates may lead to changes in the physical nature of the river bed or channel.

River flows are normally protected from the impacts of abstraction by the inclusion of prescribed flow conditions in abstraction licences. Under the Water Resources Act 1991, a system of Water Quality Objectives are devised for each water course based upon the use of that river. Abstraction of drinking water is one of the recognised uses (Environment Agency 1996c). These prescribed flows are often set with reference to some statistical measure of low flow such as Q95 (the flow equalled or exceeded for 95% of the time, on average), with an additional allowance to protect other legal users downstream.

SSSIs which have been designated for their aquatic interest may be subject to Water Level Management Plans (WLMPs). Preparation of these plans is a MAFF initiative whereby the water level requirements for a range of activities, including agriculture, flood defence and conservation, can be balanced and integrated. It is the responsibility of the relevant operating authorities (Environment Agency, Internal Drainage Board or Local Authority) to produce and implement these plans. English Nature's role is to define the nature conservation interest of SSSIs and the water level requirements of the relevant species.

The water level requirements of wetland plants are defined as the upper and lower limits of tolerance to either soil water tables or depth of water, or as a mixture of the two. The water level requirements of rare and scarce wetland plants are given in Table 9.14-9.16.

Further information: Newbold & Mountford 1997.

Effects of over abstraction on plants and animals

Drying of edge and marginal habitats leading to the encroachment of ruderal species. Certain swamp and fen plant communities are characteristic of disturbed habitats and will tend to replace more species-rich assemblages in sub-optimal or disturbed conditions. An example is the *Phragmites australis-Urtica dioica* community, characterised by an understorey of tall dicotyledons such as great hairy willow-herb *Epilobium hirsutum* and stinging nettle *Urtica dioica*. This community of ruderal herbs will out-compete other reed-swamp communities in situations where the marginal edge of watercourses has dried out and become enriched. This will obviously affect the dependent animals.

Reduced flushing rate leading to build up of nutrients. A reduction in water levels will lead to an increased concentration of nutrients. Such an increase could enhance the production of some species at the disadvantage of others. Canadian pondweed *Elodea canadensis*, for example, often proliferates in nutrient enriched waters at the expense of other submerged species. In many cases this dominance by one particular species may only be broken by increasing water levels.

Increased sedimentation. Reduced flushing rates in eroding upland water courses will often result in the deposition of suspended material. Sedimentation will have a smothering effect on submerged animal and plant species, and may fundamentally change the balance of species. Deposition of suspended organic material may change the nature of the surface substratum, leading to a change in the plant and animal communities.

Exposure of normally submerged sub-littoral zones leading to possible reduction in submerged species. Areas normally covered by water may become exposed to the air, reducing the availability of habitat for submerged species.

Box 9.2 Managing abstraction

Abstraction

The Environment Agency is empowered to licence abstractions, to enforce conditions imposed in an abstraction licence, and to take action against illegal abstractions.

When an abstraction is being considered for a water body which has special conservation interests the following steps should be taken:

- Surveys should be carried out to determine the distribution of marginal and submerged communities/species.
- The sensitivity of communities to changes in water level can then be determined using Newbold and Mountford (1997).
- For Sites of Special Scientific Interest the Environment Agency will carry out a hydrological survey for use in the development of a Water Level Management Plan.
- A limit should be set on the extent of change in water levels, in accordance with the findings of the survey.
- The site should then be monitored for species performance and for water levels.

Where there is an existing licence abstraction affecting a water body with special conservation interest, the following steps should be taken:

- Where Water Level Management Plans are being produced, the requirements of the wildlife interest should be taken into account.
- The Environment Agency has a duty to review existing abstraction licences affecting Special Areas of Conservation (SAC), designated under the Habitats Directive, and prepare plans for remedial action.
- In any other situations, work with the Environment Agency and interested parties to develop sustainable water resource strategies on a catchment basis.

Further information: Newbold & Mountford 1997.

9.10.2 Impoundments

Water courses are impounded for a variety of purposes. Running water systems may be impounded to create reservoirs for public water supply, or for hydro-electric power generation. On a smaller scale, individual farmers may dam a stream to raise the water level sufficiently to allow abstraction for irrigation. Some standing waters are impounded to raise water levels for recreational purposes such as fishing, shooting or sailing.

Effects of impoundments on freshwater plants and animals

Impounded streams and rivers will undergo a rise in water level, leading to permanent inundation of both terrestrial and littoral communities. The existing terrestrial plant communities which are flooded may be of considerable wildlife value in themselves, such as the limestone grassland communities of Teesdale which were lost when Cow Green reservoir was created. Plant communities of the littoral zone of standing or running waters have specific habitat requirements in terms of inundation and exposure and are also likely to be lost or adversely affected. Conversely, artificial lakes and reservoirs will be subject to draw down during the summer months as demand for water exceeds supply by rainfall. In this case sub-littoral areas will be exposed leading to a loss of shallow rooting communities.

Impoundments can also have major impacts downstream of the dam or sluice. This includes changing the normal flow regime, which is likely to alter the physical, chemical and biological nature of the water course, and potentially leading to a lack of flushing in the downstream system.

Box 9.3 Managing impoundments

Impoundments

The Reservoirs Act 1975 states that a water body cannot be impounded without due consideration to downstream users.

- Where sites of nature conservation may be affected by impoundments water level management plans should be consulted.
- Surveys should be conducted to determine which plant communities are present at the site.
- An appraisal should be made of the likely impacts changes in water levels will have on particular plant communities and species.
- An appraisal should be made of the likely impacts changes in water levels will have on fish spawning sites.

9.10.3 Aquatic pollutants

Aquatic pollutants include sewage, industrial and farm waste. The impact of a discharge on a freshwater system will depend on the amount discharged, the nature of the pollutant, and the water quality of the receiving water course. Large volumes of pollutant discharged into a small or medium sized river may lead to a rise in water level, thereby altering flow regimes and causing eutrophication.

Organic effluent

Organic effluent such as farm waste (slurry and silage) or sewage are broken down through the action of a range of micro-organisms. This biochemical break down of complex organic molecules utilises oxygen from the surrounding water column resulting in a shortage of dissolved oxygen in the water course downstream of an outfall. The degree of de-oxygenation will depend on:

- the dilution of the effluent in the receiving water course;
- the Biochemical Oxygen Demand (BOD) of the effluent and the receiving water course;
- the nature of the organic material;
- the total organic load of the water body;
- temperature.

Farm effluent such as silage and slurry have an extremely high BOD and if discharged untreated into a water course will cause the complete elimination of the downstream flora and fauna (See Box 9.5 for methods of disposal of farm effluent). Lower strength effluent such as domestic sewage are unlikely to lead to complete elimination of the downstream biota but will tend to cause a change in the structure of the plant community.

Effects of organic effluent on plants and animals

Turbidity and sedimentation. Organic effluent often has high sediment loads associated with it. The resulting increase in the turbidity of the water column reduces the light available for photosynthesis and may lead to the elimination of submerged plants. Sedimentation caused by organic inputs to upland freshwater systems can cause deposition of organically enriched silt. This results in a limitation of the habitat available for animal species, many of which require clean, unsilted cobble or gravel substances for their survival. It can also result in a change in the plant community.

Eutrophication. Eutrophication is the increase in phosphate and nitrogen in a water system. These nutrients, particularly phosphate, are the primary limiting factors of phytoplankton production. Microbial breakdown of organic material, plus direct input of the nutrients from fertiliser run-off, increase the nutrient status of a water body. Increased nutrients cause an increase in plant production, which may block water channels and increase the risk of flooding. The plant assemblages become less diverse and light penetration is reduced, which can limit the area available for plant colonisation. The breakdown of the increased plant material can cause sediment to become silted and anoxic, resulting in the loss of invertebrates and fish. Severe eutrophication in standing water bodies can result in the production of toxic blue-green algae (cyanobacteria).

Box 9.4 Managing sewage effluent

Sewage effluent discharge

The Environment Agency is responsible for issuing numerical consents for discharges to the aquatic environment. The consent system is based on the principle that a discharge with a BOD of 30 mg/l and suspended solid (SS) load of 20 mg/l can be discharged to a water course providing the dilution therein is at least 1:8.

There are a number of inherent problems associated with this system:

- A river with a naturally high suspended solid load (derived from catchment run-off) may receive a number of point source discharges. Assuming all these discharges comply with the specified consent the total suspended solid load of the river may be sufficient to change the ecological state of the river. The problem will be further exacerbated by low flows resulting from dry weather or from abstraction.

- Conventional secondary treatment of sewage using biological filter beds or an activated sludge system facilitates the microbial breakdown of organic material; it does not remove the nitrate and phosphate which result from this break down. The input of nutrients from a number of consented discharges may be sufficient to cause eutrophication in some water courses.

- Some villages and hamlets have no sewage treatment works and rely totally on residential properties having septic tanks and soakways, which can overflow into freshwater systems. Again, there is no removal of nitrate and phosphorous involved.

Options

- For sites with particular conservation value it may be advisable to test background levels of nitrogen, phosphorous and suspended solids in the water course.

- Seek advice on whether the Environment Agency consent system is sufficient to maintain SSSI interest, based on the water quality data above and the N, P and SS loading of the proposed discharge.

Tertiary treatment

For point source discharges of organic effluent, tertiary treatment, which principally involves phosphorous removal, may be a feasible option. This process can involve the precipitation of phosphorous using coagulants of lime, or compounds of aluminium or iron and is approximately 90-95% efficient. Alternative methods are also available, such as reedbeds and lagoons. The cost of phosphate removal for a sewage treatment works is relatively small in comparison with total annual running costs. The EC Waste Water Directive requires Water Authorities to install tertiary treatment where the population is above a certain number (10,000). This usually refers to large sewage treatment works and where the water is deemed sensitive.

An alternative is to divert the phosphorous-rich effluent away from the sensitive water body. The practicality of this option depends on the proximity to a less sensitive water body. All discharges to the sea must now be treated.

Box 9.5 Managing farm waste

Farm waste

The disposal of farm waste is regulated under the Control of Pollution (Silage, Slurry and Agricultural fuel oil) Regulations 1991 (SI 1991/324). The Environment Agency is responsible for the enforcement of these regulations, and for issuing consents to discharge from farms. The Ministry of Agriculture Fisheries and Foods have produced a Code of good agricultural practice of the protection of water (MAFF 1998h).

Slurry disposal and storage

Under the Control of Pollution (Silage, Slurry and Agricultural Fuel Oil) Regulations 1991 slurry must be kept in a reception pit or slurry storage tank, unless it is temporarily in a tanker. The Regulations lay down certain rules for most new, substantially enlarged or substantially reconstructed stores, reception pits and channels. The MAFF Code (1998h) provides guidance and gives a detailed description of all the methods employed for slurry storage, such as under floor storage, above ground circular stores, and weeping wall slurry stores. It also deals with the treatment of slurry by mechanical separation, anaerobic digestion and aerobic treatment.

Silage storage

As for slurry, the Control of Pollution (Silage, Slurry and Agricultural Fuel Oil) Regulations 1991 include requirements for the storage and disposal of silage effluent. The MAFF Code (1998h) gives guidance on controlling the amount of effluent generated by silage, designing a silo to prevent the leakage of effluent and methods of disposing of effluent.

Further information: Kelly 1995; MAFF 1991b.

Toxic contaminants

Toxic contaminants, originating from a wide range of sources, can have far-reaching effects on aquatic biota if allowed to enter a water course. There is also the potential for adverse effects on humans where drinking water supplies are involved. Although heavy industry is less common in upland areas, a number of industrial processes require large quantities of fresh water, and are therefore often located on the upland reaches of rivers. An example is the processing of wool for carpets and clothing.

In some upland areas, acid drainage, resulting from the mining of coal or metal ores, is a significant source of toxicity in fresh water. In the case of coal mines, substantial amounts of the mineral pyrite are exposed to the oxidising action of the air and water. The subsequent reaction causes a lowering of pH in the receiving water course, leading to the mobilisation of toxic metals. These waters can often be recognised by a characteristic ochre colour.

Toxic chemicals used on farms, such as pesticides, can enter water courses accidentally if procedures for their correct use and disposal are not observed. (see Box 9.6). They may enter the aquatic system through drift or run-off during crop spraying or during disposal and decontamination activities and may have significant local impact on the biota.

Sheep dip is a particular concern, being the source of major pollution incidents every year (Environment Agency 1998d). All sheep dip formulations pose a hazard to animals (see below). They can also contaminate ground water, rendering it unfit for use. The increasingly used synthetic pyrethroid dip (SP) formulations are about 100 times more toxic to aquatic invertebrates than organophosphorus (OP) formulations, although both have been involved in serious pollution incidents. Sheep dipping activities and the disposal of sheep dip solution must therefore be carried out with great care. Very small quantities of any dip solution can contaminate large volumes of water. Problems can be avoided by simple precautions and planning ahead (see Box 9.6). Implementation of the Ground Water Regulations (1998) will require an assessment of siting and disposal of sheep dip by the Environment Agency. It is important that the potential risks to both aquatic and terrestrial fauna are considered in this assessment.

The use of herbicides close to a water course may lead to seepage and drift into the water and impacts on aquatic flora and fauna. Bracken spraying, for example, is common in the uplands and the herbicide involved, asulam, can cause a slight to moderate check, or even severe check in some cases, in the growth of certain aquatic and wetland plants, such as duckweed *Lemna* sp., bog pondweed *Potamogeton polygonifolius* and lesser spearwort *Ranunculus flammula* (Rhone-Poulenc 1997, see Information Note 6 regarding bracken management).

Effects of aquatic pollutants on plants and animals

Evidence for the impact of toxic chemicals on the aquatic system is often most rapidly shown by the macro-invertebrate communities. But both direct and indirect effects on other groups of organisms (eg by a reduction in the invertebrate food supply) can be significant and often more evident (eg fish kills). Pesticides, including veterinary medicines such as sheep dips, and herbicides, which enter a water course accidentally, can kill aquatic invertebrates and cause browning and death of aquatic plants. In the case of acid mine drainage from disused coal mines, decreases in pH may render the water course unsuitable for certain plants and animals. In addition, as the pH increases with distance downstream, ferric hydroxide precipitates out. This blankets the stream bed, inhibiting the growth of aquatic plants and changing the suitability of the habitat for aquatic animals.

Otter

Box 9.6 Managing toxic contaminants

Toxic contaminants

Since 1991 pollution incidents have been categorised by the Environment Agency on the basis of their severity. Category 1 incidents are the worst and may result in the closure of a source of water abstraction, or extensive fish kills. Of the total number of serious pollution incidents recorded, those resulting from industrial activities (in particular the construction industry) are the most frequent. Prosecutions are always sought when Category 1 incidents occur, if adequate evidence is available (Environment Agency 1996a). The Control of Pesticides 1986 (amended 1997) requires users "to take all reasonable precautions to protect.....creatures and plants.....and in particular to avoid the pollution of water".

Different statutory requirements, codes of practice and guidance is required or available for users of veterinary medicines and pesticides, including:

- the label recommendations;
- the requirements of the Control of Substances Hazardous to Health Regulations (COSHH) 1998;
- the Control of Pesticides Regulations 1986 (as amended 1997);
- the Guidelines for the use of herbicides on weeds in or near watercourses or lakes (MAFF 1995);
- the Code of practice for the safe use of pesticides on farms and holdings (The Green Code, MAFF 1998j);
- the Guidance on storing pesticides for farmers and other professional users (Health and Safety Executive 1997);
- the Sheep dipping: Pollution prevention guidelines no. 12 (Environment Agency 1998d) and sheep dipping leaflet (Health and Safety Executive 1998).

Sheep dip

Careful siting of new dipping facilities, proper use and maintenance of existing dipping facilities, correct management and handling of sheep after dipping, and correct disposal of spent solution and empty containers are all important to prevent water pollution. Some guidelines are provided below, but see Environment Agency 1998c and HSE 1998 for further details on all these aspects. The Ground Water Regulation 1998 will require assessment and authorisation of dipping facilities to prevent entry to ground water of List I and List II substances, including both OP and SP dips. Guidance on the implementation of the Regulation is expected during 1999.

Dip chemicals may also enter rivers through the contamination of effluent from the wool scouring industry. Label withdrawal periods must be observed for the product used, but it is good practice not to shear sheep for three months after dipping.

Box 9.6 Managing toxic contaminants cont.

Siting and design of sheep dips

- See Health and Safety Executive leaflet (1998) for siting and design of sheep dip facilities.
- The dip bath should not have a drainage hole and drip pens should be constructed with impervious floors which drain back into the bath. They should be large enough to hold sheep for at least 10 minutes so that they are not actively dripping when released to secondary holding pens.
- New facilities should be located as far away from any water course or drain as possible, but never less than 10 m, and at least 50 m from any well, spring or borehole.
- For mobile dip facilities, the appropriate place to let sheep drain and the correct method of disposal must be decided beforehand.

Disposal of spent dip

- Before disposal, the EA must be consulted so that they can consider measures needed to protect ground water and issue an authorisation.
- Spent dip must not be tipped into sewers, drains, cesspools or septic tanks and must not be able to run off or seep into any river, stream or ground water.
- Soakaways must not be used for the disposal of used dip and an alternative must be sought.
- One possibility is to use a registered waste disposal contractor.
- In certain circumstances spent dip can be spread thinly onto grassland at certain application rates, but see EA 1998c for further details and conditions. Consult English Nature if within an SSSI because some such areas may be very important for wildlife.

Further information: Environment Agency 1998d; Health and Safety Executive 1998; Veterinary Medicines Directorate publications 1991, 1992, 1993.

Box 9.6 Managing toxic contaminants cont.

Pesticides

The Environment Agency and statutory conservation agencies must be consulted at least 72 hours before any aerial spraying is undertaken. In the case of the conservation agencies, this applies to any aerial spraying application within 1,500 m of an SSSI. Failure to consult may result in prosecution. For ground spraying, follow the Code of practice for the safe use of pesticides on farms and holdings (The Green Code, MAFF 1998j).

- Wherever possible, control weeds by mechanical means.
- A certificate of competence is required for users of pesticides.
- Always follow the label instructions.
- To avoid unnecessary damage to non-target plants apply herbicide by spot treatment or weed wiper where possible.
- Avoid spraying pesticides close to aquatic habitats and follow any label instructions on no-spray zones.
- Avoid spraying in high winds and follow the Green code recommendations on wind speed.
- Use appropriate no-spray buffer zones when spraying adjacent to sites of nature conservation importance (see Cooke 1993 and Information Note 6 Managing bracken).
- Dispose of pesticides and washings safely and follow the Green code.

Further information: Control of Pesticides Regulations 1986 (as amended) (COPR); Cooke 1986, 1993; Control of Substances Hazardous to Health Regulations 1994 (as amended) (COSHH); Information Note 6 Managing bracken; MAFF 1995 & 1998j.

9.10.4 Structural modification of water courses

River channels have been modified in the UK for many purposes including: flood alleviation, agricultural drainage, reducing bank erosion and maintaining navigation. The methods include widening, deepening, straightening and embanking. Although large-scale engineering projects are less common in upland areas, a significant number of upland rivers and streams have undergone some small-scale engineering, usually in the form of channelisation. These types of modifications often result in loss or change of aquatic and riparian habitats.

Re-sectioning is the mechanical re-profiling of river banks and/or bed to produce a larger, more uniform cross-section, which can carry flood flows more effectively. This will usually involve dredging to maintain the cross-section and mowing of bank vegetation. The result is, in general, a loss of physical features, such as riffles, point bars and eroding cliffs.

Bank reinforcement is usually associated with urban areas and major rail or road links, although it can occur wherever there is a danger of bank erosion. On a smaller scale banks may be subject to reinforcement following flooding. Reinforcement may involve the whole bank or just the bottom section. Various materials are used, including concrete, sheet piling, brick, laid stone, rip-rap and rock filled gabion baskets. The immediate result of bank reinforcement is the loss of bank features and vegetation; there may also be an associated change in sediment transport.

Weirs and sluices are used as a means of harnessing the power of rivers to drive milling machinery, for water-level, flood control and in conjunction with locks for navigation. These fixed structures hold back water upstream, with a resulting reduction in velocity. Their impact on habitat features is dependent on the nature of the river section. In upland areas weirs appear to have little impact on the physical elements of the stream, such as pools, riffles and point bars. However, the fall in velocity caused by the weir may result in some sedimentation in the upstream section.

Further information: Boon, Calow & Petts 1992; Calow & Petts 1992, 1996a,b,c; Newbold, Purseglove & Holmes 1983; National Rivers Authority 1996; RSPB, NRA & RSNC 1994.

Effects of river engineering on plants and animals

Reduction in channel diversity. River engineering techniques which result in a loss of in-stream physical features will lead to a loss of species diversity. For example, upland riffle systems are normally characterised by a small number of higher plants, such as alternate-flowered water milfoil *Myriophyllum alterniflorum*, shore-weed *Littorella uniflora*, and a wider range of moss and liverwort species such as *Fontinalis antipyretica* and *Solenostoma triste*. In contrast pools or slacks support a broader range of higher plants, such as intermediate water star-wort *Callitriche hamulata*, common water star-wort *C. stagnalis*, floating club rush *Eleogeton fluitans* with a narrower range of non-vascular plnts eg *Sphagnum* moss. Similarly, the wide range of bank and marginal habitats support a characteristic assemblage of species, the diversity of which may be reduced by bank reinforcement.

River engineering may reduce the river margin width, remove or alter shoal and riffle structures and severely alter riparian and aquatic invertebrate communities. This is especially the case for sand and shingle structures, above and below water. Regulating the flow of rivers and streams, especially reducing the periodicity of flow, flash flooding and so on, allows shoal structures to stabilise, or they may remain permanently submerged, potentially wiping out the invertebrate communities. Rivers downstream of reservoirs rarely have shoal faunas of note.

Sedimentation. The physical disturbance associated with any structural modification of the banks or bed of a river will tend to increase levels of suspended solids, and hence increase deposition in the downstream reaches. This problem may be further exacerbated in rivers subject to abstraction (see 9.10.1). Similarly, changes in the flow regime may lead to erosion of the bank and bed downstream of the modified channel. The result in both cases will be a smothering of submerged vegetation. The problems of deposition will be particularly acute where the affected river flows into a lake where the sudden fall in water velocity will cause sediment to settle out. In extreme cases the nature of the substratum may be altered significantly, both in physical structure and trophic status, resulting in a change in the rooted macrophyte flora and the fauna.

Box 9.7 Structural modifications of river channels

The Environment Agency is responsible for balancing the use of water resources in England. However, water courses which are not designated SSSIs are afforded no statutory protection against structural modifications, such as channelisation. The following points aim to provide guidance on the methods available for dealing with the problems which commonly affect upland rivers.

River Bank Erosion

- **Fence off riparian areas**
  Stock fences should be sited some distance from the bank edge to allow establishment of bank vegetation. If vegetation begins to encroach into the channel some cutting or controlled grazing may need to be implemented.

- **Construct vegetated revetments**
  A revetment is a sloping bank protected by stone or some other durable material. The bank should be re-graded to a stable angle. Shelves and shallow berms planted with appropriate marginal species will protect the bank against erosion. For example, grasses will retard flows whilst reeds will consolidate the lower part of the bank.

- **Plant native trees**
  Planting of trees such as alder *Alnus glutinosa* and willow *Salix* spp help to stabilise river banks. However, there are regulations which control how close to the water's edge this is allowed. Note also that alder is subject to a fungal disease (*Phytophora*) and in areas where this is prevalent, use of alder should be avoided (see Environment Agency 1997).

Flood Alleviation

- **Retain the flood plain**
  Avoid any development of or modification to flood plains.

- **Establish distant flood banks**
  Distant flood banks allows a degree of flooding to occur but enables the river to meander naturally. This method of flood prevention is generally the most appropriate in upland gravel bed rivers as it results in minimum impact on the river environment.

- **Partial dredging**
  This option is preferable to full dredging for removal of high spots in the river bed, as it retains areas of undisturbed bed and creates less spoil (RSPB, NRA & RSNC 1994). It does, however, still destroy valuable habitat and does not address the problem of sediment loading to the system.

- **Gravel traps**
  High energy, upland rivers often carry elevated sediment loads, which may cause bank erosion and scouring. Gravel traps are designed to reduce stream velocity over a designated stretch, thereby causing sedimentation. They may take the form of two concrete sills located some distance apart.

  High sediment loads can be caused by overgrazing, a lack of riparian vegetation and moorland drainage. Reducing sediment loading is preferable to managing the sediment once it is in the river. River management should aim to retain the natural fluvial processes wherever possible.

Further information: Environment Agency 1998c; RSPB, NRA & RSNC 1994; MAFF 1997c & 1999b.

Box 9.8 Managing drainage ditches

Drainage ditches

Ditch systems in the uplands include those in moorland and grassland situations. Managing these to maintain the wildlife interest of the surrounding habitat is covered in Chapters 6 and 7 respectively. Towards the lower reaches of water catchments in the uplands, drainage ditches themselves may be of wildlife value. They may support the remnants of ancient wetland communities, and may be the richest wildlife habitats in many agricultural landscapes, supporting a diversity of water plants, invertebrates, amphibians and fish.

Drainage channels are often managed solely to ensure the prevention of flooding. However, small changes in management could also benefit wildlife. For example, management can prevent emergent vegetation such as reeds invading open water areas and out competing submerged aquatic plants.

Options for drainage ditches

- Deeper channels can be re-profiled and a shallow berm or shelf created along selected lengths.
- Generally management should be carried out 'little and often' using hand tools such as scythes and peat spades where possible.
- On-going cycles of ditch dredging on a three to five-year rotation will create areas for recolonisation of water plant species

Further information: Newbold, Honnor & Buckley 1989.

9.10.5 Recreation

The use of natural areas for recreation has increased significantly in recent years, and freshwaters provide a focus for a range of recreational activities. Fishing is an extremely widespread and popular activity, and boating is also popular, especially on many of the larger lakes in Cumbria, and has increased substantially since the 1970s.

Effects of boat activity on freshwater plants and animals

Power boating in particular can have an adverse impact on freshwater plants and is more disruptive than any other recreational activity for the following reasons.

- Physical turbulence caused by wash and propeller action may lead to the loss of rooted macrophyte species and the prevention of their re-establishment.
- Floating and submerged species may also be cut by propeller action.
- Wave action may cause erosion of banks and bank side vegetation.
- Turbidity may be increased in shallow water courses through disturbance of the substrate.

- Marginal and emergent plants may be removed to enable access to the water's edge. The result of their loss may be accelerated bank erosion.

Further information: MacNee & Harvey 1996

Effects of fishing on freshwater plants and animals

Fishing and fisheries management has the potential to provide many practical conservation benefits (Environment Agency 1998b). Most fisheries have some conservation value and this can be readily increased, both for fishing and wildlife, through simple management of habitats, fish and the activities of the anglers themselves. However, some fisheries management procedures can be detrimental both to fisheries and conservation.

Potential problems that may arise from fishing are given below, although it is recognised that angling is often only one of a range of activities which can result in the problems identified.

- Cutting or removing marginal vegetation to allow access to the water's edge can alter the bank profile, and marginal vegetation may be removed and replaced by a grass sward.

- Clearing vegetation and physical structures in river channels can adversely affect plant, fish and invertebrate communities.

- Invasive plant species, such as the Canadian pondweed *Elodea canadensis*, can be introduced into water courses as a result of fishing activity. *E. canadensis* grows rapidly under suitable conditions and may out-compete other submerged species, alter animal communities and hamper future fishing activity.

- Diseases, such as crayfish plague, can be introduced as fungal spores on fishing gear. The recommendation is to sterilise fishing gear with an iodine-based disinfectant when moving between catchments and water bodies.

- Species which are not endemic to that water body may be introduced, either for sport or as live bait, eg roach and pike, and these can prey on and out-compete other species.

- Discarded fishing line and hooks can cause problems for birds, and fishing may disturb breeding and resting birds and other wildlife.

- Conflict with wildlife interests may arise where fish-eating birds are thought to be affecting fishery interests.

- Sensitive macrophyte species may be threatened as a result of grazing by introduced exotic fish species.

- Many fish populations are genetically distinct, and restocking with fish from different populations can have a detrimental effect on the local population. The recommendation is to stock with fish which are genetically similar to the wild stocks, ie non-genetically distinct sources of fish, in order to reduce the possible impacts.

Further information: Environment Agency 1998b

9.10.6 Fish farming

Fish farming has undergone a rapid expansion since 1990, and although much of this expansion has occurred in Scotland, a number of the larger lakes and rivers in the English uplands now support fish farms.

Rainbow trout are the most popular farmed species throughout northern Europe, and can be farmed in fresh or salt water, although they must spawn in fresh water. The brown trout is also farmed, largely to re-stock fishing ponds. Fish farms can be divided into those which are land-based and abstract water from a nearby water body, and those which use cages anchored some distance from the lake shore. In the former case effluent from the production process is normally discharged to the nearest water course.

Farming of crayfish also occurs in England to supply the restaurant and hotel trade. It involves the introduction of larger, non-native crayfish species to ponds and lakes, the most common being the North American signal crayfish *Pacifastacus leniuculus*. These are either retained by some means in a part of the water body or merely added to the pond or lake and not contained at all.

Effects of fish farming on fresh water plants and animals

Eutrophication. Effluent from fish farms has a high organic content in the form of faeces and excess food. Several studies have shown increases in organic and inorganic nitrogen in fresh waters used for cage culture (Phillips 1985). Similarly, localised increases in phosphorous resulting from excretion or leachate from solid waste have been found to occur close to fish cages. Elevated levels of nutrients may in the long term lead to eutrophication of nutrient-poor oligotrophic lakes and running waters, whilst the sediment underneath fish cages may undergo some localised enrichment.

Where nitrogen and phosphorous inputs to oligotrophic systems are elevated as a result of other activities, the additional input from fish farms will contribute to changes in trophic status. In extreme cases increases in nutrients may result in blooms of micro-algae, which increase the turbidity of the water and reduce light penetration. There may also be a long-term change in higher plant and animal communities.

Sedimentation. Organic matter such as faeces and excess food material will be deposited below fish cages. Blanketing of the substratum by organic material will cause changes in the chemical nature of the sediment, and may lead to a change in the rooted macrophyte flora and aquatic fauna. Species characteristic of oligotrophic systems will be out-competed by species that favour more enriched sediments and eutrophic conditions. Sediment loads are very high; 1 tonne of fish (trout) produced/ annum is equivalent to the suspended solid load from 854 people (Newbold, Hambrey & Smith 1986).

Introduced species. The escape of farmed fish into the environment can affect native fish stocks. It can introduce inappropriate genetic differences in native stocks, ie non-native genotypes, and may lead to a loss of the native genetic diversity. In addition, there may be a transfer of pathogens and parasites, eg sea lice, to native stock. Chemicals, such as antibiotics, used to combat fish parasites and diseases may also exert some toxicity on freshwater biota.

The import of the signal crayfish for farming purposes has had an enormous impact on the native white-clawed crayfish. Signal crayfish are a vector for crayfish plague which is caused by the fungi *Aphanomyces astaci* and is thought to have been introduced into the country in the 1970s (Holdwich, Rogers & Reader 1995). It is spread by signal crayfish escaping from fish farms, by fishermen using live signals as bait and on fishing gear. Crayfish plague has destroyed many native populations. MAFF have identified 'no-go' areas and permissible areas for crayfish farms, to protect river systems unaffected by the disease (MAFF 1996a).

9.10.7 Controlling nuisance vegetation

The majority of upland rivers and lakes are oligotrophic, and the growth of native plants usually causes few problems. Exceptions occur where upland waters receive organic enrichment such as fertiliser run-off, or slurry effluent, or where invasive plants are present. Impacts may include the development of algal blooms, including blooms of blue-green algae which may produce toxins (such as *Anabaena* spp.). Excessive growth of vascular plants may also result. These changes may interfere with other uses of the water body, such as water abstraction or hydroelectric power generation. Problems associated with excessive plant growth include an inability to use the water for drinking purposes, impeded flows, siltation, the blockage of pumps and filters and interference with recreational activity. The ecosystem may change as a result of competition for light by the invasive species and de-oxygenation of the water column by decaying plant material. (See Boxes 9.10 and 9.11.)

A number of exotic plant species were introduced to Britain during the nineteenth century, largely for ornamental purposes. Some of these species are highly invasive and will out-compete native species. Himalayan balsam *Impatiens glandulifera*, for example, occurs throughout the British Isles and forms extensive stands on river banks. It changes the riparian vegetation by shading out native plants and also threatens the invertebrate communities which the native flora supports, as well as those reliant on the open sand, silt or shingle shoals and bars which the plant invades. Introduced and invasive species are listed under Schedule 9 of the Wildlife and Countryside Act 1981 and as such it is an offence to plant or cause these species to grow in the wild.

Further information: National Rivers Authority 1994; Dawson 1992

Box 9.9 Managing fish farms

Several authorities have responsibility for the control of fish farming activity. Planning permission must be sought from the local authority, licences are required from MAFF for the purposes of disease control and a discharge consent must be obtained from the Environment Agency.

Treatment of effluent from land based fish farms

Options

- **Settlement treatment system**
  These systems are effective in removing solid waste from fish farm effluent. Retention time within the system is important as small less dense particles will require longer to settle out.

- **Filtration or screening system**
  Where solid levels are low a single stationary mesh may be sufficient. Effluent with a higher solid content may require a self-cleaning or rotating filter.

Treatment of effluent from cage fish farms

Options

- **Collection of solids**
  Solid waste can be prevented from reaching the substratum by suspending a funnel device below fish cages. The waste accumulates in the collection apparatus and is pumped out at intervals for treatment.

- **Feeding regime**
  Careful feeding minimises waste and reduces cost. Hand feeding produces less waste than mechanical hoppers.

- **Use of antibiotics**
  Use of prophylactic antibiotics in food should be minimised. Dead/ill fish should be removed daily. Antibiotics should only be applied to treat diseases.

- **Use of chemicals**
  Follow manufacturers' instructions. Ensure correct dilution is used.

Preventing spread of crayfish plague

- Ensure non-native crayfish cannot escape from the water body.

- Ensure waste water is not discharged to water bodies capable of supporting native crayfish.

- Ensure fishing gear is sterilised with iodine when transferring between water bodies.

Further information Environment Agency 1998b; MAFF 1996a; Nature Conservancy Council 1990c; Newbold, Hambrey & Smith 1986; Phillips 1985.

Box 9.10 Controlling nuisance vegetation

Nuisance vegetation

A range of techniques exist for the control of nuisance aquatic vegetation. These can be divided broadly into physical, chemical and biological techniques.

Physical control

A range of techniques are available of which **cutting, dredging** and **shading** are the most widely used. Although mechanical control achieves immediate results these methods only produce a relatively short-term solution to the problem.

Cutting

- Cutting of native species can be carried out either by hand or mechanically from a boat, depending on water depth.
- Cut or dredged material should be removed from the watercourse and disposed of carefully to avoid damaging riparian vegetation and any release of nutrients back into the water course.
- Cutting should be timed appropriately to avoid damaging any wildlife interests. For example, avoiding bird nesting times, the flowering time of desirable plants, the emergence time of desirable invertebrates, and the spawning times for fish.
- Cutting may need to be repeated frequently as it tends to stimulate re-growth.

Note: **Cutting alien species can make the problem worse rather than better.**

Dredging

- Dredge alternate lengths to allow recolonisation by plants and animals.
- Leave patches of weed on the margins of the channel, or mid-stream, to act as refuges for recolonisation.

Shading

- By reducing light penetration into the water column the biomass of nuisance species can be reduced.
- For small areas material such as black plastic sheeting can be used to cover the water body.
- A more long-term (although possibly less effective) solution is to plant trees and tall plants on the south side of a water course or encourage the growth of floating leaved plants.

Box 9.10 Controlling nuisance vegetation cont.

Chemical control

Chemical control of vegetation is achieved through the use of herbicides, most of which are broad spectrum herbicides and not specific to individual plant species. The results may last longer than physical methods, but may be less predictable. Great care should be taken to avoid unacceptable effects on non-target species. Use of chemicals may not be possible for all watercourses, depending upon the use of the site. Use of herbicides requires a specialist knowledge if damage to other vegetation is to be avoided. A certificate of competence is also required for users of pesticides.

Only herbicides approved for use in or near water may be used in rivers or on banks (see HSE Pesticides Safety Directorate booklet 500, published annually). The Environment Agency must always be consulted. Some locations are unsuitable for herbicide application (eg close to a public drinking water supply, see National Rivers Authority 1995).

- Use herbicide only when strictly necessary.
- Identify the target weed and check that it is susceptible to the product and that the product is approved for use (MAFF booklet B 2078, MAFF 1995, Pesticides Safety Directorate booklet 500 (MAFF/Health and Safety Directive - annual publication) and product label).
- Consult the pollution control department of the EA to obtain permission for use of the product in the circumstances of the proposed use.
- Check that the application site is not an SSSI, that there is no risk to any SSSIs from applications (eg downstream) and that rare plants or other species are not present and likely to be affected.
- Where an SSSI is involved in any way, consult English Nature.
- Check that there are no poisonous plants to which livestock may have access; these may become palatable after treatment.
- Only undertake at times which avoid damaging the wildlife interest present.
- Never spray more than a third of the vegetation at any one time.
- Do not repeat the spraying on an area either within the same or the next year.
- Avoid any rare species which might be harmed by the herbicide.
- Ensure operators are fully trained and certificated, and that all applications are carried out within the rules laid down by the relevant regulations and legislation (see below).

Relevant regulations and codes

Control of Pesticides Regulations 1986
The Control of Substances Hazardous to Health Regulations (COSHH) 1998
Wildlife and Countryside Act 1981
The code of practice for the safe use of pesticides on farms and holdings (the Green code, MAFF 1998j).

Further information: MAFF 1995; Newbold, Honnor & Buckley 1989; National Rivers Authority 1994; Tuffnell 1995.

Biological control

Biological control may involve the use of grazing animals, or other plant species. Cattle, ducks and geese, and some species of fish can provide effective control of aquatic and marginal vegetation. The introduction of the exotic grass carp requires a licence and is only endorsed within water bodies which are totally enclosed so that the species cannot escape. Grazing animals, such as cattle, can cause extensive damage to some aquatic habitats and it is impossible to target nuisance species. As such their use in sensitive sites is not recommended.

Box 9.11 Control techniques for a range of invasive plant species		
Species	**Habitat**	**Appropriate control**
New Zealand pygmy-weed (also known as Australian swamp stonecrop) *Crassula helmsii*	Damp soil in or near water at depths of 0.5 m above water level to 3 m water depth. Can tolerate wide range of pH and alkalinity.	• Ensure that the plant has been accurately identified. Expert advice may need to be sought. Associated species should also be identified to ensure that vulnerable species can be safeguarded. • Where small areas of land are affected (<20 m^2) opaque material can be used to cover the area, thereby excluding light. • Medium sized areas (20-100 m^2) and large areas (>2,000m^2) should be treated with herbicide. Diquat is recommended for both submerged and emergent plants. • When spraying emergent plants a wire mesh should be placed around the affected area to prevent reinfection by small pieces of shoot released after treatment. • In all cases the area should be monitored for the re-appearance of *C. helmsii* and areas of re-growth spot treated. • Management may be needed for several years.
Canadian pondweed *Elodea canadensis*	Submerged, in mesotrophic waters, but will tolerate oligotrophic situations.	• Direct removal. • Herbicide used to control re-growth. • Control of nutrients. • Management may be needed for several years.

Box 9.11 Control techniques for a range of invasive plant species cont.

Species	Habitat	Appropriate control
Japanese knotweed *Fallopia japonica*	Can colonise most habitats, eg river banks, woodlands, grasslands	• Control can either be by mechanical means such as cutting or grazing, or by chemical means through the use of herbicides. • Glyphosate is the most effective and commonly used herbicide, but will damage non-target plants and so in areas of wildlife interest its use as a spray is only advisable when dealing with dense stands of the target plant. • Control should be started in the upper most reaches. • Priority should be given to areas which have been recently colonised. • Ensure that all vehicles, equipment and clothing is free of seed and plant fragments before leaving the site. • Do not dump any cut material or spread any soil contaminated with seed or plant fragments. • Management may be needed for several years.
Himalayan balsam *Impatiens glandulifera*	Occurs throughout the British Isles; forms extensive stands on river banks	• As for Japanese knotweed.
Giant hogweed *Heracleum mentagazzianum*	Occurs widely throughout the British Isles especially along river banks NOTE: The sap can cause severe skin burns in reaction with sunlight and this plant should be managed with great care.	• As for Japanese knotweed, plus the following. • Cut large plants before they set seed, taking care to ensure sap does not come into contact with the skin. • Weed wipe smaller plants with glyphosate. • Spray seedlings with glyphosate, this herbicide will damage non-target plants and so in areas of wildlife interest its use as a spray is only advisable when dealing with dense stands of the target plant. • Management may be needed for several years.

9.10.8 Managing small water bodies

Small oligotrophic standing waters in upland areas are known as tarns. Because of their reduced dilution capacity and low nutrient status tarns are vulnerable to changes in water quality. Managing tarns therefore incorporates a number of the issues discussed in 9.9 and 9.10. These are summarised in Box 9.12.

Further information: Biggs *et al* 1994; Drake *et al* 1996.

Box 9.12 Oligotrophic tarns

Nutrient enrichment

The introduction of nutrients into small water bodies, either through catchment run-off or from cattle faeces, can have a profound effect on trophic status. Depending on the source of enrichment a number of methods can be used to combat the causes and effects of eutrophication.

Catchment run-off

- Reduce fertiliser applications within the catchment (see Boxes 9.1 and 9.3).
- Establish a buffer area around the water body.

Poaching by stock

- Fence pond/tarn margins (see MAFF 1999b).
- Stock may need to be excluded from margins if poaching or enrichment from dunging is severe. This will also mitigate the problems of erosion and puddling of tarn edges by cattle.

Managing vegetation

- Where changes in trophic status owing to enrichment have led to domination by one species a cutting regime may need to be introduced to restore the balance of species.
- If alien species appear (in an oligotrophic tarn this may include *Potamogeton pectinatus* or *Elodea canadensis*) seek advice regarding total removal of that species.

9.11 Techniques to create freshwater habitats

The protection of existing freshwater habitats is normally preferable to the creation of new ones as established habitats generally offer a larger number of ecological niches and therefore support a wider diversity of species. Standing water habitats, such as reservoirs and gravel pits, are created for purposes other than nature conservation, but appropriate management will maximise their wildlife value. There are a number of publications which provide advice on construction techniques. These are listed in Chapter 11.

9.11.1 Creating a standing water habitat

Several points should be considered when planning a standing water habitat. First, care should be taken not to destroy any existing wetland habitats with their associated flora and fauna. Marshy grasslands, swamps and fens will be located at the lowest point in the drainage basin. Flooding to create a standing water body will result in the loss of these potentially more valuable marginal habitats. Naturally wet hollows, flushes and so on are intrinsically valuable for certain groups of invertebrates, notably craneflies, soldier flies, some ground beetles and spiders. Many are specific to these habitats and are easily eliminated if they are excavated to create standing water. Equally, the creation of a standing water body diverts water from other aquatic habitats within the catchment and may lead indirectly to their loss.

The topography and hydrological conditions of an area will determine its suitability for a standing water habitat. Some sites will naturally hold water if excavated to a sufficient depth, eg to the water table, or to impermeable strata. Alternatively, an artificial liner can be used to prevent seepage. Liners can be made from a variety of materials, including clay, concrete and PVC. The source of water should be established at the planning stage. Potential fluctuations in water level and the periodicity of flooding will determine the type of habitat that may be created and the plant species that will establish. For example, in sites where there is considerable summer draw-down edge species, such as six-stamened waterwort *Elatine hexandra*, that benefit from frequent wetting and drying may establish.

The length of the shoreline can be maximised by creating an irregularly shaped water body, and the diversity enhanced by leaving surfaces uneven rather than smoothly graded. The incorporation of bays and inlets will allow for the establishment of vegetation which may be sensitive to erosion or wave-washing.

Local water quality should be investigated for sources of pollution. In particular, high nutrient levels in catchment run-off can lead to eutrophication of standing waters. Suspended solid loads will affect the rate at which siltation occurs, and will determine whether silt traps should be incorporated into the design of a new habitat.

Water depth is fundamental in determining which plant species will establish. Emergent species can grow in up to 1 m of water. By creating areas of variable depth invasive emergent species, such as reed *Phragmites australis*, can be controlled. The growth of submerged plants is controlled by the level of light penetration, but in general they will grow in depths of up to 2 m.

The size of the water body is also important. Small sites are likely to become choked with emergent vegetation more rapidly than larger sites. Larger sites may also provide greater potential for a range of wildlife including fish, birds and plants.

9.11.2 Creating marginal habitats

In association with running or standing waters marginal habitats increase the structural diversity of a site and as such increase its value for other wildlife. Various techniques have been developed for establishing emergent and bank side vegetation. If natural recolonisation is not appropriate, material derived from a variety of sources can be planted and established by various methods, to be followed by appropriate aftercare and management. Reedbeds have been successfully re-created and this is well documented. Re-creation techniques for other wetland habitats, however, are less well developed.

Further information: Hawke & José 1995; International Waterfowl Research Bureau 1972; RSPB, NRA & RSNC 1994.

9.11.3 Creating conservation features in running water habitats

Traditionally, managing river channels for purposes such as land drainage and flood defence has resulted in the loss of river habitat features, and hence reduced their value for nature conservation. However, more recently a number of 'soft' engineering techniques have been adopted. Features such as shoals and islands, pools and riffles, vegetated margins and backwaters can be created in existing river channels to enhance structural diversity. Upland rivers tend to carry large quantities of suspended material and therefore have a much greater erosive power. As a result river restoration schemes in upland areas must be carefully planned with due consideration to the hydrology of each individual site. A summary of features is presented in Box 9.13.

Further information: Brookes & Agate 1997; RSPB, NRA & RSNC 1994.

Water vole

Box 9.13 Conservation features in running water habitats

Shoals and islands

- Increase structural diversity.
- Provide refuges for animals and plants away from human disturbance and grazing.
- Current velocity tends to increase around islands thereby creating silt free conditions, favourable for submerged plants.
- Islands can be created from spoil dredged from adjacent stretches of river and protected from erosion by planting emergent vegetation such as reeds on the upstream end.

Pools and riffles

- Pools and riffle systems are characteristic features of upland gravel-bed rivers.
- They occur as a result of variations in the profile of the river bed which causes changes in current speed and water depth.
- Pools and riffles support markedly different assemblages of both plant and invertebrate species and are therefore extremely valuable structural features.

The following guidelines have been developed for reinstating pools and riffles (Brookes 1990):

- Channel and flow characteristics should be assessed to determine if pools and riffles are appropriate features.
- The size and spacing should be determined; typically six times the channel width for riffles.
- Identify and locate the size of the bed material to be used in riffle formations.
- Riffles should be 300 - 500 mm above the natural gradient, pools should be a minimum of 300 mm deep.
- Individual pools and riffles should be between one and three channel widths long.
- Use should be made of the natural meandering of the channel so that pools are formed on the outside of bends with diagonal riffles at the exit.

Unvegetated point bars

- Several invertebrates are totally dependent on the exposed riverine sediments of unvegetated point bars, which is why it is important to retain the natural fluvial geomorphology of a river.

Table 9.3 Nationally rare and scarce aquatic and wetland plants associated with upland freshwater habitats in England

Plant species	Status	Distribution in upland Natural Areas of England
Aquatics		
Elatine hexandra six-stamened waterwort	LR-ns	Cumbria Fells & Dales, Bodmin Moor, Dartmoor
Isoetes echinospora spring quillwort	LR-ns	Cumbria Fells & Dales, Bodmin Moor, Dartmoor
Luronium natans floating water-plantain	Annex IIb Sched. 8 of WCA LR-ns Priority	Cumbria Fells & Dales, Southern Pennines
Najas flexilis slender naiad	Annex IIb Sched. 8 of WCA LR-ns Priority	Cumbria Fells & Dales
Pilularia globulifera pillwort	LR-ns Priority	Cumbria Fells & Dales, Dartmoor, Black Mountains and Golden Valley
Potamogeton coloratus fen pondweed	LR-ns	Cumbria Fells & Dales, Exmoor and the Quantocks
Potamogeton compressus grass-wrack pondweed	LR-ns Priority	Border Uplands
Potamogeton trichoides hairlike pondweed	LR-ns	Cumbria Fells & Dales, Exmoor and the Quantocks
Marginal / inundation		
Calamagrostis purpurea ssp *phragmitoides* Scandinavian small-reed	LR-nt	Cumbria Fells & Dales
Calamagrostis stricta narrow small-reed	LR-nt	Yorkshire Dales, Southern Pennines
Carex appropinquata fibrous tussock-sedge	LR-ns	Yorkshire Dales
Carex elongata elongated sedge	LR-ns	Cumbria Fells & Dales
Circuta virosa cowbane	LR-ns	Border Uplands
Eleocharis austriaca northern spike-rush	LR-nt	Forest of Bowland, Yorkshire Dales, Border Uplands, Southern Pennines
Juncus filiformis thread rush	LR-ns	Forest of Bowland, Yorkshire Dales, North Pennines, Cumbrian Fells & Dales
Limosella aquatica mudwort	LR-ns	Cumbrian Fells & Dales, South West Peak
Mentha pulegium pennyroyal	Vu Priority Sched. 8 of WCA	Exmoor and the Quantocks

Plant species	Status	Distribution in upland Natural Areas of England
Persicaria mitis tasteless water-pepper	LR-ns	Border Uplands, Shropshire Hills
Teucrium scordium water germander	VU	Exmoor and the Quantocks
Thelypteris palustris marsh fern	LR-ns	North Pennines, Cumbria Fells & Dales, Dark Peak

Key to Table 9.3

Annex IIb - listed on Annex IIb of the EC Habitats and Species Directive

Sched. 8 of WCA - listed on schedule 8 of the Wildlife & Countryside Act.

Red list categories

EN - endangered

VU - vulnerable

LR - nt - Lower risk - near threatened

LR - ns - Lower risk - nationally scarce.

Biodiversity Action Plan (BAP)

Priority - Priority species from UK Steering Group 1995 and UK Biodiversity Group 1998.

Sources

Most information from Hodgetts, Palmer & Wigginton 1996; Porley & McDonnell 1997; Stewart, Pearman & Preston, 1994 and Wigginton 1999

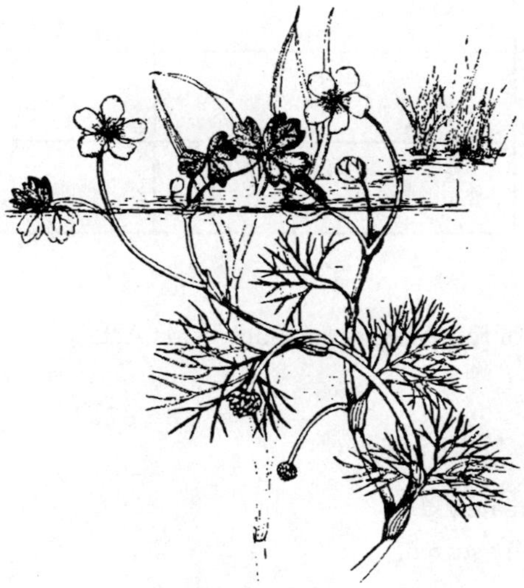

Table 9.4 Nationally rare and scarce bryophytes and lichens associated with upland freshwater habitats in England

Bryophyte and lichen species	Status	Distribution in upland Natural Areas of England
Bryum gemmiparum a moss	EN	Exmoor and the Quantocks
Collema dichotomum river jelly lichen	Sched. 8 of WCA VU Priority	Cumbria Fells & Dales
Fissidens monguillonii a moss	LR-nt	Dartmoor
Fissidens polyphyllus a moss	LR-ns	Dartmoor, Bodmin Moor
Fissidens rufulus a moss	LR-ns	Border Uplands, North Pennines, Yorkshire Dales, Cumbria Fells & Dales, Pennine Dales Fringe
Fissidens serrulatus a moss	VU	Dartmoor
Hygrohypnum dilatatum a moss	LR-ns	Border Uplands, Cumbria Fells & Dales
Jubula hutchisiae a liverwort	LR-ns	Southern Pennines, Dartmoor
Porella pinnata a liverwort	LR-ns	Cumbria Fells & Dales, Exmoor and the Quantocks, Dartmoor, Bodmin Moor
Radula voluta a liverwort	LR-nt	Cumbria Fells & Dales
Rhynchostegium alopecuroides a moss	LR-ns	South West Peak, Exmoor and the Quantocks, Dartmoor, Bodmin Moor
Schistidium alpicola var. alpicola a moss	LR-ns	Yorkshire Dales
Thamnobryum cataractarum a moss	VU Priority	Yorkshire Dales

Key to Table 9.4

Sched. 8 of WCA - listed on schedule 8 of the Wildlife & Countryside Act.

Red list categories

EN - endangered
VU - vulnerable
LR - nt - Lower risk - near threatened
LR - ns - Lower risk - nationally scarce.

Biodiversity Action Plan (BAP)

Priority - Priority species from UK Steering Group 1995 and UK Biodiversity Group 1998.

Sources

Most information from Hodgetts, Palmer & Wigginton 1996; Porley & McDonnell 1997; Stewart, Pearman & Preston 1994 and Wigginton 1999.

Table 9.5 Aquatic plant communities associated with upland freshwater habitats in England (ordered according to standing water types)

Standing water type[1]	Description	Inclusion in Annex 1 of the EC Habitats Directive[2]	Upland Natural Areas of England where community occurs
2	Small, oligotrophic, upland tarns in the Lake District. Typical species: *Juncus bulbosus, Potamogeton polygonifolius.*	Oligotrophic to mesotrophic standing waters of plains to subalpine levels of the Continental and Alpine Region and mountain areas of other regions, with vegetation belonging to *Littorelletea uniflorae* and/or *Isoeto-Nanojuncetea.*	Cumbria Fells & Dales
3	Large oligotrophic lakes on base-poor rock. Typical species: As Type 2 plus *Myriophyllum alterniflorum, Isoetes lacustris.*	Oligotrophic to mesotrophic standing waters of plains to subalpine levels of the Continental and Alpine Region and mountain areas of other regions, with vegetation belonging to *Littorelletea uniflorae* and/or *Isoeto-Nanojuncetea.*	Cumbria Fells & Dales
4	Mesotrophic lakes with some acid and calcareous influence. Often marl sites with species-rich assemblage of water plants, eg *Potamogeton filiformis, Potamogeton praelongus.*	-	Cumbria Fells & Dales Bodmin Moor
5	Mesotrophic lakes on slightly base-rich rock. Species include: *Littorella uniflora, Elodea canadensis, Nymphaea alba.*	Oligotrophic to mesotrophic standing waters of plains to subalpine levels of the Continental and Alpine Region and mountain areas of other regions, with vegetation belonging to *Littorelletea uniflorae* and/or *Isoeto-Nanojuncetea.*	Cumbria Fells & Dales
8	Meso-oligotrophic waters typified by meres of glacial origin. Poor in open water species, rich in emergents. Typical species *Lemna minor, Callitriche stagnalis.*	-	Cumbria Fells & Dales, North York Moors
9	Meso-eutrophic sites generally dominated by water lilies (*Nuphar lutea, Nymphaea alba*).	-	Cumbria Fells & Dales

Standing water type[1]	Description	Inclusion in Annex 1 of the EC Habitats Directive[2]	Upland Natural Areas of England where community occurs
10	Eutrophic water bodies based on fine substrates often calcareous in nature. Typical species; *Myriophyllum spicatum, Potamogeton pectinatus.*	-	Cumbria Fells & Dales, Yorkshire Dales

Key

1. Taken from Palmer, Bell & Butterfield 1992.
2. Taken from Brown *et al* 1997.

* Priority habitat.

Table 9.6 River types of upland Natural Areas in England

River type[1]	Description
Group A	
2	Lowland, clay-dominated rivers.
Group B	
5	Sandstone, mudstone and hard limestone rivers of England and Wales
6	Sandstone, mudstone and hard limestone rivers of Scotland and northern England
Group C	
7	Mesotrophic rivers dominated by gravels, pebbles and cobbles
8	Oligo-mesotrophic rivers
Group D	
9	Oligotrophic, low-altitude rivers
10	Ultra-oligotrophic rivers

1. Taken from Holmes 1983 & Holmes, Boon & Rowell 1998.
Distribution information for these river types for upland Natural Areas is not available owing to the recent revision of this classification system.
This classification system is not referred to the interpretation of Annex 1 of the EC Habitats Directive (Brown *et al* 1997).

Table 9.7 Swamp and fen communities of upland Natural Areas in England

NVC code	NVC name[1]	Inclusion in Annex 1 of the EC Habitats Directive[2]	Upland Natural Areas of England where community occurs
S1	*Carex elata* swamp	-	Cumbria Fells & Dales
S2	*Cladium mariscus* swamp and sedge beds	-	Cumbria Fells & Dales
S4	*Phragmites australis* swamp and sedge bed	-	Border Uplands Cumbria Fells & Dales
S5	*Glyceria maxima* swamp	-	Southern Pennines
S8	*Schoenoplectus lacustris* spp. *lacustris* swamp	-	Cumbria Fells & Dales
S9	*Carex rostrata* swamp	-	Border Uplands Cumbria Fells & Dales
S10	*Equisetum fluviatile* swamp	-	Border Uplands Cumbria Fells & Dales
S12	*Typha latifolia* swamp	-	Border Uplands Yorkshire Dales Southern Pennines Cumbria Fells & Dales
S14	*Sparganium erectum* swamp	-	Southern Pennines Cumbria Fells & Dales
S19	*Eleocharis palustris* swamp	-	Cumbria Fells & Dales
S23	Other water margin vegetation. *Glyceria sparganion*	-	Southern Pennines
S24	*Phragmites australis - Peucedanum palustre* tall-herb fen	-	Southern Pennines
S27	*Carex rostrata-Potentilla palustre* tall-herb fen	Transition mires and quaking bogs	Border Uplands Cumbria Fells & Dales, South West Peak
S28	*Phalaris arundinacea* tall-herb fen	-	Cumbria Fells & Dales

Key

1. Taken from Rodwell 1995.
2. Taken from Brown *et al* 1997.

Table 9.8 Breeding birds associated with upland freshwater habitats in England

(Note: See also Chapters 6 and 7 for species predominantly of moorland or grassland)

Bird species[1]	Birds of conservation concern in the UK[2]	Listed on Schedule 1 of the 1981 Wildlife & Countryside Act	Listed on Annex 1 of the EC Birds Directive	No. of British 10 km squares with breeding records 1988-90	% of breeding records in upland ITE squares[3]	Main upland habitat associations	Principal upland Natural Areas supporting the species *= major/important areas[4]
Wigeon *Anas penelope*	Amber list	-	-	128	74.2	Moorland and Fresh waters	2, 4*, 8*, 14
Teal *Anas crecca*	Amber list	-	-	571	52.5	Moorland and Fresh waters	2*, 4*, 8*, 12*, 14, 25
Goosander *Mergus merganser*	-	-	-	398	68.1	Fresh waters	2*, 4*, 8*, 10*, 12, 15, 17
Osprey *Pandion haliaetus*	Red list	•	•	39	64.1	Fresh waters	None as yet
Common sandpiper *Actitis hypoleucus*	-	-	-	1,057	69.5	Fresh waters	2*, 4*, 8*, 10*, 12*, 14*, 15*, 25*, 29*, 30, 41, 42, 58, 60, 92
Black-headed gull *Larus ridibundus*	-	-	-	671	46.2	Moorland and Fresh waters	2*,4*,8*,10*,12*,14,17
Common gull *Larus canus*	Amber list	-	-	577	62.4	Moorland and Fresh waters	2*, 4
Grey wagtail *Motacilla cinerea*	-	-	-	1,657	39.6	Fresh waters	All areas
Dipper *Cinclus cinclus*	-	-	-	1,097	56.2	Fresh waters	2*, 4*, 8*, 10*, 12*, 14*, 15, 17, 25*, 29, 30, 41, 42, 58, 60, 87*, 92*, 94*

Key to Table 9.8

1. Upland breeding bird species as identified in Stillman & Brown 1994.
2. From RSPB 1996.
3. From Bunce & Barr 1988, using the 13 ITE land classes which were regarded as upland (information not available on an English basis).
4. The following 18 Natural Areas are classed as upland by English Nature:

No	Natural Area name		
2	Border Uplands	29	South West Peak
4	North Pennines	30	White Peak
8	Yorkshire Dales	41	Oswestry Uplands
10	Cumbria Fells & Dales	42	Shropshire Hills
12	Forest of Bowland	58	Clun and North West Herefordshire Hills
14	Southern Pennines	60	Black Mountains and Golden Valley
15	Pennine Dales Fringe	87	Exmoor and the Quantocks
17	North York Moors and Hills	92	Dartmoor
25	Dark Peak.	94	Bodmin Moor

Table 9.9 Nationally rare and scarce invertebrates associated with upland freshwater habitats in England

Invertebrate species		Nature conservation status	Typical habitat	Distribution in upland England (not currently available in terms of NaturalAreas)
Scientific name	**English name**			
Bugs				
Saldula fucicola	Shore bug	Nationally Scarce	Bare gravel and sand beside lakes, rivers and streams	Northumberland, Cumbria
Flies				
Agrypnia crassicornis	Caddis fly	RDB1	In *Chara* beds in large lakes	Malham Tarn
Chelifera astigma	Small dance fly	RDB1	Wooded upland streams	Herefordshire, Yorkshire
Cyrnus isolutus	Caddis fly	RBDK	Rocky shore of large water bodies	Blelham Tarn, Cumbria; Berkshire
Dicranota gracilipes	Cranefly	Nationally scarce	Stony rivers and streams with *Phalaris* at the margins	Peak District, Gloucestershire, Herefordshire, Westmorland
Dicranota guerini	Cranefly	Nationally scarce	Springs, streams, boggy flushes, usually with well vegetated margins	Northern England to Cheshire
Dicranota simulans	Cranefly	RDB3	Upland streams with shingly margins	Northern England, Peak District
Eristalis rupium	Hoverfly	Nationally scarce	Pools, flushes	Northern England
Glossosoma intermedium	Caddis fly	RDB3	Fast-flowing stony streams	Lake District
Hilara barbipes	Dance fly	Nationally Scarce	Banks of streams and rivers	Herefordshire (Monnow)
Hydroptila sylvestris	Caddis fly	RDBK	Unknown	Lake District
Ichthytrichia clavata	Caddis fly	RDB3	Fast-flowing rivers	Lake District, Hampshire
Limonia stylifera	Cranefly	RDB2	Base-rich flushes	Moor House, Westmorland
Limnophila mundata	Cranefly	Nationally Scarce	Upland streams, usually with alders but also unshaded	Northern England to the Forest of Dean
Rhamphomyia obscura	Dance fly	Nationally Scarce	Moorland and pools, lowland bogs	Shropshire, Yorkshire, Cumbria
Setodes argentipunctellus	Caddis fly	RDB3	Shores of large stony lakes	Windermere, Coniston
Tachydromia acklandi	Small dance fly	RDB3	Shingle banks of uplands streams and rivers	Herefordshire, Rivers North and South Tyne, Northumberland

Invertebrate species		Nature conservation status	Typical habitat	Distribution in upland England (not currently available in terms of NaturalAreas)
Scientific name	**English name**			
Tachydromia woodi	Small dance fly	RDB1	River shingle and sandy banks	Herefordshire (R. Monnow), Yorkshire (R. Wharfe)
Tipular cheethami	Cranefly	Nationally Scarce	Flushes, moorland; larvae in wet mossy rock-faces on streams and waterfalls	North-west England to Cheshire
Tipula gimmerthali	Cranefly	RDB3	Flushes and margins of base-rich streams	Moor House, Westmorland
Triogma trisulcata	Cranefly	RDB3	Seepage bog and upland streams	Yorkshire, Lancashire
Beetles				
Elaphrus lapponicus	Ground beetle	Nationally Scarce A	Margins of swift montane streams, bogs	Yorkshire, Cumbria
Oreodytes davisii	Diving beetle	Nationally Scarce B	Shallow margins of fast streams and rivers	Yorkshire, Northumberland
Spiders				
Erigone capra	Money spider	Nationally Scarce B	In moss or grass at the edge of open water	Yorkshire, Cumbria, Northumberland
Erigone psychrophila	Money spider	Nationally Scarce A	Montane, in *Sphagnum* at the edge of bog pools	Cheviot, Northumberland
Crustacea				
Austropotamobius pallipes	White-clawed crayfish	HSD, Priority	Stony streams, rivers, lakes and large ponds	Widespread
Mysis relicta	Opossum shrimp	RDB1, SCC	Lake bottom and pelagic	Ennerdale Water
Molluscs				
Catinella arenaria	Sandbowl snail	RDB1, Priority	Base-rich flushes	Crumbria, Devon
Margaritifera margaritifera	Freshwater pearl mussel	HSD, Priority	Unpolluted, well oxygenated rivers with clean gravels	R. Ehen, Cumbria
Pisidium conventus	Pea mussel	Nationally Scarce A, SCC	Lakes and tarns	Lake District

Invertebrate species		Nature conservation status	Typical habitat	Distribution in upland England (not currently available in terms of NaturalAreas)
Scientific name	English name			
Pisidium tenuilineatum	Fine-lined pea mussel	RDB3, Priority	Rivers, streams, springs	Yorkshire (R. Wharfe) and lowland sites in southern England
Vertigo genesii	Round-mouthed whorl snail	RDB1, HSD, Priority	Base-rich flushes	Durham
Vertigo geyeri	Geyer's whorl snail	RDB1, HSD, Priority	Base-rich	Cumbria

Key to Table 9.9

Status

HSD	Included in the Habitats Directive
RDB1	Red Data Book category 1 Endangered
RDB2	Red Data Book category 2 Vulnerable
RDB3	Red Daa Book category 3 Rare
RDB4	Red Data Book category 4 Out of Danger
RDB5	Red Data Book category 5 Endemic
RDBI	Red Data Book category Indeterminate
RDBK	Red Data Book category Insufficiently known
Nationally Scarce A	15-30 km squares of national grid
Nationally Scarce B	30-100 km squares of national grid
Priority	Priority species in the UK Biodiversity Action Plan (UK Biodiversity Group 1998; UK Steering Group 1995)
SCC	Species of concern in the UK Biodiversity Action Plan (UK Biodiversity Group 1998; UK Steering Group 1995)

Table 9.10 Fish of conservation significance in upland freshwater habitats in England

	Biodiversity Action Plan[1]	Included in the EC Habitats Directive	Included in Schedule 5 of the W & C Act 1981
Fish			
Bullhead *Cottus gobio*	SCC	Annex IIa	-
Brook lamprey *Lampetra planeri*	SCC	Annex IIa	-
River lamprey *Lampetra fluviatilis*	SCC	Annexes IIa & Va	-
Sea lamprey *Petromyzon marinus*	SCC	Annex IIa	-
Salmon *Salmo salar*	SCC	Annexes IIa & Va (in fresh water only)	-
Allis shad *Alosa alosa*	Priority	Annexes IIa & Va	Section 9(1) & (4a) only
Twaite shad *Alosa fallax*	Priority	Annexes IIa & Va	Section (4a) only
Vendace *Coregonus albula*	Priority	Annex Va	Full protection
Schelly *Coregonus lavaretus*	SCC	Annex Va	Full protection
Arctic char *Salvelinus alpinus*	SCC	-	-
Grayling *Thymallus thymallus*	SCC	Annex Va	-

Key

1. Priority species and Species of conservation concern (SCC) from UK Steering Group 1995 and UK Biodiversity Group 1998.

Table 9.11 Conservation objectives for standing waters

Conservation objectives	Management activities likely to affect conservation objective
Restore or maintain the appropriate nutrient status.	• Run-off of fertiliser applications/slurry effluent. • Discharge of effluent, eg sewage, fish farms. • Domestic/industrial discharges. • Grazing leading to local enrichment from dunging.
Improve or maintain water quality other than nutrient status.	• Accidental and deliberate discharges of oil, chemicals, eg sheep dip. • Additions of water from different catchments. • Activities which increase siltation, eg ploughing. • Processes leading to acid rain.
Restore or maintain water levels and flushing rates.	• Drainage/moor gripping. • Abstraction directly from water source or water table. • Impoundment.
Maintain or enhance desirable marginal communities.	• Agricultural activities such as fertiliser/slurry applications, grazing/watering of stock, drainage. • Impoundment.
Restore, maintain or enhance the naturalness of the freshwater habitats.	• Introduction of artificial edges to the water body.
Limit and, where possible, eliminate introduced species.	• Deliberate introductions, eg of fish, wildfowl, plants. • Accidental introductions, eg from fishing gear.
Ensure land use within the catchment does not adversely affect the nature conservation value.	• Shading, eg development or planting of woodland and scrub. • Activities which increase siltation, eg ploughing. • Physical damage or change to the edge of water course, eg poaching, bank protection. • Recreational pressure, especially sailing.
Prevent abnormal sediment accretion.	• Activities which increase siltation, eg ploughing, drainage.
Restore or maintain the desirable balance of plant species.	• Vegetation control methods, eg cutting, spraying.
Maintain or enhance populations of rare and scarce species.	• Many of the activities covered above, depending on the species and their requirements.

Table 9.12 Conservation objectives for running waters

Conservation objectives	Management activities likely to affect conservation objective
Restore or maintain the appropriate nutrient status.	• Run-off of fertiliser applications/slurry effluent. • Discharge of effluent, eg sewage, fish farms. • Domestic/industrial discharges. • Grazing leading to local enrichment from dunging.
Improve or maintain water quality other than nutrient status.	• Accidental and deliberate discharges of oil, chemicals, eg sheep dip. • Activities which increase siltation, eg ploughing. • Additions of water from different catchments.
Restore or maintain water levels and flow regimes.	• Drainage/moor gripping/abstraction. • Abstraction directly from water source or water table. • Impoundment.
Maintain or enhance desirable marginal communities.	• Agricultural activities such as fertiliser/slurry applications, grazing/watering of stock, drainage. • Impoundment.
Restore or retain the natural channel profile.	• Introduction of artificial edges to the water body, or straightening of channels.
Restore, maintain or enhance the naturalness of the freshwater habitats.	• Introduction of artificial edges or straightening of channels.
Protect associated physical features, such as meanders, cut-off channels.	• Channel straightening, flood defence measures, land reclamation.
Restore or retain optimum shading of the channel.	• Planting or growth of woodland and scrub.
Limit and, where possible, eliminate introduced species.	• Deliberate introductions, eg of fish, wildfowl. • Accidental introductions, eg on fishing gear.
Ensure land use within the catchment does not adversely affect the nature conservation value.	• Shading, eg development or planting of woodland and scrub. • Activities which increase siltation, eg ploughing. • Physical damage or change to the edge of water course, eg poaching, bank protection. • Recreational pressure, especially sailing.
Prevent abnormal sediment accretion.	• Activities which increase siltation, eg ploughing, drainage.
Restore or maintain the desirable balance of plant species.	• Vegetation control methods, eg cutting, if particular types of vegetation start to dominate.
Maintain or enhance populations of rare and scarce species.	• Many of the activities covered above, depending on the species and their requirements.

Table 9.13 Conservation objectives for swamp and fen

Conservation objectives	Management activities likely to affect conservation objective
Maintain the current extent of swamp, fen and carr.	• Drainage, cutting, burning, over-grazing.
Improve all existing areas of swamp, fen and carr habitat by appropriate management.	• Selective cutting/grazing.
Re-establish swamp, fen and carr around existing freshwater habitats.	• Impeding drainage/provide conditions for seasonal flooding.
Establish linkage between smaller areas to enhance value to wildlife.	• Creation/enhancement of habitats of value to wildlife.
Improve or maintain nutrient status and water quality.	• Liming/addition of fertilisers. • Pollution of area. • Run-off of fertiliser from surrounding land.
Manage water levels to ensure occasional flooding, where appropriate.	• Drainage/moor gripping/abstraction.
Ensure that marginal communities do not dry out.	• Drainage/moor gripping/abstraction.
Maintain or enhance desirable marginal communities.	• Agricultural activities such as fertiliser/slurry applications, grazing/watering of stock.
Limit and, if possible, eliminate introduced species.	• Fish farming and fishery management.
Maintain or enhance populations of rare and scarce species.	• Many of the activities covered above, depending on the species and their requirements.

Table 9.14 Habitat requirements of upland freshwater plants

Depth requirements are measured in cm. A minus sign indicates that the water table is below ground level, the plus sign indicates water level above ground level, ie depth of water. Figures in brackets refer to extreme records where species may have been found on one or two occasions (Newbold & Mountford 1997).

Freshwater plants	Habitat requirements
Elatine hexandra	Soft, sandy mud; periodic exposure; shallow edges; can tolerate nutrient enrichment. **Depth requirements**: Preferred water level: +50 +100cm Limit of 'dryness': -150 Limit of 'wetness': +200(300) *E. hexandra* is well adapted to tolerate extremes of this range. **Preferred pH range**: pH5.5-pH6.0
Isoetes echinospora	Acid, gravelly, nutrient-poor substrate; depths to around 2 m; disturbance through wave action etc to dislodge spores. **Preferred pH range**: pH6.0 - pH7.0
Luronium natans	Slightly acidic, oligotrophic, standing waters, with depth of as much as 2 m. **Depth requirements**: Preferred water level: +10-100 Limit of 'dryness': +5 Limit of 'wetness': +150 **Preferred pH range**: pH5.5-pH7.0
Najas flexilis	Silty substrates, mesotrophic lowland lakes; grows in water more than 1.5 m deep. **Depth requirements**: Preferred water level: +50+100 Limit of 'dryness': +20 Limit of 'wetness': +150 **Preferred pH range**: pH5.5-pH6.5
Calamagrostis stricta	Neutral bogs and marshes; shallow canal edges
Eleocharis austriaca	Sandy substrate on upland river margins Depth requirements Preferred water level: -5+5
Juncus filiformis	Lake margins; marshy grassland or lake shore sand and gravel.

Table 9.15 Habitat requirements of lowland freshwater plants which occur in upland areas

Depth requirements are measured in cm. A minus sign indicates that the water table is below ground level, the plus sign indicates water level above ground level, ie depth of water. Figures in brackets refer to extreme records where species may have been found on one or two occasions (Newbold & Mountford 1997).

Fresh water plant	Habitat requirements
Potamogeton compressus	Slow-flowing lowland rivers and ox-bows; calcareous, mesotrophic lowland lakes. **Depth requirements**: Preferred water level: +10+100 cm Limit of 'dryness': (+2) Limit of 'wetness': +150
Potamogeton trichoides	Shallow, still, slow moving water; meso-eutrophic conditions; tolerated disturbance readily, eg drainage. **Depth requirements**: Preferred water level: +20+75 Limit of 'wetness': +100
Pilularia globulifera	Lowland, non-calcareous, silty or peaty standing water. **Depth requirements**: Preferred water level: +10+20 Limit of 'dryness': 0+5 Limit of 'wetness': (+75)
Carex elongata	Lowland ponds; winter flooding and drying in summer; stagnant ditches; minimal shading; undisturbed banks.
Circuta virosa	Lake shores, pond margins, mires and ditches; shallow water or vegetation mats; restricted to lowlands.
Equisetum variegatum	Open habitats; base-rich flushes.

Dipper

Table 9.16 Management prescriptions for *Luronium natans*

Habitat requirements for *L. natans*	Management prescriptions for *L. natans*
L. natans occurs naturally in upland oligotrophic lakes and lowland canals. However, it is an extremely rare species in the English uplands, with only two recent records in Derwent Water and Bassenthwaite Lake (Cumbria Fells & Dales Natural Area). This species tends to occur in oligotrophic water bodies that have undergone some disturbance, hence its success in lightly dredged canals. However, the increasing density of boat traffic on many canals has been one of the principal causes of the species' decline. The turbulence caused by intense boat activity leads to shallow rooted stolons becoming detached. Water acidification is another factor causing loss or decline of this species.	• Seek to minimise the effects of acidification on waters containing the species in acid-sensitive areas. • Prevent the encroachment of emergent vegetation likely to out-compete this plant. • In disused and little used canals, seek a programme of dredging and other maintenance work to produce the open habitat necessary for this plant. • Seek to dissuade planting of coniferous forests in sensitive lake catchments and around river headwaters important for this species. • Where high volumes of boat traffic may damage beds of this species, seek to develop 'refuges' near the banks protected by barriers such as piling. • Where canals containing the plant are subject to unavoidable restoration schemes, consider creating reserves (either as widened areas or secondary channels or ponds) and manage them to maintain healthy populations. *L. natans* should be translocated to the reserve in advance of the restoration works. • Where such forests already exist, encourage the creation of buffer zones around lake shores and river margins to allow deciduous woodland to develop. • In areas with records of the species but where it is no longer apparently present, experiment with dredging small areas of water bodies to give any remaining seed a chance to germinate.

Table 9.17 Habitat requirements of birds associated with upland freshwater habitats

Species	Habitat requirements
Wigeon *Anas penelope*	See Chapter 6.
Teal *Anas crecca*	See Chapter 6.
Goosander *Mergus merganser*	• Present late February to end July. • Strong association with rivers and lakes. • Nests placed in holes in larger riverside trees. • Adults and young forage for aquatic invertebrates in rivers, lakes and pools.
Osprey *Pandion haliaetus*	• Present April to September. • Strong association with lakes and large rivers. • Nest in trees. • Adults bring fish to dependent young in nest.
Common sandpiper *Actitus hypoleucos*	• Present late April to end July. • Strong association with shallow, swift-flowing rivers and reservoir sides with exposed substrates. • Nest placed on ground within stream or lake-side heather, bracken or grass tussocks, appears to avoid areas regularly used by anglers and others engaged in waterside recreation. • Adults forage for aquatic and aerial invertebrates amongst exposed gravels along stream and lake-sides and amongst wet and exposed riparian zone for invertebrates. • Chicks forage for invertebrates as adults.
Black-headed gull *Larus ridibundus*	See Chapter 6.
Common gull *Larus canus*	See Chapter 6.
Grey wagtail *Motacilla cinerea*	• Present throughout the year. • Strong association with upland streams and rivers, lake shores and other fresh waters. • Nest placed under rock overhang, tree root or bridge, usually in association with streams, rivers or lake shores. • Adults forage for terrestrial invertebrates along stream sides, exposed lake shore and riparian grasslands and around outbuildings. • Adults bring food to dependent young in nest.
Dipper *Cinclus cinclus*	• Present throughout the year. • Strong association with riffle zone of calcareous to circumneutral upland streams. • Extremely susceptible to acidification - favoured mayfly larvae food does not survive acid conditions. • Nest placed beneath bridge or other overhang in stream or, less commonly, at lake sides. • Adults take aquatic invertebrates from riffles along mountain streams and lake shores. • Adults bring food to dependent young in nest.

Table 9.18 Management guidelines for birds associated with upland freshwater habitats

Running water	Standing water	Surrounding land
• Retain and enhance the naturalness of running waters and fringing habitats. • Maintain water quality. • Maintain water levels and flow regimes. • Retain or re-establish natural channel profile. • Retain or re-establish features such as meanders, bluffs, channels and flood plains. • Retain or re-establish native bank side vegetation. • Establish areas that are not disturbed by recreation (boats, anglers, walkers).	• Retain and enhance the naturalness of standing waters and fringing habitats. • Maintain water quality. • Maintain water levels. • Retain or re-establish natural shore profile. • Retain or re-establish swamp, fen and carr. • Establish areas that are not disturbed by recreation (boats, anglers, walkers).	• Prevent deterioration of water quality because of eutrophication, siltation, toxic contaminants, etc. • Prevent deterioration of quality of fringing habitats because of grazing, etc. • Prevent reduction in water levels because of over abstraction, etc. • Maintain natural drainage systems and avoid new drainage. • Retain wetland features such as pools, fens and mires. • Create small, wet areas by blocking existing drains and grips. • See Chapters 6 & 7 for further details.

Table 9.19 Habitat management requirements of invertebrates associated with upland freshwater habitats in England

As many of these habitats are not man-made or dependent upon traditional land use for their continued existence, most of the management recommendations are necessarily phrased in negative terms, since non-intervention is the most beneficial management.

Freshwater invertebrates	Habitat requirements	Management requirements
Freshwater pearl mussel *Margaritifera margaritifera*	Clear, cool, fast-flowing, unpolluted, acid waters that are well oxygenated and low in nutrients. Require fish host for parasitic phase. Also mosaic of habitat for feeding and shelter, and clean gravels for reproducing.	• Avoid enrichment by point and diffuse sources of pollution. • Retain overhanging trees, undercut banks for shade. • Maintain healthy fish stocks. • Ensure sheep dips used in accordance with good practice and not disposed on rivers. • Avoid physical alteration of river course.
White-clawed crayfish *Austropotamobius pallipes*	Unpolluted, calcium-rich water with high levels of oxygen and low siltation levels. Also mosaic of habitats for feeding and shelter, including gravels, tree roots, stone walls, bridges, etc.	• Avoid input of silt. • Maintain diversity of physical habitat in particular bank structure.
Species of open flushes	Mainly sunny, well-lit trickles that can warm up. Not too much overgrowth of tall grasses or thatch of litter. Isolated scrub (especially sallow). Permanent water supply (no summer drought). Even small flushes can support good assemblages, provided they are permanent. Calcareous seepages support more scarce species than neutral or acid ones. Flowering plants to provide nectar and pollen sources.	• Maintain light grazing and very light trampling. • Prevent drainage or water abstraction from springs. • Keep scrub to a small proportion of the site, with only a small amount over shading the trickles.
Species of carr woodland	High humidity. Deep organic soil that is permanently saturated to ground level. Seepages and shallow pools. Old trees and dead wood.	• Avoid gaps in the canopy, coppicing or rides. • Prevent drainage.
Species of small pools.	Various - see Kirby 1992.	• As specified in Kirby 1992.
Species of small fast streams	Leaf litter input from overhanging vegetation (trees, grasses, etc).	• Avoid intensive grazing which reduces the potential for litter input.

Freshwater invertebrates	Habitat requirements	Management requirements
Aquatic species of larger streams and rivers	Natural pool and riffle to provide contrasting conditions of current. Marginal emergents (eg *Phalaris*) along some sections as shelter for adults of species with aquatic larvae (eg mayflies, stoneflies, caddis). Intermittently spaced trees, especially alder, to provide shelter, submerged roots as underwater shelter, and coarse woody debris (important food source). No unnatural silt load.	• Prevent river canalisation or artificial steepening of banks. • Limit forestry operations that increase silt loads. • Maintain some trees along the banks.
Terrestrial species of vegetated margins of unshaded larger streams and rivers.	Vegetation mosaic with margins having mostly tall plants and a smaller proportion of short to bare vegetation. Limited shading by tree with some litter input from leaf-fall. Accumulations of pockets of leaf litter and strand lines. Flowering plants to provide nectar and pollen sources.	• At most, maintain light grazing and trampling, and preferably none. • Fence fields with heavy grazing pressure.
Species of exposed riverine sediments (gravel beds)	Natural flow regime that allows the development and annual redistribution of gravels and stones, and natural erosion of river banks to provide this material. Bars of sediments with a range of particle sizes from large stones to sand. Absence of colonisation by vegetation on exposed sediments.	• Prevent trampling by livestock, by fencing sections with large sediment banks. • Avoid gravel winning, impoundments or bank stabilisation.
Aquatic species of tarn and lake shores	Shelter above and below water, and provision of litter (food supply) by a dense fringing stands of emergent vegetation (eg reeds *Phalaris*), or trees lining the shore. Some areas of wave-washed stony shore. Dense submerged aquatic plants that provide refuge from fish predation.	• Ensure minimal destruction of the marginal vegetation (eg no burning from camp fires, or excessive trampling). • Fish stocking should be at no more than the natural carrying capacity of the water body.
Terrestrial species of tarn and lake shores	Similar to above. Accumulations of pockets of leaf litter and strand lines. Partial natural drop in water level in summer to expose a bare shoreline.	• Leave plant litter, avoid tidying up. • Ensure minimal trampling of shoreline gravels.

Table 9.20 Habitat and management requirements of certain mammals, amphibians and reptiles associated with upland freshwater habitats[1]

Species	Habitat requirements	Management requirements in freshwater habitats
Otter *Lutra lutra*	Large home ranges (perhaps 10's of km across); therefore need for large / inter-connected habitats. Dependent on water (which can be fresh, estuarine or marine); requires good water quality and presence of animal (fish, some invertebrates, eg crayfish) food. It is vulnerable to disturbance, pollution or river management. Requires secure lying-up (eg wet woodland carr) and breeding sites (often associated with riverside trees, particularly mature oak, ash and sycamore) and their availability may influence distribution.	• Ensure good water quality, unaffected by pollution, pesticides and fertilisers, to maintain fish prey species and prevent accumulations of toxins. • Manage river sides to ensure a range of habitats extending back from the river margin, and with a good vegetation structure up to the river edge. • Allow vegetation to grow along river and canal banks. • Maintain existing fens, wet woodland and carr vegetation for holts and lying up areas. • Encourage or create fens where appropriate. • Ensure river engineering is sensitive when regrading banks, straightening rivers or devising erosion control methods. • Ensure connectivity of habitats over the large home ranges, eg maintain or create linear features to connect different areas. • Ensure infrastructure projects, eg road building, are designed to maintain connections between habitats, eg via wildlife tunnels or bridges. • See Species Action Plan (UK Steering Group 1995).
Water vole *Arvicola terrestris*	Steep banks; high vegetational structural diversity; absence of mink or extensive width of marginal vegetation	• Ensure good water quality, unaffected by pollution, pesticides and fertilisers, to prevent direct toxicity. • Manage river sides to ensure a range of habitats extending back from the river margin. • Allow vegetation to grow along river and canal banks. • Ensure river engineering is sensitive when regrading banks, straightening rivers or devising erosion control methods. • Encourage fen habitats, the larger the better. • Ensure connectivity of habitats, eg maintain or create features such as hedgerows, marshes and woodland margins, to connect different areas. • Ensure infrastructure projects, eg road building, are designed to maintain connections between habitats, eg via wildlife tunnels or bridges. • See Species Action Plan (UK Steering Group 1995).

Species	Habitat requirements	Management requirements in freshwater habitats
Water shrew *Neomys fodiens*	Unknown; while often associated with clear, fast-flowing, unpolluted water are also found by ponds and drainage ditches, rocky beaches and even some distance from water; linear features such as hedges valuable for connecting populations.	• Ensure good water quality, unaffected by pollution, pesticides and fertilisers, to maintain invertebrate prey species and prevent direct toxicity. • Maintain existing fens, wet woodland, carr vegetation and small water bodies such as ponds, streams and ditches. Encourage or create them where appropriate.
Great crested newt *Triturus cristatus*	Unshaded, fish-free ponds; generally between 100 - 300 m^2 in surface area with depths around 1-2 m maximum, with good cover of aquatic and emergent vegetation. Associated with these is a structurally diverse terrestrial habitat which may be grasses, hedgerows, woodland or even open or well grazed land provided that the ground itself is deeply fissured and has a range of invertebrate species for prey. Structures, such as log piles, for hibernation are required.	• Maintain and create appropriate pond habitats for breeding, with suitable surrounding terrestrial habitat. • Create small clusters of ponds in different locations; pond clusters (more than two ponds within a few hundred metres of each other) are preferable for safeguarding amphibian populations than single, isolated ponds. • Ensure connectivity between populations, by maintaining or providing suitable terrestrial habitat between ponds and pond clusters. • Do not drain wetlands. • Ensure good water quality, unaffected by pollution, pesticides and fertilisers, to maintain populations and their invertebrate prey species. • Fish eat newt larvae and may need to be removed from ponds which are permanent, but the Environment Agency must be consulted and a licence obtained to do this. • See Species Action Plan (UK Steering Group 1995).
Natterjack toad *Bufo calamita*	Shallow, often ephemeral ponds, that hold water between April and late July. Generally these are relatively free of weed. Terrestrial habitat associated with this is often fairly open in structure with very short turf (eg close-grazed by sheep or rabbits) or bare ground over which the animals actively forage. Structures, such as log piles, for hibernation or a sandy soil or soft rock substrate in which to burrow are required.	• Maintain and create appropriate pond habitats for breeding, with suitable surrounding terrestrial habitat. • Create small clusters of ponds in different locations; pond clusters (more than two ponds within a few hundred metres of each other) are preferable for safeguarding amphibian populations than single, isolated ponds. • Ensure connectivity between populations, by maintaining or providing suitable terrestrial habitat between ponds and pond clusters. • Do not drain wetlands where they occur. • Ensure good water quality, unaffected by pollution, pesticides and fertilisers, to maintain populations and invertebrate prey species. • See Species Action Plan (UK Steering Group 1995).

Species	Habitat requirements	Management requirements in freshwater habitats
Grass snake *Natrix natrix*	Structurally diverse, but generally open vegetation, such as open grassland (with no or very low grazing levels), open woodlands/woodland rides, hedgerows; that offer a range of different 'thermal' environments during the day. Banks and slopes are especially favoured. Egg laying sites of rotting vegetation, compost heaps, piles of wood chips, manure piles are important for breeding. Structures, such as log piles, banks, cracked ground are required for hibernation and as lying up areas over night and during extremes of temperature.	• Maintain and create pond habitats for amphibians and fish for feeding. • Create small clusters of ponds in different locations; pond clusters (more than 2 ponds within a few hundred metres of each other) are preferable for safeguarding amphibian populations than single, isolated ponds. • Ensure connectivity between amphibian and snake populations, by maintaining or providing suitable terrestrial habitat between ponds and pond clusters. • Promote the conservation of grass snakes in areas with good populations of amphibians (where this does not jeopardise any over-riding conservation interests, eg natterjack toad conservation). • Ensure good water quality, unaffected by pollution and pesticides, to maintain their amphibian and fish prey species. • Do not drain wetlands.

Key

1. Arnold 1995; Beebee 1996; Harris *et al* 1995; Hilton-Brown & Oldham 1991; Morris 1993; Swan & Oldham 1993a & b.

Table 9.21 Habitat and management requirements of fish of conservation significance in upland freshwater habitats in England

Species	Habitat requirements	Management requirements
Bullhead *Cottus gobio*	• Clean gravels. • Fast flowing clean water.	• Maintain water quality particularly oxygen. • Limit, nutrients and siltation. • Avoid habitat modification. • Maintain bank structure.
Salmon *Salmo salar*/sea trout/ brown trout adults	• Deep water with plenty of cover such as undercut banks, overhanging vegetation, weed or rock to lie up in.	• Maintain access up through the catchment to spawning beds. • Avoid obstructions and where obstructions occur incorporate appropriate fish passes.
spawners	• Clean gravels with low levels of silt and well oxygenated unpolluted water.	• Maintain water quality, particularly oxygen and nutrients. • Limit siltation.
fry	• Bank side cover, good supply of food.	• Avoid insensitive habitat modification which removes mosaic of pools and riffles.
parr	• Fast riffles and runs. • Plenty of cover such as weeds, rocks, banks. • Cool clean well oxygenated water.	• Maintain bank structure, overhanging trees, scrubs. • Maintain river flows and spates.
Grayling *Thymallus thymallus*		
spawners	• Clean gravel.	• Maintain water quality, particularly oxygen and nutrients. • Limit siltation.
juveniles	• Shallow flowing water.	• Avoid habitat modification.
adults	• Deeper water in glides.	
Lampreys *Lampetra* spp and *Petromipon marinus*		
spawners	• Clean gravels, fast flows.	• Maintain mosaic of habitats. • Ensure gravels do not become silted.
juveniles	• Silts or fine sands with low organic matter for ammocoete larvae to bury in.	• Avoid total removal of silt beds. • Maintain bank structure. • Maintain access through estuaries. • Avoid obstructions, incorporate appropriate fish passes where obstructions occur.

Species	Habitat requirements	Management requirements
Vendace *Coregonus albula* and schelly *Coregonus lavaretus* spawners juveniles and adults	 • Clean littoral gravels for spawning • Deep nutrient poor lakes. • High levels of oxygen.	 • Maintain good water quality in particular reduce enrichment, maintain high levels of oxygen. • Maintain gravels free of silt. • Avoid fluctuating water levels which can leave littoral spawning beds stranded. • See Vendace Species Action Plan (UK Steering Group 1995).
Allis shad *Alosa alosa* Twaite shad *Alosa fallax*	• Clean gravels adjacent to deep pools for spawning.	• Maintain gravel shoals and deep pools in areas where fish spawn. • Maintain water quality, in particular oxygen levels with special emphasis on estuaries. • Maintain flows during migration period (April to August). • Do not obstruct migration route and where possible remove or modify existing obstructions. • See Species Action Plan (UK Steering Group 1995).

Crags & pave

Crags, scree and limestone pavement **10**

Tables

Definition and location of crags, scree and limestone pavement

10.1 Definition of crags, scree and limestone pavement

This chapter is concerned with the biological interest of rock exposed at the surface. Rock exposures occur as features such as cliffs or crags, gullies and ravines, boulders and scree, and limestone pavements. The geological and geomorphological interest of these features is dealt with in Chapter 4 Earth heritage features.

Exposures may occur in rocks of sedimentary, volcanic or metamorphic origin. The base status of the exposure varies from high to low, although areas of base-poor rock may contain thin strata or veins of calcareous material to give localised variation.

Limestone pavement is a particular type of rock habitat which occurs from sea level to mountain top. It is defined in law as "an area of limestone which lies wholly or partly exposed on the surface of the ground and has been fissured by natural erosion" (Wildlife and Countryside Act 1981, Section 34 (6)). This past natural weathering has formed a complex of deep crevices known as grikes interspersed with massive blocks known as clints.

The vegetation of rock habitats is characteristically discontinuous and often sparse. Soil cover is thin, skeletal or absent altogether. The vegetation includes two distinct types:

- Vegetation that uses the physical structure or form of the rock as a shelter from the extremes of climate or grazing. This includes ledge flora, scree communities, the flora of grikes of limestone pavement and remnant woodland on upland crags.

- Vegetation consisting of species that are poor competitors but can withstand or tolerate the stress caused by thin or absent soil, low nutrient levels, poor shelter and drought. This is true 'chasmophytic' vegetation, and includes the flora of cracks and fissures of rock faces, and the surface of clints of limestone pavement.

10.2 Location and extent of crags, scree and limestone pavement

Rock habitats are widespread throughout upland areas. They can occur in all situations within the landscape, from unenclosed mountain summits to enclosed valley grassland and all agricultural and other land in between. Calcareous rock faces and scree, especially those consisting of limestone, are particularly well represented in the uplands of northern England. Acidic rock exposures are present throughout the upland areas of England.

The physical and chemical nature of the parent rock determines the morphology and longevity of the rock exposure, as well as influencing the rates of weathering and erosion. The English uplands are characterised by harder rock types such as Carboniferous limestone, volcanic rocks, granites and hard sandstones, which tend to form permanent rock exposures.

The nature of the rock exposure is also determined by the mechanism creating the exposure. These geomorphological agents include glacial erosion, rivers, deep weathering, land slips and the actions of man. As these processes are responsible for erosion they are also agents of deposition. For this reason the uplands show a disproportionate amount of exposed rock and much of the lowlands mantled by a thick cover of soil, alluvium or glacial drift. Glacial and fluvial erosion are particularly centred on the uplands.

Limestone pavement is a type of rock exposure which, in Britain, is largely restricted to the north west of England, with small pockets in Wales, Scotland and Northern Ireland. This habitat has been thoroughly surveyed by Ward & Evans (1976) and English Nature (Webb 1995). It is restricted to areas of hard limestone which have been glacially scoured during the last ice age more than 10,000 years ago. The area of British limestone pavement is small and it is a scarce resource (Ward & Evans 1976), covering 3,000 ha in Britain, with 2,350 ha of this in England. British limestone pavements have been extensively damaged to meet the demand for decorative rockery stone. Stone has also been robbed historically from pavements to produce lime, build dry stone walls and to supply local building materials. Only 3% of the pavements surveyed by Ward & Evans (1976) were undamaged. About half of all the remaining limestone pavement in England occurs on the Craven District of North Yorkshire, with the remainder largely in Cumbria and north Lancashire.

There have been no comprehensive surveys of the extent of other forms of rock exposure (inland cliffs, crags and scree) in Britain, although some land cover surveys have produced estimates of bare rock. Surveys of the plant communities associated with these features are also scarce. Recent surveys of plant communities associated with rock exposures in three Cumbrian candidate Special Areas for Conservation, however, found that tall herb ledge communities were far more restricted in extent and distribution than had hitherto been suspected (Jerram 1997a, b & c).

Examples of calcareous chasmophytic vegetation (defined in these surveys as vegetation growing in fissures, crevices and directly on the rock), while relatively widespread over the sites as a whole, tended to be represented by very small 'stands' of vegetation. These were often no more than a metre in length or covering a couple of square metres at the most and were usually much smaller. They often consisted of only a few individuals of one or two vascular plant species. Siliceous (base-poor) chasmophytic vegetation was widespread, however, as was siliceous scree, but large areas of this scree was unvegetated owing to the continuance of natural scree forming processes. Eutric (base-rich) scree communities were confined to areas of limestone scree (Jerram 1997a, b and c).

Man-made rocky habitats also occur in the uplands. Quarries, for example, provide rock exposures and ledges as habitats for plants and animals. Mine spoil, for example from lead mines, supports specialised and often rare plants and animals (see Chapter 6 Moorland for more details).

Habitats and species of crags, scree and limestone pavement

10.3 Why crags, scree and limestone pavement are important

10.3.1 Crags and scree

Exposures of bare rock such as crags and scree support rare plant communities found only in these situations. Many of the communities are important in an international context and this is recognised by their inclusion in the Habitats and Species Directive (see 10.4.3). These plant communities contain nationally rare and scarce vascular plants, bryophytes and lichens (Tables 10.1, 10.2 and 10.4). Crags and scree also provide essential habitats for a variety of animals, including scarce invertebrates (Table 10.8) and birds of conservation concern (Table 10.6), such as peregrine falcon *Falco peregrinus*, golden eagle *Aquila chrysaetos* and ring ouzel *Turdus torquatus* that nest there. Several species associated with crags and scree are included in the UK Biodiversity Action Plan (UK Biodiversity Group 1998; UK Steering Group 1995).

In addition to species specifically associated with rock exposures, these features often provide important refugia for species intolerant of high grazing levels. In many locations these species, which include stands of high altitude woodland and scrub, have become restricted to ledges inaccessible to livestock.

10.3.2 Limestone pavement

Limestone pavements are a rare habitat in Europe. The UK holds a significant proportion of the resource within the EU and England has 78% of the British resource. Their special interest lies in the unusual plant assemblages they support (Table 10.5), together with their geomorphological and geological features and the unique landscape features they create. Their significance is recognised by the inclusion of limestone pavement in Annex 1 of the EC Habitats and Species Directive as a priority habitat. This means that this habitat is in danger of disappearance and its natural range mainly falls within the territory of the European Union (European Commission 1996).

The plant assemblages of limestone pavement include many rare and scarce vascular and non-vascular plant species (Tables 10.1 and 10.2). Certain rare lichens are also associated with this habitat (Table 10.4) and pavements provide habitats for rare and scarce invertebrate species (Table 10.8). In addition, areas of limestone pavement support various woodland and scrub types which are considered to be of international importance (Table 10.5).

Limestone pavement and some of the species associated with it are also included in the UK Biodiversity Action Plan (UK Biodiversity Group 1998; UK Steering Group 1995).

Ring ouzel

Limestone pavements are also of interest for their geological and geomorphological features, which reflect the glacial scouring of the last ice age and the post glacial weathering processes that have operated over the last 10,000 years. Pavements are well recognised for their scenic beauty and their contribution to the landscape.

Pavements often occur in a mosaic of other features of interest such as calcareous grassland, limestone scars and cliffs, scree, limestone woodland and scrub. These are often features of interest in their own right.

Further information: Chapter 4 Earth heritage features

10.4 Habitats and species of rock features, their nature conservation status and distribution

10.4.1 Vascular plants

Crags, scree and limestone pavement support a wide range of nationally rare and scarce plant species (Table 10.1). Crags shelter relict Arctic-alpine plants like mountain avens *Dryas octopetala*, alpine enchanter's nightshade *Circaea alpina* and alpine cinquefoil *Potentilla crantzii*. Crags and screes are important for their rich fern flora and because they act as a refugia for a number of rare species, including oblong woodsia *Woodsia ilvensis*, forked spleenwort *Asplenium septentrionale* and Killarney fern *Trichomanes speciosum*. Many of the British species of whitebeam *Sorbus* spp., several of which are endemic, are confined to cliffs, particularly on rocks of a calcareous nature. One example is the nationally rare Lancashire whitebeam *Sorbus lancastriensis*, which only occurs around Morecambe Bay. Most of the records of this species are from cliffs and rocks of the Carboniferous limestone (Rich & Baecker 1986, 1992).

Many species associated with ledges are found in the montane zone and are covered in Chapter 5. Examples of these include alpine catchfly *Lychnis alpina*, glaucous meadow-grass *Poa glauca*, alpine saxifrage *Saxifraga nivalis* and alpine mouse-ear *Cerastium alpinum*.

Grikes and other solution features of limestone pavement support rare and scarce plant species such as rigid buckler-fern *Dryopteris submontana*, downy currant *Ribes spicatum*, baneberry *Actaea spicata* and dark-red helleborine *Epipactis atrorubens*. Gilbert (1970) considers that 80% of the rigid buckler-fern population is confined to limestone pavement. It was formerly more widespread, occurring in upland areas with no limestone pavement, and its present dependence on the clefts of pavements is thought to be because these offer protection from grazing (Jermy 1994). Limestone pavements in Yorkshire are known to contain a significant proportion of the UK baneberry population (Usher 1980, 1986). Other plant species of note associated with limestone pavements include fingered sedge *Carex digitata*, bird's-foot sedge *Carex ornithipoda*, pale St. John's-wort *Hypericum montanum*, angular Solomon's-seal *Polygonatum odoratum*, narrow-leaved bitter-cress *Cardamine impatiens* and limestone fern *Gymnocarpium robertianum*. The grikes provide a cold humid microclimate where shade-tolerant plants, as well as species typical of calcareous woodland, occur.

10.4.2 Bryophytes and lichens

Rock exposures, particularly base-rich ones, support a large number of specialist bryophytes and lichens. Tables 10.2 and 10.4 show the nationally rare and scarce bryophytes and some examples of rare lichen species associated with rock exposures. Several of the bryophyte species are included in the UK Biodiversity Action (UK Biodiversity Group 1998; UK Steering Group 1995).

10.4.3 Plant communities

Table 10.5 shows the National Vegetation Classification (NVC) communities associated with rock exposures, together with their conservation status and distribution in upland Natural Areas.

Crags support plant communities of rock faces (chasmophytic vegetation), particular bryophyte and lichen assemblages, and species-rich tall-herb communities on montane and sub-montane cliff ledges. Screes are important for their rich fern flora and both crags and scree support common juniper *Juniperus communis* scrub, which is a very variable, local and unevenly distributed habitat type within Europe. All these habitats are important in an international context and this is recognised by the EC Habitats and Species Directive, which lists in Annex I six types of crag and scree habitat: eutric and siliceous screes, calcareous and siliceous types of chasmophytic vegetation on rocky slopes, eutrophic tall-herb communities and juniper formations (Brown *et al* 1997, Table 10.5).

It should be noted that the NVC only partially covers these habitat types. The communities described are frequently derived from very small numbers of samples, and these samples are often restricted geographically. The results of recent surveys suggest that more detailed sampling of scree, chasmophytic and ledge vegetation would reveal a number of sub-communities, and possibly new communities in addition to those described by Rodwell (1992 and in press; Jerram 1997a, b & c). In addition, the NVC does not distinguish communities of limestone pavements from other limestone woodland, grassland and open vegetation (rock) communities.

Limestone pavements support particular plant assemblages containing elements of these other limestone communities. It seems likely that most limestone pavements originally carried a cover of woodland, even in upland areas (Pigott & Pigott 1959). The woodland would probably be accompanied by a soil cover on the surface of the limestone. Tree cover was lost from the Craven Pennines by Iron Age times, with soil loss following. The present day general absence of trees on limestone pavements is maintained by grazing and climatic pressures. Tree-covered pavements are at present largely confined to north-east Wales and around Morecambe Bay. Here they include two internationally important woodland types, one composed of ash *Fraxinus excelsior*, wych elm *Ulmus glabra* and small-leaved lime *Tilia cordata*, and the other containing yew *Taxus baccata* (Table 10.5). Both these woodland types are included in the Habitats and Species Directive as priority habitats. Juniper scrub also occurs on some areas of limestone pavement.

In the continuum from wooded through scrubby to open pavements, their morphology offers a variety of microclimates, allowing the establishment of complex vegetation consisting of a mosaic of different communities (European Commission 1996). The transitions between these communities, as well as where pavements grade into other habitats such as species-rich limestone grassland, support a particularly diverse flora and fauna.

10.4.4 Birds

Rock exposures are used by a relatively small number of bird species. Ledges provide nest sites for raven *Corvus corax*, buzzard *Buteo buteo* and peregrine falcon, which use these situations because they are less disturbed and in some cases because of the lack of alternative sites, such as mature trees. Holes and crevices in scree provide nest sites for wheatear *Oenanthe oenanthe* and ring ouzel. All these birds forage elsewhere in the vicinity of the rock feature.

Birds characteristic of other upland habitats become associated with rock features where the habitat is integral to the interest of the area. For example wintering thrush flocks exploit autumn and winter berry crops on scrub and woodland associated with rock exposures and limestone pavement. Some species, for example raven and twite *Carduelis flavirostris*, may also use rock features for roosting. Table 10.6 lists bird species associated with rock exposures.

10.4.5 Invertebrates

Rock exposures provide habitats for a number of species of rare and scarce invertebrate species (Table 10.8). Molluscs such as *Vitrea subrimata, Clausilia dubia, Pyramidula rupestris* and *Pomatias elegans*, which inhabit moist places and are often nocturnal, occur in crevices and under loose rocks on limestone rocks, as does the pill woodlouse *Armadillidium pictum*. The shelter and humidity in the grikes of limestone pavement favour certain invertebrates, such as particular spiders and molluscs.

The high brown fritillary butterfly *Argynnis adippe*, which is listed in the UK Red Data Book as a vulnerable species and is included in the UK Biodiversity Action Plan (UK Steering Group 1995; Barnett & Warren 1995a), is associated with coppiced limestone pavement in north Lancashire and south Cumbria.

Important microhabitats are small pockets of soil, loose stones, moss and seepages of water over the rock surface. For a few species, the high temperatures and dry conditions associated with the exposed rock are of particular importance.

Solution hollows on limestone pavement have a very specialised aquatic fauna of species that are capable of tolerating the desiccation and high temperatures that occur when they dry out, including the midge *Dasyhelea saxicola*.

Yellow mountain saxifrage

10.5 Habitat and management requirements of species of rock features

The habitat and management requirements of key plant and animal species associated with crags, scree and limestone pavement are shown in Tables 10.1 (vascular plants), 10.3 (bryophytes), 10.7 (birds) and 10.9 (invertebrates).

Grazing-intolerant plant species of crags require a reduction in the grazing pressure on the surrounding land if they are to spread from their refugia. However, some plants of rocky terrain require certain levels of grazing. This may be because they are poor competitors, or they require bare ground to germinate or are intolerant of the shade cast by encroaching scrub.

To maintain populations of species associated with limestone pavement, the most important factor is to prevent damage or destruction of the pavement. In addition, many of the rare and scarce plant species thrive only where grazing is light or absent, and on wooded pavements some plants and animals benefit from woodland management such as coppicing.

Plants and animals associated with crags, scree and limestone pavement may require protection from damage or disturbance by walkers or rock climbers. Species associated with limestone pavement and screes and birds which nest on crags particularly require the habitat to remain intact and undisturbed.

Raven

Management of crags, scree and limestone pavement

10.6 Managing crags, scree and limestone pavement

Agricultural practices which occur on or around rock features include grazing, stone removal, applying surface treatments such as fertilisers or herbicides, and stock feeding. Other activities affecting rock features include recreation, such as walking and rock climbing, and woodland management. To maintain, and where necessary enhance, the nature conservation interests of crags, scree and limestone pavement, all these activities need to be at appropriate levels, locations or times, depending on the particular interest present.

10.6.1 Managing limestone pavement

Limestone pavements vary in their appearance, geological features and the flora they support. The differences reflect the geological structure of the rock and its formation during the ice ages, as well as climate, altitude and the more recent impact of man.

Pavements may be split into three broad types: open, scrubby and wooded. Open pavements have bare clints with vegetation largely confined to the grikes, although they may have scattered trees. These are largely the result of a long history of grazing management. Wooded pavements have vegetation cloaking the clint tops and a more continuous tree cover, although clearings may be frequent. These types of pavement have usually developed where grazing is low or absent. Woodland cover is the natural climax vegetation type on limestone pavement. Scrubby pavements form part of a continuum between open and wooded pavement. All three types are of conservation value because they form part of the complex mosaic of vegetation which is characteristic of limestone pavements (see 10.4.3) and areas of each should be retained. Features considered favourable for each type of pavement are given in Box 10.1.

Stone removal and disturbance

The first step in maintaining the interest of limestone pavement is to ensure that the pavement clints are not removed. Removing clints for use as decorative garden stone has been the major cause of loss of, and damage to, limestone pavement in Britain. Historically, stone has also been removed from pavements to produce lime, build dry stone walls and to supply local building materials. All limestone pavements will be covered by Limestone Pavement Orders (LPOs), which prohibit the removal of limestone from pavements (Webb 1995).

Disturbing and removing stone from limestone pavements is extremely detrimental to their geomorphological and geological interest. These landforms need initial glacial scouring to form, followed by thousands of years of sub-soil weathering to create the grikes and other solution features. Once damaged they will not re-form.

Disturbing and removing stone from pavements is also extremely detrimental to the plants and invertebrates of these habitats.

- Where clints are removed the grikes are reduced in depth and offer less shelter to plants. Most ferns, for example, die immediately.

- The clint top solution features (runnels, pits, pans, etc) offer a variety of niches and microclimates to plants with different requirements, and these are immediately lost when clints are removed.

- Removal of clints is equally detrimental to invertebrate populations. It reduces cover, destroys the architecture of the grikes, which are important for web-building spiders, and changes the humidity, which will negatively affect the mollusc fauna.

- The debris from the extraction process fills the remnants of the grikes with chips of stone and rubble, and destroys these habitats.

- Lichens on the pavement, which grow very slowly indeed, are also lost with the extracted stone.

- All that remains when limestone pavement has been removed is horizontal scree, which cannot support the rare and specialised flora of intact pavement.

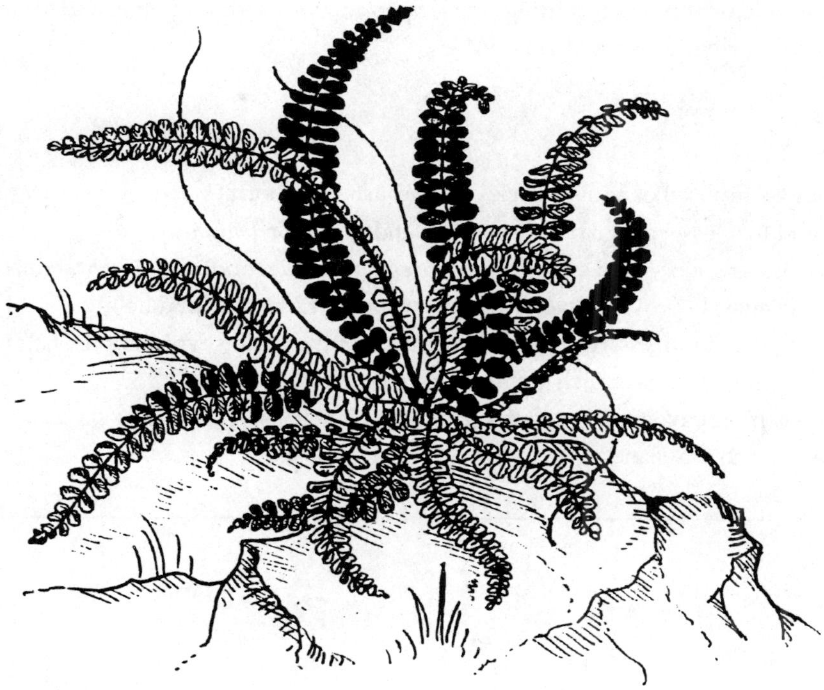

Maidenhair spleenwort

Box 10.1 Favourable features of limestone pavement

Open pavement

- A diversity of characteristic plant species, eg herb-robert *Geranium robertianum*, hart's-tongue fern *Phyllitis scolopendrium*, rigid buckler fern *Dryopteris submontana*, angular Solomon's-seal *Polygonatum odoratum*, downy currant *Ribes spicatum*, baneberry *Actea spicata*, dark-red helleborine *Epipactis atrorubens* and limestone fern *Gymnocarpium robertianum*.
- Wild flowers and ferns growing beyond the grikes and onto the clint tops, and producing flowers, seeds and spores, including species intolerant of grazing, eg bloody crane's bill *Geranium sanguineum* and baneberry.
- Scattered trees and shrubs of native species, eg hazel *Corylus avellana*, ash *Fraxinus excelsior* and juniper *Juniperus communis*.
- Abundant vegetation to encourage butterflies, spiders, snails and other invertebrates, eg fritillary butterflies.
- Transitions from pavement vegetation to other valuable habitats such as scrub, woodland, heath and species-rich grassland.

Scrubby pavement

- Scrub composed of native shrub species typical of the habitat, including abundant juniper and hazel stands.
- Frequent transitions between open and wooded pavement, because these are botanically the richest.
- A mosaic of habitat types, including scrub, open and wooded pavement, and species-rich grassland, to provide habitat diversity.

Wooded pavement

- Woodland composed of native species such as ash, hawthorn *Crataegus monagyna*, hazel, yew *Taxus baccata* and to a lesser extent oak *Quercus* sp and rowan *Sorbus aucuparia*.
- Open glades and woodland edges, to encourage butterflies and other invertebrates.
- Trees of all ages, to provide diversity in the woodland structure and height.
- Yew groves and juniper scrub, because these are native species typical of the habitat.
- Areas with mossy clints, which are important for invertebrates.
- Transitions from pavement vegetation to other valuable habitats such as scrub, woodland, heath and species-rich grassland.

Managing open limestone pavement

The majority of the higher altitude limestone pavement in England has been subject to heavy grazing, especially where it falls within common land, and this has led to an open nature. The lower altitude limestone pavements, which in England occur around Morecambe Bay, tend to be ungrazed and wooded and are dealt with below.

Heavy grazing generally lowers the species diversity of limestone pavements as it results in the vegetation being restricted to deep, narrow grikes. Plant species which are vulnerable to grazing or favour the top of the grikes, such as bloody crane's-bill *Geranium sanguineum*, lesser meadow rue *Thalictrum minus* and rigid buckler fern, are suppressed. Sheep are the main grazers of limestone pavements, but rabbits have a significant impact on some sites, not least because they are small enough to run along grikes and graze species not accessible to sheep.

Heavy grazing disturbs loose stones on and around pavements, and this reduces the likelihood of them being used by invertebrates which rely on stones for cover.

Restoration management of open limestone pavement

Restoration of heavily grazed pavements by total stock exclusion, for a limited period of five to ten years, may be the most effective way of improving the nature conservation interest of these pavements. This is likely to require fencing, and if so the impact of the fencing on adjacent grassland, as well as on agricultural and other land uses, should be considered. In many areas, a temporary exclusion of grazing could be beneficial to the nature conservation interest of the adjacent grassland because it is often heavily grazed. On many higher altitude pavements an additional complication is that they lie on common land, so permission to fence them will need to be sought from the Secretary of State for the Environment, once the commoners and all other relevant interest groups have been consulted.

Where the number of rabbits is significant and their grazing is restricting the abundance and diversity of plant species, rabbit *Oryctolagus cuniculus* control may be necessary (see Information Note 8).

Once the pavement has been returned to favourable condition the long-term maintenance regime of stocking at less than 1 ewe/ha (or cattle equivalent) should be introduced.

Maintenance management of open limestone pavement

Where pavements are considered to be in good (favourable) condition a maintenance management regime should be implemented. The optimum long-term stocking level to maintain the interest of English upland limestone pavements is less than 1 ewe/ha (or cattle equivalent).

For nature conservation interests, cattle are the preferred grazers for limestone pavement areas because they tend not to venture on to the uneven surface and hence the pavement remains little grazed. However, the pattern of land use around higher altitude pavements, at least, makes sheep grazing a more likely practice.

A stocking rate of less than 1 ewe/ha will generally involve a reduction in grazing for higher altitude limestone pavements. This will:

- increase species populations and species diversity;
- encourage grazing intolerant species, eg baneberry, lesser meadow rue;
- encourage species that favour grike top or clint top positions, eg bloody crane's bill;
- give more structure to the vegetation, with plants growing above the clints, including woody species such as hazel, hawthorn, yew and juniper;
- provide shelter for invertebrates, eg butterflies such as fritillaries and the northern brown argus *Aricia artaxerxes;*
- support a mosaic of species-rich grassland, heathland and pavement, with associated transitions and habitat edges.

Some grazing, however, is considered beneficial as it:

- prevents 'scrubbing up';
- maintains the interest of surrounding pasture;
- keeps geological and geomorphological interest features accessible.

A range of grazing regimes, from less than 1 ewe/ha, to some very lightly grazed situations and other areas completely ungrazed, is desirable to increase the diversity of the limestone pavement resource as a whole.

Rabbit control may be necessary in areas of limestone pavement where numbers are significant and rabbit grazing is restricting plant species abundance and diversity. See Information Note 8 on rabbit control in the uplands for more details.

Grazing does not harm the geomorphological or geological interest of limestone pavement. It is unlikely that even in the absence of grazing limestone pavements will become covered with scrub to such an extent that the geomorphological or geological interest will be harmed. It takes many years for vegetation to establish on pavements and, although grikes are warm, humid and stable environments, plants do not always survive beyond these niches.

Stock feeding

Stock feeding in areas of nature conservation interest can lead to nutrient enrichment and poaching of the ground, resulting in the loss of characteristic plants and animals. The following recommendations apply to stock feeding on limestone pavement and the surrounding habitats.

- seek to avoid stock feeding wherever possible but if unavoidable keep it to a minimum and normally in severe weather;

- do not place feed on areas of limestone pavement or any other areas of wildlife interest;

- where stock feeding is undertaken do not cause poaching to surrounding habitats (other than in sacrificial areas);

- locate a permanent feeder in a place with no conservation value and treat this as a sacrificial area;

- where this is not possible, feed in small quantities at widely scattered sites, avoiding using the same sites;

- or rotate the feeding sites to avoid excessive pressure on any one area.

Application of surface treatments and infilling

Fertilisers, slurry and farmyard manure can all seriously damage the flora and fauna of limestone pavements and associated semi-natural habitats. They should not be applied to limestone pavements or surrounding grasslands.

Limestone pavement and other karst (limestone) landforms are vulnerable to damage by dumping and infilling. Shakeholes and cave entrances are all too convenient dumps for farmyard rubbish. Many of the shakeholes and depressions on the Mendip Plateau, for example, have been lost in this way.

Managing scrubby limestone pavement

Scrubby limestone pavement may have features of both open and wooded pavement, with shrub species reaching a height of around 3 m. This habitat, especially where dominated by native species such as hazel or juniper, is valuable in its own right and it should be retained rather than changed into either wooded or open pavement.

Management of scrubby pavement involves removing invasive species such as bramble, *Rubus fruticosa* blackthorn *Prunus spinosa*, gorse *Ulex* spp and cotoneaster *Cotoneaster* spp where they are shading out the pavement flora. Where woodland cover threatens to dominate the pavement, coppice management or stock reintroduction at less than 1 ewe/ha should be considered.

Managing wooded limestone pavement

Wooded pavements have a closed canopy of trees and shrubs covering the clints, which are often cloaked with a dense moss carpet. Clearings and glades may be present, and the lower branches of yews and junipers may have developed into a broad skirt of foliage. While these pavements may not be open to domestic stock, wooded pavements may still be grazed or browsed by deer or rabbits.

In wooded pavements, management is required to maintain some open glades, both for plants of woodland edges and invertebrates, particularly butterflies. Many wooded pavements were traditionally managed as coppice woodland, but this practice has declined in recent decades, resulting in reduced species diversity in many cases (UK Steering Group 1995). Chapter 8 Woodland and scrub considers the pros and cons of different woodland management regimes in greater detail.

- Coppice or woodland management should be maintained where it is currently practised and should be reintroduced where it has lapsed. The introduction of coppicing to wooded pavements where it was not previously practised may enhance their nature conservation value, but there is probably some value in long-term rotations or maintaining high forest on some sites to provide diversity.

- Where pavements are managed as high forest, heavy thinning and selective felling should be used in rotation to open up the canopy and create glades. Where present, rides should be widened or at least maintained (Guest 1997).

- Yew and juniper should be retained and not felled or coppiced because they are native species characteristic of this habitat. Similarly, hazel should not be cleared, although it may be appropriate to coppice this species. Veteran trees, some of which may be very small because of the stressed conditions for growth, should also be retained.

- Many wooded pavements have been planted with, or invaded by, alien species such as sycamore *Acer pseudoplatanus*, beech *Fagus* spp, conifers and cotoneaster. Beech and conifers should be removed from pavements because they have an adverse effect on the underlying flora through shading, acidification and smothering, resulting from leaf or needle fall (Guest 1997). Cotoneaster should be removed because it ousts native species. Sycamore should also be removed where its presence is thought to threaten the nature conservation interest of a pavement.

- Deer control or fencing may be required on some wooded pavements, particularly where they are managed as coppice. Heavy deer browsing may prevent coppice re-growth.

- Dense growth of shrubs, such as blackthorn or bramble, can shade out a number of the more uncommon species associated with pavements, such as baneberry. Where this is occurring, or threatening to occur, scrub clearance should be carried out.

- Mossy clints support rare invertebrates such as the whorl snail *Vertigo augustior*. Such clints should be protected and the moss cover maintained.

Further information: English Nature 1993a; Craven Limestone Grassland Wildlife Enhancement Scheme (WES); Mercer & Evans 1997; Boxes 10.1 - 10.4.

Box 10.2. English Nature Craven limestone grassland Wildlife Enhancement Scheme (WES)

The standard (Tier 1) Craven limestone grassland WES prescription is given below. This largely relates to areas of pavement within areas of limestone grassland.

- Graze at 1 ewe/ha (or equivalent or lower) for a continuous eight week period between 1 May and 31 August.
- At other times graze at 2 ewes/ha or equivalent.
- Cattle grazing in summer is preferable as they spend less time on the pavement than sheep.
- Lambs (to 31 October) and calves at foot are included.
- Stock feeding only in agreed areas of low nature conservation value.
- No applications of manure, fertiliser or lime.
- Fence at least one area of ungrazed land (preferably pavement) on the holding.
- Control rabbits if necessary.

As part of this scheme land owners are encouraged to exclude stock from areas of limestone pavement to promote woodland regeneration.

Examples of the effects of various stocking regimes are given in Box 10.3 and Mercer & Evans 1997.

Wheatear

Box 10.3 Examples of management on limestone pavement areas under the EN Craven limestone grassland WES

Malham-Arncliffe SSSI (Knotts)

Habitats:	A mixture of limestone pavement, calcareous grassland and acid grassland.
Management:	2 ewes/ha April No stock May-August *c* 1.25 ewe/ha September-October No stock November-March Cattle and sheep stocked.
Effects:	Limestone fern *Gymnocarpium robertianum* showed a 100% increase in shoot numbers in the pavement between 1994 and 1996. Northern brown argus *Aricia artaxerxes* butterflies appeared on the site in 1996.

Malham-Arncliffe SSSI (Clowder)

Habitats:	A mixture of limestone pavement, calcareous grassland and acid grassland, with scattered ash.
Management:	0.5 ewes/ha May-August 1 ewe/ha approx. September-October No stock November-April Cattle and sheep. Some protection of ash from grazing using 1.2 m tree shelters.
Effects:	Significant regrowth of ash in grikes, together with a probable increase in limestone fern abundance.

Malham-Arncliffe SSSI (West Gordale)

Habitats:	A mixture of limestone pavement, calcareous grassland and acid grassland.
Management:	
1993-1995:	1 ewe/ha for eight weeks between May-August 2 ewes/ha at other times Sheep only
1995 onwards:	2 ewes/ha May 4 ewes/ha September-November No stock at other times Sheep only
Effects:	Baneberry *Actaea spicata* showed increased fruiting and suspected increased patch size and number of plants. Lily of the valley *Convallaria majalis* re-recorded after 20 years absence.

Box 10.4 Further examples of management on limestone pavement areas

Southerscales Yorkshire Wildlife Trust Reserve, Ingleborough

A nature reserve of 43 ha with large areas of grassland amongst the pavement.
Stocking:

1 June-31 July	10 cattle	(equivalent to 1.1 ewes/ha)
1 August-31 August	10 cattle + 20 ewes	(equivalent to 1.5 ewes/ha)
1 September-31 October	100 ewes	(equivalent to 2.3 ewes/ha)
1 November-30 April	40 ewes	(equivalent to 0.9 ewes/ha)

If the site consisted of pavement alone stocking levels would need to be lower.

Gait Barrows National Nature Reserve, Lancashire

This low altitude site has no stock grazing, but deer control is carried out to protect areas of coppice regrowth. A programme of active coppicing is carried out to benefit both butterflies and the ground flora. Some areas of coppice are protected by deer-proof fences.

Whitbarrow National Nature Reserve, Cumbria (Cumbria Wildlife Trust Hervey Reserve)

A low altitude limestone grassland and pavement reserve. Grazing has recently been reintroduced at 0.7 ewes/ha from August to November.

Underlaid Wood, Marble Quarry & Hale Fell and Middlebarrow (Forest Enterprise woodlands in Cumbria with limestone pavement)

All these areas are actively managed as coppice. Areas of Corsican pine *Pinus nigra*, spruce *Picea* spp, beech and red cedar *Thuja plicata* are being progressively cleared to leave open pavement or limestone grassland.

Yew

Public access

At low levels public access is unlikely to have a significant effect on the nature conservation interest of limestone pavements. High levels of public pressure could result in trampling damage to the pavement flora, especially lichens and mosses, solution features and, on pavements where the clints are loose, could result in the dislodging of clints.

In situations where the encouragement of public access is thought to be beneficial serious consideration should be given to the public liability aspects of such action. This is because limestone pavements can provide a very unstable surface for walking, so there is a significant risk of visitors tripping or falling into grikes, which could result in serious injury. They are also very slippery when wet, in frost and when polished smooth by the passage of many feet.

10.6.2 Managing crags and scree

Grazing

Crags and cliffs are often the only areas free from grazing in upland situations, both above and below the fell wall. Even so, traditional upland breeds of sheep are remarkably agile and only the most inaccessible ledges remain totally free of grazing, particularly where stocking levels are high. Tall-herb ledge communities such as U17 *Luzula sylvatica – Geum rivale* community and the majority of plant species associated with ledges and rock faces are highly sensitive to grazing and are largely restricted to situations which are almost entirely free of grazing. Even on the largest upland sites this can mean that these communities and species are restricted to a few individual ledges and rock faces.

As a result of the high grazing pressures on many montane and moorland situations in England, many species and communities are frequently restricted to those rock exposures where the grazing pressure is lower (because of reduced accessibility to stock), in addition to those species which are truly associated with rock faces and ledges. In some circumstances the only areas of dry heath or woodland present are confined to these locations. In England, high altitude willow scrub (W20 *Salix lapponum-Luzula sylvatica* scrub) is reduced to a few isolated bushes of downy willow *Salix lapponum* on ledges inaccessible to sheep (Jerram 1997d). Under reduced grazing intensities this community extends on to hillsides away from rock ledges and the latter are indeed considered to be a sub-optimal habitat for this species (Mardon 1990 & 1996).

In situations where species or communities of nature conservation interest are restricted to inaccessible ledges by grazing, grazing levels on the surrounding land or management unit should be reduced to a level that will allow the spread of the species and/or community concerned. Chapter 6 Moorland, and Chapter 7 Meadows and enclosed pasture, give guidelines for appropriate stocking levels. Where it is not possible to reduce grazing levels in the grazing unit as a whole, consideration should be given to fencing off sections of hillside containing suitable habitat/conditions into which the species or community can spread (see Information Note 7 on fencing).

Fencing can be a contentious issue in moorland or montane situations, largely because of potential implications for access and other land uses, and the potential for its visual intrusion on the landscape. Where fencing is required on common land permission from the Secretary of State for the Environment is required, once the commoners and all other relevant interest groups have been consulted and have agreed the proposal.

Heavy grazing of rocky habitats makes disturbance of individual stones and screes more likely. This reduces the likelihood of them being used as cover by invertebrates that live under stones (lapidocolous species). As with other upland habitats low, rather than high, stocking levels will be beneficial to the nature conservation interest of scree. It is not thought that scree requires a different management regime from that for the surrounding land. However, where scree forms a high proportion of the land cover, the stocking rate should be calculated for the vegetated area only.

Stone removal and disturbance

Use of stone for wall construction and repair is widespread and in most instances has had little impact on the nature conservation interest of rock features. However, the extensive use of stone and scree for major new projects such as footpath stone pitching and new wall construction could harm fragile plant and animal communities and destroy geological and geomorphological features.

Public access, recreation and human disturbance

Recreational activities and human disturbance can have significant, localised effects on the nature conservation interest of crags and screes.

Frequent disturbance by rock climbers can cause cliff-nesting birds, for example, peregrine, to abandon nests, either permanently, or for long enough for eggs to go cold, resulting in breeding failure. Such incidents are thought to be uncommon and there have been occasional examples of peregrines successfully rearing young on cliffs that are regularly climbed. It seems likely, however, that the small number of records for climbers disturbing peregrines is at least partly due to peregrines avoiding nesting on regularly climbed cliffs (King 1989).

Where climbing is considered to be a significant threat to the breeding success of peregrines, voluntary restrictions on climbing during the breeding season have been introduced by nature conservation organisations in conjunction with the British Mountaineering Council (BMC). These have by and large been successful and are respected by the majority of climbers, providing that they have been well publicised. King (1989) recommends that:

- Restrictions should only be imposed where peregrines are nesting on a climbed cliff.
- They should not be imposed in situations where birds might nest on a cliff or because a cliff is close to one on which peregrines nest.
- Publicity is essential and should be in the form of on-site signs, both at the base of the cliff and on the approach routes.
- In seasons where nesting fails or birds do not take up residency at all restrictions should be lifted for the remainder of that season.

Rock climbing, especially the establishment of new routes, can also damage the botanical interest of cliffs and ledges. The removal of vegetation from ledges ('gardening') can have a serious impact on the vegetation of crags. Evidence from Borrowdale in Cumbria shows that vegetation re-establishing after gardening is of significantly less interest than the vegetation present before the disturbance (Karen Slater, pers comm). This remains a significant issue in England.

Concern has recently been expressed about the effects of winter, or ice, climbing on rare arctic-alpine plants and an evaluation of this is currently being undertaken by the Lake District National Park (Lake District National Park Authority 1997a). The principal concern has been for climbing when snow and/or ice conditions are poor, that is there is only a very thin layer of snow/ice over the rock. The main reason for this concern is where there are only very small numbers (often fewer than ten) of individual plants present of some of the rarer species, which makes them highly susceptible to chance extinctions which could be exacerbated by plants being accidentally kicked off by a climber. Should a problem be found then restrictions on climbing in poor snow or ice conditions may be introduced (P. Davies, pers comm). Such restrictions should only be introduced following a detailed survey of plant locations and a study of climbing routes.

Scree is highly unstable in many situations and the fragile plant communities which develop within it are easily damaged by frequent trampling. Wherever possible new footpaths should be routed around, rather than across scree. This is particularly important on limestone scree as this can support a number of nationally rare and scarce plant species.

10.6.3 Managing bracken

Limestone pavements, other rock exposures and scree support many species of fern susceptible to the chemicals used to control bracken. Other plants of these habitats may also be adversely affected by chemical treatments for bracken control. With aerial spraying, even the drift of chemicals used on adjacent areas can be harmful to rock habitats, and large no-spray buffer zones are required around pavements, crags and scree to ensure that no adverse effects occur. Weed wiping chemicals directly onto the bracken or hand spraying are preferable to aerial spraying, but again buffer zones should be identified and adhered to. For further information on bracken management, see Information Note 6.

Table 10.1 Nationally rare and scarce vascular plants associated with crags, scree and limestone pavement in England

(Note: See also Chapter 5 for species predominantly of montane areas)

Plant species	Status	Habitat requirements	Management requirements	Distribution by upland Natural Area
Actaea spicata baneberry	LR-ns	Shaded sites on soils over calcareous rocks, such as on ledges of scars, in deciduous woods and in grikes in limestone pavement. It will tolerate dense shade but not competition from more vigorous plants.	• In sites where the plant is threatened by the growth of vigorous species, these should be controlled.	Cumbria Fells & Dales North York Moors and Hills Yorkshire Dales
Alchemilla glomerulans	LR-ns	A variety of ungrazed or lightly grazed habitats on base-poor rocks in mountains. In Teesdale, also in species-rich hay-meadows and roadsides.	• Prevent heavy grazing.	Border Uplands North Pennines Yorkshire Dales
Alchemilla wichurae	LR-ns	Damp, basic soils or rocks. See Table 6.1.	• Where it grows on track sides, it needs protection from trampling by walkers and off-road vehicles. • Roadside populations need to be protected from agricultural enrichment which promotes the growth of coarse grasses.	Cumbria Fells & Dales North Pennines Yorkshire Dales
Allium ampeloprasum var. *babingtonii* Babington's leek	LR-ns	Rank vegetation on road verges or field edges which are not often cut or grazed. It can become quite invasive[1] and has increased its range.	• It is likely to benefit from moderate disturbance. • It should not be cut and grazing should be at most light. • At some sites, the growth of scrub may need to be controlled.	Dartmoor
Allium schoenoprasum chives	LR-ns	On thin soil in sparsely vegetated, rocky habitats which fluctuate between very wet and bone dry, often over limestone with winter annuals.	• Prevent destruction of the habitat, which otherwise requires little management.	Border Uplands Cumbria Fells & Dales
Arenaria norvegica ssp *anglica* English sandwort	Sched. 8 of WCA VU, EE	A stress-tolerant species of bare substrates, either on shallow, dry soils on the edge of limestone pavement or on frequently flushed slopes around the edges of flushes and mires. See Table 6.1.	• Where necessary, protect the sites from recreational damage by walkers and off-road vehicles. • Control grazing at the sites to moderate levels. Levels of less than 1.5 ewes per hectare during the growing season have allowed populations to thrive. Moderate grazing is preferable to no grazing.	Yorkshire Dales

Plant species	Status	Habitat requirements	Management requirements	Distribution by upland Natural Area
Asplenium obovatum lanceolate spleenwort	LR-ns	Frost-free, sheltered, shady crevices and ledges on exposures of non-calcareous rocks, cliffs and dry stone walls. Also where a slight seepage of permanent moisture occurs with very free drainage and good air movement.[2] It is intolerant of competition from dense flowering plants and heavy grazing by snails.[3]	• It is thought that this species may be sensitive to pollution of ground water and of air (Page 1982). Therefore sites should be protected from pollution, including agricultural run-off.	Bodmin Moor Cumbria Fells & Dales Dartmoor Exmoor and the Quantocks
Asplenium septentrionale forked spleenwort	LR-ns	Steep or vertical faces of hard, base-poor, dark-coloured volcanic and metamorphic rocks. Also on old earthy, unmortared walls on dry, south facing, unshaded slopes. It is intolerant of shade, waterlogging and competition from gorse and other shrubs.	• Landscaping or reclamation should avoid damage to the habitat. • Where necessary, shrubs should be cleared away.	Cumbria Fells & Dales Dartmoor North Pennines
Asplenium trichomanes subsp. *pachyrachis* lobed maidenhair spleenwort	DD	Perpendicular calcareous rocks, in crevices or under overhangs or on walls where non-calcareous rock is used with calcareous mortar. Normally in well shaded sites with relatively high humidity. It seems to be intolerant of water retained in the crown and favours sites where it is sheltered from direct rain.	• Plants on walls are vulnerable to destruction when walls are cleaned or maintained and should be protected from this.	Border Uplands North York Moors and Hills Pennine Dales Fringe
Cardamine impatiens narrow-leaved bitter-cress	LR-ns	Shaded places including grikes in limestone pavement, deciduous woodland, scree, riverbanks and damp roadsides, often on calcareous rocks.	• Prevent the destruction of limestone pavement.	Clun and North West Herefordshire Hills Cumbria Fells & Dales Dark Peak White Peak Yorkshire Dales
Carex digitata fingered sedge	LR-ns	Open woods and on scree and the shaded ledges of limestone quarries. Always on soil with a high calcium content, high pH (7.3-8.0), good drainage and some protection from drying-out. Some shade is required but the plants will die out under dense shade, leaving dormant seed which will germinate following disturbance.	• Prevent destruction of limestone pavement and afforestation. • Woodland management such as lopping, felling, clearing of rides or coppicing would benefit this species at some sites.	Cumbria Fells & Dales North York Moors and Hills Pennine Dales Fringe Shropshire Hills White Peak

Plant species	Status	Habitat requirements	Management requirements	Distribution by upland Natural Area
Carex muricata muricata prickly sedge	CR Priority	Bushy and grassy areas on steep, dry limestone slopes. It may be intolerant of heavy grazing and is found in rather scrubby sites.[4] But may also be out-competed in the absence of grazing.[5]	• Prevent succession towards woodland. • Avoid heavy grazing, but do not eliminate grazing. • See Species Action Plan (UK Biodiversity Group 1998).	Yorkshire Dales
Carex ornithopoda bird's-foot sedge	LR-nt	Open, calcareous grassland on Carboniferous limestone, often on thin, parched soils, which require light grazing to maintain the open character of the vegetation. See Table 6.2.	• Maintain light or moderate levels of grazing.	Cumbria Fells & Dales North Pennines White Peak Yorkshire Dales
Circaea alpina Alpine enchanter's nightshade	LR-ns	Open and usually shaded or north-facing seepage areas or stream sides. The main method of reproduction is probably by rhizome but it does fruit freely. It may have declined owing to competition with the closely related and much more vigorous hybrid, *C.* x *intermedia*. See Table 8.1.	• Protect sites from drainage.	North Pennines White Peak Yorkshire Dales Cumbria Fells & Dales
Dianthus deltoides maiden pink	LR-ns	In sandy grassland or heath and amongst detritus on rocky exposures, especially on sunny slopes on soils with some base content, such as those derived from Silurian sandstones, basalt, mica-schist or Carboniferous limestone. Usually growing where the sward is broken by bare rock or soil. In Derbyshire it grows in fairly tall species-rich vegetation on metalliferous spoil. Although susceptible to heavy grazing, at many sites it requires some grazing to maintain an open sward.	• Control levels of grazing and other disturbance to moderate levels. • See Species Action Plan (UK Biodiversity Group 1998).	Border Uplands Clun & North West Herefordshire Hills Dark Peak North Pennines North York Moors and Hills Shropshire Hills White Peak
Draba muralis wall whitlow grass	LR-ns	An overwintering annual of Carboniferous limestone, growing on open, unstable soils with a pH of more than 6.5, on stony ground such as the edges of screes or quarry debris where there is enough soil to support it, sometimes in very open ash woodland. It avoids the shallowest and driest soils.[6]	• Protect sites from habitat destruction.	Border Uplands Dark Peak Forest of Bowland White Peak Yorkshire Dales

Plant species	Status	Habitat requirements	Management requirements	Distribution by upland Natural Area
Dryas octopetala mountain avens	LR-ns	Shallow, well drained soil over limestone or base-rich rock. See Table 5.1.	• At some sites, the populations need to be protected from erosion caused by walkers or heavy grazing by livestock or rabbits.	North Pennines Yorkshire Dales Cumbria Fells & Dales
Dryopteris submontana rigid buckler-fern	LR-ns	Pockets of moist, freely draining soils in Carboniferous limestone pavement, cliffs or rough screes. It needs some protection from grazing and from strong winds, thriving best where there is a layer of at least 15-20 cm of reasonably sheltered but not stagnant air above its rhizome. Such conditions are usually found in the bigger grikes or amongst large boulders but some plants grow on the surface amongst scrubby wood of yew, juniper or hawthorn. It is intolerant of heavy shade.[2]	• Sites should be protected from limestone quarrying and removal of limestone pavement. • Grazing levels should be controlled to preferably light, or moderate, levels to encourage the establishment of young plants.	Cumbria Fells & Dales Forest of Bowland North Pennines White Peak Yorkshire Dales
Epipactis atrorubens dark-red helleborine	LR-ns	Carboniferous or magnesian limestone scree or pavement. Sites include exposed, bare scree, well wooded limestone pavement and especially wide, shallow grikes filled with small, broken scree in thinly wooded situations. Damage by deer and rabbits reduces its reproductive capacity, and often only inaccessible spikes set seed. It does not tolerate deep shade, nor heavy browsing or grazing, particularly in summer.	• Limestone pavement, cliffs and some screes may not require management. • Some sites need protection from quarrying of limestone. • Light grazing or cutting of scrub may benefit some populations; grazing by sheep between September to April to leave a sward of about 10 cm tall with up to 10% bare ground is suggested for grazed sites. • See Rich (1997) for more details.	Cumbria Fells & Dales North Pennines White Peak Yorkshire Dales
Euphrasia ostenfeldii	LR-ns	Exposed and very well drained habitats, usually with very limited cover of vascular plants, including limestone rock ledges and fine gravel screes.	• Protect sites from habitat destruction.	Cumbria Fells & Dales

Plant species	Status	Habitat requirements	Management requirements	Distribution by upland Natural Area
Gymnocarpium robertianum limestone fern	LR-ns	Broken ground, usually cracks and fissures, on limestone screes and pavement. It thrives on sunny, exposed rocks and can tolerate light woodland cover, sometimes occurring in shady grikes, but not dense shade or stagnant air. It seems to be sensitive to pressure of grazing, especially by sheep but also rabbits and deer; it can be slowly excluded if dense growths of dog's mercury or hawthorn develop.[2]	• Protect sites from limestone quarrying and removal of limestone pavement. • Prevent excessive growth of dense woodland. • Some sites may require grazing to be controlled if this species is to thrive.	Black Mountains and Golden Valley Cumbria Fells & Dales Exmoor and the Quantocks North Pennines Oswestry Uplands Southern Pennines White Peak Yorkshire Dales
Helianthemum canum hoary rock-rose	LR-ns	Limestone exposures and cliffs, especially in exposed south-facing sites prone to summer drought. Often on the upper parts of exposures and in sparse vegetation on shallow soil near the edges of cliffs. Moderate grazing may allow the species to colonise adjacent grassland.[4]	• Protect sites from habitat destruction.	Cumbria Fells & Dales North Pennines
Helianthemum canum spp *laevigatum* hoary rock-rose	VU, EE	On granular sugar limestone, on loose and open gravel and in more open grassland. Often on humus-rich but skeletal soil on a broken rocky slope. Growth and reproduction are suppressed by heavy grazing by sheep or rabbits.	• Those parts of the population currently protected from grazing should continue to be fenced. • Grazing in other areas should if possible be reduced.	North Pennines
Hornungia petraea Hutchinsia	LR-ns	In open vegetation with bare soil which is dry in summer and moist in winter, on south or southwest facing slopes on Carboniferous limestone. A certain amount of disturbance by grazing can be beneficial.	• Protect sites from habitat destruction.	Cumbria Fells & Dales Oswestry Uplands White Peak Yorkshire Dales
Hypericum linariifolium toadflax-leaved St. John's-wort	LR-nt	Steep rocky slopes with a southerly aspect in open areas surrounded by woodland in steep inland valleys, where thin soils have developed over acid rocks. It is a poor competitor and needs patches of bare soil to germinate. Past declines have been associated with invasion of scrub onto formerly open habitats and fire is also considered to be a risk to the species. It may be that the species is also vulnerable to introgression with *Hypericum humifusum*.	• Where relevant, scrub removal should be used to keep the vegetation open. • So far as possible sites should be protected from fire damage.	Dartmoor

Plant species	Status	Habitat requirements	Management requirements	Distribution by upland Natural Area
Meconopsis cambrica Welsh poppy	LR-ns, I	Moist, shady, rocky places, often under trees and usually on base-rich soils.	• Protect sites from destruction	Exmoor and the Quantocks
Minuartia hybrida fine-leaved sandwort	LR-ns	Dry, weathered, calcareous rocky slopes, also quarries, old walls, road verges and railway banks and sidings. In arable and grassland sites it is susceptible to agricultural 'improvement'.	• Protect sites from destruction. • Where relevant, protect sites from damaging agricultural practices.	Pennine Dales Fringe White Peak Yorkshire Dales
Minuartia verna spring sandwort	LR-ns	Open or semi-open short grassland over calcareous rocks, among limestone rocks and scree or on old lead and zinc mine spoil, often associated with sites liable to soil erosion. Also on base-rich rock ledges and gullies, often at high altitude. The distribution is mainly restricted to sites with an annual rainfall of at least 100 cm and the species is susceptible to summer drought.[7] It is threatened by insufficient grazing, which allows the sward to become too closed for the species.[4]	• Protect major sites from destruction. • Where possible, sites should be heavily grazed. Other forms of disturbance may be required where heavy grazing cannot be arranged.	Cumbria Fells & Dales Dark Peak North Pennines Pennine Dales Fringe South West Peak White Peak Yorkshire Dales
Orobanche alba thyme broomrape	LR-ns	Parasitic on plants of thyme on rocky slopes below low cliffs. Newly germinated seedlings can be damaged by grazing, especially by rabbits.	• Protect sites from destruction.	Yorkshire Dales

Plant species	Status	Habitat requirements	Management requirements	Distribution by upland Natural Area
Polemonium caeruleum Jacob's-ladder	LR-nt	Cool, moist, north-facing slopes of Carboniferous limestone. It is sensitive to drought and relies on a damp microclimate, often on damp north-facing slopes with a light canopy of trees or scrub, on thin organic soils. Grazing suppresses flowering and is thought generally to be undesirable, but on those sites prone to succession to woodland, very light and occasional grazing might be needed to maintain the appropriate structure of the vegetation. Cattle are thought to cause less damage than sheep.[8] See Table 8.1.	• The following management prescriptions are thought appropriate but are still experimental. • Where sites are part of grazing units, grazing by cattle between early September and the end of December for one in every three years; density of stock should be low enough to prevent poaching. • Occasional mowing or strimming, for example once every three years may be a substitute where grazing is not practicable. • Where populations are confined by grazing to ledges, fencing off the adjacent vegetation and reducing grazing there may allow the population to expand. • Where plants grow in dense shade, thinning of the canopy may benefit the plants. • For more details, see Rich (1997).	Border Uplands Yorkshire Dales Dark Peak
Polygonatum odoratum angular Solomon's-seal	LR-ns	Limestone in ancient woodland or limestone pavement, preferring well drained steep slopes or small cliffs. Plants do not appear readily able to colonise new sites.	• Protect sites from quarrying of limestone and removal of limestone pavement.	Yorkshire Dales Cumbria Fells & Dales White Peak
Potentilla crantzii alpine cinquefoil	LR-ns	Steep, dry faces and ledges of calcareous and base-rich rocks or close-grazed calcareous grassland. See Table 5.1.	• Populations which are accessible to stock should be protected from heavy grazing.	Cumbria Fells & Dales North Pennines White Peak Yorkshire Dales
Potentilla fruticosa shrubby cinquefoil	LR-ns	In Teesdale, in cracks between boulders in the bedrock of river banks and islands and on silty stabilised shingle banks and islands. In the Lake District on rock ledges and cracks in rock faces. See Table 5.1.	• Protect sites from habitat destruction. • Protect from grazing.	Cumbria Fells & Dales North Pennines Pennine Dales Fringe
Potentilla neumanniana spring cinquefoil	LR-ns	Open vegetation on seasonally parched, skeletal soils in base-rich habitats, such as limestone crags and scree. It can persist under light scrub but disappears with prolonged exposure to shade. Some, mainly lowland, sites have been lost as rank vegetation and scrub develops with the cessation of grazing.	• Some sites may require control of rank grasses or scrub, by cutting or grazing.	Cumbria Fells & Dales Oswestry Uplands White Peak Yorkshire Dales

Plant species	Status	Habitat requirements	Management requirements	Distribution by upland Natural Area
Ribes spicatum downy currant	LR-ns	Rocky woods on basic soils. The species is hard to identify except when in flower and is thought to be under-recorded.	• Protect major sites from habitat destruction.	Border Uplands Yorkshire Dales North Pennines Pennine Dales Fringe Cumbria Fells & Dales
Sedum forsterianum rock stonecrop	LR-ns	Open grassland on rocks and scree, usually in open, dry situations such as rock faces and broken cliffs, although occasionally in wet woodland. It seems to have become more common and may benefit from increased grazing.	• Protect major sites from destruction.	Clun & North West Herefordshire Hills Exmoor and the Quantocks Oswestry Uplands Shropshire Hills
Sesleria caerulea blue moor-grass	LR-ns	Open communities on shallow, well drained rendzina soils in areas of Carboniferous or Permian limestone. Also in scree, crevices and ledges of scars, extending some way onto the usually non-calcareous overlying drift so long as this is shallow. Sometimes found in the light shade of limestone ash woodland. Moderate grazing seems to benefit the species.[4]	• Protect major sites from destruction. • Moderate grazing should be maintained.	Border Uplands Cumbria Fells & Dales Pennine Dales Fringe North Pennines White Peak Yorkshire Dales
Sibthorpia europaea Cornish moneywort	LR-ns	Humid microclimates in sheltered sites on acidic soils and rocks. Often growing above small streams and ditches, usually shaded, also at the edge of granite massifs where there are numerous streams.	• Protect sites from changes in the hydrology and water regime.	Bodmin Moor Dartmoor Exmoor and the Quantocks
Sorbus lancastriensis	LR-nt, EE	Rocky scrub and woodland on Carboniferous limestone.	• Protect major sites from habitat destruction and damage to individual trees.	Cumbria Fells & Dales
Sorbus porrigentiformis	LR-ns, E	Rooted into the crevices of cliffs and exposures of Carboniferous limestone or Old Red Sandstone, usually in well lit places, sometimes under a canopy of trees.	• Protect sites from destruction.	Exmoor and the Quantocks

Plant species	Status	Habitat requirements	Management requirements	Distribution by upland Natural Area
Sorbus rupicola	LR-ns	Steep rocky slopes or cliffs of limestone.	• Protect major sites from destruction.	Cumbria Fells & Dales Exmoor and the Quantocks North Pennines Oswestry Uplands White Peak Yorkshire Dales
Sorbus vexans	VU, EE	Open woodland of sessile oak *Quercus petraea* on steep slopes of Old Red Sandstone or slate.	• Protect sites from destruction. • If the populations become threatened by the spread of rhododendron, then this should be controlled.	Exmoor and the Quantocks
Thlaspi caerulescens alpine penny-cress	LR-ns	A pioneer colonist of metalliferous mine wastes and river gravels contaminated with lead, zinc and cadmium, often in limestone areas but also on shales. Usually in open vegetation but able to persist in a more closed turf. It is threatened by insufficient grazing, which allows the sward to become too closed for the species.[4] See Table 5.1.	• Protect major sites from destruction. • Where possible, sites should be heavily grazed. Other forms of disturbance may be required where heavy grazing cannot be arranged.	Border Uplands North Pennines White Peak Yorkshire Dales
Trichomanes speciosum Killarney fern	Sched. 8 of WCA Annex IIb VU Priority	The larger, vascular form of this fern, or sporophyte, is extremely rare and grows in conditions of high humidity, permanent running groundwater and extreme shelter, often in very low light. Typically it is found in wet caves, steep-sided ravines or under over-hanging rocks, occasionally it is epiphytic on tree-boles. The gametophyte has been discovered to be much more common and new sites are still found regularly, in very dark, damp recesses in natural rock, often sandstone or shales. It reproduces asexually and persists at very low levels of light where competition, even from bryophytes and algae, is minimal.[3]	Research into the management needs of this species is on-going. **Sporophyte:** • Maintain the microclimate, particularly the water regime and water quality. • Protect sites from the attentions of collectors by maintaining strict confidentiality. **Gametophyte:** • Protect known sites from habitat destruction until the autecology and distribution of the species are better understood. • See Species Action Plan (UK Steering Group 1995).	**Sporophyte**: Cumbria Fells & Dales, Pennine Dales Fringe. **Gametophyte**: Border Uplands, Cumbria Fells & Dales, Dark Peak, Dartmoor, Exmoor and the Quantocks, North York Moors and Hills, Pennine Dales Fringe, Southern Pennines, South West Peak, Yorkshire Dales[9]

Plant species	**Status**	**Habitat requirements**	**Management requirements**	**Distribution by upland Natural Area**
Veronica spicata ssp. *hybrida* spiked speedwell	LR-ns	On rocks or shallow soil on cliff ledges, in crevices, on cliff tops and exposures mostly of Carboniferous limestone. It is moderately tolerant of shade and competition but can be out-competed by the development of scrub of native or introduced species. It will tolerate but not flower under heavy grazing.	• Protect sites from destruction. • Where necessary, control the spread of scrub. • Stock should be excluded from grazed sites from June to September to optimise seed production (Rich 1997).	Cumbria Fells & Dales Yorkshire Dales
Woodsia ilvensis oblong woodsia	Sched. 8 of WCA LR-nt Priority	Among hard, neutral igneous rocks facing north. See Table 5.1.	• Populations of this species have been damaged by collecting in the past and are still considered to be vulnerable. Site confidentiality should be maintained. • See Species Action Plan (UK Biodiversity Group 1998).	Cumbria Fells & Dales

Key to Table 10.1

Annex IIb	- listed on Annex IIb of the EC Habitats and Species Directive
Sched. 8 of WCA	- listed on schedule 8 of the Wildlife & Countryside Act.

Red list categories

CR	- critically endangered
EN	- endangered
VU	- vulnerable
DD	- data deficient
LR -nt	- Lower risk - near threatened
LR-ns	- Lower risk - nationally scarce
E	- endemic to Great Britain
EE	- endemic to England.

Biodiversity Action Plan (BAP)

Priority	- Priority species from UK Steering Group 1995 and UK Biodiversity Group 1998.
SCC	- Species of conservation concern from UK Steering Group 1995 and UK Biodiversity Group 1998.

Sources

Most information from Hodgetts, Palmer & Wigginton 1996; Porley & McDonnell 1997; Stewart, Pearman & Preston 1994; Wigginton 1999.

1. K. Hearn, pers comm
2. Page 1982.
3. R. Cooke, pers comm
4. I. Taylor, pers comm
5. R. Goodison, pers comm
6. Rich 1991.
7. Grime, Hodgson & Hunt 1990.
8. Rich 1997.
9. F. Rumsey, pers comm.

Table 10.2 Nationally rare and scarce bryophytes associated with crags, scree and limestone pavement in England

Plant species	Status	Typical habitat	Distribution by upland Natural Area
Aloina ambigua	LR-ns	Floors of limestone quarries, also on banks, soil, crumbling mortar on walls and on base-rich sandstone.	Bodmin Moor Cumbria Fells & Dales
Amblyodon dealbatus	LR-ns	Cliffs and gravel where flushed by calcareous water. See Table 6.2.	Border Uplands Cumbria Fells & Dales North Pennines Yorkshire Dales
Amblystegium compactum	LR-ns	In extensive, dense mats on limestone in deep shade, including damp rocks and soil below overhanging crags.	Border Uplands Pennine Dales Fringe South West Peak
Amblystegium confervoides	LR-ns	A calcicolous species typically occurring on limestone rock in shaded sites, usually in woodland. It is found in deep clefts in rock-faces, or on vertical faces of rock-scars or boulders, often amongst or shaded by robust bryophytes. Also growing on lumps of limestone on the ground in woodland and on damp basic rocks in the hills.	Forest of Bowland Pennine Dales Fringe South West Peak
Andreaea rothii subsp. *rothii*	LR-ns	On more-or-less exposed, periodically wet, acid rock.	Dark Peak
Anomobryum filiforme var. *concinnatum*	LR-ns	Montane and lowland rocks. See Table 5.2.	Border Uplands Yorkshire Dales
Anomodon longifolius	EN	On shaded, steep or vertical limestone or basic sandstone rocks, often in wooded valleys and ravines and on limestone rock-ledges.	Pennine Dales Fringe
Barbilophozia atlantica	LR-ns	Dry acid block-screes, rocky ravines, loch-side boulders and shady sandstone crags and river gorges.	Cumbria Fells & Dales Dark Peak Border Uplands South West Peak Yorkshire Dales
Bartramia hallerana	LR-ns	On usually dry, moderately calcareous rock crevices and overhangs in wooded ravines and on mountain cliffs.	Cumbria Fells and Dales Yorkshire Dales
Brachydontium trichodes	LR-ns	On vertical or slightly overhanging faces of ravines, mountain cliffs and boulders, on the sides of small boulders in stony flushes and on stones in stable screes and old quarries. Unshaded sites probably always have a north to east aspect. The substrate, which may be moderately calcareous to strongly acid, is most commonly sandstone but can be any of a wide range of soft siliceous rocks, including the crumbling weathered surfaces of igneous rocks such as granite and basalt.	Cumbria Fells & Dales Bodmin Moor Border Uplands North Pennines South West Peak

Plant species	Status	Typical habitat	Distribution by upland Natural Area
Bryum elegans	LR-ns	Limestone rocks and turf. See Table 5.2.	Forest of Bowland Yorkshire Dales
Bryum intermedium	LR-ns	A calcicole forming green tufts on bare damp soil in sand dunes and quarries, on roadsides and waste ground, sometimes also on rock ledges and walls. This species is widely overlooked and probably occurs in many upland Natural Areas.	Border Uplands Cumbria Fells & Dales (and probably others)
Bryum pallescens	LR-ns	In dense tufts, green above and reddish-brown below, on soil in quarries, in crevices in rocks and walls, on concrete and mine-waste. It is tolerant of heavy metals. This species is widely overlooked and probably occurs in many upland Natural Areas.	Cumbria Fells and Dales Forest of Bowland (and probably others)
Bryum riparium	LR-ns	Crevices in rocks in stream-beds and other habitats. See Table 6.3.	Cumbria Fells and Dales Forest of Bowland
Calypogeia integristipula	LR-ns	Sandstone and gritstone rocks, and sandy or peaty banks in woodland and other shaded lowland and montane places. See Table 5.2.	Border Uplands North Pennines South West Peak Yorkshire Dales
Campylium calcareum	LR-ns	A strong calcicole, growing on limestone rocks and earth. See Table 8.2.	Border Uplands North Pennines North Yorkshire Moors & Hills White Peak Yorkshire Dales
Campylopus schwarzii	LR-ns	Among and on wet rocks. See Table 6.2.	Cumbria Fells & Dales
Campylopus setifolius	LR-ns	Found in a variety of moist acid habitats including on rock ledges and in block-screes. See Table 6.2.	Cumbria Fells & Dales
Campylopus subulatus	LR-ns	Unshaded, acid, gravelly and sandy places. See Table 6.2.	Forest of Bowland Cumbria Fells & Dales Bodmin Moor
Campylostelium saxicola	LR-ns	Wet or periodically flushed, acid or mildly basic sandstone, shale or slate blocks and stones in low-lying shaded ravines, gullies and wooded rivulets; also in damp crevices in bedded sandstone walls of shaded wooded ravines.	Border Uplands Cumbria Fells & Dales
Cephaloziella massalongi	VU	Confined to copper-bearing rocks and associated soils, chiefly on stony slopes of mine waste or the silt washed from it and in wall crevices around disused copper mines, in moist to wet situations.	Bodmin Moor

Plant species	Status	Typical habitat	Distribution by upland Natural Area
Cephaloziella nicholsonii Greater copperwort	LR-nt, E Priority	Confined to copper-bearing rocks and associated soils, chiefly on stony stream-sides influenced by copper-rich rocks.	Bodmin Moor Exmoor and the Quantocks
Cephaloziella stellulifera	LR-ns	Most records are from mine-waste or from coastal sites, where it grows on heathland, soil in rock crevices on cliffs and in turf on cliff-tops. Also occasionally on heathy tracks or sandy ditch-banks inland, especially in plantations.	Bodmin Moor Exmoor and the Quantocks North Pennines Pennine Dales Fringe
Cololejeunea rossettiana	LR-ns	On shaded basic rocks, often limestone, in gorges, streams and woods and amongst other bryophytes or as pure patches on sheltered limestone rocks, cliffs and caves. Typically on dry rocks in humid situations but occasionally epiphytic on other bryophytes.	Cumbria Fells & Dales Forest of Bowland North Pennines Pennine Dales Fringe White Peak Yorkshire Dales
Colura calyptrifolia	LR-ns	Forming small dense pure patches or as scattered stems amongst other liverworts on damp, shaded rocks and boulders in humid situations including sheltered ravines, rocky gorges, low-lying wooded stream sides, lake sides and damp north- or east-facing montane cliffs. Also epiphytic on heather stems on steep, shaded block-strewn slopes and on conifer trunks. Favours mildly basic rocks.	Cumbria Fells & Dales Yorkshire Dales
Coscinodon cribrosus	LR-ns	On dry, very acidic, frequently friable slate or shale, in exposures or on walls. Also sometimes on harder rocks such as granite.	Cumbria Fells & Dales North York Moors and Hills Yorkshire Dales
Cynodontium jenneri	LR-ns	Acid rocks, usually sheltered or in light shade, rarely on stone walls, occasionally on sandy soils in woodland.	Cumbria Fells & Dales
Dicranella crispa	LR-ns	In a wide variety of habitats but apparently absent from markedly acid or basic substrates. Most typical on disturbed open soil on banks of gravel, clay, loam or sand by roads, rivers and streams. Also on rocks, especially vertical sandstone.	Yorkshire Dales
Dicranodontium uncinatum	LR-ns	On acid humus in sheltered moist north- to east-facing sites such as under heather on rocky slopes and on mountain cliff-ledges. At lower altitudes, locally abundant on north-facing periodically irrigated near-vertical rock-faces and in similar sites in wooded ravines.	Cumbria Fells & Dales Forest of Bowland

Plant species	Status	Typical habitat	Distribution by upland Natural Area
Didymodon nicholsonii	LR-ns	Stones and tree roots on the banks of streams and rivers where subject to periodic flooding, sometimes embedded in alluvial sand or detritus.	Cumbria Fells & Dales Border Uplands Forest of Bowland Yorkshire Dales
Ditrichum cornubicum Cornish path-moss	CR, EE Priority	Only known location in the world is from copper-mine waste in two granite areas of Cornwall. See Species Action Plan (UK Steering Group 1995).	Bodmin Moor
Ditrichum plumbicola	LR-nt	Restricted to lead-mine spoil that is largely devoid of vascular plants, occurring in small pure patches or as scattered plants.	North Pennines
Encalypta rhaptocarpa	LR-ns	Dry or seasonally moist crevices and crumbling earthy ledges on limestone, highly calcareous schists or basalt or other soft, basic igneous rocks. See Table 5.2.	North Pennines Yorkshire Dales
Eurhynchium striatulum	LR-ns	A strict calcicole, confined in the uplands to areas of limestone where it occurs on dry shaded stones, rocks, walls and tree-roots, often forming quite extensive patches.	Yorkshire Dales
Fissidens limbatus	LR-ns	On compacted soil or on thin soil over rock. See Table 8.2.	Cumbria Fells & Dales Exmoor and the Quantocks Forest of Bowland White Peak
Funaria muhlenbergii	LR-ns	A calcicole forming yellowish green patches or found as scattered shoot on bare soil among rocks, in turf, on anthills or on thinly earth-covered rocks.	Cumbria Fells & Dales Oswestry Uplands White Peak Yorkshire Dales
Glyphomitrium daviesii	LR-ns	On dry, exposed, often sun-exposed or periodically irrigated south- or west-facing exposures or boulders of basic igneous rocks-such as basalt, gabbro and peridotite.	Cumbria Fells & Dales
Grimmia arenaria	LR-nt	In crevices of hard slatey rocks, especially on roadside walls.	Cumbria Fells & Dales
Grimmia atrata	LR-ns	Heavy-metal-bearing rocks. See Table 5.2.	Cumbria Fells & Dales
Grimmia laevigata	LR-ns	On exposed acidic to slightly basic rock, on cliffs, on exposures, by rivers and on roofing slates.	Dartmoor Exmoor and the Quantocks Oswestry Uplands White Peak

Plant species	Status	Typical habitat	Distribution by upland Natural Area
Grimmia lisae	LR-ns	Forming tufts, usually silt- and grit-encrusted, on rocks below flood-level beside streams and rivers and by lakes. Also found occasionally on rock exposures away from water. Sometimes locally abundant.	Cumbria Fells & Dales
Grimmia montana	LR-ns	On hard, exposed granite.	Cumbria Fells & Dales Dartmoor Shropshire Hills
Grimmia orbicularis	LR-ns	Usually on exposed dry rocks, especially Carboniferous limestone and on walls; commonly associated with rocks with a high heavy-metal content. It is apparently susceptible to atmospheric pollution.	Border Uplands Cumbria Fells & Dales White Peak
Grimmia ovalis	VU	Forming tufts or cushions on dry exposed basic to neutral rocks, especially basalt and dolerite.	North Pennines Cumbria Fells & Dales[1]
Gymnostomum calcareum	LR-ns	On limestone rocks or calcareous basalt, particularly where soft, slightly moist and shaded; very rarely on the mortar of walls. Usually in low-lying, sheltered situations.	Pennine Dales Fringe White Peak Yorkshire Dales
Hedwigia integrifolia	LR-ns	On dry, acid or mildly basic angular detached boulders, usually sun-exposed with a south to west aspect, in block screes, on moorland and below cliffs. Most frequent on basic igneous rocks of gabbro, basalt, dolerite, tuff and peridotite and is absent from cliff-faces and artificial habitats except, rarely, dry stone walls. Mainly at low and moderate altitudes.	Cumbria Fells & Dales
Hypnum hamulosum	LR-ns	A calcicole of sheltered rocks. See Table 5.2.	Cumbria Fells and Dales
Jungermannia subelliptica	LR-ns	In moist habitats on rocks. See Table 5.2.	Border Uplands Cumbria Fells & Dales Exmoor and the Quantocks Forest of Bowland
Lophozia gillmanii	LR-nt	Mossy, constantly-irrigated basic rock ledges and in mossy base-rich flushes and rocks by streams.	Yorkshire Dales
Lophozia heterocolpos	LR-ns	On damp calcareous rocks. See Table 5.2.	North Pennines Yorkshire Dales
Mielichhoferia mielichhoferiana var. *elongata*	VU	On vertical faces of shale in a series of narrow, steep gullies with constantly trickling streams.	North Yorkshire Moors & Hills

Plant species	Status	Typical habitat	Distribution by upland Natural Area
Mnium thomsonii	LR-ns	In dense, pale green/red tufts or patches on basic rock-ledges and in crevices in basic rocks.	Cumbria Fells & Dales White Peak Yorkshire Dales
Myurella julacea var. *julacea*	LR-ns	Usually as scattered shoots growing amongst other base-loving bryophytes on dry or slightly irrigated soil in cracks on calcareous rock ledges, usually of north to east aspect.	Yorkshire Dales
Nardia geoscyphus	LR-ns	On moist basic soil on rock ledges and at the foot of mountain cliffs; also on sandstone rocks or on sandy or peaty soil in wet heaths or by water, often on banks. The habitat ranges from relatively dry to very wet, including stream sides and lake shores, sometimes submerged for most of the winter.	Border Uplands Dark Peak Dartmoor Forest of Bowland North Pennines Oswestry Uplands Southern Pennines South West Peak
Orthothecium rufescens	LR-ns	Forming dense, vinous-red silky patches on damp, periodically flushed north- to east-facing steep, often vertical sheltered montane or sub-montane cliff-faces of limestone, calcareous mica-schist, basalt or other basic volcanic rocks; also on damp, shaded limestone walls of low-lying ravines.	Cumbria Fells & Dales Yorkshire Dales
Pedinophyllum interruptum	LR-ns	On sheltered moist Carboniferous limestone rock ledges and ravine walls, less often on boulders. In one site, on Millstone Grit which receives basic floodwater.	Cumbria Fells & Dales North Pennines Yorkshire Dales
Philonotis arnellii	LR-ns	Circum-neutral non-calcareous soil and rock crevices in intermittently flooded or flushed places, typically on crumbling earth on rocky banks in light shade; also woodland rides, heathy tracks, mud, floors of quarries and basic mountain-cliffs.	Border Uplands Cumbria Fells & Dales Forest of Bowland Shropshire Hills
Philonotis caespitosa	LR-ns	On moist or wet non-calcareous soil and rocks, where flushed or flooded by slightly basic mineral-rich water, for example in springs, stream sides, ditches, marshes, boggy fields, margins of lakes and reservoirs, track sides, quarries and dripping rocks.	Bodmin Moor Border Uplands Cumbria Fells & Dales Dark Peak Exmoor and the Quantocks Forest of Bowland Pennine Dales Fringe Southern Pennines Yorkshire Dales

Plant species	Status	Typical habitat	Distribution by upland Natural Area
Plagiopus oederiana	LR-ns	On basic rock-ledges and in crevices, such as gills, ravines and valley woods, wooded limestone scars and north-facing crags. It grows mostly on hard calcareous rocks, typically at moderate altitudes on the Carboniferous Limestone of northern England, but sometimes ascending to high mountain cliffs and gullies.	Cumbria Fells & Dales North Pennines White Peak Yorkshire Dales
Plagiothecium cavifolium	LR-ns	On moist, basic mountain rock-ledges, where it may be associated with a wide variety of other calcicoles. Less often on siliceous rock-ledges at lower altitudes, sometimes where the basic influence is only slight.	Cumbria Fells & Dales Yorkshire Dales
Plagiothecium laetum	LR-ns	Woodland and among boulders. See Table 8.2.	Cumbria Fells & Dales Border Uplands Clun & North West Herefordshire Hills North Yorkshire Moors & Hills Shropshire Hills South West Peak
Pleurochaete squarrosa	LR-ns	In limestone grassland, in turf on sea-cliffs and on stony limestone ground, rarely on limestone pavement. It may grow in scrubby ground and in light shade, but is most common in open habitats. Inland it is most common on open, stony, unproductive calcareous soils.	Bodmin Moor Cumbria Fells & Dales Exmoor and the Quantocks South West Peak
Pohlia filum	LR-ns	A calcifuge species almost exclusively confined to soils of very low organic content. It grows mostly on damp sandy or gravelly soils, by streams and rivers, on rocks, on sandy tracks and roadsides.	Border Uplands
Pohlia flexuosa	LR-ns	On moist sandy or gritty soils in rocky places by streams and waterfalls in montane regions, often in very sheltered locations which are noted for hygrophilous liverworts. Also steep sandy riverbanks and less frequently in rock crevices.	Bodmin Moor Dark Peak Cumbria Fells & Dales Forest of Bowland Southern Pennines
Pseudoleskea catenulata var. *catenulata*	LR-ns	Forming dense dark- or olive-green patches on calcareous rocks in the hills on Carboniferous limestone, preferring dry open sites, often south-facing, where there is little competition. See Table 5.2.	North Pennines Yorkshire Dales
Racomitrium affine	LR-ns	On moist or intermittently moist acid rocks, walls and roof tiles.	Cumbria Fells & Dales

Plant species	Status	Typical habitat	Distribution by upland Natural Area
Racomitrium sudeticum	LR-ns	On dry or moist acid rocks, occasionally on soil in the mountains.	Cumbria Fells & Dales Dark Peak Dartmoor North Pennines Yorkshire Dales
Radula aquilegia	LR-ns	Most frequently as pure patches growing on mildly basic boulders and vertical rock-walls in wet, wooded ravines, in the submontane or even montane zone.	Cumbria Fells & Dales
Rhabdoweisia crenulata	LR-ns	On shaded ledges and crevices of siliceous rock in humid or damp situations, often under overhangs. Typically on north-facing crags, among boulders in scree and in ravines, especially near waterfalls. Usually on acid substrates but occasionally on basic rock. See Table 5.2.	Border Uplands Cumbria Fells & Dales Yorkshire Dales
Rhynchostegiella curviseta	LR-ns	Damp stones, tree-roots, walls and banks. See Table 8.2.	Exmoor and the Quantocks
Rhytidium rugosum	LR-ns	Open grassland and on limestone rock-ledges. See Table 6.3.	Cumbria Fells & Dales North Pennines White Peak Yorkshire Dales
Riccia subbifurca	LR-ns	On moist, thinly vegetated soil on rock-ledges and rocky slopes, banks of lanes, streams and ditches, the edges of pools and reservoirs and in gardens and arable fields. Usually on acidic soils but also over limestone and basic igneous rocks.	Bodmin Moor Yorkshire Dales
Scapania praetervisa	VU	Wet limestone boulders and rock exposures on river banks.	Yorkshire Dales
Schistidium agassizii	LR-nt	On rocks and stones at or near the flood-zone of fast-flowing rivers and large streams.	Cumbria Fells & Dales North Pennines
Schistostega pennata	LR-ns	A calcifuge species of shaded soil and rocks. See Table 8.2.	Bodmin Moor Dartmoor Exmoor and the Quantocks Shropshire Hills Southern Pennines South West Peak Yorkshire Dales

Plant species	Status	Typical habitat	Distribution by upland Natural Area
Seligeria acutifolia	LR-ns	On moist, shaded limestone rocks, where it grows in crevices and under overhanging rocks.	North Pennines White Peak Yorkshire Dales
Seligeria brevifolia	VU	A single small tuft on Millstone Grit in a moist, shaded situation under overhanging rock.	Dark Peak
Seligeria donniana	LR-ns	On shaded or well-sheltered calcareous rocks, usually limestone, most often on cliffs but also in crevices, under overhangs, in the entrances to pot-holes and on small limestone fragments on the ground in woodland.	Dark Peak North Pennines Oswestry Uplands White Peak Yorkshire Dales
Seligeria pusilla	LR-ns	A minute plant of shaded basic rocks such as the vertical and overhanging surfaces of cliffs and ravine walls, especially on limestone but also sometimes on basalt and calcareous sandstone.	Border Uplands Cumbria Fells & Dales Dark Peak Forest of Bowland North Pennines White Peak Yorkshire Dales
Seligeria trifaria	LR-ns	On lightly shaded, vertical or overhanging Carboniferous limestone rocks down which water seeps. Occasionally in similar situations on other hard limestone.	North Pennines Yorkshire Dales
Targionia hypophylla	LR-ns	On earthy, sandy or rocky roadside banks and on thin layers of soil over walls and rocks; usually in sites which dry out in summer. Although not a strict calcicole, it is often associated with limestone or basic igneous rocks.	White Peak Cumbria Fells & Dales[1]
Thamnobryum angustifolium Derbyshire feather-moss	CR, EE Priority	On a shaded limestone rock in a ravine, growing by a calcareous spring, where it is inundated in winter but dry in summer. See Species Action Plan (UK Steering Group 1995).	White Peak
Tortella densa	LR-ns	In the crevices of limestone rocks and more rarely on bare soil among rocks and in grassy flushes. A strong calcicole, it occurs on various types of limestone, but especially on the Carboniferous. Most stations are at moderate altitude in exposed situations. Also on heavy metal mine-waste in northwest England.	Cumbria Fells & Dales North Pennines Yorkshire Dales
Tortula subulata var. *graeffii*	LR-ns	Soil and rocks. See Table 8.2.	Yorkshire Dales
Trichostomopsis umbrosa	LR-ns	Damp, shady, calcareous places, often on mortar at the base of walls that are backed by earth, such as railway arches. Also recorded from shaded soil in old limestone quarries.	White Peak
Trochobryum carniolicum	CR	Damp calcareous sandstone or impure limestone rocks beside streams.	Border Uplands

Plant species	Status	Typical habitat	Distribution by upland Natural Area
Weissia controversa var. *crispata*	LR-ns	A calcicole of bare soils which are relatively stable and not frequently disturbed, found on cliffs, in quarries and among limestone and other calcareous rocks including limestone pavement.	Cumbria Fells & Dales
Weissia controversa var. *densifolia*	LR-ns	Open ground rich in heavy metals, especially on spoil heaps and diggings around old lead mines but also in natural habitats, such as on rotten rock-ledges in the Lake District and river gravels with high levels of zinc in Northumberland.	Bodmin Moor Exmoor and the Quantocks Forest of Bowland North Pennines
Zygodon gracilis Nowell's limestone moss	EN Priority	On Carboniferous rocks and dry stone walls in the Craven Pennines.	Yorkshire Dales

Key to Table 10.2

Annex IIb - listed on Annex IIb of the EC Habitats and Species Directive
Sched. 8 of WCA - listed on schedule 8 of the Wildlife & Countryside Act.

Red list categories
CR - critically endangered
EN - endangered
VU - vulnerable
DD - data deficient
LR-nt - Lower risk - near threatened
LR-ns - Lower risk - nationally scarce
E - endemic to Great Britain
EE - endemic to England.

Biodiversity Action Plan (BAP)
Priority - Priority species from UK Steering Group 1995 and UK Biodiversity Group 1998.
SCC - Species of conservation concern from UK Steering Group 1995 and UK Biodiversity Group 1998.

Sources
Most information from Hill, Preston & Smith 1991, 1992, 1994, and Hodgetts, Palmer & Wigginton 1996.
1. D. Ratcliffe, pers comm.

Table 10.3 Bryophytes of upland rock habitats in England: general habitat and management requirements

Plants	Habitat requirements	Management requirements
Plants growing on tors, cliffs and in gorges.	Such sites generally require minimal interference.	• Climbing and walking may need to be controlled, where important populations of bryophytes are threatened by disturbance.
Plants growing on walls, including soil-capped walls.	Relatively undisturbed walls of suitable substrate.	• Repair of walls, where unavoidable, should be carried out with care by workers who have been made aware of the whereabouts of important areas for bryophytes and using compatible materials. • Some sites may require protection from excessive trampling.
Plants growing on block screes, rock crevices and limestone pavement.	Such sites generally require minimal interference.	• Protect sites from quarrying.
Plants growing on heavy-metal-bearing rocks and soil or in quarries.	Such sites generally require minimal interference.	• Protect important sites from further excavation, either commercially or by amateurs. • Protect sites from inappropriate reclamation or landscaping.
Plants growing on rocks in and by rivers, streams and tarns.	Many such species rely on fluctuating levels and flows of unpolluted water.	• Protect important sites from regulation of flows and from drainage or forestry operations upstream which would change the yearly pattern of flows. • Protect sites from pollution by agricultural or other chemicals.

Sources

P. Lambley, pers comm and Species Action Plans (UK Biodiversity Group 1999 and UK Steering Group 1995).

Table 10.4 Examples of red list lichens of crags, scree and limestone pavement in England

Plant species	Status	Typical habitat	Distribution
Bryoria nadvornikiana	VU	Sandstone cliffs.	Northumberland
Collema fragile	VU	Limestone.	Northwest Yorkshire
Collema parvum	VU	River gorge on limestone.	Yorkshire Dales
Endocarpon adscendens	EN	Rocks by rivers.	Mid-west Yorkshire
Gyalecta ulmi elm gyalecta	Sched.8 of WCA, EN	Now only on limestone, formerly on elms.	Northumberland
Ionaspis heteromorpha	VU	Limestone at high altitudes.	Northern Pennines
Ionaspis melanocarpa	VU	Limestone pavement at about 750 m altitude.	Teesdale
Lecanora achariana tarn lecanora	Sched.8 of WCA, CR	Nutrient-enriched boulders by a tarn.	Cumbria
Lecanora epibryon	VU	Turf and dry stone walls.	North Yorkshire
Lecidea inops copper lecidea	Sched.8 of WCA, EN	Copper-rich mine waste.	Lake District
Peltigera venosa	VU	Basic soil often near waterfalls, mine-tips, cliff-ledges, and turf-capped walls.	North Pennines
Pertusaria melanochlora	EN	Sheltered boulders of dolerite.	Dartmoor
Stereocaulon symphycheilum	EN	Mine waste.	Cumbria
Umbilicaria crustulosa	VU	Crags.	Cumbria

Key to Table 10.4

Annex IIb - listed on Annex IIb of the EC Habitats and Species Directive
Sched. 8 of WCA - listed on schedule 8 of the Wildlife & Countryside Act.

Red list categories

CR - critically endangered
EN - endangered
VU - vulnerable
DD - data deficient
LR-nt - Lower risk - near threatened
LR-ns - Lower risk - nationally scarce
E - endemic to Great Britain
EE - endemic to England.

Biodiversity Action Plan (BAP)

Priority - Priority species from UK Steering Group 1995 and UK Biodiversity Group 1998.
SCC - Species of conservation concern from UK Steering Group 1995 and UK Biodiversity Group 1998.

Sources

P. Lambley, pers comm and Church *et al* 1996.

Table 10.5 Plant communities associated with crags, scree and limestone pavement in England

NVC code	NVC name[1]	Inclusion in Annex 1 of the Habitats Directive[2]	Significance in England[3]	Upland Natural Areas where community occurs
Tall-herb communities				
U15	*Saxifraga aizoides-Alchemilla glabra* banks	--	L	Cumbria Fells & Dales
U16	*Luzula sylvatica-Vaccinium myrtillus* tall-herb community	--	UK	Border Uplands North Pennines Cumbria Fells & Dales
U17	*Luzula sylvatica-Geum rivale* tall-herb community	Eutrophic tall herbs	L	Border Uplands North Pennines Yorkshire Dales/Pennine Dales Fringe Cumbria Fells & Dales
Fern communities				
U19	*Thelypteris limbosperma-Blechnum spicant* community	--	L	North Pennines Yorkshire Dales/Pennine Dales Fringe Cumbria Fells & Dales Exmoor & the Quantocks
U20	*Pteridium aquilinum-Galium saxatile* community See Chapter 6: Moorland	--	I	All upland Natural Areas except White Peak Oswestry uplands
U21	*Cryptogramma crispa-Deschampsia flexuosa* community	Siliceous scree	L	Border Uplands North Pennines Yorkshire Dales/Pennine Dales Fringe Cumbria Fells & Dales

NVC code	NVC name[1]	Inclusion in Annex 1 of the Habitats Directive[2]	Significance in England[3]	Upland Natural Areas where community occurs
Calcareous grassland				
CG9#	*Sesleria albicans-Galium sterneri* grassland See Chapter 7: Meadows and enclosed pasture	Semi-natural dry grasslands and scrubland facies on calcareous substrate (*Festuco brometalia*) (important orchid sites*)	I	Border Uplands North Pennines Yorkshire Dales/Pennine Dales Fringe Cumbria Fells & Dales Southern Pennines
Acid grassland				
U4	*Festuca ovina-Agrostis capillaris - Galium saxatile* grassland See Chapter 6: Moorland	--	L	All upland Natural Areas except Oswestry Uplands
U5	*Nardus stricta-Galium saxatile* grassland See Chapter 6: Moorland	--	L	All upland Natural Areas except Oswestry Uplands
Open vegetation				
OV37	*Festuca ovina-Minuartia verna* metalliferous grassland See Chapter 6: Moorland	--	Not specified	Yorkshire Dales/Pennine Dales Fringe White Peak
OV38#	*Gymnocarpium robertianum-Arrhenatherum elatius* community	Eutric scree	Not specified	Cumbria Fells & Dales Yorkshire Dales/Pennine Dales Fringe White Peak Oswestry Uplands
OV39#	*Asplenium trichomanes-Asplenium ruta-muraria* community	Chasmophytic vegetation on rocky slopes: Calcareous sub-types	Not specified	Cumbria Fells & Dales Yorkshire Dales/Pennine Dales Fringe White Peak
OV40#	*Asplenium viride-Cystopteris fragilis* community	Chasmophytic vegetation on rocky slopes: Calcareous sub-types	Not specified	Cumbria Fells & Dales Yorkshire Dales/Pennine Dales Fringe

NVC code	NVC name[1]	Inclusion in Annex 1 of the Habitats Directive[2]	Significance in England[3]	Upland Natural Areas where community occurs
Woodland and scrub				
W8#	*Fraxinus excelsior-Acer campestre-Mercurialis perennis* woodland See Chapter 8: Woodland and scrub	*Tilio acerion ravine* forests*	Not specified	Not specified
W9#	*Fraxinus excelsior-Sorbus aucuparia-Mercurialis perennis* woodland See Chapter 8: Woodland and scrub	*Tilio acerion ravine* forests*	Not specified	Not specified
W21#	*Crataegus monogyna-Hedera helix* scrub See Chapter 8: Woodland and scrub	*Juniperus communis* formations on heaths or calcareous grasslands	Not specified	Not specified

Key to Table 10.5

1. National Vegetation Classification (NVC) from Rodwell 1992 and 2000, status and distribution from Drewitt & Manley 1997

2. Taken from Brown *et al* 1997
   - * Priority habitat

3. Taken from Drewitt & Manley 1997
   - I Internationally scarce with UK representation
   - UK Well developed in UK but represented elsewhere
   - L Well developed in Europe
   - Note At the time of the production of this document, the two Natural Areas now known as the Yorkshire Dales (no 8) and the Pennines Dales Fringe (no 15) were combined as one Natural Areas.

\# The flora of limestone pavement is best described as encompassing elements of these community types, and limestone pavement is a priority habitat in Annex 1 of the Habitats Directive.

Table 10.6 Breeding birds associated with crags, scree and limestone pavement in England

(Note: See also Chapters 5, 6 and 7 for species predominantly of montane areas, moorland or grassland)

Bird species[1]	Birds of conservation concern in the UK[2]	Listed on Schedule 1 of the 1981 Wildlife & Countryside Act	Listed on Annex 1 of the EC Birds Directive	No of British 10 km squares with breeding records 1988-90	% of breeding records in upland ITE squares in Britain[3]	Main upland habitat associations	Principal upland Natural Areas supporting the species (including those not containing montane areas) *= major/important areas[4]
Buzzard *Buteo buteo*	-	-	-	1,174	47.6	Woodland and enclosed land	2, 4*, 8, 10*, 41*, 42*, 58*, 60*, 87*, 92*, 94*
Golden eagle *Aquila chrysaetos*	Amber list	•	•	216	88.9	Moorland and montane areas	10* extinct elsewhere
Peregrine *Falco peregrinus*	Amber list	•	•	719	61.6	Moorland and montane areas	4, 8, 10*, 12, 14, 15, 25, 87*, 94
Wheatear *Oenanthe oenanthe*	-	-	-	1,339	60.6	Montane areas, moorland and enclosed land	2*, 4*, 8*, 10*, 12, 14, 15, 17, 25, 29, 30*, 41, 42, 58, 60, 87, 92*, 94
Ring ouzel *Turdus torquatus*	Amber list	-	-	401	93.5	Moorland and scrub	2, 4*,8*, 10*, 12, 14*, 15(?), 17, 25, 29, 30, 42, 87, 92*
Raven *Corvus corax*	-	-	-	783	52.0	Moorland and montane areas	4*, 10*, 41*, 42*, 58*, 60*, 87*, 92*, 94*, extinct elsewhere but recolonising.

Key to Table 10.6

1. Upland breeding bird species as identified in Stillman & Brown 1998.
2. Birds of conservation concern from RSPB 1996.
3. From Bunce & Barr 1988, using the 13 ITE land classes which were regarded as upland (information not available on an English basis).
4. The following 18 Natural Areas are classed as upland by English Nature:

No	Natural Area name	No	Natural Area name
2	Border Uplands	29	South West Peak
4	North Pennines	30	White Peak
8	Yorkshire Dales	41	Oswestry Uplands
10	Cumbria Fells & Dales	42	Shropshire Hills
12	Forest of Bowland	58	Clun and North West Herefordshire Hills
14	Southern Pennines	60	Black Mountains and Golden Valley
15	Pennine Dales Fringe	87	Exmoor and the Quantocks
17	North York Moors and Hills	92	Dartmoor
25	Dark Peak	94	Bodmin Moor.

Table 10.7 Habitat and management requirements of birds associated with crags, scree and limestone pavement in England

Species	Habitat requirements	Management requirements relevant to crags, scree and limestone pavement
Buzzard *Buteo buteo*	• Strong association with woodland and enclosed grassland at the moorland fringe. • Nest placed in isolated or woodland trees or occasionally on rock ledges, usually within woodland. • Adults feed over all types of open country - moors, acid grasslands, tilled land and pastures and meadows - taking earthworms from pastures and tilled land and small mammals, road kills and other carrion from hill and roadsides. • Adults bring food to dependent young in nest. • Present throughout the year.	• Maintain natural drainage & wetland features such as pools & flushes. • Create small wet areas by blocking existing drains & grips. • Do not re-seed or plough permanent pastures. • Do not apply surface applications unless this has been a traditional practice. • Retain scrub & scattered trees on steep slopes. • On gentle slopes graze or cut scrub in rotation. Provide a range of habitats by clearing 10% of scrub each year once it is 10 years old. • Scarify ground where old scrub stands have been cleared to promote regeneration. • Plant native tree species on areas of low nature conservation interest. • Fence off areas where there is some scrub to allow natural regeneration.
Golden eagle *Aquila chrysaetos*	• Associated with remote, open country with cliffs or widely scattered woodland. • Nest placed on rock ledge on tall cliff or in large forest tree. • Adults forage on grouse, rabbits and carrion found mainly on moorland but also over enclosed land, particularly in winter. • Adults bring food to dependent young in nest. • Birds present throughout the year, nesting February to July.	• Manage to encourage grouse and rabbit abundance, and to increase the amount of carrion available.
Peregrine *Falco peregrinus*	• Nest placed on undisturbed steep crags, cliff ledge, chimney or ledge on tall building. • Adults forage on waders, grouse and pigeons caught over moorland, enclosed grasslands and urban areas. • Adults bring food to dependent young in nest. • Present throughout the year.	• Limit recreational disturbance during February-June to nest sites and potential nest sites.

Species	Habitat requirements	Management requirements relevant to crags, scree and limestone pavement
Wheatear *Oenanthe oenanthe*	• Nest in hole in ground or wall, in bracken clump, beneath stones, on enclosed farmland, moorland or scree. • Adults forage for invertebrates over bare ground or short swards on heather moors, stream sides, lake shores and enclosed farmland. • Adults bring food to dependent young in nest. • Birds usually present during extended breeding season, March to September.	• Maintain natural drainage and wetland features such as pools and flushes. • On steep slopes retain scrub such as gorse and juniper and scattered trees such as hawthorn and rowan. • Where burning is desirable use a rotation of at least 20 years on steep slopes, at the moorland edge and in gullies and cloughs so that the heather can grow tall. • Where bracken is controlled, cut or spray after the breeding season in late July/early August and leave a buffer zone near streams and gullies. • Leave areas of bracken on steep slopes or gullies. Only spray areas where the underlying sward is still intact and likely to recover and target the invading edge for control.
Ring ouzel *Turdus torquatus*	• Preference for nesting in areas of sloping land, particularly ghylls and stream sides and, rarely, trees. • Nest on ground in tall heather or bracken litter or in hole in wall or rock crevice. • Adults forage in short swards in enclosed fields, unenclosed moors, especially *Vaccinium* when fruiting. • Adults bring mainly invertebrate food to the nest for the chicks. • Relatively heavily grazed areas near to nest sites, with damp, short, earthworm-rich swards for feeding, may be important but key feeding habitats and foods require further study. • Birds present early April to end September Absent from uplands in non-breeding season.	• On steep slopes retain scrub such as gorse and juniper and scattered trees such as hawthorn and rowan. • Fence off areas where there is some scrub to allow natural regeneration. • Where burning is desirable use a rotation of at least 20 years on steep slopes, at the moorland edge and in gullies and cloughs so that the heather can grow tall. • Leave some areas unburnt to allow scrub and scattered trees to grow. • Where bracken is controlled, cut or spray after the breeding season in late July/early August and leave a buffer zone near streams and gullies. • Leave areas of bracken on steep slopes or gullies. Only spray areas where the underlying sward is still intact and likely to recover, and target the invading edge for control.

Species	Habitat requirements	Management requirements relevant to crags, scree and limestone pavement
Raven *Corvus corax*	• In the uplands, nest on ledges on cliff or quarry faces, and less frequently in trees (preferably conifers) which are isolated, in small woods or at the edges of plantations (not deep in large forests), and on buildings. • Adults forage over open country for a variety of food, particularly carrion but also living animals, on moorland, enclosed and cultivated land, and roadsides. • Opportunist feeders, scavenging carrion such as sheep, rabbit, hare, other small mammals and birds. Also take live animal prey such as small rabbits and other small mammals, reptiles, amphibians and invertebrates. Can be major predators of eggs and chicks of other birds. Some vegetable material, such as seeds, buds, berries and cereal grains, is also eaten. • Food brought to dependent young in nest by adults. • Early nesters and disturbance to nests when young present can affect growth. • Present throughout the year.	• Maintain moorland trees and undisturbed cliffs for nesting. • Manage to encourage rabbit and carrion availability.

Table 10.8 Nationally rare and scarce invertebrates associated with crags, scree and limestone pavement in England

Invertebrate species		Nature conservation status	Typical habitat	Distribution in England (not currently available in terms of Natural Areas)
Scientific name	**English name**			
Moths				
Entephria flavicincta	Yellow-ringed carpet moth	Nationally Scarce A	Feeds on *Saxifraga hypnoides* on rock ledges, but in gorges and ravines.	Yorkshire Dales
Butterflies				
Argynnis adippe	High brown fritillary	RDB2	Breeds in sunny, sheltered areas containing a warm, sparse ground flora with violets. The two main habitats are bracken-dominated areas and limestone rock exposures, usually where scrub or woodland has recently been cleared.	Three main strongholds in north Lancashire, south Cumbria, Dartmoor and Exmoor. Also a few populations in the southwest midlands (Herefordshire, Worcestershire and Shropshire)
Flies				
Dactylolabis sixmaculata	Cranefly	Nationally Scarce B	Limestone soil and open soils with moss - larvae develop in moss.	Cumbria, Yorks, Durham and Peak District limestone. Also Somerset
Dasyhelea lithotelmatica	Midge	RDB2	Larvae live in water filled (temporarily) solution hollows on the surface of limestone pavement.	Southern Cumbria and Yorkshire limestone pavements
Platyparaea discoidea	Picture-winged fly	RDB3	Stem miner in giant bell flower in woods or limestone pavement.	A few woods in Yorkshire Dales (and single wood on magnesian limestone in South Yorkshire)
Beetles				
Eudectus whitei	Rove beetle	Nationally Scarce A	Under stones and in moss on mountain summits.	On summits of Three Peaks in Yorkshire Dales, although possibly now extinct there
Geodromicus longipes	Rove beetle	Nationally Scarce B	In *R. lanuginosum* and under stones on mountain tops.	Cumbria and perhaps Staffordshire

Invertebrate species		Nature conservation status	Typical habitat	Distribution in England (not currently available in terms of Natural Areas)
Scientific name	**English name**			
Leistus montanus	Ground beetle	Nationally Scarce A	Under stones on mountain tops.	Lake District
Notiophilus neothuans	Ground beetle	Nationally Scarce B	Under stones, especially in mineral-rich sites such as land mire spoil.	Yorkshire Dales
Oxypoda soror	Rove beetle	Nationally Scarce B	In moss and under stones on mountains.	Old records from Skiddaw in Cumbria
Spiders				
Entelecara errata	Money spider	Nationally Scarce B	Under stones on mountain tops.	Northumberland
Erophrys jpetrensis	Jumping spider	Nationally Scarce B	Under rocks in uplands (and under stones in lowland heath).	North Yorkshire - also southern heaths
Lepthyphantes pinicola	Money spider	Nationally Scarce B	Mainly under stones on mountains but also on moorland.	Yorkshire, Cumbria and Staffordshire
Lepthyphantes whymperi	Money spider	Nationally Scarce B	In cavities among rocks on mountains.	Lake District
Pardosa trailli	Wolf spider	Nationally Scarce B	Under stones and in scree on mountains.	Lake District
Rugathodes bellicosus	Comb-footed spider	Nationally Scarce B	Under stones on high ground (but at sea level in Scotland). Mountain tops and moorland in England.	Yorkshire Pennines and the Lake District
Theridion belliosum	Comb-footed spider	Nationally Scarce B	Among boulders (also on rocky coasts).	Pennines, Lake District and Northumberland
Tiso aestivus	Money spider	Nationally Scarce B	Under stones above 600 m.	Lake District
Snails				
Clausillia dubia	Door snail	Nationally Scarce B SCC	Bare limestone rocks (and walls) and scree.	Craven Pennines - just extends to East Cumbrian limestone
Vertigo alpestris	Whorl snail	Nationally Scarce A	Screes, rocks, dry stone walls, also stones in woods.	South Cumbria, northeast England
Vertigo angustior	Narrow-mouthed whorl snail	Annex II RDB1 Priority	Limestone pavement and damp grassland.	Gaitbarrows, Lancashire

Invertebrate species		Nature conservation status	Typical habitat	Distribution in England (not currently available in terms of Natural Areas)
Scientific name	**English name**			
Vitraea subrimata	Glass snail	Nationally Scarce A	Limestone scree, walls, rocks, in limestone grassland.	Limestone areas in Cumbria/S lakes, Craven Pennines and County Durham
Crustacea				
Armidillidium pictum	Pill woodlouse	RDB3	In moss and leaf litter on limestone and other base rich rocks (eg Dolerite) pavements, exposures and gorge.	Cumbria and Dales Carboniferous limestone

Key to Table 10.8

Annex II	Annex II of the Habitats and Species Directive
RDB	Red Data Book (Hyman & Parsons 1992)
RDB1	Red Data Book category 1 Endangered
RDB2	Red Data Book category 2 Vulnerable
RDB3	Red Data Book category 3 Rare
Nationally Scarce A	15-30 10 km squares of national grid
Nationally Scarce B	30-100 10 km squares of national grid
Priority	Priority species in the UK Biodiversity Action Plan (UK Biodiversity Group 1998; UK Steering Group 1995)
SCC	Species of conservation concern in the UK Biodiversity Action Plan (UK Biodiversity Group 1998; UK Steering Group 1995).

Table 10.9 Habitat and management requirements of invertebrates associated with crags, scree and limestone pavement in England

Invertebrates	Habitat requirements	Management requirements
Species of limestone pavement	• Molluscs and some other invertebrates require moist, sheltered places such as rock crevices, grikes and under loose rocks. • Certain specialised aquatic species require water-filled solution hollows. • Certain species require particular or abundant limestone pavement vegetation as food or shelter. • Certain species, particularly butterflies, require coppiced woodland or scrubby pavement.	• Prevent disturbance or removal of the pavement. • Maintain light or no grazing. • Maintain woodland and scrub management, such as coppicing, to provide open glades and woodland edges. • Encourage non-intervention areas.
Species of micro habitats on the rock surfaces	Pockets of soil, moss, leaf litter and seepages of water over the rock surface.	• Prevent disturbance or removal of rock habitats. • Maintain light or no grazing. • Encourage non-intervention areas.
Species which live under stones (lapidicolous)	Undisturbed stony areas, fairly stable screes.	• Prevent disturbance or removal of rock habitats. • Maintain light or no grazing. • Encourage non-intervention areas.

Further reading

Bibliography & further reading 11

ADAS. 1991. *Heather moorland grazing management.* London: ADAS.

ALLANSON, P. & WHITBY, M. eds. 1996. *The rural economy and the British countryside.* London: Earthscan Publications Ltd.

ANDERSON, P. 1986. *Accidental moorland fires in the Peak District.* Peak District moorland restoration project. Bakewell: Peak District National Park.

ANDERSON, P. 1990. *Moorland recreation and wildlife in the Peak District: summary.* Bakewell: Peak District National Park.

ANDERSON, P. 1997. *Hareden moorland restoration.* Chinley: Penny Anderson Associates.

ANDERSON, P. & GILBERT, O.L. 1998. *Habitat creation and repair.* Oxford: Oxford University Press.

ANDERSON, P. & RADFORD, E. 1988. *Moorland restoration: a review of experience in the Peak District and elsewhere.* Bakewell: Peak Park Joint Planning Board (Moorland Management Project).

ANDERSON, P. & RADFORD, E. 1992. A review of the effects of recreation on woodland soils, vegetation and fauna. Peterborough: *English Nature Research Reports,* No. 27.

ANDERSON, P. & RADFORD, E. 1994. Changes in vegetation following reduction in grazing pressure on the National Trust's Kinder Estate, Peak District, Derbyshire, England. *Biological Conservation,* **69**, pp. 55-63.

ANDERSON, P. & YALDEN, D.W. 1981. Increased sheep numbers and the loss of heather moorland in the Peak District, England. *Biological Conservation,* **20**, pp. 195-213.

ANDERSON, P., TALLIS, J.H. & YALDEN, D.W. 1997. *Restoring moorlands.* Peak District moorland management project phase III report. Over Haddon: English Nature.

ANDREWS, J. & KINSMAN, D. 1990. *Gravel pit restoration for wildlife: a practical manual.* Sandy: RSPB.

ANDREWS, J. & MACDONALD, A. 1996a. Heather re-establishment on mechanically-disturbed areas. *Information and advisory note* No. 44. Battleby: Scottish Natural Heritage.

ANDREWS, J. & MACDONALD, A. 1996b. Fences and upland conservation management. *Information and advisory note* No. 59. Battleby: Scottish Natural Heritage.

ANDREWS, J. & REBANE, M. 1994. *Farming & Wildlife: a practical handbook for the management, restoration and creation of wildlife habitats on farmland.* Sandy: RSPB.

ANTONOVICS, J., BRADSHAW, A.D. & TURNER, R.G. 1971. Heavy metal tolerance in plants. *Advances in Ecological Research*, **7**, pp. 1-85.

APPLEBY, M. 1994. Agriculture and the environment: opportunities in the UK under the Agri-environment Regulation. *RSPB Conservation Review*, **8**, pp. 10-18.

ARMSTRONG, H.M. 1993. The MLURI Hill grazing model: using a computer to help set stocking rates. *Enact*, **1(4)**, pp. 7-9.

ARMSTRONG, H.M. 1996. The grazing behaviour of large herbivores in the uplands. *Information and advisory note* No. 47. Battleby: Scottish Natural Heritage.

ARMSTRONG, H.M. 1998. The grazing behaviour of large herbivores in the uplands. *In*: F.E. Stewart & S.G. Eno, *Grazing management planning for upland Natura 2000 sites: a practical manual*. Edinburgh: The National Trust for Scotland, pp. 101-110.

ARMSTRONG, H.M. & MILNE, J.A. 1995. The effects of grazing on vegetation species composition. *In*: D.B.A. Thompson, A.J. Hester & M.B. Usher, eds. *Heaths and moorland: cultural landscapes*. Edinburgh and London: HMSO, pp. 162-173.

ARNOLD, H.R. 1995. *Atlas of amphibians and reptiles in Britain*. London: HMSO.

ASH, H.J., BENNETT, R. & SCOTT, R. 1992. *Flowers in the grass: creating and managing grasslands with wild flowers*. Peterborough: English Nature.

ATHERDEN, M. 1992. *Upland Britain: a natural history*. Manchester: Manchester University Press.

AUSDEN, M. & TREWEEK, J. 1995. Grasslands. *In*: W.J. Sutherland & D.A. Hill, eds. *Managing habitats for conservation*. Cambridge: Cambridge University Press, pp. 197-229.

BACON, J. 1996. Tussling with turves: a review of turf-stripping techniques. *Enact*, **4** (2), pp. 12-16.

BACON, J. & LORD, R. 1996. Troublesome trees: taking trees off bogs. *Enact*, **4** (3), pp. 12-15.

BADDELEY, J.A. 1991. *Effects of atmospheric nitrogen deposition on the ecophysiology of* Racomitrium lanuginosum. PhD thesis. Manchester: Manchester University.

BAINES, D. 1988. The effects of improvement of upland, marginal grasslands on the distribution and density of breeding wading birds (Charadriiformes) in Northern England. *Biological Conservation*, **45**, pp. 221-236.

BAKER, A.J.M. 1987. Metal tolerance. *New Phytologist*, **106** (Suppl.), pp. 93-111.

BARDGETT, R.D. & MARSDEN, J.H. 1992. *Heather condition and management in the uplands of England and Wales*. Peterborough: English Nature.

BARDGETT, R.D., MARSDEN, J.H., HOWARD, D.C. & HOSSELL, J.E. 1995. The extent and condition of heather in moorland, and the potential impact of climate change. *In*: D.B.A. Thompson, A.J. Hester & M.B. Usher, eds. *Heaths and moorland: cultural landscapes*. Edinburgh and London: HMSO, pp. 43-50.

BARKMAN, J.J. 1992. Plant communities and synecology of bogs and heaths pools in the Netherlands. *In*: J.T.A. Verhoeven, ed. *Fens and bogs in the Netherlands: vegetation, history, nutrient dynamics and conservation*. The Netherlands: Kluwer Academic Publishers, pp. 173-235.

BARNETT, L.K. & WARREN, M.S. 1995a. *Species Action Plan: high brown fritillary* Argynnis adippe. Wareham: Butterfly Conservation.

BARNETT, L.K. & WARREN, M. 1995b. *Species Action Plan: marsh fritillary* Eurodryas aurinia. Wareham: Butterfly Conservation.

BARNETT, L.K. & WARREN, M. 1995c. *Species Action Plan: pearl-bordered fritillary* Boloria euphrosyne. Wareham: Butterfly Conservation.

BARNETT, L.K. & WARREN, M. 1995d. *Species Action Plan: small pearl-bordered fritillary* Boloria selene. Wareham: Butterfly Conservation.

BARNETT, L.K. & WARREN, M. 1995e. *Species Action Plan: heath fritillary* Mellicta athalia. Wareham: Butterfly Conservation.

BARR, C.J., BUNCE, R.G.H., CLARKE, R.T., FULLER, R.M., FURSE, M.T., GILLESPIE, M.K., GROOM, G.B., HALLAM, C.J., HORNUNG, M., HOWARD, D.C. & NESS, M.J. 1993. *Countryside Survey 1990*. Main Report. Department of the Environment.

BARRETT, J. 1997. Regenerating juniper. *Enact*, **5(1)**, pp. 8-9.

BARRY, R.C. 1981. *Mountain weather and climate*. London: Methuen.

BATTARBEE, R.W., LOGAN, N.A., MURPHY, K.J., RAVEN, P., ASTON, R.J. & FOSTER, G.N. 1985. Other aquatic biology: flora and fauna. *In:* G. Howells & T.R.K. Dalziel, eds. *Restoring acid water: Loch Fleet 1984-1990*. London: Elsevier Applied Science.

BATTEN, L.A., BIBBY, C.J., CLEMENT, P., ELLIOT, G.D. & PORTER, R.F. 1990. *Red data birds in Britain*. London: Poyser.

BAYFIELD, N.G. 1976. Impact of trampling on montane vegetation. *Institute of Terrestrial Ecology: Annual Report 1976*. Grange-over-Sands: Institute of Terrestrial Ecology.

BAYFIELD, N.G. 1979. Recovery of four montane heath communities on Cairngorm, Scotland, from disturbance by trampling. *Biological Conservation*, **15**, pp. 165-179.

BAYFIELD, N.G. 1980. Replacement of vegetation in disturbed ground near ski lifts in the Cairngorm Mountains, Scotland. *Journal of Biogeography*, **7**, pp. 249-260.

BAYFIELD, N.G. 1985. Effects of extended use of footpaths in mountain areas in Britain. *In*: N.G. Bayfield & G.C. Barrow, eds. *The ecological impacts of outdoor recreation in mountain areas in Europe and North America.* Ashford: Recreation Ecology Research Group, pp. 100-111.

BAYFIELD, N.G. 1987. Approaches to reinstatement of damaged footpaths in the Three Peaks area of the Yorkshire Dales National Park. *In*: M. Bell & R.G.H. Bunce, eds. *Agriculture and conservation in the hills and uplands.* ITE Symposium No. 23. Grange-over-Sands: Institute of Terrestrial Ecology, pp. 78-87.

BAYFIELD, N.G. & BARROW, G.C. eds. 1985. *The ecological impacts of outdoor recreation in mountain areas in Europe and North America.* Ashford: Recreation Ecology Research Group.

BAYFIELD, N.G. & MILLER, G.R. 1988. *Restoration of vegetation in the Scottish uplands: a review.* Banchory: Institute of Terrestrial Ecology.

BAYFIELD, N.G., URGUHART, U.H. & COOPER, S.M. 1981. Susceptibility of four species of *Cladonia* to disturbance by trampling in the Cairngorm mountains, Scotland. *Journal of Applied Ecology,* **18,** pp. 303-10

BAYFIELD, N.G., WATSON, A. & MILLER, G.R. 1988. Assessing and managing the effects of recreational use on British hills. *In*: M.B. Usher & D.B.A. Thompson, eds. *Ecological change in the uplands.* Oxford: Blackwell Scientific Publications, pp. 399-414. (British Ecological Society Special Publication No. 7).

BEEBEE, T.J.C. 1996. *Ecology and conservation of amphibians.* London: Chapman and Hall.

BEEBEE, T.J.C. & DENTON, J. eds. 1996. *The natterjack toad conservation handbook.* Peterborough: English Nature.

BELL, M. & BUNCE, R.G.H. 1987. *Agriculture and conservation in the hills and uplands.* ITE Symposium No. 23. Grange-over-Sands: Institute of Terrestrial Ecology.

BIGGS, J., CORFIELD, A., WALKER, D., WHITFIELD, M. & WILLIAMS, P. 1994. New approaches to the management of ponds. *British Wildlife,* **5,** pp. 273-287.

BIRKS, H.J.B. 1988. Long-term ecological change in the British uplands. *In*: M.B. Usher & D.B.A. Thompson, eds. *Ecological change in the uplands.* Oxford: Blackwell Scientific Publications, pp. 37-56.

BIRSE, A.S. 1980 Plant communities of Scotland: a preliminary phytocoenonia. *Soil Survey of Scotland Bulletin* No. 4. Aberdeen: Macaulay Institute for Soil Research, pp. 158-172.

BOBBINK, R., HORNUNG, M. & ROELOFS, J.G.M. 1998. The effects of air-borne nitrogen pollutants on species diversity in natural and semi-natural European vegetation. *Journal of Ecology,* **86,** pp. 717-729.

BOGGIE, R., HUNTER, R.F. & KNIGHT, A.H. 1958. Studies of the root development of plants in the field using radioactive tracers. *Journal of Ecology,* **46,** pp. 621-639.

BOON, P.J., CALOW, P. & PETTS, G.E. eds. 1992. *River conservation and management*. Chichester: Wiley.

BOURN, N.A.D. & WARREN, M. 1998a. *Species Action Plan: Duke of Burgundy* Hamearis lucina. Wareham: Butterfly Conservation

BOURN, N.A.D. & WARREN, M. 1998b. *Species Action Plan: large heath* Coenonympha tullia. Wareham: Butterfly Conservation

BRATTON, J.H. ed. 1991. *British red data books: 3. Invertebrates other than insects*. Peterborough: Nature Conservancy Council.

BROOKES, A. 1990. Restoration and enhancement of engineered river channels: some European experiences. *Regulated Rivers Research and Management*, **5**, pp. 45-56.

BROOKES, A. & AGATE, E. 1997. *Waterways and wetlands: a practical conservation handbook*. Wallingford: British Trust for Conservation Volunteers.

BROOKS, S. & STONEMAN, R. 1997. *Conserving bogs: the management handbook*. Edinburgh: The Stationery Office.

BROUWER, F.M. & VAN BERKUM, S. 1996. *CAP and environment in the European Union. Analysis of the effects of the CAP on the environment and assessment of existing environmental conditions in policy*. Agricultural Economics Research Institute (LEI-DLO). The Hague: Wageningen Press.

BROWN, A.E., BURN, A.J., HOPKINS, J.J. & WRAY, S.F. eds. 1997. *The Habitats Directive: Selection of Special Areas of Conservation in the UK*. JNCC Report No. 270. Peterborough: JNCC.

BROWN, A.F. 1996. Upland management for breeding birds. *In:* English Nature. *Species conservation handbook*. Peterborough: English Nature.

BROWN, A.F. & BAINBRIDGE, I.P. 1995. Grouse moors and upland breeding birds. *In*: D.B.A. Thompson, A.J. Hester & M.B. Usher, eds. *Heaths and moorland: cultural landscapes*. Edinburgh and London: HMSO, pp. 51-66.

BROWN, A.F. & GRICE, P.V. 1993. Birds in England: context and priorities. Peterborough: *English Nature Research Reports*, No. 62.

BROWN, A.F., STILLMAN, R.A. & GIBBONS, D.W. 1995. Use of breeding bird atlas data to identify important bird areas: a northern England case study. *Bird Study*, **42**, pp. 132-143.

BROWN, M. & FARMER, A. 1996. Excess sulphur and nitrogen deposition in England's Natural Areas. Peterborough: *English Nature Research Reports*, No. 201.

BROWN, R. 1997. The biology and ecology of bracken. *The Heather Trust Annual Report*. Kippen: The Heather Trust.

BUCKLEY, G.P. 1989. *Biological habitat reconstruction.* London: Belhaven Press.

BUCKLEY, G.P. & FRASER, S. 1998. *Locating new lowland woods.* Peterborough: *English Nature Research Reports* No. 283.

BULLOCK, D.J. & GUNN, S. eds. 1998. The impact, use and control of fire: a joint workshop organised by English Nature and the National Trust. March 1998. Dartmoor National Park Authority, Bovey Tracey, Devon. Peterborough: *English Nature Research Reports,* No. 297.

BULLOCK, D.J., CLUNAS, A. & DAVIES, M. 1997. Grading the grazing; using the Grazing Index for heather moorland. *Enact,* **5** (1), pp. 20-22.

BULLOCK, J.M. & WEBB, N.R. 1995. Responses to severe fires in heathland mosaics in southern England. *Biological Conservation,* **73**,pp. 207-214.

BUNCE, R.G.H. & BARR, C.J. 1988. The extent of land under different management regimes in the uplands and the potential for change. *In:* M.B. Usher & D.B.A. Thompson, eds. *Ecological change in the uplands.* Oxford: Blackwell Scientific Publications, pp. 415-426. (British Ecological Society Special Publication No. 7).

BUNCE, R.G.H., BARR, C.J. & WHITTAKER, H.A. 1983. A stratified system for ecological sampling. *In:* R.M. Fuller, ed. *Ecological mapping from ground, air and space.* ITE Symposium No. 10. Cambridge: Institute of Terrestrial Ecology, pp. 39-46.

BUNCE, R.G.H., TRANTER, R.B., THOMPSON, A.M.M., MITCHELL, C.P. & BARR, C.J. 1984. Models for predicting changes in rural land use in Great Britain. *In:* D. Jenkins, ed. *Agriculture and the environment.* ITE Symposium No. 13. Abbots Ripton: Institute of Terrestrial Ecology, pp. 37-44.

BURGESS, N., WARD D., HOBBS, R. & BELLAMY, D. 1995. Reedbeds, fens and acid bogs. *In:* W.J. Sutherland & D.A. Hill, eds. *Managing habitats for conservation.* Cambridge: Cambridge University Press, pp. 149-196.

BURT, T.P., HEATHWAITE, A.L. & LABADZ, J.C. 1990. Runoff production in peat-covered catchments. *In:* M.G. Anderson & T.P. Burt, eds. *Process studies in hillslope hydrology.* Chichester: Wiley, pp. 463-500.

BUTTERFIELD, J., COULSON, J.C. & WANLESS, S. 1981. Studies in the distribution, food, breeding biology and relative abundance of pygmy and common shrews *Sorex minutus* and *S. araneus* in upland areas of northern England. *Journal of the Zoological Society of London,* **195**, pp. 169-180.

BUTTERFLY CONSERVATION. 1998. *Bracken for butterflies.* Wareham: Butterfly Conservation.

BYRNE, S. 1991. Botanical monitoring methods for terrestrial habitats with particular reference to grasslands and habitat transplantation sites. *England Field Unit Project No. 103.* Peterborough: Nature Conservancy Council.

CADBURY, J. 1993. Grazing and other management of upland vegetation for birds in the UK. *RSPB Conservation Review*, **7**, pp. 12-21.

CALOW, P. & PETTS, G.E. eds. 1992. *The rivers handbook: hydrological and ecological principles*. Oxford: Blackwell Scientific Publications.

CAREW-REID, J., PRESCOTT-ALLEN, R., BASS, S. & DALAL-CLAYTON, B. 1994. *Strategies for national sustainable development: a handbook for their planning and implementation.* London: International Union for Conservation of Nature and Natural Resources (IUCN) & International Institute for Environment and Development (IIED).

CARROLL, J. & ROBERTSON, P. 1997. *Integrating pheasant management and woodland conservation.* Fordingbridge: Game Conservancy.

CHALMERS, A.J. 1993. *New horizons for upland environments, Scientific Seminar, ADAS Pwllpeiran, September 1993*. Pwllpeiran: ADAS.

CHAMBERS, F.M., DRESSER, P.Q. & SMITH, A.G. 1979. Radiocarbon dating evidence on the impact of atmospheric pollution on upland peats. *Nature*, **282**, pp. 829-832.

CHURCH, J.M., COPPINS, B.J., GILBERT, O.L., JAMES, P.W. & STEWART, N.F. 1996. *Red data books of Britain and Ireland: lichens. Volume 1: Britain.* Peterborough: Joint Nature Conservation Committee.

CLARKE, R. & WATSON, D. 1997. The hen harrier winter roost survey: thirteen winters' data reveal serious declines. *The Raptor*, **24**, pp. 41-45.

CLIFTON, S.J., RANNER, D.S. & WARD, L. 1995. The conservation of juniper in Northumbria. Peterborough: *English Nature Research Reports*, No. 152.

CLIFTON, S.J., WARD, L.K. & RANNER, D.S. 1997. The status of juniper *Juniperus communis* L. in north-east England. *Biological Conservation*, **79**, pp. 67-78.

CLIMATE CHANGE IMPACTS REVIEW GROUP. 1996. *Review of potential effects of climate change in the United Kingdom.* Second report. London: HMSO.

COLE, L., KERNON, T. & KNIGHTBRIDGE, R. 1996. Identifying and describing farm character and structure in the Natural Areas. Peterborough: *English Nature Research Reports*, No. 206.

COOKE, A.S. 1986. *The use of herbicides on nature reserves.* Focus on nature conservation No. 14. Peterborough: Nature Conservancy Council.

COOKE, A.S. ed. 1993. *The environmental effects of pesticide drift.* Peterborough: English Nature.

COOKE, A.S. 1997. *Avermectin use in livestock.* Peterborough: English Nature.

COOPER, E. 1996. *The basis and effectiveness of designation in the countryside.* Lancaster: Unit of Vegetation Science, Lancaster University & Worldwide Fund for Nature - UK.

CORBET, G.B. & HARRIS, S. 1991. *The handbook of British mammals.* Oxford: Blackwell Scientific Publications.

CORKHILL, P. 1997. *Ingleborough bibliography.* Leyburn: English Nature.

COTE, I.M. & SUTHERLAND, W.J. 1995. The scientific basis for predator control for bird conservation. Peterborough: *English Nature Research Reports,* No. 144.

COULSON, J.C. 1988. The structure and importance of invertebrate communities on peatlands and moorlands, and effects of environmental and management changes. *In:* M.B. Usher & D.B.A. Thompson, eds. *Ecological change in the uplands.* Oxford: Blackwell Scientific Publications, pp. 365-380. (British Ecological Society Special Publication No. 7.)

COULSON, J.C. & BUTTERFIELD, J.E.L. 1985. The invertebrate communities of peat and upland grasslands in the north of England and some conservation implications. *Biological Conservation,* **34,** pp. 197-225.

COULSON, J.C. & WHITTAKER, J.B. 1978. The ecology of moorland animals. *In:* O.W. Heal & D.F. Perkins, eds. *Production ecology of British moors and montane grasslands.* Berlin: Springer-Verlag, pp. 53-93.

COULSON, J.C., BUTTERFIELD, J.E.L. & HENDERSON, E. 1990. The effect of open drainage ditches on the plant and invertebrate communities of moorland and the decomposition of peat. *Journal of Applied Ecology,* **27,** pp. 549-561.

COULSON, J.C., FIELDING, C.A. & GOODYEAR, S.A. 1992. The management of moorland areas to enhance their nature conservation interest. JNCC Report No. 134. Peterborough: Joint Nature Conservation Committee.

COUNCIL OF EUROPE. 1996. *Biodiversity: questions and answers.* Strasbourg: Council of Europe.

COUNTRYSIDE COMMISSION. 1983. *What Future for the Uplands?* Cheltenham: Countryside Commission.

COUNTRYSIDE COMMISSION & COUNTRYSIDE COUNCIL FOR WALES. 1997. *National Park management plans guidance.* Cheltenham: Countryside Commission.

COUNTRYSIDE COUNCIL FOR WALES. 1992. *Tir Cymen management guidelines.* Bangor: Countryside Council for Wales.

COUNTRYSIDE COUNCIL FOR WALES. 1998. *Tir Gofal: a new agri-environment scheme for Wales.* Bangor: Countryside Council for Wales.

CROCKFORD, N.J. 1992. *A review of the possible impacts of wind farms on birds and other wildlife.* JNCC Report No. 27. Peterborough: Joint Nature Conservation Committee.

CROFTS, A. & JEFFERSON, R.G. eds. 1994. *The lowland grassland management handbook.* Peterborough: English Nature and The Wildlife Trusts.

CROFTS, A. & JEFFERSON, R.G. eds. 1999. *The lowland grassland management handbook. Second edition.* Peterborough: English Nature and The Wildlife Trusts.

CURRIE, F. & ELLIOT, G. 1997. *Forests and birds.* Edinburgh: RSPB and Forestry Authority.

DANIELS, R.E. 1991. Management of Sphagnum on lowland heaths. *In*: M.H.D. Auld, B.P. Pickess & N.D. Burgess, eds. *Proceedings of heathland conference II: History and management of southern lowland heaths.* Sandy: RSPB, pp. 52-60.

DASMANN, R.F & POORE, D. 1979. *Ecological guidelines for balanced land use, conservation and development in high mountains.* Gland, Switzerland: UNEP, IUCN and WWF.

DAVIES, P., LOXHAM, J. & HUGGON, G. 1996. *Repairing upland path erosion: a best practice guide.* Kendal: Lake District National Park Authority, National Trust and English Nature.

DAWSON, F.H. 1992. Crassula helmsii: *focus on control.* Wareham: Institute of Freshwater Ecology & English Nature.

DEARNLEY, T.C. & CDUCKETT, J.G. 1999. Juniper in the Lake District National Park. A review of condition and regeneration. *Watsonia*, 22, pp. 261-267.

DEPARTMENT OF THE ENVIRONMENT. 1994a. *Biodiversity: the UK Action Plan.* London: HMSO.

DEPARTMENT OF THE ENVIRONMENT. 1994b. *Sustainable development: the UK strategy.* London: HMSO.

DEPARTMENT OF THE ENVIRONMENT. 1996a. Land use change in England No. 11. London: *Department of the Environment Statistical Bulletin.*

DEPARTMENT OF THE ENVIRONMENT. 1996b. *Reclamation of damaged land for nature conservation.* London: HMSO

DEPARTMENT OF THE ENVIRONMENT, TRANSPORT AND THE REGIONS. 1998a. Access to the open countryside in England and Wales: a consultation paper. London: Department of the Environment, Transport and the Regions.

DEPARTMENT OF THE ENVIRONMENT, TRANSPORT AND THE REGIONS. 1998b. Climate change impacts in the UK: the agenda for assessment and action. London: Department of the Environment, Transport and the Regions.

DEPARTMENT OF THE ENVIRONMENT, THE SCOTTISH OFFICE & JOINT NATURE CONSERVATION COMMITTEE. 1995. *The Habitats Directive: how it will apply in Great Britain.* London: HMSO.

DODDS, G.W., APPLEBY, M.J. & EVANS, A.D. 1995. *A management guide to birds of lowland farmland.* Sandy: RSPB.

DODDS, G.W., APPLEBY, M.J. & CAMPBELL, L. 1996. *A management guide to birds of upland farmland.* Sandy: RSPB.

DRAKE, M., CLEMENTS, D., EYRE, M., GIBBS, D. & KIRBY, P. 1998. Invertebrates and their habitats in Natural Areas. Volume 1: Midland and Northern Areas. Peterborough: *English Nature Research Reports,* No. 298.

DRAKE, M., WILLIAMS, P., BIGGS, J. & WHITFIELD, M. 1996. *Managing ponds for wildlife.* Peterborough: English Nature.

DREWITT, A.L. & MANLEY, V.J. 1997. The vegetation of the mountains and moorlands of England: national assessment of significance. Peterborough: *English Nature Research Reports,* No. 218.

DRYDEN, R., HORTON, P. & HALL, J. 1997. Habitat restoration project: fact sheets and bibliographies. Peterborough: *English Nature Research Reports,* No. 260.

ECONOMIC COMMISSION FOR EUROPE. 1993. *Protection of water resources and aquatic ecosystems.* Water Series, no.1. United Nations.

EDGINGTON, M. & STOCKS, P. 1993. The Quantocks. *Enact,* **1(4)**, pp. 17-18.

EDWARDS, H.M. & MARSDEN, J.H. 1991. *Flock performance and stocking rate models in hill sheep farming systems in England and Wales.* ADAS report to the Nature Conservancy Council. Peterborough: English Nature.

EGDELL, J., SMITH, S. & TAYLOR, J. 1993. Agricultural policy in the uplands: the move to extensification. *RSPB Conservation Review,* **7**, pp. 27-34.

EGGELSMANN, R. 1990. Moor und wasser. *In*: K. Gottlich, ed. *Moor- und Torfkunde.* Stuttgart: E. Schweizerbart'sche Verlagsbuchhandlung, pp. 288-320.

ELLIS, N.V., BOWEN,D.Q., CAMPBELL, S., KNILL, J., McKIRDY, A.P., PROSSER, C.D., VINCENT, M.A. & WILSON, R.C.L. 1996. *An introduction to the Geological Conservation Review.* Peterborough: Joint Nature Conservation Committee.

ENGLISH NATURE. 1992. *Enjoying our natural heritage.* Peterborough: English Nature.

ENGLISH NATURE. 1993a. *Wildlife enhancement scheme for the Craven Limestone Grassland.* Peterborough: English Nature.

ENGLISH NATURE. 1993b. *Strategy for the 1990's: Natural Areas.* Peterborough: English Nature.

ENGLISH NATURE. 1994a. *Sustainability in practice.* Internal staff manual. Peterborough: English Nature.

ENGLISH NATURE. 1994b. *Position statement on: Environmentally sustainable forestry and woodland management.* Peterborough: English Nature.

ENGLISH NATURE. 1994c. *Natural Areas: responses to English Nature's consultation document.* Peterborough: English Nature.

ENGLISH NATURE. 1994d. *Natura 2000 European Habitats Directive; European wildlife sites in England.* Peterborough: English Nature.

ENGLISH NATURE. 1994e. *Species conservation handbook.* Peterborough: English Nature.

ENGLISH NATURE. 1995a. *Conservation in catchment management planning - a handbook.* Peterborough: English Nature.

ENGLISH NATURE. 1995b. *The grazing index for heather moorland.* Peterborough: English Nature.

ENGLISH NATURE. 1995c. *The grazing index: field notes.* Peterborough: English Nature.

ENGLISH NATURE. 1996. *Position statement on: Fossil collecting.* Peterborough: English Nature.

ENGLISH NATURE. 1996a. *Land management for upland birds.* Peterborough: English Nature.

ENGLISH NATURE. 1996b. *Grazing in upland woods: managing the impacts.* Peterborough: English Nature.

ENGLISH NATURE. 1996c. *Natural Area core profiles.* Peterborough: English Nature. Unpublished.

ENGLISH NATURE. 1997a. *Position statement on: Non-aggregate mineral extraction.* Peterborough: English Nature.

ENGLISH NATURE. 1997b. *Windows in time.* Peterborough: English Nature.

ENGLISH NATURE. 1997c. *Deer management and woodland conservation in England.* Peterborough: English Nature.

ENGLISH NATURE. 1997d. *Wildlife and freshwater: an agenda for sustainable management.* Peterborough: English Nature.

ENGLISH NATURE. 1997e. *Habitat creation for wildlife: fact sheets.* Peterborough: English Nature. Folder containing 7 fact sheets.

ENGLISH NATURE. 1997f. *Cumbria Fells and Dales Natural Area Profile.* Kendal: English Nature.

ENGLISH NATURE. 1997g *Position statement on: Environmentally sustainable agriculture and nature conservation.* Peterborough: English Nature.

ENGLISH NATURE. 1998a. *Position statement on: Aggregate extraction and nature conservation.* Peterborough: English Nature

ENGLISH NATURE. 1998b. Lake SSSIs subject to eutrophication - an environmental audit. *English Nature Freshwater Series,* No. 3. Peterborough: English Nature.

ENGLISH NATURE. 1998c. *Conserving your local geological heritage.* Peterborough: English Nature.

ENGLISH NATURE. 1998d. *Managing your local geological heritage.* Peterborough: English Nature.

ENGLISH NATURE. 1998e. *Management choices for ancient woodland: getting it right.* Peterborough: English Nature.

ENGLISH NATURE. 2000a. *Position statement on: Access to the countryside and urban greenspace.* Peterborough: English Nature.

ENGLISH NATURE. 2000b. *Position statement on: Countryside recreation.* Peterborough: English Nature.

ENGLISH NATURE. 2000c. *Position statement on: Electricity generation, transmission and use.* Peterborough: English Nature.

ENGLISH NATURE, THE COUNTRYSIDE AGENCY & COUNTRYSIDE COUNCIL FOR WALES. 1999. *Agenda 2000: Implementing the CAP reforms 1999.* Working papers from the staff of the wildlife and countryside agencies of England and Wales.

ENGLISH NATURE & COUNTRYSIDE COMMISSION. 1996. *The character of England: landscape, wildlife and natural features.* Peterborough: English Nature.

ENGLISH NATURE, COUNTRYSIDE COMMISSION, JOINT NATURE CONSERVATION COMMITTEE, SCOTTISH NATURAL HERITAGE & COUNTRYSIDE COUNCIL FOR WALES. 1998. *Agenda 2000: CAP draft regulations 1998.* Working papers from the countryside agencies of Great Britain.

ENGLISH NATURE & RSPB. 1995. *The lowland heathland inventory.* Peterborough: English Nature.

ENVIRONMENT AGENCY. 1996a. *The environment of England and Wales: a snapshot.* Bristol: Environment Agency.

ENVIRONMENT AGENCY. 1996b. *Understanding buffer strips: an information booklet.* Exeter: Environment Agency.

ENVIRONMENT AGENCY 1996c. *Local Environment Agency plan: Tees consultation report.* Leeds: Environment Agency NE Region.

ENVIRONMENT AGENCY. 1997. *Phytophthora disease of alder.* Bristol: Environment Agency.

ENVIRONMENT AGENCY. 1998a. *Understanding riverbank erosion: an information booklet.* Bristol: Environment Agency.

ENVIRONMENT AGENCY. 1998b. *Freshwater fisheries and wildlife conservation: a good practice guide.* Bristol: Environment Agency.

ENVIRONMENT AGENCY. 1998c. *Understanding riverbank erosion: an information booklet.* Bristol: Environment Agency.

ENVIRONMENT AGENCY. 1998d. *Sheep dipping. Pollution prevention guidelines no. 12.* Bristol: Environment Agency.

ETHERIDGE, B., SUMMERS, R.W. & GREEN, R. 1997. The effects of human persecution on the population dynamics of hen harriers *Circus cyaneus* nesting in Scotland. *Journal of Applied Ecology*, **34**, pp. 1081-1106.

EUROPEAN COMMISSION. 1996. *Interpretation manual of European Union habitats.* Version EUR 15. Brussels: European Commission.

EUROPEAN COMMISSION DG XI. 1996. Interpretation manual of European Union habitats. European Commission DG XI.

EUROPEAN COMMUNITIES. 1992. *Special Protection Areas: areas designated under Article 4 of Directive 79/409/EEC on the conservation of wild birds.* Luxembourg: EC.

EVANS, J. 1984. *The silviculture of broadleaved woodland.* Forestry Commission Bulletin 62. London: HMSO.

EVANS, S. & FELTON, M. 1987. Hill livestock compensatory allowances and upland management. *In*: M. Bell & R.G.H. Bunce, eds. *Agriculture and conservation in the hills and uplands.* ITE Symposium No. 23. Grange-over-Sands: Institute of Terrestrial Ecology, pp. 66-72.

FARMER, A.M. 1992. Catchment liming and nature conservation. *Land Use Policy*, **9**, pp. 8-10.

FEDERATION OF NATURE AND NATIONAL PARKS OF EUROPE. 1992. Loving them to death? Sustainable tourism for Europe's nature and national parks. Federation of Nature and National Parks of Europe.

FELTON, M. & MARSDEN, J.H. 1990. *Heather regeneration in England and Wales. A feasibility study for the Department of the Environment.* Peterborough: Nature Conservancy Council.

FERGUSON, J.A. 1982. *Pollution and the growth of Sphagnum in the southern Pennines - I. The role of sulphur*. Paper presented to the British Ecological Society winter meeting, acid rain and atmospheric pollution session, Durham, 14 December 1982.

FISHPOOL, M. & USHER, M.B. 1989. Association between Carabid beetle distribution and vegetation in the North York Moors. *The Naturalist*, **114**, pp. 41-50.

FOLEY, M.J.Y. 1987. The current distribution and abundance of *Orchis ustulata* L. in northern England. *Watsonia*, **16**, pp. 409-415.

FORESTRY AUTHORITY. 1993. *Environmental assessment of new woodlands*. Edinburgh: Grants and Licences Division, Forestry Authority.

FORESTRY COMMISSION. 1993. *Forest and water Guidelines*. 3rd edition. London: HMSO.

FORESTRY COMMISSION. 1994. *The management of semi-natural woodland*. Edinburgh, Forestry Commission (Forest Practice Guides 1-8).

FORESTRY COMMISSION. 1998. *England Forestry Strategy: A new focus for England's woodlands* Cambridge.

FORREST, G.I. 1971. Structure and production of north Pennine blanket bog vegetation. *Journal of Ecology*, **59**, pp. 453-579.

FRCA. 1997. Bilberry project first interim report 1996/7. Wolverhampton: FRCA.

FRY, M. 1997. *A manual of environmental protection law: the pollution control functions of the Environment Agency and SEPA*. Oxford: Clarendon Press.

FULLER, R.J. 1982. *Bird habitats in Britain*. Calton: Poyser.

FULLER, R.J. 1992. Effects of coppice management on woodland breeding birds. *In*: G.P. Buckley, ed. *Ecology and management of coppice woodlands*. London: Chapman and Hall, pp. 169-192.

FULLER, R.J. 1995. *Bird life of woodland and forest*. Cambridge: Cambridge University Press.

FULLER, R.J. 1996. *Relationships between grazing and birds with particular reference to sheep in the British uplands*. BTO Research Report. Thetford: British Trust for Ornithology.

FULLER, R.J. & PETERKEN, G.F. 1995. Woodland and scrub. *In*: W.J. Sutherland & D.A. Hill, eds. *Managing habitats for conservation*. Cambridge: Cambridge University Press.

FULLER, R.J. & WARREN, M.S. 1993. *Coppiced woodlands: their management for wildlife*. Second edition. Peterborough: Joint Nature Conservation Committee.

FULLER, R.J. & WARREN, M.S. 1995. Management for biodiversity in British woodlands - striking a balance. *British Wildlife*, **7**, pp. 26-37.

FULLER, R.M. 1987. The changing extent and conservation interest of lowland grasslands in England and Wales: a review of grassland surveys 1930-1984. *Biological Conservation*, **40**, pp. 81-300.

GALBRAITH, H., MURRAY, S., DUNCAN, K., SMITH, R., WHITFIELD, D.P. & THOMPSON, D.B.A. 1993a. Diet and habitat use of the dotterel *Charadrius morinellus* in Scotland. *Ibis*, **135**, pp. 148-155.

GALBRAITH, H., MURRAY, S., RAE, S., WHITFIELD, D.P. & THOMPSON, D.B.A. 1993b. Numbers and distribution of Dotterel *Charadrius morinellus* breeding in Great Britain. *Bird Study*, **40**, pp. 161-169.

GARDINER, A.J. 1996. *Freshwater wetlands in England: a Natural Areas approach*. Peterborough: *English Nature Research Reports*, No. 204.

GARDNER, S.M. & USHER, M.B. 1989. Insect abundance on burned and cut *Calluna* heath. *The Entomologist*, **108**, pp. 147-157.

GARDNER, S.M., HARTLEY, S.E., DAVIES, A. & PALMER, S.C.F. 1997. Carabid communities on heather moorlands in northeast Scotland: the consequences of grazing pressure for community diversity. *Biological Conservation*, **81**, pp. 275-286.

GARDNER, S.M., LIEPERT, C. & REES, S. 1993. Managing heather moorland: impacts of burning and cutting on *Calluna* regeneration. *Journal of Environmental Planning and Management*, **36** (3), pp 283-293.

GENT, A. & GIBSON, S. 1998. *Herpetofauna workers' manual*. Peterborough: Joint Nature Conservation Committee.

GIBBONS, D., GATES, S., GREEN, R.E., FULLER, R.J & FULLER, R.M. 1994. Buzzards *Buteo buteo* and ravens *Corvus corax* in the uplands of Britain: limits to distribution and abundance. *Ibis*, **137**, pp. S75-S84.

GIBBONS, D.W., REID, J.B. & CHAPMAN, R.A. 1993. *The new atlas of breeding birds in Britain and Ireland: 1988-1991*. London: Poyser.

GILBERT, O.L. 1970. *Dryopteris villarii*. Biological flora of the British Isles. *Journal of Ecology*, **58**, pp. 301-314.

GILBERT, O.L. & GIAVARINI, V.J. 1993. The lichens of high ground in the English Lake District. *Lichenologist*, **25 (2)**, pp. 147-164.

GILBERT, D., HORSFIELD, D. & THOMPSON, D.B.A. eds. 1997. The ecology and restoration of montane and subalpine scrub habitat in Scotland. *Scottish Natural Heritage Review*, No. 83. Battleby: Scottish Natural Heritage

GILL, J.P. 1990. A guide to the Moor House collection. In: *Aspects of the ecology of the Northern Pennines, Moor House Occasional Paper*, No. 13. Grange-over-Sands: Institute of Terrestrial Ecology.

GILL, J.P., TOWNSLEY, M. & MUDGE, G.P. 1996. *Review of the impacts of wind farms and other aerial structures upon birds*. Scottish Natural Heritage Review No. 21. Battleby: Scottish Natural Heritage.

GILLINGHAM, A.G. 1980. Phosphorus uptake and return in grazed steep hill pastures. I. Pasture production and dung and litter accumulation. *New Zealand Journal of Agricultural Research,* **23,** pp. 313-321.

GILLINGS, S. & FULLER, R.J. 1998. *Breeding bird communities in upland scrub and woodland: a preliminary report on work undertaken in Scotland in 1996 and 1997.* Thetford: British Trust for Ornithology.

GIMINGHAM, C.H. 1972. *Ecology of heathlands.* London: Chapman and Hall.

GIMINGHAM, C.H. 1975. *An introduction to heathland ecology.* Edinburgh: Oliver and Boyd.

GIMINGHAM, C.H. 1988a. Introduction: ecological change in the uplands. *In*: M.B. Usher & D.B.A. Thompson, eds. *Ecological change in the uplands.* Oxford: Blackwell Scientific Publications, pp. 1-6. (British Ecological Society Special Publication No. 7.)

GIMINGHAM, C.H. 1988b. A reappraisal of cyclical processes in *Calluna* heath. *Vegetatio,* **77,** pp. 61-64.

GIMINGHAM, C.H. 1992. *The lowland heathland management handbook.* English Nature Science No. 8. Peterborough: English Nature.

GIMINGHAM, C.H. 1995. Heaths and moorland: an overview of ecological change. *In*: D.B.A. Thompson, A.J. Hester & M.B. Usher, eds. *Heaths and moorland: cultural landscapes.* Edinburgh and London: HMSO, pp. 9-19.

GODWIN, H. 1975. *The history of the British flora. A factual basis for phytogeography. Second edition.* Cambridge: Cambridge University Press.

GOOD, J.E.G., NORRIS, D., MCNALLY, S. & RADFORD, G.L. 1997. Developing new native woodland in the English uplands. Peterborough: *English Nature Research Reports,* No. 230.

GORE, A.J.P. 1961. Factors limiting plant growth on high-level blanket peat II. Nitrogen and phosphate in the first year of growth. *Journal of Ecology,* **49,** pp. 605-616.

GORE, A.J.P. ed. 1983. *Mires: swamp, bog, fen and moor: general studies.* Amsterdam: Elsevier.

GORE, A.J.P. & GODFREY, M. 1981. Reclamation of eroded peat in the Pennines. *Journal of Ecology,* **69,** pp. 85-96.

GORE, A.J.P. & OLSON, J.S. 1967. Preliminary models for accumulation of organic matter in an *Eriophorum/Calluna* ecosystem. *Aquilo, Ser. Botanica,* **6,** pp. 297-313.

GRANT, M. 1997. Breeding curlews in the UK: RSPB research and implications for conservation. *RSPB Conservation Review*, **11**, pp. 67-73.

GRANT, S.A. & ARMSTRONG, H.M. 1993. Grazing ecology and conservation of heather moorland: the development of models as aids to management. *Biodiversity and Conservation*, **2**, pp. 79-94.

GRANT, S.A., BARTRAM, G.T., LAMB, W.I.C & MILNE, J. 1978. Effect of season and level of grazing on the utilisation of heather by sheep. I. Responses of the sward. *British Grassland Society Journal*, **33**, pp. 289-300.

GRANT, S.A., BOLTON, G.R. & TORVELL, L. 1985. The responses of blanket bog vegetation to controlled grazing by hill sheep. *Journal of Applied Ecology*, **22**, pp. 739-751.

GRANT, S.A., HUNTER, R.F. & CROSS, C. 1963. The effects of muir burning *Molinia*-dominant communities. *British Grassland Society Journal*, **18**, pp. 249-257.

GRANT, S.A., LAMB, W.I.C., KERR, C.D. & BOLTON, G.R. 1976. The utilisation of blanket bog vegetation by grazing sheep. *Journal of Applied Ecology*, **13**, pp. 857-869.

GRANT, S.A., MILNE, J.A., BARTRAM, G.T. & SOUTER, W.G. 1982. Effects of seasons and level of grazing on the utilisation of heather by sheep. 3. Longer term responses and sward recovery. *Grass Forage Science*, **37**, pp. 311-320.

GRANT, S.A., SUCKLING, D.E., SMITH, H.K., TORVELL, L., FORBES, T.D.A. & HODGSON, J. 1985. Comparative studies of diet selection by sheep and cattle: the hill grasslands. *Journal of Ecology*, **73**, pp. 1987-2004.

GRANT, S.A., TORVELL, L., ARMSTRONG, R.G. & BEATTIE, M.M. 1987. The manipulation of mat-grass pasture by grazing management. *In*: M. Bell & R.G.H. Bunce, eds. *Agriculture and conservation in the hills and uplands*. ITE Symposium No. 23. Grange-over-Sands: Institute of Terrestrial Ecology, pp. 62-64.

GRANT, S.A., TORVELL, L., COMMON, T.G., SIM, E.M. & SMALL, J.L. 1996. Controlled grazing studies on *Molinia* grassland: effects of different seasonal patterns and levels of defoliation on *Molinia* growth and responses of swards to controlled grazing by cattle. *Journal of Applied Ecology*, **33**, pp. 1267-1280.

GREEN, R.E. 1986. *The management of lowland wet grasslands for breeding waders*. Unpublished report. Sandy: RSPB.

GREGORY, M. 1994. *Conservation law in the countryside*. Croydon: Tolley.

GRICE, P., BROWN, A.F., CARTER, I.C. & RANKIN, C.A. 1994. Birds in England: a Natural Areas approach. Peterborough: *English Nature Research Reports*, No. 114.

GRIME, J.P., HODGSON, J.G. & HUNT, R. 1990. *The abridged comparative plant ecology*. London: Unwin Hyman.

GUEST, R. 1997. *Great Britain Plan for Limestone Pavement on Forestry Commission Land*. York: Forest Enterprise. Unpublished.

GUTHRIE, I. 1997. The whole-moor tick study. Kippen: *The Heather Trust Annual Report*.

HADLEY CENTRE. 1997. *Climate change and its impacts: a global perspective*. Bracknell: Meteorological Office.

HAGGAR, R.J. & PEEL, S. eds. 1994. *Grassland management and nature conservation*. Proceedings of a joint meeting held at Leeds University, September 1993. Reading: British Grassland Society, Occasional Symposium No. 28.

HAINES, M. 1982. *An introduction to farming systems*. London: Longman.

HAINES-YOUNG, R.H., BARR, C.J., BLACK, H.I.J., BRIGGS, D.J., BUNCE, R.G.H., CLARKE, R.T., COOPER, A., DAWSON, F.H., FIRBANK, L.G., FULLER, R.M., FURSE, M.T., GILLESPIE, M.K., HILL, R., HORNUNG, M., HOWARD, D.C., McCANN, T., MORECROFT, M.D., PETIT, S., SIER, A.R.J., SMART, S.M., SMITH, G.M., STOTT, A.P., STUART, R.C. & WATKINS, J.W. 2000. *Accounting for nature: assessing habitats in the UK countryside*. London: Department of the Environment, Transport and the Regions.

HALL, J. E. 1997. *An analysis of woodland NVC survey data*. JNCC Report, No. 272. Peterborough, Joint Nature Conservation Committee

HARRIS, S., MORRIS, P., WRAY, S. & YALDEN, D. 1995. *A review of British mammals*. Peterborough: Joint Nature Conservation Committee.

HARRISON, A.F. & TAYLOR, K. 1989. Phosphorus in grasslands: its understanding, control and use. *In*: M. Bell & R.G.H. Bunce, eds. *Agriculture and conservation in the hills and uplands*. ITE Symposium No. 23. Grange-over-Sands: Institute of Terrestrial Ecology, pp. 50-55.

HASLAM, S.M. 1987. *River plants of Western Europe*. Cambridge: Cambridge University Press.

HAWKE, C.J. & P.V. JOSÉ. 1995. *Reedbed management for commercial and wildlife interests*. Sandy: RSPB.

HEAL, O.W. & PERKINS, D.F. eds. 1978. *Production ecology of British moors and montane grasslands*. Berlin: Springer-Verlag.

HEALTH AND SAFETY EXECUTIVE. 1997. Guidance on storing pesticides for farmers and other professional users. Agricultural information sheet No. 16. Suffolk: Health and Safety Executive Books.

HEALTH AND SAFETY EXECUTIVE. 1998. *Sheep dipping*. Leaflet AS29 (revision 2). Suffolk: Health and Safety Executive Books.

HEATHWAITE, A.L. & GOTTLICH, K. eds. 1993. *Mires: process, exploitation and conservation.* Chichester: Wiley.

HEIL, G.W. & DIEMONT, H. 1993. Raised nutrient levels change heathland into grassland. *Vegetatio,* **53**, pp. 113-120.

HESTER, J.A. 1996. Overgrazing in upland habitats: a literature review. *Countryside Council for Wales Science Report,* No 152. Bangor: Countryside Council for Wales.

HESTER, J.A. & BAILLIE, J. 1999. Spatial and temporal patterns of heather use by sheep and red deer within natural heather/grass mosaics. *Journal of Applied Ecology,* **35**, pp. 772-784.

HESTER, A.J. & SYDES, C. 1992. Changes in burning of Scottish heather moorland since the 1940s from aerial photographs. *Biological Conservation,* **60**, pp. 25-30.

HESTER, A.J., KIRBY, K J., MITCHELL, F J G., GILL, R.M., LATHAM, J. & ARMSTRONG, H. 1998. Ungulates and forest management use in Great Britain and Ireland. *In Grazing as a management tool in European Forest Systems,* Forestry Commission Technical Paper 25, Edinburgh, pp. 24-35.

HESTER, A.J., MITCHELL, F.J.G. & KIRBY K.J. 1996. Effects of season and intensity of sheep grazing on tree regeneration in a British upland woodland. *Forest Ecology and Management* **88**, pp. 99-106.

HILL FARMING RESEARCH ORGANISATION. 1979. *Science and hill farming.* Edinburgh: Hill Farming Research Organisation.

HILL, D., PETERKEN, G., RICH, T. & TUCKER, G. 1997. *Generic guidelines for favourable condition of features of conservation interest under the EC Habitats Directive and Wild Birds Directive. Second stage report - 2nd revision: 8/1/97 - Ecoscope Applied Ecologists.* Peterborough: Joint Nature Conservation Committee.

HILL, M.O., EVANS, D.F. & BELL, S.A. 1992. Long-term effects of excluding sheep from hill pastures in North Wales. *Journal of Ecology,* **80**, pp. 1-13.

HILL, M.O., PRESTON, C.D. & SMITH, A.J.E. eds. 1991. *Atlas of the bryophytes of Britain and Ireland. Volume 1 Liverworts Hepaticae and Anthocerotae.* Colchester: Harley Books.

HILL, M.O., PRESTON, C.D. & SMITH, A.J.E. eds. 1992. *Atlas of the bryophytes of Britain and Ireland. Volume 2 Mosses (except Diplolepideae).* Colchester: Harley Books.

HILL, M.O., PRESTON, C.D. & SMITH, A.J.E. eds. 1994. *Atlas of the bryophytes of Britain and Ireland. Volume 3 Mosses (Diplolepideae).* Colchester: Harley Books.

HILLIER, S.H., WALTON, D.W.H. & WELLS, D.A. eds. 1990. *Calcareous grasslands: ecology and management.* Huntingdon: Bluntisham Books.

HILTON-BROWN, D. & OLDHAM, R.S. 1991. The status of the widespread amphibians and reptiles in Britain, 1990, and changes during the 1980's. *Contract surveys no. 131*. Peterborough: Nature Conservancy Council.

HIRONS, G., GOLDSMITH, B. & THOMAS, G. 1995. Site management planning. *In*: W.J. Sutherland and D.A. Hill, eds. *Managing habitats for conservation.* Cambridge: Cambridge University Press.

HISTORIC SCOTLAND. 1996. *Managing Scotland's archaeological heritage: a guide to the management of archaeological sites for owners, land managers and others.* Edinburgh: Historic Scotland.

HMSO. 1976. *The Convention on Wetlands of International Importance especially as Waterfowl Habitat, Ramsar, Iran.* Command Paper 6465. Treaty Series no. 34 (1976). London: HMSO.

HMSO. 1994a. *Sustainable forestry: the UK programme.* London: HMSO.

HMSO. 1994b. *The Conservation (Natural Habitats, &c.) Regulations.* London: HMSO.

HMSO. 1997. *Agriculture in the United Kingdom 1996.* London: MAFF, SOAEFD, DANI & WOAD.

HOBBS, A. & SYDES, C. 1988. The upland vegetation survey. *Nature Conservancy Council Chief Scientist Directorate Note,* No. 56. Peterborough: Nature Conservancy Council.

HOBBS, N.B. 1986. Mire morphology and the properties and behaviour of some British and foreign peats. *Quarterly Journal of Engineering Geology,* **19**, pp. 7-80.

HOBBS, R.J. 1984. Length of burning rotation and community composition in high-level *Calluna-Eriophorum* bog in N. England. *Vegetatio,* **57**, pp. 129-136.

HOBBS, R.J. & GIMINGHAM, C.H. 1984. Studies on fire in Scottish heathland communities. II. Post fire vegetation development. *Journal of Ecology,* **72**, pp. 585-610.

HOBBS, R.J. & GIMINGHAM, C.H. 1987. Vegetation, fire and herbivore interactions in heathland. *Advances in Ecological Research,* **16**, pp. 87-193.

HODGETTS, N.G. 1992. *Guidelines for selection of biological SSSIs: non-vascular plants.* Peterborough: Joint Nature Conservation Committee.

HODGETTS, N.G. 1993a. Atlantic bryophytes on the western seaboard. *British Wildlife,* **4**, pp. 287-295.

HODGETTS, N.G. 1993b. *The conservation of lower plants in Britain & Ireland.* Peterborough: Joint Nature Conservation Committee.

HODGETTS, N.G. 1996. *The conservation of lower plants in woodland.* Peterborough: Joint Nature Conservation Committee.

HODGETTS, N.G., PALMER, M. & WIGGINTON, M. 1996. *The pink book of plants: Lists of vascular and non-vascular plant species which are nationally threatened, localised or protected in Great Britain. First version June 1996 (unpublished).* Peterborough: Joint Nature Conservation Committee.

HOLDICH, D.M., ROGERS, W.D. & READER, J.P. 1995. Crayfish conservation. *Research and development project* No. 379. Bristol: National Rivers Authority.

HOLMES, N. 1983. *Typing British rivers according to their flora.* Focus on Nature Conservation No. 4. Peterborough: Nature Conservancy Council.

HOLMES, N. & NEWBOLD, C. 1984. *River plant communities: reflectors of water and substrate chemistry.* Focus on Nature Conservation No. 9. Peterborough: Nature Conservancy Council.

HOLMES, N., BOON, P.J. & ROWELL, T.A. 1998. A revised classification system for British rivers based on their aquatic plant communities. *Aquatic Conservation: Marine and Freshwater Ecosystems,* **8**, pp. 555-578.

HOOPER, S. 1996. The Wildlife Enhancement Scheme in the uplands. Peterborough: *English Nature Research Reports,* No. 199.

HOPKINS, A. & HOPKINS, J.J. 1993. UK grasslands today: agricultural production and nature conservation. *In:* R.J. Haggar & S. Peel, eds. *Grassland management and nature conservation.* British Grassland Society, Occasional Publication, No. 28. pp. 10-19.

HOPKINS, J.J. 1996. Scrub ecology and conservation. *British Wildlife,* **8**, pp. 28-36.

HORSFIELD, D. & THOMPSON, D. 1996. The uplands: guidance on terminology regarding altitudinal zonation and related terms. *Information and Advisory Note No. 26.* Edinburgh: Scottish Natural Heritage.

HOWARTH, W. 1992. *Wisdom's law of watercourses.* Crayford: Shaw.

HOWELLS, G. & DALZIEL, T.R.K. eds. 1992. *Restoring acid waters: Loch Fleet 1984 - 1990.* London: Elsevier Applied Science.

HUDSON, P.J. 1984. Some effects of sheep management on heather moorlands in northern England. *In*: D. Jenkins, ed. *The impact of agriculture on wildlife and semi-natural habitats.* Institute of Terrestrial Ecology Symposium No. 13, What ecological research is necessary?, held at Monkswood Experimental Research Station, pp. 143-149.

HUDSON, P. & NEWBORN, D. 1995. *A manual of red grouse and moorland management.* Fordingbridge: The Game Conservancy Trust.

HULME, M. & JENKINS, G.J. 1998. *Climate change scenarios for the UK: scientific report.* UKCIP Technical Report No. 1. Norwich: Climate Research Unit.

HYMAN, P.S. & PARSONS, M.S. 1992. *A review of the scarce and threatened Coleoptera of Great Britain. Part 1.* UK Nature Conservation, No. 3. Peterborough: Joint Nature Conservation Committee.

ILBERY, B. 1992. *Agricultural change in Great Britain.* Oxford: Oxford University Press.

INESON, P. 1989. The nitrogen cycle in upland agriculture: its understanding, control and use. In: M. Bell & R.G.H. Bunce, eds. *Agriculture and conservation in the hills and uplands.* ITE Symposium No. 23. Grange-over-Sands: Institute of Terrestrial Ecology, pp. 44-49.

ING, B. 1992. A provisional Red Data list of British fungi. *Mycologist*, 6, pp. 124-128.

INGROUILLE, M. 1995. *Historical ecology of the British flora.* London: Chapman and Hall.

INTERNATIONAL WATERFOWL RESEARCH BUREAU. 1972. *Manual of wetland management.* International Waterfowl Research Bureau.

IVANOV, K.E. 1981. *Water movement in mirelands (Vodoobman v bolotnykh landshaftakh).* London: Academic Press.

JEFFERSON, R.G. 1996. Lowland grassland in Natural Areas: national assessment of significance. Peterborough: *English Nature Research Reports*, No. 171.

JEFFERSON, R.G. & ROBERTSON, H.J. 1994. Lowland grassland. *In*: A. Moffat, ed. *Habitat conservation in England.* Peterborough: English Nature.

JEFFERSON, R.G. & ROBERTSON, H.J. 1996a. Lowland grassland: wildlife value and conservation status. Peterborough: *English Nature Research Reports*, No. 169.

JEFFERSON, R.G. & ROBERTSON, H.J. 1996b. Lowland grassland: a strategic review and action plan. Peterborough: *English Nature Research Reports*, No. 163.

JEFFERSON, R.G., ROBERTSON, H.J., MARSDEN, J. & FRASER, A.J.L. 1994. Lowland dry neutral grassland in England. The conservation of a declining resource with particular reference to Worcestershire. *In*: R.J. Haggar & S. Peel, ed. *Grassland management and nature conservation.* Proceedings of a joint meeting held at Leeds University, September 1993. Reading: British Grassland Society, Occasional Symposium No. 28.

JERMY, A.C. 1994. *Dryopteris submontana. In:* A. Stewart, D.A. Pearman & C.D. Preston, eds. *Scarce plants in Britain.* Peterborough: JNCC.

JERMY, A.C., ARNOLD, H.R., FARRELL, L. & PERRING, F.H. 1978. *Atlas of ferns of the British Isles.* London: Botanical Society of the British Isles and British Pteridological Society.

JERRAM, R. 1992. *Montane lichen and moss heath in the Lake District.* Contract report to English Nature. Bowness-on-Windermere: English Nature. Unpublished.

JERRAM, R. 1997a. *Helvellyn and Fairfield cSAC. Survey of SAC feature communities.* Contract report to English Nature. Kendal: English Nature. Unpublished.

JERRAM, R. 1997b. *Wasdale Screes cSAC. Survey of SAC feature communities.* Contract report to English Nature. Kendal: English Nature. Unpublished.

JERRAM, R. 1997c. *Moorhouse and Crossfell SSSI. Survey of National Vegetation Classification communities.* Contract report to English Nature. Kendal: English Nature. Unpublished.

JERRAM, R. 1997d. *Helvellyn Massif. The Conservation of Downy Willow (*Salix lapponum*).* Contract report to Lake District National Park Authority. Kendal: Lake District National Park Authority. Unpublished.

JOINT NATURE CONSERVATION COMMITTEE. Ongoing. Invertebrate Site Register. Peterborough: Joint Nature Conservation Committee. Unpublished.

JOINT NATURE CONSERVATION COMMITTEE. Ongoing. Geological Conservation Review. Peterborough: Joint Nature Conservation Committee. Unpublished.

JOINT NATURE CONSERVATION COMMITTEE. 2000. *Looking to the hills.* Newsletter of the Uplands Lead Co-ordination Network. Issue No. 9.

JOYCE, C.B. & WADE, P.M. eds. 1998. *European wet grasslands: biodiversity, management and restoration.* Landscape ecology series. Chichester: Wiley.

KEENE, P. & HARLEY, M. 1987. *Burrator, Dartmoor landform trail.* Peterborough: Nature Conservancy Council.

KELLY, M. ed. 1995. *Design and construction guidelines for farm waste storage.* Edinburgh: Scottish Agricultural College & Scottish Farm Waste Liaison Group.

KELLY, P.G. & PERRY, K.A. 1990. *Wildlife habitat in Cumbria.* Research and survey in nature conservation No. 30. Peterborough: English Nature.

KING, A., GLASSER, N., LARWOOD, J., LITTLEWOOD, A., MOAT, T. & PAGE, K. 1996. Earth heritage conservation in England: a Natural Areas perspective. Peterborough: *English Nature Research Reports,* No. 158.

KING, C.A.M. 1976. *The geomorphology of the British Isles - Northern England.* London: Methuen & Co. Ltd.

KING, J. 1960. Observations on the seedling establishment and growth of *Nardus stricta* in burned Callunetum. *Journal of Ecology,* **48**, pp. 667-677.

KING, S. 1989. *Peregrines and rock climbing.* Manchester: British Mountaineering Council. Unpublished.

KIRBY, K.J. 1984. *Forestry operations and broadleaf woodland conservation.* Focus on nature conservation No. 8. Peterborough: Nature Conservancy Council

KIRBY, K.J. 1993. Assessing nature conservation values in British woodland: a review of recent practice. *Arboricultural Journal* **17**, pp. 253-276.

KIRBY, K.J. 1996a. The importance of native woods for nature conservation in the National Parks of England and Wales. *Quarterly Journal of Forestry,* **90**, pp. 31-38.

KIRBY, K. J. ed. 1996b. Sustainable forestry and nature conservation in England. Peterborough: *English Nature Research Reports,* No. 195.

KIRBY, K.J. & MAY, J 1989. The effects of enclosure, conifer planting and the subsequent removal of conifers in Dalavich oakwood (Argyll). Scottish Forestry, **43**, pp. 280-288.

KIRBY, K.J. & PATTERSON, G. 1993. Ecology and management of semi-natural tree mixtures. *In*: M.G.R. Cannell, D.C., Malcolm & P.A. Robertson, eds. *The ecology of mixed species stands of trees.* Oxford: Blackwell, pp. 189-210.

KIRBY, K.J. & REID, C. 1997. Preliminary nature conservation objectives for Natural Areas: woodland and forestry. Peterborough: *English Nature Research Reports,* No. 239.

KIRBY, K.J. & RUSH, A. 1994. Sustainable forestry and nature conservation: slow steps in the right direction. Peterborough: *English Nature Research Reports,* No. 122.

KIRBY, K.J., MITCHELL, F.G. & HESTER, A.J. 1994. A role for large herbivores (deer and domestic stock) in nature conservation management in British semi-natural woods. *Arboricultural Journal,* **18**, pp. 381-399.

KIRBY, P. 1992. *Habitat management for invertebrates: a practical handbook.* Sandy: RSPB.

KIRKBRIDE, C. 1996. Managing for sustainable leisure in the countryside - have we begun? *Ecos,* **17**, pp. 10-17.

KIRKHAM, F.W., MOUNTFORD, J.O. & WILKINS, R.J. 1996. The effects of nitrogen, potassium and phosphorus addition on the vegetation of a Somerset peat moor under cutting management. *Journal of Applied Ecology,* **33**, pp. 1013-1029.

LAKE DISTRICT NATIONAL PARK AUTHORITY. 1997a. *Helvellyn Management Plan.* Kendal: Lake District National Park Authority.

LAKE DISTRICT NATIONAL PARK AUTHORITY. 1997b. *Skiddaw Massif Management Plan.* Kendal: Lake District National Park Authority.

LANCE, A.N. 1983. Performance of sheep on unburned and serially burned blanket bog in western Ireland. *Journal of Applied Ecology,* **20**, pp. 767-775.

LANGBEIN, J. 1995. The red deer of Exmoor and the Quantocks. *Deer*, **9**, pp. 492-498.

LANGBEIN, J. 1997. *The ranging behaviour, habitat-use and impact of deer in oak woods and heather moors of Exmoor and the Quantock Hills.* Fordingbridge: The Deer Society.

LARWOOD, J. & MARKHAM, D. 1995. *Roads and geological conservation: a discussion document.* Peterborough: English Nature.

LAVERS, C.P. & HAINES-YOUNG, R.H. 1997. Displacement of dunlin *Calidris alpina schinzii* by forestry in the Flow Country and an estimate of the value of moorland adjacent to plantations. *Biological Conservation*, **79(1)**, pp. 87-90.

LEE, J.A. 1998. Unintentional experiments with terrestrial ecosystems: ecological effects of sulphur and nitrogen pollutants. *Journal of Ecology*, **86**, pp. 1-12.

LEE, J.A., TALLIS, J.H. & WOODIN, S.J. 1988. Acid deposition and British upland vegetation. *In*: M.B. Usher & D.B.A. Thompson, eds. *Ecological change in the uplands.* Oxford: Blackwell Scientific Publications, pp. 151-164.

LEGG, C. 1995. Heathland dynamics: a matter of scale. *In*: D.B.A. Thompson, A.J. Hester & M.B. Usher, eds. *Heaths and moorland: cultural landscapes.* Edinburgh and London: HMSO, pp. 117-134.

LIMESTONE PAVEMENT ACTION GROUP. 1998. *Limestone pavement: our fragile heritage.* Windermere: Limestone Pavement Action Group.

LIMESTONE PAVEMENT ACTION GROUP. 1999. *Limestone pavement: managing our fragile heritage.* Windermere: Limestone Pavement Action Group.

LINDSAY, R.A. 1995. *Bogs: the ecology, classification and conservation of ombrotrophic mires.* Perth: Scottish Natural Heritage.

LINDSAY, R.A., CHARMAN, D.T., EVERINGHAM, F., O'REILLY, R.M., PALMER, M.A., ROWELL, T.A. & STROUD, D.A. 1988. *The Flow Country: the peatlands of Caithness and Sutherland.* Peterborough: Nature Conservancy Council.

LISTER, C. 1996. *European Union environmental law: a guide for industry.* Chichester: John Wiley.

LOH, J. 1997. *Ecological impacts of climate change on national parks and protected areas of the world.* Gland: World Wide Fund for Nature.

LONGWORTH, A. 1992. *Water: a landowner's guide to water law.* London: Country Landowners' Association.

LOWDAY, J.E. 1984. The restoration of heathland vegetation after control of dense bracken by asulam. *Aspects of Applied Biology*, **5**, pp. 283-290.

LOWE, D.J. & WALTHAM, A.C. 1995. *A dictionary of karst and caves.* British Cave Research Association, Cave Studies 6.

MACDONALD, A. 1993. *Heather damage: a guide to types of damage and their causes.* Second edition. Research & survey in nature conservation No. 28. Peterborough: JNCC.

MACDONALD, A. 1996a. Heather layering and its management implications. *Information and advisory note* No. 35. Battleby: Scottish Natural Heritage.

MACDONALD, A. 1996b. Cutting of heather as an alternative to muirburn. *Information and advisory note* No. 58. Battleby: Scottish Natural Heritage.

MACDONALD, A. & ARMSTRONG, H. 1989. *Methods of monitoring heather cover.* Research & survey in nature conservation No. 27. Peterborough: Nature Conservancy Council.

MACDONALD, A.J. & HAYSOM, K. 1997. Heather moorland management for lepidoptera. *Information and advisory note* No. 78. Battleby: Scottish Natural Heritage.

MACDONALD, A.J., IMMIRZI, P., ARMSTRONG, H. & REYNOLDS, P. 1998. *A field guide to upland habitat condition.* Edinburgh: Scottish Natural Heritage.

MACDONALD, A.J., KIRKPATRICK, A.J., HESTER, A.J. & SYDES, C. 1995. Regeneration by natural layering of heather (*Calluna vulgaris*); frequency and characteristics in upland Britain. *Journal of Ecology*, **32**, pp. 85-99.

MACDONALD, A.J., STEPHENS, P., ARMSTRONG, H., IMMIRZI, P. & REYNOLDS, P. 1998. *A guide to upland habitats: surveying land management impacts. Vols 1 & 2.* Edinburgh: Scottish Natural Heritage.

MACEWEN, M. & SINCLAIR, G. 1983. *New life for the hills: policies for farming and conservation in the uplands.* London: Council for National Parks.

MACKAY, A.W. & TALLIS, J.H. 1996. Summit-type blanket mire erosion in the Forest of Bowland, Lancashire, UK: predisposing factors and implications for conservation. *Biological Conservation*, **76**, pp. 31-44.

MACKAY, J.W. 1995. People, perceptions and moorland. *In*: D.B.A. Thompson, A.J. Hester & M.B. Usher, eds. *Heaths and moorland: cultural landscapes.* Edinburgh and London: HMSO, pp. 102-111.

MACNEE, K. & HARVEY, J. 1996. *Water and recreation: a guide to managing the recreational use of water in Scotland.* A report to the Scottish Office. Edinburgh: Cobhams Resource Consultants & the Scottish Office.

MACPHERSON, H.A. & DUCKWORTH, W. 1886. *The birds of Cumberland including some notes on the birds of Westmorland.* Carlisle: Thurnam and Sons.

MAFF. 1988. *Agricultural Land Classification of England and Wales.* London: HMSO.

MAFF. 1991a. *Environmental aspects of support for hill farming*. London: MAFF.

MAFF. 1991b. *Farm waste storage: guidelines on construction.* Construction Industry Research and Information Association (CIRIA) Report No. 126. London: MAFF.

MAFF. 1992a. *The heather and grass burning code*. London: MAFF.

MAFF. 1992b. *The Pennine Dales ESA: guidelines for farmers*. London: MAFF.

MAFF. 1995. *Guidelines for the use of herbicides on weeds in or near watercourses or lakes*. London: MAFF. (Reprinted 1996)

MAFF. 1996a. *Prohibition of keeping of live fish (crayfish) Order 1996*. London: MAFF.

MAFF. 1996b. *Your livestock and your landscape: a guide to the environmental conditions attached to livestock subsidy schemes*. London: MAFF.

MAFF. 1997a. *Conservation grants for farmers*. London: MAFF.

MAFF. 1997b. *The Countryside Stewardship Scheme management guidelines directory*. London: MAFF Publications.

MAFF. 1997c. *Controlling soil erosion. An advisory booklet for the management of agricultural land*. London: MAFF.

MAFF. 1998a. *Clun ESA: guidelines for farmers*. London: MAFF Publications.

MAFF. 1998b. *Dartmoor Environmentally Sensitive Area: guidelines for farmers*. London: MAFF Publications.

MAFF. 1998c. *Exmoor ESA: guidelines for farmers*. London: MAFF Publications.

MAFF. 1998d. *Lake District ESA: guidelines for farmers*. London: MAFF Publications.

MAFF. 1998e. *The Shropshire Hills Environmentally Sensitive Area: guidelines for farmers*. London: MAFF Publications.

MAFF. 1998f. *South West Peak ESA: guidelines for farmers*. London: MAFF Publications.

MAFF. 1998g. *Code of good agricultural practice for the protection of soil*. London: MAFF.

MAFF. 1998h. *Code of good agricultural practice for the protection of water*. London: MAFF.

MAFF. 1998i. *Code of good agricultural practice for the protection of air*. London: MAFF.

MAFF. 1998j. *The code of practice for the safe use of pesticides on farms and holdings* (The Green Code). London: MAFF.

MAFF. 1999a. *The Countryside Strewardship Scheme. Information and how to apply.* London: MAFF.

MAFF. 1999b. *Controlling soil erosion. An advisory leaflet for preventing erosion caused by grazing livestock in lowland England.* London: MAFF.

MAFF. 2000. *England Rural Development Programme 2000-2006.* MAFF.

MAFF & HSC. 1990. *Code of practice for the safe use of pesticides on farms and holdings.* London: MAFF.

MAFF & WELSH OFFICE. 1991. *Code of good agriculture practice for the protection of water.* London: MAFF.

MAITLAND, P.S. 1996. *Spawning habitat of the vendace* Coregonus albula*: a review and management options for Bassenthwaite Lake and Derwentwater.* Contract report to English Nature. Kendal: English Nature.

MANLEY, V.J. & SMITH, C.A. 1994. Uplands. *In*: A.M. Moffat, ed. *Habitat conservation in England.* Peterborough: English Nature, pp. 187-243.

MARCHANT, J.H., HUDSON, R., CARTER, S.P. & WHITTINGTON, P.A. 1990. *Population trends in British breeding birds.* Tring: British Trust for Ornithology.

MARDON, D.K. 1990. Conservation of montane willow scrub in Scotland. *Transactions of the Botanical Society of Edinburgh,* **45,** pp. 427-436.

MARDON, D.K. 1996. *Eight years of montane scrub restoration at Ben Lawers NNR.* Unpublished conference paper.

MARRS, R.H. & FROST, A.J. 1996. Techniques to reduce the impact of asulam drift from helicopter sprayers on native vegetation. *Journal of Environmental Management,* **46,** pp. 373-393.

MARRS, R.H. & PAKEMAN, R.J. 1995. Bracken invasion: lessons from the past and prospects for the future. *In*: D.B.A. Thompson, A.J. Hester & M.B. Usher, eds. *Heaths and moorland: cultural landscapes.* Edinburgh and London: HMSO, pp. 180-193.

MARRS, R.H. & WELCH, D. 1991. *Moorland wilderness: the potential effects of removing domestic livestock, particularly sheep.* Huntingdon: Institute of Terrestrial Ecology.

MARSDEN, J.H. 1990. More sheep and less heather in the Lake District: what should be done? *In*: D.B.A. Thompson & K.J. Kirby, eds. Grazing research and nature conservation in the uplands: proceedings of a seminar, 1988. *Research & survey in nature conservation,* No. 31. Peterborough: Nature Conservancy Council, pp. 19-31.

MASON, C.F. 1991. *Biology of fresh water pollution.* 2nd edition. Essex: Longman Scientific and Technical.

MASON, C.F. & MACDONALD, S.M. 1999. Habitat use by lapwings and golden plover in a largely arable landscape. *Bird Study,* **46 (1)**, pp. 89-99.

MATTHEWS, J.R. 1937. Geographical relationships of the British flora. *Journal of Ecology,* **25**, pp. 1-90.

MATTHEWS, J.R. 1955. *Origin and distribution of the British flora.* London: Hutchinson.

MAXWELL, T.J., EADIE, J. & HODGSON, J. 1989. Land use in the hills and uplands: the work of the Hill Farming Research Organisation. *In:* M. Bell & R.G.H. Bunce, eds. *Agriculture and conservation in the hills and uplands.* ITE Symposium No. 23. Grange-over-Sands: Institute of Terrestrial Ecology, pp. 56-62.

McLUSKY, D.S. 1994. Tidal Fresh Waters. *In:* P.S. Maitland, P.J. Boon, & D.S. McLusky, eds. *The fresh waters of Scotland: a national resource of international significance.* Chichester: John Wiley & Sons.

McGILVRAY, J. 1996. *An economic study of grouse moors.* Fordingbridge: Game Conservancy Scottish Research Trust.

MERCER, B. & EVANS, P. 1997. *A review of the Craven Limestone Grassland Wildlife Enhancement Scheme.* Leyburn: English Nature.

MILES, J. 1971. Burning *Molinia*-dominant vegetation for grazing by red deer. *British Grassland Society Journal,* **26**, pp. 247-250.

MILES, J. 1987. Effects of man on upland vegetation. *In:* M. Bell & R.G.H. Bunce, eds. *Agriculture and conservation in the hills and uplands.* ITE Symposium No. 23. Grange-over-Sands: Institute of Terrestrial Ecology, pp. 22-31.

MILES, J. 1988. Vegetation and soil change in the uplands. *In:* M.B. Usher & D.B.A. Thompson, eds. *Ecological change in the uplands.* Oxford: Blackwell Scientific Publications, pp. 57-70.

MILLER, G.R. 1986. *Ecological impact of downhill skiing developments in north-east Scotland.* Natural Environment Research Council contract report to the Nature Conservancy Council. Banchory: Institute of Terrestrial Ecology.

MILLER, G.R., GEDDES, C. & MARDON, D.K. 1994. Response of the alpine gentian (*Gentiana nivalis*) and other montane species to protection from grazing. *Scottish Natural Heritage Review,* No. 32. Edinburgh: Scottish Natural Heritage.

MILNE, J.A., BIRCH, C.P.D., HESTER, A.J., ARMSTRONG, H.M. & ROBERTSON, A. 1998. *The impact of vertebrate herbivores on the natural heritage of the Scottish uplands - a review.* Scottish Natural Heritage Review No. 95. Battleby: Scottish Natural Heritage.

MITCHELL, F.J.G. & KIRBY, K.J. 1990. The impact of large herbivores on the conservation of semi-natural woods in the British uplands. *Forestry*, **63**, pp. 333-353.

MITCHELL, F.J.G., HESTER, A.J. & KIRBY K.J. 1996. Effects of season and intensity of sheep grazing on a British upland woodland: browsing damage to planted saplings. *Botanical Journal of Scotland*, **48**, pp. 199-207.

MITCHELL, K. & BALDOCK, D. 1996. Glossary of agri-environmental terms. Peterborough: *English Nature Research Reports*, No. 159.

MITCHELL-JONES, A.J. 1996. *Mammals in England: a conservation action priority list.* English Nature Science No. 26. Peterborough: English Nature.

MITCHELL-JONES, A.J. & GENT, A.H. 1997. Priority Natural Areas for mammals, reptiles and amphibians. Peterborough: *English Nature Research Reports*, No. 242.

MOFFAT, A.M. ed. 1994a. Priorities for habitat conservation in England. Peterborough: *English Nature Research Reports*, No. 97.

MOFFAT, A.M. ed. 1994b. *Habitat conservation in England.* Peterborough: English Nature.

MOORE, N.W. & CORBETT, P.S. 1990. Guidelines for monitoring dragonfly populations. *Journal of the British Dragonfly Society*, **6(2)**, pp. 21-23.

MOORLAND WORKING GROUP. 1998. *Good practice for grouse moor management.* Battleby: Scottish Natural Heritage.

MORRIS, P.A. 1993. *A red data book for British mammals.* London: The Mammal Society.

MORTIMER, S.R., TURNER, A.J., BROWN, V.K., FULLER, R.J., GOOD, J.E.G., BELL, S.A., STEVENS, P.A., NORRIS, D., BAYFIELD, N. & WARD, L.K. 2000. *The nature conservation value of scrub in Britain.* JNCC Report No. 308.

MOUNTFORD, E. 2000. A provisional minimum intervention woodland reserve series for England with proposals for baseline recording and long-term monitoring therein. Peterborough: *English Nature Research Reports*, No. 385.

MOWFORTH, M.H. & SYDES, C. 1989. *Moorland management: a literature review.* Nature Conservancy Council Research & survey in nature conservation No. 25. Peterborough: Nature Conservancy Council.

NATIONAL CAVING ASSOCIATION. 1995. *Cave conservation policy.* London: National Caving Association, London.

NATIONAL CAVING ASSOCIATION. 1997. *Cave conservation handbook.* London: National Caving Association.

NATIONAL CONSUMER COUNCIL. 1995. *Agricultural policy in the European Union.* London: National Consumer Council.

NATIONAL FARMERS UNION. 1997. *The 1997 Hill Review.* London: NFU.

NATIONAL RIVERS AUTHORITY. 1996. *River habitats in England and Wales: a national overview.* Bristol: National Rivers Authority.

NATIONAL RIVERS AUTHORITY. 1994. *Guidance for the control of invasive plants near watercourses.* Bristol: National Rivers Authority.

NATIONAL RIVERS AUTHORITY. 1995. *The use of herbicides in or near water.* Bristol: National Rivers Authority.

NATIONAL SHEEP ASSOCIATION. 1989. *Sheep naturally!* Malvern: National Sheep Association.

NATIONAL SHEEP ASSOCIATION. 1994. *British sheep.* Malvern: National Sheep Association.

NATURE CONSERVANCY COUNCIL. 1984. *Nature conservation in Great Britain.* Shrewsbury: Nature Conservancy Council.

NATURE CONSERVANCY COUNCIL. 1986a. *Nature conservation and afforestation in Britain.* Peterborough: Nature Conservancy Council.

NATURE CONSERVANCY COUNCIL. 1986b. *Potentially damaging operations manual.* Peterborough: Nature Conservancy Council.

NATURE CONSERVANCY COUNCIL. 1987. Changes in the Cumbria countryside. *Research and survey in nature conservation,* No. 6. Peterborough: Nature Conservancy Council.

NATURE CONSERVANCY COUNCIL. 1988. *Site management plans for nature conservation: a working guide.* Peterborough: Nature Conservancy Council.

NATURE CONSERVANCY COUNCIL. 1989. *Guidelines for the selection of biological SSSIs.* Peterborough: Nature Conservancy Council.

NATURE CONSERVANCY COUNCIL. 1990a. *Handbook for phase I habitat survey: a technique for environmental audit.* Peterborough: Nature Conservancy Council.

NATURE CONSERVANCY COUNCIL. 1990b. Nature conservation and agricultural change. *Focus on nature conservation,* No. 25. Peterborough: English Nature.

NATURE CONSERVANCY COUNCIL. 1990c. *Fish farming and the Scottish fresh water environment.* Peterborough: Nature Conservancy Council.

NATURE CONSERVANCY COUNCIL. 1991. *Earth Science Conservation in Great Britain, A Strategy.* Peterborough: Nature Conservancy Council.

NATIONAL ECONOMIC DEVELOPMENT COUNCIL. 1990. *Understanding the Less Favoured Areas: the importance of farming in the rural economy.* National Economic Deveopment Council.

NEW PHYTOLOGIST. 1998. Major biological issues resulting from anthropogenic disturbance of the nitrogen cycle. The third *New Phytologist* symposium, Lancaster University, UK, 3-5 September 1997. Vol. 139.

NEWBOLD, C. & MOUNTFORD, O. 1997. *Water level requirements of wetland plants and animals.* English Nature Freshwater Series No. 6. Peterborough: English Nature.

NEWBOLD, C., HAMBREY, J.B. & SMITH, I.R. 1986. *Nature conservation and fresh water fish farming.* Unpublished internal report. Peterborough: Nature Conservancy Council.

NEWBOLD, C., HONNOR, J. & BUCKLEY, K. 1989. *Nature conservation and the management of drainage channels.* Peterborough: Nature Conservancy Council and Association of Drainage Authorities.

NEWBOLD, C., PURSEGLOVE, J. & HOLMES, N. 1983. *Nature conservation and river engineering.* Peterborough: Nature Conservancy Council.

NICHOLSON, I.A., PATTERSON, I.S. & CURRIE, A. 1970. A study of vegetational dynamics: selection by sheep and cattle in *Nardus* pasture. *In*: A. Watson, ed. *Animal populations in relation to their food resources.* Oxford: Blackwell Scientific Publications, pp. 129-143. British Ecological Society Symposium No. 10.

NINNES, R.B. 1995. Bracken, heath and burning on the Quantock Hills, England. *In*: D.B.A. Thompson, A.J. Hester & M.B. Usher, eds. *Heaths and moorland: cultural landscapes.* Edinburgh and London: HMSO, pp. 194-199.

NIX, J. Annual publication. *Farm management pocket book.* Wye: Wye College, University of London.

NOLAN, A.J., HENDERSON, D.J. & MERRELL, B.G. 1995. *In*: D.B.A. Thompson, A.J. Hester & M.B. Usher, eds. *Heaths and moorland: cultural landscapes.* Edinburgh and London: HMSO, pp. 174-179.

NORTH WEST WATER. 1996. *Code of practice for bracken control.* Warrington: North West Water.

NORTH YORK MOORS NATIONAL PARK. 1986. *Moorland management.* Helmsley: North York Moors National Park.

NORTH YORK MOORS NATIONAL PARK. 1991. *Moorland management programme 1985-1990.* Helmsley: North York Moors National Park.

NORTH YORK MOORS NATIONAL PARK. 1993a. *Advice Note: heather cutting guidelines.* Helmsley: North York Moors National Park.

NORTH YORK MOORS NATIONAL PARK. 1993b. *Advice Note: bracken control, follow up treatments and after care.* Helmsley: North York Moors National Park.

NORTH YORK MOORS NATIONAL PARK. 1996. *Advice Note: heather cutting guidelines.* Helmsley: North York Moors National Park.

O'HALLORAN, D., GREEN, C., HARLEY, M., STANLEY, M. & KNILL, J. eds. 1994. *Geological and landscape conservation.* London: The Geological Society.

OLIVER, P.G. & KILLEEN, I.J. 1996. Report on the 1995 survey of the freshwater pearl mussel (*Margaritifera margaritifera* L., 1758). Peterborough: *English Nature Research Reports,* No. 162.

ORMEROD, S.J. & BUCKTON S.T. 1994. Catchment source areas and the ecological effects of catchment liming - phases I and II. *Research and development project* No. 281. Bristol: National Rivers Authority.

PAGE, C.N. 1982. *The ferns of Britain and Ireland.* Cambridge: Cambridge University Press.

PAKEMAN, R.J. & HAY, E. 1996. Heathland seed banks under bracken *Pteridium aquilinum* (L.) Kuhn and their importance for re-vegetation after bracken control. *Journal of Environmental Management,* **47**, pp. 329-339.

PAKEMAN, R.J. & MARRS, R.H. 1992. The conservation value of bracken *Pteridium aquilinum* (L.) Kuhn-dominated communities in the UK, and an assessment of the ecological impact of bracken expansion or its removal. *Biological Conservation,* **62**, pp. 101-114.

PAKEMAN, R.J. & MARRS, R.H. 1993. Bracken. *Biologist,* **40**, pp. 105-109.

PAKEMAN, R.J. & MARRS, R.H. 1996. Modelling the effects of climate change on the growth of bracken (*Pteridium aquilinum*) in Britain. *Journal of Applied Ecology,* **33**, pp. 561-575.

PAKEMAN, R.J., MARRS, R.H. & JACOB, P.J. 1994. A model of bracken (*Pteridium aquilinum*) growth and the effects of control strategies and changing climate. *Journal of Applied Ecology,* **31**, pp. 145-154.

PALMER, M.A. 1989. A botanical classification of standing waters in Great Britain. *Research and Survey in Nature Conservation,* No. 19. Peterborough: Nature Conservancy Council.

PALMER, M.A. 1994. *A UK plant conservation strategy.* Peterborough: Joint Nature Conservation Committee.

PALMER, M.A. 1996. A strategic approach to the conservation of plants in the United Kingdom. *Journal of Applied Ecology,* **33**, pp. 1231-1240.

PALMER, M.A. & BRATTON, J.H. eds. 1995. *A sample survey of distribution.* The Botanical Society of the British Isles Monitoring Scheme 1987-1988. UK Nature Conservation, No. 8. Peterborough: Joint Nature Conservation Committee.

PALMER, M.A., BELL, S.L., BUTTERFIELD, I. 1992. A botanical classification of standing waters in Britain: applications for conservation and monitoring. *Aquatic Conservation: Marine and Freshwater Ecosystems*, **2**, pp. 125-143.

PARKER, D.M. 1995. *Habitat creation: a critical guide.* English Nature Science No. 21. Peterborough: English Nature.

PARKYN, L., STONEMAN, R.E. & INGRAM, H.A.P. eds. 1997. *Conserving peatlands.* Wallingford: CAB International.

PARR, R. 1992. The decline to extinction of a population of golden plover in north-east Scotland. *Ornis Scandinavica*, **23**, pp. 152-158.

PARR, R. 1993. Nest predation and numbers of golden plover *Pluvialis apricaria* and other moorland waders. *Bird Study*, **40**, pp. 223-231.

PARRY, M., BRUCE, A. & HARKNESS, C. 1981. The plight of British moorlands. *New Scientist*, **28**, pp. 550-551.

PARRY, M., PORTER, J.H. & CARTER, T.R. 1990. Climatic change and its implication for agriculture. *Outlook on Agriculture*, **19**, pp. 9-15.

PARSISSON, D., & MOXEY, A. 1999. Modelling the impact of the agencies proposals for financial support within the Less Favoured Areas of England and Wales. Unpublished report to English Nature.

PAYNE, N.F. & BRYANT, F.C. 1994. *Techniques for wildlife habitat management of uplands.* New York: McGraw-Hill, Inc.

PEAK DISTRICT NATIONAL PARK 1990. *Code of practice for bracken control in the peak District National Park (Provisional).* Bakewell: Peak District National Park.

PEARSALL, W.H. 1920. The aquatic vegetation of the English Lakes. *Journal of Ecology*, **8**, pp. 163-201.

PEARSALL, W.H. 1950. *Mountains and moorlands.* The New Naturalist Series. London: Collins.

PEARSALL, W.H. & PENNINGTON, W. 1973. *The Lake District.* London: Collins.

PEPPER, H. W. 1992. Forest fencing. *Forestry Commission Bulletin*, 102. HMSO.

PERRING, F.H. & FARRELL, L., 1983. *British Red Data books: 1 Vascular Plants.* Lincoln: Royal Society for Nature Conservation.

PERRING, F.H. & WALTERS, S.M. eds. 1990. *Atlas of the British flora.* East Ardsley: Botanical Society of the British Isles.

PERRING, F.H. & WALTERS, S.M. eds. 1990. *Atlas of the British flora.* Oundle: Botanical Society of the British Isles.

PETERKEN, G.F. 1977. Habitat conservation priorities in British and European woodland. *Biological Conservation* **11**, pp. 223-236.

PETERKEN, G.F. 1993. *Woodland conservation and management* (2nd edition). London: Chapman and Hall.

PETERKEN, G.F. 1996. *Natural woodland.* Cambridge: Cambridge University Press.

PETERKEN, G.F. 2000. Natural reserves in English woodlands. Peterborough: *English Nature Research Reports,* No. 384.

PETERSEN, R.C. JR, PETERSEN, L. & LACOURSIERE, J. 1992. A building block model for stream restoration. *In:* P. Boon, P. Calow & G. Petts, eds. *River conservation and management.* New York: John Wiley & Sons, pp. 293-309.

PETTS, G.E. & CALOW, P. eds. 1996a. *River restoration: selected extracts from the river handbook.* Oxford: Blackwell Science.

PETTS, G.E. & CALOW, P. eds. 1996b. *River biota: diversity and dynamics: selected extracts from the river handbook.* Oxford: Blackwell Science.

PETTS, G.E. & CALOW, P. eds. 1996c. *River flows and channel forms: selected extracts from the river handbook.* Oxford: Blackwell Science.

PETTY, S.J. & AVERY, M.I. 1990. *Forest bird communities: a review of the ecology and management of forest bird communities in relation to silvicultural practices in the British uplands.* Forestry Commission Occasional Paper 26. Edinburgh: Forestry Commission.

PHILLIPS, J. 1993. The white moorland programme. *Joseph Nickerson Reconciliation Project Annual Report,* **9**, pp. 23-26.

PHILLIPS, J. 1997a. The white moorland programme. *The Heather Trust Annual Report.* Kippen: The Heather Trust.

PHILLIPS, J. 1997b. Bringing back the black grouse. *Enact,* **5(1)**, pp. 12-14.

PHILLIPS, J. & WATSON, A. 1993. The whole-moor tick study. *Joseph Nickerson Reconciliation Project Annual Report,* **9**, pp. 28-29.

PHILLIPS, J. & WATSON, A. 1995. Key requirements for management of heather moorland: now and for the future. *In*: D.B.A. Thompson, A.J. Hester & M.B. Usher, eds. *Heaths and moorland: cultural landscapes.* Edinburgh and London: HMSO, pp. 344-361.

PHILLIPS, M.J. 1985. *The environmental impact of cage culture on Scottish fresh water lochs.* Unpublished report to the Highlands and Islands Development Board. Stirling: Institute of Aquaculture, University of Stirling.

PIETERSE, A.H. & MURPHY, K.J. 1990. *Aquatic weeds: the ecology and management of nuisance aquatic vegetation.* Oxford: Oxford University Press.

PIGOTT, M.E. & PIGOTT, C.D. 1959. Stratigraphy and pollen analysis of Malham Tarn and Tarn Moss. *Field Studies,* **1**, pp. 84-101.

PITCAIRN, C.E.R., FOWLER, D. & GRACE, J. 1991. *Changes in species composition of semi-natural vegetation associated with the increase in atmospheric inputs of nitrogen.* Nature Conservancy Council Chief Scientist (CSD) Report No. 1246. Peterborough: Nature Conservancy Council.

POLDEN,. M. & JACKSON, S. 1994. *The environment and the law: earth, air, fire and water: a practical guide.* London: Longman.

POLLARD, E. 1977. A method for assessing changes in the abundance of butterflies. *Biological Conservation,* **12**, pp. 115-134.

POORE, D. 1992. *Guidelines for mountain protected areas.* Cambridge: IUCN, The World Conservation Union.

PORLEY, R. & MCDONNELL, A. 1997. Rare and scarce vascular plants and bryophytes in Natural Areas. Peterborough: *English Nature Research Reports,* No. 267.

PORTER, M. 1990. *Pennine Way management project.* Bakewell: Peak District National Park.

PRESS, M.C., POTTER, J.A., BURKE, M.J.W., CALLAGHAN, T.V. & LEE, J.A. 1998. Responses of a subarctic dwarf shrub heath community to simulated environmental change. *Journal of Ecology,* **86**, pp. 315-327.

PRESTON, C.D. & CROFT, J.M. 1997. *Aquatic plants in Britain and Ireland.* Peterborough: Joint Nature Conservation Committee.

PURVIS, O.W. & JAMES, P.W. 1985. Lichens of the Coniston copper mines.. *Lichenologist,* **17 (3)**, pp. 221-237.

PURVIS, O.W., COPPINS, B.J., HAWKSWORTH, D.L., JAMES, P.W. & MOORE, D.M. eds. 1992. *The lichen flora of Great Britain and Ireland.* London: Natural History Museum and British Lichen Society.

PUTMAN, R.J. 1996. *Deer management on National Nature Reserves.* Peterborough: English Nature (Research Report 173).

PYATT, D.G. 1987. Afforestation of blanket peatland: soil effects. *Forestry and British Timber,* March, pp. 15-16.

PYWELL, R.F., WEBB, N.R. & PUTWAIN, P.D. 1996. Harvested heather shoots as a resource for heathland restoration. *Biological Conservation*, **75**, pp. 247-254.

RACKHAM, O. 1980. *Ancient woodland.* London, Arnold.

RACKHAM, O. 1986. *The history of the countryside.* London, Dent.

RACKHAM, O. 1990. *Trees and woodland in the British landscape (2nd edition).* London: Dent.

RADFORD, E. 1998. *The restoration of replanted ancient woodland.* Peterborough: *English Nature Research Reports*, No. 269.

RAMBLERS ASSOCIATION. 1998. *Managing conflict over access to open country: a case study of the Peak National Park.* London: Ramblers Association.

RATCLIFFE, D.A. 1959. Vegetation of the Carneddau, North Wales: 1. Grasslands, heaths and bogs. *Journal of Ecology*, **47**, pp. 371-413.

RATCLIFFE, D.A. 1968. An ecological account of Atlantic bryophytes in the British Isles. *New Phytologist*, 67, pp. 365-439.

RATCLIFFE, D.A. 1973. The dotterel as a breeding bird in England. *In*: D. Nethersole-Thompson, *The Dotterel.* Collins: London, pp. 190-197.

RATCLIFFE, D.A. 1977. *A Nature Conservation Review. Vol. 1 and 2.* Cambridge: Cambridge University Press.

RATCLIFFE, D.A. 1982. Will this wilderness remain? *Natural World*, **4**, pp. 26-29.

RATCLIFFE, D.A. 1983. *The future of nature conservation in Britain.* Peterborough: Nature Conservancy Council.

RATCLIFFE, D.A. 1988. The British upland scene. *In*: D.B.A. Thompson, S. Whyte & P.H. Oswald, eds. *Nature Conservancy Council research in the uplands: proceedings of a seminar, 1986.* (Nature Conservancy Council Research & survey in nature conservation No. 16.) Peterborough: Nature Conservancy Council, pp. 7-14.

RATCLIFFE, D.A. 1990a. Upland birds and their conservation. *British Wildlife*, **2**, pp. 1-12.

RATCLIFFE, D.A. 1990b. *Bird life of mountains and uplands.* Cambridge: Cambridge University Press.

RATCLIFFE, D.A. 1991. The mountain flora of Britain and Ireland. *British Wildlife*, **3(1)**, pp. 10-19.

RATCLIFFE, D.A. 1993. The mountain flora of Britain and Ireland. *British Wildlife*, **4(6)**, pp. 10-19.

RATCLIFFE, D.A. & THOMPSON, D.B.A. 1988. The British uplands: their ecological character and international significance. *In*: M.B. Usher & D.B.A. Thompson, eds. *Ecological change in the uplands.* Oxford: Blackwell Scientific Publications, pp. 9-36. (British Ecological Society Special Publication No. 7.)

RAVENSCROFT, N.O.M. & WARREN, M. 1996a. *Species Action Plan: northern brown argus* Aricia artaxerxes. Wareham: Butterfly Conservation.

RAVENSCROFT, N.O.M. & WARREN, M. 1996b. *Species Action Plan: the mountain ringlet* Erebia epiphron. Wareham: Butterfly Conservation

RAWES, M. 1971. Aspects of the ecology of the northern Pennines 1. The influence of agriculture. *Moor House Occasional Papers,* **1**, pp. 1-15.

RAWES, M. 1981. Further results of excluding sheep from high-level grasslands in the North Pennines. *Journal of Ecology,* **69**, pp. 651-669.

RAWES, M. 1983. Changes in two high altitude blanket bogs after cessation of sheep grazing. *Journal of Ecology,* **71**, pp. 219-235.

RAWES, M. & HEAL, O.W. 1978. The blanket bog as part of a Pennine moorland. *In*: O.W. Heal & D.F. Perkins, eds. *Production ecology of British moors and mountain grasslands.* Berlin: Springer-Verlag, pp. 224-243.

RAWES, M. & HOBBS, R. 1979. Management of semi-natural blanket bog in the northern Pennines. *Journal of Ecology,* **67**, pp. 789-807.

RAWES, M & WELCH, D. 1964. Studies on sheep grazing in the North Pennines. *British Grassland Society Journal,* **19**, pp. 403-411.

RAWES, M. & WELCH, D. 1972. Trails to recreate floristically rich vegetation by plant introduction in the northern Pennines, England. *Biological Conservation,* **4**, pp. 135-140.

RAWES, M. & WILLIAMS, R. 1973. Production and utilisation of *Calluna* and *Eriophorum*. In: Potassium Institute Ltd., Hill pasture improvement and its economic utilisation. *Papers presented at the 3rd Colloquium of the Potassium Institute Ltd.,* **3**, pp. 115-119.

REDPATH, S.M. & THIRGOOD, S.J. 1997. *Birds of prey and red grouse.* London: The Stationery Office.

REID, C.M., KIRBY, K.J. & COOKE, R. 1996. A preliminary assessment of woodland conservation in England by Natural Areas. Peterborough: *English Nature Research Reports,* No. 186.

REYNOLDS, P. 1998. Red deer. *In*: F.E. Stewart & S.G. Eno, *Grazing management planning for upland Natura 2000 sites: a practical manual.* Edinburgh: The National Trust for Scotland, pp. 111-116.

RHONE-POULENC. 1997. *Bracken management handbook: Integrated bracken management - a guide to best practice.* Essex: Rhone-Poulenc.

RICH, T.C.G. 1991. *Crucifers of Great Britain and Ireland.* BSBI Handbook No. 6. London: Botanical Society of the British Isles.

RICH, T.C.G. 1997. The management of semi-natural lowland grassland for selected rare and scarce vascular plants: a review. Peterborough: *English Nature Research Reports,* No. 216.

RICH, T.C.G. & BAECKER, M. 1986. The distribution of *Sorbus lancastriensis* E.F. Warburg. *Watsonia,* **16,** pp. 83-85.

RICH, T.C.G. & BAECKER, M. 1992. Additional records of *Sorbus lancastriensis* E.F. Warburg (Rosaceae). *Watsonia,* **19,** pp. 139-140.

ROBERTS, J., MACDONALD, A. & WOOD-GEE, V. 1996a. Bracken control. *Information and advisory note* No. 24. Battleby: Scottish Natural Heritage.

ROBERTS, J., MACDONALD, A. & WOOD-GEE, V. 1996b. Supplementary feeding. *Information and advisory note* No. 13. Battleby: Scottish Natural Heritage.

ROBINSON, C.H., WOOKEY, P.A., LEE, J.A., CALLAGHAN, T.V. & PRESS, M.C. 1998. Plant community responses to simulated environmental change at a high arctic polar semi-desert, Svalbard (79 °N). *Ecology,* **79(3),** pp. 856-866.

ROBINSON, R.C. 1986. Practical herbicide use for bracken control. *In*: R.T. Smith & J.A. Taylor (eds), *Bracken: Ecology, land use and control technology.* Carnforth: Parthenon Press, pp. 331-240.

RODWELL, J. ed. 1991a. *British plant communities. Volume 1. Woodlands and scrub.* Cambridge: Cambridge University Press.

RODWELL, J. ed. 1991b. *British plant communities. Volume 2. Mires and heaths.* Cambridge: Cambridge University Press.

RODWELL, J. ed. 1992. *British plant communities. Volume 3. Grasslands and montane communities.* Cambridge: Cambridge University Press.

RODWELL, J. ed. 1995. *British plant communities. Volume 4. Aquatic communities, swamps and tall herb fens.* Cambridge: Cambridge University Press.

RODWELL, J. ed. 2000. *British plant communities. Volume 5. Maritime and weed communities and vegetation of open habitats.* Cambridge: Cambridge University Press.

RODWELL, J. & PATTERSON, G. 1994. *Creating new native woodland.* Forestry Commission Bulletin 112. London: HMSO

ROTHERAY, G.E. & HORSFIELD, D. 1995. Insects of Scottish mountains. *British Wildlife*, **6(3)**, pp. 160-167.

ROWELL, T.A. 1988. *The peatland management handbook.* Nature Conservancy Council Research & survey in nature conservation No. 14. Peterborough: Nature Conservancy Council.

RSPB. 1984. *Hill farming and birds: a survival plan.* Sandy: RSPB.

RSPB. 1995. *Conservation management on blanket bog: a review.* A report commissioned from Rob Stoneman of the Scottish Wildlife Trust. Sandy: RSPB.

RSPB. 1996. *Birds of conservation concern.* Sandy: RSPB.

RSPB. 1998. *A future for grouse moors: a call to action.* Sandy: RSPB.

RSPB, ENGLISH NATURE & INSTITUTE OF TERRESTRIAL ECOLOGY. 1997. *The wet grassland guide: managing floodplain and coastal wet grasslands for wildlife.* Sandy: RSPB.

RSPB, NRA & RSNC. 1994. *The new rivers and wildlife handbook.* Sandy: RSPB.

SANDERSON, J., RUSHTON, P.S., CHERRIL, A.J. & BYRNE, J.P. 1995. Soil, vegetation and space: an analysis of their effects on the invertebrate communities of a moorland in north-east England. *Journal of Applied Ecology*, **32(3)**, pp. 506-518.

SAUNDERS, C.M. & MOXEY, A. 1994. Livestock movement and location in England. Peterborough: *English Nature Research Reports*, No. 88.

SCANDRETT, E. 1989. *Regenerating heather moorland: a study of methods to encourage regeneration from seed.* Aberdeen: MLURI.

SCHUMAKER, R., HODGETTS, N.G., MARTIGNY, P. & STEWART, N.F. 1993. *Red data book of European bryophytes.* Gland: Unpublished report to the Worldwide Fund for Nature.

SCOTTISH AGRICULTURAL COLLEGE. Annual publication. *Farm management handbook.* Edinburgh: Scottish Agricultural College.

SCOTTISH AGRICULTURAL COLLEGE. 1997. The European Union sheepmeat and goatmeat regime and its effects on the environment. Report for the English Nature Land Use Policy Group. Peterborough: English Nature.

SCOTTISH NATURAL HERITAGE. 1993. *A Muirburn Code.* Perth: Scottish Natural Heritage.

SCOTTISH NATURAL HERITAGE. 1995. *Boglands.* Perth: Scottish Natural Heritage.

SCOTTISH NATURAL HERITAGE. 1997. *Countryside recreation and access strategies: guidance for Local Authorities.* Battleby: Scottish Natural Heritage.

SEAWARD, M.R.D. 1984. Census catalogue of Irish lichens. *Glasra*, **8**, pp. 1-32.

SELLERS, B. & BAKER, A.J.M. 1988. *Review of the metallophyte vegetation and its conservation.* (Nature Conservancy Council CSD Report No. 797). Peterborough: Nature Conservancy Council.

SHAW, S., WHEELER, B. & BACKSHALL, J. 1997. Review of effects of burning and grazing of blanket bogs: conservation issues and conflicts. *In*: J.H. Tallis, R. Meade & P.D. Hulme, eds. *Blanket mire degradation: causes, consequences and challenges.* Aberdeen: The Macaulay Land Use Research Institute on behalf of the Mires Research Group of the British Ecological Society.

SHAW, S.C., WHEELER, B.D., KIRBY, P., PHILIPSON, P. & EDMUNDS, R. 1996. Literature review of the historical effects of burning and grazing of blanket bog and upland wet heath. Peterborough: *English Nature Research Reports*, No. 172.

SHIRT, D.B. ed. 1987. *British red data books: 2. Insects.* Peterborough: Nature Conservancy Council.

SIBBALD, A.R., GRANT, S.A., MILNE, J.A. & MAXWELL, T.J. 1987. Heather moorland management - a model. *In*: M. Bell & R.G.H. Bunce, eds. *Agriculture and conservation in the hills and uplands.* ITE Symposium No. 23. Grange-over-Sands: Institute of Terrestrial Ecology, pp. 107-108.

SIDAWAY, R. & THOMPSON, D.B.A. 1991. Upland recreation: the limits of acceptable change. *Ecos*, **12**, pp. 31-39.

SIMMONS, I.G. 1990. The mid-Holocene ecological history of the moorlands on England and Wales and its relevance for conservation. *Environmental Conservation*, **17**, pp. 61-69.

SIMPSON, N. 1993. A summary review of information on the autoecology and control of six grassland weed species. Peterborough: *English Nature Research Reports*, No. 44.

SKEMPTON, A.W., LEADBEATER, A.D. & CHANDLER, R. J. 1989. The Mam Tor landslide, North Derbyshire. *Philosophical Transactions of the Royal Society*. A329, pp. 503-547.

SMALLSHIRE, D., SHORROCK, D..J. & HALSHAW, L. 1997. Sustainable grazing practices on the South West moors of England. Peterborough: *English Nature Research Reports*, No. 253.

SMITH, I. & LYLE, A. 1979. *Distribution of fresh waters in Great Britain.* Edinburgh: Institute of Freshwater Ecology.

SMITH, R.S. 1989. The effects of fertilisers on the conservation interest of traditionally managed upland meadows. *In*: M. Bell & R.G.H. Bunce, eds. *Agriculture and conservation in the hills and uplands.* ITE Symposium No. 23. Grange-over-Sands: Institute of Terrestrial Ecology, pp. 38-43.

SMITH, R.S. 1994. Effects of fertilisers on plant species composition and conservation interest of UK grassland. *In:* R.J. Haggar & S. Peel, eds. *Grassland management and nature conservation.* Occasional Symposium No. 28. Reading: British Grassland Society.

SMITH, R.S. 1997. Upland meadow grasslands in the Pennine Dales ESA. *In:* R.D. Sheldrick ed. *Grassland management in Environmentally Sensitive Areas*. Occasional Symposium No. 32. Reading: British Grassland Society.

SMITH, R.T. & TAYLOR, J.A. eds. 1986. *Bracken: ecology, land use and control technology*. Carnforth: Parthenon Publishing.

SNOW, C.S.R. & MARRS, R.H. 1997. Restoration of *Calluna* heathland on a bracken *Pteridium*-infested site in North West England. *Biological Conservation*, **81**, pp 35-42.

SPENCER, J.W. & KIRBY, K.J. 1992. An ancient woodland inventory for England and Wales. *Biological Conservation* **62**, pp. 77-93.

SPORTS COUNCIL & COUNTRYSIDE COMMISSION. 1995. *Good practice in the planning and management of sport and active recreation in the countryside.* Cheltenham: Countryside Commission.

STACE, C. 1997. *New flora of the British Isles.* 2nd Edition. Cambridge: Cambridge University Press.

STANTON, W. 1992. There I was surveying this hole. *New Scientist*, 30, pp. 5-92.

STEVENSON, A.C. & THOMPSON, D.B.A. 1992. Long-term changes in the extent of heather moorland in upland Britain and Ireland: palaeoecological evidence for the importance of grazing. *The Holocene*, 3, pp. 70-76.

STEVENSON, A.C., RHODES, A.N., KIRKPATRICK, A.H. & MACDONALD, A.J. 1996. The determination of fire histories and an assessment of their effects on moorland soils and vegetation. *Scottish Natural Heritage Research, Survey and Monitoring Report*, No. 16. Edinburgh: Scottish Natural Heritage.

STEWART, A. & DREWITT, A. 1989. *Botanical survey of the Yorkshire Dales National Park (N. Yorks) 1985-86*. Peterborough: Nature Conservancy Council.

STEWART, F.E. & ENO, S.G. 1998. *Grazing management planning for upland Natura 2000 sites: a practical manual*. The National Trust for Scotland

STEWART, A., PEARMAN, D.A. & PRESTON, C.D. 1994. *Scarce plants in Britain.* Peterborough: Joint Nature Conservation Committee/Institute of Terrestrial Ecology/Botanical Society of the British Isles.

STEWART, J.M. & LANCE, A.N. 1983. Moor draining: a review of impact on land use. *Journal of Environmental Management*, **17**, pp. 81-89.

STEWART, J.M. & LANCE, A.N. 1991. Effects of moor-draining on the hydrology and vegetation of northern Pennine blanket bog. *Journal of Applied Ecology*, **28**, pp. 1105-1117.

STEWART, N.F. 1995. *Red Data Book of European bryophytes.* Trondheim: European Committee for the Conservation of Bryophytes.

STEWART, N.F. & CHURCH, J.M. 1992. *Red Data Books of Britain and Ireland: stoneworts.* Peterborough: Joint Nature Conservation Committee.

STILLMAN, R.A. 1995. Bird associations with heather moorland in the Scottish and English uplands. *In:* D.B.A. Thompson, A.J. Hester & M.B. Usher, eds. *Heaths and moorland: cultural landscapes.* Edinburgh and London: HMSO, pp. 67-73.

STILLMAN, R.A. & BROWN, A.F. 1994. Population sizes and habitat associations of upland breeding birds in the south Pennines, England. *Biological Conservation,* **69**, pp. 307-314.

STILLMAN, R.A. & BROWN, A.F. 1998. Pattern in the distribution of Britain's upland breeding birds. *Journal of Biogeography,* **25**, pp. 73-82.

SUTHERLAND, W.J. 1996. *Ecological census techniques: a handbook.* Cambridge: Cambridge University Press.

SUTHERLAND, W.J. & HILL, D.A. eds. 1995. *Managing habitats for conservation.* Cambridge: Cambridge University Press.

SWAN, M.J.S. & OLDHAM, R.J. 1993a. Herptile sites: Volume 1. National amphibian survey. Peterborough: *English Nature Research Reports,* No. 38.

SWAN, M.J.S. & OLDHAM, R.J. 1993b. Herptile sites : Volume 2. National common reptile survey. Peterborough: *English Nature Research Reports,* No. 39.

TABBUSH, P.M. & WILLIAMSON, D.R. 1987. *Rhododendron as a forest weed.* Forestry Commission Bulletin, 73. HMSO.

TAIT, J., LANE, A. & CARR, S. 1988. *Practical conservation: site assessment and management planning.* London: Hodder & Stoughton.

TALLIS, J.H. 1964. Studies on Southern Pennine peats III. The behaviour of *Sphagnum. Journal of Ecology,* **52**, pp. 345-353.

TALLIS, J.H. 1985. Mass movement and erosion of a Southern Pennine blanket peat. *Journal of Ecology,* **73**, pp. 283-315.

TALLIS, J.H. 1987. Fire and flood at Holme Moss: erosion processes in an upland blanket mire. *Journal of Ecology,* **75**, pp. 1099-1129.

TALLIS, J.H. 1997. Peat erosion in the Pennines: the badlands of Britain. *Biologist,* **44**, pp. 277-279.

TALLIS, J.H., MEADE, R. & HULME, P.D. eds. *Blanket mire degradation: causes, consequences and challenges.* Aberdeen: The Macaulay Land Use Research Institute on behalf of the Mires Research Group of the British Ecological Society.

TANSLEY, A.G. 1939. *The British islands and their vegetation.* Cambridge: Cambridge University Press.

TAYLOR, I. 1994. Context and priorities for plant conservation in England: the international importance of the English Flora. *In:* English Nature, *Species Conservation Handbook.* Peterborough: English Nature.

TAYLOR, J. 1997. Perceptions of bracken. *The Heather Trust Annual Report.* Kippen: The Heather Trust.

TAYLOR, K. & MARKS, T.C. 1971. The influence of burning and grazing on the growth and development of *Rubus chamaemorus* L. in Calluna-Eriophorum bog. *In*: E.A. Duffy & A.S. Watt, eds. *The scientific management of plant and animal communities for conservation.* Oxford: Blackwell, pp. 153-166.

THE ACCESS FORUM & SCOTTISH NATURAL HERITAGE. 1997. *Care for the hills: guidance on the careful use of Scotland's hills and mountains.* Edinburgh: Scottish Natural Heritage.

THOMAS, J.A. 1983. A quick method for estimating butterfly numbers during surveys. *Biological Conservation,* **27**, pp. 195-211.

THOMPSON, D.B.A. & BADDELEY, J. 1991. Some effects of acidic deposition on montane *Racomitrium* heaths. *In*: S.J. Woodin & A. Farmer, eds. *The effects of acid deposition on nature conservation in Great Britain.* Peterborough: Nature Conservancy Council, pp. 17-28.

THOMPSON, D.B.A & BROWN, A. 1992. Biodiversity in montane Britain: habitat variation, vegetation diversity and some objectives for conservation. *Biological Conservation,* **1**, pp. 179-208.

THOMPSON, D.B.A. & HORSFIELD, D. 1990. Towards an assessment of nature conservation criteria in the British uplands. *In*: D.B.A. Thompson & K.J. Kirby, eds. *Grazing research and nature conservation in the uplands: proceedings of a seminar, 1988.* Nature Conservancy Council Research & survey in nature conservation No. 31. Peterborough: Nature Conservancy Council, pp. 9-18.

THOMPSON, D.B.A. & KIRBY, K.J. eds. 1990. *Grazing research and nature conservation in the uplands: proceedings of a seminar, 1988.* Nature Conservancy Council Research & survey in nature conservation No. 31. Peterborough: Nature Conservancy Council.

THOMPSON, D.B.A. & MILES, J. 1995. Heaths and moorland: some conclusions and questions about environmental change. *In*: D.B.A. Thompson, A.J. Hester & M.B. Usher, eds. *Heaths and moorland: cultural landscapes.* Edinburgh and London: HMSO, pp. 362-385.

THOMPSON, D.B.A. & SYDES, C. 1992. The British uplands. *In*: I.F.G. McLean, ed. *Our natural heritage.* Peterborough: Nature Conservancy Council/Joint Nature Conservation Committee.

THOMPSON, D.B.A., GALBRAITH, H. & HORSFIELD, D. 1987. Ecology and resources of Britain's mountain plateaux: land use conflicts and impacts. *In*: M. Bell & R.G.H. Bunce, eds. *Agriculture and conservation in the hills and uplands.* ITE Symposium No. 23. Grange-over-Sands: Institute of Terrestrial Ecology, pp. 22-31.

THOMPSON, D.B.A., HESTER, A.J. & USHER, M.B. eds. 1995. *Heaths and moorland: cultural landscapes.* Edinburgh and London: HMSO.

THOMPSON, D.B.A., HORSFIELD, D., BROWN, A., AVERIS, A., KIRKPATRICK, H., ROBSON, M. & SYDES, C. In press. *Objectives for nature conservation in the British uplands.* Peterborough: Joint Nature Conservation Committee.

THOMPSON, D.B.A., MACDONALD, A.J & HUDSON, P.J. 1995. Upland moors and heaths. *In:* W.J. Sutherland & D.A. Hill, eds. *Managing habitats for conservation.* Cambridge: Cambridge University Press, pp. 292-326.

THOMPSON, D.B.A., MACDONALD, A.J., MARSDEN, J.H. & GALBRAITH, C.G. 1995. Upland heather moorland in Great Britain: a review of international importance, vegetation change and some objectives for nature conservation. *Biological Conservation,* 71, pp. 63-178.

THOMPSON, D.B.A., WHYTE, S. & OSWALD, P.H. (eds.) 1988. *Nature Conservancy Council research in the uplands: proceedings of a seminar, 1986.* (Nature Conservancy Council Research & survey in nature conservation No. 16.) Peterborough: Nature Conservancy Council.

THOMPSON, J., MOUNTFORD, E., PRESTWOOD, W., MILLS, E., & JERRAM, R. 1999. Creating native woodland in upland England. Peterborough: *English Nature Research Reports,* No. 307.

TODD, P.A. 1997. The MAFF *Molinia* contract - Year 2. *The Heather Trust Annual Report.* Kippen: The Heather Trust.

TORVELL, L., COMMON, T.G. & GRANT, S.A. 1988. Seasonal patterns of tissue flow and responses of *Molinia* to defoliation. *In:* M.B. Usher & D.B.A. Thompson, eds. *Ecological change in the uplands.* Oxford: Blackwell Scientific Publications, pp. 219-222. British Ecological Society Special Publication No. 7.

TREWEEK, J., JOSÉ, P. & BENSTEAD, P. (eds.) 1997. *The Wet Grassland Guide: managing floodplain and coastal wet grasslands for wildlife.* Sandy: RSPB.

TUFFNELL, S. (ed.) 1995. *The registration handbook: pesticides, biocides, plant protection products: a guide to the policies, procedures and data requirements relating to their control within the United Kingdom.* York: Health and Safety Executive.

UK BIODIVERSITY GROUP. 1998. *Tranche two action plans. Volume 1 - vertebrates and vascular plants. Volume II - terrestrial and freshwater habitats.* Peterborough: English Nature.

UK BIODIVERSITY GROUP. 1999. *Tranche two action plans. Volume II1 - plants and fungi. Volume IV - invertebrates. Volume VI - terrestrial and freshwater species and habitats.* Peterborough: English Nature.

UK CLIMATE CHANGE IMPACTS REVIEW GROUP. 1991. *The potential effects of climate change in the United Kingdom. First report.* London: HMSO.

UK STEERING GROUP. 1995. *Biodiversity: the UK Steering Group Report*. London: HMSO.

USHER, M.B. 1980. An assessment of conservation values within a large Site of Special Scientific Interest. *Field Studies*, **5**, pp. 323-348.

USHER, M.B. 1986. Wildlife conservation evaluation: attributes, criteria and values. *In:* M.B. Usher, ed. *Wildlife conservation evaluation.* London: Chapman and Hall, pp. 3-44.

USHER, M.B. 1992. Management and diversity of arthropods in *Calluna* heathlands. *Biodiversity and Conservation*, **1**, pp. 63-79.

USHER, M.B. & SMART, L.M. 1988. Recolonization of burnt and cut heathland in the North York Moors by arachnids. *The Naturalist*, **113**, pp. 103-111.

USHER, M.B. & THOMPSON, D.B.A. eds. 1988. *Ecological change in the uplands.* British Ecological Society Special Publication No. 7. Oxford: Blackwell Scientific Publications.

USHER, M.B. & THOMPSON, D.B.A. 1993. Variation in the upland heathlands of Great Britain: conservation importance. *Biological Conservation*, **66**, pp. 69-81.

VARVARIGOS, P. & LAWTON, J.H. 1991. Farmers' perceptions of the scale of the bracken problem on farms in Less Favoured Areas in England and Wales. *Journal of Applied Ecology*, **28**, pp. 988-1003.

VETERINARY MEDICINES DIRECTORATE. 1991. *Handle sheep dips with care.* Guidance sheet on disposal.

VETERINARY MEDICINES DIRECTORATE. 1992. *The safe handling and disposal of sheep dips: advisory note for farmers*.

VETERINARY MEDICINES DIRECTORATE. 1993. *Safe use of organophosphorus sheep dips: important instructions for farmers and operators*.

VOLLENWEIDER, R.A. 1968. *Scientific fundamentals of the eutrophication of lakes and flowing waters, with particular reference to nitrogen and phosphorous factors in eutrophication.* Paris: OECD Water Management Research Group.

WALTHAM, A.C., SIMMS, M.J., FARRANT, A.R. & GOLDIE, H.S. 1997. *Karst and caves of Great Britain.* London: Chapman and Hall.

WARD, L.K. 1990. Management of grassland - scrub mosaics. *In*: S.H. Hillier, D.W.H. Walton and D.A. Wells, eds. *Calcareous grasslands - ecology and management.* Huntingdon: Bluntisham Books.

WARD, S.D. & EVANS, D.F. 1975. *A botanical survey and conservation assessment of British limestone pavements.* 10 Vols. Bangor: Institute of Terrrestrial Ecology (unpublished).

WARD, S.D. & EVANS, D.F. 1976. Conservation assessment of British limestone pavements based on floristic criteria. *Biological Conservation*, **9**, pp 217-233.

WARD, S.D., MACDONALD, A.J. & MATTHEW, E.M. 1995. Scottish Heaths and moorland: how should conservation be taken forward? *In*: D.B.A. Thompson, A.J. Hester & M.B. Usher, eds. *Heaths and moorland: cultural landscapes*. Edinburgh and London: HMSO, pp. 319-333.

WARREN, M.S. & BOURN, N.A.D. 1997. The impact of grassland management on threatened butterflies in ESA's. *In:* R.D. Sheldrick ed. *Grassland Management in Environmentally Sensitive Areas*. Occasional Symposium No. 32. Reading: British Grassland Society.

WARREN, M.S. & FULLER, R.J. 1993. *Woodland rides and glades: their management for wildlife*. Second edition. Peterborough: Joint Nature Conservation Committee.

WARREN, M.S. & OATES, M.R. 1995. The importance of bracken habitats to fritillary butterflies and their management for conservation. *In*: R.T. Smith & J.A. Taylor, eds. *Bracken: An Environmental Issue*. International Bracken Group Special Publication No 2. Aberystwyth: Aberystwyth University, pp 178-181.

WATKINS, C. 1990. *Woodland management and conservation*. Newton Abbott: David & Charles.

WATKINS, C. 1991. *Nature conservation and the new lowland forests*. Peterborough: Nature Conservancy Council.

WATSON, A. 1979. Bird and mammal numbers in relation to human impact at ski lifts on Scottish hills. *Journal of Applied Ecology*, **16**, pp. 753-764.

WATSON, A. 1981. Effects of human impact on ptarmigan and red grouse near ski lifts in Scotland. *Annual Report Institute of Terrestrial Ecology*, 1981, p. 51.

WATSON, A. 1985. Soil erosion and vegetation damage near ski lifts at Cairngorm. *Biological Conservation*, **33(4)**, pp. 363-381.

WATSON, A. 1988. Dotterel numbers in relation to human impact in Scotland. *Biological Conservation*, **43**, pp. 245-256.

WATSON, A., MILLER, G.R., & GREEN, F.H.W. 1966. Winter browning of heather and other moorland plants. *Transactions of the Botanical Society of Edinburgh*, **40**, pp. 195-203.

WATSON, J. ed. 1997. *Guidelines for cave and karst protection*. Gland: International Union for Conservation of Nature and Natural Resources/World Commission on Protected Areas/Working Group on Cave and Karst Protection.

WATT, A.S. 1955. Bracken versus heather, a study in plant sociology. *Journal of Ecology*, **43**, pp. 490-506.

WEAKE, C. & HARPER, I. 1993. Heather matters: redressing the balance. *Enact*, **1(4)**, pp. 10-11.

WEBB, N. 1986. *Heathlands*. New Naturalist Series. London: Collins.

WEBB, S. 1995. Conservation of limestone pavement. *Cave and Karst Science*, **21**, pp. 97-100.

WEBB, S. & GLADING, P. 1998. The ecology and conservation of limestone pavement in Britain. *British Wildlife*, **10**, pp. 103-113.

WELCH, D. 1974. The floristic composition of British upland vegetation in relation to grazing. *Land*, **1**, pp. 59-68.

WELCH, D. 1984a. Studies in the grazing of heather moorland in north-east Scotland. I. Site descriptions and patterns of utilisation. *Journal of Applied Ecology*, **21**, pp. 179-195.

WELCH, D. 1984b. Studies in the grazing of heather moorland in E. Scotland. II. Response of heather. *Journal of Applied Ecology*, **21**, pp. 197-207.

WELCH, D. 1984c. Studies in the grazing of heather moorland in E. Scotland. III. Floristics. *Journal of Applied Ecology*, **21**, pp. 209-225.

WELCH, D. 1985. Studies in the grazing of heather moorland in E. Scotland. IV. Seed dispersal and plant establishment in dung. *Journal of Applied Ecology*, **22**, pp. 461-471.

WELCH, D. 1986. Studies in the grazing of heather moorland in E. Scotland. V. Trends in *Nardus stricta* and other unpalatable graminoids. *Journal of Applied Ecology*, **23**, pp. 1047-1058.

WELCH, D. & RAWES, M. 1966. The intensity of sheep grazing on high-level blanket bog in Upper Teesdale. *Irish Journal of Agricultural Research*, **5**, pp. 185-196.

WELCH, D. & SCOTT, D. 1995. Studies in the grazing of heather moorland in north-east Scotland. VI. 20 year trends in botanical composition. *Journal of Applied Ecology*, **32**, pp. 596-611.

WELCH, D., SCOTT, D., MOSS, R. & BAYFIELD, N.G. 1994. *Ecology of blaeberry and its management in British moorlands*. Banchory: Institute of Terrestrial Ecology.

WELLS, T.C.E., COX, R. & FROST, A. 1989. *The establishment and management of wild flower meadows*. (Nature Conservancy Council Focus on nature conservation No. 21.) Peterborough: English Nature.

WELSH, P. 1994. *Yorkshire Dales Natural Area: mesotrophic grassland management principles for SSSI*. Leyburn: English Nature unpublished report.

WELSH OFFICE, COUNTRYSIDE COUNCIL FOR WALES, FARMING AND RURAL CONSERVATION AGENCY & SNOWDONIA NATIONAL PARK. 1999. *Tir Gofal: farmer's handbook*. Welsh Office.

WHITTAKER, E. & GIMINGHAM, C.H. 1962. The effect of fire on regeneration of *Calluna vulgaris* (L) Hull from seed. *Journal of Ecology*, **50**, pp. 815-82.

WHITTOW, J.B. 1984. *The Penguin dictionary of physical geography.* Middlesex: Penguin Books.

WIGGINTON, M. ed. 1999. *British red data books: 1 Vascular plants.* Third edition. Peterborough: Joint Nature Conservation Committee.

WILLBY, N.J. & EATON, J.W. 1993. The distribution, ecology and conservation of *Luronium natans* (L). Raf. in Britain. *Journal of Aquatic Plant Management,* **31**, pp. 70-76.

WILLEMS, J.H. 1990. Calcareous grasslands in continental Europe. *In:* S.H. Hillier, D.W.H. Walton & D.A. Wells, eds. *Calcareous grasslands: ecology and management.* Huntingdon: Bluntisham Books, pp. pp. 3-10.

WILLIAMS, G. & GREEN, R. 1993. Towards an upland habitat action plan. *RSPB Conservation Review,* **7**, pp. 5-11.

WILLIAMS, P., BIGGS, J., CORFIELD, A., FOX, G., WALKER, D. & WHITFIELD, M. 1997. Designing new ponds for wildlife. *British Wildlife,* **8**, pp. 137-151.

WILSON, D. 1993. Ten years on: Kinder Scout. *Enact,* **1(4)**, pp.4-6.

WILSON, R.C.L. ed. 1994. *Earth heritage conservation.* Milton Keynes: The Geological Society in association with The Open University.

WOLF, S. & WHITE, A. 1997. *Principles of environmental law.* London: Cavendish.

WOLTON, R.J. 1994. *Wildlife enhancement scheme: management guidelines for Culm grasslands.* Peterborough: English Nature.

WOODIN, S.J. & FARMER, A. eds. 1991. *The effects of acid deposition on nature conservation in Great Britain.* Peterborough: Nature Conservancy Council.

WOODIN, S.J. & FARMER, A.M. 1993. Impacts of sulphur and nitrogen deposition on sites and species of nature conservation importance in Great Britain. *Biological Conservation,* **63**: pp. 23-30.

WOOD-GEE, V. 1996. *Environmentally sensitive farming in the Southern Uplands: a practical guide for farmers, land owners and managers.* Edinburgh: Scottish Natural Heritage.

WOODS, R.G. 1993. *Flora of Radnorshire.* Cardiff: National Museum of Wales and the Bentham-Moxon Trust.

WWF-UK. 1996. *Sustainable agriculture report.* Godalming: WWF-UK.

Glossary

Glossary

accompanying measures - three regulations introduced in the MACSHARRY REFORM of the CAP: AGRI-ENVIRONMENTAL REGULATION; EARLY RETIREMENT REGULATION (not implemented in the UK); FORESTRY REGULATION

acid grassland - grassland occurring on soils which have a pH below 5, often on unenclosed hillsides

acidophilic - species preferring acidic conditions

ADAS - commercial providers of consultancy to agriculture, horticulture, food and drink and environment, to UK and international land based industries

aftermath - a term associated with grazed grassland describing the new growth of the sward after management, eg cutting or burning

Agenda 2000 - in July 1997 the European Commission (EC) published *Agenda 2000: for a stronger and wider Europe.* The primary aim was to deepen the reforms of the CAP started in 1992 (MACSHARRY REFORM), in preparation for the next round of WTO negotiations and the enlargement of the EU. This round of reforms was agreed in Berlin on 26 March 1999. The UK Government published draft regulations for reform in this country in 1998 and a consultation process followed. Agenda 2000 is intended to run from 1 January 2000 through to 2006-7

Agenda 21 - international action plan for sustainable development arising from the Rio EARTH SUMMIT in 1992. Local Agenda 21 is essentially about community involvement and partnerships to get consensus and action toward sustainable development

agistment - grazing of farm stock on land on the basis of payment per head per day/week/month, usually away from the home farm

Agri-environment regulation - one of the three ACCOMPANYING MEASURES introduced in the MACSHARRY REFORM. It obliges all Member States to offer farmers a set of incentive payments for pursuing environmental management and extensification of production by means of a number of possible schemes (see ENVIRONMENTALLY SENSITIVE AREA, COUNTRYSIDE STEWARDSHIP SCHEME). Now replaced by the RURAL DEVELOPMENT REGULATION

allotment/new take - pasture taken in and fenced from the hill, generally used for grazing and holding stock, they may or may not be improved

alpine plant species - plants which are more normally associated with a central and south European montane distribution, but are absent from arctic regions (see also MONTANE)

anaerobic - in the absence of free oxygen (O_2)

ancient woodland - woodland with continuous cover since at least AD 1600

anthropogenic - originated by man

Arctic plant species - plant species which are entirely absent from central and southern Europe and have their chief continental area lying north of the Baltic

Arctic-alpine plant species - plants which display a central and southern European montane distribution and also appear at high latitudes, often with a circumpolar distribution

asulam - a fern-specific herbicide used for the control of bracken

Asulox - the trade name for the fern-specific herbicide, ASULAM, used for the control of bracken

away winter/tack - send livestock to lowland pasture for the winter

Beef Special Premium (BSP) - a headage based support payment available on male beef cattle (at 10 and 22 months old) subject to stocking density limits and 'regional ceilings'

berm - shallow shelf at the base of the bank of a ditch that is at the level of normal flow and gives extra channel width at high flows

Biochemical Oxygen Demand (BOD) - the amount of oxygen needed to break down organic material within a system

biodiversity - "the variability among living organisms from all sources including, *inter alia*, terrestrial, marine and other aquatic ecosystems and the ecological complexes of which they are part; this includes diversity within species, between species and of ecosystems." as defined in Article 2 of the Convention on Biological Diversity

Biodiversity Action Plan (BAP) - originating from the Rio EARTH SUMMIT and taken to a national level, the overall goal of the Plan is to conserve and enhance biological diversity within the UK and to contribute to the conservation of global diversity through all appropriate mechanisms

blanket bog or mire - term to describe a wide range of OMBROTROPHIC and RHEOTROPHIC peatlands

bog - OMBROTROPHIC MIRE generally with a low nutrient status

Bronze Age - the period in human history when bronze was the main metal used to make implements. In Britain, approximately 2000 to 500 years ago

BSP - see BEEF SPECIAL PREMIUM

cairn - pile of stones used as way-marker or to denote high point of a hill. Also archaeological term for grave

calcareous - growing on soil derived from the decomposition of calcareous rocks, such as limestone

calcareous grassland - grasslands typically found on soils with a pH range between 6.5 and 8.5, usually found over calcareous substrates

calcifuge - a plant species that does not thrive on soils of high pH, preferring more acid conditions

carr - wet woodland composed of trees such as willow and alder, which is a successional stage between open water and dry woodland

ceilings - maximum level of payment which may be made to an individual farm business

channelisation - artificial modification of channels by widening, deepening, straightening, embanking or concrete lining for the purpose of flood alleviation, drainage of agricultural land or stabilisation

chasmophyte - a plant which grows in the crevices of rocks

chasmophytic - of rocks

climatic climax - a plant community determined and maintained in a given area by the prevailing climatic conditions

climax vegetation - the stable vegetation of an area under the prevailing environmental conditions

clough - a steep-sided gully/valley in northern England

Common Agricultural Policy (CAP) - provides the principal framework for agricultural policy in all countries belonging to the European Union

conserved fodder - fodder conserved for feeding stock over the winter, usually hay or silage

CORINE - Co-ordination of Information on the Environment - an experimental project to collect, co-ordinate and ensure consistency of information on the state of the environment and natural resources in the EC

coppice - a form of woodland management where trees or shrubs are cut regularly at the base to promote regrowth

Countryside Stewardship Scheme (CSS) - a voluntary scheme of annual payments for ten years where participant agreements contain conditions protecting, enhancing and restoring landscape-based features. The scheme is administered by FRCA for MAFF and covers a wide range of habitats - see RURAL DEVELOPMENT REGULATION

critical load - a quantitative estimate of exposure to one or more pollutants below which significant harmful effects on sensitive elements of the environment do not occur according to present knowledge

Culm grasslands/Rhôs pastures - local name given to the unimproved pasture of Dartmoor, northern Devon, northeast Cornwall and south Wales, some of which overlies the Carboniferous slates and shales of the Culm Measures

Disadvantaged Areas (DAs) - see LESS FAVOURED AREAS

draft ewe - breeding ewes removed from the flock. Associated with hill flocks where ewes are 'drafted' at 4-5 years old to lowland farms for further breeding, because they are considered too old for harsh mountain life

dystrophic - freshwater systems with very poor nutrient levels

Early Retirement Regulation - one of the three ACCOMPANYING MEASURES introduced in the MACSHARRY REFORM. Member States may obtain funding for schemes to promote early retirement of farmers. Not taken up in England. Now incorporated into the RURAL DEVELOPMENT REGULATION

Earth Summit - United Nations Conference on Environment and Development held in Rio de Janeiro in June 1992. Here the UK Government signed the Biodiversity Convention which brought about the BIODIVERSITY ACTION PLAN

emergent vegetation - plants that grow in water but have leaf structures that emerge above the surface

environmental audit - gathers information on features of environmental interest and may also include a qualitative assessment of condition

environmental conditions - used in the EU to refer to the attachment of environmental conditions to agricultural support payments under the CAP commodity regimes. Sometimes known as cross-compliance

Environmentally Sensitive Area (ESA) - areas of high landscape and conservation value, designated under EC regulations where 'traditional' farming is under threat, in which farmers enter into ten-year management agreements and receive incentive payments for positive environmental management - see also RURAL DEVELOPMENT REGULATION

epiphyte - a plant growing upon another, though not parasitic

epilimnium - the surface water layer of a standing water body

ericoid / ericaceous - pertaining to plants of the Heath family (Ericaceae)

European Union (EU) - formally created by the Maastricht Treaty and supported by three pillars, including the European Community, Common Foreign and Security Policy, and Home Affairs and Justice Policy

eutrophic - nutrient enriched

eutrophication - the process of nutrient enrichment

extensification premium - incentive mechanism under the EU beef regime to encourage lower stocking rates for cattle production

fell - northern term for hill

fen - a term that includes all MINEROTROPHIC MIRES, though is often only associated with nutrient-rich tall-herb vegetation

finished - term applied to animals which have been fattened and are ready for slaughter

flush - wet area irrigated by a spring or soak-way

fodder / foddering - animal food/provision of animal food

Forestry regulation - one of the three ACCOMPANYING MEASURES introduced in the MACSHARRY REFORM. It obliges Member States to offer farmers incentive payments to encourage tree planting and forestry management on farmland. Now replaced by the RURAL DEVELOPMENT REGULATION

FRCA - Farming and Rural Conservation Agency. A science-based organisation which is the Executive Agency of MAFF and the Welsh Office. It manages agri-environment schemes and advises MAFF on agricultural issues. From April 2001 FRCA will be known as The Rural Development Service when it becomes part of the Environment Group of MAFF.

geotextiles - natural or synthetic permeable fabrics used in conjunction with soil for the function of erosion protection

General Agreement on Tariffs and Trade (GATT) - a multilateral agreement between trading nations to promote global trade liberalisation, by acting as a forum for international trade negotiations. Now replaced by WORLD TRADE ORGANISATION

gill/ghyll - name for a valley or mountain stream, especially deeply cut, steep streams liable to drying out in the summer

gimmer - a female sheep from weaning to shearing (ie 6-15 months old), or from first clipping for a further year (ie 15-27 months old, see HOGG/HOGGET)

grip - moorland drainage ditch

hagg / hagging - gullying in blanket bogs

hay meadow - enclosed grassland managed for the purpose of gathering hay, usually cut once a year in the summer

Habitats and Species Directive - an EC Directive that seeks to encourage the maintenance of BIODIVERSITY by establishing a 'favourable conservation status' for specific natural habitat types and species considered to be of community interest

heft - a piece or parcel of land in unenclosed hill and mountain pasture to which sheep are attached, usually because they have been bred on it.

heifer - a female cow more than a year old which has not calved

high forest - forest where the majority of trees are allowed to reach maturity

hill farm - a farm of the highest altitudes of which the majority of land comprises open moorland with little IN-BYE land. Typically, sheep are the main enterprise

Hill Livestock Compensatory Allowance (HLCA) - headage payment available to beef and sheep farmers within LESS FAVOURED AREAS. Now replaced by area-based payments under a Hill Farming Allowance (HFA) Scheme

hill sheep - hardy purebred sheep with an ability to thrive in the harsh conditions of the high moorlands and open hills. The mainstay of the HILL FARM

hogg/hogget - a male or female sheep between being weaned and being shorn for the first time (ie 6-15 months)

hypolimnium - the lower water layer of a standing water body

igneous - rock formed from the cooling of molten magma

improved grassland - grassland which has been agriculturally improved by the application of fertilisers or herbicides, by drainage or by ploughing and reseeding. Such swards generally contain a very limited range of plant species, mainly those which either demand or tolerate high nutrient levels and grazing. They have lost many of the species characteristic of unimproved semi-natural grassland

in-bye - enclosed grassland, often surrounding farm buildings

injurious weeds - weeds listed in the Weeds Act 1959: creeping thistle *Cirsium arvense*, spear thistle *Cirsium vulgare*, broad-leaved dock *Rumex obtusifolius*, curled dock *Rumex crispus* and ragwort *Senecio jacobaea*

instream - occurring within the confines of a river channel

intake - improved pasture taken in and fenced from the hill

karst - geomorphological features created by the weathering of limestone by solution

lamb - male or female sheep from birth to weaning (ie 0-6 months)

lambing percentage - number of lambs born and reared per 100 ewes put to the ram

lapidicolous - living under stones

lentic - freshwater system of standing water

Less Favoured Areas (LFAs) - areas originally designated under EU Directive 75/268. In the UK these are split into DISADVANTAGED AREAS and SEVERELY DISADVANTAGED AREAS . Compensation payments now made under RURAL DEVELOPMENT REGULATION through the Hill Farm Allowance Scheme - see Hill Livestock Compensatory Allowance

ley - a short-term pasture, often cut for SILAGE or hay, sown to last for one or more years, after which it is ploughed and another crop sown

LIFE fund (***L'instrument Financier pour l'Environnement***) **(EU)** - a financial instrument, established to assist the development and implementation of the EU's environmental policy

limestone pavement - a karst feature of weathered limestone bedding surfaces, consisting of smooth blocks (clints) separated by deep solution crevices (grykes)

littoral zone - zone in a water body colonised by macrophytes

livestock quota - rights for beef and sheep subsidies linked to the holding and tradable between producers

livestock unit (LU) - method of describing different stock types and age groups based on their energy requirements. Standard ratios are used, commonly based on one livestock unit equalling one Friesian dairy cow

	Livestock units (LSU)		**Livestock units (LSU)**
Cattle		***Sheep***	
Dairy cow	1.00	Ewes:	
Dairy bull	0.65	Light	0.06
Beef cow	0.75	Medium	0.08
Beef bull	0.65	Heavy	0.11
Heifers in calf	0.80		
Other cattle (not intensive beef):			
0-12 months	0.34	Breeding ewe hoggs (½-1 year)	0.06
12-24 months	0.65		
Over 24 months	0.80	Other sheep over 1 year	0.08
Horses	0.80	Rams	0.08
		Lambs	0.04-0.08
		Store lambs under 1 year	0.04

These figures are from the MAFF Farm Business Survey (FBS). NB: Not all schemes for the calculation of Livestock Units are comparable.

For example, MAFF definitions include:

- Exmoor pony = 1.00 LU
- 1 sheep = 0.15 LU

Local Nature Reserve (LNR) - areas designated by the local authority, often owned by them and managed by other bodies, such as wildlife trusts

lotic - freshwater system of flowing water

macrophyte - aquatic plant (vascular and non-vascular) that can be seen with the naked eye and is therefore not microscopic

MacSharry reform - unofficial term often used for the CAP reform package adopted in 1992

MAFF - Ministry of Agriculture, Fisheries and Food

management agreement - contractual term used to describe documented agreements completed with land owners and occupiers regarding their management of land, often within an incentive scheme for example ENVIRONMENTALLY SENSITIVE AREAS, COUNTRYSIDE STEWARDSHIP SCHEME, WILDLIFE ENHANCEMENT SCHEME

marl - calcareous mudstone or clay

marl sites - said of freshwater bodies with concentrations of dissolved calcium carbonate greater than 100 mg/l

meadow - enclosed grassland not permanently grazed and cut once a year for CONSERVED FODDER

meristem - a localised group of cells, which are actively dividing and undifferentiated, but which ultimately give rise to permanent tissue

metamorphic - rock that has been changed in texture, structure or composition owing to the effects of temperature and/or pressure

mesotrophic - of a moderate nutrient status

minerotrophic - to be fed by ground water, often used when describing mires

milk quota - production limit per holding above which a superlevy is charged. Can be traded

mire - a general term applied to peat producing ecosystems which develop in sites of abundant water supply. Some workers also include some mineral-based wetland within the compass of 'mire'

MLURI - Macaulay Land Use Research Institute

montane - used to describe the zone above the altitude at which trees naturally occur. Equivalent to the term 'alpine' used by many European ecologists

moorland - the unenclosed land of the uplands supporting upland heath (wet and dry), blanket and other upland mires and upland grassland

Moorland Scheme - UK scheme under the EU agri-environment programme which closed in 1998 and was incorporated into the COUNTRYSIDE STEWARDSHIP SCHEME. It was aimed at protecting and improving moorland environments by providing incentive payments for farmers in defined areas to reduce livestock grazing

national envelope - funds available under AGENDA 2000 beef reforms which can be used to support particular aspects of the UK beef industry

National Nature Reserve (NNR) - designated areas of national or international importance which are owned or leased by the UK statutory nature conservation agencies or are managed by means of Nature Reserve Agreements with land owners and managers

National Trust - a constituted charity, established for the purpose of promoting the permanent preservation of buildings and land of beauty or historical interest and for the preservation of their natural aspect features and animal and plant life

National Vegetation Classification (NVC) - a classification used to describe British plant communities

nationally rare plants - plant species recorded nationally in 15 or fewer 10km squares of the national grid

nationally scarce plants - species recorded nationally in 16 to 100 10km squares of the national grid

Natural Areas - tracts of countryside which are readily recognised by their characteristic land forms, wildlife and land use. English Nature has divided the whole of England into Natural Areas. They are not designations and they are not confined by traditional administrative boundaries. Natural Areas are intended to provide a framework to identify the priorities and objectives for nature conservation at a local level. They have a key role to play in the translation of national targets for habitats and species into action at the local level, and for setting targets for species and habitats which are important and characteristic locally

Net Farm Income (NFI) - reward to farmer and spouse for their own labour, management and interest on tenant-type capital invested in the farm

new take - see ALLOTMENT

neutral grasslands - grasslands that are mostly found within enclosed field systems on moist mineral soils with a pH between 5 and 6.5

nivation - the localised erosion of a hill slope by post-action, mass-wasting and erosion by meltwaters at the edges of, and beneath, welling snowdrifts

NPK - an abbreviation for nitrogen, phosphorous and potassium in describing the composition of a fertiliser

off-winter - remove stock from ground for the winter to allow vegetation to recover

oligotrophic - nutrient poor (not necessarily base poor)

ombrotrophic - supplied solely by water derived from the atmosphere (such as rain, snow and fog)

ombrogenous - generated by precipitation

orogeny - major phase of fold-mountain building

overgrazing regulation - an environmental condition of livestock premia in the UK such as SAPs, BSPs and SCPs. Defined in SI No. 1500/1996 The HILL LIVESTOCK (COMPENSATORY ALLOWANCES) Regulation 1996 as: "grazing land with livestock in such numbers as adversely to affect the growth, quality or species composition of vegetation (other than vegetation normally grazed to destruction) on that land to a significant degree" (see also UNSUITABLE SUPPLEMENTARY FEEDING). Also attached to the new Hill Farm Allowance Scheme

passerine - a perching bird (literally a 'sparrow-like' bird)

pasture - enclosed grassland for the sole purpose of grazing STOCK

patterned ground - a collective term for the approximately symmetrical forms that are characteristic of, but not necessarily confined to, that part of the ground surface is subject to intensive frost action. It requires a combination of moderate moisture and frequent cycles of freeze-thaw action and also depends on the susceptibility of the soil to frost sorting. Includes POLYGONS, circles and STRIPES

peat - soil of partially decomposed vegetable matter, accumulated under waterlogged (anaerobic) conditions, sometimes made up entirely of *Sphagnum* mosses

perennial - a plant living for three or more seasons, and normally flowering and fruiting at least in the second and subsequent seasons

periglacial - applied to an area bordering the edge of an ice sheet, to the climate of that area and the physical processes associated with it. Perma-frost is often prevalent in the area

ploughing-back - a boulder that moves downslope by frost creep and/or SOLIFLUCTION in a PERIGLACIAL environment

poaching - the trampling of land when wet, by stock, so the soil becomes churned and muddy, often to the detriment of the vegetation

podzolisation - the process which forms podzolic soils (podzols). Podzols are soils which are freely drained and in which iron and aluminium are moved down the profile as organic salts by the downward movement of water (leaching) which occurs when precipitation exceeds evaporation

point bar - bar formed on the convex side of a channel bed

poll - to de-horn cattle or sheep

pollard - woodland management whereby mature trees are cut to promote regrowth above the reach of browsing stock

polled - term for cattle or sheep naturally lacking in horns

polygons - a collection of many-sided geometric figures, occurring as a type of patterned ground, usually formed by frost action in the PERIGLACIAL environment

potable - water which is fit for human consumption

rake - small scale open-cast excavation for early lead extraction. Usually linear, following a rich surface vein. Often rich in plant species

Ramsar Site - wetlands of international importance designated under the Ramsar Convention 1971, which requires signatory countries to protect internationally important wetlands, especially those used by migratory water birds, and to use wetlands wisely

raptor - a bird of prey

Red Data Book - lists nationally rare species; for example see NATIONALLY RARE PLANTS

Regionally Important Geological/ Geomorphological Site (RIGS) - geological and geomorphological sites, excluding SSSIs, that are considered worthy of protection for their educational, research, historical or aesthetic importance

rheotrophic - influenced by ground water

rhôs grasslands - see CULM GRASSLANDS

ride - cleared area in woodland, often linear, for access, fire breaks and to provide open areas for game and wildlife

riparian - relating to or situated on the bank of a river or stream

rip-rap - stones or similar material laid on a river bank to stabilise it and prevent erosion

riffle - a depositional bar in a stream, over which the water flows rapidly with a 'rippled' surface

Rural Development Regulation - "second pillar of the CAP" under AGENDA 2000. Brings together instruments for LESS FAVOURED AREAS, AGRI-ENVIRONMENT, forestry,

EARLY RETIREMENT, rural development and STRUCTURAL FUNDS

SAP - see SHEEP ANNUAL PREMIUM

saproxylic - living on dead or decaying wood

SCP - see SUCKLER COW PREMIUM

scree - angular rock debris, often mobile, formed from weathering of parent material, mainly by frost action, and often located below the parent outcrop

sedimentary rock - a rock formed by sediments laid down in layers

semi-improved grassland - grassland which has been modified by the application of fertilisers (generally at a low level over a long period of time), herbicides, intensive grazing or drainage such that its species-richness and diversity is lower than that of unimproved semi-natural grassland but still retains some characteristics of the semi-natural grassland from which it has been derived

semi-natural vegetation - plant associations often created by direct or indirect effects of man - see CLIMAX VEGETATION

Severely Disadvantaged Areas (SDAs) - see LESS FAVOURED AREAS

shakehole - steep sided depression found commonly in limestone, usually resulting from a collapsed cave roof

shearling - a young sheep between its first and second shears

Sheep Annual Premium (SAP) - headage support payment for eligible ewes kept on the farm, limited by quota

sheep walk - upland areas which have been used long term for sheep management

silage - partially fermented conserved fodder

siliceous - rich in silica. Quartz-rich rocks eg granites are likely to be siliceous. Siliceous rocks are generally base-poor, with low concentrations of irons, magnesiums, etc.

silviculture - the growing and tending of trees as a branch of forestry

SINC - Site of importance for nature conservation. A non-statutory designation of sites at the county/district level. Sites are generally assessed by either local authorities or county wildlife trusts

sinkhole - a steep-sided depression found commonly in limestone, usually the result of solution weathering

Site of Special Scientific Interest (SSSI) - designated best examples of habitat types and sites with notable species or groups of species, notified under the Wildlife and Countryside Act 1981

slurry - liquefied animal manure

snowfield - area of permanent snow accumulated in a basin-shaped hollow

solifluction - the downhill viscous flow of surface deposits saturated with water, especially when released by thaw, often over still frozen ground beneath

soligenous mire - MINEROTROPHIC MIRE with a constant through-put of water

southern-continental - the large number of European plants whose chief area of distribution is central and southern Europe (Matthews, 1937)

Special Area of Conservation (SAC) - areas designated under the EC HABITATS DIRECTIVE. Sites important for habitats or species listed in the Directive which contribute to the maintenance of 'a favourable conservation status'

Special Protection Area (SPA) - areas designated under the EC Birds Directive 1979 as important habitats for those species either listed on Annex I of the Directive or those regularly occurring on migration species

steer - a castrated male bovine animal more than a year old

stock - term used to refer to livestock

stock (livestock) density - LIVESTOCK UNITS per unit area

store cattle (stores) - animals kept on a low level of growth for later fattening or sold for fattening

store lambs - lambs requiring finishing (fattening) prior to slaughter

stripes - a type of PATTERNED GROUND oriented down the steepest slope gradient of a terrain influenced by marked thermal activity in the soil

Structural Funds - measures to aid economic and social development in the EU. Objective 5b areas covered large tracts of the English uplands but have been replaced by smaller Objective 1 and 2 areas under AGENDA 2000

submerged vegetation - plants rooted to the bed of a water body and either completely submerged or with only part of their shoots floating or emergent

suckler cow - a cow which is allowed to rear its own calf which is then used for beef production (suckler beef)

Suckler Cow Premium (SCP) - a subsidy to be paid on breeding cows used for beef calf production. This is subject to 'stocking density limits'

supplementary feed - feed used to supplement livestock dietary requirements usually during the winter. This often consists of CONSERVED FODDER, such as hay or SILAGE, feed blocks or concentrates

swale - to winter burn grass or heathland

swamp - a broad term covering mostly tall, emergent vegetation that fills the seral stage between open water and FEN

sward - above ground components of grassland vegetation

tarn - small upland water body

terminal sire - breed of ram mated with crossbred ewes to produce slaughter lambs

thufur - an Icelandic term for an earth hummock, a mound of earth in a PERIGLACIAL environment, having either a core of mineral soil or stones

top - to cut grass sward or selected plant species to favour growth of palatable shoots or for weed control

tor - an isolated exposure of much jointed rock, eg granite, standing as a prominent castellated mass above the general surface of a plateau, notably in Cornwall and Devon

tup - colloquial name for a ram

tupping - when tups mate with ewes

turbidity - reduced transparency in water, caused by suspended solids, giving it a murky appearance

unimproved grassland - grassland that has not been subjected to agricultural improvement through the use of fertilisers, herbicides, intensive grazing or drainage. Such grasslands are often species-rich

upland farm - a marginal farm with both open hill grazing and IN-BYE land, as distinct from a HILL FARM

unsuitable supplementary feeding - (as defined by SI No. 1500/1996 The HILL LIVESTOCK (COMPENSATORY ALLOWANCES) Regulations 1996) "providing supplementary feed (other than to maintain livestock during abnormal weather conditions) in such a manner as to result in damage to vegetation through excessive trampling or POACHING of the land by animals or excessive rutting by vehicles" (see also OVERGRAZING REGULATION)

viviparous - giving birth to live young

weir - an obstacle preventing maximum river flow, used as a means of harnessing the power of rivers to drive milling machinery, for water level/flood control and in conjunction with locks for navigation

wether - a castrated male sheep

wet heath - heath community on peat soils less than 0.5 m deep

whole farm plan - integrated management plan for a whole farm which incorporates physical characteristics, information on agricultural activities and environmental features. May include management objectives.

Wildlife Enhancement Scheme (WES) - voluntary and flexible scheme run by English Nature providing positive incentives in the form of annual and standard capital payments for the sensitive management of SITES OF SPECIAL SCIENTIFIC INTEREST in certain parts of England

Woodland Grant Scheme - provides support for the establishment, by planting or regeneration, and management of woodland

World Trade Organisation (WTO) - body established during the Uruguay Round of the GENERAL AGREEMENT ON TARIFFS AND TRADE (GATT) to supervise and adjudicate implementation of international trading agreements and arrangements

Index

Index

Location references are to page numbers. Page references to tables are in **bold**. Page references to INFORMATION NOTES are prefixed by IN, e.g. IN2.4 refers to page 4 of INFORMATION NOTE 2.

Information notes

Information note 1 — Assessing vegetation condition in the English uplands

Introduction

Please note that this Information Note supersedes the method published by English Nature as: Jerram, R. & Drewitt, A. 1998. Assessing vegetation condition in the English uplands. Peterborough: *English Nature Research Reports*, No. 264.

The English uplands support a wealth of wildlife habitats, such as heather moors and blanket bogs with all their associated plants and animals. For future generations to enjoy the wildlife of these areas and to secure their conservation interest, they need to be managed in an environmentally sustainable way. For these reasons English Nature has devised a method for assessing the condition of the vegetation for the four most extensive habitats in the English uplands which is described in this note. Work has recently been completed on some of the more discrete vegetation types in the English uplands including flushes, ledge vegetation and screes, and will be published in due course, as will methodology covering woodlands, grasslands and freshwater habitats in the English uplands.

The method describes how upland heath and mire vegetation in good condition will look, principally in terms of the plant species present and the structure of the vegetation. Areas that fit this description are then considered to be in 'favourable condition'. The aim has been to encompass the range of variation in vegetation composition, structure and management found in different parts of upland England within our definitions of favourable condition, not to impose a homogeneous look to upland habitats. Field methods for making an assessment of vegetation condition at various levels of detail are also described.

The method is intended to be rapid and repeatable and useful for initial assessments of the condition of the vegetation types covered. It was originally developed as a consistent way of assessing the condition of Sites of Special Scientific Interest (SSSIs) and Special Areas of Conservation (SACs) and is used by English Nature for this purpose. However, it is equally applicable to any land and will provide a better understanding of the vegetation condition of these upland habitats in the wider countryside. It is hoped that it will aid general assessments of vegetation condition within agri-environment schemes such as the Countryside Stewardship and Environmentally Sensitive Area schemes. It will also feed into the Biodiversity Action Plan process for the habitats concerned. The method can be used as a crude monitoring tool, as it is capable of detecting gross changes in vegetation, provided it is used in a standardised way for all site visits, but it is not suitable for detailed monitoring.

Assessing favourable condition

The upland vegetation condition assessment method described in this document is used to assess and monitor vegetation interest features[1] on upland SSSIs and the wider countryside. The attributes and targets[2] set here are the national standard and are applicable to all Natural Areas of England. Conservation objectives for individual sites will be set within this standard. English Nature is required to report on the condition of the interest features for which the SSSI was notified. However, English Nature also has responsibilities for these habitats under the Habitats Directive and through the Biodiversity Action Plan process and will also use the techniques described in this note to determine the overall condition of these habitats in the wider countryside.

Common Standards (Joint Nature Conservation Committee 1998) require that site features are assessed against the following categories:

Favourable - maintained
Favourable - recovered
Unfavourable - recovering
Unfavourable - no change
Unfavourable - declining
Partially destroyed
Destroyed

The first two categories equate to favourable vegetation condition as defined in this document, the remaining five categories equate to unfavourable vegetation condition. Whether the unfavourable vegetation is recovering, declining or showing no signs of change will depend on the dynamics of the situation and comparison with its condition on previous assessments.

Principles

Favourable vegetation condition is defined in this note for the four most extensive habitats found in the English uplands:

- Sub-montane dry dwarf-shrub heath
- Wet heath
- Blanket and upland raised mires
- Montane moss and lichen heath

Other upland vegetation types not listed above, such as hay meadows, other enclosed grasslands, limestone grasslands and semi-natural woodlands, are covered by other guidelines.

---

[1] **Interest features** are those features for which an SSSI, SAC or SPA has been designated. They may include features such as the presence of a particular vegetation type, such as H12 heather-bilberry dry heath, or the presence of particular species or groups of species, for example breeding hen harrier.

[2] An **attribute** is a measurable feature of the vegetation, such as sward height. A **target** is a level of the attribute (eg >3 cm for sward height) which has to be met for the vegetation to be in favourable condition.

These definitions are expressed as a series of attributes with target levels for each habitat. These identify the features which characterise vegetation in favourable condition. They focus on the effects of management on the condition of the vegetation, rather than on whether there is evidence that a particular management practice is, or has been, in operation. All attributes and targets must be met for the vegetation to be judged to be in favourable condition.

Box IN1.1 Definitions of terms of abundance and distribution (see also Figure IN1.5)

Abundance terms (DAFOR)	**Definition**
Dominant	A single species which prevails over other species in terms of the ground cover of a stand of a particular habitat
Abundant	Found regularly throughout a stand of a particular habitat and contributing significa ntly to the ground cover of that stand (>5% cover)
Frequent	Scattered plants or small clumps of plants found regularly throughout a stand (found on at least one in every three footfalls when walking through vegetation) and making a modest contribution to the ground cover of that stand (<5% cover)
Occasional	Scattered plants found on less than one in three footfalls and generally not making a contribution to the ground cover of that stand
Rare	No more than a few individual plants or clumps of a species recorded in a stand
Distribution terms	
Widespread	Widely distributed throughout a stand
Local	Restricted to particular areas or parts of a stand

Definitions of favourable condition

Definitions of favourable condition for each of the four habitat types covered are given below. A number of terms are used throughout to describe specific levels of abundance and distribution. These terms are in common usage in ecology but can be given a variety of meanings. To avoid confusion their usage and meaning in the context of the assessment of upland vegetation condition is defined in Box IN1.1.

Sub-montane dry dwarf-shrub heath

Habitat definition

Dry dwarf-shrub heath is defined as vegetation in which ericoid dwarf-shrubs (heather *Calluna vulgaris*, bell heather *Erica cinerea*, bilberry *Vaccinium myrtillus*, cowberry *Vaccinium vitis-idaea* and crowberry *Empetrum nigrum*) or western gorse *Ulex gallii* form a significant component of the vegetation in relatively dry situations. Species-poor acid grassland is a vegetation type where species such as mat-grass *Nardus stricta*, wavy hair-grass *Deschampsia flexuosa*, bristle bent *Agrostis curtisii*, common bent *Agrostis capillaris* and sheep's fescue *Festuca ovina* are abundant and in which dwarf-shrubs are scarce. These two vegetation types can form an intricate mosaic but species-poor acid grassland is generally derived from dwarf-shrub heath via grazing and/or burning and where dwarf-shrub cover falls below a certain threshold should be regarded as degraded dry heath in this context.

Sub-montane dry heath is sub-divided into two types for the purposes of vegetation condition assessment: 'typical' *Calluna* dry heath and dry heaths with *Ulex gallii*. These are differentiated simply on the presence or absence of *Ulex gallii*.

Table IN1.1 NVC communities covered by upland vegetation condition assessment: Sub-montane dry heath

H4	*Ulex gallii-Agrostis curtisii* heath
H8	*Calluna vulgaris-Ulex gallii* heath
H9	*Calluna vulgaris-Deschampsia flexuosa* heath
H10	*Calluna vulgaris-Erica cinerea* heath
H12	*Calluna vulgaris-Vaccinium myrtillus* heath
H18	*Vaccinium myrtillus-Deschampsia flexuosa* heath
H21	*Calluna vulgaris-Vaccinium myrtillus-Sphagnum capillifolium* heath
U2	*Deschampsia flexuosa* grassland
U3	*Agrostis curtisii* grassland
U4	*Festuca ovina-Agrostis capillaris-Galium saxatile* grassland
U5	*Nardus stricta-Galium saxatile* grassland
U20	*Pteridium aquilinum-Galium saxatile* community

Exclusions

Exceptionally, species-rich grasslands can occur on moorlands in England: for example, where base-rich strata lie close to the soil surface or where there is slight base-rich flushing. Where present, the condition of these grasslands should be assessed on a site specific basis as species-rich grassland rather than heath.

Agrostis-Festuca grasslands which retain a relic woodland flora (eg wood anemone *Anemone nemorosa* or bluebell *Hyacinthoides non-scripta*), and hence show clear signs of having been derived from woodland, are also excluded and should be assessed on a site specific basis.

Any vegetation on blanket or raised peat bodies deeper than 0.5 m should be assessed as blanket/raised mire.

Heath over 600 m, particularly on or just below mountain summits, in which pleurocarpous mosses like *Hypnum jutlandicum* and *Pleurozium schreberi* are replaced by species such as woolly hair moss *Racomitrium lanuginosum* and *Polytrichum alpinum*, and montane species such as alpine clubmoss *Diphasiastrum alpinum*, Iceland moss *Cetraria islandica* (a lichen), stiff sedge *Carex bigelowii* or dwarf willow *Salix herbacea* are present, should be assessed as montane heath. Grasslands with abundant *Deschampsia flexuosa*, *Festuca ovina* or *Agrostis capillaris* on or just below mountain summits over 600 m should also be assessed as montane heath as they are likely to have been derived from montane heath via grazing.

Stands of bracken *Pteridium aquilinum* with a more or less continuous cover of litter (>90% cover) should be mapped as bracken and should not normally be included in the dry heath assessment.

Table IN1.2 Typical *Calluna* sub-montane dry dwarf-shrub heath
Attributes and targets for favourable vegetation condition
(for vegetation to be favourable all targets listed below must be met)

Dwarf-shrub cover

- Dwarf-shrubs are dominant over grass species.
  Minimum of 75% cover of dwarf-shrubs, excluding recently burnt stands.

Dwarf-shrub diversity

- At least two dwarf-shrub species should be frequent and widespread in the sward. No one dwarf-shrub species should be dominant to the exclusion of all others. Where there is a dominant species one or more species must also be frequent and widespread. Where three or more species are present, but only one is frequent and widespread, the abundances of the less abundant species may be combined and treated as if they are a single species.

Bryophyte/lichen abundance

- Bryophytes (excluding *Polytrichum* spp and/or *Campylopus* spp) and/or 'bushy' *Cladonia* spp. lichens (eg *C. impexa* and *C. arbuscula*) should be at least frequent and forming patches below or, in more open swards, between the dwarf-shrubs.

Age structure

- Either: all age classes of *Calluna* present with at least 25% of the management unit in the late mature/degenerate age class or 25% or more excluded from the burning rotation
  or: the whole management unit is unburnt.
  Stands which are never burnt should be present on level or gently sloping ground, not entirely confined to steep slopes.
  [Note that in stands which are never or infrequently burnt *Calluna* may regenerate through layering. Where this occurs the pioneer phase may not be present and it may be difficult to distinguish between the building, mature and degenerate phases. Stands where layering of *Calluna* is frequent and widespread should be included in the late mature/degenerate age class.]

Grazing impact

- Grazing impacts should be light
  (An absolute maximum of 5% of the grazing unit may show signs of current moderate or heavy grazing).

Indicators of light grazing: * * Field indicators taken from MacDonald *et al* 1998	• Where stands of dwarf-shrubs lie adjacent to stands of preferentially grazed vegetation such as grassland, flushes, or recently burnt heath, any marginal band of distinctly grazed dwarf-shrubs should not exceed 1 m in width. • < 33% of long shoots of *Calluna vulgaris* or *Vaccinium myrtillus* showing signs of having been grazed where average shoot growth is >4 cm, or, where average shoot growth is <4 cm then <16% of shoots grazed. [Note that this indicator may only be reliable in late winter and early spring as *Calluna* in particular is mainly grazed in autumn and winter] • Only shoot tips (most recent years growth) removed by grazing. • Abundant and conspicuous flowering of *Calluna* and/or *Vaccinium myrtillus*. • Upright growth of *Calluna vulgaris*. Bush canopy open, not a tightly packed mass of contorted shoots. Very few or no instances of 'drumstick', 'topiary' or 'carpet' growth forms. • Little or no signs of grazing of *Empetrum nigrum*, *Vaccinium vitis-idaea* or *Nardus stricta*, if present. • No uprooted dwarf-shrub seedlings in areas regenerating after fire. • Herbivore dung should be rare and very difficult to find in short vegetation. • Negligible bare ground attributable to grazing pressure.

Guidance notes for assessing Calluna sub-montane dry dwarf-shrub heath

Attribute	Notes
Dwarf-shrub cover	• It should be assumed that recent controlled burns (areas burnt within the last two years) will regenerate good dwarf-shrub cover unless there is good evidence to the contrary.
	• The area to assess for dwarf-shrub cover will include species-poor acid grassland, scattered trees or shrubs and open bracken stands, but will exclude other habitat types, such as dense bracken stands, flushes, woodland (including plantations) and stands of the other habitats covered by the assessment system.
	• The presence of trees and shrubs, both native and non-native, does not in itself render an area of dry heath unfavourable. However, where shading by trees or shrubs reduces dwarf-shrub cover below the target level then it is judged as being in unfavourable vegetation condition. Where non-native trees are seeding in to an area of heath and becoming established this should be highlighted and brought to the attention of the site manager even if dwarf-shrub cover currently meets the target level.
	• Similarly bracken is a natural component of dry heath, but where the presence of scattered bracken within a stand of heath reduces the cover of dwarf-shrubs below the target level the stand will be in unfavourable condition.
Dwarf-shrub diversity	• In most dwarf-shrub heaths there is a dominant species; generally this is heather *Calluna,* although occasionally it may be bilberry *Vaccinium myrtillus.*
	• Stands in favourable condition will also have one or more additional dwarf-shrub species present. To be favourable two or more dwarf-shrubs (including the dominant species) must be frequent and widespread throughout the sward. Where only two species are present this must be strictly interpreted. However, where three or more species are present a slightly less strict interpretation is allowed. In this circumstance one species *must* be frequent and widespread, but the other species may be combined and their abundance assessed as if they were a single species. Where this is done the species that are combined must be truly frequent and widespread.
Frequency of bryophytes and lichens	• Generally only bryophytes (mosses and liverworts) figure in this assessment, but occasionally bushy lichens can also be a prominent feature of the vegetation.

Attribute	Notes
Frequency of bryophytes and lichens (continued)	• Bryophytes which count positively towards the assessment can be described as 'feather mosses' (MacDonald *et al* 1998) or pleurocarpous mosses. These are mosses with much branched shoots, often regularly branched, which form loose, horizontally layered mats (Figure IN1.1b). Typical heathland examples include *Hylocomium splendens, Pleurozium schreberi* and *Hypnum cupressiforme/ jutlandicum*. Liverworts tend to be less conspicuous.
	• Certain *Polytrichum* and *Campylopus* spp mosses are typical colonisers of bare ground following very hot fires and possibly also frequent fires. They tend to form short mats, generally less than 1.5 cm deep and are small spiky mosses, often with white hairs and an upright growth form. Note that *Polytrichum commune,* a large (3-10 cm+ bright green moss) can be frequent in favourable heath vegetation, particularly in damp humid conditions (Figure IN1.1b).
	• 'Bushy' *Cladonia* lichens have a growth form reminiscent of bushes or trees (arbuscular). Typical species are *Cladonia impexa* (*C. portentosa*) and *C. arbuscula* (Figure IN1.1a).
Age structure	• The growth phases of *Calluna* (from Gimingham, 1992):

Pioneer phase: This is the period of establishment, either of seedlings or of sprouts from stem bases surviving after fire. In both cases the young plants are neatly pyramid shaped, but seedlings are scattered whereas stem-base sprouts are clustered. Flowering usually begins in the second growing season after establishment, and from about this time growth is no longer concentrated in a leading shoot but takes place in a number of radiating branches.

Building phase: Radiating growth gives rise to a dome-shaped bush in isolated individuals, or to a closed canopy in dense stands. This is the most vigorous growth-phase, with abundant production of shoots near the periphery of the branches as well as flowers and seed. Very little light penetrates the canopy.

Mature phase: In time, extension growth becomes rather less vigorous while the woody parts of the branches continue to increase in girth. The canopy becomes more irregular and inclined to open up. In isolated plants a central gap may form in the canopy.

Degenerate phase: Gaps in the canopy increase as the older central frame-branches become moribund and die. Branches tend to collapse sideways, increasing the gaps, but any lateral branches which have rooted in the moist humus may remain alive for long periods.

These phases merge gradually into one another without sharp transitions. The rate at which the whole process takes place varies considerably according to habitat and geographical location, but to give a general indication the pioneer phase may last until plants are

Attribute	Notes
Age structure (continued)	from two to six years of age, the building phase up to about 10 to 15 years of age and the mature phase up to 20 to 25 years of age, when the plants pass gradually into the degenerate phase and die back progressively from the central branches outwards.
	• Stands that are never or infrequently burnt may be found to be layering (vegetative regeneration via the production of adventitious roots from prostrate stems). Examine the underside of a live branch which is lying on the ground and look for roots.
	• Where layering is occurring the pioneer phase may not be present and it can be difficult to distinguish between the building, mature and degenerate phases.
	• Stands where layering of *Calluna* is frequent and widespread should be included in the late mature/degenerate age class.
	• Age structure should be assessed over whole burning management units.
Grazing impacts: General	• See record card for impact levels for moderate and heavy grazing for each indicator. Examination of these targets will aid an assessment of whether the grazing impact is light or otherwise.
	• The indicators are just that, they are designed to help a surveyor assess the grazing impact. It is not necessary for all the indicators to be recorded as light to assess the overall grazing level as light. It is permissible for one or more indicators to be recorded as moderate or heavy, but these must not outnumber light indicators recorded.
	• Grazing impact should be assessed over the whole assessment unit. This will require impacts to be averaged out.
Width of grazing zone	• Width of heavy grazing zone refers to a zone of obviously heavily grazed dwarf-shrubs which may be present at the interface of stands of dwarf-shrubs and preferentially grazed vegetation, such as limestone grassland, flushes or stands of pioneer/early building phase *Calluna*. Where grazing impact is light there may be no such grazing zone evident. The zone is the result of increasing herbivore density on the preferred vegetation forcing animals to graze the less palatable taller dwarf-shrubs surrounding it.
Percentage long shoots grazed	• 'Long shoots' refers to the current or most recent year's growth (Figure IN1.2).
	• Strictly speaking this indicator should be used only in early spring (March/April), when an entire season of grazing and growth can be assessed. However, obvious summer grazing of *Calluna* indicates a heavy grazing impact.

Attribute	Notes
Percentage long shoots grazed (continued)	• The two annual shoot growth lengths relate to the vigour of the bush and refer to long shoots (Figure IN1.2). Vigorously growing bushes will put on an average of >4 cm growth per year, while less vigorous plants will put on an average of <4 cm growth per year. Several factors influence the vigour of dwarf-shrubs: ❑ vigour declines with increased altitude and exposure; ❑ soil dampness/waterlogging reduces vigour; ❑ vigour declines with plant age. Both sets of thresholds may need to be used in a single assessment unit. Vigorously growing plants can tolerate higher grazing levels than less vigorous plants. From record card: ❑ <33% - the sward will not normally be obviously grazed. Grazed shoots will be difficult to find without both intensive and extensive searching; ❑ 33-66% - the sward will be clearly grazed in general appearance, although effects may be patchy; ❑ >66% - grazing of the sward will be very conspicuous and it will be difficult to find ungrazed shoots. Grazing impacts may be harder to assess in stands of low vigour, but any obvious evidence of grazing will tend to indicate heavy grazing here.
Type of shoot material removed	• As grazing intensity increases the type of shoot material eaten changes. At low grazing levels only the most nutritious shoot tips are removed, but under heavy grazing levels there will be frequent evidence of grazing of woody material older than the most recent year's growth.
Amount of flowering of dwarf-shrubs	• This indicator can be used in the late summer (late August/September) and autumn, when the previous indicator is less reliable. • Some knowledge of the seasonal grazing pattern is required. If grazing only occurs in winter then new flowering shoots can be produced during the flowering season. However, if there is heavy summer grazing of dwarf-shrubs most flowering shoots will be removed. • Note that the amount of flowering can be affected by weather patterns and may be reduced at high altitude (550 m+).

Attribute	Notes
Frequency of grazing induced *Calluna* growth forms	• Continued moderately heavy and heavy grazing over several years results in changes to the growth form of *Calluna*. The repeated removal of the lead shoot results in side shoots repeatedly becoming the lead shoot, such that the main axis of growth along a branch changes every 1-2 cm, producing bushes with twisted contorted growth forms and tightly packed branches. During the summer this may be obscured by a surface of new growth which is removed over winter. This is particularly the case where grazing of *Calluna* mainly occurs in winter.
	• The tightly packed branches of a heavily grazed bush will prevent one from pushing ones fingers into the centre of the bush.
	• Lightly grazed bushes will have an open structure with straight, upright shoots. It will be possible to see into the middle of the bush and one will be able to push one's fingers deep into the bush unhindered.
	• 'Drumstick', 'topiary' and 'carpet' or 'prostrate' heather describe the appearance of the suppressed growth forms produced by continued heavy grazing. These growth forms give no indication of the relative intensity of the heavy grazing, rather they are indicative of the age of the *Calluna* when heavy grazing started. 'Drumstick' is the result of heavy grazing of late mature/degenerate plants, 'topiary' of building early/mature plants and 'carpet/prostrate' of pioneer *Calluna* (Figure IN1.3).
	• Note that this indicator may reflect past grazing impacts rather than the current grazing impact.
Signs of grazing on *Empetrum nigrum*, *Vaccinium vitis-idaea*, *Erica tetralix* or *Nardus stricta*	• These four species are unpalatable to livestock and are rarely grazed, except under heavy stocking levels when other, more palatable, species have been grazed down; or at times of high snow cover when other food may be unavailable. Any signs of these species being grazed is evidence of heavy grazing levels in the immediate vicinity.
Uprooting of dwarf-shrub seedlings	• Large numbers of uprooted, but largely uneaten dwarf-shrub seedlings, particularly *Calluna*, in recently burnt patches are a good sign of heavy grazing.
Herbivore dung in short vegetation	• This only relates to the ease of finding dung in short vegetation. It will be hard to find dung in tall vegetation regardless of the grazing impact.
Trampled bare ground	• Look for hoof prints to determine the origin of the bare ground. Note that heavily burnt patches may retain bare ground for several years after being burnt, regardless of the grazing impact.

Figure IN1.1a. 'Bushy' lichens
a: *Cladonia arbuscula* and
b: *Cladonia impexa* (*C. portentosa*)

Reproduced from Alvin (1977)

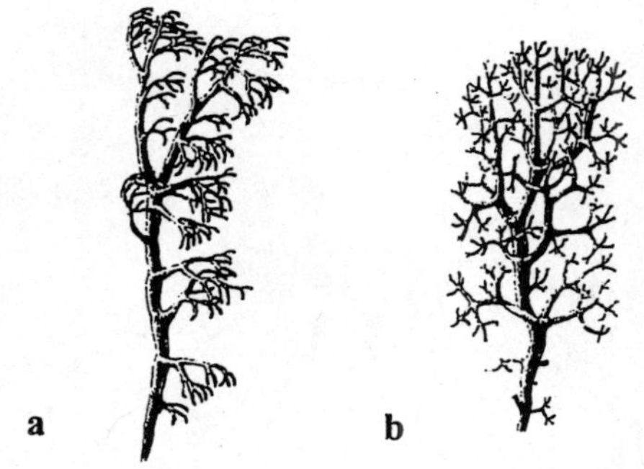

Figure IN1.1b. Mosses
a: *Campylopus* sp (dry and moist);
b: *Polytrichum* sp;
c: *Polytrichum commune*
d: a feather moss

Reproduced from Watson (1969)

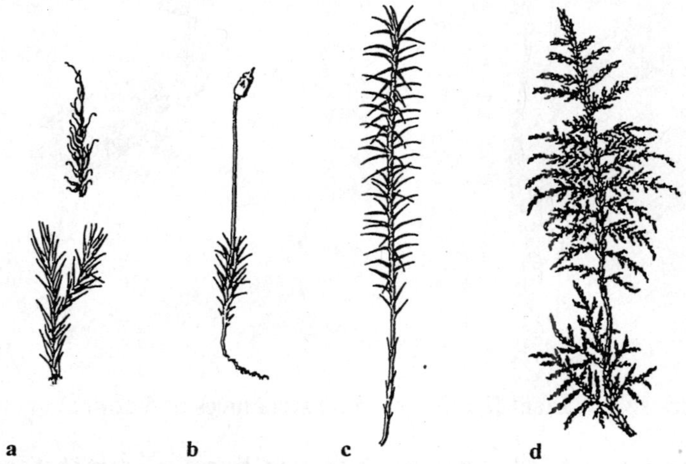

Grading unfavourable *Calluna* dry heath

Table IN1.3. *Calluna* Dry heath
Vegetation condition grading system (see Box IN1.2)

Attribute	Favourable scores	Unfavourable scores		
	0 points	1 point	2 points	6 points
Dwarf-shrub cover	>75%	26-75%	5-25%	<5%
Dwarf-shrub diversity	2 or more spp widespread & frequent	no more than 1 spp widespread & frequent		
Bryophyte/lichen abundance	frequent patches	occasional	rare	
Age structure	>25% late mature/degenerate or excluded from burning	<25% late mature/degenerate or excluded from burning		
Grazing impact	light	moderate	heavy	

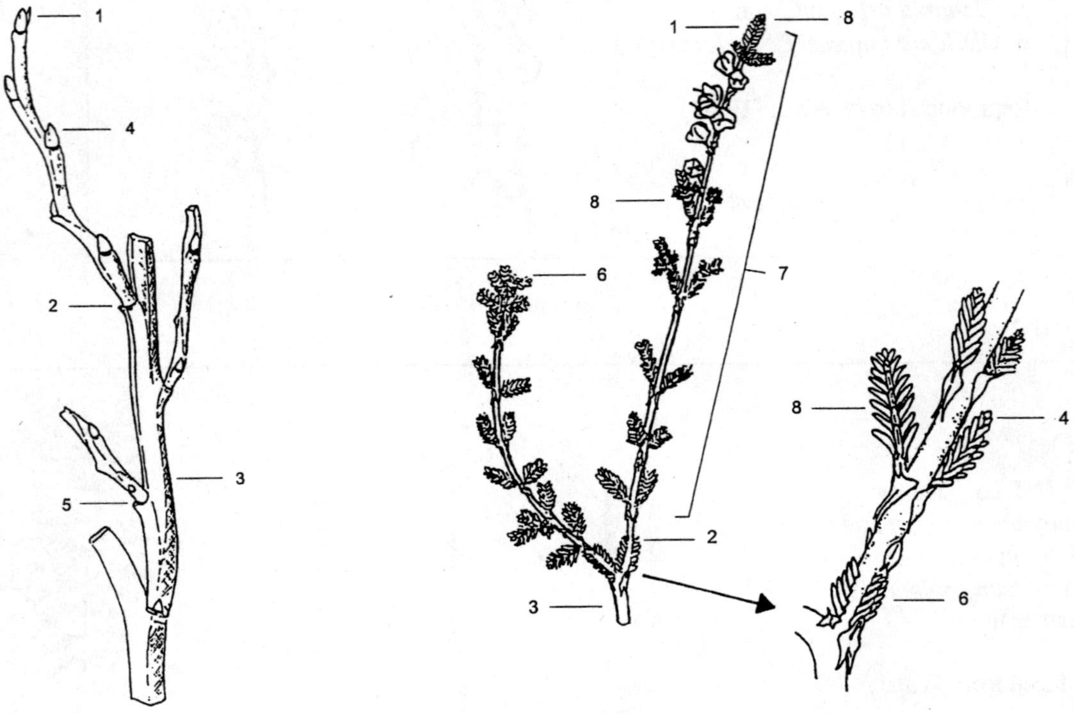

Figure IN1.2. Identification of shoot structures and annual growth in bilberry (left) and heather

Features as seen in late winter/early spring, before the start of shoot extension in the new growing season:

1 End of previous season's growth
2 Start of previous season's growth
3 Old shoot material (as in grazing into old material)
4 Bud
5 'Joint' formed by bowl-shaped seat of bud/shoot
6 Closely spaced small leaves
7 Long shoot
8 Short shoot

Reproduced from MacDonald *et al* (1998)

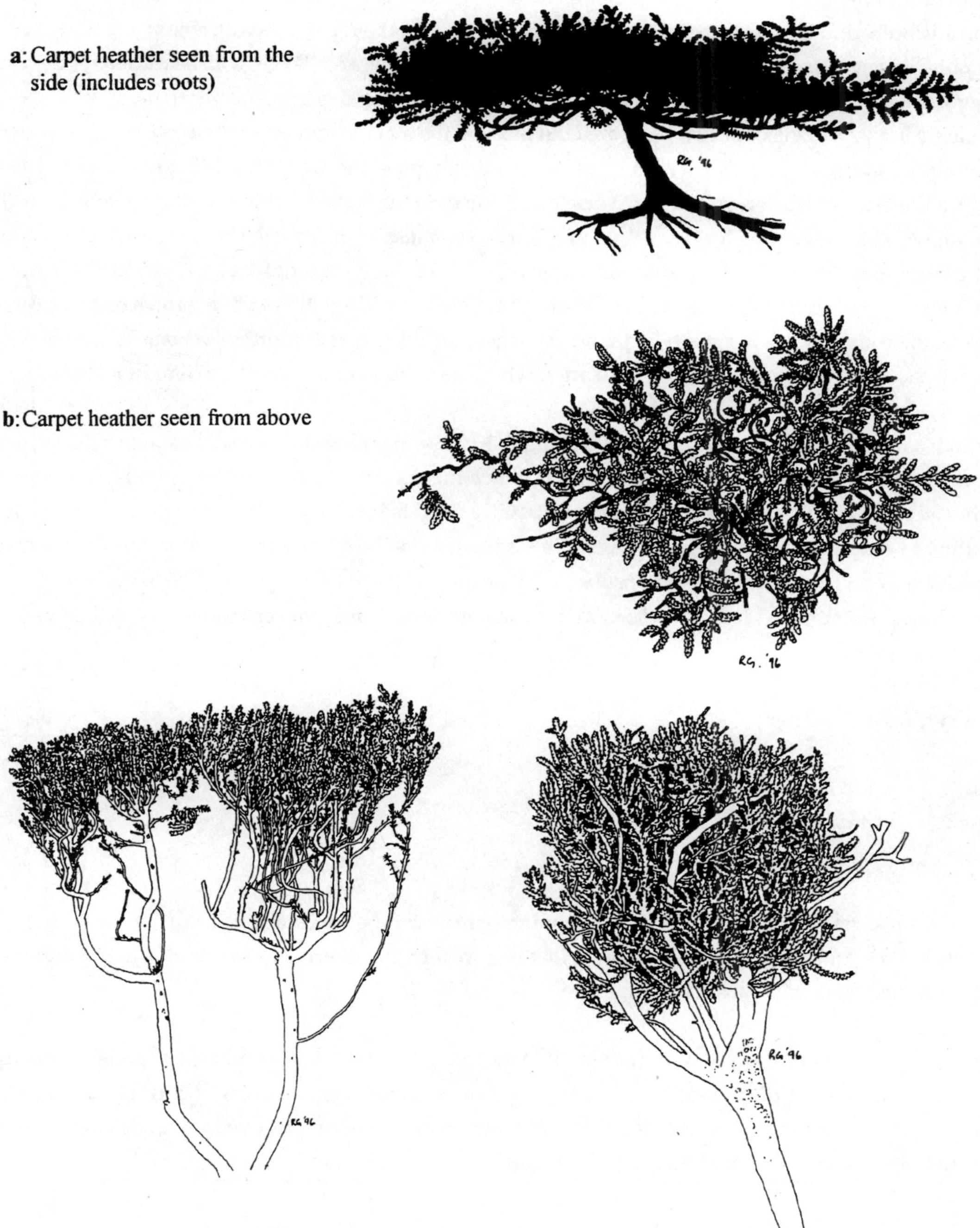

a: Carpet heather seen from the side (includes roots)

b: Carpet heather seen from above

c: Topiary heather, cross-section and bush

d: Drumstick heather

Figure IN1.3. Heather growth forms
Drawings by Robert Goodison ©

Box IN1.2. Grading unfavourable vegetation

Where stands, survey units or entire management units fail to meet one or more of the favourable vegetation condition attributes and targets then the vegetation unit is classed as being in unfavourable vegetation condition. Clearly not all vegetation in unfavourable condition is the same and there will be different degrees of 'unfavourableness'. If we take dry heath as an example, one unfavourable management unit may exhibit signs of moderately heavy grazing over 20% of its area but meet all the other attributes and targets, while another unit may have formerly been dry heath but is now species-poor acid grassland with dwarf-shrubs present. The latter area of degraded dry heath is clearly in far worse condition than the former, which could probably be restored to favourable condition within a few years by fairly modest changes in the grazing regime. However, to restore the acid grassland to heath in favourable condition would take many decades and a considerable amount of management intervention, which even then might not be successful. The ability to distinguish between different degrees of unfavourability will greatly aid land managers and conservation organisations in directing scarce resources at those areas of unfavourable vegetation where the resources are likely to be of most benefit.

A weighted scoring system has been devised to distinguish between different degrees of unfavourable vegetation condition. Points are awarded for each attribute on which the vegetation fails, so that favourable stands score zero points, a stand failing one attribute scores one point, a stand failing two attributes scores two points and so on. Additional weighting is given to those attributes considered to be of particular importance in determining vegetation condition (eg cover of dwarf-shrubs in dry heath, or *Sphagnum*/bryophyte cover in blanket mires). These attributes are sub-divided and additional points are scored for poorer examples of that vegetation condition component.

Scores are graded as follows:

0 points:	favourable
1-5 points:	unfavourable
>5 points:	severely unfavourable

Within the unfavourable grade, the number of points scored can be used to give a further indication of the relative level of the unfavourability of a stand. However, within the severely unfavourable grade there is little value to be gained from comparing scores.

This grading system can be applied to individual stands or parts of stands of a habitat (polygon mapping), sample squares (raster mapping), facets (facet mapping) or whole management units. It must be noted, however, that in the first three situations the age structure attribute can only be assessed over a whole management unit and should not be applied to individual sample squares, stands or facets.

ENGLISH NATURE

Upland Vegetation Condition Assessment

Field record card

Site Name:		Grid/square reference:		Date:	
Management unit:				Surveyor:	

***CALLUNA* DRY HEATH** (without *Ulex gallii*) Is this card for a whole management unit, raster square or facet?

ATTRIBUTES AND TARGETS:

Attribute	pass (✓)		(circle)			
>75% cover of dwarf-shrubs		Cover of dwarf-shrubs:	>75%	25-75	5-25	<5%
At least 1 dwarf-shrub species other than the dominant species frequent & widespread		Species present & their abundance (DAFOR):	Y / N			
Bryophytes &/or bushy *Cladonia* at least frequent & forming carpets		Cover of bryophytes/lichens:	Freq	Occ	Rare	
Age Structure			(see Age Structure section below)			
Grazing impact (see indicators below)		Impact:	Light	Moderate	Heavy	

AGE STRUCTURE:

Calluna regenerating by layering ? Y / N (If yes count layering areas as late mature/degenerate)

	Pioneer & newly burnt	Building & early mature	Late mature & degenerate
% cover of *Calluna* growth phases:			

GRAZING IMPACTS*:

Impact level (circle indicators & overall impact)

Indicator	**Light**	**Moderate**	**Heavy**
Width of zone of heavy grazing of dwarf-shrubs on interface with preferentially grazed vegetation	<1 m or absent	1 m-10 m	>10 m
% of long shoots grazed (a) if shoot growth >4 cm/yr	<33%	33-66%	>66%
(b) if shoot growth <4 cm/yr	<16%	16-33%	>33%
Shoot material removed	tips only	mainly tips	tips & older woody growth
Amount of flowering of dwarf-shrubs	abundant and conspicuous	obvious but patchy	sparse
Frequency of grazing induced *Calluna* growth forms ('drumstick', 'topiary' or 'carpet')	hard to find	localised	widespread
Signs of grazing of *Empetrum nigrum*, *Vaccinium vitis-idaea* or *Nardus stricta*, if species present	hard to find		some
Uprooting of dwarf-shrub seedlings in recent burns	hard to find	present but not conspicuous	conspicuous
Herbivore dung in short vegetation	rare and difficult to find	easy to find but not conspicuous	very conspicuous
Trampled bare ground	none, other than sporadic sheep scars or rabbit scrapes in recent burns		widespread

Vegetation condition (✓): Favourable | Unfavourable

Outlook:

[briefly outline your assessment of the short, medium and long-term outlook for the area you have assessed and give reasons]

Land-use & management

Grazers (✓)					
	sheep	cattle	deer	rabbits	grouse
	horses	other			

Stock feeding points present ? Y / N

Native trees & shrubs:	None	Local	Widespread	Species:	
Non-native trees & shrubs:	None	Local	Widespread	Species:	

Burn patch size	**small (<2 ha)**	**medium (2-5 ha)**	**large (>5 ha)**	**no evidence of being in a burning rotation**
None, Local, Widespread?:	L / W	L / W	L / W	L / W

* Field indicators taken from MacDonald *et al.* (1998) *A Guide to Upland Habitats. Surveying Land Management Impacts.* Vol. 2

Table IN1.4. *Ulex gallii* sub-montane dry dwarf-shrub heath **Attributes and targets for favourable vegetation condition** (for vegetation to be favourable all targets listed below must be met)	
Dwarf-shrub cover • Dwarf-shrubs (*Calluna, Erica* spp, *Vaccinium* spp, *Empetrum* and *Ulex gallii*) are dominant over grass species. Minimum of 75% cover of dwarf-shrubs, excluding recently burnt stands. [Note that when grazing is light *Agrostis curtisii*, where present, can be dominant for the first few years following burning.]	
Dwarf-shrub diversity • At least two dwarf-shrub species should be frequent and widespread in the sward. No one dwarf-shrub species should be dominant to the exclusion of all others. Where there is a dominant species one or more species must also be frequent and widespread. Where three or more species are present, but only one is frequent and widespread, the occurrence of the less abundant species may be combined and treated as if they are a single species.	
Cover of *Ulex gallii* • *Ulex gallii* should not exceed 50% cover, neither over a whole stand of *Ulex gallii* dry heath nor within individual age class stands where burning is practised.	
Age structure • All age classes of dwarf-shrub present with at least 25% of the management unit in the late mature/degenerate age class or 25% or more excluded from the burning rotation. Stands which are never burnt should be present on level or gently sloping ground, not entirely confined to steep slopes. [Note that in stands which are never or infrequently burnt *Calluna* may regenerate through layering. Where this occurs the pioneer phase may not be present and it may be difficult to distinguish between the building, mature and degenerate phases. Stands where layering of *Calluna* is frequent and widespread should be included in the late mature/degenerate age class.]	
Grazing impact • Grazing impacts should be light. (An absolute maximum of 5% of the grazing unit may show signs of current moderate or heavy grazing.)	
Indicators of light grazing*: *Field indicators taken from MacDonald *et al* (1998).	• Where stands of dwarf-shrubs lie adjacent to stands of preferentially grazed vegetation such as grassland, flushes, or recently burnt heath, any marginal band of distinctly grazed dwarf-shrubs should not exceed 1 m in width. • < 33% of long shoots of *Calluna vulgaris* or *Vaccinium myrtillus* showing signs of having been grazed where average shoot growth is >4 cm, or, where average shoot growth is <4 cm then <16% of shoots grazed. [Note that this indicator may only be reliable in late winter and early spring as *Calluna* in particular is mainly grazed in autumn and winter.] • Only shoot tips (most recent years growth) removed by grazing. • Abundant and conspicuous flowering of *Calluna* and/or *Vaccinium myrtillus*. • Upright growth of *Calluna vulgaris*. Bush canopy open, not a tightly packed mass of contorted shoots. Very few or no instances of 'drumstick', 'topiary' or 'carpet' growth forms. • Little or no signs of grazing of *Erica tetralix, Empetrum nigrum, Vaccinium vitis-idaea* or *Nardus stricta*, if present. • No uprooted dwarf-shrub seedlings in areas regenerating after fire. • Herbivore dung should be rare and very difficult to find in short vegetation. • Negligible bare ground attributable to grazing pressure.

Guidance notes for assessing *Ulex gallii* dry dwarf-shrub heath

Attribute	Notes
Dwarf-shrub cover	• *Ulex gallii* is included as a dwarf-shrub. • *Agrostis curtisii*, where present, can be dominant in the first few years after a burn, but under light grazing such burns will regenerate with good dwarf-shrub cover. • Otherwise as *Calluna* dry heath guidance notes.
Dwarf-shrub diversity	• In most dwarf-shrub heaths there is a dominant species, in *Ulex gallii* dry heath *Erica cinerea, Calluna* or *Ulex gallii* may become dominant. • Otherwise as *Calluna* dry heath guidance notes.
Cover of *Ulex gallii*	• When *Ulex gallii* becomes dominant in the sward species diversity tends to decline.
Age structure	• See *Calluna* dry heath guidance notes.
Grazing impacts	• See *Calluna* dry heath guidance notes.

Grading unfavourable *Ulex gallii* dry heath

Table IN1.5. *Ulex gallii* dry heath
Vegetation condition grading system (see Box IN1.2)

Attribute	Favourable scores	Unfavourable scores		
	0 points	1 point	2 points	6 points
Dwarf-shrub cover	>75%	26-75%	5-25%	<5%
Dwarf-shrub diversity	2 or more spp widespread & frequent	no more than 1 spp widespread & frequent		
Cover of *Ulex gallii*	<50%	>50%		
Age structure	>25% late mature/degenerate or excluded from burning	<25% late mature/degenerate or excluded from burning		
Grazing impact	light	moderate	heavy	

ENGLISH NATURE

Upland vegetation condition assessment **Field record card**

Site Name: | Grid/square reference: | Date:

Management unit: | Surveyor:

***ULEX GALLII* DRY HEATH** Is this card for a whole management unit, raster square or facet ?

ATTRIBUTES AND TARGETS:

	pass (✓)		(circle)			
>75% cover of dwarf-shrubs		Cover of dwarf-shrubs:	>75%	25-75	5-25	<5%
At least 1 dwarf-shrub species other than the dominant species frequent & widespread		Species present & their abundance (DAFOR):	Y / N			
Ulex gallii cover <50%		Cover of *U. gallii*:	<50%		>50%	
Age structure			(see Age Structure section below)			
Grazing impact (see indicators below)		Impact:	Light	Moderate	Heavy	

AGE STRUCTURE:

Calluna regenerating by layering ? Y / N (If yes count layering areas as late mature/degenerate)

% cover of *Calluna* growth phases or height classes of other dwarf-shrub spp if *Calluna* absent:	Pioneer & newly burnt (<15 cm)	Building & early mature (15-35 cm)	Late mature & degenerate (>35 cm)

GRAZING IMPACTS*:

Impact level
(circle indicators & overall impact)

Indicator	**Light**	**Moderate**	**Heavy**
Width of zone of heavy grazing of dwarf-shrubs on interface with preferentially grazed vegetation	<1 m or absent	1 m-10 m	>10 m
% of long shoots grazed			
(a) if shoot growth >4 cm/yr	<33%	33-66%	>66%
(b) if shoot growth <4 cm/yr	<16%	16-33%	>33%
Shoot material removed	tips only	mainly tips	tips & older woody growth
Amount of flowering of dwarf-shrubs	abundant and conspicuous	obvious but patchy	sparse
Frequency of grazing induced *Calluna* growth forms ('drumstick', 'topiary' or 'carpet')	hard to find	localised	widespread
Signs of grazing of *Erica tetralix*, *Empetrum nigrum*, *Vaccinium vitis-idaea* or *Nardus stricta*, if present	hard to find		some
Uprooting of dwarf-shrub seedlings in recent burns	hard to find	present but not conspicuous	conspicuous
Herbivore dung in short vegetation	rare & difficult to find	easy to find but not conspicuous	very conspicuous
Trampled bare ground	none, other than sporadic sheep scars or rabbit scrapes in recent burns		widespread

Vegetation condition (✓): Favourable | Unfavourable

Outlook:

[briefly outline your assessment of the short, medium and long-term outlook for the area you have assessed and give reasons]

Land-use & management

Grazers (✓): sheep | cattle | deer | rabbits | grouse | horses | other

Native trees & shrubs: None | Local | Widespread Species:

Non-native trees & shrubs: None | Local | Widespread Species:

Stock feeding points present ? Y / N

Burn patch size	small (<2 ha)	medium (2-5 ha)	large (>5 ha)	no evidence of being in a burning rotation
None, Local, Widespread?:	L / W	L / W	L / W	L / W

* Field indicators taken from MacDonald *et al.* (1998) *A Guide to Upland Habitats. Surveying Land Management Impacts.* Vol. 2

Wet heath

Habitat definition

Wet heath is defined by the presence of an ericoid dwarf-shrub cover of more than 25% in wet situations where peat depth does not exceed 0.5 m. However, dwarf-shrubs may be scarce or absent in degraded stands. Cross-leaved heath *Erica tetralix* is generally frequent in wet heath whereas it is usually no more than occasional in dry heath. Bryophytes, including *Sphagnum* spp, are generally abundant, although again they may be absent in degraded stands. Purple moor-grass *Molinia caerulea*, heath rush *Juncus squarrosus* and deer grass *Scirpus cespitosus* may also be frequent or abundant, and where any of these are dominant or abundant in the absence of frequent hare's-tail cotton-grass *Eriophorum vaginatum* on peat less than 0.5 m deep, the vegetation should be assessed as wet heath. Note, however, that herb-rich *Molinia* grasslands should not be categorised as wet heath and are not covered by this scheme.

Table IN1.6. NVC communities covered by upland vegetation condition assessment: Wet heath

M15	*Scirpus cespitosus-Erica tetralix* wet heath
M16	*Erica tetralix-Sphagnum compactum* wet heath
M25	*Molinia caerulea-Potentilla erecta* mire
U6	*Juncus squarrosus-Festuca ovina* grassland

Exclusions

Any vegetation on blanket or raised mire peat greater than 0.5 m in depth should be assessed using the blanket and raised mire attributes and targets.

Sphagnum moss
Reproduced from Watson (1969)

Favourable wet heath

Table IN1.7 Wet dwarf-shrub heath

Attributes and targets for favourable vegetation condition

(For vegetation to be favourable all targets listed below must be met)

Dwarf-shrub cover

- Sward composed of a variety of higher plants and bryophytes. Dwarf-shrubs should not dominate the sward and there should be a minimum of 25% cover of species other than dwarf-shrubs.

Dwarf-shrub diversity

- At least two dwarf-shrub species should be frequent and widespread in the sward. No one dwarf-shrub species should be dominant to the exclusion of all others. Where there is a dominant species one or more species must also be frequent and widespread. Where three or more species are present, but only one is frequent and widespread, the occurrence of the less abundant species may be combined and treated as if they are a single species.

Bryophyte abundance

- Bryophytes (excluding *Polytrichum* spp and/or *Campylopus* spp) should be at least frequent and forming patches below or, in more open swards, between the dwarf-shrubs.

Age structure

- Either: all age classes of *Calluna* present with at least 33% of the management unit in the late mature/degenerate age class or 33% or more excluded from the burning rotation

  or: the whole management unit is unburnt.

  Stands which are never burnt should be present on level or gently sloping ground, not entirely confined to steeper slopes.

  [Note that in stands which are never or infrequently burnt *Calluna* may regenerate through layering. Where is occurs the pioneer phase may not be present and it may be hard to distinguish between the building, mature and degenerate phases. Stands where layering of *Calluna* is frequent and widespread should be included in the late mature/degenerate age class.]

Graminoid cover

- Purple moor-grass *Molinia caerulea*, deer grass *Scirpus cespitosus*, wavy hair-grass *Deschampsia flexuosa*, heath rush *Juncus squarrosus* or other graminoids should not dominate over other species.
  Total cover of graminoids should not exceed 50%.

Grazing impact

- Grazing impacts should be light.

  (An absolute maximum of 5% of the grazing unit may show signs of current moderate or heavy grazing.)

Indicators of light grazing: * * Field indicators taken from MacDonald *et al* (1998)	• Where stands of dwarf-shrubs lie adjacent to stands of preferentially grazed vegetation such as grassland, flushes, or recently burnt heath, any marginal band of distinctly grazed dwarf-shrubs should not exceed 1 m in width. • < 33% of long shoots of *Calluna vulgaris* or *Vaccinium myrtillus* showing signs of having been grazed where average shoot growth is >4 cm, or, where average shoot growth is <4 cm then <16% of shoots grazed. [Note that this indicator may only be reliable in late winter and early spring as *Calluna* in particular is mainly grazed in autumn and winter.] • Only shoot tips (most recent years growth) removed by grazing. • Abundant and conspicuous flowering of *Calluna*. • Upright growth of *Calluna vulgaris*. Bush canopy open, not a tightly packed mass of contorted shoots. Very few or no instances of 'drumstick', 'topiary' or 'carpet' growth forms. • Little or no signs of grazing of *Erica tetralix*, *Empetrum nigrum*, *Vaccinium vitis-idaea* or *Nardus stricta*, if present. • No uprooted dwarf-shrub seedlings in areas regenerating after fire. • Herbivore dung should be rare and very difficult to find in short vegetation. • Negligible bare ground attributable to grazing pressure.

Guidance notes for assessing wet dwarf-shrub heath

Attribute	Notes
Dwarf-shrub cover	• See *Calluna* dry heath guidance notes.
Dwarf-shrub diversity	• In most dwarf-shrub heaths there is a dominant species, in wet heath this is generally heather *Calluna*, although occasionally it may be cross-leaved heath *Erica tetralix*.
	• Otherwise as *Calluna* dry heath guidance notes.
Frequency of bryophytes	• Positive bryophytes include *Sphagnum* spp as well as 'feather mosses' (see *Calluna* dry heath guidance notes).
	• See also *Calluna* dry heath guidance notes.
Age structure	• See *Calluna* dry heath guidance notes, but note increased cover of late mature/degenerate *Calluna* required for wet heath.
Graminoid cover	• Graminoids are plants which look like grasses and include true grasses, sedges and rushes.
Grazing impacts	• See *Calluna* dry heath guidance notes.

Grading unfavourable wet heath

Table IN1.8. Wet heath

Vegetation condition grading system (see Box IN1.2)

Attribute	Favourable scores	Unfavourable scores		
	0 points	1 point	2 points	4 points
Dwarf-shrub cover	51-75%	>75% or 26-50%	5-25%	<5%
Dwarf-shrub diversity	2 or more spp widespread & frequent	no more than 1 spp widespread & frequent		
Bryophyte abundance	frequent patches		occasional patches	rare
Age structure	>33% late mature/degenerate or excluded from burning	<33% late mature/degenerate or excluded from burning		
Graminoid cover	<50%	50-75%	>75%	
Grazing impact	light	moderate	heavy	

ENGLISH NATURE

Upland Vegetation Condition Assessment

Field record card

Site Name: ______ Grid/square reference: ______ Date: ______

Management unit: ______ Surveyor: ______

***CALLUNA* DRY HEATH** (without *Ulex gallii*) Is this card for a whole management unit, raster square or facet? ______

ATTRIBUTES AND TARGETS:

Attribute	pass (✓)		(circle)			
>75% cover of dwarf-shrubs		Cover of dwarf-shrubs:	>75%	25-75	5-25	<5%
At least 1 dwarf-shrub species other than the dominant species frequent & widespread		Species present & their abundance (DAFOR):	Y / N			
Bryophytes &/or bushy *Cladonia* at least frequent & forming carpets		Cover of bryophytes/lichens:	Freq	Occ	Rare	
Age Structure			(see Age Structure section below)			
Grazing impact (see indicators below)		Impact:	Light	Moderate	Heavy	

AGE STRUCTURE:

Calluna regenerating by layering ? Y / N (If yes count layering areas as late mature/degenerate)

	Pioneer & newly burnt	Building & early mature	Late mature & degenerate
% cover of *Calluna* growth phases:			

GRAZING IMPACTS*:

Impact level (circle indicators & overall impact)

Indicator	Light	Moderate	Heavy
Width of zone of heavy grazing of dwarf-shrubs on interface with preferentially grazed vegetation	<1 m or absent	1 m-10 m	>10 m
% of long shoots grazed (a) if shoot growth >4 cm/yr	<33%	33-66%	>66%
(b) if shoot growth <4 cm/yr	<16%	16-33%	>33%
Shoot material removed	tips only	mainly tips	tips & older woody growth
Amount of flowering of dwarf-shrubs	abundant and conspicuous	obvious but patchy	sparse
Frequency of grazing induced *Calluna* growth forms ('drumstick', 'topiary' or 'carpet')	hard to find	localised	widespread
Signs of grazing of *Empetrum nigrum*, *Vaccinium vitis-idaea* or *Nardus stricta*, if species present	hard to find		some
Uprooting of dwarf-shrub seedlings in recent burns	hard to find	present but not conspicuous	conspicuous
Herbivore dung in short vegetation	rare and difficult to find	easy to find but not conspicuous	very conspicuous
Trampled bare ground	none, other than sporadic sheep scars or rabbit scrapes in recent burns		widespread

Vegetation condition (✓): Favourable | Unfavourable

Outlook:

[briefly outline your assessment of the short, medium and long-term outlook for the area you have assessed and give reasons]

Land-use & management

Grazers (✓): sheep | cattle | deer | rabbits | grouse | horses | other

Stock feeding points present ? Y / N

Native trees & shrubs: None | Local | Widespread Species: ______

Non-native trees & shrubs: None | Local | Widespread Species: ______

Burn patch size	**small (<2 ha)**	**medium (2-5 ha)**	**large (>5 ha)**	**no evidence of being in a burning rotation**
None, Local, Widespread?:	L / W	L / W	L / W	L / W

* Field indicators taken from MacDonald *et al.* (1998) *A Guide to Upland Habitats. Surveying Land Management Impacts*. Vol. 2

Blanket and upland raised mire

Habitat definition

Any vegetation on blanket or raised peat bodies deeper than 0.5 m should be assessed using these attributes and targets. This will include not only typical ombrotrophic mire vegetation composed of a mix of hare's-tail cotton-grass *Eriophorum vaginatum*, deer grass *Scirpus cespitosus*, purple moor-grass *Molinia caerulea*, bog mosses *Sphagnum* spp and ericoid dwarf-shrubs (heather *Calluna vulgaris*, cross-leaved heath *Erica tetralix*, bilberry *Vaccinium myrtillus*, cowberry *Vaccinium vitis-idaea* and crowberry *Empetrum nigrum*), but also vegetation superficially resembling dry heath on deep peat and other degraded forms where Sphagna and/or dwarf-shrubs may be absent. In addition to this, any vegetation in which *Eriophorum vaginatum* is more than occasional should be assessed as blanket and raised mire.

The following discussion deals mainly with blanket mires as these are by far the most widespread of the mire types in the uplands. However, much of what is said should also be applicable to upland raised mires.

The majority of English blanket mire is found on the Pennines and belongs to the relatively dry *Calluna vulgaris-Eriophorum vaginatum* type and its degraded derivatives. The wetter *Scirpus cespitosus-Eriophorum vaginatum* type is largely confined to the extreme west, principally the moors of SW England and the western Lake District. As a result, the attributes and targets tend to be biased towards favourable Pennine blanket mires. However, trials have shown that these will also identify the better areas of western blanket mires and should also apply to upland raised mires.

Table IN1.9 NVC communities covered by upland vegetation condition assessment: Blanket and upland raised mire

M17	*Scirpus cespitosus-Eriophorum vaginatum* blanket mire
M18	*Erica tetralix-Sphagnum papillosum* raised and blanket mire
M19	*Calluna vulgaris-Eriophorum vaginatum* blanket mire
M20	*Eriophorum vaginatum* blanket mire
M25	*Molinia caerulea-Potentilla erecta* mire
H9	*Calluna vulgaris-Deschampsia flexuosa* heath
H12	*Calluna vulgaris-Vaccinium myrtillus* heath
H18	*Vaccinium myrtillus-Deschampsia flexuosa* heath
U6	*Juncus squarrosus-Festuca ovina* grassland

Table IN1.10. Blanket and upland raised mires
Attributes and targets for favourable vegetation condition
(for vegetation to be favourable all targets listed below must be met)

Bryophyte abundance • Bryophytes should be abundant and must include *Sphagnum* spp. *Sphagnum* spp must be both frequent and widespread in the stand and not restricted to hollows, forming at least occasional lawns or hummocks.	
Dwarf-shrub cover • Except in wetter areas where *Sphagnum* spp are abundant and forming lawns, cover of dwarf-shrubs must be greater than 33%.	
Dwarf-shrub diversity • At least two dwarf-shrub species should be frequent and widespread in the sward. No one dwarf-shrub species should be dominant to the exclusion of all others. Where there is a dominant species one or more species must also be frequent and widespread. Where three or more species are present, but only one is frequent and widespread, the occurrence of the less abundant species may be combined and treated as if they are a single species.	
Graminoid cover • Hare's-tail cotton-grass *Eriophorum vaginatum*, purple moor-grass *Molinia caerulea*, deer grass *Scirpus cespitosus*, wavy hair-grass *Deschampsia flexuosa*, heath rush *Juncus squarrosus* or other graminoids should not dominate over dwarf-shrubs. The cover of graminoids should not exceed 50%, unless *Sphagnum* spp are abundant/co-dominant and forming lawns below the graminoids.	
Extent of bare ground or ground covered by algal mats etc. • Little or no bare ground, or bare ground carpeted by *Racomitrium lanuginosum*, *Polytrichum* spp, *Campylopus* spp, crust forming lichens or algal mats (found only after widespread and intensive searching) *.	
Erosion features associated with human impacts • No erosion, other than very localised instances, associated with human impacts (eg drainage, fires, peat extraction, livestock grazing, recreational activities or military training).	
Active peat extraction • Peat extraction absent (areas of cut peat which have revegetated with good mire vegetation which meets the other attributes for favourable vegetation condition may be acceptable).	
Grazing impact • Grazing impacts should be light. (An absolute maximum of 5% of the grazing unit may show signs of current moderate or heavy grazing.)	
Indicators of light grazing: * * Field indicators taken from MacDonald *et al* (1998)	• Widespread and abundant flowering of cotton-grasses *Eriophorum* spp. [Note that this indicator may only be reliable in spring.] • No evidence of encroachment by graminoid species such as *Juncus squarrosus*, *Deschampsia flexuosa* or *Nardus stricta*. • Upright growth of *Calluna vulgaris*. Bush canopy open, not a tightly packed mass of contorted shoots. Very few or no instances of 'drumstick, topiary or carpet growth forms. • No obvious grazing of *Calluna vulgaris* or *Vaccinium myrtillus*. Grazed shoots difficult to find without both intensive and extensive searching. • Little or no signs of grazing of *Erica tetralix*, *Empetrum nigrum* or *Vaccinium vitis-idaea*, if present. • Little or no evidence of trampling of *Sphagnum* hummocks or carpets. • At most only very localised occurrence of trampled bare ground, including animal paths and enhanced hagging.

Guidance notes for assessing blanket and upland raised mires

Attribute	Notes
Bryophyte abundance	• In many Pennine blanket mires *Sphagna* do not make up as high a proportion of the bryophyte component as they do in more northern and western mires. In these Pennine mires, other mosses, particularly pleurocarpous or 'feather mosses' (see *Calluna* Dry Heath guidance notes and Figure IN1.1b), can make up a significant proportion of to the bryophyte layer. These mires will be favourable, provided that bryophytes as a group are abundant and that *Sphagnum* spp are at least frequent and widespread throughout the mire vegetation. The presence of Sphagna indicates that these mires are still active in that they are forming peat. • Note that patches of *Polytrichum* spp, *Campylopus* spp (see *Calluna* dry heath guidance notes and Figure IN1.1b) and *Racomitrium lanuginosum* which have colonised bare ground resulting from hot fires do not count towards the bryophyte abundance for this attribute. Note, however, that *Racomitrium* can be present on hummocks within the mire and in this situation it will contribute to bryophyte abundance.
Dwarf-shrub cover	• In wetter mires dwarf-shrub cover may be reduced owing to the reduced vigour of these species in these conditions. This does not detract from the favourability of a mire, provided that there is high cover of *Sphagnum* mosses. Indeed high *Sphagnum* cover is of greater importance than high dwarf-shrub cover in blanket and raised mires.
Dwarf-shrub diversity	• See *Calluna* dry heath guidance notes, but note that both *Empetrum nigrum* and *Erica tetralix* can be locally dominant.
Graminoid cover	• Generally graminoids (plants that are grass-like - see wet heath guidance notes) should not be the dominant component of mire vegetation. However, in very wet mires, where there is a high cover of *Sphagnum* this is allowable as dwarf-shrub vigour will be greatly reduced by waterlogging.
Extent of bare ground	• This refers to bare ground resulting from fires, rather than erosion, although fire can lead to erosion as well (see below). • While there are examples of blanket mires in favourable condition which are burnt; hot fires can, particularly at high altitude (500 m+), result in loss of mire vegetation and its replacement either by bare ground or ground covered by colonisers of bare peat such as those listed.
Erosion associated with human impacts	• Erosion is a natural feature of blanket mires, particularly marginal fretting on breaks of slope. However, where natural erosion is exacerbated by human impacts such as heavy livestock grazing impacts; or where erosion is the direct result of human impacts, such as loss of vegetation cover following overly hot fires or use of

Attribute	**Notes**
Erosion (continued)	vehicles, the mire will not be in favourable condition, except where such erosion is very localised in nature.
Active peat extraction	• Current active peat extraction is uncommon on blanket mires and upland raised mires, but examples do exist. All current examples of this practice, together with examples of abandoned peat workings which have not recolonised with mire vegetation that meets the other attributes for favourable vegetation condition will be unfavourable.
Grazing impacts: General	• See *Calluna* dry heath guidance notes for general comments on grazing indicators.
Flowering of *Eriophorum* spp	• This indicator is only reliable in spring and early summer, during the cotton-grass *Eriophorum* flowering season. At other times of year flowers may be inconspicuous.
Encroachment by graminoids	• Species such as *Nardus, Deschampsia flexuosa* or *Juncus squarrosus* tend to have low abundance and cover in mire vegetation in favourable condition. However, they can become more prominent in mire vegetation when it is subject to high grazing impacts over a long period of time. • Widely scattered individual plants of these species may be acceptable, but areas where they are frequent or abundant, except on the very margins of a mire, will be unfavourable. • These species may also become more prominent in mires which are drying out.
Frequency of grazing induced *Calluna* growth forms	• See *Calluna* dry heath guidance notes.
Conspicuousness of grazing on dwarf-shrubs	• Where grazing is having a moderate or heavy impact on the vegetation grazed dwarf-shrub shoots will be easy to find. Of particular importance is grazing during the summer or removal of older woody material as opposed to the most recent year's growth (see *Calluna* dry heath guidance notes). • Blanket and raised mires are generally avoided by livestock if more palatable vegetation is available.
Trampling damage to *Sphagnum*	• Look for hoof prints in areas of *Sphagnum*, broken surfaces on hummocks and lawns and loose, bleached *Sphagnum* plants or parts of plants.
Presence of trampled bare ground	• Look for hoof prints in bare peat.

Grading unfavourable blanket mire

Table IN1.11. Blanket mire
Vegetation condition grading system (see Box IN1.2)

Attribute	Favourable scores	Unfavourable scores		
	0 points	1 point	2 points	4 points
Bryophyte abundance	abundant, including frequent & widespread *Sphagnum* spp	frequent to abundant but *Sphagnum* spp occasional - rare	occasional, *Sphagnum* spp more-or-less absent	rare
Dwarf-shrub cover	>33% except in wetter areas	<33% except in wetter areas	<5%	
Dwarf-shrub diversity	2 or more spp widespread & frequent	no more than 1 spp widespread & frequent		
Graminoid cover	<50%	51-75%	>75%	
Extent of bare ground or ground covered by algal mats etc	none	present	extensive	ubiquitous
Erosion features associated with human impacts	none	present	extensive	ubiquitous
Active peat extraction (excluding areas revegetated with mire spp)	none	present	extensive	ubiquitous
Grazing impact	light	moderate	heavy	

ENGLISH NATURE

Upland vegetation condition assessment

Field record card

Site Name:		Grid/square reference:		Date:	
Management unit:			Surveyor:		

BLANKET & UPLAND RAISED MIRE

Is this card for a whole management unit, raster square or facet?

ATTRIBUTES AND TARGETS:	**pass (✓)**		(circle)			
Bryophytes abundant, inc. frequent & widespread *Sphagnum*		Bryophyte/ *Sphagnum* cover	Bryos A Sph F & W	Bryos F/A Sph R/O	Bryos O Sph R/abs	Bryos R Sph abs
Dwarf-shrub cover >33% except where *Sphagnum* abundant & forming carpets		Dwarf-shrub cover	>33%	5-33%	<5%	
At least 1 dwarf-shrub species other than the dominant species frequent & widespread		Species present & their abundance (DAFOR):	Y / N			
Total cover of graminoids <50% unless *Sphagnum* abundant/ co-dominant & forming lawns beneath		Cover of graminoids	<50%	>50%	>75%	
Little or no bare ground, or ground covered by *Racomitrium lanuginosum*, *Polytrichum* spp, *Campylopus* spp, crust forming lichens or algal mats*		Cover of bare ground etc.	none	pres[nt]	extens	ubiq.
No erosion assoc. with human impacts (other than very localised impacts)		Extent of bare peat	none	pres[nt]	extens	ubiq.
No active peat extraction (Old works reveg. with mire spp are OK)		Extent of peat extraction	none	pres[nt]	extens	ubiq.
Grazing impact		Impact:	Light	Moderate	Heavy	

GRAZING IMPACTS*:

Impact level (circle indicators & overall impact)

Indicator	**Light**	**Moderate**	**Heavy**
Amount of flowering of *Eriophorum* spp	widespread & abundant	patchy or thinly scattered	inconspicuous/absent
Encroachment by *Juncus squarrosus*, *Deschampsia flexuosa* or *Nardus stricta*	hard to find	localised	widespread
Frequency of grazing induced *Calluna* growth forms ('drumstick', 'topiary' or 'carpet')	hard to find	localised	widespread
Conspicuousness of grazing on *Calluna* & *Vaccinium myrtillus*	hard to find	Grazed shoots easy to find (may be patchy)	
Signs of grazing of *Empetrum nigrum*, *Vaccinium vitis-idaea* or *Nardus stricta*, where species present	hard to find		some
Trampling damage to *Sphagnum* hummocks or carpets	hard to find	localised	widespread
Presence of trampled bare ground, paths & enhanced hagging	hard to find	localised	conspicuous & extensive

Vegetation condition (✓) | Favourable | Unfavourable |

Outlook: [briefly outline your assessment of the short, medium and long-term outlook for the area you have assessed and give reasons]

Land-use & management

Grazers (✓)	sheep	cattle	deer	rabbits	grouse
				horses	other

Stock feeding points present? Y / N

Drainage (✓)	None	Inactive (blocked)	Active	
Erosion (✓)	sheep/deer scars	sheet	gully	other
Burning (✓)	Absent	Controlled	Uncontrolled	
Native trees & shrubs:	None	Local	Widespread	Species:
Non-native trees & shrubs:	None	Local	Widespread	Species:

Age structure:

Calluna regenerating by layering? Y / N (If yes count layering areas as late mature/degenerate)

	Pioneer & newly burnt (<10 cm)	Building & early mature (10-25 cm)	Late mature & degenerate (>25 cm)
% cover of *Calluna* growth phases:			

Burn patch size	**small (<2 ha)**	**medium (2-5 ha)**	**large (>5 ha)**	**no evidence of being in a burning rotation**
None, Local, Widespread?:	L / W	L / W	L / W	L / W

* Field indicators taken from MacDonald *et al* (1998) *A Guide to Upland Habitats. Surveying Land Management Impacts*. Vol. 2

Montane moss and lichen heath

Habitat definition

Montane vegetation occurs above the natural tree line. This limit varies regionally according to climatic conditions but is generally taken to be around 600 m. However, local climatic conditions may lead to considerable variation between individual hills.

There is inevitably a gradation between sub-montane and montane heath. As a general guide, the two habitats can be distinguished floristically by the replacement of pleurocarpous or feather mosses (see *Calluna* dry heath guidance notes), such as *Hypnum jutlandicum* and *Pleurozium schreberi*, by species such as woolly hair moss *Racomitrium lanuginosum* and *Polytrichum alpinum*. Stiff sedge *Carex bigelowii*, *Racomitrium* or "bushy" lichens, notably *Cladonia arbuscula* and *C. impexa* (see *Calluna* dry heath guidance notes), form a significant part of the vegetation in montane heath. Dwarf-shrubs are represented by bilberry *Vaccinium myrtillus*, cowberry *V. vitis-idaea* and crowberry *Empetrum nigrum* but heather *Calluna vulgaris*, cross-leaved heath *Erica tetralix* and bell heather *E. cinerea* tend to be absent (note that the general absence of *Calluna* from this type of vegetation in England is probably grazing induced rather than climatic).

Grassland with wavy hair-grass *Deschampsia flexuosa*, sheep's fescue *Festuca ovina* or common bent *Agrostis capillaris* over the altitudinal limits above should be assessed as montane heath unless there are strong indications that sub-montane attributes should apply.

Montane heath has been identified on Lake District peaks, the North Pennines and Cheviots and may be present elsewhere, particularly in the Yorkshire Dales. Although much of the land above 600 m is likely to be blanket mire over the southern Pennines and Dartmoor, some summits may support grasslands on mineral soils and, where such stands are encountered, they should be assessed as montane heath.

Table IN1.12. NVC communities covered by upland vegetation condition assessment Montane moss and lichen heath	
U10	*Carex bigelowii-Racomitrium lanuginosum* moss-heath
H19	*Vaccinium myrtillus-Cladonia arbuscula* lichen-heath

Exclusions

Areas of peat deeper than 0.5 m above these altitudinal limits should be assessed as blanket mire (see also definition of sub-montane dry dwarf-shrub heath).

Table IN1.13. Montane moss and lichen heaths **Attributes and targets for favourable vegetation condition** (for vegetation to be favourable all targets listed below must be met)	
Cover of *Racomitrium* • In *Carex bigelowii-Racomitrium lanuginosum* moss-heath the cover of *Racomitrium* should exceed 66% over the whole stand.	
Mean depth of moss/lichen/dwarf-shrub mat • Mean depth of moss/lichen/dwarf-shrub mat, should exceed 5 cm in *Carex bigelowii-Racomitrium lanuginosum* moss-heath.	
Cover of *Cladonia* spp • In *Vaccinium myrtillus-Cladonia arbuscula* lichen-heath 'bushy' *Cladonia* lichens (eg *C. impexa, C. arbuscula, C. uncialis* and *C. rangiferina*) should contribute >50% of the vegetation cover over the whole stand.	
Mean depth of moss/lichen/dwarf-shrub mat • Mean depth of moss/lichen/dwarf-shrub mat, should exceed 7 cm in *Vaccinium myrtillus-Cladonia arbuscula* lichen-heath.	
Grazing impact • Grazing impacts should be light.	
Indicators of light grazing: * * Field indicators taken from MacDonald *et al* (1998)	• No signs of grazing of any dwarf-shrubs present. • Very little or no signs of grazing of plant parts, except on leaves of *Carex bigelowii* or fine-leaved grasses such as *Deschampsia flexuosa, Festuca ovina* and *F. vivipara* and then less than 10% of green leaves grazed (grazed leaves hard to find after intensive and extensive searching). • Very little or no signs of grazing on leaves of broad-leaved grasses such as *Agrostis capillaris, A. vinealis, Anthoxanthum odoratum* or *Poa* spp. • Fine-leaved grasses such as *Deschampsia flexuosa, Festuca ovina* and *F. vivipara* contribute less than 10% of the vegetation cover in total. • Negligible collective cover of broad-leaved grasses such as *Agrostis capillaris, A. vinealis, Anthoxanthum odoratum* or *Poa* spp. • No more than sporadic occurrence of either *Galium saxatile* or *Potentilla erecta*. (Where grazing intensity has been heavy in past but has now been reduced to favourable levels these two species may be present at more than negligible ground cover but other indicators will suggest light grazing.) • *Juncus squarrosus* absent or very scarce. • No uprooting of plants. • Dung of grazing animals sparse or absent - fewer than five groups of sheep pellets per 100 m^2.

Guidance notes for assessing montane moss and lichen heath

Attribute	Notes
Cover of *Racomitrium* and bushy *Cladonia*	• Either *Racomitrium lanuginosum* or bushy *Cladonia* lichens (see *Calluna* dry heath guidance notes and Figure IN1.1a) must form a major part of the ground cover for the vegetation to be in favourable condition.
Mean depth of moss/lichen/dwarf-shrub mat	• The minimum depths for favourable condition are based on the mean vegetation heights recorded in the NVC data for the two communities (Rodwell 1991 and 1992) and lie in the upper range of vegetation heights recorded in a survey of Lake District montane heath (Jerram 1992). • Depth should be recorded by measuring the vertical distance a pencil, finger or ruler can be inserted into the vegetation mat until the ground is met. Exclude grass flower spikes from the depth measurement.
Grazing impacts: General	• See *Calluna* dry heath guidance notes for general comments on grazing indicators, but note that only light and heavy impacts are distinguished in montane heath.
Grazing of dwarf-shrubs, if present	• Where heavy grazing occurs evidence of grazing of dwarf-shrubs (see *Calluna* dry heath guidance notes) will be noticeable, but may not necessarily be conspicuous. However, where the grazing impact is light such evidence will be very difficult to find.
Grazing of sedges and fine-leaved grasses	• Where heavy grazing occurs evidence of grazing of species such as *Carex bigelowii*, *Deschampsia flexuosa* and *Festuca ovina/vivipara* will be easily seen. But where the grazing impact is light there will be little or no signs of grazing of green leaves.
Grazing of broad-leaved grasses, where present	• When present these species will be preferentially grazed as they are more palatable than other species. The principal broad-leaved grasses involved are common bent *Agrostis capillaris*, brown bent *A. vinealis*, sweet vernal-grass *Anthoxanthum odoratum* and meadow grasses *Poa* spp.
Cover of *Galium* and *Potentilla*	• The presence of either of these species indicates that heavy grazing has been present for many years. These species are not a natural component of this vegetation type.
Collective cover of fine-leaved grasses	• High cover (>10%) of these species (see above) indicates that heavy grazing has been present for many years. Although a natural component of the vegetation they generally only occur at low cover under light grazing levels.
Collective cover of broad-leaved grasses	• These species are not a natural component of this vegetation type. The presence of any of these species at abundances of anything other than very occasional indicates that heavy grazing has been present for many years.
Presence of *Juncus squarrosus*	• *Juncus squarrosus* is not normally a component of montane vegetation, but it may become frequent under chronic heavy grazing where there are shallow peat deposits, and it can spread into mineral soils.
Uprooting of plants	• Uprooted plants both of grasses and dwarf-shrubs lying on the ground are a good indicator of current grazing.
Frequency of sheep dung pellet groups	• The threshold density applies to pellet groups not individual pellets. A dung pellet group is an aggregation of more than six individual pellets.

Grading unfavourable montane moss and lichen heath

Table IN1.14 ***Carex bigelowii–Racomitrium lanuginosum*** **montane heath**
Vegetation condition grading system
(see Box IN1.2)

Attribute	Favourable scores	Unfavourable scores		
	0 points	**1point**	**2 points**	**4 points**
Cover of *Racomitrium*	>66%	33-66%	5-33%	<5%
Mean depth of moss/ lichen/dwarf-shrub mat	>5 cm	2.5-5 cm	<2.5 cm	
Grazing impact	light		heavy	

Table IN1.15 ***Vaccinium myrtillus-Cladonia arbuscula*** **montane heath**
Vegetation condition grading system (see Box IN1.2)

Attribute	Favourable scores	Unfavourable scores		
	0 points	**1 point**	**2 points**	**4 points**
Cover of *Cladonia* spp	>50%	25-50%	5-25%	<5%
Mean depth of moss/ lichen/dwarf-shrub mat	>7 cm	2.5-7 cm	<2.5 cm	
Grazing impact	light		heavy	

ENGLISH NATURE

Upland Vegetation Condition Assessment

Field record card

Site Name:		Grid/square reference:		Date:	
Management unit:				Surveyor:	

WET HEATH

Is this card for a whole management unit, raster square or facet?

ATTRIBUTES AND TARGETS:	pass (✓)		(circle)			
50-75% cover of dwarf-shrubs		Cover of dwarf-shrubs:	50-75	>75% or 25-75	5-25%	<5%
At least 1 dwarf-shrub species other than the dominant species frequent & widespread		Species present & their abundance (DAFOR):	Y / N			
Bryophytes (excluding *Polytrichum* & *Campylopus* spp) at least frequent & forming patches		Bryophytes abundance:	Freq	Occ	Rare	
Age structure			(see Age Structure section below)			
Total cover of graminoids <50%		Cover of graminoids:	<50%	50-75%	>75%	
Grazing impact		Impact:	Light	Moderate	Heavy	

AGE STRUCTURE:

Calluna regenerating by layering? Y / N (If yes count layering areas as late mature/degenerate)

	Pioneer & newly burnt	Building & early mature	Late mature & degenerate
% cover of *Calluna* growth phases:			

GRAZING IMPACTS *:

Impact level (circle indicators & overall impact)

Indicator	Light	Moderate	Heavy
Width of zone of heavy grazing of dwarf-shrubs on interface with preferentially grazed vegetation	<1 m or absent	1 m-10 m	>10 m
% of long shoots grazed			
(a) if shoot growth >4cm/yr	<33%	33-66%	>66%
(b) if shoot growth <4cm/yr	<16%	16-33%	>33%
Shoot material removed	tips only	mainly tips	tips & older woody growth
Amount of flowering of dwarf-shrubs	abundant and conspicuous	obvious but patchy	sparse
Frequency of grazing induced *Calluna* growth forms ('drumstick', 'topiary' or 'carpet')	hard to find	localised	widespread
Grazing of *Erica tetralix*, *Empetrum nigrum*, *Vaccinium vitis-idaea* or *Nardus stricta*, if present	hard to find		some
Uprooting of dwarf-shrub seedlings in recent burns	hard to find	present but not conspicuous	conspicuous
Herbivore dung in short vegetation	rare and difficult to find	easy to find but not conspicuous	very conspicuous
Trampled bare ground	none, other than sporadic sheep scars or rabbit scrapes in recent burns		widespread

Vegetation condition (✓) | Favourable | Unfavourable |

Outlook:

[briefly outline your assessment of the short, medium and long-term outlook for the area you have assessed and give reasons]

Land-use & management

Grazers (✓)	sheep	cattle	deer	rabbits	grouse
	horses	other			

Stock feeding points present ? Y / N

Drainage (✓)	None	Inactive (blocked)	Active

Native trees & shrubs:	None	Local	Widespread	Species:	
Non-native trees & shrubs:	None	Local	Widespread	Species:	

Burn patch size	**small (<2 ha)**	**medium (2-5 ha)**	**large (>5 ha)**	**no evidence of being in a burning rotation**
None, Local, Widespread?:	L / W	L / W	L / W	L / W

* Field indicators taken from MacDonald *et al* (1998) *A Guide to Upland Habitats. Surveying Land Management Impacts.* Vol. 2

Field survey techniques

This assessment technique can be applied at several levels of detail. Which method is used will be determined by the amount of detail required and the resources available:

1. The walk-over survey method will provide a general overview of vegetation condition on a site;

2. The raster and facet methods both divide the site up into survey units, across which vegetation condition is averaged out. This avoids the need to record every stand of vegetation and will provide quite detailed information as to how management impacts vary across the site, although some small scale detail may be lost.

1. Field method for a quick walk-over survey

(time required: half a day to one day)

To assess the condition of vegetation for an area of land using these attributes and targets, a minimum of 20% of both the management unit and the habitat within that unit must be covered on foot by doing a 'W-walk' over the site. An assessment of vegetation condition should be made in at least 10 randomly located points along the walk in the main habitat present and at five points in any subsidiary habitats (Figure IN1.4). Where habitats cover similar proportions of the square ten stops should be made in each habitat. It is important that both the core area of the unit/habitat and the margins of the unit/habitat are covered during the assessment walk as impacts are likely to differ across the site. To take this into account, the assessor must cover both 20% of the unit margin and 20% of the core area of the unit.

When a baseline (first) assessment is being made using this method the route walked should be recorded as accurately as possible on a 1:25,000 scale map or larger. Subsequent assessments must follow the same route if the method is to be used as a monitoring tool to indicate broad changes in structure and vegetation composition.

Prior to making an assessment of a habitat, it is necessary to define the extent of the habitat in the unit as shown in Box IN1.3.

2. Methods for more detailed site/management unit surveys

(time required: one to many days - survey rate: 4 km^2 per day)

Both nature conservation bodies and land managers often wish to assess how the impacts of various land management practices vary across a management unit prior to formulating management prescriptions. On moorland sites in the past, this has frequently involved undertaking a Heather Condition Survey, which maps burning patterns and grazing impacts (Bardgett, Marsden & Howard 1995). The attributes presented here for assessing vegetation condition can be used in a similar manner, particularly if the attributes on which stands, or parts of stands, classified as unfavourable are mapped as well, rather than simply mapping which areas meet the attributes for favourable vegetation condition. Maps of vegetation condition will not only help to target management action but will also aid the zoning of moors where there are potential conflicts between nature conservation objectives. For example, golden plover require short vegetation to breed, but maintaining high proportions of short vegetation can usually involve burning at a frequency that is too high to maintain a botanically diverse sward.

Box IN1.3. Defining the extent of the habitat	
The following definitions of extent are broad so that they will incorporate the marginal areas of the habitats. It is in these marginal areas where change in condition is most likely to occur, so it is essential that these areas are included in any assessment.	
Dry and wet heaths:	For both these habitats the heath to be assessed will include all heath and acid grassland where the abundance of dwarf-shrubs is more than occasional. Areas of acid grassland where dwarf-shrub abundance is more than occasional can be disregarded for the purposes of assessing heath for a walkover assessment but for whole site/unit surveys they should be mapped as the appropriate heath in unfavourable condition.
Blanket and upland raised mires:	The area to be assessed includes the whole of the main peat body plus any satellite areas of deep peat. Any grassland or heath between the main peat body and these satellites should be included in the assessment area.
Montane heath:	The assessment area should include all the heath and grassland above the tree line in the unit.

Modifications to vegetation condition attributes required to facilitate site/management unit surveys

Several of the attributes and targets as defined above require assessments to be made taking into account whole management units. These are inappropriate for surveys designed to map variation in vegetation condition across a management unit and modifications are required:

All habitats:

- Attributes and targets should refer to the stand, square or facet being assessed not the management unit;

- Grazing impacts must be assessed for each stand (or parts of larger stands), square or facet and the allowance for 5% of the assessment area to be either moderately heavily or heavily grazed is dropped.

Dry and wet heaths:

- The percentage cover of each age class in the stand, square or facet should be recorded so that the age class attributes can be assessed for the site as a whole once the survey is completed.

Methodology

Two potential methods for mapping vegetation condition are considered here.

2a. *Raster mapping*

The area to be surveyed is divided into a series of squares based on the National Grid. 25 ha (5 km^2) squares have been used by Scottish Natural Heritage for surveys using their field indicators (MacDonald *et al* 1998) and by English Nature staff testing this English Nature assessment methodology. This allows for increased coverage rates in comparison to recording every stand, while still retaining a sufficient level of detail to pick out local variation of impacts. Imposing a fixed grid for recording acts as a filter and helps to reduce the amount of between observer variability which all field survey is prone to. English Nature staff found that the maximum coverage rate using this method was four square kilometres per day per surveyor.

A 'W-walk' is made through each square and an overall assessment of the vegetation condition (favourable or unfavourable) is made for each habitat within the square. An assessment of vegetation condition should be made in at least ten randomly located points along the walk in the main habitat present in the square and at five points in any subsidiary habitats. Where habitats cover similar proportions of the square ten stops should be made in each habitat (Figure IN1.4). A minimum of 20% of both the square and each habitat present in the square must be walked through, including both core areas and the margins of stands of habitats present. When making the overall assessment, it is important not to give undue weight to small, local patches of an impact. The assessment should be based on the proportion of the habitat over which that condition occurs, not the proportion of the square with the condition. Habitats should be recorded only where they constitute more than 10% of the total area of a sample square. Likewise, where a sample square extends beyond the site boundary, it should be recorded only if more than 10% of the square lies within the site. Again, the attributes on which any unfavourable squares fail are also recorded. Recording can be done simply on to a map, but a considerable amount of additional information on the vegetation in each square can be collected if standardised record cards, such as those included in this information pack, are completed for each habitat present in each square surveyed.

Results can be presented as a habitat map with overlays of vegetation condition for each habitat present. The use of record cards is strongly recommended as it allows comparisons to be made if further surveys are carried out in subsequent years and facilitates input of survey data into a Geographical Information System (GIS) computer mapping/database programme. If data are entered into a GIS then further data analysis can be carried out as it is a relatively simple task to produce maps showing the distribution of particular impacts, light, moderate and heavy grazing for example, or the distribution of other features recorded, such as bryophyte abundance, or the distribution of active drains on a blanket mire.

2b *Facet mapping*

The Northern Ireland Environment and Heritage Service have used a modified version of the raster technique for a monitoring exercise in a large upland site in 1997. The main modifications to the raster technique are:

The survey area is subdivided into 'facets' (physical units that have been identified from aerial photographs) usually on the basis of physical features such as rivers or breaks in slope which are readily identified in the field. Facet size can vary from 40 to 100 ha.

The variability of the vegetation in a facet is assessed prior to the field visit using aerial photographs. The route the surveyor is to walk through each facet is drawn onto the map or aerial photograph so that it takes the surveyor through the full range of vegetation types and conditions present in the facet.

A minimum of 20% of both the facet and each habitat present in the facet must be walked through including core areas of the facet/habitat and the margins of the facet/habitat.

Periodic stops are made throughout the walk through the facet to assess the attributes on the relevant recording card in a 10 × 10 m quadrat. At least 20 such stops should be made for the dominant habitat in the facet and between five to 10 stops for other habitats present.

The area of each facet must be measured before calculations can be made to assess whether the age structure attributes for dry and wet heaths are met.

The record cards used here to record vegetation condition in each habitat are the same as for the raster sampling technique. However, an additional record card for each habitat is required to record the quadrat data and surveyors also completed a summary card for each facet which recorded estimates of the area of the facet covered by each habitat and general comments on its management and vegetation condition. Again, the information recorded can be entered into a GIS database and presented as a map or series of maps.

The pros and cons of each sampling technique

Both sampling techniques can provide maps showing the range of vegetation condition by habitat across a site. The facet method will provide assessments related to recognisable geographical/vegetation units while the raster method provides an overview of the site as a whole which cannot be directly related to individual stands of vegetation.

The facet method has the higher degree of repeatability for monitoring purposes, as it has the most easily identifiable sample unit boundaries in the field. Determining where the edge of a sample raster grid square can be difficult on featureless terrain. While this may not be particularly important in some instances, where this vegetation condition survey method is used as a regular monitoring technique an error of one or two hundred metres could change the grading of an attribute simply by including or excluding a stand which had been critical to a previous assessment. This problem could be alleviated by the use of a Global Positioning System (GPS) in the field.

In terms of data input to GIS databases, the production of maps and subsequent analysis, the raster method may have the advantage over the facet method because the use of a grid system and uniform sample sizes allows maps to be generated quickly and simply as data can be displayed using symbols generated from a grid reference. The stand and facet sampling methods will require the drawing of polygons on the map, linked to a grid reference to represent the facets in order to produce a meaningful map.

General guidance on field survey and filling out record cards

- The record cards can be used for any of the three survey methods described. Always specify whether the record card is for a management unit, raster unit (0.25 km^2 grid square) or facet.

- All sections should be completed so that the maximum amount of data is collected from a site visit.

- Borderline situations should always be placed in the lower (less favourable) category; ie the vegetation should be considered to fail to meet an attribute if there is doubt.

- Always fill out the grading box as well as the pass tick box. Circle the appropriate grade level for each attribute.

- For grazing impacts always circle the impact level for each indicator as well as filling in the grading box.

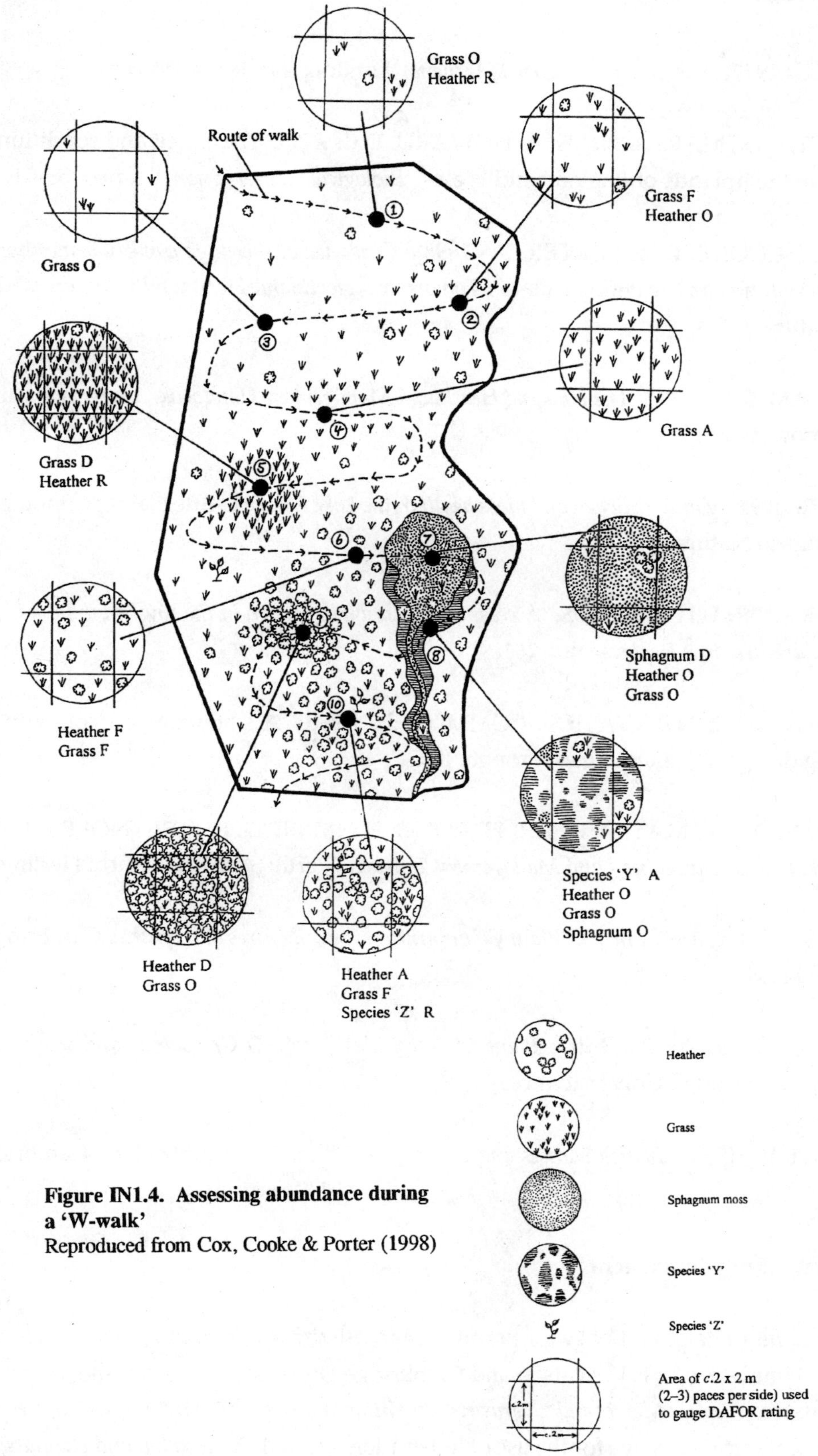

Figure IN1.4. Assessing abundance during a 'W-walk'
Reproduced from Cox, Cooke & Porter (1998)

Figure IN1.5 Assessing abundance during a 'W-walk'
Reproduced from Cox, Cooke & Porter (1998)

References

ALVIN, K.L. 1977. *The Observer's Book of Lichens.* London: Frederick Warne.

BARDGETT, R.D., MARSDEN, J.H. & HOWARD, D.C. 1995. The extent and condition of heather on moorland in the uplands of England and Wales. *Biological Conservation,* **71**, pp. 155-61.

COX, J.H.S., COOKE, R. & PORTER, K. 1998. *Guidance on heritage condition monitoring of lowland heathland restoration and re-creation sites in Tomorrow's Heathland Heritage Project areas.* Peterborough: English Nature.

GIMINGHAM, C.H. 1992. *The Lowland Heathland Management Handbook.* English Nature Science No. 8. Peterborough: English Nature.

JERRAM, R. 1992. *Montane lichen and moss heath in the Lake District.* Internal report for English Nature. Kendal: English Nature.

JERRAM, R & DREWITT, D. 1998. *Assessing vegetation condition in the English uplands.* Peterborough: *English Nature Research Reports,* No. 264.

JOINT NATURE CONSERVATION COMMITTEE. 1998. A statement on common standards for monitoring designated sites. Peterborough: JNCC.

MACDONALD, A.J., MAYER, P., ARMSTRONG, H., IMMIRZI, P. & REYNOLDS, P. 1998. *A Guide to Upland Habitats; Surveying Land Management Impacts.* Perth: Scottish Natural Heritage.

RODWELL, J.S. ed. 1991. *British Plant Communities. Vol. 2 Mires and heaths.* Cambridge: Cambridge University Press.

RODWELL, J.S. ed. 1992. *British Plant Communities. Vol. 3 Grasslands and montane communities.* Cambridge: Cambridge University Press.

WATSON, E.V. 1969. *British Mosses and Liverworts, 2nd edition.* Cambridge: Cambridge University Press.

Illustration acknowledgements

We are grateful to Penguin Books for permission to use drawings from K. Alvin's *The Observer's Book of Lichens* (Figure IN1.1); E.V. Watson and Cambridge University Press for allowing us to reproduce illustrations from *British Mosses and Liverworts, 2nd edition* (Figures IN1.1b & page 20)); Angus MacDonald and Scottish Natural Heritage for the use of illustrations from *A Guide to Upland Habitats; Surveying Land Management Impacts* (Figure IN1.2); Robert Goodison for the use of his drawings of heather growth forms (Figure IN1.3); and Messrs Cox, Cooke and Porter for allowing us to use their diagram in Figure IN1.4.

Information note 2 — Sheep breeds of the English uplands and their characteristics

Introduction

The total sheep flock in England consists of some 19.9 million sheep, of which 7.9 million are breeding ewes (1998 MAFF census). This consists of 73 breeds and 12 recognised crosses. The variety of breeds and crosses can be narrowed down to six main types:

- hardy/hill breeds;
- longwools (for crossing with hill breeds);
- crossbreds;
- lowland meat breeds (terminal sires);
- specialist breeds (eg for milk production and early lambing);
- rare breeds.

The hardy or hill breeds that graze the rough terrain of the UK's uplands account for approximately 50% of the national flock. One of the most important products of the hill farming system is the crossbred ewe, which accounts for a further 40% of the national flock and features highly in the prime lamb producing systems of the more fertile lowland farms. This interaction between upland and lowland practices gives rise to the stratified system on which UK sheep farming is based (see Information note 3). The upland's role in this system is the breeding of hardy hill ewes with longwool rams to produce crossbred ewes (all males of this resulting generation are reared as slaughter lambs).

Sheep in the uplands

The majority of sheep found in the uplands are from the hill breed, longwool or crossbred categories. Historically, sheep would have stayed relatively local to their breed origins, indicated by their names ie Swaledale, Lleyn, Wensleydale, etc. This is still true to some extent today although examples of the breed will tend to spread throughout the UK as producers seek the particular characteristics exhibited by that breed.

Hill breeds

The main factor differentiating the hill breeds from those found in more lowland areas is the hill breeds' ability to thrive in difficult, unfertile terrain, often under prolonged periods of adverse weather and still provide their owners with a live lamb and wool to sell. To do this they have to be hardy, have good mothering instincts and be able to convert rough vegetation and heathland plants into milk to sustain young lambs.

Sheep breeds and nature conservation

The Grazing Animals Project (GAP), involving a partnership of many organisations, will shortly be publishing details of breeds of sheep, cattle, ponies and goats used for nature conservation management.

Badgerface Welsh Mountain

Also known as the Torddu, meaning 'black belly'. Occasionally an individual occurs in which the colour pattern is reversed, which is called the Torwen or 'white belly'. These are varieties of the Welsh Mountain breed and produce good quality purebred and crossbred lambs. Rams are horned and weigh up to 80 kg. Ewes are polled (hornless) and weigh up to 50 kg.

Beulah Speckled Face

Developed over the past century on the hills west of Builth Wells in Mid-Wales. Mature rams and ewes weigh around 86 kg and 52 kg respectively and are larger and less hardy than the Welsh Mountain breed. They also produce a finer fleece than many hill breeds. Beulah ewes are crossed with the Blue-faced Leicester to produce the Welsh Mule.

Blackface

The Blackface evolved to graze the exposed uplands of Scotland and Northern England, particularly the 'black' or heather covered hills. Several distinct types have developed and ewes may be crossed to produce Mules or Greyface lambs. The sheep are hardy and thrifty with a coarse fleece that is much used in the carpet industry. Both sexes are horned and mature rams may weigh as much as 70 kg, the ewes about 55 kg. The ewe population of this breed is one of the largest in the UK.

Brecknock Hill Cheviot

Cheviot sheep were introduced in Breconshire in the mid-nineteenth century. Since then, this hardy breed has adapted to the wet upland and hills of south and west Wales to produce this newer strain of Cheviot. Rams are used to improve the size and quality of native mountain breeds. The rams are usually horned, and may weigh up to 90 kg. Ewes are polled and weigh up to 60 kg.

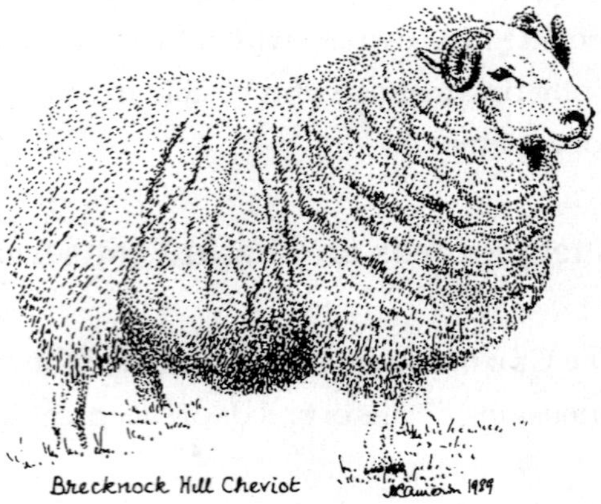

Cheviot

The breed originated in the Border Hills of southern Scotland but can now be found throughout the world. The rams may be horned or polled and weigh up to 105 kg. The ewes are always polled and weigh up to 60 kg.

Clun Forest

This breed originates in the upland area of southwest Shropshire adjoining the Welsh border. Clun flocks are found at up to 460 m but also thrive in the lowlands of England. Mated with a Border Leicester ram, the Clun ewe produces the English Halfbred. They are a long-lived, productive breed with an average lambing rate of 175%. Rams may weigh up to 90 kg and ewes 65 kg.

Dalesbred

This breed is indigenous to the central area of the Pennine Hills bordering North Yorkshire, Lancashire and Cumbria. In later life the ewes are mated to other breeds to produce Mashams and Mules. The wool is used in tweed and carpet making. Both sexes are horned and the face is black with a white patch on each side of the nostrils. Ewes may weigh up to 60 kg and rams 75 kg.

Derbyshire Gritstone

One of the oldest British hill breeds originating in the Peak District of Derbyshire. They are good rangers and have a weatherproof jacket of wool which is the finest of all grown by Blackface-type sheep. Rams are used to sire polled lambs on other horned hill breeds. Both sexes are polled, the ewes weighing up to 74 kg and the rams 110 kg.

Exmoor Horn

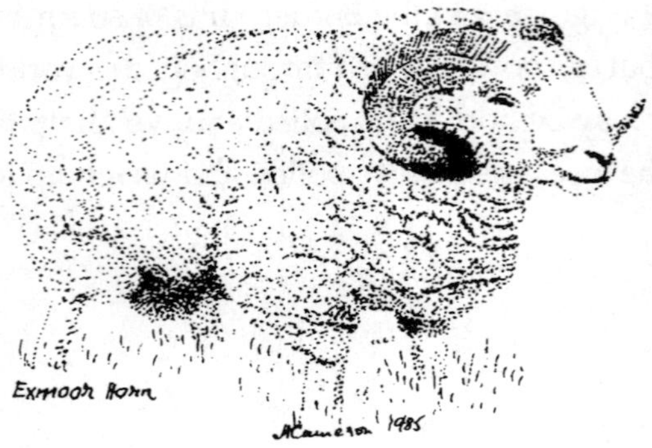

This breed is native to the exposed upland grazings of Exmoor. It produces both a pure and crossbred lamb of high quality. It is also one of the very few hill breeds to produce fine quality wool. Crossing with the Blue-faced Leicester produces the Exmoor Mule. Both sexes are horned; mature rams weigh up to 85 kg and ewes up to 65 kg.

Herdwick

This is Britain's hardiest breed of sheep and is native to the Cumbrian Lake District. The kemp (hair) in the fleece assists in waterproofing. The lambs are born black and the head and legs gradually become white. The fleece lightens to a pale, steel-grey with age. The rams may be horned and weigh around 80 kg. Mature ewes are always polled and weigh about 50 kg.

Hill Radnor

These sheep have a light brown face and legs which are free from wool. The breed was developed in Radnorshire and the central region of the Welsh Marches. It is more docile than some of the other hill breeds and its wool is used to produce speciality fabrics. The ewes are polled and weigh around 50 kg. The rams are horned and weigh about 75 kg.

Kerry Hill

This breed from Powys is named after the village of Kerry near Newtown, where the breed has been recorded since 1809. These hardy sheep are adaptable and much used for cross-breeding. Both the sexes are polled and the rams may weigh around 85 kg, with the ewes around 55 kg.

Llanwenog

Llanwenogs are a semi-lowland breed with a high lambing percentage. The breed was developed in west Wales at the end of the last century by using Shropshire rams on local sheep and was used as one of the foundation breeds to produce the Cambridge. The head is black with a prominent tuft of wool on the forehead. The wool is considered amongst the finest in the UK. Both sexes are polled, rams weighing around 90 kg and ewes 56 kg.

Lleyn

This breed was developed on the Lleyn Peninsula in North Wales. The ewes are prolific and multiple births are relatively common with lambing percentages regularly above 200%. The sheep and lambs are hardy and well adapted to thrive in the exposed area of the Lleyn Peninsula and in similar conditions. Ewes may be crossed to produce the Welsh Bleu and rams are used to improve the prolifacy and wool quality of other breeds. Both sexes are polled. Mature rams weigh up to 72 kg, ewes to 60 kg.

Lonk

This breed, which is one of the largest native hill breeds, originated on the hill ranges of Lancashire and Yorkshire. The sheep are nimble and hardy and can survive in the heather of the exposed Pennines. Lonk rams are used on other hill breeds to produce bigger lambs. Both sexes are horned, with ewes weighing about 50 kg and rams 80 kg.

North Country Cheviot

This is the largest UK upland breed. Developed in the far north of Scotland from the Cheviot, these hardy hill sheep carry a quality fleece and are also ideal for crossing with other breeds. The ewes, crossed with the Border Leicester, produce the famous halfbred. Both sexes are polled. Mature rams weigh up to 100 kg and ewes up to 85 kg.

Rough Fell

This is one of the larger bodied mountain breeds. It is particularly hardy and will thrive on the poor grasses and heathers on the moors and fells of Cumbria and the Pennine areas of North Lancashire and Yorkshire. It is exceptionally docile and has a lambing percentage of around 150%. Both sexes are horned. Mature rams weigh around 80 kg and ewes 50 kg.

Shetland

These small sheep formed the basis of the woollen industry of the Shetland Islands. Fleeces occur in a range of colours and the wool is very fine and soft. Ewes are polled and weigh up to 35 kg. Rams are horned and weigh up to 45 kg.

South Wales Mountain

This breed may also be known as the Nelson type of Glamorgan Welsh. The sheep are the largest of the Welsh Mountain breeds and have distinctive tan markings in the face and legs. They are left to range the open hills but have good hefting instincts. The ewes are polled and weigh up to 55 kg. The rams are usually horned and weigh up to 75 kg.

Swaledale

This distinctive breed thrives on the exposed moors of North Yorkshire and other uplands of the north of England. These sheep often produce quality lambs from land unable to support other breeds. The draft ewes are much sought after and when mated with the Teeswater produces the Masham and with the Blue-faced Leicester produces the Mule. Both sexes are horned. Rams may weigh up to 73 kg and ewes 54 kg.

Welsh Hill Speckled Face

This breed originated in the Devils Bridge and Powys Hills area of Mid Wales derived from crossing the Kerry Hill with the Welsh Mountain. The sheep are larger than the traditional Welsh Mountain sheep and the face is distinctly speckled. The Speckled Face has increasingly displaced more traditional hill breeds, especially in North Wales. Crossed with the Blue-faced Leicester, ewes produce the Welsh Mule. Ewes are polled and weigh around 50 kg. The rams may be horned or polled and weigh about 70 kg.

Welsh Mountain

These thrifty and hardy sheep were developed to exploit the available grazing in highland Wales. Welsh Mountain ewes form one of the largest purebred sheep populations in the UK. The rams are horned and may weigh as much as 80 kg. Ewes are polled and weigh about 35 kg, but when moved to lowland grazing may increase in weight by as much as 25%.

Whiteface Dartmoor

These hardy sheep are native to Dartmoor where they graze up to 600 m and the flocks are kept on the Moor from May to December. The sheep used always to be horned, but this feature has tended to disappear, particularly among the ewes. The ewes weigh up to 54 kg and the rams up to 75 kg.

White-faced Woodland

A large hill breed originating in the Pennine Hills of South Yorkshire and Derbyshire. There are two forms: the White-faced Woodland and the Penistone White-faced Woodland. Its remarkably fine wool is likely to be due to the introduction of Merino blood to the breed in the eighteenth century. Rams are frequently used on other hill breeds to improve size and the breed has been spreading to other parts of the UK.

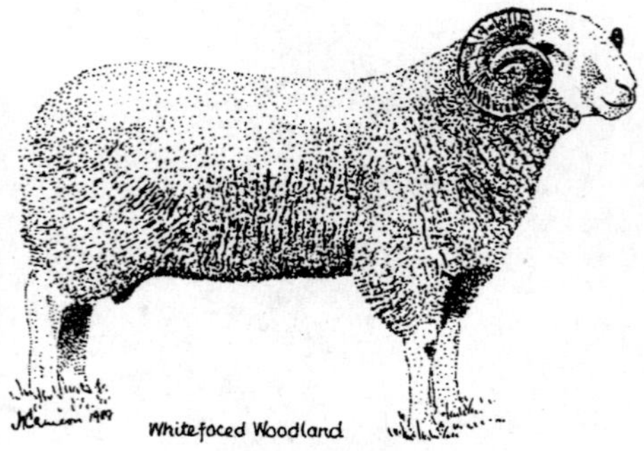

Longwool breeds

The longwool breeds originate from the areas of Britain where the growing conditions of the sloping valley sides are not so harsh as those on the exposed hills. However, the climate is still wet and windy and the sheep are protected by a long warm fleece. As a result of better pasture, they are slightly bigger and will produce more lambs than the breeds on the sparse upland pastures. The ewes have plenty of milk and are able to feed the extra lambs that are born.

Bluefaced Leicester

This breed evolved around Hexham at the beginning of the century. The breed is prolific with lamb crops often exceeding 250%. The rams are crossed with hill ewes to produce the Mule which is valued as the best commercial breeding ewe on the market. The wool of the Bluefaced Leicester is the finest of any native breed. Both sexes are polled. Rams weigh around 115 g and ewes about 80 kg.

Border Leicester

These are direct descendants of Robert Bakewell's Dishley Leicesters which were introduced into Northumberland in 1767. The breed has been recognised as being distinct from Leicesters since the 1850s. Rams crossed with hill breeds produce Halfbreds and the Greyface. The Border Leicester is also used on lowland breeds for early prime lamb production. Both sexes are polled. Mature rams weigh up to 150 kg and ewes to 100 kg.

British Milksheep

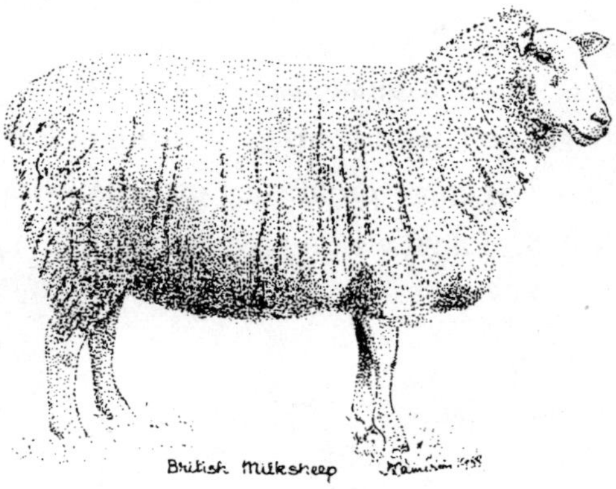

This new breed was developed by Lawrence Alderson to produce a crossing ram and a high yield dairy ewe. The ewes are prolific and produce sufficient milk to rear triplets. Both sexes of these white-faced sheep are polled. Mature rams weigh on average 110 kg and ewes around 80 kg.

Cotswold

The native breed of the Cotswolds was improved by crossing with Lincoln and Leicester rams to produce the breed of today. A longwool breed which is now used to produce heavyweight lambs, mature ewes will weigh up to 85 kg and rams may exceed 135 kg. Both sexes are polled.

Dartmoor Greyface

Descended from the original moorland sheep, the Greyface was 'improved' during the last century by crossing with local longwool breeds as well as 'Notts' and Leicester. Dartmoor ewes are generally put to Down or Continental rams to produce early prime lambs. Now a minority breed, it is in danger of extinction. Both sexes are polled. Mature rams weigh up to 102 kg and ewes 68 kg.

Devon and Cornwall Longwool

The head and body of this breed are well-covered with long, curly, white wool. The ewes, on grass, will produce 160% lamb crop and the lambs are shorn when 6 months old. Adult fleeces average between 8 and 9 kg but can be up 18 kg. Both sexes are polled. Mature rams weigh 136 kg and ewes 100 kg.

British Friesland

These large-framed sheep originated in Holland and are famous for milk yield and quality, up to 700 litres at 6.5% butterfat. The breed average prolificacy exceeds 240%. Both sexes are polled. Rams weigh an average of 82 kg and ewes 65 kg.

Leicester Longwool

Today's Leicesters are the direct descendants of the Dishley Leicesters developed by Robert Bakewell more than two centuries ago. These large sheep are very hardy and produce a heavy lustrous fleece. Both sexes are polled. The rams weighing an average of 150 kg and the ewes 100 kg.

Lincoln Longwool

Lincoln Longwool

Sheep and wool have been associated with Lincoln City and Shire for very many years. Lincoln sheep were well known by 1750 and it is possible that Robert Bakewell used them in his foundation stock. Both sexes are polled and mature rams weigh around 150 kg and ewes around 85 kg. These sheep have been exported in large numbers to South America, Australia and New Zealand where they have been used to create new wool breeds such as the Corriedale and the Polworth.

British Oldenburg

These docile longwool sheep were first imported to the UK in 1964 from West Germany. The breed was developed on the North Sea Marshes by crossing North German Marsh sheep with local milk sheep and various British longwool sheep, including Cotswolds. The main commercial use of this breed is for crossing with hill breeds such as the Scottish Blackface, the Cheviot and the Swaledale. The resulting half-bred, the Oldenbred, produces prime lamb quickly in both intensive and extensive conditions. Both sexes are polled, ewes weighing around 84 kg and rams 110 kg.

Oldenburg

Romney

Romney

The original Romney Marsh sheep were developed on low lying land along the channel coast of Kent and Sussex. The breed has spread world wide and formed the basis of the sheep industry in New Zealand and other Countries. The Romney ewe is put to the Lleyn ram to produce the Kent Halfbred which is then put to a terminal sire for the prime lamb market. Both sexes are polled and rams weigh up to 100 kg and ewes 72 kg.

Teeswater

These medium size sheep originated in Teesdale. The rams have been used for crossing on Dalesbred, Swaledale, Rough Fell and Scottish Blackface ewes to produce the Masham ewes for commercial lamb production. Both sexes are polled. Rams weigh an average of 100 kg and ewes 80 kg.

Wensleydale

A blue-faced longwool breed producing a fleece with very long staple (up to 30 cm) and weighing up to 5 kg. This breed was developed in North Yorkshire to produce rams for crossing on to hill ewes to produce a breeding ewe (the Masham). The Wensleydale's wool is recognised as the finest lustre longwool. A slow maturing breed, ewes weigh about 113 kg and rams may exceed 136 kg. Both sexes are polled.

Cross breeds (ie mule or halfbred)

These terms are given to recognised first crosses (F1 hybrids) of established breeds as described under the section on stratification in Information Note 3. Usually the term 'mule' is given to a female animal which has been produced by mating a Blue-faced Leicester ram on a hill ewe. The term 'half bred' is given to a similar product which has been produced by using the Border Leicester on a hill ewe. There are also Mashams, Greyfaces and other recognised crosses.

Scottish Greyface

Crossbred ewes are produced by crossing the Border Leicester ram on Blackface ewes.

North of England Mule

Crossbred ewes are produced by crossing the Bluefaced Leicester ram with Swaledale or Blackface ewes.

Masham

Produced by crossing the Teeswater or Wensleydale ram on Dalesbred or Swaledale ewes.

Scottish Half-Bred

Produced by crossing the Border Leicester ram on South or North Country Cheviot ewes.

Welsh Half-Bred

Produced by crossing the Border Leicester ram on Welsh Mountain ewes.

Welsh mule

Welsh mule ewes are produced by crossing Bluefaced Leicester ram on one of three hardy hill breeds - the Welsh Mountain, Welsh Hill Speckled Face or Beulah Speckled Face ewes.

Other cross breeds

Ram	Ewe	Progeny
Border Leicester	Clun Forest	English Halfbred
Blue-faced Leicester	Scottish Blackface	Scottish Mule
Lleyn	Romney	Kent Halfbred
North country Cheviot	Shetland	Shetland-Cheviot
Bleu du Maines	Welsh Mountain Welsh Hill Speckled Face Beulah Speckled Face Lleyn	Welsh Bleu

Hill Farm Allowance Scheme and Specially Qualified Flock

Within Less Favoured Areas, sheep producers can claim the new Hill Farm Allowance (HFA) (which has replaced the Hill Livestock Compensatory Allowance (HLCA)) help maintain extensive livestock systems. Temporary arrangements are in place for 2000-01 and final details of the new scheme were confirmed during 2000. There is an additional sum available to producers who have flocks which meet the 'Specially Qualified Flock' requirements. This is limited to flocks of the following breeds:

Balwen
Black Welsh Mountain
Cheviot - All Types
Dalesbred
Derbyshire Gritstone
Exmoor Horn
Gotland
Herdwick
Icelandic
Kerry
Llanidloes
Lonk
Manx Loghtan
Nelson
Radnor
Ronaldsay
Rough Fell
St Kilda (Hebridean)
Scottish Blackface
Shetland
Soay
Speckled Face (Beulah or Welsh Hill)
Swaledale
Torddu
Torwen
Welsh Mountain
Whitefaced Dartmoor
Whitefaced Woodland
Whitefaced Woodland (Penistone)

This information has been derived from *British Sheep* published by the National Sheep Association.

Information note 3

Sheep farming systems of the English uplands

Introduction

Upland sheep farming in England can be classed as two distinct systems; hill/mountain and upland/marginal. Both are extensive systems and differ chiefly in the amount of in-bye land or improved pasture held in the valleys. This determines the numbers and type of stock that the farm can sustain throughout the year. It is difficult to draw distinct boundaries between the two systems as gradation obviously occurs. The sheep flock totals some 19.9 million at peak summer numbers, of which 7.9 million are breeding ewes (1998 MAFF census). Purebred hill ewes account for 50% of the national breeding flock, while crossbred ewes (a product of the hill/upland system) account for a further 40%.

Hill sheep farming

The farm

Traditional hill farming systems occur where little or no fenced or improved in-bye is available around the farm. This is one of the simplest farming systems and is almost entirely based on grass and other native vegetation. True hill farms are confined to northern Scotland, North Wales, the Pennines, the North York Moors, the Lake District and areas of the southwest such as Dartmoor and Exmoor. They possess little or no improved pasture. Often relying totally on sheep, some hill farms may keep a small herd of suckler cows on in-bye land (enclosed pastures).

Climatic conditions are often harsh on the open hillsides with high winds, high rainfall and extreme cold in winter. The available grazing usually consists of agriculturally poor grasslands and areas of dwarf shrubs which can have a low nutritional value. Stocking rates are therefore low and the breeds used must be able to feed on this range of plants and, not only survive, but produce viable offspring in such harsh conditions.

It is often impossible or unfeasible to fence areas of open fell and moorland owing to constraints of land ownership, common land, grazing rights or land use (eg shooting). Stock are often free to roam over wide areas. A hefted flock is therefore necessary to keep stock within a manageable regime. Hefting is where the sheep are acclimatised to, and use a certain area of hillside, knowing the best places to graze and shelter. This hefting instinct aids survival and is passed from ewe to lamb while on the hill. A hefted flock is an important asset to the hill farmer and a flock is usually sold together with the land or grazing rights.

The severe constraint of little in-bye land can be off-set by using buildings to house stock in the winter (although these may have adverse impacts on the landscape) or by the practice of away-wintering ewe lambs. The nutritional value of open fell-side grassland is very poor, especially out of the growing season, with stock relying on taller dwarf shrubs in snowy conditions. Coupled with the severe weather conditions, this is too hard for newly weaned lambs, which are transferred to the in-bye land and either sold as stores or finished for the meat market, depending on how much keep is available. Lack of in-bye, even with housing space, means little conserved fodder (hay or silage) is available and supplementary feed would need to be bought in.

Stock

The mainstay of the hill farming system are the purebred hardy 'hill breeds'. These are often specific to a certain area of the country, as suggested by their names, such as Swaledale, Dalesbred and Welsh Mountain (see Information note 2). These breeds possess hardy characteristics giving them an inherent ability to thrive in the harsh mountain conditions. They are good 'milky' ewes and have strong mothering instincts. They often possess the ability to twin, but this is not usually exploited, owing to the lack of hardiness in the lambs produced. Twins also put a strain on the ewe and when kept on the hill are too small to be commercial in the autumn.

Ewes are put to the ram (tupped) in the late autumn, November/December, and lamb in the late spring from mid-April to May, depending on the breed and location. In harsh conditions, stock may be brought onto in-bye land or to the lower slopes for shelter or possibly supplementary feeding (feed blocks or hay). The sheep will normally be brought down from the hill again only for clipping and dipping in July and the weaning of male lambs in the autumn. To reduce winter grazing some of the ewe lambs (gimmer hoggs) to be used as replacements may be wintered away (tack or agistment) on the more fertile pastures of farms in the lowlands. Winter housing is often cheaper than tacking, if space and capital are available, and housing can be used in addition to tacking. The cost of housing can be partially offset by finishing male (wether) lambs indoors in autumn and then selling them direct to the meat buyer.

Production

Most male lambs (wether hoggs) are sold at the autumn sales to marginal and lowland farms where they will be finished on grass or as store lambs over the winter. Ewes of four to five years old are considered too old for the rough conditions of the hill farm, although they are still healthy. These are sold as draft ewes to the marginal and lowland farms to be bred with 'longwool' rams to produce meatier hardy half-breds or 'mules' (see Information note 2). Some of the ewes may be crossed with lowland meat breeds (eg Texel, Suffolk) to produce fat lambs. Healthy ewe lambs are retained as replacements for the draft ewes, keeping the flock sustainable and maintaining the hefting instinct. Wool production also brings in some income, although the fleece of the hill breeds is not of the best quality.

The low stocking levels, harsh environment and farm size mean that income from traditional hill farming systems is relatively low. To try to preserve hill farming and to stop the movement of people from rural areas, support payments and grant schemes have been made available for farms within the Less Favoured Areas through the Hill Livestock Compensatory Allowance (now replaced by the Hill Farm Allowance Scheme). For hill farming, 45-60% of the gross income per ewe can come from subsidies, the majority of this from the Sheep Annual Premium Scheme (see Chapter 2).

Upland sheep farming

The farm

Usually situated in the valleys of upland areas, these farms will account for the majority of farms in the Less Favoured Areas. As with the hill farm system, the amount and type of stock is often dependent upon the size of in-bye/improved pasture and the availability of buildings. The availability of generally larger areas of in-bye give the farmer a greater flexibility in stocking rates, and dictates the amount of conserved fodder available for over-wintering. The availability of buildings determines the amount of over-wintering store space and accommodation for cattle. As well as in-bye, in-take or allotment which has been land enclosed from the open fell, may be improved, providing land for a more substantial cattle enterprise.

Stock

Marginal farms often keep two flocks of sheep. Hardy hill ewes are run on the open hillside and are made up of hefted flocks of purebred hill breeds, as described above. In addition to these, the older drafted ewes are kept on in-bye land in the valleys, where they are crossed with 'longwool rams' such as Bluefaced Leicester or Border Leicester (see Information note 2). The crossbred progeny of this mating are 'mules' or half-breds. The fast growth rates, prolificacy and larger carcase characteristics of the 'longwool' breeds and the hardiness and good mothering instincts of the hill breeds combine to give a desirable ewe. If good grazing and/or conserved fodder is available in quantity, then the crossbreds may be bred for lowland sheep meat production with large, fast-growing meat breeds of the lowlands and the resulting 'fat lambs' will go to slaughter. A suckler cow or dairy herd will normally be kept as well (see Information note 5).

Production

As with the hill farm, male (wether) lambs will be sold as stores or finished for slaughter. In the marginal system, finishing will usually take place on the farm, which will then benefit from the higher value of finished lambs. 'Mules' or half-bred ewes will normally be sold to lowland farms where they are then crossed with terminal meat sires. If these sires are kept on the marginal farm, the resulting fat lambs will be finished and sold for slaughter. Wool sales will make up a slightly larger proportion of the income than on the hill farms, owing to the higher quality of the wool produced by half-breds, but in percentage terms this is still small. Suckler calves may be sold as store calves or finished on the farm for slaughter if sufficient food is available.

Stratification

All elements of sheep production from the hill farm to the lowlands are linked by the stratification of the sheep industry which is a system unique to the UK. Cross breeding allows for selection of preferable characteristics and enables the optimum use of poor grazing to produce quality meat lambs for both the home and export markets. Figure IN3.1 explains the stratified system.

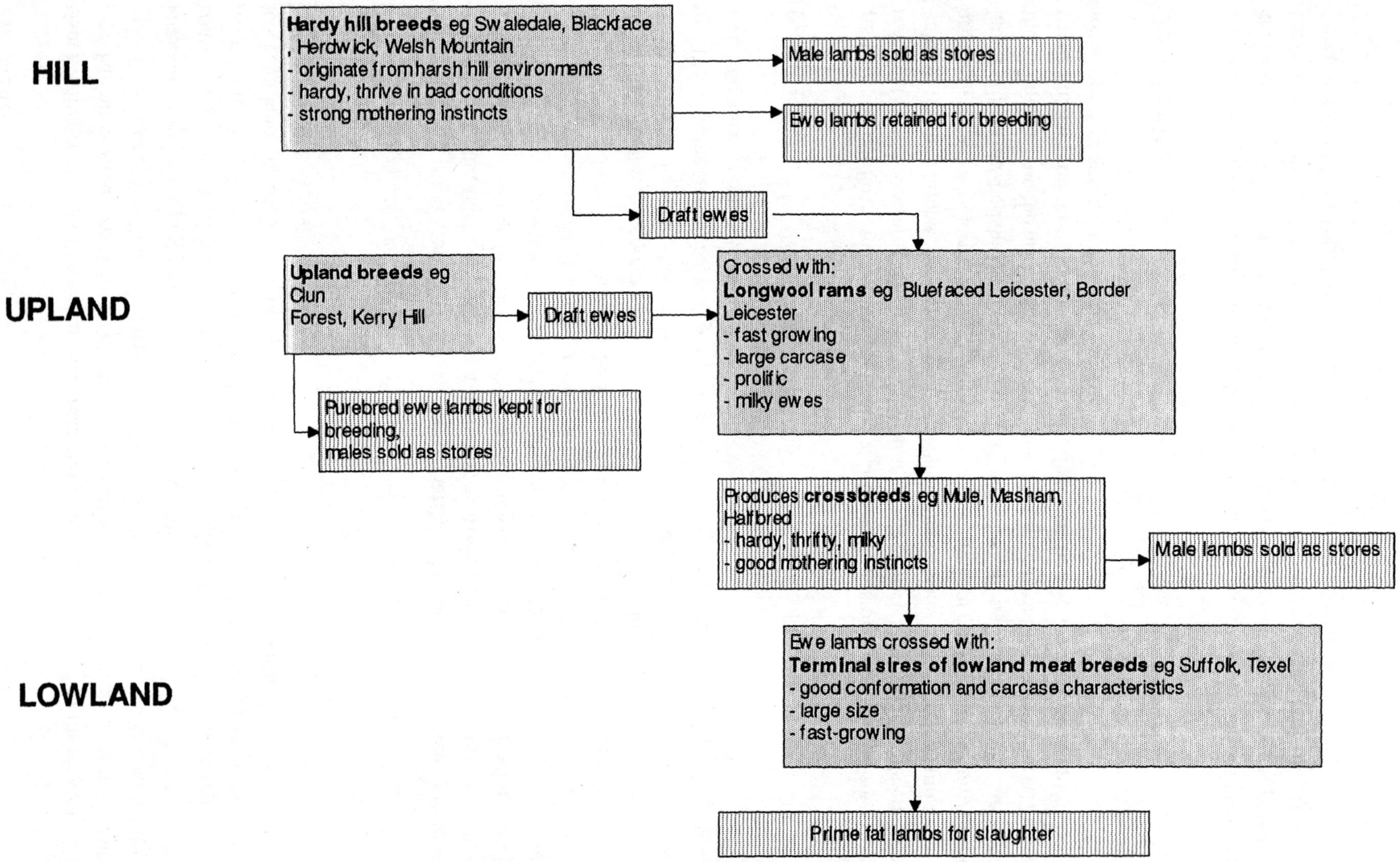

Figure IN3.1 Stratification of the British sheep industry

A typical farming year for hill/upland ewe flocks

Early November:	Draft ewes (4/5-shear and older) mated with Longwool crossing ram on in-bye.
Late November:	Hill ewes gathered onto in-bye for tupping by purebred ram.
1 January:	Ewes may be returned to the hill.
Mid-February:	Ewes (especially drafts) scanned and those carrying twins retained on enclosed low ground with supplementary feed until lambing. Those carrying singles returned to the hill.
February/March:	Blocks and supplementary feed available to hill ewes.
Mid-April/May:	Draft and hill ewes lamb on in-bye. Hoggs return to hill after away-wintering.
Mid-May:	Ewes with single lambs at foot return to hill. Ewes with twins remain on enclosed ground until weaning.
July:	Ewes and followers gathered off hill for clipping and dipping.
Late July:	Lambs weaned off draft ewes. (These 5/6-shear ewes may then be turned out onto the hill until late October).
August/September:	Lambs weaned off hill ewes.
September/October:	Wether lambs/surplus ewe lambs sold as stores or retained on in-bye or inside for finishing.
Mid-October:	4/5-shear hill ewes 'drafted' onto lower ground for cross breeding or sale.
Late October:	Gimmer hoggs (ewe replacements) sent away to lowland pasture over winter.

Note: In a typical hill system, ewes will remain on the hill for approximately 36 weeks on average each year. The main periods off the hill are tupping (4-6 weeks), lambing (4-6 weeks) and clipping/dipping and weaning.

Information note 4 Cattle breeds of the English uplands and their characteristics

Introduction

Upland cattle farming is mostly made up of 'suckler' herds of crossbred cows that are then crossed with beef bulls (terminal sires) to produce calves for finishing in the lowlands (see Information note 5). Hardy hill breeds are used to a lesser extent for the production of suckled calves. Dairy production does take place in the uplands, though in more marginal areas. A description of the main breeds and their positions within this structure are discussed below.

Cattle breeds and nature conservation

The Grazing Animals Project (GAP), involving a partnership of many organisations, will shortly be publishing details of breeds of cattle, sheep, ponies and goats used for nature conservation management.

Dairy cows

Although there are a number of dairy herds in the uplands, milk production often requires intensive farming methods and is not usually associated with upland areas. Dairy breeds play a large part in the production of calves for suckling within the beef industry. The most widely used breeds are included here.

British Friesian

British Friesian cow

This used to be the most widespread and popular breed in the UK dairy industry. This was due to the breed's commercial excellence, primarily for high and economic yields of milk, but also the bonus of quickly grown, lean meat production. The Friesian was the biggest producer of home killed beef in Britain, mainly from the male calves produced by the dairy system. This is a dual purpose breed, with good milk production and beef characteristics. As a dairy cow, the Friesian has now been largely surpassed by the Holstein.

In the uplands, the calves from Friesian dams (cows) crossed with beef breed sires, such as the Hereford, Aberdeen Angus and continental breeds, are very popular as suckler cows.

British Holstein

Now the most popular dairy cow, the Holstein is a prolific milk producer. Originally from Friesland Island, as are Friesians, the British Holstein has been bred to be a more effective milk producer and have less of the original beef characteristics of the Dutch strain. As with Friesians, Holstein cows are crossed with beef sires to produce suckler cows.

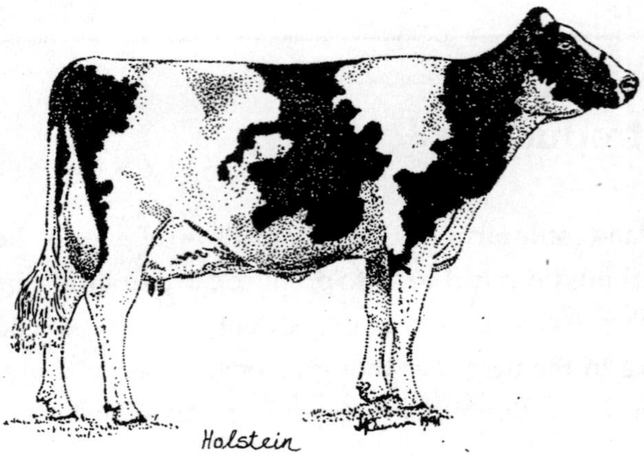

Ayrshire

From its origins in west Scotland in the early seventeenth century, the Ayrshire has spread worldwide as a viable dairy breed that can tolerate extremes of climate. The cows are of medium size and are capable of producing good yields of high butterfat milk (good for cheese making) from poorer pastures than the Friesian or Holstein. Females make top class suckler dams. Ayrshires tend to be a thin-fleshed breed, but crossing with Charolais, Hereford, Friesian or Beef Shorthorn bulls produces beef-type calves.

Beef sires

Purebred beef bulls are important in all aspects of suckled calf production. They are often used to produce the first cross suckler cow, either with a dairy dam or another beef breed. They are then used again to produce the suckled calves as the second cross. Choice of breed depends on many factors, including climate and food availability. The large continental breeds have the advantage of increased weight, and high rate of weight gain, but the disadvantages of higher nutritional requirements, and a higher percentage of difficult births and consequent calf mortality.

Aberdeen Angus

The Aberdeen Angus is renowned throughout the world for the economic production of quality beef. These bulls are largely used as terminal sires for crossing on crossbred cows such as the Blue-Grey (Shorthorn x Galloway) or Hereford x Friesian. Purebred Aberdeen Angus and Aberdeen Angus x Friesian cows are increasingly popular in beef suckler herds. Aberdeen Angus bulls are often used on Holstein or Friesian heifers to give an easy first calving because the calves' heads and shoulders are small. The Aberdeen-Angus breed combines medium size (and therefore ease of calving) with early maturity and high carcase yield despite a slow growth rate.

Beef Shorthorn

The Shorthorn is one of the oldest native British breeds and was established about 200 years ago. The Scotch or Beef Shorthorn has its origins in Aberdeenshire. The Shorthorn cow can be out-wintered in almost any condition and maintained on modest rations. This factor makes the Shorthorn or first-cross cow particularly suited to the uplands. Commercial breeders in these areas use the Shorthorn bull to produce thrifty calves for finishing in upland conditions and also to produce replacement females with good mothering qualities for breeding. The Shorthorn bull, particularly of Cumberland origin, has played an important part in producing first-class commercial suckler cows when put to the pure-bred Ayrshire, Galloway or Highland cow. The Blue Grey is the product of a white Shorthorn bull crossed with a black Galloway cow.

Simmental

This continental beef breed is the most numerically dominant in Europe and originates from the Simmen valley in Switzerland. The Simmental is classed as a big beef breed and can be used both as terminal sire and as a first cross for suckler herd female replacements eg Simmental x Galloway, Simmental x Blue-Grey. Here it imparts size and added milk to the dam, while retaining the important qualities of these indigenous breeds.

Charolais

The Charolais was introduced to Britain in the 1960s from France. It is the largest beef breed and is used predominantly as a terminal sire. The exceptional growth rates, food conversion and production of quality lean carcase beef has made the Charolais very popular. However, there is a high incidence of assisted calvings and calf mortality associated with this breed.

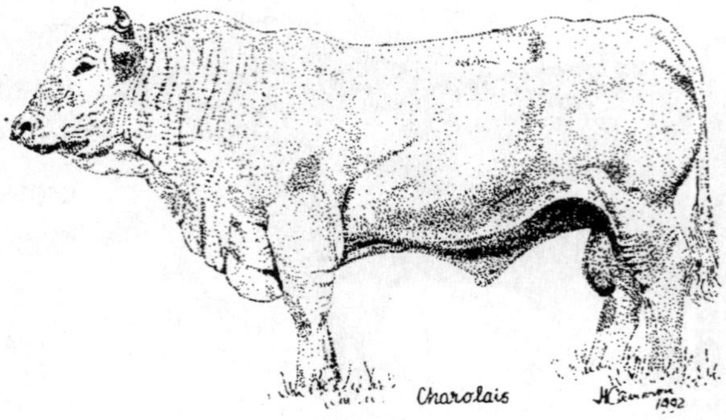

Hereford

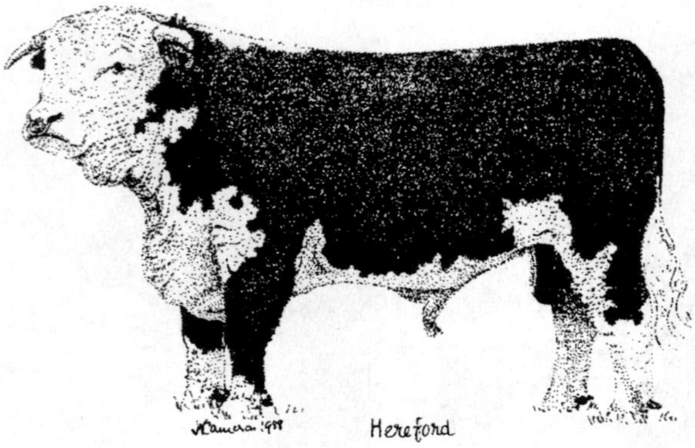

This is the most widespread beef breed in the world. Herefords are extensively used for cross breeding with beef suckler herds. The Hereford has a good reputation for ease of calving. The Hereford x Friesian cross is one of the most popular in Britain and produces hardy calves capable of high growth rates and early maturity.

Limousin

This continental medium/heavy beef breed has its origins on the edge of the Massif Central in France, where 7,000 year old cave paintings depict a very similar beast. Limousin are hardy animals and out-winter well. A Limousin bull on Friesian cows gives male calves that produce a high yield of quality beef for comparatively low food inputs. The heifer calves make first-class hardy suckler cows. A Limousin bull on these suckler cows (to produce three-quarter bred animals), gives most of the commercial advantages in carcase quality and production of the purebred. The Limousin bull on Angus x Friesian, Hereford x Friesian, Blue-Grey or Welsh Black cows will give equal carcase advantage.

Lincoln Red

The Lincoln Red may descend from cattle brought to Britain by the Vikings. Used in the past for both meat and milk, today the Lincoln Red is essentially a beef breed. Bulls are sometimes used as terminal sires on crossbred suckler cows. Resulting calves are born easily, mature early and have a rapid growth rate.

South Devon

The earliest mention of this breed goes back 230 years when they were known as the 'Big Red Cattle' which grazed the pastures in 'the South Hams' area of southern Devon. The economic value of this breed is that they are well adapted to the conversion of grass to meat at a fast growth rate. This breed is often used locally as a first and second cross in the production of suckled calves.

Sussex

Sussex cattle are generally accepted as being descended from the red cattle that inhabited the dense forests of the Weald land of Sussex and Kent, and were recorded at the time of the Norman conquest. Sussex bulls are widely used as sires in the dairy and suckler herds, producing calves of good growth potential and excellent beef quality. The most popular of these crosses is the Sussex x Friesian.

Blonde D'Aquitaine

A French breed imported in the early 1970s, it is native to southwestern France. It is superficially similar to the Charolais and has many of that breed's characteristics.

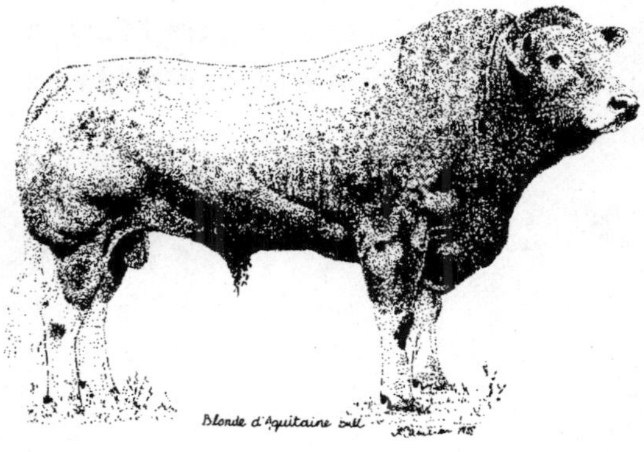

Belgian Blue

A beef breed which is notable for enormous hind-quarters. The breed has a quiet temperament and has been widely used by dairy farmers to impart fleshing characteristics to milk cows of poor beef conformation, such as Jerseys.

Hardy hill breeds

These are often old breeds which originated in the mountain and hill districts of Britain and Ireland and are often direct decendants of wild cattle once found in these areas. Their hardy constitutions, the greatest attributes of these breeds, mean that they can survive and even thrive in extreme climatic conditions. The ability to turn poor forage into beef, with little need for extra feed or housing is also an advantage. Advances in housing and conserved fodder systems mean that much suckled calf production uses the more profitable dairy x beef cross to the detriment of the hardy hill breeds. Only in the extreme conditions of the hill farm, where these animals thrive, are they still utilised to the full. For conservation purposes, they have the added benefit of being small animals and consequently tend to do less damage through poaching on wet grazings. The use of hill beef breeds to produce crossbred cows is common especially in the marginal upland areas.

Dexter

Dexters originated in the south or southwestern regions of Ireland and they are believed to have descended from the original wild Irish mountain cattle. They are the smallest British cattle breed and were first introduced into England in 1882. Being a mountain breed, they are extremely hardy and can be kept out of doors all the year round, even through the severest winters. Many animals are kept as suckler cows for which they are well suited, although their small size limits the growth potential in their calves.

Highland

This breed is a native of Scotland and the Western Isles. The cattle are hardy, largely due to their long shaggy coat. The long hairs of the outer coat shed water, while a short under coat provides insulation. These cattle possess an ability to forage efficiently and can travel far in harsh conditions in search of food. Highland females are in demand as crossing animals due to their good mothering abilities and easy calving. However, they are slow to mature and are often poor milkers.

Belted Galloway

A hardy hill breed with a distinctive white belt. This breed originated in southwest Scotland and is a race of the Galloway.

Galloway

The Galloway is one of the oldest beef breeds in the UK and has been a keystone in prime beef production in Britain for many generations. Owing to its hardy characteristics, the Galloway has been able to thrive in extreme conditions and help to turn acres of mountain moor and poor pasture into economically viable farmland. The Galloway is the foundation breed in the production of the crossbred Blue-Grey (see below) which is so popular as a suckler cow.

Welsh Black

Welsh Blacks have been the native cattle of Wales since pre-Roman times and are referred to in the earliest Welsh literature. The modern breed is a much improved animal which makes a hardy suckler herd producing first class beef. Although traditionally a dual purpose breed, nowadays beef production is regarded as its primary role. This breed is extremely hardy, able to stand the harshest winters with very little shelter. It probably originates from the same foundation stock as the Galloway.

Cross breeds

Suckled calf production relies heavily on crossbred cows, which are then crossed again to produce the suckler calf. Many variations of cow and bull are used, depending on the conditions on the farm (housing, conserved fodder, amount of in-bye, etc), climatic conditions and the preferences of the producer. Other factors that must be taken into account are ease of birth, calf mortality and growth rate of the calf.

Blue-Grey

This progeny of the mating of a Cumberland (sometimes termed Whitebred) Shorthorn sire on a Galloway dam is very popular as a suckler cow. These cows possess sufficient milkiness to produce fast-growing calves, particularly when crossed with large continental beef breeds. The name 'Blue-Grey' sometimes embraces breeds and crosses other than Cumberland Shorthorn x Galloway.

Adapted from *The British cattle book,* published by the National Cattle Association.

Information note 5

Cattle farming systems of the English uplands

Introduction

Upland cattle farming is usually based on the rearing of beef calves for sale to lowland farms for finishing. This is a low intensity system of one calf per cow where the calf is suckled by its mother until it is weaned at between 6 and 10 months. Finished beef is still produced to a lesser extent, but in the harsh conditions found on hill farms it requires the hardy purebred hill breeds. However, the introduction of the 'Over Thirty Months Scheme' in response to the BSE crisis has put pressure on beef finishing systems based on slow-maturing, mainly upland breeds. Dairy farming also takes place in the more marginal areas. This is a much more intensive system relying heavily on housing and supplementary feed. As with sheep production, the type and number of stock kept is dependent on the amount of in-bye land and the availability of buildings for housing stock over winter.

Suckler cow production

This is the most commonly used cattle farming system in the English uplands and forms the upper tier of the beef stratification system. Calves born and weaned in the uplands can be sold in the autumn sales to lowland farms to be fattened for slaughter. Alternatively, many herds are summer to autumn calvers with calves sold in the spring. Replacement stock for suckler herds may be reared in the lowlands as a by-product of the dairy system.

Hill farms

The size of herd depends on a number of factors. The main constraint on cattle numbers is the ability to grow and store sufficient conserved fodder (hay or silage). This is dependent on the amount of in-bye land available. Suckler cows may be housed over the winter period. The buying-in of large amounts of supplementary feed may not be economically viable. Housing space may also provide a constraint on the numbers kept. Normally, hill calves will be born in the spring and put to grass for the spring and summer. They would be then sold at the autumn sales to provide store calves (finished indoors) for the lowlands.

Marginal upland farms

Here herd sizes may be bigger owing to the availability of more improved grassland and housing space. Most calves will be sold for fattening to lowland farms, as in the hill system. Where feed and housing are available some calves may be kept and finished on the farm, therefore bringing in higher returns. Another option available to the marginal farm is that of double or multiple suckling. Extra calves are bought-in for suckling, thereby increasing productivity, but housing may be necessary and the price of calves can be prohibitive.

The major difference between the hill and marginal systems is the greater choice of options available to those with adequate feed and housing resources. These options are discussed below.

Calving seasons

Suckler cows can be calved at any time of the year. The principal calving times are spring and autumn. When to calve depends upon feed supplies and storage facilities, housing, other farm enterprises and plans for calf sales or finishing.

Autumn calving produces a more mature, heavier calf that is more saleable in the following year's autumn sales. This greater output is balanced by the high input of feed needed to sustain lactation and produce sufficient milk to suckle the calf over the winter. Calves are normally born at grass in September/October and housed in November for the winter. They are then weaned and turned out onto grass in the spring or turned out with their mothers to be weaned later in July/August. In some hill systems, weaned calves are turned out onto in-bye pastures while the cows are run on rough hill grazings for the summer.

Spring calving is a lower cost system, with peak feed demands coinciding with peak grass growth. Over-wintered cows require less food and are fed on hay, silage and small amounts of concentrates. Care must be taken to raise the dietary standards of the cows after winter housing to be sure of conception after calving. The lower input is reflected in the lower value of spring-born calves sold in the autumn, because they are smaller (and younger) than the autumn-born calves. Spring calving cows will normally be calved outside in April/May/June. Though the systems differ in cost terms, there is little difference between the gross margins of autumn and spring calving systems.

Summer and winter calving - to calve every year, a cow must conceive within three months of calving. Low nutrition can lead to failure to conceive and create 'slippage' in the calving time. Summer calving in July/August is similar to the autumn system although less grass will be available as conserved fodder and the good early grazing of spring has been missed. Winter calving must take place indoors. This creates a risk of disease, particularly calf scour, and vaccines may be needed. To avoid slippage and to manage calving times, late calvers or barren cows are often culled and replacements bought in. It is sometimes possible to move an autumn calver into the spring calving herd, though not vice versa.

The suckler cow

Crossbred cows are most often used in the suckler system because hybrid vigour brings the benefits of longevity and reproductive efficiency. Dairy crosses are the most common foundation cows. These are usually Friesian or Friesian Holstein crossed with a beef sire such as Angus, Hereford or South Devon (see Information note 4). More producers are now using to continental crosses with beef breeds such as Charolais, Simmental or Limousin. These crossbred cows are then crossed again with a beef bull (often kept on the farm) to exploit further the advantages of hybrid vigour and improve fleshing characteristics. The introduction of the dairy Holstein into the Friesian breed has had detrimental effects on the quality of suckled calves.

Hill farms sometimes use crossbred cows obtained from hardier breeds, eg the Blue-Grey, which comes from a White Shorthorn sire and a Galloway dam (see Information note 4). These crosses cope better with harsh conditions than crosses derived from dairy breeds.

The sire

The choice of bull is very important, both for productivity and the quality of the calf. A heavy meat breed will be the most productive, producing the heavier and faster growing calves. This is offset by the fact that calves from these bulls are more likely to have difficult births and mortality rates can be higher. Charolais, Simmental and South Devon are examples of heavy beef breeds. Smaller beef breeds such as Aberdeen Angus and Hereford produce smaller and lighter calves. Choice of sire depends on the climatic conditions of the farm with smaller hardier breeds more able to thrive under poor conditions. One strategy is to put a smaller breed of bull on the heifers and a continental sire on the adult cows.

Compatibility

Suckled calf production and upland sheep farming are compatible systems with little conflict between them. Rotational grazing of both sheep and cattle keeps the grazing in good condition, with cattle eating what the sheep will not. In winter hill sheep can graze the open hill sides, and draft ewes can graze the in-bye while cattle are housed. Problems may occur if spring calving coincides with lambing of a large sheep flock. This can be remedied by splitting calving between spring and autumn, or calving only in the autumn if there is capacity to over-winter the whole herd inside.

Income

The suckler cow system produces only one calf per cow with no by-products. This means the calf's survival and wellbeing are of paramount importance to the farmer. Certain subsidies are available to the beef farmer. The Beef Special Premium provides support payments for young male animals, while the Suckler Cow Premium is based on non-milk producing cows of a beef cross. Both of these subsidies are subject to Stocking Density Limits. Extensification premiums are available to producers stocking at less than 1.6 livestock units per hectare or between 1.6 and 2 LU/ha. For farms lying within the Less Favoured Areas, the Hill Livestock Compensatory Allowance (replaced by the Hill Farm Allowance Scheme) is also available now (see Chapter 2). Different amounts are paid depending on whether the land is classified as Disadvantaged or Severely Disadvantaged.

Dairy production

Dairy farming does not play as large a role in upland farming as sheep or suckler cows, but is quite often found in marginal upland areas. The dairy system does not have the same degree of stratification as the beef system, though it does provide the main source of beef calves in England. Replacement dairy stock comes from within the herd. Surplus calves from the dairy farms will be sold on for finishing on grass or intensive cereal systems in the lowlands.

Due to breeding advances, over 90% of dairy herds have been standardised around the Friesian or Holstein breeds. These can be crossed with beef bulls to produce cows of good beef shape and milkiness, making them suitable for use as suckler cows later on. Calves are usually artificially reared, weaned at six weeks and fattened on concentrates. Male calves are fattened for slaughter while females may either be finished for the market or reared as stock cows for future breeding.

A typical farming year for hill/upland suckler cow herds (spring calving)

November/December:	On in-bye, fed outside on hay or silage. Time of housing is weather dependent, eg wet weather = early housing.
December/March:	Inside, fed on hay, silage or straw and perhaps a small amount of concentrates.
March/April/May:	Calving. Usually outside. Turnout depends on season and altitude of the farm.
April/May:	Cows and calves on in-bye. (Possible competition with ewes and lambs, depending on numbers and land available.)
May/June:	Cattle to improved hill. In-bye meadows closed up for hay/silage.
July:	Bull run with cows on in-bye.
August/September:	Cows and calves on in-bye. (Possible competition with weaned lambs, depending on numbers and land available.)
October:	Calves fed some concentrates then sold.
November:	Cows on in-bye, prior to housing. Fed on hay or silage if necessary as quality can be poor and weather can deteriorate.

Modified from Haines, M. 1992. *An introduction to farming systems.* London: Longman.

Introduction

Bracken *Pteridium aquilinum* was originally a woodland fern but locally it has become an invasive weed of marginal land (Pakeman & Marrs 1992; Smith & Taylor 1986). Once established, it is aggressive, supremely competitive, and extremely difficult and expensive to control. There are continuing concerns about the spread of bracken in the UK where bracken cover is thought to have doubled during the twentieth century (Birnie *et al* 1998; Brown 1997; Pakeman *et al* 1996; Rhone-Poulenc 1997; Taylor 1997).

The reasons for and against managing bracken are many and varied. These concern nature conservation, agriculture, forestry, management for grouse, human and animal health, recreation and archaeology. From a wildlife point of view, bracken can be of great value, particularly where it occurs as a mosaic with other vegetation types, and significant areas should be retained in appropriate locations. However, bracken-dominated areas may be less important for wildlife than the communities displaced by invasion (Marrs & Pakeman 1995).

The single most important factor in managing bracken is to adhere to the guidance developed by a number of organisations and described in the following text (Environment Agency 1998; North West Water 1996; Peak District National Park 1997; Rhone-Poulenc 1997; Roberts, MacDonald & Wood-Gee 1996).

Reasons for managing bracken

Nature conservation

- Loss of species and communities of wildlife value, such as heaths, species-rich grasslands and their associated plants and animals.

- Increased grazing pressure on habitats of wildlife value, such as heaths and species-rich grassland.

- Presence of 'woodland' fritillary butterflies, most notably two rare and declining species, high brown fritillary *Argynnis adippe* (RDB2 & Schedule 5) and pearl bordered fritillary *Boloria euphrosyne* (Nationally Scarce), but also the commoner dark green fritillary *Argynnis aglaia*, which utilise violets *Viola* spp under appropriately managed bracken (see Butterfly Conservation 1998).

- Reduced diversity of natural vegetation and associated fauna (although bracken may also add diversity).

Agriculture

- Reduced availability of grazing on bracken-infested land.

- ✓ Increased numbers of sheep ticks which can cause disease in stock.
- Problems with stock movement and gathering.
- ✓ Poisoning and even death of animals owing to powerful poisons in bracken, including some carcinogens (Taylor 1989).

Forestry

- Increased competition with and damage to young trees.

Grouse

- Loss of heather moorland.
- Increased numbers of sheep ticks which create problems for grouse (eg louping ill)

Human health

- Increased numbers of sheep ticks which can lead to Lyme disease in humans (Brown 1993).
- Presence of powerful poisons in bracken, including some carcinogens, leading to fears for human health (Taylor 1989).

Recreation

- Loss of amenity land.
- Problems with access for recreation.

Archaeology

- Damage to archaeological sites and features by the rhizomes.

Reasons against managing bracken

Nature conservation

Plants

- Plants which could be harmed by bracken management, eg rare ferns, may be present in the vicinity of bracken stands, particularly in gills, cloughs, rocky and limestone areas.
- Bracken supports a woodland ground flora in some areas, including violets and bluebells *Hyacinthoides non-scripta*, by acting as a substitute woodland canopy (but see also previous page).

- Bracken protects some plants from grazing, such as chickweed wintergreen *Trientalis europaea* and lesser butterfly-orchid *Platanthera bifolia* (Rhone-Poulenc 1997).

- It enables some plants growing under its shade to survive drought summers better than would the same species growing outside the bracken stand (A. MacDonald, pers comm).

Birds

Bracken provides sheltered roost sites and nesting habitat for birds such as twite *Carduelis flavirostris*, whinchat *Saxicola rubetra*, skylark *Alauda arvensis*, ring ouzel *Turdus torquatus*, merlin *Falco columbarius*, short-eared owl *Asio flammeus*, curlew *Numenius arquata*, stonechat *Saxicola torquata* and meadow pipit *Anthus pratensis*, many of which are birds of conservation concern (RSPB 1996).

- Whinchat, for example, are positively associated with bracken (Allen 1995), and twite are particularly associated with bracken in the South Pennines, where they prefer larger stands (A. Brown, pers comm).

- It provides song posts and perches from which stonechat and whinchat forage, and the litter can provide sheltered roosting sites for red and black grouse in winter.

- It supports small birds, which provide food for raptors such as merlin and hen harrier.

- It provides good habitat for additional birds such as redstart and tree pipit where it occurs with scattered shrubs.

- It provides a diversity of vegetation structure where scattered bracken occurs in a mosaic of other vegetation types, such as with acid grassland, mires, heather moorland, scrub and at woodland margins, and this is important for birds.

Invertebrates

- A high diversity of invertebrate species feed on bracken, particularly flies and sawflies, including some that are specific to it and many generalist fern or broad spectrum plant feeders.

- Bracken provides a significant nectar source early in the year (spring and early summer) when its extra-floral nectaries (low down on the frond, on the stalk at the bases of the pinnae) are producing nectar which is used in particular by ants, small flies and parasitic wasps.

- It provides shelter for one of Britain's few endemic invertebrates, the weevil *Procas granulicollis* which, although feeding specifically on climbing corydalis *Ceratocapnos claviculata*, normally a woodland plant, seems to do so preferentially when this plant grows among bracken.

- It supports an assemblage of arthropods, many of which are specific or largely dependent on bracken.

Forestry

- A light bracken layer can provide shelter for young trees from wind and frost.

Soil

- Bracken can improve the texture and stability of some soils, especially on sandy slopes.

Landscape

- Bracken provides autumn colour in the landscape.

Managing bracken

Bracken control can be an expensive, difficult and long-term process and it should not be undertaken lightly. It can also lead to considerable problems of erosion. Extensive, blanket control of this species is neither practical nor desirable.

A carefully constructed plan, taking into account all land uses and interests, is required for effective bracken management. The plan must be based on the long-term land management and wildlife objectives for the area concerned. It should identify priority areas for treatment, as well as areas to be left, and take into account all the recommendations contained here. It should include both initial and follow-up treatments . Subsequent follow-up treatment is usually essential, although the form this takes will vary. In some cases this will involve, for example, successive, larger scale aerial or ground-based herbicide applications, while in others annual spot-treatment may be more appropriate.

General recommendations concerning bracken management are contained in Box IN6.1, with further advice on specific methods in the following boxes.

Preventing bracken invasion

As a general rule, prevention is better than cure, so efforts should be focused on preventing bracken invasion of valued habitats, followed by carefully targeted treatment of selected areas where removal of bracken is a priority.

Bracken is an extremely competitive species. Vegetation which is growing vigorously should be able to hold its own against bracken, but where the vegetation is suppressed for some reason then bracken can spread. High grazing pressure, for example, may encourage bracken invasion, and preventing the overgrazing of swards will help prevent the spread of bracken. In some areas, too little grazing (under grazing) or the type of stock used is more of a problem. For example, cattle trampling is more effective in reducing the spread of bracken than sheep trampling.

Bracken often occurs in mixtures with heather on moorlands. When dwarf shrub species are in the building phase of growth they are able to compete successfully with bracken. However, when the competitiveness of dwarf shrubs is reduced, which occurs during the pioneer or degenerate growth phases, or when the land is severely grazed or burnt, bracken may have the advantage (Watt 1955). Here burning can lead to either a reduction or an increase in the cover of bracken, depending on how well the other vegetation regenerates after the fire (A. MacDonald, pers comm). This in turn depends on a number of variables such as the age of the heather before burning, the intensity of the fire and the climate. For example, young heather can regenerate relatively rapidly after a light to moderate fire and so compete successfully with bracken. Where heaths with bracken are burnt, some follow-up treatment of the bracken may be needed if it is subsequently found to be invading.

Box IN6.1 General recommendations on managing bracken

Only manage bracken where:

- there are definite benefits, for example for agriculture, wildlife, recreation or archaeology;
- there will be no harm to these interests;
- there is a properly resourced, long-term plan in place, including follow-up treatment;
- there is an understorey of heather, bilberry or grass and favoured moorland or grassland vegetation can be restored as a result;

Do NOT manage bracken:

- where the resulting harm to wildlife outweighs the benefits to other land uses;
- on steep slopes, cloughs and gullies where treatment is likely to lead to erosion;
- where other plant communities, such as in limestone pavement and mires, may be adversely affected;
- where other plant species, such as ferns, may be adversely affected;
- on unenclosed land where bracken is in competition merely with mat-grass;
- in areas known to be important for bracken-breeding birds;
- in areas known to be important for bracken-dependent invertebrates;
- along the sides of water courses and water bodies;
- on ancient stands with thick litter and no other vegetation beneath (unless tree planting is planned);
- where there will be significant, adverse impacts on the landscape.

Additional considerations

- Assess all sites before and after treatment so that appropriate further action may be planned.
- Consider the option of planting with native trees and shrubs.
- Consult the Environment Agency. There might be a legal requirement to do so before chemical treatment.
- Consult English Nature if the land to be treated is within or adjacent to a Site of Special Scientific Interest (SSSI). Within 1.5km if aerial application is being proposed.
- Consult the National Park Authority if the land to be treated is within a National Park.
- Consult the National Park archaeologist in National Parks and the County archaeologist elsewhere if the land to be treated involves a site of archaeological interest.
- Consider seeding of resulting bare areas with heather or other appropriate moorland species where necessary.
- Control stocking levels or remove stock following bracken treatment to avoid overgrazing of recolonising plants and seedlings.

Planting native trees in bracken areas

An ecologically sound solution to the problem of unwanted bracken-dominated areas in the uplands is to target them for tree planting. This could be part of the planned long-term expansion of woodland area in England. Much of the bracken land is particularly suitable for the expansion of existing woodlands or the planting of new woods. However, careful survey is needed prior to the approval of particular planting proposals, to ensure that bracken areas of high wildlife value are not lost.

Planting bracken-dominated areas with native trees is an important way of reducing the vigour of bracken stands. It also increases the diversity of the habitat and benefits various animals. Areas with dense litter cover, moorland edges, gills, cloughs and sloping ground which can be fenced from stock are particularly appropriate. It will frequently be more desirable than trying to remove bracken with chemicals, although this may be required in the first instance to allow trees to become established. It has been conducted in various areas, and provides a return to open, patchy native shrub and woodland cover (North York Moors National Park 1991, 1993). Where it is undertaken, only tree and shrub species typical of the area and of local provenance should be used.

Mechanical methods

Mechanical methods of management inflict physical damage on the plant and can be achieved by:

- cutting;
- crushing;
- trampling;
- ploughing;
- rotovating (smaller areas).

The first three methods work on the fronds when they are actively growing and have the effect of starving the surviving rhizomes. Ploughing and rotovating breaks up the rhizomes and exposes them to the action of frost (Gimingham 1992), but in the uplands this is rarely appropriate.

Effective mechanical management of bracken, like chemical methods, involves a long-term approach and is unlikely to eradicate bracken completely. However, mechanical methods are sometimes cheaper and less dependent on weather conditions than chemical treatment. It is most appropriate for small, relatively level areas of bracken or light infestations and is also a useful option in conjunction with other treatments. But mechanical methods are often not feasible in the uplands because of the topography and ground conditions.

Cutting the fronds in late summer (July-August) prevents food reserves being moved to the rhizomes, with the ultimate aim of exhausting the rhizome system (Marrs & Pakeman 1995). Cutting on two occasions during the growing season (mid-late June and mid-August) and for at least three successive years is much more effective than carrying out the process just once (North York Moors National Park 1986, 1993). However, even long-term, annual cutting may not completely destroy the rhizome system (R. Brown, pers comm.).

Crushing by roller or bracken-breaker machines is normally recommended to be undertaken twice a year, particularly during early frond growth when the stems are still brittle (North York Moors National Park 1986, 1993). Its effectiveness reduces as the stems mature. Crushing or 'bruising' squashes the bracken stems against the ground as the machine passes over. It does not cut off the stems but leaves them attached to the root to bleed the sap, so denying next year's buds essential food energy. Each bruising operation reduces vigour and shoot numbers by about one third, quickly reducing a dense stand of bracken into more scattered fronds (J. Bacon, pers comm). This process not only reduces bracken regeneration but the machine action also encourages the breakdown of bracken litter. It is not as effective as cutting but is useful as a follow-up treatment on sprayed areas. However, the use of rollers can lead to erosion of peaty soils on sloping ground.

Ploughing and **rotovating** are rarely an option in the uplands because the slope and thin soil usually make these methods impractical. It can also can disrupt the fragile soils, damage other plant communities and lead to erosion. However, it can be effective for managing bracken where practical. A method known as chisel ploughing can be used, which is a deep ploughing technique reaching to a depth of 45 cm. This operation damages the soil profile and should only be used in areas where there is an established monoculture of bracken and no risk of erosion. It imposes maximum stress on the fern by direct mechanical damage and by exposure of the rhizome system to frosts and drought. But bracken re-growth will occur even after a vigorous procedure such as ploughing.

Trampling by stock also inflicts damage on the fronds, particularly in the spring, thus depleting rhizome reserves (North York Moors National Park 1993). Cattle are much more effective than sheep, but care should be taken to avoid the risk of poisoning by providing adequate fodder for the animals. Foddering on dense bracken beds can help to break them up and create a seed bed for grass and heather to re-establish. Feeding sites may need to be moved regularly to avoid poaching. Stock treading also increases the rate of breakdown of dense bracken litter.

Information and recommendations concerning mechanical management of bracken are given in Box IN6.2.

Box IN6.2 Managing bracken with mechanical methods

Do **NOT** use this method on:

- very stony and steep areas which are not suitable for vehicles;
- peat soils;
- areas supporting nesting birds, where mechanical management must be delayed until late August, or other methods used;
- archaeological sites, which can be easily damaged by the movement of vehicles.
  - ❑ Records of known sites are held by Local Authorities and National Parks.
  - ❑ These areas can be marked and dealt with by hand.

Do:

- target management at the invading edge of the bracken (where there is sufficient frond density for treatment to be effective);
- check the area for large stones as these can damage machinery;
- exercise due care for health and safety, eg use a face mask when cutting bracken with spores, cover arms and legs to reduce the likelihood of sheep tick bites.
- repeat the mechanical method for at least three years to give reasonable results.

Box IN6.2 Managing bracken with mechanical methods (cont)

Cutting bracken

- Cut the fronds twice annually, in mid to late June and mid-August, for at least three successive years.
  - ❑ A tractor and rotary swipe can be used, setting the height of the cut to about 10 cm.
  - ❑ Cutting once will produce an even stand with more active buds which will increase the efficiency of chemical treatment carried out the following year.

Crushing bracken

- Crush emerging, brittle bracken fronds at least twice a year, in the first weeks of June and again in the first weeks of August, for at least three successive years.

Ploughing of bracken beds

- Only plough areas with deeper soils (at least 60 cm) and no risk of erosion, on slopes less than 15-20°, and where there is an established monoculture of bracken.
- Precede ploughing by two cuts to weaken the rhizomes.
- Chisel plough to a depth of 45 cm.
- Ideally plough in very hot weather to maximise damage to the plant.

Stock trampling of bracken

- Use cattle trampling in spring as an effective and cheap option, for example for follow-up treatment.
- Provide sufficient fodder to prevent animals eating the bracken.
- Stocking rates of between 0.125 and 0.25 cattle/ha, or between one and 2 sheep/ha if cattle are not available, may be appropriate, depending on the percentage cover of bracken.
- This is only appropriate where there is no risk of overgrazing adjacent heather or other habitats.
- Do not employ this method on archaeological sites as damage may occur.

Dealing with bracken litter

- Where vehicular access is possible, the grazing pressure and the soil are light, and the slope is less than 15°, then raking, chain harrowing or light rotovation of the litter beds can break them up and accelerate the development of new vegetation.
- Treading by stock will also help, provided sufficient fodder is provided to prevent animals eating the bracken. Feed can be positioned on bracken stands.
- Burning of bracken litter should only be undertaken with extreme care, and in accordance with the *Heather and Grass Burning Code* (MAFF 1992). Burning promotes vigorous bracken regrowth and so further treatment will be required.
- Do not undertake any of these activities on steep slopes where erosion may occur, or where populations of high brown or pearl-bordered fritillaries occur.

Preventing bracken invasion

- Do not overgraze areas of heath, grassland or former bracken stands.
- Graze with cattle rather than sheep.
- Manage heather, by appropriate burning or cutting, to keep it in the building phase.

Chemical methods

Effective management of bracken with chemicals is a long-term process because multiple applications and/or some other form of follow-up treatment such as mechanical management is required. Even then bracken may well return and require constant attention.

Asulam (methyl {4-aminobenzenesulphonyl} carbamate), obtained as the product Asulox, is the most widely used herbicide for bracken management (Rhone-Poulenc 1997). At the recommended application rate it is relatively specific to ferns and to a relatively narrow range of higher plants. Docks *Rumex* spp. are highly susceptible and there is some evidence that some bryophytes may also be susceptible. This of course means that all fern and some higher plant and bryophyte species which are sprayed, and not just bracken, may be affected. Asulam can also check the growth of other plant species. Species shown to be susceptible to Asulox to varying degrees include a number of grass species, heather *Calluna vulgaris*, bilberry *Vaccinium myrtillus*, saxifrages *Saxifraga* spp, eyebright *Euphrasia anglica*, common bird's-foot trefoil *Lotus corniculatus*, certain plantains *Plantago* spp, and tree and shrub species including gorse *Ulex gallii* and *U. europaeus*, willows *Salix* spp and silver birch *Betula pendula* (Rhone-Poulenc 1997). Therefore, when considering the use of chemicals for bracken management, it must be remembered that ferns and other plants of nature conservation value may be present and could be adversely affected (see effects on plants below).

Asulam is translocated into the rhizomes of bracken, where it effects a lethal action on the rhizome buds. The effects of treatment will not be seen until the following season, but there is usually at least a 95% reduction in fronds in the year after spraying, provided the Asulox is properly applied.

The herbicide can be applied to the bracken by a variety of means. These include:

- aerial spraying from a helicopter;
- tractors, quad-bikes or all terrain vehicles (ATVs) with mounted
    - spray booms;
    - roller-wiping equipment;
    - hoses and lances;
    - spinning-disc applicators;

- portable methods
    - knapsack sprayers;
    - Micron Ulva+;
    - spot-guns.

Helicopter spraying is the most commonly used and cost effective method for large areas. Tractors, quad-bikes and ATVs are used on suitable, even terrain, but areas of land too steep or rocky for vehicle access require portable methods instead. Hoses, lances and spray-guns are often used for follow-up work. Information and advice on chemical treatment of bracken are included below and in Box IN6.3.

Aerial spraying

- May be carried out only by helicopter.
- Applies chemicals in flight lanes 8-12 m wide (such precise targeting is possible when conducted by helicopters fitted exclusively with raindrop nozzles)
- May lead to missed strips.
- May lead to chemical drift. Drift is likely to be more severe if raindrop nozzles are not used, if the wind speed is greater than 10 mph (16 km/h) and if the operator is late in shutting off the chemical at the ends of runs.

Tractors, quad-bikes or all-terrain vehicles (ATVs) with mounted applicators

Conventional spray booms

- Short, stubby booms (2-3 m long) are best suited to use on ATVs and quad-bikes.
- Longer booms (usually up to 12 m for bracken spraying) are used on tractors.
- This method is not cost effective on sparse bracken.
- Volume rates can be reduced by fitting anvil nozzles or Turbo TeeJets to the booms at 1 m spacing;
- These nozzles will also produce coarser sprays which reduce drift.
- It is an advantage to employ reduced volume rates to avoid constant re-filling and to enhance work rates.
- Booms should be set high enough to ensure uniform coverage of the fronds.
- Also causes risk of drift and spraying of herbicide is not recommended if wind speed exceeds 6 mph (9.6 km/h).

Powered roller-wiping equipment

- Can be effective for both primary and secondary treatments but effectiveness decreases as the roughness of the land increases or as frond density decreases.
- Wiping is not suited to the final eradication phase of bracken clearance when small fronds will be encountered.
- Hand-held wiping gear is not generally effective on bracken.

Hoses and lances

- A rack of up to four powered hoses and lances mounted on the rear of an ATV or quad-bike can be used for highly effective follow-up treatment on rougher ground.
- A team of four, walking behind the vehicle, can achieve spot-treatment of bracken regrowth over a width of up to 20 m, thereby achieving high work rates.
- This equipment is not recommended for primary treatment.

Boom-mounted spinning-disc applicators

- Boom-mounted disc units set to give coarse droplets (>250 µm) can be very effective.
- Waterless applications are possible.

Portable methods of application

Knapsack sprayers

- Require an easy access to a water supply.
- Motorised knapsack mistblowers are not suitable for use on bracken.
- Manual, lever-operated knapsack sprayers and compression sprayers are suitable only for the smallest areas, and mostly used for spot-treatments.
- Motorised knapsack sprayers may be used to treat larger areas of shorter bracken when fitted with a short boom up to 3 m long.
- Volume rates can be reduced by fitting flooding nozzles and Turbo TeeJets to the booms at 1 m spacing.
- These nozzles will also produce coarser sprays which reduce drift.
- It is an advantage to employ reduced volume rates to avoid constant re-filling and to enhance work rates.

Micron Ulva+

- Hand-held spinning disc sprayer, operating on torch batteries.
- Can be used for primary treatment or follow-up treatment on dense patches of regrowth and missed strips.
- It is useful to treat tall, dense or inaccessible bracken which cannot be treated by other means.
- Waterless applications are possible.

- This is a skilled operation requiring a specialised spray method, with the operator walking across the wind and applying swaths at 3 m intervals.

- Best results are obtained in a steady, light breeze.

Spot-guns

- These are able to deliver 0.5-1.0 ml per shot and used on foot are a practical means to achieve follow-up treatment of sparse bracken fronds on extended areas of rough ground (sometimes known as the 'gardening' stage at the end of a programme eradication scheme).

- Higher capacity, conventional drench guns (minimum output of 5 ml/shot) are not usually suitable for this work.

- A red foodstuffs dye (eg Eurocert Red) may be used to help identify treated fronds.

Further information: Cooke 1986, 1993; North York Moors National Park 1986; Rhone-Poulenc 1997.

Timing of chemical treatments

Timing the application of herbicide is particularly important in bracken eradication. The aim is not to kill the fronds but to use them as a mechanism for translocating the herbicide to the underground rhizome. This is maximised during late summer when there is movement of photosynthetic products from the fronds to the rhizome. The producers of Asulox suggest that at least three pairs of pinnae (bracken 'leaves' or fronds) should be fully open before applying the herbicide. This refers to untouched bracken stands, not regrowth and is usually during late July or early August, although it will vary with the location, altitude and the season. In some areas, applications will be effective in September.

Use of additives

Additives (or adjuvants) can enhance the activity of asulam applied to bracken by increasing the rate and quantity of translocation to the rhizome buds, achieving a higher mortality for a given dose. The same effects can also offer a measure of protection against rain washing or poor application (under dosing). However, care is required when additives are used because they can amplify the damaging effects of spraying on other, non-target species and may alter the drift characteristics and the spectrum of activity of asulam. They should also not be used when over-spraying of trees is to be attempted (forestry uses).

Where Asulox is sprayed using water as a carrier, a wetting agent such as Agral is usually employed at 0.1%. For waterless carriers, applied by spinning-disc equipment, Asulox is usually mixed with an emulsifiable oil such as Adder (11:7 ratio). A wetting agent or an emulsifiable oil will also enhance the activity of asulam applied by wiping equipment. Certain forms of wiping gear will require the additional use of a polymer to adjust the viscosity of the mixture.

'Stickers' may help to prevent rain-washing of Asulox after application to bracken but the effect is not proven.

Use of chemicals other than asulam

Other chemicals are available for bracken management but are not specific to bracken. These include glyphosate, which is sold under the product name 'Roundup' and other products. The lack of specificity limits the potential location and method of application of such chemicals. For example, they should be applied only with weed wipers or spot treatment, so that the chemical is not applied to plants other than bracken. Non-specific chemicals are best used in areas of dense bracken monoculture because they will kill all non-target plant species. Care should be taken to avoid risks to other non-target organisms, although glyphosate has a fairly low toxicity to animals and is effectively inactive once it reaches the soil. This chemical also has the advantage of producing a general yellowing of vegetation within a few weeks, enabling evenness of application to be judged and any additional treatment to be carried out where necessary.

Follow-up treatment

Most bracken management programmes will involve some degree of follow-up management and this is often more expensive than the primary treatment (Rhone-Poulenc 1997). In the year following the initial herbicide treatment, it is likely that at least a sparse cover of individual fronds will emerge in areas formerly covered by dense stands. If helicopter spraying has been used there may also be strips or areas of bracken which were missed. The type of follow-up treatment used to manage this regrowth will depend on such factors as financial and labour resources, the suitability of the ground for machines and the density of the regrowth.

The response of bracken to chemical treatment is determined by the number of dormant buds and the structure and volume of the rhizome system (Rhone-Poulenc 1997). Generally speaking, the smaller the total rhizome bulk, the simpler the rhizome system, the fewer the total number of buds and the fewer the number of dormant buds, the easier the bracken will be to manage. Complex, layered rhizome beds with large numbers of dormant buds are very likely to require a prolonged programme of aftercare to ensure eradication. An assessment of the rhizome system should ideally be undertaken before a management programme is initiated.

Secondary treatment using herbicides is probably the most straight forward means of follow-up management. Repeated, annual follow-up and spot spraying is highly effective, if expensive and time consuming. Alternatively, cutting or crushing can be conducted as a follow-up (or pre-) treatment for dense stands.

The vegetation that replaces bracken

After it has been removed by spraying, the vegetation that replaces bracken is influenced by (Brown 1986; North York Moors National Park 1991):

- slope;
- aspect;
- altitude;
- soil wetness;
- management practices such as grazing and burning;

- the state of the vegetation beneath the bracken;
- region and locality (ie east coast versus west coast).

In general, where moorland species such as grasses, heather and bilberry are present beneath a stand of bracken, their recovery can be achieved after spraying with Asulox, provided erosion does not result and grazing is sufficiently low or absent. Follow-up spraying is normally required immediately or within two-three years of primary treatment to control the regrowth of fronds. However, recovery of other vegetation may be much slower or may not occur at all if a dense bed of bracken litter prevents seedling germination or establishment. Such litter needs to be broken down by frost, by stock trampling or physically removed. Regeneration of native grasses or heather can be achieved by sowing grass seed or by applying cut heather brash (North York Moors National Park 1986). The stocking density will then need to be greatly reduced, or preferably removed using fencing, to allow seedling establishment.

Applying lime and fertilisers

Applying lime and fertilisers following bracken spraying on areas of grass moorland is sometimes proposed, with the intention of improving the sward and allowing an increase in stocking levels. However, on unimproved land this is not usually compatible with nature conservation objectives, because it prevents successful regeneration of heather and may adversely affect areas such as species-rich mires. On enclosed, improved grassland some follow-up treatment using lime and phosphate may be desirable.

Box IN6.3 Recommendations concerning chemical treatment of bracken

Legislation and safety

- The landowner and operator must ensure that any use of sprays is in accordance with health and safety regulations.
- *Control of Pesticides Regulations* 1986 set out the qualifications required by those involved.
- These also require prior (at least 72 hours) consultation with English Nature before aerial spraying any land within 1,500 m of an SSSI, and with the Environment Agency before spraying any land adjacent to a water course, lake or reservoir.
- *Control of Substances Hazardous to Health Regulations* must be followed by the owner or manager of the land and the persons doing the work, who must be suitably qualified.
- All users of pesticides (including herbicides) are required to take all reasonable precautions to protect the health of human beings, animals and plants, to safeguard the environment and in particular to avoid pollution of water.
- At all times when spraying *The Green Code* (*The code of practice for the safe use of pesticides on farms and holdings*, MAFF 1998) must be complied with.
- The statutory conditions of use on the product label must be adhered to when using any chemicals for bracken management.

Timing of application

- Asulam should be applied when the fronds are fully open and before they have started to die back, for example when at least three pairs of pinnae are fully open (untouched bracken stands, not regrowth). This is usually during late July or early August, although it will vary with the location and the season. In some areas, applications will be effective in September.
- Spraying should not occur until late August where whinchat and twite are present because these species may still be breeding in the bracken.
- A rain-free period of 12 hours must follow application for maximum effect.

Box IN6.3 Recommendations concerning chemical treatment of bracken cont.

Other considerations

- Check the area for the presence of other susceptible plant species of nature conservation interest when using asulam.
  - ❑ No spraying should take place on or close to sites containing susceptible plants of conservation importance.
- Establish buffer zones around all areas to be avoided.
  - ❑ See areas to be avoided above and size of buffer zones below.
- Target management at the invading edge of the bracken.
- Mark out areas clearly, to assist even coverage and ensure buffer zones are adhered to.
- Certain additives may be employed when treating bracken (see *Use of additives* in text).
- Plan secondary treatment.
  - ❑ This is essential, and repeated, annual follow-up and spot spraying is highly effective.
  - ❑ Alternatively, cutting or crushing can be conducted as a follow-up (or pre-) treatment for dense stands.
- Only use chemicals other than asulam where no other vegetation is present, eg areas with deep bracken litter, and then only with weed wipers.
  - ❑ The vicinity must first be checked for the presence of important plant and animal species.
  - ❑ If these are present the area containing the interest should not be treated.
    An appropriate buffer zone must be left around these areas when treating adjacent land (see below).

Aerial spraying of bracken

- Follow all the legal and safety requirements laid out above.
- Conduct aerial spraying in accordance with Civil Aviation Authority licence conditions.
- Publicise aerial spraying operations to avoid hazards to neighbouring properties, livestock and the general public.
- Asulam is the only herbicide cleared for aerial application for bracken management.
- Helicopters should be fitted exclusively with Delavan RD raindrop nozzles to minimise drift.
- No spraying should occur directly on to areas with susceptible, rare plant species beneath the bracken canopy.
- The following no-spray buffer zones must be used:
  - ❑ with helicopters fitted with RD raindrop nozzles:
    - 50 m from water courses (where susceptible, rare plant species are absent);
    - 100 m from areas with susceptible, rare plant species or particularly sensitive habitats, eg limestone pavement;
  - ❑ with helicopters fitted with conventional hydraulic nozzles:
    - 160 m from water courses (where susceptible, rare plant species are absent);
    - 180 m and up to 250 m from areas with susceptible, rare plant species or particularly sensitive habitats, eg limestone pavement.

- Spraying is not permitted when wind speed exceeds 11.5 mph (18.5 km/h).
- Mark out areas to be sprayed and avoided on the ground prior to spraying.
- When spraying outside of an SSSI, spray parallel to the boundary where possible, to reduce the risk of chemical drift from overshooting or wind changes.
- If a buffer zone is not in use, spray when the sensitive site is upwind of the area to be treated.
- Plan secondary treatment, usually by other methods.

Ground spraying of bracken
- Do not spray within the following distances of valuable wildlife features or water courses (Environment Agency 1998; North West Water 1996; Rhone-Poulenc 1997):
  - ❑ wiping systems: 1 m
  - ❑ tractor and knapsack boom systems with conventional, hydraulic nozzles:
    - 10 m for protection of established plants
    - 20 m for protection of seedlings
  - ❑ hand held Micron Ulva drift sprayer: 50 m
- Spraying is inadvisable above wind speeds of 6-9 mph (9.6-14.4 km/h) (Green Code, MAFF 1998)
- Where buffer zones are not in use, spray when the sensitive site is upwind of the area to be treated.
- Only use glyphosate where no other vegetation is present, eg areas with deep bracken litter, and then only on suitable terrain and with a tractor- or ATV-mounted weed wiper.

The effect of bracken management on other plants

Plants of nature conservation value may be present in areas where bracken occurs (Marrs & Pakeman 1995) and bracken management may adversely affect them, particularly when chemicals are involved. Conversely, removing bracken may benefit nature conservation by encouraging the expansion of dwarf shrub heath or species-rich grassland.

Asulam can be toxic to all fern species and can also adversely affect several moorland shrubs, grasses and herbs, causing a temporary check in growth or slight die back (Rhone-Poulenc 1997). This chemical is also sold to control docks *Rumex* spp. in pasture and, therefore, certain members of the Polygonaceae are highly susceptible to it. Lists of species shown to be susceptible to the chemical, as well as those shown to have some resistance to it, are available (Cooke 1986; English Nature 1999; Rhone-Poulenc 1997).

Bracken spraying should not take place on or close to areas containing susceptible plants of nature conversation importance. Where there is concern about the effects of bracken spraying, a suitable buffer zone around the area of interest must be left unsprayed. Spray deposition tends to fall off logarithmically, but it should be remembered that chemical drift can cause adverse effects or death to ferns and other plants beyond the immediate treatment area. Recommended buffer zones are contained in Box IN6.3 above.

Limestone and rocky areas, gills and cloughs are particularly likely to support susceptible plants of nature conservation interest which could be harmed by bracken spraying. Caution should also be exercised when dealing with plant communities which are diverse in both species and groups, because even if plants are not killed, the balance of species across a community could change if one or more species is weakened. In all these situations, appropriate buffer zones are required.

The effect of bracken management on animals

Birds

Any mechanical method must be timed to avoid disturbance to ground-nesting birds, which can be present until late July or early August. Chemical methods involving spraying should not occur until late August where whinchat and twite are present because these species may still be breeding in the bracken until then. Significant areas of bracken should be retained for breeding birds (Brown & Bainbridge 1995).

Invertebrates

A high diversity of invertebrate species depends on bracken or the habitats associated with it (see *Reasons for retaining bracken*). Managing bracken may lead to the loss of species of nature conversation importance. However, bracken also supports pest species such as sheep tick in high densities (Sheaves & Brown 1995), and removing bracken may be desirable for controlling these invertebrates.

In areas where fritillary butterflies occur, particular conditions and management regimes are required to maintain the populations. This is because the butterflies feed in spring and early summer on violets growing in the warm microclimate provided by the developing bracken canopy. However, as bracken stands become more dense the violets are lost and the value to the butterflies declines. Appropriate bracken management, for example grazing with cattle or ponies to break up the bracken litter, spot-spraying or crushing, is then necessary to retain the required conditions (see Butterfly Conservation 1998; Warren & Oates 1995).

Bracken management should also take into account the weevil *Procas granulicollis* which, although feeding specifically on climbing corydalis *Ceratocapnos claviculata*, normally a woodland plant, seems to do so preferentially when this plant grows among bracken. When not feeding, the weevil spends most of its time sheltering within dead bracken stalks with bracken litter. The distribution of this species is unclear, but it has been found in Cumbria, Northumberland, North Yorks, Wales (Ceredigion) and Scotland.

Amphibians and reptiles

Managing bracken is beneficial for reptiles in some areas. Dense bracken creates problems for these animals because it shades the ground too heavily. Where bracken management is considered in areas with reptiles, the methods used should be sensitive to the needs of these species. Consequently rolling bracken or forage harvesting should be avoided, or at least carried out with caution, in areas that are good for reptiles. Hand spraying using Asulox is recommended.

Bibliography & further reading

ALLEN, D. 1995. Habitat selection by whinchats: a case for bracken in the uplands? *In*: D.B. Thompson, A.J. Hester, & M.B. Usher, eds. *Heaths and moorland: cultural landscapes*. Edinburgh and London: HMSO.

BIRNIE, R.V., HORNE, P.L., MILLER, D.R. & MACDONALD, A. 1998. *Potential impacts of bracken spread on natural heritage features in Scotland*. Aberdeen: MLURI.

BROWN, A.F. & BAINBRIDGE, I.P. 1995. Grouse moors and upland breeding birds. *In*: D.B.A. Thompson, A.J. Hester & M.B. Usher, eds. *Heaths and moorland: cultural landscapes*. Edinburgh and London: HMSO, pp. 51-66.

BROWN, R.W. 1986. Bracken in the North York Moors: its ecological and amenity implications in National Parks. *In:* R.T. Smith & J.A. Taylor, eds. *Bracken: ecology, land use and control technology*. Carnforth: Parthenon Publishing.

BROWN, R.W. 1993. Breaking the cycle: environmental control of *Borrelia*. *Annals of rheumatic diseases*, **52**, pp. 407.

BROWN, R.W. 1997. The biology and ecology of bracken. *The Heather Trust Annual Report*. Kippen: The Heather Trust.

BUTTERFLY CONSERVATION. 1998. *Bracken for butterflies*. Wareham: Butterfly Conservation.

COOKE, A.S. 1986. *The use of herbicides on nature reserves*. Nature Conservancy Council Focus on nature conservation No. 14. Peterborough: English Nature.

COOKE, A.S. ed. 1993. *The environmental effects of pesticide drift*. Peterborough: English Nature.

ENGLISH NATURE 1999. *Aerial spraying using Asulam: Buffer Zones*. Advisory note.

ENVIRONMENT AGENCY. 1998. *Aerial spraying with asulam to control bracken: guidance notes for Environment Agency staff*. Wallingford: Environment Agency.

GIMINGHAM, C.H. 1992. *The lowland heathland management handbook*. English Nature Science No. 8. Peterborough: English Nature.

KIRBY, P. 1992. *Habitat management for invertebrates: a practical handbook*. Sandy: RSPB.

LOWDAY, J.E. 1984. The restoration of heathland vegetation after control of dense bracken by asulam. *Aspects of Applied Biology*, **5**, pp. 283-290.

MAFF. 1992. *Heather and grass burning code*. London: HMSO.

MAFF. 1998. *Code of practice for the safe use of pesticides on farms and holdings*. London: HMSO.

MARRS, R.H. & FROST, A.J. 1996. Techniques to reduce the impact of asulam drift from helicopter sprayers on native vegetation. *Journal of Environmental Management*, **46**, pp. 373-394.

MARRS, R.H. & PAKEMAN, R.J. 1995. Bracken invasion: lessons from the past and prospects for the future. *In*: D.B.A. Thompson, A.J. Hester & M.B. Usher, eds. *Heaths and moorland: cultural landscapes*. Edinburgh and London: HMSO, pp. 180-193.

NINNES, R.B. 1995. Bracken, heath and burning on the Quantock Hills, England. *In*: D.B.A. Thompson, A.J. Hester & M.B. Usher, eds. *Heaths and moorland: cultural landscapes*. Edinburgh and London: HMSO, pp. 194-199.

NORTH WEST WATER. 1996. *Code of practice for bracken control*. Warrington: North West Water.

NORTH YORK MOORS NATIONAL PARK 1986. *Moorland management*. Helmsley: North York Moors National Park.

NORTH YORK MOORS NATIONAL PARK. 1991. *Moorland management programme*. Helmsley: North York Moors National Park.

NORTH YORK MOORS NATIONAL PARK. 1993. *Advice Note: bracken control, follow up treatments and after care*. Helmsley: North York Moors National Park.

PAKEMAN, R.J. & HAY, E. 1996. Heathland seed banks under bracken *Pteridium aquilinum* (L.) Kuhn and their importance for re-vegetation after bracken control. *Journal of Environmental Management*, **47**, pp 329-339.

PAKEMAN, R.J. & MARRS, R.H. 1992. The conservation value of bracken *Pteridium aquilinum* (L.) Kuhn-dominated communities in the UK, and an assessment of the ecological impact of bracken expansion or its removal. *Biological Conservation*, **62**, pp. 101-114.

PAKEMAN, R.J. & MARRS, R.H. 1993. Bracken. *Biologist*, **40**, pp. 105-109.

PAKEMAN, R.J. & MARRS, R.H. 1996. Modelling the effects of climate change on the growth of bracken (*Pteridium aquilinum*) in Britain. *Journal of Applied Ecology*, **33**, pp 561-575.

PAKEMAN, R.J., MARRS, R.H. & JACOB, P.J. 1994. A model of bracken (*Pteridium aquilinum*) growth and the effects of control strategies and changing climate. *Journal of Applied Ecology*, **31**, pp 145-154.

PAKEMAN, R.J., MARRS, R.H., HOWARD, D.C., BARR, C.J. & FULLER, R.M. 1996. The bracken problem in Great Britain: its present extent and future changes. *Applied Geography*, **16 (1)**, pp. 65-86.

PEAK DISTRICT NATIONAL PARK. 1997. *Code of practice for bracken control in the Peak District National Park*. Bakewell: Peak District National Park.

ROBERTS, J., MACDONALD, A. & WOOD-GEE, V. 1996. Bracken control. *Information and advisory note* No. 24. Battleby: Scottish Natural Heritage.

ROBINSON, R.C. 1986. Practical herbicide use for bracken control. *In*: R.T. Smith & J.A. Taylor, eds. *Bracken: Ecology, land use and control technology*. Carnforth: Parthenon Press, pp. 331-240.

ROBINSON, R.C. 1998. *Helicopter applications of asulox to bracken: drift-monitoring study for buffer-zone assessment*. York: Rhone-Poulenc.

RHONE-POULENC. 1997. *Bracken management handbook: Integrated bracken management - a guide to best practice*. Essex: Rhone-Poulenc.

RSPB. 1996. *Birds of conservation concern in the United Kingdom, Channel Islands and Isle of Man*. Sandy: RSPB

SHEAVES, B.J. & BROWN, R.W. 1995. Densities of *Ixodes ricinus* ticks (Acari: Ixodidae) on moorland vegetation communities in the UK. *Experimental & Applied Acarology*, **19**, pp. 489-497.

SMITH, R.T. & TAYLOR, J.A. eds. 1986. *Bracken: ecology, land use and control technology*. Carnforth: Parthenon Publishing.

SNOW, C.S.R. & MARRS, R.H. 1997. Restoration of *Calluna* heathland on a bracken *Pteridium*-infested site in North West England. *Biological Conservation*, **81**, pp 35-42.

TAYLOR, J. ed. 1989. *Bracken toxicity and carcinogenicity as related to animal and human health*. International Bracken Group special publication. Aberystwyth: International Bracken Group.

TAYLOR, J. 1997. Perceptions of bracken. *The Heather Trust Annual Report*. Kippen: The Heather Trust.

VARVARIGOS, P. & LAWTON, J.H. 1991. Farmers' perceptions of the scale of the bracken problem on farms in Less Favoured Areas in England and Wales. *Journal of Applied Ecology*, **28**, pp. 988-1003.

WARREN, M.S. & OATES, M.R. 1995. The importance of bracken habitats to fritillary butterflies and their management for conservation. *In*: R.T. Smith & J.A. Taylor, eds. *Bracken: An Environmental Issue*. International Bracken Group Special Publication No 2. Aberystwyth: Aberystwyth University, pp 178-181.

WATT, A.S. 1955. Bracken versus heather, a study in plant sociology. *Journal of Ecology*, **43**, pp. 490-506.

Introduction

Upland fencing is usually aimed at controlling grazing livestock, although it is also used for other purposes such as managing people and access. It is often related to nature conservation objectives, such as protecting vegetation from grazing pressure or restoring eroded areas. It can also assist with stock management over large sites, prevent damage by wild animals such as rabbits or deer, allow vegetation to recover and trees and shrubs to regenerate, and encourage stock to graze relatively unpalatable areas.

In many areas, walls have traditionally been used to control stock numbers and movement, and for biodiversity, building up delapidated walls is preferable to erecting fencing. Where this is not possible, fencing alongside walls is generally preferable to new fences.

Upland areas are highly valued for their open landscape character and recreational use. Both are easily diminished by insensitive fencing and, therefore, new fence lines are unpopular with many organisations. Some National Park Authorities, for example, have policies to resist fencing over open land. Alternatives to new fences should always be explored first, such as reducing stock, shepherding or using individual shelters for protecting trees and shrubs. Where new temporary or permanent stock proofing is still felt to be necessary, it must take into consideration potential visual impacts and effects on recreational access (Andrews & MacDonald 1996).

Many upland areas are registered common land, and the consent of the Secretary of State must be obtained for temporary or permanent fencing. There is a standard procedure to follow and applications must demonstrate the benefits of fencing. The precedent for temporary fencing to restore degraded, damaged or eroded areas has been well established, but the support of common rights holders is essential.

Siting the fence

Terrain

- It is more difficult to erect fencing over sloping and uneven ground, as more materials are needed.
- Animals can often squeeze beneath fences where dips occur, therefore gaps must be blocked with netting or post and rails.
- Sharp rises may make it easier for animals to jump the fence.
- Not siting the fence above, below or on unstable slopes will help to prolong the life of the fence.
- It is wise to try to find the best substrate. Rocky or stony areas for the straining posts should be avoided, if possible.

- If the soil is very soft (ie peaty ground) then mineral soil or rocky ground may be preferable, if available.
- Waterlogged areas may not hold the posts and should be avoided.

Land management factors

- Fencing can hinder as well as help stock movement and should be sited so that is does not unnecessarily impede existing shepherding and gathering practices.
- Where burning is conducted, the impact of fencing on the burning regime will need to be considered.

Appearance

- Where possible, the existing scale and pattern of enclosure should be maintained.
- Siting the fence along the line of existing boundaries, stream lines and breaks of slope helps to minimise the landscape impact.
- Fencing against the sky line should be avoided, if possible.
- Although it may be the most economical option, straight fences should be avoided, especially up steep slopes.
- Oblique angles should be used on steeply sloping ground wherever possible.
- A fence may produce contrasts in vegetation which in the longterm may be more obvious than the fence itself.

Recreation

- Recreational interests should be consulted where enclosures of significant size are considered in popular access areas.
- Rights of way and other similar through-routes must not be blocked and appropriate means of access will be required.
- Explaining the purpose of the enclosure, by descreet interpretative signing or leaflets at appropriate nearby points, will help visitors to understand the situation.
- Fences may displace or concentrate recreational impacts, and this may have adverse environmental or management impacts.

Biotic Factors

- It is best to avoid wild animal and stock tracks. Badgers *Meles meles* may undermine the stock proofness, as may deer in the rutting season. Stock may cause heavy grazing and poaching along fence lines.

- The tops and bases of slopes should be avoided, to limit erosion from animals and humans which may follow the fence line.

- Displaced animals may unacceptably increase the grazing pressure outside the fenced enclosure.

- Stock will still need access to water and adequate shelter in bad weather, whether inside or outside of the fenced area.

- Any fenced enclosure which animals might get into should have a gate. This will also allow vehicular access.

- Birds such as black grouse *Tetrao tetrix* and, to a lesser extent, red grouse *Lagopus lagopus* can collide with fences. Fences should not be sited in particular locations, such as following ridges, and should be positioned so that they are easily flown over without avoiding action being necessary. Attaching markers, such as the traditional twists of heather, or more modern markers such as bright orange plastic strips/nets or metal reflectors, at intervals on the top wire should help. Making the fence more visible by bringing the stock netting up to the height of the top wire (and adding a wire below to compensate) may also reduce fatalities.

- On mires, treated timbers can leach chemical preservatives into the system and cause loss of *Sphagnum*. Treated timbers should not be used in sensitive locations.

Snow

- Drifting snow can break the fence. Site away from hollows and breaks of slope to avoid snow drifts, or seek local advice about where snow accumulates.

- Avoid acute corners in the fence where snow and stock may gather as the stock may be trapped by snow lie.

- Close netting or mesh gathers more snow. Single wire fencing is therefore preferable.

- High tensile wire fencing is better than mild steel because it uses fewer posts, farther apart. High tensile electric fencing may be an alternative.

Choosing the most appropriate type of fence

To choose the most appropriate type of fence, it is necessary to consider the type of stock and vegetation involved, the terrain and ease of access to the area, and the effects of climate (including snow lie, see above). On top of these considerations are the cost of labour and materials, the intended life span of the fence, and the maintenance and appearance of the fence.

Stock proof fencing will vary depending on the type of stock involved and whether they are to be kept in or out. Different types of fence for different kinds of stock are discussed below. The effectiveness of stock fencing is dependent on the contentedness of the stock as much as the competence of the fence. Content animals with sufficient grazing have less inducement to break out. However, in some instances, fencing is aimed at forcing animals to eat coarse vegetation.

Stock are likely to break out of enclosures when:

- insufficient feed or grazing is present;
- the grazing is better on the other side of the fence, and they force their heads through the fence;
- they seek shade in hot conditions;
- certain mountain and rare breeds are kept, which are more likely to jump;
- they are being herded by dogs;
- they are kept on their own and get bored.

The type of vegetation and the terrain to be fenced will also determine the requirements. For example, when fencing trees or shrubs on difficult terrain, it may be more effective and economical to use individual fences or tree protectors.

Concerning access to the area, issues to consider include the following:

- getting tools and materials to and from the site;
- the weight of materials;
- high tensile wire is much lighter than stock netting;
- size of stock netting rolls (some rolls are too big and heavy for people to carry);
- electric fencing is light and cheap but supply of power and maintenance in remote areas may be difficult;
- solar and wind power may be an option.

Types of fencing

Post and wire strained fencing

This is a very common form of fencing consisting of wire stretched between straining posts with intermittent stakes to stiffen the fence and keep the wires apart. It is:

- easy to erect;
- versatile;

- relatively low cost;
- good for covering long distances;
- best suited to smooth terrain;
- less easy and more expensive if the terrain is uneven and/or has many changes in direction.

Types of post and wire fences include:

- wire with stock netting - good, stock proof fence - sheep and cattle;
- three line wires - cattle only - conforms to MAFF specifications;
- five line wires - cattle and sheep;
- seven line wires - cattle and sheep;
- high tensile seven line wires - very strong stock proof fence - conforms to MAFF specifications;
- rabbit fencing - wire and rabbit meshing - cattle, sheep and rabbits (see Information note 8 Rabbit Control);
- deer fencing - 1.85 m fence of line with netting - deer, sheep and goats;
  - wire and netting with rabbit mesh below - deer, sheep, goats and rabbits (see Information note 8 Rabbit Control).

Post and rail fencing

This type of fencing is:

- not usually sheep proof;
- adequate for light use with cattle;
- usually amenity fencing.

Electric fencing

Commonly used as temporary fencing, and useful for managing open habitats and zoning grazing. It is:

- used as a psychological barrier;
- lighter and cheaper than other fencing;
- liable to short out on growing vegetation or snow;
- likely to need frequent supervision and maintenance;
- easily breached by stock if inoperative.

Types of electric fence include:

- cattle fence - temporary single wired fence for cattle control only - can be used to compartmentalise grazing;

- reel system fence - similar to cattle fence - capability of more than single wire;
  - single strand - cattle and horses;
  - three strand - cattle, horses, sheep and goats;
- electric netting - temporary - different heights for rabbits/sheep/horses;
- scare wire - addition of single live wire to existing stock proof fence;
  - prolongs life of fence by lessening damage by animals;
  - located on the interior of the fence for stock and on the exterior for wild animals such as deer or goats;
- permanent five strand - sheep/cattle;
  - high tensile version for extreme conditions.

A comprehensive guide to fencing, including siting, choice of fence and construction details is given in Agate (1986).

Examples of upland fencing specifications

Five line strained wire fencing

Strained line wire fencing should be not less than 1.05 m high from ground level to the top wire and can be constructed to the following specifications.

- Preservation Treatment

  All timber should be pressure impregnated with Tanalith C.
  Note: All timber should be dried prior to treatment in order to gain maximum penetration.

- Straining Posts

  Straining posts should be equivalent in strength and durability to:
  - ❑ 125 mm top diameter round timber, or
  - ❑ 125 × 125 mm sawn timber,

  and at least 2.17 m long when not set in concrete and at least 1.87 m long when set in concrete. Straining posts should be spaced at centres appropriate for the ground conditions and in any case not exceeding 100 m where mild steel line wire is used or not exceeding 200 m for high tensile line wire.

- Struts

  Struts should be equivalent in strength and durability to:
  - ❑ 80 mm top diameter round timber, or
  - ❑ 75 × 75 mm sawn timber,

  and at least 1.9 m long when not set in concrete and at least 1.6 m long when set in concrete.

- Intermediate Posts

  Intermediate posts should be equivalent in strength and durability to:
  - ❑ 80 mm top diameter round timber, or
  - ❑ 75 × 75 mm sawn timber,

  and at least 1.72 m long.
  Intermediate posts should be at centres not exceeding 3 m.

- Line Wire

  Wire should be galvanised and equivalent in strength and durability to:
  - ❑ 4 mm steel wire, or
  - ❑ 2.5 mm mild steel 2 ply twisted barbed wire, or
  - ❑ oval section 13 gauge barbed wire.

Woven wire stockproof fencing

Woven wire fencing should be not less than 1.05 m high from ground level to the top wire and can be constructed to the following specifications.

- Preservation Treatment

  All timber should be pressure impregnated with Tanalith C.
  Note: All timber should be dried prior to treatment in order to gain maximum penetration.

- Straining Posts

  Straining posts should be equivalent in strength and durability to:
  - ❑ 125 mm top diameter round timber, or
  - ❑ 100 × 100 mm, or equivalent cross section sawn timber,

  and at least 2.15 m long when not set in concrete and at least 1.85 m long when set in concrete. Straining posts should be spaced at centres appropriate for the ground conditions and in any case not exceeding 100 m where mild steel line wire is used, or not exceeding 200 m for high tensile line wire.

- Struts

  Struts should be equivalent in strength and durability to:
  - ❑ 80 mm top diameter round timber, or
  - ❑ 75 × 75 mm sawn timber,

  and at least 1.9 m long when not set in concrete and at least 1.6 m long when set in concrete.

- Intermediate Posts

Intermediate posts should be equivalent in strength and durability to:
- ❑ 80 mm top diameter round timber, or
- ❑ 75 × 75 mm sawn timber,

and at least 1.8 m long where 1.15 m woven wire is used, otherwise not less than 1.7 m. Intermediate posts should be at centres not exceeding 3 m.

- Woven wire

Woven wire should be galvanised and should comply with British Standard (BS) 4102. Where the width of the woven wire selected is less than 1.05 m the required fence height should be obtained by fixing plain or barbed wire above or below the woven wire. The use of heavyweight woven wire is recommended in areas subject to atmospheric pollution.

Woven wire BS reference: C8/115/30
C6/90/30
C8/80/15 OR C8/80/30

- Barbed wire

This should be galvanised barbed wire to BS 12.5 g two strand.

- Plain wire

This should be galvanised plain wire 10 g (3.15 mm).

- Staples

These should be galvanised wire staples 40 mm × 4 mm (8 g).

One strand of plain wire should be fixed 2" (50 mm) above ground level. The bottom of the woven wire should be fixed 2" (50 mm) above the plain wire, ie 4" (100 mm) above ground level. The bottom strand of any wire fence deteriorates most quickly and a single strand below the woven wire can be replaced cheaply and quickly, thereby prolonging the life of the fence.

One strand of barbed wire should be fixed 4" (100 mm) above the top of woven wire. The wire should be properly strained and fastened to the posts with galvanised staples. To allow for future adjustments and to prevent damage to the galvanising, staples should be driven in obliquely but not driven fully home.

Bibliography & further reading

AGATE, E. 1986. *Fencing: a practical handbook.* British Trust for Conservation Volunteers.

ANDREWS, J. & MACDONALD, A. 1996. Fences and upland conservation management. *Information and Advisory Note* No. 59. Battleby: Scottish Natural Heritage.

MAFF. 1984. *Electric fencing for sheep.* London: Leaflet 709. HMSO.

MAFF. 1996. *Fencing to prevent damage to crops by rabbits.* York: MAFF Central Science Laboratory.

PEPPER, H.W. 1992. *Forest fencing.* London: HMSO.

Rabbit grazing

The rabbit *Oryctolagus cuniculus*, which was introduced to Britain in the twelfth century, can be a significant grazer in some areas. Rabbits became a major agricultural pest until myxomatosis almost wiped out the population in 1954. This decline had a dramatic impact on certain grassland types, especially over limestone, where rabbit grazing often maintained the conservation value. However, in many areas rabbits have since returned to, or close to, their pre-myxomatosis levels and can adversly affect valuable wildlife habitats. Plant communities can be prevented from flowering and species may be lost, for example in limestone pavement and grassland areas. The natural regeneration of trees and shrubs can also be prevented by rabbit grazing. They are common on land grazed by domestic stock and therefore their impacts are additional to those of grazing livestock. Their populations tend to fluctuate from year to year and this should be taken into account when considering agricultural stocking rates. The advent of the disease, Viral Haemorrhagic Disease (VHD) may influence rabbit numbers in the future, although to what extent is not fully known.

Rabbit control is an important issue in nature conservation and should be considered in any grazing strategy. The main problem faced by conservationists is that rabbits are difficult to control.

Rabbit control methodology

Non-lethal control methods: barriers

Rabbits may be fenced in or out depending on the prevailing circumstances. Rabbit fencing is based upon the specifications for post and wire fencing given in Information Note 7, with 31 mm, 18 gauge mesh held to line wires above and below by netting rings. Barbed wire may be used as the top strand if stock is also relevant. A further mid-wire is also recommended for additional strength for stock fencing. The bottom 150 mm of the netting may either be turned outwards at an angle of 45° to the vertical and buried in a shallow trench or be laid out at 90° to lay flat on the ground. This should be pegged out with wire loops and turfs may be placed on top. In all cases the netting should face in the direction from which the rabbits are expected to dig. Electric net fencing (Flexinet) can also be effective particularly where there is a temporary need to exclude rabbits.

Individual tree saplings may be protected using tree guards if fencing is inappropriate or unfeasible.

Lethal direct control methods

In certain situations the use of lethal control methods for rabbits may be unavoidable. In situations where rabbits are causing damage to crops, pasture, animal or human foodstuffs there may be a legal responsibility for landowners to eradicate rabbits. Severe degradation of a site's conservation value may also warrant such action. When considering a methodology, efficacy and humaneness must be taken into consideration. Where rabbit control is required, local landowners and farmers may be a useful source of advice when seeking persons who are able to undertake such control.

The optimum time to commence any form of direct control is when the population is at its lowest, prior to the breeding season. A concerted effort should therefore be made between the months of November and March.

Gassing

Gassing is considered to be the most effective direct control method where burrows are accessible. After a single treatment, rabbit numbers can be reduced by as much as 90%.

This method involves the use of either sodium cyanide powder (marketed by ICI as Cymag) or aluminium phosphide pellets (Talunex). These produce, respectively, hydrogen cyanide gas and hydrogen phosphate gas, are both lethal to rabbits. In both methods the chemicals react with moisture and air to produce the gas. Use of both methods is extremely hazardous and great care must be taken to ensure the safety of humans and wildlife. Aluminium phosphide should only be employed by an operator trained in its use. This method is purportedly safer and quicker than using sodium cyanide.

The powder or pellets is/are introduced at the entrance to a burrow. The other exits to the burrow must be blocked and made sufficiently airtight that there is no risk of a major gas escape. Gas must not be employed where the porosity of the soil or substrata will allow leakage of the gas. This is most apparent in limestone areas where gas could leak into cave and ground water systems.

Shooting

Shooting with a shotgun or .22 rifle is a widely used, though relatively inefficient, method of dealing with surface-living rabbits. Shooting at night with lights (lamping) is considered a more effective method. Both methods are confined to authorised persons, ie owners, occupiers and those possessing the shooting rights.

Possession of firearms, shotguns and ammunition is all governed by legislation which should be consulted (see Parkes 1991).

Snares

Snares should be set on rabbit runs away from cover, preferably on windy, moonlit nights, lacking frost. The 1981 Wildlife and Countryside Act prohibits the use of self-locking snares except under licence and requires that other types should be inspected every 24 hours. Snares should not be sited where livestock or domestic animals have access.

Traps

Spring Traps

Spring traps must be of a type approved by legislation for use on rabbits (see Crofts and Jefferson 1994). They must, according to law, be placed in burrows, at least within the overhang of the hole, to reduce the risk of catching other species. This method of trapping is labour intensive, requires considerable skill and is not widely used.

Drop Traps (Drop Boxes)

This is a much more effective method of trapping with consistent results. Drop traps exploit the behaviour of the rabbits, catching them while they move from rough pasture to more fertile grassland to feed at night. Drop traps consist of a tunnel, below which is a box. The floor of the tunnel acts as a trap door letting the rabbit fall in the box for retrieval later (see Figure IN8.1). The specification of a wooded trap is given below, but metal designs also exist.

It is a legal requirement that the traps are checked daily, but to set the trap at night and check first thing in the morning is probably more acceptable.

Rabbit drop trap specification

- Traps should be placed about 75 m apart.
- Where possible traps should be placed in the paths of identified existing rabbit runs.
- Traps should be dug in at the same time as rabbit mesh is erected, so rabbits will continue to use the same runs.
- Traps should be dug in so that the top is flush with the ground surface.
- Traps need to be locked shut for a period while the rabbits become used to using the tunnels.
- Trap bottoms should be porous to prevent water build up.
- Trap doors should be made loose fitting to allow for swelling of the wood in damp conditions. There can also be a problem with doors freezing shut in winter.
- Correct building specifications are important:
  - ❑ the correct gauge wood must be used to make sure the trap is not too springy or fast acting;
  - ❑ tunnel length must be sufficient for rabbits to be fully inside before the flap falls.
- If wood preserver is used, try to avoid a strong vapoured brand. 'Bartoline' shed and fence treatment is ideal, being harmless to plants and animals.

(Adapted from *Focus on rabbits* in the Craven Wildlife Enhancement Scheme newsletter).

Ferreting

This is a useful follow-up method, or for small scale problems. It is advisable to allow at least a week before ferreting in a gassed area. Ferrets are used to bolt rabbits which are either shot as they emerge or caught in nets and killed. It is possible that somebody local will be able to carry out the work, often just for the rabbits caught.

Long Netting

Where rabbits are abundant, large numbers may be taken in long nets. These nets are usually 45 to 135 m long, 1 m wide with a 5 cm mesh. Nets are run out at night, downwind from feeding rabbits, about 13 m from the nearest cover. There is a line along the top of each net which is supported by 1 m sticks at 4 m intervals (smaller hazel pegs are also effective and lighter to transport). The slack of the net is allowed to lie loosely on the ground weighted with a leaded line below. Once the net is erected rabbits can be driven into the net at speed by dogs and beaters, or more quietly at night by herding rabbits toward the net with a slow zig-zag walk. Netting can be used in conjunction with ferreting by setting long nets around and across a warren. Ferrets are then sent down the burrows and the rabbit are caught escaping.

'Trammel' nets work in a similar way to long nets though two nets are involved. A fine mesh front net is pulled by the fleeing rabbit through a hole in the much coarser netting behind. This creates a 'purse net' effect making it difficult for the rabbit to escape.

Whichever method is utilised, care must be taken to minimise the impact on the nature conservation resource. The eventual method chosen should account for this, as no method will fit all situations. All methods should be practised in as humane a manner possible and discretion should be paramount where public attention may be drawn to the operation.

Adapted from Crofts and Jefferson (1994).

Bibliography & further reading

CROFTS, A. & JEFFERSON, R.G. 1994. eds. *The lowland grassland management handbook.* Peterborough: English Nature and The Wildlife Trusts.

MAFF CENTRAL SCIENCE LABORATORY. 1996. *Fencing to prevent damage to crops by rabbits.* York: MAFF Central Science Laboratory.

PARKES, C. 1991. *Law of the countryside.* 4th edition. Bakewell: Association of Countryside Rangers.

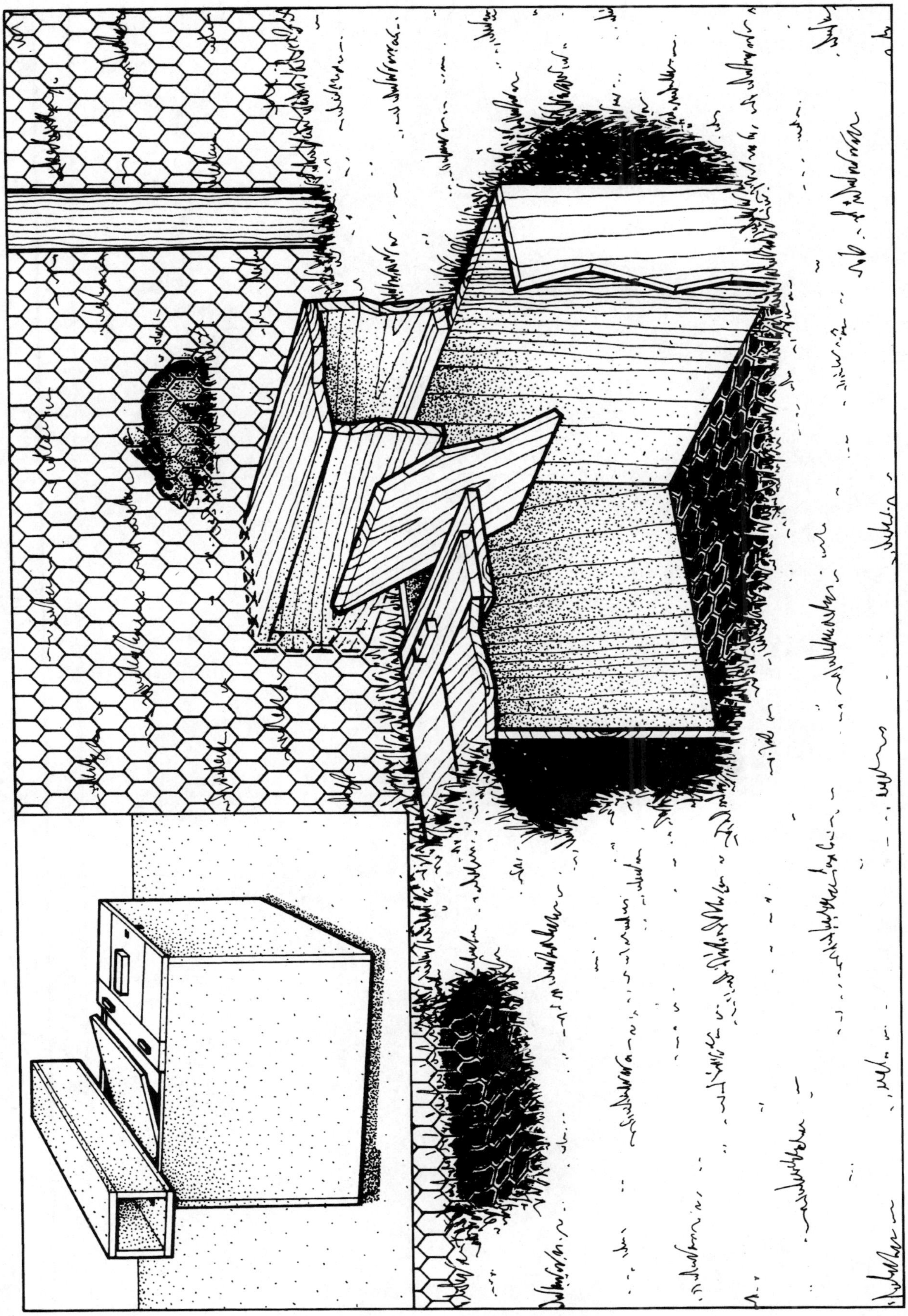

Figure IN8.1. Rabbit drop traps (drop boxes)

Background

Moorland gripping is the practice of digging ditches with the intention of draining wet areas of heath and blanket bog. Gripping was especially prevalent in the uplands of northern England from the 1960s to the mid-1980s and was often grant-aided. In the Yorkshire Dales about 60% of the peat moorlands in the National Park were subjected to machine gripping. Gripping generally consists of a herring bone pattern of ditches cut into the bog at approximately 20 m intervals.

Apart from the obvious destruction of vegetation caused by gripping, drainage can change the vegetation structure and composition, and the exposed peat surfaces are extremely susceptible to erosion. Subsequent increased runoff can greatly affect flow downstream of the catchment. Increased siltation and a greater likelihood of flash flooding are both associated with an increase in runoff. During dry periods reduced flow can be caused by the bog having reduced capacity to retain water.

Objectives of grip blocking:

- to restore natural drainage patterns;
- to encourage revegetation of the bog surface;
- to reduce erosion;
- to minimise the knock-on effect of hydraulic change downstream.

Achieved by:

- blocking eroding grips (and those feeding into hagged areas);
- blocking 'active' grips that are maintaining themselves;
- blocking grips across level and basin/raised mire areas;
- allowing grips to infill naturally where possible;
- designing works to avoid danger to stock.

Construction

Dams should be constructed using a plug of peat and retaining the surface vegetation where possible. This will allow the vegetation plug to knit together with adjacent vegetation, thus creating a stronger structure. Material should be scooped out of the adjacent ground immediately up slope of the dam, but must not be taken from undisturbed bog. The peat should not be allowed to dry out before it is well compacted into the grip. The breadth of the dam should normally be one to two times the width of the grip (but more where the grip is deep). The dam height should normally be level with, or slightly higher than the surrounding vegetation surface. It is important that water behind the dam should not exceed a depth of 60 cm, as this would create a potential hazard for livestock. In this situation dam height should not exceed 60 cm. Overflow seepage should be directed laterally away from the grip into low points or runnels, where they exist. Dams in wider more eroded grips may be strengthened by the insertion of timber posts or boards, with peat compacted behind. Boards may also be required to stop leakage in the less consolidated peats of raised mires.

Situation

Dams should always be included at the uphill end of a grip system, not just in the highly eroding middle or lower sections. They should be spaced so that the water level reaches the base of the next dam up slope or at 10 -20 m intervals where the ground is level or shallow sloping. On steeper ground this may not be practical, and here high feeder grips should be blocked so as to slow down the water flow. Wherever possible grips should be blocked at the junction with natural drainage runnels. This is preferable to blocking at regular intervals, as it restores natural flow patterns.

Practicalities

Dams should be built in the autumn and should start to revegetate in the spring. Use of excavation machines is likely to be cost effective for any significant number of dams in one area. This should be a low ground pressure, tracked excavator to avoid damage to the vegetation (a Kubota 151 on 60 cm wide tracks has been used in the North Pennines). Access for machines is easier and less damaging at drier times, but the peat may not be wet enough to compact well during these periods. A balance therefore must be sought, to minimise damage while installing effective dams. Hand working is likely to be more appropriate for inserting a small number of dams or for work in steep or eroded situations too dangerous for machines. Care must always be taken to minimise hazards to livestock and wildlife.

Further reading

BARRETT, J. 1997. Moor gripping in the uplands. *Enact*, **5 (1)**, pp. 16-17.

BROOKS, S. & STONEMAN, R. 1997. *Conserving bogs: the management handbook.* Edinburgh: The Stationery Office.

MAWBY, F. 1997. Peat dams. *Enact*, **5 (1)**, pp. 18-19.

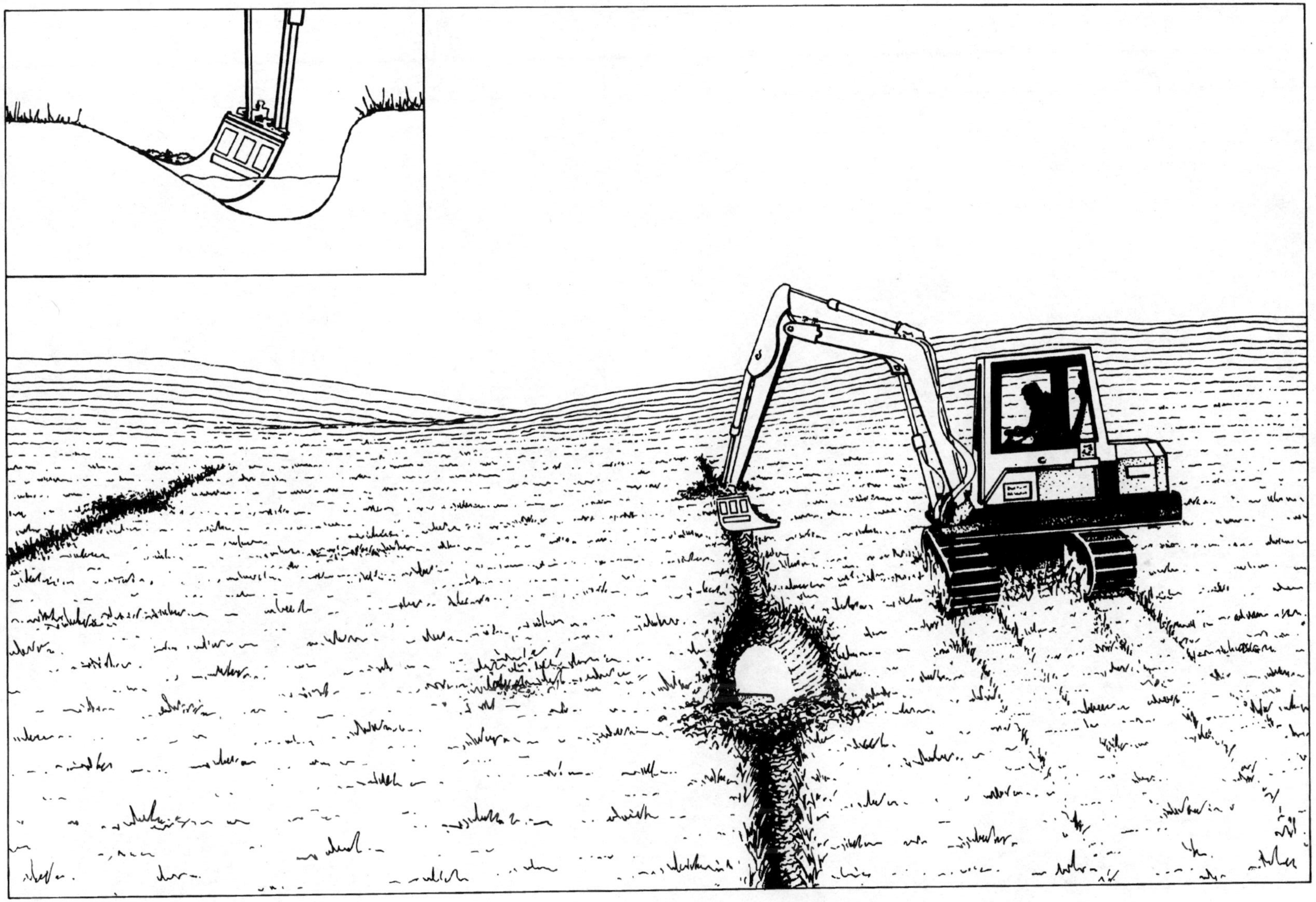

Figure IN 9.1. Moorland grip blocking

Material is scooped out up slope of the proposed obstruction to form the dam itself, but must not be taken from undisturbed bog. As the use of machinery can seriously damage bogs and wet heath, alternative methods should always be considered.

Information note 10 Managing public access and footpaths in the uplands

Introduction

The uplands are popular areas for public access and recreation. They are extremely valuable for providing enjoyment and appreciation of the countryside. In some areas visitor pressure may cause problems for wildlife, landscape interests or land managers, but generally the effects are localised. Public access can take place without causing problems, provided that it is well planned and managed. Where there are localised problems, these can usually be resolved, through the cooperation of interested parties and the type of management being related to the type of access and use, and the area concerned.

Much of upland England is already open to the public to varying degrees and appropriate management here can benefit all concerned. In other areas public access is not permitted, but the extent of the uplands open to the public will increase as a result of the Countryside and Rights of Way Act.

Managing public access is a well documented subject. The detail covered in this Information note merely aims to provide some practical guidance on methods which could be employed.

Why access management is necessary

Management of access may be deemed necessary for varying reasons, for example where:

- areas/species that are susceptible to damage/disturbance need to be protected from public interference;
- public safety may be jeopardised;
- an area of relative seclusion may lose its attraction if over used;
- erosion of a footpath necessitates re-routing of the path to a more sustainable position.

Once the specific motives for management have been identified, then strategies for the implementation of the management can be considered.

Car parking

Practical control of access in many instances begins in the car park. Ease of access to a site is often the most influential factor in determining visitor popularity. In the car orientated environment of today, car parking is a primary consideration for many visitors. The size of a car park dictates the approximate number of visitors during peak periods. This is especially true of nature reserves, view points and other areas of high interest.

Provision of 'lay-by' type car parking along a linear feature (eg a lake shore) will spread visitor pressure. The provision of larger car parks at selected sites and the absence of 'lay-bys' means intensified visitor pressure in those areas, but also containment to specified sites where remediation of adverse effects may be more easily implemented. In the same way, development of a new car park at a similar, though less used, site may ease pressure from a 'honey pot' location and spread visitor impacts. It must be remembered that if areas are to be formally turned into car parks, planning permission may be needed.

Car parking should ideally be on free-draining soils, to reduce the cost of resurfacing. Care should be taken to minimise the visual impact of the site and screening with trees should be considered. Maximisation of space is important, but this should not be at the expense of visual acceptance. Straight lines of vehicles will look out of place in a rural environment. Small enclosed bays are often more visually acceptable though they are difficult to police and may encourage theft or vandalism (Vickery 1995).

A proportion of spaces should also be specifically allocated for people with special needs such as wheelchair users or visitors with walking difficulties, located near facilities such as toilets and visitor centres and in more scenic parts of the car park. The parking spaces must be wide enough to allow easy movement in and out of the car (minimum width of 3 m, preferably 3.6 m - a standard bay is 2.4 m) and with level access to footpaths (Vickery 1995).

Owing to the significance of the car park as the initial visitor access point, guidance from the car park is an important measure in controlling the movements of visitors from the outset. Strategies for this type of manipulation are discussed below.

Zoning

Zoning is the prioritisation of areas for visitors, either by direct or indirect manipulation. These areas can be represented by parts of a National Park or even county, or small areas of a nature reserve with different access requirements/needs. An example is the designation of quiet areas within the Lake District National Park Authority's policies. Zoning can involve encouragement of visitors to use a certain area, as much as discouragement. It may be that the only way to divert attention from a site would be to offer an alternative, comparative site elsewhere.

In the Derbyshire Dales National Nature Reserve (NNR) zoning is practised on a sliding scale by the amount of publicity and maintenance given to each Dale. Lathkill Dale is advertised in the local press and visitors are actively encouraged by ease of access and the availability of interpretive material (there are eight leaflets published about this dale). Situated close to Bakewell, this is an ideal place of focus for people when out for a day in the Dales. Cressbrook Dale has a public access path running through it. Paths are maintained and waymarking is provided, making access reasonably easy. Monks Dale is a more isolated valley and attracts fewer visitors. Here the path can be quite difficult to walk on as it passes along the edge of the stream. The path has deliberately not been improved and there is little or no publicity of the Dale because it has been decided that increased recreational use of this dale will not be actively encouraged. The fourth dale in the suite has access by permit only, and completes the range of accessibility from easy to less so (B le Bas, pers comm).

Zoning within smaller areas is also useful. Zoning of access on a reserve can be achieved by active manipulation (eg waymarkers, good paths, interpretive material) and also by inactivity (eg non-removal of scrub/undergrowth, leaving paths to deteriorate).

The zoning of recreational activities and wildlife interests is a well practised formula for inland water bodies. Sizable water bodies can be compartmentalised to allow for recreational activities to be zoned from 'noisy to quiet', therefore minimalising conflicts between users. Refugia can also be created to maintain a site's wildlife interest, though wildlife often does not comply with boundaries and time tables. On smaller water bodies zoning may prove more of a problem. Where there is a series of smaller water bodies, for example disused gravel pits, individual water bodies could cater for different activities. However, zoning may be difficult to police and may need wardening.

Interpretation

Interpretive material supplied at a discrete site, such as on a nature reserve, or before a site visit, can be a valuable tool in influencing visitor movements and activities. This can be done in a number of ways, from simply showing the main routes of access at the entrance to a site, to directing people toward areas of special interest. The main uses of interpretation in visitor management are:

- to direct people to areas where the manager would prefer them to go;
- to try to prevent people from visiting areas that are sensitive, or where the manager does not want them to go;
- to provide information on safety and fulfill public liability requirements;
- to increase awareness and a sense of responsibility toward a site or area;
- to enhance the enjoyment of an area.

Interpretive material can come in many different forms. **Information boards** are the most often used and can be very useful in directing the movement of people at a site. As mentioned above, even a simple map showing the main routes around a site is often enough to keep people from wandering. Further explanation of conservation issues and reasons for not straying from waymarked areas are also very effective. Signs and information boards should be made as unobtrusive as possible and usually confined to the site entrance, preferably where visitors leave the car park. Elsewhere signs should be avoided, unless absolutely necessary.

Leaflets detailing general or specific information about a site can be used in a similar manner to information boards. They are especially useful when dealing with visitors with specialist interests. Leaflets about birdwatching, botany and geology can be used to direct visitors to areas chosen by the manager, and to try to deflect interest away from sensitive areas which may suffer from increased visitor pressure. Leaflets of this kind are very helpful in situations where access is limited to permit only. Those applying for permits will probably have some special interest in the site and additional information can be sent with the permit. As well as information detailing where to go, safety information can also be included.

Codes of Conduct are often employed to raise awareness and as a means of access management. These can be conveyed in all forms of interpretive material and can be targeted to certain users and certain recreational activities. Dartmoor National Park Authority, for example, produces Codes of Conduct for many specialist user groups to try to strike a balance between recreational access and wildlife interests.

Nature trails can also be used to concentrate interest, and direct the movement of visitors. At a privately owned reserve such as Upper Teesdale NNR, where access is by footpath only, the provision of nature trails and the explanation that all interest features can be seen from the path helps to ensure trespass is kept to a minimum (C. McCarty, pers comm).

Footpaths

The provision of footpaths is one of the simplest and most effective forms of access management. Many statutory rights of way already exist in the uplands and it is important to remember that there is a legal procedure for altering them. Information on public rights of way is available from County and District councils and National Park Authorities. Societies such as Ramblers Associations will also have information.

In upland areas especially, the majority of visitors will tend to follow recognisable routes. The provision of an easier walking surface than that of the surrounding land (eg a flagged path over wet peat, or a pitched path in a boulder field) will also encourage visitors not to stray. However, the purpose of constructing paths in the uplands is to protect or repair the vegetation - it is not to make access easier, although indirectly this may occur. The problems associated with footpath construction, maintenance and user management are discussed below.

Waymarking

Waymarking is very much a part of footpath management and is a useful technique for preventing accidental digressions from the intended route. Care must be taken not to allow waymarkers to become obtrusive or be placed unnecessarily. Many valley paths across agricultural land are not well defined on the ground. In these instances waymarking allows continued use of a right of way which may otherwise fall into disuse, especially for people without a map.

Waymarks can consist of coloured **dots** or **logos**, displayed on signs, fences, walls and so on, or **arrows** dictating changes in direction. Standard waymark arrows recommended by the Countryside Agency indicate both direction and status of the right of way. A yellow arrow indicates a footpath and a blue arrow a bridlepath. A white arrow indicates a permitted route. Waymarkers should, wherever possible, be placed at or on existing structures, such as stiles or fences and only when absolutely necessary should structures be created for this purpose.

Waymarking in upland areas is often deemed unnecessary by some hill users, who consider a thorough knowledge of navigation techniques a prerequisite to leaving the valley floor. One method of upland waymarking used in the Lake District and other areas, is the **cairn** (pile of stones). Traditionally these marked the tops of passes and high points along routes. Recreational walking has produced a multitude of modern cairns that are often obtrusive and in some cases misleading. Strategically placed cairns can be employed to direct users on to certain path lines and can be a great asset in combatting footpath erosion. Other types of waymarking include the discreet use of boulders, vegetation, and so on. However, in upland areas no waymarking should be the general policy.

Wardening

In certain situations and for certain access management strategies the deployment of wardening staff may be necessary. At Upper Teesdale NNR in the Pennines, wardens are deployed at peak visitor times, in an advisory capacity and to discourage trespass of visitors onto sensitive land. Voluntary wardening staff may be used.

In Dartmoor National Park emphasis is placed upon guided walks for the public led by National Park Wardens. By highlighting and publicising the walks, many visitors get to know certain areas chosen by the Park Authorities. In this way the public's attention is focused on these areas when independent visits are planned.

Public access management plans and access agreements

This can be a useful way of balancing the requirements of all parties involved. It is a consultative method, whereby all parties with an interest in the access rights of a certain area agree to an Access Management Plan, which then becomes the basis for an Access Agreement. To be successful it has to offer potential benefits to all parties (landowners, farmers, conservationists and those involved in recreation) and recognise that each has a legitimate interest in the area. All parties involved should have an increased awareness of each other's position and recognise the common goals of maintaining the area's interest features. Direct involvement of all parties in the plan should reassure each that they can safeguard the qualities that are important to them.

The key to these plans is to include provision for access points, car parks and the other people management mechanisms discussed previously.

Constructing and maintaining footpaths in the uplands

This Information note sets out to cover the basic principles of constructing and maintaining paths in upland settings, including types of path and suggestions for sighting and remediation. Thorough coverage of this subject is given in Davies and Loxham (1996). A comprehensive guide to general footpath issues, construction and maintenance in both the uplands and the lowlands is given in Agate (1996). Visitor pressure has increased substantially since the 1960s and footpath erosion is a problem in all upland areas of England.

Constructing footpaths

Methods for footpath construction can be split into two main categories: paths over rocky substrates, as in the Lake District, and those over deep peat deposits, as in the Dark Peak area of the Peak District and across the Pennines. The two strategies will be dealt with separately.

Paths over rocky substrates

The two main methods of path construction over this kind of substrate are **aggregate paths and stone pitching.**

Aggregate paths can appear naturally, when erosion takes the walking surface down to the mineral soil. They can also be constructed by the import of aggregate from other sources. These paths are often self sustaining at lower gradients where water erosion is not serious. Aggregate paths are best used:

- on flat or sloping ground with an angle of less than 15°;
- when linking steeper sections of a route;
- at lower levels (valleys);
- where damage requires hard surfacing.

Where aggregate is imported to a site, it should always be of a compatible colour and geological type (and therefore of the same pH) to that of the surrounding country rock. Where an aggregate path is constructed from scratch then a 'cut and fill' method is used. Here the width of path is excavated and an appropriate aggregate is then in-filled.

Stone pitching is the main technique for footpath construction on steep ground in rocky areas. This is an old technique of 'laying stones in a random manner, to create a series of small irregular steps which blend naturally into the landscape and do not look like a uniform staircase' (Davies & Loxham 1996). Materials should be gathered en route, and a good route should ensure a healthy supply of suitable stone is available. Nature conservation issues must be taken into consideration when collecting material, as must the aesthetic value of the site, ie leaving visual scars where material is gathered from.

Paths over peat

Path construction on deep peat (over 50 cm) is difficult because of its poor structure and the often waterlogged condition of the soil. This is most apparent in the bog systems which cover large areas of the northern uplands in the Pennines and north Peak District. The wet nature of the peat and the fragility of the overlying bog vegetation make these areas very susceptible to damage from even low numbers of walkers. Once bare areas appear in wet peat due to trampling, the rate of spread can be enormous, with walkers trying to stay on the drier vegetated edges. Wherever possible, new paths should not be constructed over peat.

Due to the high nature conservation value of these areas, great care must be taken not to upset the hydrological systems of the area. This means that drainage to facilitate path construction is out of the question.

Box IN10.1 General guidelines for path repair over peat

Any path repair seeking to prevent further erosion/widening or gully formation should:

- Remedy and/or inhibit further erosion.
- Integrate with and enhance the landscape.
- Be consistent with the ethos of a trail passing through wild country.
- Reduce visually intrusive impacts of earlier management.
- Be durable or offer relatively low level and inexpensive maintenance.
- Float on the peat surface, the principle being that the weight of the path and the people is spread over a wide area so that the repair does not sink.
- Follow desire lines and be smoother to walk on than any alternative beside the path and then separate the boot from the vegetated or bare peat surface.
- Remain above the water table.
- Seek to retain any remnant vegetation and encourage the revegetation of bare peat.
- Try to arrest water flow.
- Be carefully surveyed in the wettest of conditions.

Taken from Davies and Loxham (1996).

The main forms of path construction/repair on deep peat are **floated aggregate paths, 'causey'** or **'flagged' paths** and a relatively new technique called **soil reorganisation**. As well as these methods, **pitched paths, stepping stones** and **boardwalks** are also used.

Floated aggregate paths consist of aggregate filling a shallow trench, lined with a layer of man-made geo-textile or filament matting. Matting is used to combat the sinkage of parts of the path into the peat, spreading the pressure over a wide surface. The aggregate usually consists of a coarse sub-base covered above with smaller stones. Three-metre wide fabric is usually used, though the finished path need not be the full width of the fabric. A camber should always be constructed into the path surface to facilitate drainage. On steeper slopes a semi-pitched path can be constructed over the matting, using the aggregate as filling between the larger 'faced' stones.

Advantages of aggregate paths:

- a sound and proven technique;
- they can carry considerable load;

- they are smoother than the surrounding terrain and therefore more attractive to walkers than the vegetation and peat.

Disadvantages of aggregate paths:

- the paths can be uniform and road-like in character if the material and design are not carefully chosen;

- the technique is expensive and labour intensive - further damage and disturbance may be caused by the use of heavy machinery;

- the method introduces man-made materials into blanket peat areas which can become exposed at a later date;

- these paths often require regular maintenance and renewed aggregate as water flow removes material.

The construction of **'causey'** or **'flagged' paths** is a recent revival of a traditional technique used in the Pennines and North Yorkshire. A simple technique, it involves the laying of large flat 'flag' type stones over the peat surface, end-to-end. This can be an aesthetically acceptable method where path construction avoids straight lines and exhibits short sight lines. Flags are laid directly onto the peat/vegetation surface except where the ground is extremely wet. In these situations chestnut palings bound with polypropylene chord can be used to disperse the load over a wider area. Aggregate has also been used as an underlayer but should not be required for anything but extremely wet conditions. Flags should be laid so each abuts the next. This helps to stabilise the walking surface and prevent the possibility of flags sinking below the surface.

Ideally flags would be transported to the site by helicopter, minimising handling, facilitating rapid construction and, on large scale projects, being competitive in price to other approaches. The material used for the flags should always be compatible with the surrounding geology of an area. The use of flagging from the floors of old mills is in common practice, though quarried stone is readily available (see Figure 5.2).

Box IN10.2 Advantages and disadvantages of 'flagged' paths

Advantages of 'causey' or 'flagged' paths:

- The path is easily and fairly rapidly laid.
- It is a traditional and durable method.
- The finished surface is smoother and firmer than the surrounding terrain and is used by walkers.
- Requires relatively low maintenance.
- Requires no imported man-made materials.
- Maturation helps the path blend unobtrusively as the colour of the flags darkens and the vegetation covers the edges.
- There is minimum intervention with the disturbance of the hydrology and vegetation during construction.

Disadvantages of 'causey' or 'flagged' paths:

- They have a very defined, uniform and delineated feel which some people find alien and aesthetically unacceptable in broad and open landscapes.
- Flags are heavy, bulky and pose logistical storage, transport and path-making problems.
- Flags have serious health and safety implications, especially concerning strain-related injuries.
- The long-term success of flags is uncertain.
- Flags are unsuitable for steep slopes in excess of 12-15°.
- It is a regional technique and probably inappropriate outside the Pennine and Yorkshire districts.

Taken from Davies and Loxham (1996)

A relatively new method of footpath maintenance over deep peat is **soil reorganisation** or **HiMac paths.** This technique has been trialled extensively in the Yorkshire Dales National Park especially in the Three Peaks Project. The basis of this method is to excavate the peat along the line of a path (usually with a mechanical excavator, hence the name Hi Mac), down to the mineral soil below. A layer of the mineral soil is then removed, the peat is replaced and the mineral soil laid on top of the replaced peat. Peat can be removed to as deep as the machine used will extend.

This is a comparatively very cheap system of path maintenance and involves no importation of materials. Care must be taken, as with 'flagged' paths, to avoid straight lines and keep sight lines along the path to a minimum. The mineral soil surface should be cambered to allow free drainage and avoid erosion from surface water. Shallow ditches at either side of the path help the drainage process. The landscaping of the path, especially the revegetation of the path edges is very important in the appearance and the way walkers use the path. The path should be revegetated to the minimum legal width, to concentrate erosion from walkers and decrease the loss of surrounding vegetation. The positioning of large turves along the edges of the path is the preferable method for encouraging revegetation. Re-seeding and top dressing with fertiliser can also be used.

Another technique used over peat and already mentioned above, is the **pitched path.** When used over peat, a geo-textile base is needed, as with **floated aggregate paths.** These kind of paths are mainly applicable for steep slopes where **aggregate paths** and **flagged** surfaces are not suitable.

Stepping stones are useful for crossing wet areas, often where another form of path maintenance is being used, when wet hollows and flushes cannot be avoided with path alignment. This is another form of **'flagging'** which can also be useful for crossing wet areas in rocky uplands. When this is the case naturally occurring, large, flat (or nearly so), irregularly shaped stones are more desirable than the conformity of rectangular flags. By placing these in a haphazard manner, but close enough to step from one to the next, a natural effect can be obtained.

It is important that the size of the stones used is sufficient to spread out the load of use by walkers without sinking. Not excavating vegetation and placing the stones straight onto existing vegetation will facilitate this.

Owing to their visually intrusive nature **boardwalks** are considered an anathema in virtually all upland situations. The only situation where a **boardwalk** is the viable option would be where the site's nature conservation interests outweigh the aesthetic value. However, there can be problems with the timber treatment chemicals leaching into the system and harming bryophytes and aquatic systems. The use of **stepping stones**, as described above, should always be the preferred option. The construction of boardwalks is well described by Agate (1996).

Landscaping

Landscaping aims to reduce the visual impact of footpath erosion and lessen the impact of subsequent remedial work. Certain underlying principles can be employed to minimise this impact during maintenance. These include the softening of any edges and boundaries and the avoidance of abrupt changes in texture and colour. All material gathered for use in erosion rehabilitation should blend naturally with their surroundings and disturbance and visual impact to the gathering area should be kept to a minimum. Wherever possible prominent stones, especially edge stones, should be used with their weathered surfaces facing outwards. The use of lines of large boulders to try to keep people on a path should be avoided. Often a few strategically placed boulders is all that is required.

The continued erosion of rehabilitated slopes is a big problem and can undermine much hard work. Exclusion of people and, where necessary, animals from the area may be the only solution. Temporary stock netting is needed for the exclusion of sheep, where signs or barriers may be adequate for people.

For stabilisation of slopes over 15° **revetments** may be used. These can consist of untreated larch poles, kept in place by small stakes, which can be left to rot *in situ* leaving no lasting, incongruous features. Large rocks can also be used in this manner, though care should be taken to leave a natural looking formation. Any boulders or large rocks already present should always be left in place as the best form of natural stabilisation.

For all eroded areas some form of **vegetation reinstatement** must be used. The three main techniques for this are **natural recolonisation, seeding** and **transplanting turves/plants**. The practicalities of these techniques and a thorough guide to landscaping in general can be found in Davies and Loxham (1996).

Maintaining footpaths

Guiding principles

A set of principles was formulated by the Lake District Upland Access Management Group, which were adapted from a British Mountaineering Council policy statement on the repair and maintenance of upland paths.

Box IN10.3 Upland path erosion - guiding principles

The repair and maintenance of paths in open country are subject to the following considerations:

- Repairs are necessary to prevent or ameliorate visual intrusion and environmental damage.
- Works should be of a high standard of design and implementation using indigenous materials, sympathetic in colour and texture to the immediate surrounding area. Uniformity of construction should be avoided, eg steps.
- Techniques used should protect existing vegetation and, normally, only locally occurring plant species should be used in restoration. Non-local species will be acceptable only where necessary as a nurse crop and where natural succession will rapidly result in their disappearance.
- The more remote the path, the more stringently the criteria for path repairs should be applied. This will be a matter of judgement, but in general, the more remote or wild the location the less acceptable an obviously engineered path will be.
- Repaired paths should be suitable to the route's use and constructed on a scale appropriate for the intended use as a footpath, bridleway or byway.
- Before any work is agreed the question should be asked 'is there a better solution'?

The use of waymarks, cairns or other intrusive features, other than those traditionally established on summits and path junctions, will be discouraged. A sustained commitment of resources to path management will be sought, so that small scale continuous maintenance can replace infrequent major repairs as the normal method of path management.

Taken from Davies and Loxham (1996)

These principles have been accepted and adopted by the House of Commons Environment Select Committee as the best practice guidelines to establish a nationwide approach for the repair and maintenance of upland footpaths (Davies and Loxham, 1996).

Selecting a route

Box IN10.4 Route selection guidelines

As specialist advice may affect route selection, consult widely. Specialist advice can be obtained from organisations and individuals who are not representatives of statutory bodies.

- Ensure the route has minimal impact on nature conservation, archaeological and landscape features.
- Vary the width of the path, follow natural contours of the land and avoid straight alignments.
- Take advantage of natural topographic features which allow the route to blend in with its surroundings.
- Take account of desire lines (lines of walker's preferred route) and incorporate them into route design where possible.
- Try to establish a route which follows a clear line for users and discourages the development of short cuts. Choose sustainable alignments. Any diversion from the original route or re-alignment should not cause more problems.
- Avoid direct ascents where possible, as this can lead to drainage problems.
- Avoid water running down the line of the path with potential for erosion. Cross streams and water courses at right angles.
- Design the route to avoid crossing areas of excessive seepage or gullying and where possible, make use of well drained slopes.
- Try to use natural landscape features to contain the path and its users, eg boulder fields, tall vegetation.
- Make sure route alignment and width are compatible with the intended or designated use, eg bridleway.

Taken from Davies and Loxham (1996)

Combatting upland footpath erosion

Preventing erosion

It is much better to prevent the erosion of footpaths than to spend large amounts of time and money on repairing erosion damage. The recognition of early stages in the erosion process mean that preventative measures can be deployed before more severe erosion takes hold. Methods for preventing erosion include:

- reduction of grazing pressure;
- resting a route, ie temporarily changing to an adjacent alignment;

- fertilising and reseeding;
- keeping people on the desired route;
- permanently re-aligning the path to a more sustainable route;
- drainage (see below);
- fencing (usually temporary).

All these techniques can be employed separately, although combinations of preventative measures are often complementary. Fertilising and reseeding an eroded area may need a reduction in grazing pressure or fencing to allow the seeds to grow and surrounding natural vegetation to rejuvenate.

Drainage

Erosion becomes more damaging as a slope steepens, because the erosive power of water increases with increased slope. Soils also tend to be thinner on steeper slopes. The erosive potential of water also increases with decreased vegetation, with robust vegetation being more resilient than sparse cover.

Types of drainage system used in upland path construction include:

- off-path drainage — using natural drainage patterns to divert water from path lines;
- on-path drainage — **water breaks** - barriers or open drains at regular intervals, to divert water to the side of the path;
  rock barriers - help contain aggregate from being carried away therefore reducing scouring and gullying;
  open culverts - often simple open trenches or stone lined features at path edge, or angled across the path;
  closed culverts - small covered box drain angled across the path (for larger volumes of water this may need a rock or 'clapper' bridge).

Techniques and strategies for the diversion of water and drainage on and around footpaths is covered in greater detail by Davies and Loxham (1996).

Bibliography & further reading

AGATE, E. 1996. *Footpaths: a practical handbook*. Wallingford: British Trust for Conservation Volunteers.

BAYFIELD, N.G. & AITKEN, R. 1992. *Managing the impacts of recreation on vegetation and soils: a review of techniques*. Banchory: Institute of Terrestrial Ecology.

COUNTRYSIDE COMMISSION & COUNTRYSIDE COUNCIL FOR WALES. 1997. *National Park management plans guidance*. Cheltenham: Countryside Commission..

COUNTRYSIDE COUNCIL FOR WALES. 1995. *Managing public access: a guide for farmers and landowners*. Bangor: Countryside Council for Wales.

DAVIES, P. 1997. Maintaining Lakes footpaths. *Enact*, **5 (1)**, 4-7.

DAVIES, P. & LOXHAM, J. 1996. *Repairing upland path erosion: a best practice guide.* Kendal: Lake District National Park Authority, National Trust and English Nature.

DENMAN, R. 1994. *Delivering countryside information: a good practice guide for promoting enjoyment of the countryside.* Cheltenham: Countryside Commission & Tourism Company.

ENGLISH SPORTS COUNCIL & COUNTRYSIDE COMMISSION. 1995. *Good practice in the planning and management of sport and active recreation in the countryside.* London: English Sports Council.

SCOTTISH NATURAL HERITAGE. 1997. *Countryside recreation and access strategies: guidance for Local Authorities.* Battleby : Scottish Natural Heritage.

SIDAWAY, R. 1991. *Good conservation practice for sport and recreation.* London: The Sports Council, Countryside Commission, Nature Conservancy Council and World Wide Fund for Nature.

SIDAWAY, R. 1994. Recreation and the natural heritage: a research review. Battleby: *Scottish Natural Heritage Review*, No. 25.

VICKERY, J. 1995. Access. *In*: W.J. Sutherland & D.A. Hill, eds. *Managing habitats for conservation.* Cambridge: Cambridge University Press.